DATE DUE

OC 27 '95			
AP 5 '96			
DE 17 '98			
AP 20 '98			
MR 29 '99			
OC 27 '00			
JY 31 '02			
NOV 24 2003			
MAY 17 2004			
OC 04 '05			
OC 25 '05			
NO 13 '06			
NO 7 '07			

DEMCO 38-296

CONSTRUCTIVE EVOLUTION

CONSTRUCTIVE EVOLUTION

ORIGINS AND DEVELOPMENT OF PIAGET'S THOUGHT

MICHAEL CHAPMAN

University of British Columbia

and

Max Planck Institute for Human Development and Education

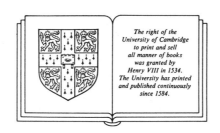

The right of the
University of Cambridge
to print and sell
all manner of books
was granted by
Henry VIII in 1534.
The University has printed
and published continuously
since 1584.

CAMBRIDGE UNIVERSITY PRESS

Cambridge

New York   New Rochelle   Melbourne   Sydney

Published by the Press Syndicate of the University of Cambridge
The Pitt Building, Trumpington Street, Cambridge CB2 1RP
32 East 57th Street, New York, NY 10022, USA
10 Stamford Road, Oakleigh, Melbourne 3166, Australia

First published 1988

Printed in the United States of America

Library of Congress Cataloging-in-Publication Data
Chapman, Michael, 1947–
Constructive evolution.
Bibliography: p.
Includes index.
1. Cognition in children.   2. Piaget, Jean,
1896–1980.   I. Title.
BF723.C5C484   1988   155.4′13′0924   87–21816

British Library Cataloguing in Publication Data
Chapman, Michael
Constructive evolution: origins and development
of Piaget's thought.
1. Piaget, Jean   2. Developmental psychology
I. Title
155′.092′4   BF713

ISBN 0 521 33163 3 hard covers
ISBN 0 521 36712 3 paperback

Contents

Preface

I did not start out to write a book on Piaget. Rather, in reading his works for other purposes, I discovered a different thinker than I had been led to expect from textbook presentations of his theory. His autobiographical remarks on the importance of the problem of universals for his early thinking had impressed me, being a former student of philosophy, but as yet I did not know what to make of this connection. Later, in searching through his books looking for a clear statement of the relation between the concept of *structures d'ensemble* and the hypothesis of general developmental synchrony, I was surprised to discover that I could not find any. Instead, I found statements to the contrary: Piaget apparently did not believe in the hypothesis of general developmental synchrony commonly attributed to him. This discovery led me to reexamine the notion of *structures d'ensemble* and ultimately back to the problem of universals.

In my subsequent encounter with his adolescent novel *Recherche* and his early writings on religion, I discovered that the original problem motivating his work had been the attempt to reconcile science and values. His interest in psychology now appeared in a different light. Psychological research had been less an end in itself than a way of addressing the problem of values with scientific means. By observing the development of increasingly more powerful forms of reasoning in children, he had hoped to discover a principle underlying development progress. In this way, scientific observation could provide a basis, not for deciding judgments of relative value, but for distinguishing the relative values of different forms of judgment.

The question was how to communicate this new understanding of Piaget's work to others. I could think of no better way than the developmental method he had used himself. The most intuitive way of illuminating the organic structure of this thought was to trace its evolution from the inception of his basic ideas to their full fruition in his later writings. In so doing, I hoped to present a more full-bodied picture of Piaget as a thinker than had been previously available.

Acknowledgments

I would like to thank Victoria Watters, James Youniss, and Paul B. Baltes for their encouragement, and Susan Milmoe, Helen Wheeler, and Katharita Lamoza at Cambridge University Press for their commitment to the book. Thanks also to Harry Beilin, Augusto Blasi, Daniel Bullock, Jonas Langer, Ulman Lindenberger, Irving Sigel, Ellen Skinner, and Karl Wahlen for reading and commenting on drafts of various chapters. I benefited from attending the 8th Annual Advanced Course at the Piaget Archives in Geneva in 1986 and from my discussions and correspondence with Fernando Vidal regarding Piaget's early thought. Finally, I would like to thank Linda Buechner for her care in preparing the manuscript.

I would also like to express my appreciation to the following copyright holders for permission to quote from the sources indicated.

Allen & Unwin, for material from: G. W. F. Hegel, *The phenomenology of mind,* New York: Harper Torchbooks, 1967.

Basic Books, for material from: B. Inhelder & J. Piaget, *The growth of logical thinking from childhood to adolescence,* 1958; J. Piaget, *The construction of reality in the child,* New York: Ballantine, 1971; J. Piaget & B. Inhelder, Mental images. In H. E. Gruber & J. J. Vonèche (Eds.), *The essential Piaget,* 1977.

Cambridge University Press, for material from: K. W. Fischer, Open peer commentary. *The Behavioral and Brain Sciences, 2,* 1978; P. M. Churchland, *Scientific realism and the plasticity of mind,* 1979; T. S. Kuhn, Reflections on my critics. In I. Lakatos & A. Musgrave (Eds.), *Criticism and the growth of knowledge,* 1970; C. J. Brainerd, The stage question in cognitive-developmental theory. *The Behavioral and Brain Sciences, 2,* 1978.

Columbia University Press, for material from: J. Piaget & R. Garcia, *Psychogenèse et histoire des sciences,* Paris: Flammarion, 1983.

Delachaux et Niestlé, for material from: J. Piaget & A. Szeminska, *La genèse du nombre chez l'enfant* (3rd ed.), 1964; J. Piaget, *Le jugement et le raisonnement chez l'enfant* (3rd ed.), 1978; B. Inhelder, R. Garcia, & J. Vonèche, *Epistémologie génétique et équilibration,* 1977; J. Piaget, *The origins of intelligence in children,* New York: Norton, 1963.

Dunod, for material from: J. Piaget, *Essai de logique opératoire* (2nd ed., *Traité de logique*), 1972.

Editions Medicine et Hygiene, for material from: J. Piaget, Le mécanisme du développement mental et les lois du groupement des opérations. *Archives de Psychologie, 28,* 1941; J. Piaget, Une forme verbale de la comparaison chez l'enfant: Un cas de transition entre le jugement prédicatif et le jugement de relation. *Archives de Psychologie, 18,* 1923.

Encyclopaedia Britannica, for material from: R. M. Hutchins (Ed.), *Great books of the Western world* (vol. 42), 1952.

Gallimard, for material from: J. Piaget, *Les formes élémentaires de la dialectique,* 1980.

Harvard University Press, for material from: M. Piattelli-Palmarini (Ed.), *Language and learning: The debate between Jean Piaget and Noam Chomsky,* London: Routledge & Kegan Paul, 1980.

Hermann, for material from: J. Piaget, *Adaptation and intelligence,* 1980.

Holt, Rinehart & Winston, for material from: H. Bergson, *Creative evolution,* New York: Modern Library, 1944.

Humanities Press International, for material from: B. Inhelder & J. Piaget, *The early growth of logic in the child,* New York: Norton, 1969; J. Piaget, *The child's conception of physical causality,* London: Routledge & Kegan Paul, 1966; J. Piaget, *Judgment and reasoning in the child,* London: Routledge & Kegan Paul, 1928; J. Piaget & B. Inhelder, *The child's conception of space,* New York: Norton, 1967; J. Piaget, *The language and thought of the child,* Cleveland: Meridian, 1955.

International Universities Press, for material from: J. Piaget, *The origins of intelligence in children,* New York: Norton, 1963.

McGraw-Hill Book Co., for material from: D. R. Green (Ed.), *Measurement and Piaget,* 1971.

Macmillan, for material from: J. Piaget, *The moral judgment of the child,* New York: Free Press, 1965.

W. W. Norton & Co., for material from: J. Piaget, *Play, dreams and imitation in childhood,* 1962.

Oxford University Press, for material from: P. Kitcher, *The nature of mathematical knowledge,* 1984; W. D. Ross (Ed.), *The works of Aristotle* (Vols. 1 & 2), 1955; J. Locke, An essay concerning human understanding. In R. M. Hutchins (Ed.), *Great books of the Western world* (Vol. 35), Chicago: Encyclopaedia Britannica, 1952.

Pantheon Books, for material from: J. Piaget, *Etudes sociologiques* (D. Smith, Trans.), Geneva: Droz, 1977.

Presses Universitaires de France, for material from: J. Piaget, Essai sur quelques aspects du développement de la notion de partie chez l'enfant. *Journal de Psychologie, 18,* 1921; J. Piaget, *Recherches sur l'abstraction réfléchissante* (2 vols.), 1977; J. Piaget, *Recherches sur la généralisation,* 1978; J. Piaget, *Recherches sur les correspondances,* 1980; P. Osterrieth, J. Piaget, R. de Saussure, J. M. Tanner, H. Wallon, R. Zazzo, B. Inhelder, & A. Rey, *Le problème des stades en psychologie de l'enfant,* 1956; J. Piaget, *The equilibration of cognitive structures,* Chicago: University of Chicago Press, 1985.

Rand McNally & Co., for material from: L. Kohlberg, Stage and sequence: The cognitive developmental approach to socialization. In D. A. Goslin (Ed.), *Handbook of socialization theory and research*, 1969.

Random House, Inc., for material from: J. Piaget, *Six psychological studies* (A. Tenzer, Trans.), New York: Vintage, 1967.

D. Reidel Publishing Co., for material from: J. Piaget, J.-B. Grize, A. Szeminska, & Vinh Bang, *Epistemology and psychology of functions*, 1977.

Revue Internationale de Philosophie, for material from: L. Apostel, The future of Piagetian logic. *Revue Internationale de Philosophie*, 1982.

Revue de Théologie et de Philosophie, for material from: J. Piaget, Pour l'immanence. *Revue de Théologie et de Philosophie, 17,* 1929.

Routledge & Kegan Paul, for material from: J. Piaget & B. Inhelder, *The child's construction of quantities*, 1974; A. C. Ewing, *The fundamental questions of philosophy*, 1952; M. Piattelli-Palmarini (Ed.), *Language and learning: The debate between Jean Piaget and Noam Chomsky*, 1980; J. Piaget, Explanation in psychology and psychophysiological parallelism. In P. Fraise & J. Piaget (Eds.), *Experimental psychology, its scope and method*, 1968; J. Piaget & B. Inhelder, *Mental imagery in the child*, 1971; J. Piaget, *The mechanisms of perception*, 1969; B. Inhelder & J. Piaget, *The early growth of logic in the child*, New York: Norton, 1969; J. Piaget, *The child's conception of time*, New York: Ballantine, 1971; J. Piaget, *The moral judgment of the child*, New York: The Free Press, 1965; J. Piaget, *The child's conception of physical causality*, 1966; J. Piaget, *Introduction à l'épistémologie génétique, 1: La pensée mathématique,* 1973; J. Piaget, *Introduction à l'épistémologie génétique, 2: La pensée physique,* 1974; J. Piaget, *Introduction à l'épistémologie génétique, 3: La pensée biologique, la pensée psychologique, et la pensée sociologique,* 1950; J. Piaget, *Play, dreams and imitation in childhood*, New York: Norton, 1962; J. Piaget, *The child's conception of the world*, London: Granada, 1973; J. Piaget, *Etudes sociologiques* (3rd ed.), 1977; J. Piaget, Autobiographie. *Revue Européenne des Sciences Sociales, 14,* 1976; J. Piaget, *Judgment and reasoning in the child*, 1928; J. Piaget, *The psychology of intelligence*, 1950.

Russell & Russell Publishers, for material from: J. Piaget, (untitled autobiography). In E. G. Boring (Ed.), *A history of psychology in autobiography* (Vol. 4), 1952.

Society for Research in Child Development, for material from: R. Corrigan, Cognitive correlates of language: Differential criteria yield differential results. *Child Development, 50,* 1970.

Tavistock Publications, Ltd., for material from: J. Piaget, The general problems of the psychobiological development of the child. In M. Tanner & B. Inhelder (Eds.), *Discussions on child development* (Vol. 4), 1960.

S. Toulmin, for material from: S. Toulmin, *Human understanding*, Princeton, NJ: Princeton University Press, 1972.

University of Chicago Press, for material from: J. Piaget, *Biology and knowledge,* 1971; J. Piaget, *Experiments in contradiction*, 1980; J. Piaget, *The equi-*

libration of cognitive structures, 1985; D. Hume, A treatise of human nature. In T. V. Smith & M. Grene (Eds.), *Philosophers speak for themselves: Berkeley, Hume, and Kant*, 1957; J.-C. Bringuier, *Conversations with Jean Piaget*, 1980; J. Piaget, *Adaptation and intelligence*, 1980.

University of Minnesota Press, for material from: J. Piaget, *Le possible et la nécessaire, Vol. 1: L'évolution des possibles chez l'enfant*, 1981; J. Piaget, *Le possible et la nécessaire, Vol. 2: L'évolution du nécessaire chez l'enfant*, 1983.

R. J. Van Iten, for material from: R. J. Van Iten (Ed.), *The problem of universals*, New York: Appleton-Century-Crofts, 1970.

J. Vrin, for material from: J. Piaget, *Classes, relations et nombres*, 1942.

Wadsworth Publications, for material from: J. H. Flavell, *The developmental psychology of Jean Piaget*, 1963.

Introduction: Piaget from within

Jean Piaget is widely recognized as one of the greatest child psychologists of all time. His ideas are taught in psychology courses around the world and are mentioned in every textbook on child development. But to view Piaget solely as a psychologist of child development is to betray a fundamental misunderstanding of the issues that informed his work. He was a development psychologist and more. Among his many accomplishments, he was the founder of a new discipline called genetic epistemology. The goal of this discipline was investigation of the origins of knowledge. As such, it overlapped both with child psychology and with philosophical epistemology, without being coextensive with either one. Also belonging to the field of genetic epistemology are topics in biology, sociology, and the history of science and mathematics.

It was perhaps because of such a narrow focus on the psychological aspects of his work that Piaget complained, in an otherwise friendly foreword to Flavell's (1963) comprehensive survey of his work, of having been understood "more from without than from within" (Piaget in Flavell, 1963, p. viii). In evaluating Piaget's theory, Flavell had remarked that there was perhaps too great a gap between the theory and the facts available to support it. Piaget replied that there were basic differences between Flavell's outlook and his own, consisting in the fact that "his approach is perhaps too exclusively psychological and insufficiently epistemological while the converse is true for me" (ibid., pp. viii–ix). The solution was to be found in interdisciplinary cooperation like that fostered at the Center for Genetic Epistemology in Geneva, where scholars and scientists representing the individual disciplines of psychology, logic, and mathematics could bring their expertise to bear on common problems.

If the goal of this book were to be expressed in a single phrase, it would be *to understand Piaget from within*. It is an attempt to reconstruct the original questions to which his life work was addressed and to evaluate that work in the light of those original questions. The method used is undoubtedly one of which Piaget himself would have approved. The origins of his thought will be sought in its development. Specifically, the evolution of his thinking will be traced from his precocious interests in naturalism and zoology as a child to the end of his remarkably prolific scientific career. Without such a developmental approach, one would be unable to identify the themes that motivated his work and to see how the various parts of that work fit together to form a whole. This reconstruction of Piaget's intellectual development is based on the evidence in his published work, especially his autobiographical writings (Piaget, 1918, 1952a, 1976a). These autobiographical writings provide a key for understanding the inner development of his ideas.

The picture of Piaget that emerges from this investigation differs significantly from that of the textbooks. Many of the basic ideas that informed Piaget's life work from beginning to end were conceived before he ever considered studying the development of children's thinking. The object of Piaget's epistemological orientation was the whole "circle of sciences," of which psychology formed only a single link. The study of children's thinking was a means to the end of understanding the origins of knowledge in general. But Piaget was also interested in questions concerning values, and this interest led him to reflect on problems of morality and religion. Indeed, the problem that led him as a young man to some of his original insights was the problem of reconciling the interests of truth with the interests of value, or, as he put it himself, of reconciling science and religion. In this context, he conceived his early ideas on structure, equilibrium, and the relation between action and thought. These ideas remained with him all his life and became the core-elements of his later work, although they were conceived before he became a psychologist.

THE UNKNOWN PIAGET

Piaget's inherently interdisciplinary orientation explains in part why his theory often has been misconstrued by psychologists from within the perspective of their own discipline. Assuming that his questions were the same as their own, they have frequently been disappointed in the answers that he gave. In fact, his questions were generally different from those asked by most psychologists, and it is therefore not surprising that his answers also were different. This assimilation of Piaget's goals to those of mainstream psychology has resulted in some serious misunderstandings. The portrayal of his theory in most psychology textbooks, the conventional wisdom shared by followers and critics alike, has been inaccurate on a number of important points. For example, the view that cognitive stage development is inherently linked with age and that the concept of structure implies synchrony in development across different areas of content has often been presented as the very core of Piagetian theory, and the theory has been evaluated in these terms. Study upon study has been conducted showing that the cognitive abilities studied by Piaget either do or do not develop at the ages reported by him when certain variations are introduced into the procedures or that children's structural competencies either do or do not develop in synchrony in tasks involving different content. Depending on how the weight of evidence is judged, the theory has been taken to be either supported or refuted. In fact, one searches in vain through Piaget's published writings to find any unequivocal statement of this hypothesis of global developmental synchrony. For the most part, he did not address the issue at all. Occasionally one finds explicit denials of the views commonly attributed to him. Because he never advanced many of the hypotheses commonly believed to lie at the core of this theory, much of the evidence adduced either for or against those hypotheses is irrelevant to the questions addressed by the theory in its original form. This topic is treated in detail in chapter 7 of this book.

Other common characterizations of Piaget's theory have been based on selective readings of his voluminous writings. He has often been accused, for example, of not having paid sufficient attention to specifically social factors in development. He has been criticized both for overemphasizing environmental factors and for underemphasizing them. Many such criticisms are based on limited familiarity with the entire range of Piaget's work. This circumstance can be explained in part by his very prolificity and by the fact that many key works, including the three-volume *Introduction à l'épistémologie génétique* (Piaget, 1950/ 1973a, 1950/1974a, 1950a), the three books on operatory logic (Piaget, 1942, 1949/1972a, 1952b), and the *Etudes sociologiques* (Piaget, 1965/1977a), still are unavailable in English translation. Isolated passages can indeed be found that appear to support the common interpretations, especially if they are read outside the context of his work as a whole. Given the sheer volume of his writings, one can read a great deal and still miss much that is essential. It is of no help that much of what is central to an understanding of genetic epistemology is to be found in the untranslated works cited earlier. Piaget's treatment of the effects of social, environmental, and other factors in development may or may not be adequate. But he did not simply neglect those factors to the extent that is commonly believed.

This book is inspired by a growing perception of the discrepancy between the conventional image of Piaget and the picture that emerges from a broad reading of his life's work. It is an attempt to reconstruct his original questions, not primarily a defense of his answers to those questions. Much can be found to criticize in his theory. But in order to criticize it in an informed way, one must first understand it in its own terms. The first problem is how well Piaget succeeded in answering his own questions, as opposed to the questions that others might have asked in his stead. Then one can also ask to what extent his ideas are useful in contributing to the answers current in contemporary psychology.

The reconstruction of his original questions necessitates a consideration of certain problems lying outside the boundaries of psychology as it is typically defined. But Piaget's interdisciplinary perspective is not the only difficulty to be found in his writing. Many commentators have remarked on the obscurity of his style. This impression is due in part to the fact that his habits of thinking and writing were formed in the context of a much different intellectual tradition than that of present-day professional psychology. His conventions were not necessarily our conventions, his usages not always the same as ours, and even when the same terms were employed, they often had different connotations. Piaget had a penchant for attempting to express new thoughts in existing terminology. This meant that he frequently came to use familiar terms in quite idiosyncratic ways. If such differences in meaning go unnoticed, serious misunderstandings can result.

Our task of interpreting Piaget would have been easier if his writing had more frequently taken the form of dialogues with actual or potential critics, or if he had more consistently attempted to compare and contrast his own concepts with those employed in other theoretical approaches in psychology. When he did engage in such dialogue, the results were often illuminating, but more often he continued to develop his own ideas according to their own internal logic without taking the time to interpret himself to others who did not share his basic assumptions. Given the immensity of the task he had set for himself, this procedure was perhaps inevitable, but it has made it easier for Piaget's interpreters to understand him in their terms rather than his own. Part of the task of this book is to clarify Piaget's terminology so that his theory can be understood literally "in its own terms."

The context in which Piaget conceived his basic ideas had both personal and historical dimensions. There was a strain in Piaget's early thinking that can best be described as "cosmological" – not in the sense of speculating about the ultimate nature of the universe, but in the sense of seeking in science answers to questions about the value and meaning of human life (Toulmin, 1982). This aspect of his thought was carefully subordinated to the requirements of professional rigor in his scientific writings, a fact that may have lent an added layer of ambiguity to them, for his mature theory was in part a product of this early cosmological vision. As described in chapter 1, Piaget, as a young man, envisioned a synthesis of science and values in which a new science of "types" (or "genera") would play a leading role. In the form of an empirical investigation into the foundations of knowledge, this new science would provide a means for resolving the conflict between scientific truth and ultimate value. In practice, ascribing such a role to science meant that the terms of scientific discourse became loaded with wider connotations not immediately apparent on the surface.

In this respect, Piaget's autobiography from 1952 is an important document for understanding the hidden implications of his ideas. In chapter 1, the autobiography is seen as a key for decoding the surplus meanings in many of Piaget's terms. In this autobiography, Piaget described the central formative experience of his youth: Between the ages of 15 and 17, he suffered a severe personal crisis having to do with the conflict between science and religion. This may have had something to do with the fact that his mother was a devoutly religious woman with neurotic tendencies, whereas his father was a religious skeptic. Our purpose is not to speculate on the psychological causes of this crisis, but rather to examine its intellectual content and its possible relation to his later work.

The crisis was precipitated by the young Piaget's discovery of philosophy, specifically, the philosophy of Bergson. It was overcome through the formation of an original philosophical system in which the conflicting claims of scientific knowledge and religious belief were reconciled through a new science of genera.

The fundamentals of this new science were described in detail in an autobiographical novel that Piaget wrote at the time and published in 1918 at the age of 21. This novel, entitled *Recherche,* is another key document in the interpretation of the Piagetian opus. Many of the central concepts in Piaget's later theory, including the concepts of structure, equilibrium, and action, were foreshadowed in this early system. More important, perhaps, is the fact that the system provided the young Piaget with a solution to his immediate problems of identity in the form of a life project that satisfied the conflicting sides of his personality. He would devote his life to the realization of the new science. The latter would in turn provide the basis for resolving the conflict between science and value, which he identified as the principal cause of contemporary world problems. Understood in this light, scientific research became a value-laden activity in itself, providing the young Piaget with nothing less than a mission in life.

With regard to investigating the origins of knowledge, Piaget fulfilled his adolescent ambitions to a degree he could not have foreseen. Whether or not genetic epistemology as it has evolved in practice can help to answer questions regarding the meaning of life is another question. Such questions, however, may be asked independently of questions regarding the scientific merit of Piaget's theory. The fact that this theory may have been partially motivated by adolescent aspirations of a quasi-religious nature may be useful in understanding the origins of his theory without prejudicing the evaluation of his theory as science. It is nevertheless of interest to ask how the theory fares in answering some of the questions that originally motivated it.

One such question was the age-old philosophical problem of universals. There is evidence from Piaget himself that his early conception of a new science of genera was influenced by his encounter at a crucial moment with the problem of universals, both in the philosophy of Bergson and in the lectures of A. Reymond at the University of Neuchâtel. This encounter led directly to the idea of the new science of genera as described in *Recherche.* Bergson had realized that the problem of universals recurred in modern psychology in the form of accounting for the origins of *general ideas* and in biology in terms of explaining the unity of individual organisms and their classification in genera and species. For the young Piaget, genera came to be conceived as the basic forms of organization in all life, from the structures of the human mind to the structures of the living organism. The originality of this approach consisted mainly in the fact that the problem of universals was transformed into a program of scientific research. As forms of knowing, genera could be investigated through psychological methods, and as forms of life they could be objects of biological study. Moreover, a developmental continuity was seen to exist between human cognition and other levels of biological organization. The relation between Piaget's work and the problem of universals will be treated at greater length in chapter 8. Besides playing an important role in the genesis of his core-ideas, this problem provides a convenient context for discussing the implications of his theory for some traditional issues in epistemology.

The ways in which Piaget's early conception of genera was transformed in his later work will be traced in detail in subsequent chapters of this book. In particular, his later concepts of structure and equilibrium can be seen to have developed from this source. As described in chapter 1, genera were conceived of as relational totalities, arising at all levels of reality out of the interactions among their component parts.[1] This conception of genera was a precursor of his later concepts of "total structures" and "structures-of-the-whole" (*structures d'ensemble*). The coherence of such relational totalities resulted from their particular forms of equilibrium, of which four could be distinguished: the equilibrium of the whole, the equilibrium between the parts and the whole, the equilibrium among the parts taken by themselves, and the equilibrium between the whole and the external environment. These forms of equilibrium, already outlined in *Recherche,* were the beginnings of Piaget's later attempts to explain development in terms of a principle of equilibration, a fact also noted by Inhelder, Garcia, and Vonèche (1977). In order to grasp the central importance of the notions of structure and equilibrium in Piaget's work, one must try to see how they were related to his conception of development.

STRUCTURE AND EQUILIBRIUM

Well before Piaget ever thought of investigating children's thinking, the concept of development provided him with a standard for judging the relative adequacy of different forms of knowing. According to this reasoning, more highly developed forms of knowing were by that very fact more adequate than less developed forms. In order to play this normative role, however, development had to be distinguished from mere change. Otherwise, one would be in the position of defending the dubious proposition that forms of knowing appearing later in time were necessarily preferable to forms appearing earlier. In order to distinguish developmental progress from nonprogressive change, some independent criterion was necessary.

Piaget found such an independent criterion of developmental progress in the

---

1 Kitchener (1985, 1986) argued that, for Piaget, relational totalities (e.g., structures) are composed of their parts, plus the relations among their parts. As such, they possess emergent properties relative to their parts but not relative to their internal relations. I agree with this formulation as long as one includes under the term "relations" all the *possible* or *virtual* relations among the parts and not merely those that have been realized at any given time, For Piaget, the whole is pregnant with new possibilities and is therefore more than the sum of its parts and their actual interactions. These "structural possibilities" nevertheless have real consequences (Inhelder & Piaget, 1955/1958, pp. 260–266). For example, the development of novel forms of action and thought was explained by Piaget as the realization of possibilities created in the formation of a structure. A structure develops from real interactions, but contains possibilities beyond those from which it was formed. Kitchener's formulation should therefore be amended as follows: For Piaget, relational totalities possess emergent properties with respect to their parts and with respect to the actual relations among the parts, but not with respect to all the virtual relations. The evidence for this interpretation is presented in subsequent chapters of this book.

idea of equilibrium. Like the notion of structure to which it is related, this central organizing concept runs like a thread through all of Piaget's life work. Already present in an intuitive form in his adolescent philosophical system, it provided the basic insight behind his views on developmental change, achieving its mature expression in his book on equilibration published only 5 years before his death (Piaget, 1975/1985). In this respect, Piaget's life work represents a remarkable unity from beginning to end.

In its original form, the concept of equilibrium referred to a system of dynamic compensations in which the effective forces at work were each balanced by reciprocal influences. From the standpoint of the system, such a balance was desirable, for the action of uncompensated forces could lead to disintegration of the whole. As described in *Recherche,* equilibrium referred specifically to the effects of totalities on their several parts and the reciprocal effects of those parts on the whole. In this interaction of the parts and the whole, either of them could be more or less altered or preserved. Of the various forms of equilibrium resulting from this interaction, the most advantageous was one in which the reciprocal effects of the parts and the wholes balanced each other out. The predominance of either the whole or the parts led to rigidity or disintegration, respectively. This interaction between parts and wholes played itself out "on all levels," including the biological, the psychological, and the social. On the biological level, the relation between parts and wholes could be seen in the relations of the cell to the organism and the organism to the species. On the psychological level, it could be seen in the relationship between general concepts and their individual instances. On the social level, it could be seen in the relation between the individual and society. Piaget's later contributions in all these fields would bear the marks of this early conception of the relation between parts and wholes in relational totalities.

Piaget's later concept of cognitive structure, for example, was a direct descendant of this early vision of totalities in equilibrium. In this case, the role of the "parts" is played by cognitive operations, and that of the "whole" by the *structure d'ensemble* that comprehends them. Structural equilibrium consists in the fact that each operation is reversible – that is, it is compensated by a reverse operation contained in the same structure. For example, the grouping structure called "primary addition of classes" refers to the classification of objects into a hierarchy of classes and subclasses (i.e., genera and species) on the basis of common attributes. The "components" of this structure are the operations of joining and separating (the "addition" and "subtraction" of classes). Their particular equilibrium consists in the fact that every operation of joining is compensated by an inverse operation of separating, and vice versa (see chapter 5).

But equilibrium was never conceived by Piaget as a state to be achieved once and for all. Every equilibrium was only partial; for every achieved equilibrium, there was a higher form of equilibrium toward which the existing one tended to evolve. This process was the primary motor of development. In *Recherche,* the "ideal equilibria" toward which all totalities tended were distinguished from real equilibria, which were only partial, imperfect, and therefore temporary. Even among real equilibria, lower forms of equilibrium could be distinguished from higher forms, and development was viewed as a process leading from the one to the other. In his mature theory, higher and lower forms of equilibrium could be distinguished from each other in terms of the number and scope of the compensations that they comprehended. Higher forms of equilibrium were more stable than lower forms, because they were capable of compensating for a wider scope of possible operations. They could therefore function under a broader range of possible conditions without danger of disintegration. For example, formal operational structures represented a higher level of equilibrium than concrete operational structures, because the former included two types of reversibility (negation and reciprocity) and the latter only one (negation or reciprocity, but not both).

With this concept of equilibrium, Piaget could distinguish development from mere change. Development was change that led from a lower form of equilibrium to a higher one, defined in the preceding manner. Such a formulation did not yet specify *how* higher forms of equilibrium evolved from lower ones, but it did provide Piaget with what he needed in order to make his overall project viable: a normative standard for distinguishing more adequate forms of knowing from less adequate forms. In his later work on equilibration (Piaget, 1975/1985), he addressed the question of how progressive development occurs in more detail. There the focus was on the *process* by which a higher form of equilibrium succeeds a lower one.

The concept of equilibrium further provided Piaget with a normative standard for judging forms of knowing at all levels, from the earliest forms of sensorimotor functioning to the most advanced forms of scientific thought. As an end state to which all systems tend, the notion of ideal equilibrium imbued each system with implicit value. Higher forms of equilibrium were necessarily "better" than lower forms; the "good" was the progressive realization of the ideal equilibrium. In this sense, the notion of equilibrium was relevant to the question of science and value. On the one hand, equilibria as forms of organization could be investigated scientifically at every level of life, from the single cell to human society. On the other hand, such forms of organization were themselves imbued with value. Because scientific investigation could distinguish higher and lower forms of equilibrium, certain questions of relative value potentially could be settled through scientific means.

From this point of view, research in epistemology became endowed with value in its own right. In one of his more rhapsodical moments, Piaget identified the Divine with thought itself as the condition of all existence (Piaget, 1928a). In tracing the history of forms of knowing, the genetic epistemologist became a medium by which thought became aware of itself. It is easy to imagine how genetic epistemology, so conceived, could be experienced as a form of self-transcendence. In fact, Piaget produced several works on religion from a developmental point of view (Piaget, 1922a, 1928a, 1929a, 1930). These writings will be examined in chapter 2.

From one perspective, the personal connotations that genetic epistemology might have had for Piaget are irrelevant for the evaluation of his ideas. They were simply "personal preoccupations" that became "filtered out" of his scientific work (Toulmin, 1972). However, his interest in questions of ultimate values and their relation to science is interesting in its own right and relevant for understanding the origins of some of his basic intuitions. This is especially true for the central concepts of structure and equilibrium.

THOUGHT AND ACTION

Another of Piaget's fundamental intuitions had to do with the relation between thought and action. In this case as well, Piaget was decisively influenced by Bergson, and by pragmatism in general. But where Bergson tended to see a dichotomy between thought and action, Piaget preferred to see a developmental continuity. Thus, he viewed the very operations utilized by logical and mathematical thought as developing from the interiorization of action. Logico-mathematical operations of addition and subtraction developed from actions of joining and separating through a process of interiorization. This interiorization made possible a further characteristic of logico-mathematical operations: their *reversibility*.

For Piaget, operational reversibility was no mere return to the point of origin. The latter he called "the empirical return" or "revertibility" (*renversabilité*), as opposed to true operational reversibility (*réversibilité*). The difference between the two consists in the fact that revertibility of actions occurs in sequential time, but operational reversibility involves simultaneous coordination. Thus, the revertibility of an act of joining means that it can be undone by a subsequent act of separating. In contrast, the reversibility of a logico-mathematical operation consists in the fact that the subject, in applying that operation, realizes that it is simultaneously compensated by a potential inverse operation.

This reversible property of operations links Piaget's concept of action to his ideas on structure and equilibrium. He was fond of saying that an operation never exists in isolation, but always in relation to a whole system of operations. The child who has learned basic addition will be able to add not only 2 and 2 but also a whole range of other possible numbers. Moreover, each of these individual operations of addition will be reversible by inverse operations of subtraction. The whole system of direct operations and their inverses is an example of what Piaget called a *structure d'ensemble*. In terms of the young Piaget's conception of relational totalities and equilibria, logico-mathematical operations represent the "parts," the total structure represents the "whole," and the reversibility of operations is its particular form of equilibrium. The development of logico-mathematical operations out of sensorimotor actions represents a development from a lower form of equilibrium to a higher form, because sensorimotor actions are compensated only through sequential revertibility, whereas logico-mathematical operations are compensated both by revertibility (to the extent that they are sequentially enacted) and by operational reversibility (even if they are not sequentially enacted).

These matters will be elaborated in greater detail in subsequent chapters of this book. For the moment, one should only note that the concepts of structure, equilibrium, and action represent the core-elements of Piaget's lifelong research program (cf. Beilin, 1985). They are the basic themes developed in the symphony of his life's work. The transpositions, transformations, and modulations of these themes will be traced at the points at which they occurred in his development.

PLAN OF THE BOOK

This book is organized in eight chapters: The first six follow Piaget's intellectual development from his early preoccupations with naturalism and philosophy in adolescence to the mature expression of his ideas in the last decades of his life. Chapter 1 is primarily devoted to a description of Piaget's adolescent personality crises and the philosophical system that led him out of it. Chapter 2 follows his early career from his first works on children's thought and language to his writings on social, moral, and religious thought in the 1920s. Chapter 3 focuses on his observations of the "logic of action" in sensorimotor development that he published during the 1930s. Chapter 4 begins with the discovery of grouping structure and continues with his work on concrete operations across the decade of the 1940s. Chapter 5 covers the period from 1950 to about 1965 and describes the writings produced during this period on epistemology, logic, perception, and mental imagery. Chapter 6 completes the survey of his life's work, covering the writings on biology, equilibration, preoperational structures (functions and correspondences), and the history of the sciences.

The last two chapters undertake to provide a context for evaluating the theory from different perspectives. In chapter 7, Piaget's theory is viewed from the perspective of scientific psychology. Certain widespread misconceptions about Piaget's theory are corrected, his theory is compared to current neofunctionalist approaches (Beilin, 1983), and a possible synthesis of structural and functional approaches is proposed. In chapter 8, the implications of Piaget's theory for traditional epistemological problems, including the problem of universals, are discussed. His theory is compared to other current approaches to problems of form and structural stability. Finally, "cosmological" dimensions of Piaget's ideas are reconsidered, and the question is raised to what extent Piaget's mature views are relevant to the deeper problems of human existence that he pondered as a young man.

1

The seeker and the search

In a discussion of the relation between cognitive development and personality development in adolescence, Piaget wrote:

Personality formation begins in middle to late childhood (eight to twelve years) with the autonomous organization of rules and values, and the affirmation of will with respect to the regulation and hierarchical organization of moral tendencies. But there is more to the person than these factors alone. These factors are integrated with the self into a unique system to which all the separate parts are subordinated. There is then a "personal" system in the dual sense that it is peculiar to a given individual and implies autonomous coordination. Now this personal system cannot be constructed prior to adolescence, because it presupposes the formal thought and reflexive constructions we have just discussed. . . . One might say that personality exists as soon as a "life plan" (*Lebensplan*), which is both a source of discipline for the will and an instrument of cooperation, is formed. [Piaget, 1964/1967a, p. 65]

In an editorial footnote to this passage, Elkind informed the reader that "Piaget himself constructed such a life plan as an adolescent and published it in the form of a novel," adding, as if to explain, "the formal construction of such life plans is much more common in Europe than it is in America" (Elkind in Piaget, 1964/1967a, p. 73).

But the young Piaget's life plan is significant less for reflecting a common tendency among European adolescents than for what it reveals about the intellectual development of the man himself. As indicated by Elkind, this life plan was described in the autobiographical novel *Recherche* (Piaget, 1918), written when Piaget was 20 and published a year later. The major purpose of this chapter is to reconstruct this life plan and the philosophical system associated with it from the evidence of *Recherche* and Piaget's (1952a) autobiography. As these documents indicate, many of his most fundamental ideas can be traced back to this philosophical system, and its reconstruction is therefore useful in understanding the origins and development of his ideas.

Piaget's "system" was the product of a rather severe adolescent personality crisis that he underwent between the ages of 15 and 17. The life plan with its sense of mission was responsible, as he put it himself, for restoring his personal "equilibrium." In retrospect, this experience may easily be identified with the "identity crisis" now recognized as typical of adolescence. But the fact that the notion of identity crisis has in the meantime acquired the status of a cultural stereotype should not blind us to the acuteness of the experience for Piaget. Not only did many of his basic ideas originate at that time, but the experience itself colored his ideas of typical adolescent development years later:

Consider a group of students between 14–15 years and the *baccalaureat* [a French examination taken at the end of secondary school or about 18–19 years of age – translators' note]. Most of them have political or social theories and want to reform the world; they have their own ways of explaining all of the present-day turmoil in collective life. Others have literary or aesthetic theories and place their reading or their experiences of beauty on a scale of values which is projected into a system. Some go through religious crises and reflect on the problem of faith, thus moving toward a universal system – a system valid for all. Philosophical speculation carried away a minority, and for any true intellectual, adolescence is the metaphysical age *par excellence,* an age whose dangerous seduction is forgotten only with difficulty at the adult level. A still smaller minority turns from the start toward scientific or pseudo-scientific theories. . . . Some write down their ideas, and it is extremely interesting to see the outlines which are taken up and filled in in later life. [Inhelder & Piaget, 1955/1958, pp. 340–341]

Now it might be doubted that all adolescents would express their problems of coming of age in such lofty terms, but nearly all of the tendencies described in this passage fit Piaget's own case exactly.

In another passage on the naiveté of adolescent ambitions, the autobiographical reference is even more pointed:

We could also consider the following sample taken from the dozen or so ex-pupils of a small-town school in Rumansch Switzerland. One of them, who has since become a shopkeeper, astonished his friends with his literary doctrines and wrote a novel in secret. Another, who has since become the director of an insurance company, was interested among other things in the future of the theater and showed some close friends the first scene of the first act of a tragedy – and got no further. A third, taken up with philosophy, dedicated himself to no less a task than the reconciliation of science and religion. [ibid., p. 344]

After reading this chapter, the reader will have no difficulty in recognizing that the third of the three classmates described was Piaget himself. The major goal of the young Piaget's life plan was nothing more nor less than the reconciliation of science and religion. A scientific analysis of the principles of organization governing the activities of living things was seen as being capable of providing some answers to questions of ultimate value and the meaning of life.

This was not a privatistic vision, but one that would benefit humanity. The young Piaget's own thinking was characterized by the "Messianism" that he would later attribute to adolescent thought in general. As he put it, "the adolescent in all modesty attributes to himself an essential role in the salvation of humanity and organizes his life plan accordingly" (Piaget, 1964/1967a, pp. 66–67). The mature Piaget believed that this Messianism was a manifestation of adolescent egocentrism, a naive belief in the power of one's own thoughts and ideas to change the world. The decline of this idealistic egocentrism coincided with the young person's entry into professional life.

In attempting to reconstruct Piaget's life plan, we shall follow a method that he recommended himself: "To fully understand the adolescent's feelings, we have to go beyond simple observation and look at intimate documents such as essays not written for immediate public consumption, diaries, or simply the disclosures some adolescents may make of their personal fantasies'' (Inhelder & Piaget, 1955/1958, p. 344). Fortunately, such a document exists, in Piaget's case, in the form of the autobiographical novel already mentioned. We shall discover that he also may have had himself in mind in this statement: ''Sometimes this sort of life program has a real influence on the individual's later growth, and it may even happen that a person rediscovers in his adolescent jottings an outline of some ideas which he has really fulfilled since'' (ibid., p. 344). We begin with Piaget's (1952a) contribution to Boring's *A history of psychology in autobiography*. In this essay, Piaget literally claimed to have ''rediscovered'' in his ''adolescent jottings'' the outline of some ideas that he had since fulfilled.

THE AUTOBIOGRAPHY

Piaget began his contribution to Boring's *History* with the following remark: ''An autobiography has scientific interest only if it succeeds in furnishing the elements of an explanation of the author's work'' (Piaget, 1952a, p. 237). Piaget's short essay succeeded very well in this respect, perhaps even better than its author had intended. The central theme of the autobiography was announced in the second paragraph:

On re-reading some old documents dating from my years of adolescence, I was struck by two apparently contradictory facts. . . . The first is that I had completely forgotten the contents of these rather crude, juvenile productions; the second is that, in spite of their immaturity they anticipated in a striking manner what I have been trying to do for about thirty years. [ibid.]

Piaget took care to distance himself from these ''juvenile productions''; not only did he claim to have forgotten all about them, but he described them in an indulgent and patronizing tone. Despite their ''crudity'' and ''immaturity,'' he nevertheless admitted that they had anticipated the central themes of his professional work. This impression was reinforced in the next paragraph, where he cited a remark by Bergson to the effect that ''a philosophic mind is generally dominated by a single personal idea which he strives to express in many ways in the course of his life, without ever succeeding fully.'' He then made it clear that this principle applied in his own case as well: ''Even if this autobiography should not convey to the readers a perfectly clear notion of what that single idea is, it will at least have helped the author to understand it better himself'' (ibid.). Piaget was perhaps reluctant to provide the reader with a ''perfectly clear notion'' of the single idea animating his work. With the help of some of these same ''juvenile productions,'' however, we shall try to reconstruct it.

Piaget began by describing his childhood in Neuchâtel, his early interest in birds and mollusks, his publication at the age of 10 of an article on the albino sparrow, and his opportunity to assist the director of the Museum of Natural History in Neuchâtel in labeling specimens over a period of 4 years. He expressed the belief that these early experiences in scientific activity had helped protect him against "the philosophical crises of adolescence" that he had experienced beginning at age 15. These crises had been "due both to family conditions and to the intellectual curiosity characteristic of that productive age" (ibid., p. 239). The first crisis he described had been precipitated by his devout mother's insistence that he attend religious instruction, which he had undertaken "with a lively interest but, at the same time, in the spirit of free thinking," inspired perhaps by his father, a religious skeptic for whom "the current faith and an honest historical criticism were incompatible" (ibid.). He had been struck by the irreconcilability of religion and biology and by the "fragility" of proofs for the existence of God. About the same time, he had run across a book in his father's library on the psychological and historical bases of religion by Auguste Sabatier. This book, which treated dogmas as "symbols" and described their "evolution," had been much more to his liking. In his own words: "And now a new passion took possession of me: philosophy" (ibid., p. 240).

His subsequent encounter with the philosophy of Bergson had precipitated a second crisis. Bergson's vision of "creative evolution" had been introduced to him by his godfather, Samuel Cornut, during a vacation at Lake Annecy. It had been the first time he had heard philosophy discussed by someone who was not a theologian, and he had been profoundly shocked.

First of all, it was an emotional shock. I recall one evening of profound revelation. The identification of God with life itself was an idea that stirred me almost to ecstasy because it now enabled me to see in biology the explanation of all things and of the mind itself.

In the second place, it was an intellectual shock. The problem of knowing (properly called the epistemological problem) suddenly appeared to me in an entirely new perspective and as an absorbing topic of study. It made me decide to consecrate my life to the biological explanation of knowledge. [ibid.]

Between biology and epistemology, however, there was a missing link:

Between biology and the analysis of knowledge I needed something other than a philosophy. I believe it was at that moment that I discovered a need that could be satisfied only by psychology. [ibid.]

Inspired by this vision of a biologically based epistemology, Piaget had begun to write. Forced to spend over a year in the mountains because of his health, he had occupied himself by writing the philosophical novel mentioned earlier. The hero of this novel was a French Swiss Protestant youth between the ages of 16 and 20 named Sébastien who was tormented by the conflict between science and religion, a conflict that he also identified as lying at the root of contemporary world problems. The novel described the intellectual and emotional crises ensuing from this conflict, Sébastien's loss of faith, the depression that followed, and his eventual recovery resulting from the discovery of a new "science of types." This new science not only provided a means for resolving the conflict between science and religion but also provided the young Sébastien with a mission in life. The last part of the novel summarized the fundamental principles of the new theory, based on the equilibrium between parts and wholes in biology, psychology, and society itself. This novel, *Recherche*, is described in more detail in the following section.

In recounting this period in his life, Piaget displayed the same ambivalence we have already seen in the opening paragraphs of the autobiography. On the one hand, he distanced himself from the immaturity of these early writings, but on the other hand, he recognized in them certain themes that remained important to him throughout his life:

Now, in reading over these various writings which mark the crisis and the end of my adolescence – documents which I had completely forgotten till I reopened them for this autobiography – surprisingly I find in them one or two ideas which are still dear to me, and which have never ceased to guide me in my variegated endeavors. That is why, however unworthy such an attempt may seem at first, I shall try to retrace these early notions. [ibid., p. 241]

There follows a passage of major importance for the interpretation of Piaget's core-concepts:

I started with a rather crudely conceived essay pretentiously entitled "Sketch of a neo-pragmatism"; here I presented an idea which has since remained central for me, namely, that action in itself admits of logic (this contrary to the anti-intellectualism of James and of Bergson) and that, therefore, logic stems from a sort of spontaneous organization of acts. But the link with biology was missing. *A lesson by A. Reymond* [a professor of philosophy at the University of Neuchâtel] *on realism and nominalism within the problem area of "universals" (with some reference to the role of concepts in present-day science) gave me a sudden insight.* I had thought deeply on the problem of "species" in zoölogy and had adopted an entirely nominalistic point of view in this respect. The "species" has no reality in itself and is distinguised from the simple "varieties" merely by a greater stability. But this theoretical view, inspired by Lamarckism, bothered me somewhat in my empirical work (*viz.*, classification of mollusks). The dispute of Durkheim and Tarde on reality or non-reality of society as an organized whole plunged me into a similar state of uncertainty without making me see, at first, its pertinence to the problem of the species. Aside from this *the general problem of realism and of nominalism provided me with an over-all view: I suddenly understood that at all levels (viz., that of the living cell, organism, species, society, etc., but also with reference to states of conscience, to concepts, to logical principles, etc.) one finds the same problem of relationship between the parts and the whole;* hence I was convinced that I had found the solution. There at last was the close union that I had dreamed of between biology and philosophy, there was an access to an epistemology which to me then seemed really scientific! [ibid., pp. 241–242; emphasis added]

This passage is remarkable for what it reveals about the origins of several ideas that proved to be fundamental in Piaget's later thought. The first idea was that action and logic are intrinsically related, that there is a kind of logic inherent in action, and therefore that logic itself is derived from action. The second idea was that the problem of universals can be translated into a problem of the structure of relational totalities at multiple levels of reality. The same principles of organization may be discovered in biology, psychology, sociology, and epistemology. The originality of Piaget's approach consisted in his conception of these relational totalities in terms of certain characteristic forms of equilibrium. This concept of equilibrium can indeed be counted as a third major idea of the young Piaget that played a decisive role in his later thought:

In all fields of life (organic, mental, social) there exist "totalities" qualitatively distinct from their parts and imposing on them an organization. Therefore there exist no isolated "elements"; elementary reality is necessarily dependent on a whole which pervades it. But the relationships between the whole and the part vary from one structure to another, for it is necessary to distinguish four actions which are always present: the action of the whole on itself (preservation), the action of [the whole on] all the parts (alteration or preservation), the actions of the parts on themselves (preservation), and the action of the parts on the whole (alteration or preservation). These four actions balance one another in a total structure; but there are then three possible forms of equilibrium: (1) predominance of the whole with alteration of the parts; (2) predominance of the parts with alteration of the whole; and (3) reciprocal preservation of the parts and of the whole. To this a final fundamental law is added: Only the last form of equilibrium (3) is "stable" or "good," while the other two, (1) and (2), are less stable; though tending toward stability, it will depend on the obstacles to be overcome how closely (1) and (2) may approach a stable status. [ibid., p. 242; correction based on the original French version in Piaget, 1976a]

The concept of equilibrium was described primarily in terms of a balance between the opposing tendencies of the parts and the whole to preserve themselves and to modify each other. Piaget referred to this balance as a "total structure" (*structure totale*), foreshadowing the later concept of "structure-of-the-whole" (*structure d'ensemble*). It is no wonder that Piaget could write: "I find the re-reading of these old papers extremely interesting, inasmuch as they represent an anticipatory outline of my later research" (Piaget, 1952a, p. 242). For present purposes, these early writings are significant both because they anticipate Piaget's later work and because they make it possible to recover the context in which some of his concepts were originally conceived. This context, as Piaget described it, was closely related to the traditional problem of universals in philosophy and to his personal goal of reconciling science and a concern for ultimate values. In his later works, the original context faded into the background as the concepts themselves were elaborated in other domains. The ambivalence with which he discussed his adolescent crises and the "system" that they engendered is itself suggestive. He admitted that this system had "anticipated" his life's work in a striking fashion, but he seemed willing to admit this only if he could at the same time couple such admissions with assurances that these early writings should not be taken too seriously. Thus, he assured readers on two occasions that he had forgotten all about these documents until he had started to write this autobiography, and he took every opportunity to describe them as "crude," "juvenile," "immature," "unworthy," and "pretentious." One suspects that he protests too much.

Piaget's ambivalence on this score may have been a product of the fact that the resolution of his adolescent crisis as he described it had involved a certain compromise. Clearly, he had retained some of his early ideas only to the extent that he could make them a basis for empirical research. Their more speculative or philosophical aspects he seems to have rejected or repressed. Thus, he wrote at one point that he "always detested any departure from reality" (ibid., p. 238), an attitude that he attributed to his mother's poor mental health. Because of this situation and the "troublesome" family life that it had created, Piaget related how he had given up play activities for serious naturalist pursuits early in life so as "to take refuge in both a private and a non-fictitious world" (ibid.). In another passage, he described how these early scientific activities had helped protect him against the "demon" of philosophy (ibid., p. 239). While working on his doctorate, he had been eager to move to a larger university with a department of psychology where he could carry out experiments to verify his system, adding that as a result of his work in zoology he had "never believed in a system without precise experimental control" (ibid., p. 243). Following an encounter with the ideas of Freud, Jung, and Bleuler, he had decided, after receiving his doctorate in 1918, to abandon his system lest he should fall victim to "autism" as a result of "solitary meditation" (ibid., p. 244). One cannot help feel on reading such comments that the speculative side of his nature must have been very strong to begin with to require such vehement (for Piaget) denials.

The main point is not to speculate on Piaget's conscious or unconscious motives for abandoning his early preoccupation with questions of philosophy and religion. The point is rather to judge the precise manner in which these early preoccupations influenced his later work. There can be no doubt that his model of equilibrium in relational totalities influenced his psychological research in a direct fashion from beginning to end, but the original context of this model is not apparent in his mature work. At one extreme one could argue that his adolescent speculations served at most a heuristic purpose and that once this purpose was fulfilled, they were just as well forgotten. But a thin line separates the healthy renunciation of idle speculation and overcompensation. Another possible interpretation is that Piaget continued all his life to draw inspiration from the personal meanings of his work, but that he kept them on a close rein in order to preserve the personal equilibrium that he had established.

Whatever the truth of the matter, Piaget's abandonment of his adolescent system coincided with his entry into professional life. He perhaps had his own experience in mind in writing about the transition to adulthood:

One should not be disquieted by the extravagance and disequilibrium of the better part of adolescence. If specialized studies are not enough, once the last crises of adaptation have been surmounted, professional work definitely restores equilibrium and thus definitely marks the advent of adulthood. In general, individuals who, between the ages of fifteen and seventeen, never constructed systems in which their life plans formed part of a vast dream of reform or who, at first contact with the material world, sacrificed their chimeric ideals to new adult interests, are not the most productive. The metaphysics peculiar to the adolescent, as well as his passions and megalomania, are thus real preparations for personal creativity, and examples of genius show that there is always continuity between the formation of personality, as of eleven to twelve years, and the subsequent work of the man. [Piaget, 1964/1967a, p. 69][1]

Piaget's entry into professional life and the subsequent development of his thought will be pursued in the following chapter. For the moment, we remain with his adolescence in order to take a closer look at his personal crisis and the philo-

---

1 Recall that at age 11–12 Piaget was assisting in the Museum of Natural History in Neuchâtel and that between the ages of 15 and 17 he experienced his first adolescent crisis.

sophical ideas described in his autobiographical novel. This document fills out the rough sketch provided by Piaget in his autobiography.

RECHERCHE

The title of Piaget's novel, *Recherche,* literally means "search." In another sense, it can also mean "research," as in scientific investigation. It is an appropriate double entendre. In the person of the protagonist Sébastien, the young Piaget presented himself as a seeker after truth and ultimate value.[2] More precisely, he sought a reconciliation between the interests of truth and value as embodied in science and religion, respectively. This conflict was perceived to be at the root of contemporary world problems, as well as being a source of personal anguish. After many trials, a solution was found in the form of a new science of genera (or "types") in which the basic forms of life and knowledge are investigated. This science encompassed what could reasonably be known by the seeker after truth and what could reasonably be hoped for by the seeker after ultimate values. Sébastien found meaning in his own life through investigation of the problems opened up by this new science. The search thus ended in research.

In the remainder of this section, the story line from *Recherche* will be paraphrased. Passages especially relevant for present purposes will be quoted verbatim. Commentary will be deferred until the following section.

The first sentence of the novel expressed the identification of the young seeker with a suffering world:

While the war sustained in everyone's spirits the greatest disequilibrium ever suffered by thought, Sébastien concentrated within himself the pains of this world in labor. [Piaget, 1918, p. 11]

Penetrating the currents of thought that had moved the masses before the war, Sébastien recognized the effects of these ideas in every whirl and eddy of the fray. He had witnessed declines and renewals of faith and had seen how science had infiltrated itself everywhere to put everything in question. He had sympathized with everything, no matter how contradictory, at the risk of ending up with a superficial eclecticism. But the war had revealed a brutal reality: Intelligence had believed itself to guide humanity. Instead, it had been reduced to the service of the passions. To be sure, a few unfettered minds had retained their tolerance and idealism amidst the confusion. But these individuals could do nothing. They searched in anguish, caught in a crossfire:

They were in need of faith and in need of science. But if they attached themselves to the revealed faith, they were condemned to compromises without end that finished by drowning reason in a cloudy mysticism. And if they accepted science, they had to swear allegiance to a whole scholasticism all the more repulsive because, in paralyzing any research daring to be somewhat original, it suffocated the very organ of liberation and truth. [ibid., p. 12]

2 Any doubts about the identity of Piaget and Sébastien are removed in one of the conversations with Bringuier (1977/1980, p. 10).

Sébastien felt a profound pity at the spectacle of general misery. He passed days in solitude, burying himself in despair, and when he could bear it no longer, he burst:

> While being shaken by sobs, he would cry out to his God and compel him, as Jacob had done, to come to his aid in exchange for fulfilling the divine mission of relieving the pain. [ibid., p. 13][3]

Sébastien had diagnosed the problem. At the core of all the "contemporary disequilibrium" was the problem of reconciling science and faith. This was the problem of the century, just as reconciliation of philosophy and religion had been the problem of the 18th century (ibid., p. 21). Faith bestows affirmative value on life, whereas science portrays it as a brute reality in which good and evil, order and disorder, beauty and ugliness are indissolubly mixed (ibid., p. 22). But the answer was not to be found in the dogma of revealed religion. For the truth of that dogma rested on the authority of the Church, and the difficulty was in reconciling revelation with reality (ibid., p. 23). Nor did Protestantism have the solution. For Sébastien, the truth of Protestantism was rendered dubious by its multiplicity of sects, its tendency to individualism, and what Sébastien interpreted as a fatal compromise between Catholicism and liberalism (ibid., pp. 33– 35). In the liberalism of Protestant youth, Sébastien found only an intellectually lazy eclecticism (ibid., pp. 39–41). After examining these alternatives, he was left with the same question with which he had begun:

> Once again the poignant problem of science and religion, the torment of our contemporary generations, presents itself. How to live when our faith is paralyzed by our thought and when our thought is paralyzed by our faith? In the search for truth and the search for value, there are two cults which suffocate each other. They suffocate themselves when they cohabitate the same chapel, they die separately when one isolates them, and when one defeats the other in hand-to-hand combat, the victor retains in his heart a destructive germ that annihilates him little by little. [ibid., p. 41]

Disillusioned by religion, Sébastien turned to philosophy. Examining positivism, pragmatism, and Bergsonism, he rejected them in turn. Only Bergsonism had something unequivocally positive to offer. Bergson had seen that the time had come to reintroduce the study of genera into modern science, but he had not been able to define them within his system (ibid., p. 53). This possibility of a science of genera, however, proved to be Sébastien's salvation.

In the second part of *Recherche,* entitled "The Crisis," Sébastien had a dream in which he relived his whole struggle and was defeated. Little by little he saw the everyday world decomposing before his eyes and his illusions vanishing in the distance. Only the truth remained: a chaos in which tremendous, blind, and fatal forces clashed violently with each other, determining all reality in a hidden manner.

---

3 Years later, Piaget would write of the "Messianism" of adolescence in the following terms: "The adolescent makes a pact with his God, promising to serve him without return, but, by the same token, he counts on playing a decisive role in the cause he has undertaken to defend" (Piaget, 1964/1967a, p. 67).

Awakening from this dream, Sébastien felt an exquisite peace of a sweetness previously unknown. The forces of his being slackened and ceased to combat each other. Suddenly, he realized that he no longer existed; his person had been scattered throughout the Whole. There remained, however, a glimmer of consciousness that regarded the dissolution of the rest of itself. And when the vision was finished, this glimmer of consciousness continued to glow, fed by the memory (ibid., p. 95). It was then that Sébastien received his mission:

Sébastien saw himself again in the little room with the iron bedstead and the white-washed walls, several darkened leaves on the table, a candle causing some shadows to flicker on the bare walls. And he was on his knees before his bed, stretching his whole being toward this unknown God whom he had begun to understand. And, replete with a sacred emotion, he received with happiness but also with dread the divine mission of using his life for reconciling science and religion. [ibid., p. 96]

He began by putting the hints he had gleaned from Bergson regarding the possibility of a science of genera together with his own previous experience as a naturalist.

The problem that served him as a point of departure was that of the species, since that was the question he could treat most easily, having gathered natural history collections throughout his childhood. All disciplines could be reduced to this single point of view. To begin with, all of evolution was contained in the study of the species and with evolution all of the physiological sciences. Next, all of morality, since obligation to duty arises in the relations between the species and individuals. Finally, the same could be said for sociology, esthetics, and even religion. Everything could be reduced to this common center. . . . From the conception of the species from which he had started, he had in fact come to see an organization, that is, an equilibrium between the qualities of the whole and the qualities of the parts, in every living unity and every individual. Every real organization is in an unstable equilibrium, but by the very fact of its existence, it tends toward a total equilibrium which is an ideal organization, just as a crystal misshaped by the rock which encloses it tends toward a perfect form, or again as the irregular trajectory of a star has a regular figure for a law. There is no metaphysics or finality whatever in this conception, since it has to do simply with laws, called ideal because their realization is deferred on account of the obstacle created by other laws. And, around this so simple relation between the real organizations of life and their ideal organization all the human disciplines have come to be crystalized. The ideal organization is the good, the beautiful, the religious equilibrium, and it is toward this organization that morality, art, and mysticism tend, each in a different manner. No more need of philosophy. Science, insofar as it is a science of genera, alone provides itself with the positive foundation of these three manifestations of the spirit. On the other hand, science shows that these organizations, real or ideal, are also the laws of psychology and sociology, and the circle of the knowledge of life is thus closed, resulting in the last analysis in a positive theory of knowledge, which concludes with the incapacity of reason for breaking the circle and descending to the bottom of things. [ibid., pp. 96–99]

This vision of a new science of genera thus provided Sébastien both with a vision of the unity of all life and with a meaning for his own life in the form of a mission.

Still, something was missing. Science, even the new sciences of genera, provided knowledge about the nature of life and values, but it did not and could not in itself give life any value. It provided the means for living, but not the will to live. The problem of value thus remained irreducible and outside science (ibid., pp. 99–100). Sébastien had made progress along the path, but he had not yet arrived at his destination. In order to search for truth, he had to believe in the value of truth, but this faith still eluded him (ibid., p. 102).

Despite these doubts, Sébastien continued the battle with himself. The force that he felt within him was too great to leave him in defeat. In spite of himself, he was dominated by a new enemy in the form of "a terrible need of life" (ibid., p. 104). He would have to conquer this enemy if he wanted to follow his thought. Once again, he felt a chaos of impulsions surging up from the depths of his being without him understanding what it was that made him suffer so. In order to tire his body and to impose some order on the multitude of beings he carried within him, he took to the woods and mountains. It was then that the crisis reached its climax.

Sébastien was following a path along a mountainside dark with giant pines. The dark canopy overhead allowed a few mysterious rays to fall on the forest floor, and the music of the air was slow, solemn, and impassioned in places. Suddenly, he was seized with "brutal life," powerful and fatal. Shaken by a tumultuous force, his consciousness melted bit by bit into matter, uniting him with the All. Filled with a craving for the happiness of living intensely, he was attracted to the abyss of passion and sensation, an exultation that lifts one momentarily outside of time into the darkness of nonbeing (ibid., pp. 104–105).

Suddenly, the path he had been following left the wood and opened onto a valley with patchwork fields and a river flowing along its length. Above it in the distance rose the Alp, immobile and white, a perspective of peace and loftiness, but also of order and hierarchy in place of the dark and fascinating abyss. This immense scale of grandeur transmitted its calm to Sébastien's spirit and reestablished a normal relation of adoration and serene beauty between himself and nature (ibid., pp. 105–106).

Sébastien shuddered at this brusque contrast. It was necessary to choose between these two attitudes, passion or the Good, and to sacrifice the one for the other. Exhausted by the frenzy, he saw in an instant the lie of passion, and in this vision, the will to live, at last victorious, was the only voice to speak. This voice told him that it is mistaken to take passion for an augmentation of life, as if the torrent that overflows its banks does not destroy its own bed at the same time that it devastates the countryside. Instead, passion is a diversion of life that scatters the energies of an individual in one seething instant before extinction and death. The voice bade him further to have courage, to continue the struggle, to fight the good fight, to think, to search, and to extinguish his passion, adding, "You would not have sought me if you had not already found me" (ibid., p. 106).

That proved to be the turning point in Sébastien's crisis. From that point onward, the search itself gave life a value.

In Sébastien's search, there had been the certainty of victory, because every search is a religion [*toute recherche est une religion*]. Every search affirms by its very existence that in life, the universe, and the unknown, there is an absolute value, the source of all values of truth and goodness. If this were not the case, no search would have been possible. [ibid., p. 107]

Sébastien felt the immense joy of renewed faith welling up within him, and with this new faith in the Absolute, a renewed faith in his own mission.

Never had he been so convinced of the value of theoretical research, since by this research alone he had liberated himself from the torments of uncertainty, since by the idea alone he had emancipated his life and opened up his faith. His simmering brain spun out fantastic projects, the construction of a whole survey of the sciences, a progressive synthesis of the sciences of life, an enlarged equivalent of the progression of positive philosophy of Comte and claiming like him to contribute to the public good. [ibid., p. 113]

Thus did Sébastien's search for truth and value end in scientific research. In the idea of equilibrium he had found the key for reconciling science and religion, truth and value. Truth was to be distinguished from reality. Truth was an ideal equilibrium toward which all real disequilibria were striving. Truth was an ideal and was not to be found within reality as such. All real disequilibria tended toward an ideal equilibrium. And this ideal equilibrium was truth, biological truth as well as moral, esthetic, and religious truth. This insight had all the more force in Sébastien's eyes because it took cognizance of his orientation in biology (ibid., pp. 114–115). He realized that the life of a thinker requires the sacrifice of action and passion, but he took great joy in his new-found vocation.

The third and final part of *Recherche* is entitled "The Reconstruction" and consists primarily in a more detailed exposition of Sébastien's ideas regarding the new science of genera and its application in various areas of life. Psychology is the starting point. For example, the equilibrium of genera explains how distinct sensory qualities can be united in the perception of individual objects:

There could be no consciousness of these qualities, thus these qualities could not exist, if there were no relations between them, if they were not fused together within a total quality that contains them even while maintaining them distinct. For example, I could be conscious neither of the whiteness of this paper nor the blackness of the ink, if the two qualities were not fused in my consciousness in a certain whole, and if, despite this whole, the one did not remain white and the other black, respectively. . . . The originality of equilibria between qualities lies entirely in this: that there is equilibrium not only between the discrete parts, like that which alone obtains in material equilibria of whatever kind, but between the parts on the one hand, insofar as they are distinct and original qualities, and a whole on the other hand, insofar as it is the quality of the ensemble resulting from the partial qualities. [ibid., pp. 151–152]

The difference between purely mechanical equilibria and the equilibrium of genera is that in the former the whole is the additive result of the individual forces of which it is composed, whereas in the latter the whole constitutes a force in its own right, over and above whatever individual forces may be at work. This distinction results in two modes of scientific activity: the mode of "laws" and the mode of "genera." Whereas the mind of the physicist proceeds from the part to the whole, the genus forces the mind to proceed from the whole to the part. The reality of the whole as a force in itself gives the genus an appearance of finality, although it is not so in fact (ibid., pp. 151–153).

But the equilibrium of genera is not limited to the level of psychology. In fact, it characterizes the form of organization of all living things:

One after the other, organic chemistry has overcome the barriers that formerly separated life and matter. Nothing remains but to define life as assimilation, source of all organization. By the very fact that it lives, the living being assimilates, that is, reproduces substance identical to itself. It therefore has a stable and independent quality of the whole. On the other hand, in assimilating, it submits to the influence of the substances that it assimilates, to the environment in other words, and as such it shows variations, a certain heterogeny that constitutes qualities of the parts. [ibid., p. 155]

This organic equilibrium of genera may be described in terms of four laws, which according to the author ''govern all of biology.''

Briefly, these laws may be summarized as follows: According to the *first law,* every organization tends to preserve itself as such. This law follows from the definition of the whole as a quality existing in its own right, above and beyond the qualities of its parts. The first form of equilibrium results when the respective qualities of the parts and the whole are mutually compatible such that they tend to preserve each other. According to the *second law,* however, the environment tends to disrupt the unity of the first form of equilibrium and forces the organism to submit incessantly to new influences. This tendency represents a second form of equilibrium in which the qualities of the parts are no longer compatible with those of the whole, such that parts and whole tend to preserve themselves at the expense of the other. But this second form of equilibrium may lead to a third form, described by the *third law*: When the qualities of the parts and those of the whole are not compatible with each other, parts and whole may act on each other to modify one another. The third form of equilibrium arises when this action of the parts on the whole allies itself with the inherent tendency of the whole to preserve itself, such that it preserves itself by undergoing certain modifications. The *fourth law* is the most important of all. According to this law, all forms of equilibrium tend toward the first, characterized by mutual preservation and reciprocity between the parts and the whole. The first form thus constitutes an ideal equilibrium toward which all real equilibria tend. In effect, the organization of all life is characterized by unstable equilibria that are continuously modified by contact with the environment, but nevertheless tend toward stability even as they are modified by the environment (ibid., pp. 156–158).

One important example of such organization in biology is the relation between individual organisms and the species to which they belong. In this case, the individuals constitute the parts, and the species the whole, and evolution can be described as the progression toward stable equilibrium between the two. This approach makes it possible to reconcile Lamarck and Darwin and to deduce the known laws of biology. But the workings of equilibria are not governed by an ensemble of final causes, and a system does not pursue a predefined goal when it tends toward equilibrium. The conception of evolution in terms of equilibria is therefore not teleological (ibid., pp. 158–159).

Such a conception of the organization of life is the only conception of psychology that can be rigorously experimental while at the same time taking into account the manifestations of mind considered by metaphysical psychologies. For example, James's idea of the stream of consciousness can be interpreted as an incessant disequilibrium of qualities constantly altered by new influences producing new qualities that nevertheless preserve the old (ibid., pp. 160–161). With respect to the fundamental laws of thought, the tendency of organization to preserve itself can be viewed as the origin of the principle of identity and, by implication, the principle of noncontradiction. Likewise, the principle of sufficient reason follows from a form of organization in which the parts are preserved in their union with the whole (ibid., p. 163). As for the question of values, the only absolute value we can know is the affirmation of life. The absolute itself may be beyond our understanding, but we are linked to it by the will to live. The value of living is a direct product of the organization inherent in life. The affirmation of this value is a faith in itself (ibid., pp. 166–168).

The social order can also be interpreted in these terms. In this case, society is the whole, individuals are its parts, and morality is the equilibrium between them (ibid., p. 169). Evil may thus be equated with disequilibrium of one kind or another – either favoring society at the expense of individuals or individuals at the expense of society (ibid., p. 177). This moral equilibrium is also reflected at the individual level, for one is an equilibrium between one's own adaptation and one's realization of the social equilibrium (ibid.). One's duty is to realize a personal equilibrium, because the latter itself implies a consideration of one's relationships with others (ibid., p. 179). The two major obstacles to realization of this personal equilibrium are egoism and passion, for both tend toward an overvaluation of a part (either the self or another person) in relation to the whole (ibid., pp. 178–182). The sentiment of beauty is a sense of being in harmony with the ideal equilibrium, and in this respect it reveals its kinship with morality (ibid., pp. 185–188).

These reflections bring the discussion back to the problems of religion from which it began. The objective aspect of religion is identified with the sacrifice of individual interests for the realization of the ideal equilibrium in the social order (ibid., pp. 190–191). Because this ideal equilibrium is that of a perfect being that can be only partially realized at a given time, it is both immanent in the world and transcendent at the same time (ibid., p. 196). It is immanent as a potential that can be more or less approximated in reality; it is transcendent as an ideal that is never realized in its entirety. Only in the experience of conscience, in which individual interests are subordinated to the ideal, does the absolute value become fully incarnate in the world (ibid., pp. 199–201).

With these considerations, the task of reconciling science and religion is accomplished (ibid., p. 202). The new science of genera is based on biology and psychology, but it also provides a solid foundation for questions of ultimate value and meaning in life. Only a brief discussion of the relevance of this synthesis for the social good remains. The laws of equilibrium as applied to the social order suggest certain possibilities for social reform. The general direction of these reforms may be described by the terms "socialist cooperation" and "world federation." Both bourgeois individualism and statist collectivism are to be condemned for the different forms of disequilibrium that they represent:

The bourgeois regime is abnormal and iniquitous in not assuring in any manner the equilibrium between the good of individuals and that of society. A certain privileged class forms unto itself a common whole that alone absorbs the means of life vested in the ensemble. And, at the very center of this new partial unity reigns the disequilibrium among individuals, each of whom is concerned only with himself and his family.

The collectivist regime based on the suppression of private initiative sins by the opposite excess. The whole takes on terrible proportions.

In contrast, cooperation conforms to the ideal equilibrium. It involves a centralization of capital not by the state, but by private initiative, and in such a way that it gives to those who cooperate a share of the returns for their labor. Individual autonomy thus appears to be safeguarded. [ibid., p. 210]

With this program, *Recherche* reaches its conclusion:

We have sought to take into account the most pressing problem among those posed by the war, that of the moral personality of societies. For it is in Humanity alone that we can commune with each other in our various undertakings: It alone reconciles science and religion. [ibid.]

COMMENTARY

Recherche is indeed a revealing document, both for what it says about its author and for what it reveals about the origins of his ideas. To begin with the author, one sees in this account of crisis and recovery the origins of Piaget's professional identity. His solution of the crisis points toward a life of scientific activity, and absorption in his work leads to his recovery. But to label *Recherche* merely as the story of an adolescent identity crisis is a trivial assimilation to a preexisting scheme. It adds nothing to the excruciating detail in which the crisis is retold. What is interesting is how Piaget/Sébastien's own notion of stable equilibrium as applied to human personality considered in its totality appears to foreshadow Eriksonian notions of *ego identity*:

My personality, for example, tends to preserve its partial qualities (the believer, the philosopher, etc.), just as the latter tend to preserve the former. [ibid., p. 154]

In these same terms, the form of unstable equilibrium in which the parts preserve themselves at the expense of the whole correspond to Erikson's (1968) concept of *identity confusion*. Indeed, the incompatibility of Sébastien's partial selves ("the believer, the philosopher, etc.") was what precipitated the crisis in the first place.

Similarly, one need not be a psychohistorian to see in this account the signs of awakening sexuality. They are most apparent at that point in the narrative at which Sébastien's crisis reaches its climax. Walking through a dark wood, he is seized with a Dionysian vision of "brute life." His description of this experience is filled with barely concealed sexual imagery. He is "dominated by a terrible need of life," "a craving for the happiness of living intensely," "an attraction for the abyss of passion and sensation.'' But this vision of the abyss is abruptly replaced by the Apollonian splendor of an Alp rising majestically in the distance, the vision of order and serenity. For Sébastien, these two visions are incompatible. It is necessary to choose, and the choice is clear. The beauty of order and rationality is preferred to the frenzy of passion, now seen as a squandering of vital energy and a prime source of disequilibrium.

This interpretation is reinforced a few pages later in a passage comparing the man of action with the seeker and the place of love in the lives of each:

Action implies an acceptance of love, the search an abstinence from it, for it introduces the egoism that is the distinctive feature of all passion. The contact of two beings which destines them for marriage does not occur without a disguised contraction that only action can legitimate. From the egoism which is at its source, love can then become the absolute gift of self in harmony with the sacrifice for the sake of divine value, while for seekers the giving of oneself to a woman is in contradiction with this sacrifice. Those who are given to action place moral value in the acceptance of reality, the seekers in the rejection of reality; that is the whole difference. For the former, love can become the faith of which Amiel speaks, the faith that begets faith; for the latter, love is never only loss of consciousness and a search for personal happiness.

This is the meaning of that poignant *Kreutzer Sonata* where Tolstoy puts his finger on the problem: "sexual love is only the sign of the nonfulfillment of the law." For he understood that law is outside reality. Some are created for the accomplishment of this law – the chaste, the isolated, those who are dedicated to truth; others introduce it into reality – the pure-hearted ones, those who are confined to reality. To conclude bluntly, there are two categories: those "who are made eunuchs for the kingdom of heaven" and those who mind the concerns of the species. [Piaget, 1918, pp. 118–119]

It is hardly surprising to find evidence of some preoccupation with emerging sexuality in an account of adolescence; it would be more surprising if that were *not* the case. But the connection between this typical adolescent concern with problems of life and love and the intellectual content of this narrative is of primary interest in the present context.

Piaget/Sébastien portrayed passion as a prime source of disequilibrium. This is why at the decisive moment he decided against it. One is tempted to see a continuity between the adolescent Piaget's decisive choice of the Apollonian over the Dionysian and the direction of his later work. Although there is a place in the Piagetian system for affect, passion, and other such "disequilibrating" influences, a manifest preference for order and stability can also be discerned. This preference is reflected not only in Piaget's theoretical emphases but also in the subjects to which he devoted most of his attention. He clearly preferred to study areas such as logic and mathematics in which the development of stable structures could be demonstrated most unambiguously. He never ceased to acknowledge the importance of affect and other forms of motivation in personal development, but he simply did not spend much time on these topics, relative to the others. Still, as he perhaps would have agreed, the logic of his own theory demands disequilibrating as well as equilibrating forces. Only through continual disequilibration can the individual transcend the partial and incomplete equilibria that establish themselves along the path toward the ideal equilibrium. Disequilibrium thus appears in the ambivalent guise of Goethe's spirit that negates, which in attempting to do evil, always ends by doing good. In the logic of the theory itself, Sébastien's strict dichotomy between Dionysian and Apollonian forms of love might be too extreme.[4]

For present purposes, the major interest of *Recherche* lies in what it suggests about the origins of Piaget's ideas. The starting point was the young Piaget's concept of genera. In a revealing passage, he linked his own view of evolution in the new science of genera with the problem of universals in Greek philosophy:

> This conception of evolution was above all that of the Greek science of genera. The distended equilibrium of which we just spoke is the series discerned by Plato, the indefinite repetition of the same type that is the Idea, whereas the intensive equilibrium is the genus or Form of Aristotle! One sees in this way how the biologist Aristotle had gone straight to the extreme type of "genera," while the mathematician Plato remained with an intermediate type between pure logic and vitalism. [ibid., p. 159]

His own view was more Aristotelian than Platonic. In his emphasis on ideal equilibrium, Piaget might seem to approach a developmental Platonism. But the ideal equilibrium does not exist apart from its contents, or, rather, it exists only as an organizing *tendency*. In this, it would appear to resemble Aristotelian conceptions of potentiality or formal causality, except that the progression toward ideal equilibrium is not teleological. The outcome is not determined in advance, but by present tendencies in interaction with new qualities continuously introduced by the external environment. One might even conjecture that the ideal equilibrium toward which a given genus tends could itself change under the influence of these external factors.[5]

Likewise, the young Piaget's science of genera represented a significant departure from most treatments of the problem of universals in modern philosophy. As genera, universals became a topic for scientific investigation. In traditional terms, Piaget was both a conceptualist and realist of sorts. On a psychological level, genera exist within the mind in the form of conceptual systems. On a biological level, genera also exist in reality in the form of organic systems. Moreover, a direct continuity exists between the two. Piaget's lifelong dream

---

4 Piaget himself, or at least his unconscious, may have reached a similar conclusion. In *Play, dreams and imitation in childhood,* he cited as an example of "condensation" in dream symbolism a transparently autobiographical dream from his university days that harkened back to the rather extreme distinction between carnal and spiritual love and linked this dichotomy to the problem of genera as manifest in biology: "Take for example the case of a student of natural science dreaming of two birds and wondering whether they were two quite distinct species or merely two varieties of the same species. The presence in the dream of someone who disagreed with his conclusion showed that his preoccupation arose from an earlier situation in which a college friend maintained that the only difference between physical and ideal love is one of degree, while he supported the opposite view" (Piaget, 1945/1962, p. 210).

5 Piaget's idealism and his identification of evolutionary progress with the Good is already expressed in his prose-poem *La mission de l'idée* (Piaget, 1916). Although this work further demonstrates the religious and ethical inspiration of his early thinking, it antedates the "basic ideas" regarding action, structure, and equilibrium found in *Recherche* that were to play such an important role in his later work.

was to trace the continuity of development from the most basic forms of biological organization to the highest forms of conceptual thought. The implications of Piaget's view for traditional philosophical issues involving the problem of universals are treated in greater detail in chapter 8.

The evidence of *Recherche* is also valuable in regard to Piaget's sources. In particular, Bergson looms much larger in these pages than one would have been led to believe from Piaget's other writings. In his autobiography, Piaget described how disappointing he found Bergson when he actually came to read him and how his inspiration for the idea of a science of genera came from listening to a lecture on the problem of universals by A. Reymond at the University of Neuchâtel. In *Recherche,* both the conception of genera and the idea of equilibrium are traced back to Bergson:

Sébastien, who had always been enthused by Bergsonism, did not accept any of its particular theses, while believing himself to continue its profound logic. He was Bergsonian without the concept of duration, which is the high point of Bergsonism. . . . He delighted above all in the manner in which this philosophy had sketched a possible rehabilitation of the Greek genera. Bergson had indeed brilliantly understood that the moment had come to reintroduce genera into modern science. All of his psychology shows the effects of this ulterior motive. His biology, which remains quite superficial and verbal, supports the same interpretation.

Only Bergson had not defined the genus, and one does not see how he could have done it without altering his system rather seriously. All the work thus remained to be done, and moreover, it was much more of a scientific than a philosophical nature. Aristotle, the genius of genera, was a biologist: It is by biology that the edifice must be built. [ibid., p. 53]

With respect to the concept of equilibrium, "Our definition of equilibrium is only an advanced Bergsonism" (ibid., p. 161).

One can easily imagine how the mind of the young Piaget, already steeped in naturalism and plagued by the conflict between science and religion, could have been enthused by his first encounter with the ideas of Bergson. And one can also imagine his disappointment when he discovered that this unifying vision of life was not based on a solid scientific foundation. Possibly, the vision of the new science of genera did not in fact occur to Piaget until he heard Reymond lecture on the problem of universals, but much of the inspiration for this idea clearly came from Bergson, either the real philosopher or the one the young Piaget had constructed in his imagination. Anyone sufficiently familiar with Piaget's writings cannot help but experience a certain shock of recognition in glancing through the pages of Bergson's *Creative evolution*. One encounters not only the idea of genera in psychology and biology but also several other typically "Piagetian" notions:

The ancients, indeed, did not ask why nature submits to laws, but why it is ordered according to genera. The idea of genus corresponds more especially to an objective reality in the domain of life, where it expresses an incontestable fact, heredity. Indeed, there can only be genera where there are individual objects; now, while the organized being is cut out from the general mass of matter by [its] very organization, that is to say naturally, it is our perception which cuts inert matter into distinct bodies. It is guided in this by the interests of action, by the nascent reactions that our body indicates – that is, as we have shown elsewhere, by the potential genera that are trying to gain existence. In this, then, genera and individuals determine one another by a semi-artificial operation entirely relative to our future action on things. [Bergson, 1907/1944, pp. 248–249]

As this passage suggests, the typically "Piagetian" idea that human cognition is ultimately derived from action may also be found in Bergson. Action is the source of our knowledge of both objects and space:

Originally, we think only in order to act. Our intellect has been cast in the mould of action. [ibid., p. 50]

Our perceptions give us the plan of our eventual action on things much more than that of things themselves. The outlines we find in objects simply mark what we can attain and modify in them. [ibid., pp. 206–207]

The idea that [the mind] forms of *pure* space is only the *schema* of the limit at which this movement would end. [ibid., p. 221]

Finally, one finds in *Creative evolution* arguments for a biologically based approach to the theory of knowledge – a theme that Piaget would make very much his own:

Theory of knowledge and *theory of life* seem to us inseparable. A theory of life that is not accompanied by a criticism of knowledge is obliged to accept, as they stand, the concepts which the understanding puts at its disposal: it can but enclose the facts, willing or not, in pre-existing frames which it regards as ultimate. It thus obtains a symbolism which is convenient, perhaps even necessary to positive science, but not a direct vision of its object. On the other hand, a theory of knowledge which does not replace the intellect in the general evolution of life will teach us neither how the frames of knowledge have been constructed nor how we can enlarge or go beyond them. It is necessary that these two inquiries, theory of knowledge and theory of life, should join each other, and, by a circular process, push each other on unceasingly. [ibid., pp. xxiii-xxiv]

To point out certain resemblances between the ideas of Piaget and those of Bergson is not to attempt to reduce the one to the other. Whatever ideas Piaget may have found at Bergson's door were developed in a manner all his own. In particular, Piaget provided a scientific and empirical basis for notions that were purely speculative in Bergson's writings. The relation between the two thinkers is aptly summarized in *Recherche*: While not accepting any of Bergson's particular theses, Piaget continued the "profound logic" of Bergson's thought (Piaget, 1918, p. 53).

CONCLUSION

In this chapter, the evidence from *Recherche* has aided in reconstructing the origins of some of Piaget's basic ideas. The remainder of this book will be devoted to an exposition of their subsequent development in his thinking. Three ideas in particular have been identified as stemming from his early philosophical system: first, the idea that action lies at the basis of thought, but that action itself is characterized by a certain logic, or structure; second, the idea of genera as relational totalities underlying organization at all levels of life, from the cell to the highest levels of human thought and society; third, the idea of equilibrium as the dynamic form of development at all levels. One is astonished to think that these ideas animated Piaget's work from beginning to end, although they were conceived before it ever occurred to him to investigate cognitive development in children!

In the next chapter, Piaget's entry into professional life in the early 1920s will be reviewed, along with his early work published during the course of that decade. The unifying theme of this phase was the investigation of children's thinking and its particular structure. Although Piaget claimed in his autobiography to have abandoned his philosophical system on entry into professional life, he continued to develop and apply some of its basic ideas. In addition, he continued to be interested in problems of morality and religion, as evidenced by several publications on these topics (Piaget, 1922a, 1928a, 1929a, 1930, 1932/1965a), also examined in the next chapter.

2

The investigation of children's thinking

After Piaget received his doctorate in 1918 with a dissertation on the mollusks of Valais (Piaget, 1921a), he traveled to Zürich, where he visited Lipps's and Wreschner's psychological laboratories and Bleuler's psychiatric clinic. In his autobiography, he described the excitement awakened in him by the prospect of psychological experimentation: ''I felt at once that there lay my path and that, in utilizing for psychological experimentation the mental habits I had acquired in zoölogy, I would perhaps succeed in solving problems of structures-of-the-whole to which I had been led by my philosophical thinking'' (Piaget, 1952a, p. 243). But the experiments of Lipps and Wreschner seemed to him to have little relevance for the problems he considered fundamental. The contact with Bleuler had more lasting influence in that it brought Piaget into contact with the theories of Freud and Jung. But Bleuler had a more immediate influence on Piaget as well: ''The teachings of Bleuler made me sense the danger of solitary meditation; I decided then to forget my system lest I should fall a victim to 'autism' '' (ibid., p. 244).

In the fall of the following year, Piaget left for Paris, where he would spend 2 years at the Sorbonne. Among the courses he attended during this period were lectures on the philosophy of science by L. Brunschvicg, whose psychological orientation and historical-critical method would exert a lasting influence on him, as attested by the many references to Brunschvicg in Piaget's writings on the epistemology of science. By far the most significant event in Piaget's Paris period, however, was his encounter with Simon, an encounter that first steered Piaget toward child psychology. Simon had Binet's laboratory in Paris at his disposal, but was unable to make use of it because he was living and teaching in Rouen at the time. Instead, he made it available to Piaget for the purpose of standardizing Burt's tests of reasoning on a sample of Parisian schoolchildren. Until this time, Piaget had possessed only a very general theoretical system and a desire for experimentation, but he had lacked a concrete area of investigation. Although he had no great enthusiasm for the task of standardizing Burt's tests of reasoning, the experience provided him with what he needed. The investigation of children's thought and reasoning henceforth became his problem area.

By assimilating Burt's methods to his preexisting notion of structure, Piaget transformed the task that Simon had set for him into something quite different:

Now from the very first questionings I noticed that though Burt's tests certainly had their diagnostic merits, based on the number of successes and failures, it was much more interesting to try to find the reasons for the failures. Thus I engaged my subjects in conversations patterned after psychiatric questioning, with the aim of discovering something about the reasoning process underlying their right, but especially their wrong answers. I noticed with amazement that the simplest reasoning task involving the inclusion of a part in the whole or the coordination of relations of the "multiplication" of classes (finding the part common to two wholes), presented for normal children up to the age of eleven or twelve difficulties unsuspected by the adult. [ibid., p. 244]

Piaget continued his research in the elementary school associated with Burt's laboratory for 2 years without, as he put it, Simon being quite aware of what he was doing. Already at this early stage in his career, he had the good fortune to find a method appropriate to the theoretical ideas that he had already developed:

At last I had found my field of research. First of all it became clear to me that the theory of the relations between the whole and the part can be studied experimentally through analysis of the psychological processes underlying logical operations. This marked the end of my "theoretical" period and the start of an inductive and experimental era in the psychological domain which I always had wanted to enter, but for which until then I had not found the suitable problems. Thus my observations that logic is not inborn, but develops little by little, appeared to be consistent with my ideas on the formation of the equilibrium toward which the evolution of mental structures tends; moreover, the possibility of directly studying the problem of logic was in accord with all my former philosophical interests. [ibid., p. 245]

The research that Piaget conducted during his stay in Paris was described in three articles published between 1921 and 1923. Given his theory of part–whole structures, it comes as no surprise that the first of these articles – his first published report of original psychological research – was devoted to children's conceptions of the part (Piaget, 1921b). In this paper, Piaget described children's answers to some of Burt's tests, such as the following:

Jean says to his sisters: "Part of my flowers are yellow." Then he asks them what color his bouquet is. Marie says: "All your flowers are yellow." Simone says: "Some of your flowers are yellow." And Rose says: "None of your flowers are yellow." Which of them is right? [Piaget, 1921b, p. 450]

Piaget found that children between the ages of 10 and 14 tended to answer this question incorrectly, but their answers were nevertheless systematic. In particular, their answers could be classified into three categories that in turn could be ordered into the following stages: (a) Children ignored the quantifiers in each sentence, implicitly translating the statement "Part of my flowers are yellow" as "My flowers are yellow." Thus, Marie and Simone were held to be equally correct in their answers. (b) Children took notice of the quantifiers, but explicitly equated the part (Jean's statement) with the whole (Marie's statement). Further questioning suggested that children answering in this way understood the phrase "part of my flowers" as being equivalent to "my part of the flowers," where the part is understood merely as a quantity of flowers or as a part of some unspecified whole. (c) Children understood the quantifiers in the respective sentences, but momentarily forgot one or the other of them. The role of momentary distraction in producing this type of incorrect answer was indicated by the fact that when reminded of Jean's use of the word "part," children immediately answered the question correctly.

Several other aspects of this first psychological research report from Piaget are worth mentioning. To begin with, the classification of children's responses into developmental stages is familiar from his later works. But a slight difference also exists. With the purely verbal method that he was using then, he questioned individual children repeatedly with respect to the same problem and often reported a succession of stages *within the series of answers given by a single child*. Indeed, he used the responses of one child to illustrate all three stages. In a series of five "readings," Tard (10 years, 3 months) began at stage one, progressed to stage two, and gave one answer suggestive of stage three, only to slip back to stage two when pressed (ibid., pp. 450–452). This example indicates that from the beginning, Piaget's stages were meant as a classification of forms of thinking, not of individual children. In his later work he rarely questioned children repeatedly with respect to the same problem, and so this distinction can easily be overlooked.

The second aspect of this early paper worthy of special attention is Piaget's effort to explain the "parallelism" between the logical and psychological factors in children's reasoning. To the logical errors described in the paper correspond certain failures of attention:

Tachistoscopic experiments and the analyses of Bergson have shown that sentences are read and understood, not in detail, but straightaway as a whole [*en bloc, d'une seule venue*]. In this regard, the phenomena of narrowness in the field of attention are primary: It is in part because of these phenomena that we could characterize the three stages of our classification. Attention cuts up the totality of sentences in pieces that the logical forms have to assimilate as such. There is thus a relation of antecedent to consequent between the forms of the attentional field and the logical forms. But there is a reciprocal effect, since as we insisted above with respect to the implicit stage, the forms of the attentional field are patterned after logic itself. Each attentional field is of such a configuration that the corresponding logical form could assimilate the maximum content. The logical form thus collaborates in expanding the attentional field while attention works to constitute new logical forms. [ibid., pp. 479–480]

This passage is interesting for two reasons. First, it shows how Piaget applied Bergson's dictum that thought proceeds from the whole to the part to a concrete psychological problem. Children's conceptions of wholes are not divided into parts from the beginning; rather, their attention divides things into units that are not yet related to each other as parts to wholes. The parallel between logic and attention is the second reason why this passage is of interest, for it foreshadows later attempts to relate the development of the structures described by Piaget to attentional processes.[1]

1 Piaget's (1921b, 1923b) remarks on this topic suggest that he recognized a relation of *reciprocal implication* between children's attentional field and the logical form of their reasoning. In contrast, contemporary "neo-Piagetian" theorists (Case, 1985; Halford, 1982; Pascual-Leone, 1970, 1984) have argued that an age-related developmental increase in the capacity of children's attention is a *causal* factor in cognitive development.

The connection between logical form and the field of attention was elaborated by Piaget (1923b) in a study of children's reasoning on a verbal test of transitivity derived from C. Burt (i.e., "Edith is fairer than Olive, but she is darker than Lily. Who is darker – Olive or Lily?"). In the conclusion to this article, Piaget argued that children tend to approach this problem in terms of classes or predicates instead of relations because of the relative narrowness of their field of attention. The "breadth" of this field is described in terms of "the number of objects capable of being simultaneously associated in the field of attention, whatever the form of this association" (Piaget, 1923b, pp. 169–170). In context, the phrase "the number of objects" clearly refers to the *objects of attention,* not merely to physical objects.

The second article originating from his work in Binet's laboratory also dealt with part–whole relations in the form of logical multiplication. In this paper, Piaget studied children's ability to understand that one part can be common to two wholes (Piaget, 1922b). The third paper cited by Piaget (1952a) as stemming from the Paris period was devoted to a comparison between children's thinking and the "symbolic thought" of psychoanalysis (Piaget, 1923a).[2] According to Piaget's account, he sent this article to Claparède for publication in the *Archives de Psychologie* – whereupon the latter offered him a position as "director of studies" at the Institut J.-J. Rousseau in Geneva. This position not only gave him access to excellent research facilities but also allowed him the freedom to pursue his interests. The only problem, as he wrote in his autobiography, was that he did not yet know how to do research. That turned out not to be a problem.

Piaget took up his new post at the Institut J.-J. Rousseau in 1921. In his autobiography, he wrote that he had planned at that time to spend 2 or 3 years more investigating children's thinking and then turn to the origins of mental life in infancy. Armed with knowledge of the elementary structures of intelligence, he would then be in a position to attack the problem of thought in general in the form of a biologically and psychologically based epistemology. For the moment, however, it was necessary to forget any nonpsychological considerations and follow his empirical investigations of children's thinking wherever they might lead him.

Reality unfolded in broad outline according to this plan – although, as many other young researchers have also discovered, everything took somewhat longer than expected. Piaget devoted the next 4 years to the investigation of children's thinking, applying and extending the methods he had developed during his apprenticeship in Paris. This research, carried out with the help of more than 20 collaborators (including Valentine Chatenay, the future Mme. Piaget), provided the basis for his first four books: *The language and thought of the child* (1923/1955), *Judgment and reasoning in the child* (1924/1928b), *The child's concep-*

---

2 Actually, this article was based on research conducted at the Institut J.-J. Rousseau (Piaget, 1923a, p. 276). Perhaps Piaget meant to refer to "Une forme verbale de la comparaison chez l'enfant" (Piaget, 1923b) in this connection. The latter paper did in fact derive from the Paris period and appeared in the same volume of *Archives de Psychologie* as the paper on symbolic thought.

tion of the world (1926/1973b), and *The child's conception of physical causality* 1927/1966a). The first two of these books were devoted to a consideration of the form and function of children's thinking, and the latter two were devoted to its content. In the following sections, the contents of these early works will be reviewed in thematic fashion. *The moral judgment of the child* (1932/1965a), a fifth book also based on research dating from this period, is discussed later in the chapter.

FORM AND FUNCTION IN CHILDREN'S THINKING

The language and thought of the child

In Claparède's preface to *The language and thought of the child,* the eminent psychologist and director of the Institut J.-J. Rousseau compared Piaget's psychological work with the latter's research in biology and zoology. Just as Piaget the biologist had collected, classified, and labeled specimens of mollusks from the lakes of the Valaisian Alps, so had Piaget the psychologist collected, classified, and labeled examples of children's thinking in the Maison des Petits of the Institut J.-J. Rousseau. The comparison is illuminating. In his later works as well, Piaget's ordering of children's performances into stages can indeed be compared to a Linnaean labor of classification. Contrary to some later interpretations of his theory, his stages were from the beginning more taxonomic than explanatory. And if the classification of children's performances can be compared to the classification of biological species, his attempts to identify processes such as decentration or equilibration governing development from one stage of thought to another can be compared to biologists' attempts to identify the functional processes underlying the evolution of species.

The language and thought of the child contains examples of both descriptive classification and functional explanation. Piaget was first of all concerned to classify examples of children's speech according to function. Two major categories of child language may be distinguished: *egocentric* and *socialized.* Given the importance that the conception of egocentrism would assume in Piaget's early works, his original definition of egocentric speech is worth quoting:

When a child utters phrases belonging to the first group [i.e., the category of egocentric speech], he does not bother to know to whom he is speaking nor whether he is being listened to. He talks either for himself or for the pleasure of associating anyone who happens to be there with the activity of the moment. This talk is ego-centric, partly because the child speaks only about himself, but chiefly because he does not attempt to place himself at the point of view of his hearer. Anyone who happens to be there will serve as an audience. The child asks for no more than an apparent interest, though he has the illusion (except perhaps in pure soliloquy if even then) of being heard and understood. He feels no desire to influence his hearer nor to tell him anything: not unlike a certain type of drawing-room conversation where every one talks about himself and no one listens. [Piaget, 1923/1955, p. 32]

Three general types of egocentric speech were observed: (a) *repetition (echolalia)* – children repeated words and syllables they heard with no apparent effort to communicate with others or even in every case to make sense; (b) *monologue* – children talked to themselves without addressing anyone, as though they were thinking aloud; (c) *collective monologue* – the presence of another person served as a stimulus for utterances about ongoing thought or action, but children did not take into consideration the point of view of the other nor make any effort to determine whether or not they were heard or understood. In contrast, socialized speech took the following forms: (a) adapted *information* – children exchanged their thoughts with others, variously to influence the others' actions, to argue with them, or to collaborate in the pursuit of a common goal; (b) *criticism* – children's speech was directed to particular hearers, but its content was more affective than intellectual, generally meant to assert the superiority of the self and to deprecate others; (c) *commands, requests, threats* – children tried to influence the actions of others through the medium of language; (d) *questions* – attempts to acquire information from others; (e) *answers* – responses to others' questions or commands.

Piaget's major finding was that before the age of seven, a substantial part of children's speech was given over to egocentric speech but that the percentage of egocentric language dropped off sharply at about the age of seven or eight. In an analysis of the spontaneous conversations occurring in a class of 20 children averaging 6 years of age, a full 45% of the language used was egocentric in character. Moreover, these conversations could be classified into four progressive stages. *Stage I* consisted of collective monologues, as defined earlier. *Stage II (first type)* consisted of conversations in which the hearer was associated with the speaker's action and thought in some way, but no real collaboration occurred between them. *Stage II (second type)* consisted of conversations in which children collaborated with respect to action or nonabstract thought. *Stage III* consisted of conversations in which children collaborated with respect to abstract thought. Parallel stages could be defined for the development of arguments between children, ranging from mere quarrels (Stage II, first type) through primitive arguments (Stage II, second type) to genuine arguments (Stage III). Genuine arguments were distinguished from primitive arguments by the presence or absence of children's attempts to justify their assertions. With respect to both collaboration and argument, Piaget found that Stage III did not appear before 7–8 years of age.

The assertion that egocentric speech declines around age 7–8 years, however, does not imply that it disappears entirely. "It goes without saying that the child, as he passes through stages IIA and IIIA, does not relinquish the conversation of the earlier stages. Thus a child who has reached stage IIIA will still indulge in occasional monologues, etc." (ibid., p. 74). Piaget took it for granted that the utterances of individual children could be classified at different stages, indicating that the stages were intended to classify children's utterances, not the children themselves. Nor did Piaget suggest that individual children should begin to collaborate at the Stage III level at the same time they begin to argue at the level of Stage III. Rather, the assertion that egocentrism declines at the age of 7–8 years means that children *in general* first give evidence of more mature forms of thought and language at this age.

In another study included in *The language and thought of the child,* Piaget investigated the extent to which children understood each other when they did speak to each other. The technique was the following: The experimenter told a simple story to one child, who was then asked to communicate the same story to a second child. The second child was then questioned about the content of this twice-told tale. In this way, one could determine what the first child had retained from the experimenter's original version as well as what the second child had understood of the first's retelling. The results indicated that children understood the experimenter somewhat better than they understood each other and that there was an increase in understanding of both types from age 6–7 years to age 7–8 years. Piaget interpreted the failure of communication in both instances as another manifestation of egocentrism.

But egocentric thought was not described by Piaget as purely individualistic or asocial. Children retelling a story do not forget that they are trying to communicate with others; they simply do not differentiate their own point of view from the other's point of view. They think that what they themselves understand will automatically be understood by the other:

If children fail to understand one another, it is because they think they do understand one another. The explainer believes from the start that the reproducer will grasp everything, will almost know beforehand all that should be known, and will interpret every subtlety. [ibid., p. 116]

As such, egocentric thought represents a kind of intermediate form between *autistic thought,* which is composed primarily of private symbolism, and *communicated intelligence* (or *socialized thought*), in which the perspectives of others begin to be differentiated from that of the individual (ibid., pp. 64ff.).

In the fourth chapter of *The language and thought of the child,* Piaget compared children's egocentrism with the phenomenon of *syncretism,* identified by previous psychologists as characteristic of children's thinking. Defined by Renan as an activity of the mind in which "no distinction is made and things are heaped one upon the other" (ibid., pp. 144–145), syncretism referred fundamentally to a globality or lack of differentiation in thought and perception. Claparède had studied syncretistic perception in young children, as illustrated by the ability of a 4-year-old to recognize the printed music belonging to different songs from the global appearance of the title and page (ibid., p. 144). Similarly, linguists had found that sentences are recognized as units of language before words (ibid., p. 145). For Piaget, these were all examples of the general tendency of thought to proceed from the whole to the part, rather than the reverse. The idea of such a tendency Piaget inherited in part from Bergson, and in fact cited Bergson in his discussion of syncretism:

This movement of thought from the whole to the part is a very general one. It will be remembered how this point was emphasized by M. Bergson in his criticism of associationism. *"Associationism,"* he said, *"is not the fundamental fact; it is by *dissociation* that we begin, and the tendency of every memory to gather others around it can be explained by a natural return of the mind to the undivided unity of perception." [ibid., p. 145]

The reader informed by *Recherche* will recognize in this passage another of Piaget's attempts to express the intuitions of his early "system" in psychological terminology. The syncretism of children's thinking became the psychological embodiment of his Bergsonian intuition that thought proceeds from the whole to the part.

According to Piaget, egocentrism as the nondifferentiation of perspectives is a kind of syncretism of immediate observation. Following the decline of egocentrism at 7–8 years, a residue of syncretism is retained at the level of verbal intelligence. Two forms of syncretism may be distinguished at this level: the *syncretism of reasoning* and the *syncretism of understanding*. The former occurs when two sentences are seen to be related not because of any logical connection between them but only because they can both be subsumed under a single general scheme. The latter occurs when the meaning of either of the two sentences is distorted or elaborated in order to make it fit the general scheme. These forms of syncretism were investigated by giving children proverbs and a list of sentences, from which they were to pick one expressing the meaning of the proverb. As an example of syncretistic reasoning, Kauf (8 years, 8 months) connected the proverb "When the cat's away, the mice will play" with the sentence "Some people get very excited and never do anything." His reasoning was as follows: Some people get excited and never do anything, because they are too tired, just as cats get tired after chasing chicks or hens (ibid., p. 149). As an example of syncretism of understanding, Vau (10 years, 0 months) identified the same sentence ("Some people get very excited and never do anything") with the proverb "To each according to his works." This identification was based on the fact that Vau did not know the phrase "according to" and understood it as "coming to." In effect, he understood the two sentences taken together as expressing the thought that a group of people came to their work, but some of them never did anything.

The last chapter of *The language and thought of the child* is an investigation of a child's spontaneous questions. Over a period of 10 months, the spontaneous "whys" asked by a 6–7-year-old boy in daily conversations with the experimenter were noted and later classified. Perhaps the most important result of this study was the identification of a type of thinking that Piaget called *precausality*, characterized by a confusion between strictly causal explanations and explanations based on psychological motivation. Like egocentrism, precausality was found to decline after the age of seven. When the subject of this study, aged 7 years, 2 months, was addressed with questions he had asked himself some months before, he regarded many of them as "silly," as not making any sense because they were "so easy."

Addressing the same questions to a group of 7–8-year-old children, Piaget obtained precausal explanations as well as answers in which causal and logical forms of explanation were differentiated. One such question, for example, was the following: "Why is there a great and a little Salève?" (referring to the mountains near Geneva). Precausal answers included the following: "[The little one is] for children, and the great one for grown-ups," and "Because of people who want to go into the little or to the great one" (ibid., pp. 229–230). In the following answer, however, precausality would appear to have been overcome: "There were two mountains stuck close together, so people said that one was to be the Great Salève, and the other the Little Salève." Piaget would return to the investigation of precausality in *The child's conception of physical causality.*

In the final paragraphs of *The language and thought of the child,* Piaget attempted to provide a functional explanation of the development from precausal to more differentiated forms of explanation. He cited with approval a long passage by Claparède to the effect that the classification of different forms of judgment into *categories* is of little interest to psychology compared with identification of their functional origins. According to Claparède's "law of conscious realization," children are not likely to become conscious of the categories of thought until there occurs some failure of adaptation that forces them to reflect on factors that up until then had possessed only a functional existence. With respect to the problems of explanation, Piaget interpreted this "law" in terms of the formula "The child is cause before having any idea of cause." With respect to Piaget's own approach to functional explanation in psychology:

The study of categories is, as M. Claparède rightly maintains, a study of functional psychology, and vast new horizons are opened to it by the law of conscious realization. Here the psychologist meets on common ground with the historian of science and the modern logician. Traditional logic, whether we take the realism of the Schools or Kant's apriorism, regarded the categories as fixed, and imposed on the mind and on things once and for all, and in a definite form. This hypothesis is psychologically false, and has been brilliantly attacked by William James at a period when logicians themselves had begun to abandon it. Renouvier and Cournot have given to the theory of categories a turn which it is no exaggeration to characterize as psychological, since the task they have set themselves is to define the categories according to their genesis in the history of thought and to their progressive use in the history of the sciences. . . . From this angle the problem of categories must therefore be formulated in connexion with the intellectual development of the child himself. The genetician will therefore have to note the appearance and use of these categories at every stage of intelligence traversed by the child, and to bring these facts under the functional laws of thought. [ibid., pp. 232–233]

Piaget's functional explanation of the development of categories of thought may be summarized as follows: Around the age of three, children begin to reflect on the resistances posed by other people and things with respect to their own actions and desires. The first "whys" begin to appear at about this same time and are concerned almost entirely with intentionality – why people do things. As yet, there is no differentiation between objective causality and human agency such that children project intentionality outward into the relations between physical objects. This outward projection of intentional explanation Piaget called the *explicatory function,* and so long as intentional and causal explanation are not differentiated, it is one of the main sources of precausality in children's thinking. As subject and object become differentiated, however, the explicatory function leads to the development of the categories of causality, reality, time, and place. Parallel to the explicatory function, but directed inward toward reflection on one's own actions and intentions, is the *implicatory function*. With the differentiation of subject and object, the implicatory function leads to the categories of classification, names, number, and logical relations. Finally, a *mixed function* of explication and implication leads to the categories of the motivation for actions and the justification of rules.

These remarks on the categories of thought can be viewed as a tentative attempt on Piaget's part to translate his early philosophical intuition of genera into current psychological concepts. Such an attempt is indicated, among other things, in the proposal to investigate traditional problems of logic and epistemology from a functional psychological point of view. This project was now firmly embedded in his study of child development. Similarly, the formula "The child is cause before having any idea of cause" was a rather elliptical statement of Piaget's neo-pragmatist notion that thought develops from action. As agents, children experience themselves as causes before they are capable of reflecting on causality or of distinguishing the latter from human agency. Finally, the distinction between the "explicatory" and "implicatory" functions was perhaps the first appearance in Piaget's published writings of the notion that knowledge of the physical world develops by abstraction from the external consequences of actions, whereas knowledge of logic and mathematics develops by abstraction from the coordinations among actions themselves. All of these themes were developed further in Piaget's subsequent works.

Judgment and reasoning in the child

If *The language and thought of the child* had the character of an exploratory work in which theoretically important questions were identified, *Judgment and reasoning in the child* took those questions and pursued them more systematically. The first book ended with a classification of children's questions, and the second began with an analysis of their explanations. Where Piaget had earlier investigated children's use of the interrogative "why," he now turned to a consideration of the conjunction "because."

Children's use of "because" was studied both in spontaneous utterances of individual children, as described in *The language and thought of the child,* and in a sentence-completion task of this form: "A man fell off his bicycle, because . . ." The latter task was administered both individually and collectively to a large number of children between the ages of 6 and 10. Briefly, children's spontaneous use of "because" or "since" was found to increase with age and to be inversely related to the percentage of egocentric speech used by the individual child. These conjunctions were used to express causal, logical, or psychological (motivational) connections, of which psychological connections were by far the most frequent among children between three and seven. Both children's spontaneous speech and the sentence-completion task suggested that logical justification generally appeared only around the age of 7–8 years, the same age at which egocentric speech had previously been found to decline.

Before this age, "because" and "since" were often used to link thoughts that were semantically related, but not connected by any causal or logical relation. In the sentence-completion task, for example, children might say that the man fell from his bicycle *"because he broke his arm,"* or *"because afterwards he was ill and they picked him up in the street"* (Piaget, 1924/1928b, p. 17). It seemed clear in such examples that "because" was used in the same way as "and" or "then" might have been used: merely to link successive thoughts together, rather than to subordinate the one to the other in a causal or logical relation. This tendency Piaget called *juxtaposition,* and he compared it to what Luquet had called "synthetic incapacity" with respect to children's drawings (ibid., pp. 3–4). In each case, young children seemed unable to relate individual parts with one another to form an integral whole. In drawings, for example, children could reproduce the various parts of the human body, but had difficulty in relating them to each other in a coherent manner. In logical or causal explanation, individual thoughts were linked with each other in a successive manner, but were not related to each other as parts of a causal or logical scheme.

So defined, juxtaposition appeared to be the exact opposite of the syncretism that Piaget had found characteristic of young children's thinking in his previous book. Whereas syncretism represented a tendency to think or perceive in terms of wholes without taking into consideration the parts of which they were composed, juxtaposition represented a temporal linkage of individual thoughts that never added up to form a larger whole. One of the central questions in *Judgment and reasoning in the child* was how both of these antithetical tendencies could characterize children's thinking at the same time (ibid., p. 4).

As Piaget saw it, there was no contradiction. Both tendencies represented an inability to comprehend the *relations* between parts and wholes at the level of representational thought. Thus, children's thinking tended either to be grouped into global schemes or to be fixated on individual details; what was missing was the means for moving back and forth between them. In fact, juxtaposition and syncretism corresponded, respectively, to the two forms of unstable equilibrium described in *Recherche.* Juxtaposition represented the form of equilibrium in which the parts predominated over the whole, and syncretism the form in which the whole predominated over the parts.

We have now reached the point when we can ask what relation this phenomenon of juxtaposition bears to that of syncretism, . . . which seems to be its exact opposite. In visual perception, juxtaposition is the absence of relations between details; syncretism is a vision of the whole which creates a vague but all-inclusive schema, supplanting the details. In verbal intelligence juxtaposition is the absence of relations between the various terms of a sentence; syncretism is the all-round understanding which makes the sentence into a whole. In logic juxtaposition leads to an absence of implication and reciprocal justification between the successive judgments; syncretism creates a tendency to bind everything together and to justify by means of the most ingenious or the most facetious devices. In short, in every sphere, juxtaposition and syncretism are in antithesis, syncretism being the predominance of the whole over the details, juxtaposition that of the details over the whole. How are we to account for this paradox?

In reality these two features are complementary. As soon as perception, even in the adult, fails to analyse an object, whether on account of its novelty or its complexity, we see the two phenomena reappear. On the one hand, because of its insufficient discrimination of detail, perception creates a vague and indistinct general schema, and this constitutes syncretism. On the other hand, through having failed again to discern a sufficient amount of detail, perception cannot make the insertions and relations sufficiently precise, and this constitutes juxtaposition. The predominance of the whole over the parts or that of the parts over the whole is in both cases the result of the same lack of synthesis, synthesis being in a manner the principle of equilibrium between the formatory tendency of the schemes and the analytical tendency. [ibid., pp. 58–59]

Given the fact that syncretism and juxtaposition were both forms of thinking characterized by an insufficiency of logical relations, it made sense that Piaget should continue his investigation of children's thinking by studying the development of relational thought directly. The point of departure for this inquiry was the Simon-Binet absurdities test; children were read an absurd sentence and asked to explain why it made no sense. In several instances, the absurdity consisted in the fact that a relation was taken as a substantive, as in the sentence "I have three brothers: Paul, Ernest, and myself." This test was administered to 40 children between the ages of 9 and 11–12, and in a variation on the Simon-Binet procedure, children between 4 and 12 were asked about their own siblings.

As Piaget pointed out, solving this test presupposes that relations of *appartenance* – that is, the relations between the individual and the group of brothers of which he is a part – are differentiated from the relations existing among the brothers *as individuals*. Moreover, these two types of relations must be coordinated within a single problem. In general, the children tested did not solve this problem correctly until the age of about 11–12. Until then, they tended to emphasize one or the other of these types of relations to the exclusion of the other.

In one frequent type of answer, children did not count the narrator in the three-brothers test as a brother. Rather, the existence of only two brothers (sisters) was recognized. (Example: *"She has two sisters, she has, she's not a sister."* . . . *"Why is she not a sister?"* *"Because she is a little older than the others."* – ibid., p. 75.) In effect, the child recognized relations between the narrator as an individual and her two sisters, but did not recognize relations of appartenance between the narrator and the whole group of sisters. In another type of answer, the order was reversed: Relations of appartenance were recognized to the exclusion of relations among individuals. Thus, children would admit that there were three brothers in the family, but saw nothing wrong with the fact that the narrator counted himself as one of his brothers. (Example: *"You could have said: Paul, Ernest, and myself are my three brothers."* – ibid., p. 77.) Similar results were obtained when children were asked about their own brothers and sisters.

Several other examples of children's reasoning about relations were also investigated, including their ability to provide definitions of family and country.

Children's conceptions of nationality, for example, provided more evidence about the development of children's understanding of appartenance. Briefly, Piaget found that the understanding of country developed according to the following three stages: First, the country (e.g., Switzerland) was considered as existing alongside cities and districts; one could not be both Genevan and Swiss at the same time. Second, the country was understood as surrounding the towns and districts, without including them; Genevans still were not considered to be Swiss. Finally the correct relation was discovered; towns and districts were recognized as belonging to the country, and Genevans were necessarily Swiss as well.

In the last two chapters of *Judgment and reasoning in the child,* Piaget attempted to draw some general conclusions from the material presented in his first two books. First, he pointed out with a few examples that even when children are capable of providing correct answers to simple logical or arithmetical problems, they are generally unable to give introspective or retrospective explanations of how they arrived at those answers until they reach an age at which they also become capable of justifying those answers with rational arguments. This argument, incidentally, provides an early defense of Piaget's use of logical justifications as criteria for attainment of the respective developmental stages. For Piaget, ''understanding'' did not simply mean the ability to give a correct answer, for he recognized that correct answers could be generated in a variety of ways. The decisive questions were how and to what extent children could explain their answers.

Next, Piaget turned to a consideration of children's definitions. From his own results, as well as those of Simon and Binet, he concluded that before the age of 7–8 years, children tend to define things in terms of their uses (e.g., a mother is someone who cooks dinner). Only after the decline of precausality around this age do children begin to give definitions in terms of genus and specific difference (e.g., a mother is a lady who has children). But even then, until the age of 11–12, children tend not to give exhaustive definitions, focusing instead on the respective genus or some particular feature without generalizing. Piaget suggested that this is because of the difficulty of being simultaneously conscious of the several elements that must be synthesized in order to construct the definition. Thus, one child defined living things in terms of activity and the fact of having blood (ibid., p. 154), but he was unable to bring these two factors into relation with each other. Instead of considering them *simultaneously,* he simply applied each term *alternatively* (ibid., p. 157). This same tendency is responsible for the prevalence of contradictions in children's thinking. Because children are unable to bring contradictory judgments into relation with each other, they tend either to forget one judgment as they pass to the next (''contradiction by amnesia'') or simply to assimilate the subject matter to contrary categories without being able to resolve the opposition (''contradiction by condensation'') (ibid., pp. 164–169).

In contrast, logical thought recognizes the impossibility of simultaneously affirming contradictory propositions. But, Piaget asked rhetorically, What is the psychological equivalent of this logical principle? In the psychology of the individual, as in other natural phenomena, one can recognize antagonistic tendencies. At the level of logical thinking, such contrary tendencies manifest themselves as contradictions, as can be observed in the frequently self-contradictory character of child thought. The question is how the elimination of contradiction in logical thinking can be explained in psychological terms. According to Piaget, the contradictions characteristic of child thought constitute a form of psychological disequilibrium, and the principle of noncontradiction characteristic of logical thinking constitutes a form of equilibrium:

Non-contradiction is a state of equilibrium in contrast to the state of permanent disequilibrium which is the normal life of the mind. For, as every one knows nowadays, sensations, images, pleasure and pain, in short all the "immediate data of consciousness" are borne along on a continuous "stream of consciousness." Exactly the same thing applies to the immediate data of the external world; they constitute Heraclitus' eternal becoming. A certain number of fixed points stand out in contrast to this flux, such as concepts and the relations subsisting between them, in a word, the whole universe of logic, which in the very process of its formation is independent of time and consequently in a state of equilibrium. . . .

But this is only a rough approximation to the facts. It is not true to say that notions are immobile. Every idea grows, finds fresh application, becomes generalized and dissociated. . . . The balance we are trying to determine therefore presupposes something permanent, but it cannot be defined as the absence of all movement; it is a "moving equilibrium." [ibid., pp. 170–171]

The reference to the "immediate data of consciousness" (les données immediates de la conscience) is an allusion to a title from Bergson, and the equation of the stream of consciousness with a permanent disequilibrium in the life of the mind echoes a similar passage from Recherche.

The significant thing about this passage is not that flashes of Piaget's earlier philosophical intuitions should recur in his psychological works; rather, it is the way in which he fleshed out these early intuitions in psychological terms. In Recherche, he had already described the principle of noncontradiction as a form of psychological equilibrium. He now characterized this equilibrium in terms that would play a lasting role in his psychological theory. The reversibility of the psychological operations involved is what constitutes the psychological equilibrium corresponding to the logical principle of noncontradiction:

A non-contradictory operation is a reversible operation. This term must not be taken in the logical sense which is derivative, but in the strictly psychological sense. A mental operation is reversible when, starting from its result, one can find a symmetrically corresponding operation which will lead back to the data of the first operation without these having been altered in the process. . . . If I divide a given collection of objects into four equal piles, I can recover the original whole by multiplying one of my quarters by four: the operation of multiplication is symmetrical to that of division. Thus every rational operation has a corresponding operation that is symmetrical to it and which enables one to return to one's starting-point. Contradictions may therefore be detected in the irreversibility of any particular process, in the fact that no exactly symmetrical relation could be found whereby to control the original operation. [ibid., pp. 171–172]

In effect, this notion of reversibility enabled Piaget to bridge the gap between psychological processes, which like all natural phenomena occur in time, and logical operations, which are essentially atemporal. As the remarks quoted earlier make clear, reversibility is essentially a *simultaneous symmetry of possible operations*. Psychological processes that are reversible in this sense *can* be reversed in sequential time, but *need* not be. In nonreversible processes, a given state can be immediately succeeded by its opposite, with no connection between them. According to Piaget, this condition characterizes autistic, or nondirected, thinking, and, to some extent, the egocentric thought of children as well. Psychological processes are reversible, however, to the extent that successive moments in those processes are linked together such that in the passage from one state to another, the first state is not lost, but retained as a simultaneous *possibility* that could *potentially* be reinstated. Only because successive moments are linked together in consciousness in this way can the subject recognize when a given state has been succeeded by its contrary. And only then can the subject also eliminate them according to a regulative principle of noncontradiction.

But this raises a further question: ''What are the conditions to which the mental operations will have to be submitted in order to be really reversible?'' (ibid., p. 173). In order to answer this question, Piaget introduced two further notions that would also play a lasting role in his psychological theory:

The thought of the child, like every other kind of thought, is swayed by two fundamental interests whose interaction is precisely what determines this reversibility. These are *imitation* of reality by the organism or the mind, and *assimilation* of reality by the organism or the mind. [ibid., p. 173]

Psychologically, imitation is defined in terms of the mind's ability to reproduce or represent external events or phenomena. To the extent that these events or phenomena occur in time, imitation would already seem to imply a linkage between their successive moments. Mere imitation of such a process is not yet reversible. Only when the representation of one moment in the process is assimilated to the representations of succeeding moments does reversibility become possible. But even assimilation of present representations by previous ones is also insufficient to produce reversibility. Instead, reversibility can be achieved only through a balance between assimilation and imitation.

For Piaget, assimilation referred to a primitive recognitory activity. In assimilating elements of the environment, the organism recognizes them as assimilable. Moreover, those elements are treated as functionally identical with respect to their assimilability. In other words, assimilation alone does not entail a recognition of specific differences among the elements assimilated. For this reason, assimilation alone does not lead to reversibility. If representations of the moments of a temporal process were merely assimilated to each other, the specific *changes* that occurred from one moment to the next would not be recognized. Something of the sort happens in the case of syncretism in children's thinking. Sentences or thoughts are simply assimilated to each other or to some prior scheme, without consideration for their specific differences in meaning. Piaget called this aspect of assimilation "deforming." The element assimilated is "deformed" to the extent that its specific character is disregarded. (On the antecedents of Piaget's concept of assimilation, see Ducret, 1984.)

In contrast to this deforming nature of assimilation, imitation involves a consideration of the specific character of the phenomena imitated. This is why a balance between assimilation and imitation is necessary for reversibility. By itself, assimilation is capable of recognizing only the "eternal recurrence of the same." And imitation by itself can represent only a succession of states, without any continuity between them. Through imitation, the organism recognizes the specific character of temporal changes, and this recognition of change leads to reversibility when representations of successive moments are brought into relation with each other through assimilation. If assimilation without imitation leads to syncretism, imitation without assimilation leads to juxtaposition. Together, they make possible the continuity in change necessary for reversibility.

Expressed in this way, assimilation and imitation can be identified as the functional organismic processes corresponding to the two unstable forms of equilibrium described in *Recherche*. Assimilation alone is the predominance of the whole (in the form of a preexisting schema) over the parts (the elements assimilated), and imitation alone is the predominance of the parts (the elements imitated) over the whole (the relations among those elements). Syncretism and juxtaposition are the expression of these general functions in the specific case of children's thinking. The introduction of the notion of reversibility in *Judgment and reasoning in the child* represented Piaget's first attempt to find a psychological equivalent for the stable form of equilibrium described in *Recherche,* in which the actions of the parts and the whole balance and support each other.

The lack of a reversible equilibrium in children's thinking is also responsible for the fact that they appear to be unable to coordinate judgments involving universals and particulars:

Children's reasoning, in short, does not move from universal to particular (All voluminous objects make the water rise, therefore this pebble makes the water rise because it has volume), nor from particular to universal (This piece of wood has volume and raises the water; this pebble is smaller and raises the water less, therefore all voluminous objects raise the water-level), but from particular to particular: this pebble makes the water rise because it is heavy, therefore this other pebble will also do so because it too is heavy; this piece of wood will make the water rise because it is large, this one will therefore do so because it is also large, etc. To each object belongs a special explanation and consequently special relations which can only give rise to special reasoning. [Piaget, 1924/1928b, p. 184]

In contrast to logical thinking, characterized by deduction (reasoning from universal to particular) and induction (from particular to universal), Piaget followed W. Stern in labeling children's reasoning from particular to particular a form of *transduction*. Logical thought is characterized by a reversible equilibrium, because it is thus possible to move back and forth between universal and particulars (i.e., the whole and the parts), but transductive reasoning is nonreversible in the sense that this movement back and forth is not possible.

This formula enabled Piaget to describe the global stages in the development of children's thinking in the following way. Up until the age of 7–8 years, children reason primarily in a nonreversible, transductive manner. From 7–8 to 11–12, their reasoning is characterized by a partial reversibility that is applicable, however, only to premises given in direct observation. From 11–12 onward, children's reasoning is no longer limited to actual reality, but may also be applied to imagined, or hypothetical, situations. These stages may also be described in terms of increasing reversibility:

In conclusion, we may say that the first stage of childish reasoning is that of primitive or irreversible mental experiment, that the second is distinguished by a beginning of reversibility in the mental experiments, and that the third stage is marked by the appearance of formal deduction and logical experiment, the latter alone being capable of rendering the mental experiments completely reversible. Or again, we can say that during the first stage the reasoning mind does no more than to "imitate" reality as it is, without reaching any necessary implications; during the second stage the mind "operates upon" reality, creating partly reversible experiments and thus reaching the consciousness of implication between certain affirmations and certain results; finally, in the third stage, these operations necessitate each other in the sense that the child realizes that by asserting such and such a thing he is committing himself to asserting such and such another thing. He has at last attained to necessary implication between the various operations as such, and to a complete reversibility of thought. [ibid., pp. 194–195]

These three stages clearly prefigure Piaget's later distinction between preoperational, concrete operational, and formal operational stages in children's thought.

In the preface to the third French edition of *Judgment and reasoning in the child* from 1947, Piaget answered some early criticism of this stage scheme and anticipated many later ones by admitting that his results, and in particular the ages associated with the stages described, were relative to the methods used. This had never been in doubt. He had himself always asserted that there would be a developmental lag between children's action and their verbal reasoning. A demonstration that a certain form of reasoning developed earlier in the context of action than in a verbal context would not contradict results using verbal methods, for two very different realities are involved:

When one opposes the facts contained in this little book with other facts that appear to contradict them, the question becomes one of not mixing up the levels in the hierarchy of conduct or development. What would one say of a discussion in embryology in which, to an author showing that the development of the epidermis is incomplete, another observer replies that the mesoderm has already attained such a degree of differentiation? Everyone would agree in recognizing that the two theses are compatible and that the disputants are simply not talking about the same reality. It is exactly the same in genetic psychology, and between the levels constituted by sensorimotor intelligence, intuitive representation, concrete operations, and formal operations, the same differences exist as between the successive stages of embryology. But current psychology ignores the distinctions and treats intelligence in its formation according to the model of developed logic. [Piaget, 1924/1978a, pp. 9–10]

The controversies surrounding Piaget's global stages of cognitive development will be discussed in greater detail in chapter 7. For the moment, we continue our review of his early works. Whereas *The language and thought of the child* and *Judgment and reasoning in the child* were both devoted to the general form and functioning of children's thinking, the next two books, *The child's conception of the world* and *The child's conception of physical causality,* were focused on a consideration of its specific content.

CONCEPTIONS OF REALITY AND CAUSALITY

The child's conception of the world

In the introduction to *The child's conception of the world,* Piaget contrasted his so-called clinical method of questioning and counter-questioning with the methods of testing and direct observation. For the purpose of discovering the natural inclinations of child thought, testing has the following disadvantages: (a) It tends to neglect the context of children's thinking through a stereotyped question format. (b) It does not provide an opportunity for counter-questioning, thus making it difficult to distinguish between answers based on genuine conviction and answers influenced by the particular form of the question (Piaget, 1926/1973b, p. 15). Direct observation avoids these difficulties, but has disadvantages of its own: (a) As a consequence of children's egocentrism, they might not attempt to communicate their thoughts spontaneously, believing themselves to be understood already by those around them. (b) It is difficult, by merely observing children's spontaneous behavior, to distinguish their real beliefs from mere play.

The clinical method is an attempt to preserve both the systematic character of testing and the naturalism of direct observation. In contrast to the stereotyped method of testing, the clinical method allows the possibility for counter-questioning based on children's original answers, thereby providing more opportunity for distinguishing between genuine and suggested answers. In comparison with direct observation, the clinical method provides a context in which the natural tendencies of children's thinking are actively elicited. The remainder of the introduction to this book is devoted to explaining the rules and criteria used in the clinical method for distinguishing between answers based on genuine conviction and answers generated according to chance, spontaneous fantasy (''romancing''), or suggestion.

The book itself is an extended description of three general tendencies in children's thinking: realism, animism, and artificialism. *Realism* is the consequence of the relative nondifferentiation between the self and the external world in child thought. Specifically, it refers to children's tendency to grant objective reality to inherently subjective phenomena. *Animism* is the tendency to attribute to nonliving things some of the qualities properly reserved for living beings. As such, it represents a relative nondifferentiation between animate and inanimate nature.

Artificialism is the tendency to assume intentionality and finality in the origins of all natural phenomena. It thus represents a nondifferentiation between human creative activity and natural causes.

Piaget described the realism of children's thinking with respect to three areas: the notion of thought itself (intellectual realism), the relation between names and things (nominal realism), and the reality of dreams. With respect to thought, for example, three stages were distinguished: In the *first stage,* for which the average age was 6 years, thought was identified with the voice and was accordingly believed to take place in the mouth. In the *second stage,* around the age of eight, thinking was believed to occur in the head, but was still materialized in the form of an internal voice. Alternatively, thought was identified with air or blood. Finally, in the *third stage*, developing around the age of 11–12, thought was no longer materialized. In a stage-two answer that Piaget likened to the Platonic doctrine of recollection, one 8-year-old girl described memory as a little piece of skin that God filled with stories before she was born (ibid., p. 68).

Similarly, three stages were distinguished in the decline of realism with respect to the origin of names. In the *first stage* (age 5–6), children believed that names were located in the things themselves and that the names of things came to be known simply by looking at them. During the *second stage* (age 7–8), children thought that names were created by the makers of things (either God or the first humans), that we have learned the names of things from these personages, and that names have no particular location. In the *third stage* (age 9–10), names were recognized as having been invented by human beings, as having been handed down from generation to generation since the time they were invented, and as located in the voice, the head, or thought itself. In the first two of these stages, children tended to deny that things could exist before having a name. One child stated explicitly that something that did not exist could not possibly have a name!

The decline of realism with respect to dreaming was also described in terms of three successive stages. In the *first stage* (5–6 years), children believed the dream to come from outside and to take place externally, within the room. During the *second stage* (7–8 years), they believed that dreams originated in the head, but still took place in the room. During the *third stage*, dreams were recognized not only as having an internal origin, but also as occurring within the head. In response to direct questioning, one 5-year-old denied outright that dreaming occurred in the head: *"It is I that am in the dream: it isn't in my head(!) . . . When you dream, you don't know you are in bed. You know that you are walking. You are in the dream. You are in bed, but you don't know you are"* (ibid., p. 121).

Piaget compared children's realism with the "participation" that Lévy-Bruhl believed to characterize the magical thinking of so-called primitive peoples. According to Lévy-Bruhl's usage, "participation" is a relation recognized as existing between things that nevertheless have no spatial contact, nor any intelligible causal connection. Although Piaget believed that such magical participation could also be found in children's thinking, he acknowledged that the origins of such participation could be much different in the child as compared with the savage (ibid., p. 157). In particular, four kinds of magical participation could be found in children's thinking: (a) between actions and things, (b) between thought and things, in the form of omnipotent thinking, (c) between individual objects, in the form of magical "correspondence," and (d) between purposes and things, in the form of animism. Examples of each of these types of magical participations were described. Although Piaget adopted the idea of participation from Lévy-Bruhl, "participation" was also one of the ways in which Plato described the relationship between individual things and eternal forms. Thus, there is a certain resemblance between the participation characterizing children's realism and that characterizing Platonic realism; both may be said to involve the reification of concepts.

With respect to the animism of children's thinking, four stages were distinguished: In the *first stage,* life and consciousness were attributed to everything. *Second,* they were attributed only to things that move. In the *third stage,* they were attributed only to things that move of themselves. *Finally,* consciousness was attributed only to animals, and life to animals and plants. Another consequence of children's animism was a tendency to explain the regularities of nature with an appeal to moral necessity. Thus, one 8-year-old stated that the moon cannot choose not to come out at night, *"because it's not it who gives the orders"* (ibid., p. 256). Piaget found that this tendency persisted to about the age of seven or eight, after which age various combinations of moral necessity and physical determinism were observed.

With respect to artificialism, Piaget again found three stages. In the *first,* natural phenomena were ascribed to human (or Divine) agency. In the *second,* there was a mixture of natural and artificial explanations; clouds come from smoke, for example, but the smoke is produced by human beings. *Finally,* a purely natural explanation appeared. These same three stages were found in children's explanations for the origins of the sun, moon, and stars, the sky, night and day, clouds, thunder and lightning, rain, snow, bodies of water, trees, mountains, and the earth. But although the same three stages apply to all these contents, Piaget made it clear in a passing remark that he did not believe children should necessarily be at the same stage for all contents at the same time: "Of course, a child is not necessarily in the third stage at the same time for the stars, the sun and the moon. In general, it seems that a natural explanation of the stars is the first to appear" (ibid., p. 313). Given the fact that many contemporary psychologists believe that Piaget's stage-developmental theory necessarily implies synchrony in development in different areas of content, this remark acquires greater significance than its incidental character would suggest. Even at this early point in his own development, Piaget took it for granted that children could give answers at different levels, even with respect to such closely related contents as the origins of the sun, moon, and stars. The question of synchrony of development in current discussions of Piagetian theory will be discussed in chapter 7.

The child's conception of physical causality

In the discussion of artificialism in *The child's conception of the world,* Piaget was concerned primarily to describe children's ideas about the origins of natural phenomena. In *The child's conception of physical causality* (Piaget, 1927/1966a), he turned his attention to children's explanations of causal relations. The first section of this book was devoted to explanations of movement – the movement of the air, of wind and breath, the movements of clouds and the heavenly bodies, water currents and the effects of gravity, children's ideas of force. In the second section, predictions and explanations regarding the floating of boats, water levels, and the nature of shadows were examined. The third section describes the development of children's explanations for the functioning of machines – bicycles, the steam engine, trains, automobiles, and airplanes. For each individual inquiry, children's explanations were classified and, insofar as the material permitted, ordered according to stages. Sometimes three, sometimes four, and sometimes five stages were distinguishable. In one case, children's definitions of force, no stage development at all was noticeable. This variability of results is indicative of the fact that Piaget did not force his material into a preexisting scheme. Rather, the stages resulted from the classification of the material obtained and were therefore specific to each separate area of inquiry.

With respect to movement, children's explanations tended to evolve from a mixture of animism and artificialism to purely physical explanation. In explanations of the movement of heavenly bodies, for example, five stages could be discerned: In the *first stage* (average age 5 years), children said that the sun and moon follow around us when we walk because we make them do so by our very activity. In the *second stage* (6 years), the sun and moon were said to follow us of their own free will. During a *third stage* (7 years), the heavenly bodies were said to move because of clouds, wind, or other meteorological phenomena for reasons that are both moral and physical. During a *fourth stage* (8 years), children said that the sun and moon move because of the air, fire, or heat that they make themselves. In the *fifth stage* (9.5 years), children finally gave purely physical reasons for the movement of the sun and moon. The latter were no longer thought to follow us around when we walk.

As this example suggests, children began by conceiving physical causality in terms of human agency. In the first two stages enumerated earlier, the sun and moon were conceived of as agents, acting out of obedience or according to their own free will. According to Piaget, such a conception results from children's egocentrism, that is, from their lack of differentiation between themselves and external reality. Thus, external events are simply assimilated to preexisting notions. By virtue of children's own actions, they have a direct and immediate experience of agency, but because the boundaries between themselves and the world are not yet fixed, they immediately attribute agency to external things, including inanimate objects. That is, they assimilate those objects to the preexisting notion of agency.

Piaget's statement of this hypothesis in the context of children's ideas of force is significant for understanding the development of his ideas on the relation between action and thought. According to Piaget, the notion of force originates in children's immediate experience of effort in the context of action.

From the psychological point of view, things would seem to happen as follows. Every thought is the product of sensorial elements resulting from the pressure exercised on the organism by its immediate surrounding, and of motor schemas which organise these sensorial elements into bundles which we call perceptions, ideas, mental experiences. Thus every thought presupposes an external contribution, due to sensible reality, and an internal contribution due to the organism itself, i.e. to the movements it has made in order to perceive, to virtual movements which it carries out mentally in order to reconstruct passed scenes or to foresee future scenes, and so on. Now these two kinds of contribution are, of course, completely undifferentiated from the point of view of the subject's consciousness: Every perception and every idea will necessarily appear to be objective, so long as the mistakes and failures of action have not led the mind to discern what is subjective and what objective in a given point of view. In other words, reality is perpetually being "assimilated" by the motor schemas of the organism, without it being possible for consciousness to take part in this assimilation. . . .

Thus, reality is conceived by means of schemas which have been built up by the accumulated muscular experiences of the subject, i.e. by the residue of all those of his movements that have been accompanied by a sense of effort. The idea of object is undifferentiated from the idea of resistance. And the idea of resistance itself is undifferentiated from the ideas of activity, of will, of purpose, in short of living force. . . . Only by means of a derivative process does the mind come to dissociate the "I" from the world around it, and in the measure that this dissociation takes place, force becomes gradually withdrawn from external objects and confined within the ego. [ibid., pp. 130–132]

These statements on the sensory and motor components in thinking would be further developed in Piaget's later works on sensorimotor development.

Curiously, Piaget found that although children tended to give artificialist explanations for the origin and movement of natural phenomena, their explanations of the workings of machines, the man-made origins of which were obvious, tended to be physicalistic from the beginning. The stages of development in the understanding of the functioning of machines were defined instead by children's growing understanding of how the various parts of the mechanism were related to each other. With respect to the understanding of the steam engine, for example, three stages could be discerned: In the *first stage* (4–6 years), children believed that the fire or heat causes the wheel to move directly. In the *second stage* (6–8 years), water was believed to be the sole intermediary between the fire and the wheel. Either the fire pushed the water, which impetus was transmitted to the wheel, or the heat of the fire set the water in motion, which pushed against the wheel and moved it. In the *third stage* (8–9 years), the mediating role of steam was discovered. The fire heated the water, which turned to steam, which created a pressure, which turned the wheel.

Piaget suggested that experience with simple machines and other mechanical devices might itself be a factor in the development of physical explanations of nature. According to this view, children are less likely to attribute agency to machines precisely because they are created and set into motion through human agency. But to the extent that mechanical movements can be explained through physical causes, children discover that natural movement can also be explained in this way. Explanation in terms of physical causality is simply extended from one domain to another.

Since in the eyes of the youngest children everything in nature is manufactured, it is highly probable that progress in the knowledge of human technique will lead the child to correct his view of nature himself. Mere observation of nature is far too strongly coloured with pre-relations to account for the decline in artificialism. It is in making things and in seeing them made that the child will learn the resistance of external objects and the necessity of mechanical processes. Thus the understanding of machines would seem to be the factor which brought about the mechanisation of natural causality and the decline of artificialism in the child. [ibid., p. 234]

Piaget admitted he had little direct evidence for this hypothesis. Instead, he submitted an autobiographical anecdote that may be of some interest in itself:

At an age which through various coincidences he can place at exactly between 8 and 9, one of us remembers having played a great deal with machines. He actually invented a new means of locomotion, which he christened the "auto-steam" (Fr. *autovap*), and which consisted in applying to motor-cars the principle of the steam-engine – boiler, piston, connecting rods. The inventor of the autovap even published his discovery in an illustrated work, which, incidentally, was written in pencil. Thus machines constituted for this child his first systematic and lasting centre of interest. He liked at this period of his life to collect catalogues of motor-cars, etc., and he dreamt of nothing but factories and machines. He was conscious, however, of a certain clumsiness, and this, together with the numerous failures which attended his attempts at mechanical construction, gradually discouraged this budding vocation, so that from the age of 9–10 onwards he took up geology and zoology. He can remember very well the effort which he made at this time to understand the natural formation of mountains and the distribution of fossils of sea origin: it was after a walk, during which someone had pointed out to him some nerinea in the limestone. His naturalist's mentality had been fashioned by his games with machines, which had developed in him the desire to understand by means of mechanical schemas, and this desire, though diverted from its original object, had remained identical throughout the child's subsequent hobbies. [ibid., pp. 234–235]

Piaget suggested that the children in his study probably would not have developed notions of physical causality as quickly had they not been confronted with the artifacts of modern civilization. If the study had been repeated in some "remote country district," the results might not have been exactly the same. Even if the general form of children's thinking had remained, artificialism might have declined more slowly in comparison with that of children growing up in an urban environment.

The last chapter in *The child's conception of physical causality* is a summary of the major conclusions reached in that book and the preceding one, *The child's conception of the world*. Piaget also compared the results in these two books, on children's conceptions of reality, with the findings reported in the first two books, devoted to the logic of child thought. He prefaced the chapter with some general remarks on method, which are relevant for an understanding of Piaget's conceptions of his enterprise considered as a whole:

If we examine the intellectual development of the individual or of the whole of humanity, we shall find that the human spirit goes through a certain number of stages, each different from the other, but such that during each, the mind believes itself to be apprehending an external reality that is independent of the thinking subject. The content of this reality varies according to the stages: for the young child it is alive and permeated with finality, intentions, etc., whereas for the scientist, reality is characterized by its physical determinism. But the ontological function, so to speak, remains identical: each in his own way thinks that he has found the outer world in [itself]. [ibid., p. 237]

Reality is conceived of differently by the child and the scientist. This being so, two approaches to comparing the two standpoints are possible. The first possibility is to take the scientist's viewpoint as an arbitrary and conventional standard. Thus, reality as viewed by the child would be described in the categories of reality as viewed by the scientist, a procedure justified by the fact that the mentality of the child is developmentally prior to that of the scientist. The adoption of such a procedure, however, does not imply that the scientist's viewpoint is taken as absolute, a position reaffirmed later in the chapter: "The choice of system of reference is, we repeat, a convention, but we are making use of this convention quite consciously, and shall not allow it to lead us into epistemological realism of any kind" (ibid., p. 282). The adoption of the scientist's viewpoint is a means to an end, for it enables one to treat the problem as a psychological problem.

The alternative would be to treat both the child's notions of reality and those of the scientist as having equal epistemological status. The scientist's view, like that of the child, would be considered as just one stage among others. Both viewpoints would be described, as far as possible, without making any fixed assumptions about the nature of reality as such. This approach would be strictly epistemological, as opposed to the psychological approach described earlier. Piaget left no doubt as to which approach he proposed to follow:

For our part, we shall confine ourselves to psychology, to the search, that is, for the relations between child thought and reality as the scientific thought of our time conceives it. And this point of view, narrow and question-begging though it appear, will enable us to formulate very clearly several outstanding problems. Does the external world (and by this we shall in future mean the world as it is viewed by science) impress itself directly on the child's mind, or are childish ideas the product of the subject's own mentality? If the child's mind is active in the process of knowing, how is the collaboration effected between his thought and the data of the external world? What are the laws which this collaboration will obey? All these are the traditional problems of the Theory of Knowledge, which we shall be able to transpose into the particular sphere which we have just defined. [ibid., pp. 238–239]

In short, Piaget proposed to translate epistemological problems into psychological problems, in effect, to seek psychological answers to epistemological questions. Moreover, the psychological approach to be used is biologically oriented:

Reality, such as our science imagines and postulates, is what the biologists call Environment. The child's intelligence and activity, on the other hand, are the fruit of organic life (interest, movement, imitation, assimilation). The problem of the relation between thought and things, once it has been narrowed down in this way, becomes the problem of the relation of an organism to its environment. Is the organism entirely moulded by its environment in so far as intelligence is concerned? If so, then we have, in terms of cognition, what may be called the empirical solution of the problem. Or does the organism assimilate the actions to its environment in accordance with a structure that is independent of these actions and that resists the pressure of all modifications coming from outside? If so, then we have in terms of cognition what may be called the a priori solution. Or is it not rather the case that there is interaction between the two – the organism assimilating the environment to itself, but the environment reacting upon the structure of the organism? Such is the solution which, in the domain of cognition, would imply a capacity for transformation in the categories of thought and an increasingly delicate adaptation of thought to things or of things to thought. [ibid., p. 239]

But the investigation of children's thinking, however interesting and important it might be in its own right, is not pursued entirely for its own sake. Rather, Piaget expressed the hope that the results of this biologically oriented psychological investigation might, after all, have some implications for the theory of knowledge. By translating epistemological problems into psychological problems, Piaget acquired a method for solving them. His hope was that these solutions could then be retranslated into epistemological terms:

Let us suppose, for the sake of brevity, that intellectual growth takes place along a straight line, in a linear series such that the stages A, B, C, . . . N follow one another without either interferences or changes from one level to another. We shall take the external world corresponding to stage G as absolute, and compare to it the external world corresponding to stages C, D, E, . . . etc. Such a comparison is without any epistemological bearing, since there is nothing to prove that G is decisive. But if, now, we take into account this very possibility of variation and regard the series C, D, E, . . . G as capable of being extended, on the one hand, backwards, by the supposition of stages A and B, and, on the other hand, forwards, thanks to the future stages H, I, K, . . . N, we shall discover the following: there will obviously exist a relation between the comparison of C, D, E to G and the comparison of G to H, I, etc.; and the fragmentary conclusions obtained by the comparison of C, D, E to G will become a particular case of the general conclusions obtained by comparison of all possible stages.

To put things more concretely, it may very well be that the psychological laws arrived at by means of our restricted method can be extended into epistemological laws arrived at by the analysis of the history of the sciences: the elimination of realism, of substantialism, of dynamism, the growth of relativism, etc., all these are evolutionary laws which appear to be common both to the development of the child and to that of scientific thought. [ibid., pp. 239–240]

This passage is significant for two reasons. On the one hand it underscores the points already mentioned: that the standpoint adopted in the scientific investigation of knowledge is conventional in character and that the answers obtained by this method might possibly be retranslated into epistemological terms. On the other hand, it contains an explicit recognition of the likelihood that our present stage of scientific knowledge will itself be superseded and that the results obtained by the present method might allow us to recognize the mechanisms of further development. By following the progression of development up to the present level of knowledge, general principles of development can be derived that could enable us to explain the conditions of knowing in the present and the processes underlying future progress.

The foregoing passages resemble similar programmatic statements from *Recherche*. But where the earlier statements were highly speculative and intuitive, the present passages are informed by the psychological research that Piaget had conducted in the meantime. In a sense, Piaget's intellectual development can be interpreted in terms of his own theory: He had both assimilated his empirical results to a preexisting scheme and modified that scheme to accommodate the new information.

What, then, are the implications of Piaget's investigations of children's notions of reality for such a psychologically oriented epistemology? Piaget characterized the evolution of children's conceptions of reality between the ages of 3 and 11 as a movement from realism to objectivity, reciprocity, and relativity. According to Piaget's terminology, realism is a state of mind characterized by a certain nondifferentiation of the self and external reality. Mingled with the objects and events of the external world are subjective "adherences," including notions of magical participation, animism, artificialism, finalism, and dynamism, or subjective conceptions of force. Children attain objectivity by becoming aware of their own subjectivity. In coming to recognize their own subjectivity for what it is, they are no longer inclined to confuse it with objective facts. Children attain an awareness of their own subjectivity by recognizing the reciprocity that exists between their own viewpoints and those of other persons. Once the relation between themselves and others is properly understood, they can apply this knowledge to the relations existing between things in the world. In this way, they escape the substantialist tendency to think of relations in absolute terms and recognize the relativism of certain concepts (e.g., a brother is always a brother *of* someone).

With respect to the relation between children and their environment, Piaget came to a rather paradoxical conclusion. Children are in one sense closer to reality, and in another sense farther removed from it, than adults are. They are closer to reality in the sense that they do not draw any radical distinction between appearance and reality. For them, by and large, appearance *is* reality. But for this very reason, they are relatively unable to distinguish between subjective impressions and reality external to themselves, and in this sense they are more removed from (objective) reality than adults. Piaget argued that neither empiricism nor apriorism alone can explain this seeming paradox in a satisfactory manner.

Empiricism would appear to be insufficient for two reasons: first, because it does not explain the subjective adherences that characterize children's view of reality; second, because it also does not explain how children gradually acquire a sense of external reality. If all knowledge were directly impressed on children's minds by the external world, then their initial conception of reality would not be intermingled with subjective elements. The fact that such subjective "adherences" exist demonstrates that reality is assimilated to preexisting schemes of a subjective nature.

But although assimilation seems to point toward a priori forms of knowledge, the a priori hypothesis is unsatisfactory for quite a different reason – because it does not explain how children's conceptions of reality develop. Even though their experiences are assimilated to preexisting schemes, the results of Piaget's investigations indicate that they are also able to make use of their experiences in developing more adequate conceptions of reality.

In short, pure empiricism is contradicted by the process of assimilation, and pure apriorism by the inverse process, namely, the ability of the mind to imitate reality. According to Piaget, only a theory that acknowledges these two processes can do justice to the facts. We may recall that assimilation alone corresponds to the first form of equilibrium in Piaget's early "system" in which the whole predominated over the parts, imitation alone corresponds to the second form in which the parts predominated over the whole, and the joint workings of assimilation and imitation correspond to the third and most stable form in which the parts and the wholes functioned in harmony.

Given this scheme, children's thinking may be characterized as lacking a coordination between assimilation and imitation. On the one hand, they assimilate new data to their preexisting schemes, and on the other hand, they slavishly imitate reality to the extent that they understand it. In contrast, progress in the development of thought may be described in terms of a growing coordination between the two tendencies, a coordination that results in a more stable equilibrium:

Lacking collaboration, the two tendencies, the imitative and the assimilative, lead to no coherent result. Because he fails to imitate correctly when he is assimilating, the child deforms reality in assimilating it to himself, and because he fails to assimilate when he is imitating, he becomes the victim of direct perception instead of constructing a world of intelligible relations.

But such an equilibrium as this is unstable, and assimilation and imitation soon begin to collaborate. It may even be questioned whether the definition of the whole of thought does not lie precisely in this collaboration. [ibid., pp. 289–290]

The increasing collaboration between assimilation and accommodation also leads to progressive development in the child's understanding of causality and natural law. With respect to causality, three general stages can be discerned. During the *first*, causal explanations tend to be psychological, phenomenalistic, finalistic, and magical. During the *second*, they are artificialist, animistic, and dynamic. Only during the *third* period (after 7–8 years) do causal explanations become more rational. Piaget described this evolution as consisting of three processes: the desubjectivization of causality, the formation of sequential series in time, and the progressive reversibility of systems of cause and effect.

With respect to the understanding of natural laws, three stages can also be distinguished, although the age ranges are somewhat different. During the *first stage* (up to 7–8 years), moral necessity is not distinguished from physical determinism, and no generality at all is recognized. During the *second stage* (7–8 to 11–12 years), moral necessity is differentiated from physical determinism, and generality appears insofar as children attempt to avoid contradictions. Finally, in the *third stage* (after 11–12 years), children develop an understanding of logical necessity that is completely general.

In the concluding pages of *The child's conception of physical causality,* Piaget compared the evolution of children's thinking in regard to reality and causality with the logical or formal aspects of their thought as described in his first two books. The realism of children's thinking corresponds to their egocentrism, insofar as both terms refer to their relative inability to distinguish purely subjective realities from objective or intersubjective realities. Similarly, their relative inability to generalize with respect to physical laws corresponds to transduction, defined as reasoning from particular to particular, that is, as the inability to move from particular to universal or from universal to particular. The ability to generalize is also related to another characteristic of children's logic: the categorical character of their judgments. In a passage that echoed his earlier paper on the relativity of zoological species (Piaget, 1914), Piaget argued for a formal priority of the logic of relations over the logic of classes. In so doing, he anticipated recent ideas (Rosch, 1987) regarding the relativity of membership in natural classes in terms of "prototypes" or "family resemblances":

> One can, of course, reason with perfect correctness by making sole use of classes, as the whole of Aristotle's logic shows, but the classes themselves could only be constructed thanks to relations. Thus the biological classification which is at the root of Aristotle's logic can only be understood as the result of comparisons and relations between the characters peculiar to each species, genus, etc. . . . Thus the zoological classification had an absolute sense for Aristotle and even for Linnaeus, Cuvier, Agassiz, and others, whereas nowadays species and genera are regarded as a conventional framework by means of which we make arbitrary divisions in the continuous flux of evolution. The only reality is therefore the sum of the relations between individuals, and, strictly speaking, one should not say: "This animal is a sparrow", but: "This animal is more (or less) sparrow than this or those animals", just as we say of an object that is "more (or less) brown than . . .". [Piaget, 1927/1966a, pp. 297–298]

Piaget's psychological conception of the logic of relations was the key by which he sought to explain the phenomenon of novelty in the development of intelligence. As he had put it in *Judgment and reasoning in the child,* "the fertility of reasoning is due to our unlimited capacity for constructing new relations, two given relations being always sufficient to find a third by multiplication, and so on" (Piaget, 1924/1928b, p. 196). He would later return to this line of reasoning in explaining the phenomenon of invention as the crowning achievement of sensorimotor development, a topic to be explored in detail in the next chapter. First, the present discussion of the initial phase in Piaget's professional development will be completed with a consideration of his research on social and moral development.

SOCIAL AND MORAL THOUGHT

Piaget's first four books consist mainly of descriptive characterizations of children's thinking in terms of egocentrism, syncretism, juxtaposition, realism, artificialism, and so on. But he was also concerned to elucidate the functional processes that explain these characteristics of child thought. In *The child's conception of physical causality,* he stated that such processes are of two types, social and biological. Of these, the social factors occupied most of his attention. In *The language and thought of the child,* the decline of egocentric language was described as a consequence of parallel developments in children's social life. In *Judgment and reasoning in the child,* the understanding of reciprocity in social relations was described as extending to the understanding of reciprocity in logical relations in general. In *The child's conception of physical causality,* reciprocity between different subjective points of view was seen to contribute to the development of objectivity.

But for Piaget, children's social development was not only a functional process influencing the development of thought in other areas; it also constituted an area of content in its own right. Just as the development of children's reasoning was characterized by a growing understanding of logical relations, so was the development of their social thinking characterized by a growing awareness of social relations, and just as the development of judgment and reasoning was characterized by an increasing submission of thought to the normative rules of logic, so was the development of social thinking characterized by an increasing submission to normative rules of morality. For Piaget, as for Kant, moral thought was a form of practical reason. As he put it himself, "Logic is the morality of thought just as morality is the logic of action" (Piaget, 1932/1965a, p. 398). Moreover, the progressive development of both logical and moral rules was viewed as being governed by increasingly more stable forms of equilibrium. His research on social and moral development thus represented a realization of the belief expressed in *Recherche* that questions of value could be investigated scientifically in terms of forms of equilibrium.

The moral judgment of the child

The rules of the game. Piaget's investigation of children's moral judgments was not limited to the kinds of moral rules that children are likely to learn from their parents and other moral educators. In addition to these, he also studied children's conceptions of the rules that children follow in the context of games among themselves. Now the relevance of children's games for the study of moral thought might not be obvious at first glance. At the time that Piaget took up the problem, most social scientists had concerned themselves only with moral rules as they were handed down from one generation to the next. For Piaget, Durkheim's (1925/1973) writings on moral education provided the most conspicuous example of this tendency. But Piaget's entire book on moral judgment is an argument to the effect that the morality of constraint based on the unilateral respect between one generation and the next is only one kind of moral code. Equally important is the morality of cooperation or reciprocity, based on mutual respect between equals. Not only is this form of moral thinking to be found in children's games; it also characterizes, according to Piaget, the form of moral and legal regulations toward which modern equalitarian societies tend, however imperfectly. The study of children's understanding of rules in the context of organized games among their peers can therefore provide a key to the origins of equalitarian ethical codes in general.

Piaget's distinction between the morality of social constraint and the morality of cooperation, like many of his other psychological concepts, can be traced to the basic forms of equilibrium described in *Recherche*. As stated in his autobiography, Piaget believed that these forms of equilibrium characterized the organization of life "at all levels," biological, psychological, and sociological. In *Judgment and reasoning in the child,* he described how the three basic forms of equilibrium manifested themselves on the psychological level as syncretism, juxtaposition, and reversibility. Syncretism referred to the predominance of the whole over the parts, juxtaposition the ascendancy of the parts over the whole, and reversibility the stable equilibrium between the two tendencies. On the level of social life, these same forms of equilibrium manifested themselves as constraint, egocentrism, and cooperation (or reciprocity). According to the morality of social constraint, the younger generation is subordinated to their elders as the representatives of society. In effect, the members of society as individuals are subordinated to society as a whole. In contrast, moral egocentrism is the tendency of individuals to subordinate social concerns to their own points of view; it thus represents the ascendancy of the part over the whole. Finally, the morality of cooperation or reciprocity is a synthesis of the interests of persons considered as individuals and those persons taken together. As such, it represents a stable synthesis between the parts and the whole.

The key to this interpretation is found once again in Piaget's autobiography. There he described how in his early research he had sought characteristic structures-of-the-whole corresponding to logical operations. He had failed in this endeavor because he had not sought such structures in the context of concrete operations – that is, in the context of logical operations that are still thoroughly content bound. Instead:

I satisfied my need for an explanation in terms of structures-of-the-whole by studying the social aspect of thought (which is a necessary aspect, I still believe, of the formation of logical operations as such). The ideal equilibrium (the reciprocal preservation of the whole and of the parts) pertains here to the cooperation between individuals who become autonomous by this very cooperation. Imperfect equilibrium chracterized by the alteration of the parts in relation to the whole appears here as social constraint (or constraint of the younger by the older). Imperfect equilibrium characterized by the change of the whole as a function of the parts (and the lack of coordination of the parts) appears as unconscious egocentricity of the individual, that is, as the mental attitude of young children who do not yet know how to collaborate nor to coordinate their points of view. [Piaget, 1952a, pp. 247–248]

The *moral judgment of the child* (Piaget, 1932/1965a) provides numerous examples of this scheme. The book begins with a study of the awareness and observance of rules in the context of games. Piaget considered both boys' and girls' games, but the most space was devoted to the rules of the game of marbles. The technique employed was straightforward. Piaget simply asked a number of boys aged 4 to 13 how one played marbles. By actually playing games with them from beginning to end, he let them demonstrate the rules of the game in a concrete manner. As a check on the accuracy of information obtained from the younger children, he also observed them playing two at a time against each other. Then each child would be asked a number of questions regarding his understanding of rules in general: whether or not he could invent a new rule if he wanted to; if this new rule could actually be used in a game with other children; whether or not this new rule would be as "real" or as fair as other, existing rules; whether this new rule could be handed down to a new generation of marble-players; whether or not people had always played marbles as they do today; how the rules originated – whether they were invented by children or handed down by parents and grown-ups in general.

Piaget found that four successive stages could be distinguished in children's actual practice of the rules of the game. In the *first stage* (before the age of 3, approximately), children simply manipulated the marbles according to their own individual desires and motor habits. This led to the repetition of certain ritualized and symbolic schemes, but these "motor rules" were of an individual, not a collective, character. Only during the *second stage* (roughly between the ages of 2 and 5) did children first become aware of codified rules, but this awareness remained egocentric in the sense that children applied these rules in a distinctly idiosyncratic manner. Children either did not bother to play together or, when they did so, did not coordinate their actions according to common rules. Instead, each child played "on his own," such that everyone could win at once. In this respect, egocentric play resembled the collective monologues of egocentric language. In contrast, the *third stage* (age 7–8) was characterized by incipient co-operation. Children now coordinated their play according to mutually agreed-upon rules. Each player now played to win, and children recognized that only one player could win at a time. But although children usually could reach agreement on the rules to be followed when they were playing with each other, they often gave contradictory accounts when questioned separately. This difficulty was overcome in the *fourth stage* (after age 11–12), when the rules became thoroughly codified such that they were known to everyone. Each child was reflectively aware of the rules put into practice such that there was no discrepancy between the accounts that children gave when questioned separately. Piaget added that although development can be divided into stages for purposes of convenience and ease of exposition, development in fact occurs as a continuous process and is characterized by "minor oscillations which render it infinitely complicated in detail" (ibid., p. 28). In a significant footnote, he stated further that the age norms provided both in that book and in his previous ones applied only to the particular samples studied: "Most of our research has been carried out on children from the poorer parts of Geneva. In different surroundings the age averages would certainly have been different" (ibid., p. 46n).

As for the understanding of the rules of the game, things developed somewhat differently. Three stages could be distinguished that overlapped, but did not coincide exactly with the stages of actual usage. During the *first stage* (before the age of about 6), rules were not yet viewed as obligatory, perhaps because their collective character was not yet understood. Instead, they were viewed as "interesting examples," possible ways of acting that were not binding. During the *second stage* (from about age 6 to 9–10), however, rules came to be regarded as "sacred and untouchable," originating with adults and lasting forever without being changed. Finally, during the *third stage* (after age 9–10), rules were seen as originating in mutual consent and capable of being changed in accordance with mutual agreement.

Taken together, the development of children's understanding and practice of the rules of the game may be characterized as an evolution from egocentrism and constraint to cooperation. Children show egocentrism in the practice of rules insofar as they interpret those rules in their individual ways. This egocentrism is an excellent example of what Piaget in his earlier books had called "deforming assimilation"; in assimilating the rules to their individual schemes, children in effect deform them according to their own understanding. In regarding those rules as "sacred and untouchable," however, children conform to a morality of constraint, with the corresponding unilateral respect directed toward the supposed authors of the rules. The truly interesting thing about these findings is that children's egocentrism in the practice of rules overlaps in part with the constraint manifest in their understanding of them. That is, they begin to view rules as sacred and unchanging at the same time that they are still deforming them in an egocentric manner. This coincidence between egocentrism and the morality of constraint led Piaget to the conclusion that they are not incompatible, as they might appear at first. Instead, he argued that they complement and reinforce one another. The inequality that exists between child and adult leads to a unilateral respect of the one for the other at the same time that it prevents the child from taking the adult's perspective. Unable to take the other's perspective, the children remain imprisoned in their own – the very definition of egocentrism. To the extent that they emphasize a morality based on unilateral respect, adults only make it more difficult for children to escape from their own perspective, with the result that their native egocentrism is reinforced.

The development of cooperation is what causes the decline of both egocentrism and unilateral respect. Piaget argued (a) that constraint is not the only way in which children acquire an awareness of moral obligation, (b) that a morality of cooperation spontaneously arises among children as equals, and (c) that the latter is in some sense developmentally more advanced than the former. Children's games provide the ideal context for the study of the development of cooperation. According to Piaget, it is significant that the game of marbles tends to be dropped at the age of 14–15 at the latest. This means that 11–13-year-olds have no seniors as far as the game is concerned. Cooperation can therefore develop freely without any constraint imposed by an older generation. This situation is quite unlike that which prevails in society as a whole, in which the younger generation is always exposed more or less to the constraint of their elders. Societies themselves vary in the degree to which each generation imposes the norms of the adult world on succeeding generations. Piaget argued that such constraint is one of the major qualities distinguishing so-called primitive societies from more modern ones. In the rites and ceremonies of initiation characteristic of primitive societies, the younger generation is forced to submit to the customs and beliefs of their elders in a rather absolute fashion. In modern societies, more room generally exists for a morality of cooperation to develop, although constraint, as manifest in authoritarian pedagogical practice, for example, is by no means absent.

The blithe comparison between "primitive" and "modern" societies may appear to be an extremely simplistic anthropology. In fact, the developmental sequence separating constraint and cooperation seems to have served Piaget as a *criterion* for the "primitiveness" or "progressiveness" of societies. According to this view, it is not a question of fact whether or not "primitive" societies tend to be characterized by a gerontocratic constraint between generations; it is rather the presence of constraint that makes a society developmentally more "primitive." Theoretically, one could also order modern societies according to the same criterion. In effect, cooperation is developmentally more advanced than constraint, because it represents a more stable form of equilibrium:

Mutual respect is, in a sense, the state of equilibrium towards which unilateral respect is tending when differences between child and adult, younger and older are becoming effaced; just as cooperation is the form of equilibrium to which constraint is tending in the same circumstances. [ibid., p. 96]

Moral realism. Piaget was led to similar conclusions in investigating the understanding of rules that are more generally regarded to be moral in nature. For example, in asking children for their definitions of a lie and their ideas about what made lying wrong, he found a general evolution from "moral realism" to "subjective responsibility." Even very young children, unless they identified lies with "naughty words," were capable of understanding that "a lie is something that isn't true" (ibid., p. 142). But according to Piaget, younger children tended more than older children to interpret this proposition as meaning that a lie is a statement that is objectively untrue, regardless of the intentions of the person who makes the statement. Moreover, lies were more reprehensible to the extent that they deviated from reality. A child's statement of seeing "a dog as big as a cow" was held to be worse than another child's false statement of having received good marks in school, because the latter statement was at least plausible, whereas the former was not (ibid., pp. 150ff.). The children who gave such definitions of lies were fully capable of distinguishing between intentional and unintentional actions; they simply tended not to employ intention as a criterion for lying. A lie was not clearly distinguished from a mistake, and both were equally reprehensible to the extent that they deviated from objective truth. Thus, the statement that someone was age 30 when he was really 36 was both a lie and a mistake, and the statement that he was only 28 was even a bigger lie, *"because the difference is biggest"* (ibid., p. 143).

Between the ages of 6 and 12, however, children became increasingly more likely to consider intention in their definitions and evaluation of lies. Lying increasingly tended to be defined as willful deception, rather than simply as an objectively false statement, and the degree of deception involved was what made one lie more or less reprehensible than another. Thus, children began to favor the view that telling one's mother that one got good marks in school was worse when that was not the case than telling her that one had seen a dog as big as a cow. Oddly enough, the children who gave this answer justified it in the same way as those who answered in the opposite manner: The evaluation in each case was a function of plausibility. In the one case, the less plausible statement was taken to be worse because it deviated more from objective reality, and in the other case, the same statement was considered less bad because it was less likely to be believed in the first place. The statement that one saw a dog as big as a cow is so obviously false that the other person is likely to take it for a mistake or exaggeration right away.

Both types of answers, the interpretation of lying in terms of objective truth as well as in terms of subjective intention, were found at all ages between 6 and 12. Therefore, objective and subjective responsibility cannot be considered as bona fide developmental stages. Piaget nevertheless saw certain analogies between the gradual evolution of subjective responsibility and the development of children's conceptions of rules. Just as children believe that rules are sacred and inviolable at the same time that they distort those rules in practice, so do children tend to evaluate lies in terms of their objective validity at the same time that they display a tendency to assimilate the truth to their own needs and fantasies. On the latter point, Piaget cited W. Stern's research on the prevalence of "pseudolies" among children younger than about 7 to 8 years – that is, statements that are objectively untrue, but not uttered with any intent to deceive. This egocentric attitude toward truth cannot be overcome solely through constraint based on unilateral respect. Only through the experience of cooperation and the corresponding relations of reciprocity are children led to value the subjective intentions of telling the truth:

The need to speak the truth and even to seek it for oneself is only conceivable in so far as the individual thinks and acts as one of a society, and not of any society (for it is just the constraining relations between superior and inferior that often drive the latter to prevarication) but of a society founded on reciprocity and mutual respect, and therefore on cooperation. . . . It is as his own mind comes into contact with others that truth will begin to acquire value in the child's eyes and will consequently become a moral demand that can be made upon him. As long as the child remains egocentric, truth as such will fail to interest him and he will see no harm in transposing facts in accordance with his desires. [ibid., pp. 164–165]

As in the case of children's understanding of rules, unilateral respect can only reinforce children's native egocentrism:

One must have felt a real desire to exchange thoughts with others in order to discover all that a lie can involve. And this interchange of thoughts is from the first not possible between adults and children, because the initial inequality is too great and the child tries to imitate the adult and at the same time to protect himself against him rather than really to exchange thoughts with him. The situation we have described is thus almost the necessary outcome of unilateral respect. The spirit of the command having failed to be assimilated, the letter alone remains. Hence the phenomena we have been observing. The child thinks of a lie as "what isn't true," independently of the subject's intentions. He even goes so far as to compare lies to those linguistic taboos, "naughty words." As for the judgment of responsibility, the further a lie is removed from reality, the more serious is the offence. Objective responsibility is thus the inevitable result of unilateral respect in its earliest stage. [ibid., pp. 166–167]

These observations led Piaget to make some rather strong remarks regarding current child-rearing practices and pedagogical methods:

It looks as though, in many ways, the adult did everything in his power to encourage the child to persevere in its specific tendencies, and to do so precisely in so far as these tendencies stand in the way of social development. Whereas, given sufficient liberty of action, the child will spontaneously emerge from his egocentrism and tend with his whole being towards cooperation, the adult most of the time acts in such a way as to strengthen egocentrism in its double aspect, intellectual and moral. . . . (The "average parent" is like an unintelligent government that is content to accumulate laws in spite of the contradictions and the ever-increasing mental confusion which this accumulation leads to). . . . Unable to distinguish precisely between what is good in his parents and what is open to criticism, incapable, owing to the "ambivalence" of his feelings toward them, of criticizing his parents objectively, the child ends in moments of attachment by inwardly admitting their right to the authority they wield over him. Even when grown up, he will be unable, except in very rare cases, to break loose from the affective schemas acquired in this way, and will be as stupid with his own children as his parents were with him. [ibid., pp. 190, 192–193]

Conceptions of justice. Perhaps the clearest case of the spontaneous development of ideas of cooperation and reciprocity among children found by Piaget was in their conceptions of justice. This subject was investigated by telling children hypothetical story problems and asking what they thought should be done in the situation described. In one story involving distributive justice, for example, a mother gave each of her children a roll. The youngest, however, was careless and let his fall in the water. What should the mother do? Should she give him another roll, or not? Again, clear-cut developmental stages were not found, for the kinds of answers children gave were reported in differing proportions at all ages from 6 to 12. Nevertheless, Piaget summarized a number of inquiries regarding different aspects of justice in terms of the most frequent kinds of answers provided in three successive periods across this age range.

Before the age of 7–8, most children tended to identify justice with adult authority. In the story described, they said the mother should not give the youngest child another roll, because he was careless and deserved to be punished. Even in situations involving relations between children, the authority of adult-imposed sanctions or the greater authority of the older child outweighed considerations of equality. Between the ages of 7–8 and 11–12, however, equalitarianism predominated over every other consideration. Thus, the mother should give the youngest child another roll so that each of the children would have one. It was characteristic of this type of answer that equality was defined objectively in terms of the identity of goods to be distributed, or by some other objective criterion. Finally, after the age of 11–12, a more subtle form of equalitarianism appeared that involved a consideration of the relative circumstances of the persons involved. The mother in the story should give the youngest child another roll, because he was smaller. Piaget called this conception of equality relative to each person's particular situation a form of "equity" and considered it the developmentally most advanced conception of justice to appear in the age range studied. As in the case of children's conceptions of rules and their definitions of lying, the development of the sense of justice could be described as a progressive evolution from unilateral respect to cooperation and reciprocity.

But the very evolution of a sense of equity as defined earlier raised a certain theoretical problem: If the development of the sense of justice is marked by a progressive trend toward greater reciprocity, how do children progress beyond conceptions of exact reciprocity, that is, beyond a conception of equality based on identity? In attempting to answer this question, Piaget demonstrated most clearly the continuity of his thinking from the early system of *Recherche* to his current psychological investigations. Piaget's whole polemic against social constraint, which would appear to be the major message of *The moral judgment of the child,* was an epistemological argument against moral empiricism. Contrary to the opinions of most moral educators, Piaget argued that a genuine sense of right cannot be imposed from without through teaching or instruction. As in the case of other intellectual spheres, children do not acquire moral knowledge in a passive manner, solely from external experience. Nor are moral concepts to be regarded as innate ideas or as the result of a priori categories after the manner of the Kantian categorical imperative. Instead, children's ideas of justice and reciprocity were viewed as being actively discovered or constructed in the context of their relations with others – hence the importance of mutual respect in the relations between children as equals.

As in the case of his previous investigations, Piaget transposed the particular epistemological problems at hand into psychological problems. From an epistemological viewpoint, reciprocity represents a norm that regulates moral reasoning. "Reciprocity," wrote Piaget, "imposes itself on practical reason as logical principles impose themselves morally on theoretical reason" (ibid., p. 317). On the psychological level, however, the norm of reciprocity may be described as a form of equilibrium. In fact, "it constitutes an ideal equilibrium towards which the phenomena tend" (ibid.). We may recall that the author of *Recherche* had hoped to explain the directionality of development without recourse to teleology through this same notion of an ideal equilibrium. Thus, the a priori view is partially correct: "To speak of directed evolution and asymptotic advance towards a necessary ideal is to recognize the existence of a something which acts from the first in the direction of this evolution" (ibid., p. 399). But this a priori does not present itself in the form of innate, ready-made structures that organize the contents of consciousness in an immediate manner, but rather in the form of "a functional law of equilibrium'' that becomes manifest in structures that arise through functioning. Already at the level of sensorimotor operations an inherent tendency toward self-organization can be observed, and Piaget described this movement toward ever greater coherence and organization as the tendency toward equilibrium. Because no final state of equilibrium is ever attained, this tendency cannot be said to be teleological in character. No end state is built into the process and present from the beginning. There is only a never-ending, self-directed process, "a sum-total of functional relations implying the distinction between the existing states of disequilibrium and an ideal equilibrium yet to be realized" (ibid.).

Through such a conception of an inherent tendency in development toward equilibrium, Piaget seeks to explain the development of the higher forms of reciprocity. Against his account of cooperation and reciprocity, one can object that a morality based on such principles does not get one very far. Not only is it unclear how children develop beyond the direct reciprocity implied in the maxim, "Do unto others as they do unto you," it is also unclear how they come to apply a morality based on equalitarianism and reciprocity in circumstances in which the persons involved are in fact unequal. Yet the latter situation is what is implied in the concept of equity. Children who reason according to conceptions of equity recognize that the cause of equalitarianism is not served by treating all people in an identical manner if they are unequal in relevant ways from the beginning. Thus, the youngest child who loses his roll is accorded special consideration "because he is small." Equality is served only by taking these initial inequalities into consideration.

According to Piaget, the development of higher forms of reciprocity such as equity can be explained only by appeal to the notion of the tendency toward an ideal equilibrium:

Like all spiritual realities which are the result, not of external constraint but of autonomous development, reciprocity has two aspects: Reciprocity as a fact, and reciprocity as an ideal, as something which ought to be. The child begins by simply practicing reciprocity, in itself not so easy a thing as one might think. Then, once he has grown accustomed to this form of equilibrium in his actions, his behaviour is altered from within, its form reacting, as it were, upon its content. What is regarded as just is no longer merely reciprocal action, but primarily behaviour that admits of indefinitely sustained reciprocity. [ibid., p. 323]

Psychologically, this belief in an "indefinitely sustained reciprocity" results from children's becoming aware of the unending tendency toward an ideal equilibrium. Thus, the child replaces conceptions of "crude equality" (i.e., "Do unto others as they do unto you") with a conception of an ideal reciprocity ("Do unto others as you would have them do unto you"). Moreover, this maxim can be followed even when immediate reciprocity on the part of other persons is lacking, because it serves the cause of reciprocity in the long run. Similarly, forgiveness comes to be preferred to revenge, because (Piaget quoted a 10–year-old informant on this point) " 'there is no end' to revenge" (ibid.). When it comes to revenge, the need for exact equality can paradoxically lead to a state of perpetual disequilibrium as both parties insist on revenging themselves in turn. In contrast, forgiveness serves the cause of reciprocity in the long run, even though it means accepting a momentary inequality for the person who declines to take revenge.

In this way, Piaget attempted to apply the method first enunciated in *Recherche*: investigating questions of moral value scientifically by treating the awareness of those values as forms of psychological equilibrium. He brought *The moral judgment of the child* to a close by comparing his conclusions with those of other social theorists (Durkheim, Bovet, and Baldwin) who had considered problems of moral development. The originality of his own theory was that it recognized a morality of cooperation and mutual respect alongside the morality of constraint, or unilateral respect, recognized by previous theorists. Moreover, the higher forms of morality were seen to develop through cooperation rather than constraint. Piaget's views on questions of value will be considered further in reviewing several essays on religion also published during this period.

Essays on religion

Although Piaget claimed to have abandoned his philosophical ''system'' on entry into professional life, he did not abandon his interest in the problem of science and religion. In fact, during the period 1922 to 1930, he published three major essays on this topic (Piaget, 1922a, 1928a, 1930). These essays are of great interest, not only because they provide evidence for a thematic continuity between the concerns of his youth and his professional life but also because they demonstrate the intimate relationship that existed in his mind between questions of science and questions of value. This relationship is of central importance for interpreting the meaning of his work, as well as being of interest in its own right.

The essay ''La psychologie et les valeurs religieuses'' (Piaget, 1922a) is the text of a paper that Piaget presented to the conference of the Association Chrétienne d'Etudiants de la Suisse Romande the previous year. In it, he set out a program of psychological research on judgments of value actually carried out in *The moral judgment of the child*. The continuity between *Recherche* and the thoughts expressed in this essay are apparent in the opening paragraph: ''The problem of psychology and religious values must be conceived as a special case of the grand problem of science and religion which has impassioned people's minds so strongly, especially in the 15 or 20 years preceding the war'' (ibid., p. 38). Piaget further related how he had organized a discussion group among the members of the Association Chrétienne in Geneva for the purpose of comparing their personal religious experiences. These discussions suggested to him that among the various conceptualizations of religion, two extreme types could be distinguished. At the one extreme, some people think of God in the form of a person who is wholly external to the believer and who may be addressed as another person in the act of prayer. Others think of God as having no personal attributes whatever, but as a presence in which the categories of "internal" and "external" lose their meaning in an experience of communion. The question is, What is the psychological significance of such experiences? Is there any way of deciding if one form of religious experience is in any way superior to another (ibid., pp. 43–44)?

Piaget denied that the premises on which such judgments of value are based are in any way amenable to science. The judgments themselves, however, can be investigated by psychology. "Value eludes science, but the judgment that affirms this value is to a certain extent explicable scientifically" (ibid., p. 53). Psychology can study judgments of value in the same way that it studies logical judgment. Psychology cannot affirm the truth or falsity of the conclusions reached through logical reasoning, but it can study the psychological factors involved in logical judgment. Similarly, psychology cannot judge the ultimate worth of moral or religious values, but it can study the psychological factors bearing on the judgments by which those values are affirmed (ibid., pp. 55–57). In each case, the goal is to determine to what extent forms of judgment may be ordered in developmental stages. Such an ordering would provide a psychological criterion for determining their relative adequacy (ibid., pp. 49–50, 74). Piaget ended his address with a proposal that the Association Chrétienne establish a psychological research committee to study these problems. Although he never studied the development of religious conceptions as such, the proposed research on judgments of values was actually carried out in *The moral judgment of the child*.

The influence of this research is noticeable in "Immanence et transcendance" (Piaget, 1928a), his contribution to a book entitled *Deux types d'attitudes religieuses: Immanence et transcendance,* coauthored with J. De la Harpe. The two types of religious attitudes described in the earlier paper are in this case discussed in terms of "transcendence," defined as the anthropomorphic view of a personal Deity, and "immanence," according to which divinity is conceived as immanent in the individual's own conscience. In the first two sections of this essay, Piaget drew sociological and psychological parallels to these two religious orientations. In sociological terms, transcendence and immanence correspond to Durkheim's conformist and differentiated societies, respectively (ibid., pp. 11–12). Psychologically, transcendence corresponds to unilateral respect, and immanence to mutual respect as defined in *The moral judgment of the child*. The anthropomorphic view of God is based on the relations of authority existing between children and their parents as postulated by Bovet. In contrast, immanence is founded on transpersonal moral norms deriving from relations of equality and reciprocity among persons (ibid., pp. 20–21). According to Piaget, contemporary Protestantism was caught between these two conceptions (ibid., pp. 24–25).

In the third part of that essay, Piaget frankly expressed his own personal views. "Transcendence" was firmly rejected as an atavistic form of religious consciousness. Anthropomorphism and supernaturalism in religion were compared to the various forms of realism in children's thinking about physical reality. The belief in a personal God was compared to the Pythagorean belief in the reality of numbers or the Platonic belief in the reality of forms (ibid., pp. 31–32). Just as progress in mathematics and physical science has exposed the illusion of realism in philosophy, so has progress in social science undermined supernaturalism in religion. "In my opinion, psychology and sociology appear to have exposed the illusion of the supernatural and thus to have destroyed classical theology" (ibid., p. 26).

What is interesting in this formulation is not its iconoclasm, but the conception of the relation between science and religion that it implies. The ideas of philosophy and religion were seen to be dependent on the ideas of science; progress in the one area is correlative to progress in the other. "The true philosophy is indirect; it is reflection upon science. The more science progresses, the more thought becomes aware of itself" (ibid., p. 38). Moreover, the norms of thought are what immanentism calls divine. These norms are not merely subjective. Insofar as they involve cooperation and reciprocity among persons, they are trans-subjective. This is why immanentism cannot be described as merely individualistic. "Immanentism comes to identify God, not with the ego of psychology, but with the norms of thought itself" (ibid., p. 36). Epistemological research thus becomes a kind of religious preoccupation in its own right, a form of participation in the reflection of thought on its own activity. In conducting such research, the scientist becomes the vehicle by which Reason comes to know itself. Free intellectual search, absolute sincerity, and disregard of self-affirmation for the sake of truth imply participation in the normative activity of thought. "Wherever the unifying action of love overcomes the ego, as the unifying action of thought surmounts egocentrism and anthropomorphism, there is the realization of norms. The Spinozist identification of love and reason needs to be lived in reality. Then the conscience has that experience *sui generis* of harmony with Thought which is the mystical experience supreme" (ibid., p. 39).

The immanentist views expressed in this essay met with some opposition (Vidal, 1987), and Piaget had to defend himself in print in the years immediately following its publication. In a short article, "Pour l'immanence" (Piaget, 1929a), he replied to a previous article in which Burger (1929) had attacked his "excessive propositions."[3] This article was followed a year later by a little book entitled *Immanentisme et foi religieuse,* in which Piaget sought to explain his position in more detail. In an editor's preface, the Central Committee of the Groupe romand des Anciens Membres de l'Association Chrétienne d'Etudiants described this book as a means for allowing Piaget to clarify the views he had expressed in *Deux types d'attitudes religieuses:*

The rather lively discussion aroused by that publication in the philosophical and religious press of French-speaking Switzerland demonstrated that the educated public in our country is not left indifferent by a subject of this kind, but also that the position taken by the authors – and in particular by M. Piaget – was not well understood in certain religious

---

3 Another exchange on Piaget's immanentism involved his former teacher A. Reymond; see Reymond (1929) and Piaget (1929b).

quarters, where one appeared to consider it incompatible with the requirements of an authentic Christianity. [Piaget, 1930, p. 5]

In order to allow Piaget to explain his position further, the Groupe des Anciens Membres invited him to take part in their 1929 annual meeting, and *Immanentisme et foi religieuse* was the result.

Piaget began by attempting to find a better definition of his terms "immanence" and "transcendence." According to their customary usage in philosophy, "transcendence" refers to the property of being "outside of and superior to" a particular reality, whereas "immanence" refers to being "contained within" that reality. But Piaget thought these definitions to be too restricted by spatial metaphor, and he proposed alternative definitions in terms of causality. According to this definition, a "transcendent" God is a God who is capable of being a cause. As creator of the universe, God is the final cause of physical reality; as an actor in human history, God is the author of certain miraculous events; as a personal reality, God can be the cause of certain mystical experiences. In contrast, an "immanent" God is not conceived in causal terms at all, but in terms of *implication*. This dichotomy between causality and implication would recur throughout Piaget's works, "implication" being his term for "meaning" in the most general sense. Further, an immanent God is a God of *value*, a source of truth rather than of events, of obligations rather than of facts. An immanent God is thus thought of as affecting the sphere of human life not from without, but from within, by organizing action and experience in the form of spiritual norms (ibid., pp. 9–10).

According to Piaget, this orientation implies a new view of the relation between science and philosophy, understood in terms of the search for ultimate truth (*la recherche de l'absolu*). Three attitudes are possible: Positivism restricts itself to the truths discernible by science and does not concern itself with ultimate truth. Metaphysics attempts to define a form of knowledge above and beyond that of positive science. As opposed to either of these, critical philosophy sets out to explain science, that is, "to seek the absolute not beyond science, but in the very conditions of scientific activity" (ibid., p. 18). The attempt to delimit the boundaries of science and to seek religious values outside them is futile and self-deluding, for the boundaries of scientific knowledge are constantly changing, and one cannot know what they might be in the future (ibid., pp. 21–22). Far from seeking to define a sphere of knowledge for itself apart from science, philosophy should carry its search for truth to the depths of science itself:

The very existence of science presupposes that of the spirit and of the values that constitute it, value being the condition of thought and thought the condition of being. The existence of science thus presupposes an intimate relation between thought and the universe, unanalyzable as such, the products of which we know through different sciences and the reality of which we infer by critical reflection. [ibid., pp. 30–31]

Piaget argued for the superiority of immanence over transcendence in the context of one of the most difficult of all theological problems: the problem of evil. The historical form of this problem is well known: The belief in a supremely good and all-powerful God is not easily reconciled with the existence of evil and suffering in the world. The reality of evil appears to contradict either the omnipotence or the supreme goodness of a transcendent Deity. Immanentism does not solve the problem of evil by any means, but it does purport to remove the contradiction. If God is not a cause, then God cannot be held responsible for the existence or nonexistence of evil. Only through human action in accordance with ultimate values can the Divine enter the world. "God is not a Being who imposes Himself on us from without: His reality consists only in the intimate effort of the seeking mind" (ibid., p. 37). As before, the Divine is identified with the norms of thought. "At the very center of thought, there is thus a normative activity that imposes itself upon us and upon our whole universe, not from without as a cause produces its effect, but from within as one value entails other values" (ibid., p. 41).

In conclusion, Piaget described three affirmations of the attitude of "immanence" by which it deserves to be called religious. First, it seeks to identify values in terms of the norms of thought. Second, individuals can experience a communion with a reality greater than themselves by seeking to realize these norms in their own lives. Third, the realization of these norms transforms the lives of the individuals concerned. In this connection, Piaget drew an interesting distinction between "individuality" and "personality." The individual as such is merely an isolated unit, subject to all the egocentric illusions of a limited perspective. "Personality," however, refers to the individual's capacity for entering into relations with other persons and with the universe as a whole by means of the trans-subjective norms of thought.[4]

Immanentisme et foi religieuse was Piaget's last publication explicitly devoted to matters of religion. Whether in order to avoid being misunderstood or for other reasons, he thereafter confined himself to scientific research. But these essays serve to remind us of the personal meaning that this research must have had for him and suggest that he had achieved in his own life the synthesis of science and value to which he had aspired in *Recherche*. His view on the relation between science and religion is surely novel.[5] According to this view, no conflict between the two is necessary, because scientific research forms the very substance of a value-oriented philosophical reflection. One can therefore expect that scientific progress should force a change in how religion is conceptualized. In this respect, Piaget argued that "immanence" is developmentally more advanced than "transcendence." Just as young children's conceptions of physical causality are characterized by a lack of differentiation between objective causality and human action, so is "transcendence" characterized by a relative nondifferentiation between causes existing outside the mind and the normative activity of thought

4 This distinction between individuality and personality was further developed in a sociological essay entitled "L'individualité en histoire: L'individu et la formation de la raison," published in 1933 and included in Piaget (1965/1977a).

5 Vidal (1987) showed that it had certain roots in the liberal Protestant tradition in which Piaget grew up.

itself. Differentiating between these two realities is one of the tasks of a developmentally oriented theory of knowledge. The question remains, however, whether this view of the relation between science and value was merely the privatistic vision of a great scientist or whether it has more general implications. We shall return to this question in chapter 8.

3

From the logic of thought to the logic of action

Piaget's first five books found immediate acclaim in the fields of child psychology and education. In his autobiography he described how he had been invited to many countries to present and discuss his ideas before learned audiences. He expressed some frustration at the fact that these first works often had been taken as his last word on the subject of child psychology, although he himself had considered them only as preliminary. In particular, he mentioned two major shortcomings of his early investigations. The first limitation was that these studies were exclusively concerned with children's reasoning as expressed on a verbal level. The second was that he had thus far failed to find structures-of-the-whole corresponding to logical operations as such.

Piaget had always believed that thought proceeded from action. As described in previous chapters, this epistemological pragmatism had derived in part from Bergson. But according to his own account, he had believed that language reflected action directly and that the logic of the child could therefore be studied in the context of verbal interaction (Piaget, 1952a, p. 247). Only later, after he had studied the development of sensorimotor intelligence during the first 2 years of life, had he understood the importance of the direct manipulation of objects in the development of logical operations. This understanding had led in turn to the discovery of concrete operations – logical operations that are manifest only in concrete situations and not yet on a formal plane.

The second limitation of these early works was that he had not yet been able to explain the development of logical operations in terms of structures-of-the-whole. As described in chapter 2, he had characterized children's thinking in general terms (syncretism, juxtaposition) deriving from his early intuitions regarding relational totalities in living systems. But he had not yet succeeded in characterizing logical operations in this manner. In his own words: "I tried in vain to find characteristic structures-of-the-whole relative to logical operations themselves (again my theory of the part and the whole!), I did not succeed because I did not seek their source in concrete operations" (ibid., p. 247). Instead, he had satisfied his need for explanation by seeking a functional explanation of intellectual development in terms of the social aspects of children's thinking.

During the years 1925–1929, Piaget carried a heavy teaching load, in addition to conducting psychological research. In 1925, A. Reymond (whose lectures on the problem of universals Piaget had attended as a student) vacated his chair of philosophy at the University of Neuchâtel, and Piaget took over some of his duties. These included courses in psychology and the philosophy of science and a seminar in philosophy. In addition, he taught courses in sociology in the Institut des Sciences Sociales and continued teaching child psychology at the Institut J.-J. Rousseau. One of the most important events that occurred during this period, as far as Piaget's own development was concerned, was the birth of his daughter Jacqueline in 1925. Two other children followed in 1927 (Lucienne) and 1931 (Laurent). With the aid of his wife, he conducted extensive observations of his children's intellectual development during the first 2 years of life. These observations provided him with his first data relevant to his early Bergsonian thesis that thought develops from action. They also provided him with some confirmation of his own "neo-pragmatic" view that a logic of action exists prior to and in addition to the logic of thought. This homegrown research was collected and published in three volumes – *The origins of intelligence in children* (Piaget, 1936/1963), *The construction of reality in the child* (Piaget, 1937/1971a), and *Play, dreams and imitation in childhood* (Piaget, 1945/1962) – to be reviewed in this chapter. Piaget described the significance of these investigations in these words: "The main benefit which I derived from these studies was that I learned in the most direct way how intellectual operations are prepared by sensory-motor action, even before the appearance of language" (Piaget, 1952a, p. 249). In addition, his studies of sensorimotor development led him to change his methods of investigating children's thinking. Instead of concentrating solely on verbal inquiry as he had previously, he began to observe children's reactions toward objects that they could manipulate directly. In this way, he arrived at the notion of concrete operations – to be described in chapter 4.

While still in Neuchâtel, Piaget completed the work on mollusks that he had begun in late childhood and to which he had devoted his doctoral dissertation. The problem that preoccupied him was the relation between hereditary and environmental influences in morphogenesis. A certain species of mollusk (*Limnaea stagnalis*) found in marshlands all over Europe and Asia typically has an elongated shape. In the great lakes of Switzerland and Sweden, however, the animal is also found in a shortened, globular variety. This variation was easily explained as a phenotypical adaptation to the action of waves and movement of water that forced the organism to attach itself to stones, thus causing an enlargement of the opening of its shell and a shortening of its whorl during development. The globular variety occurred naturally only in large lakes and only in those sections of the lakes where the water was roughest, and the same phenotypic variation could be produced experimentally (by breeding the mollusks in an aquarium with an agitator). Contrary to the purely phenotypic explanation, however, the shape of the globular variety was found to be genetically fixed; they did not revert to an elongated shape when they were bred in still water. Moreover, a pure species could be bred in this way that reproduced according to the classical Mendelian laws of cross-breeding.

Taken together, these facts posed a significant theoretical problem in that they could not be easily accounted for by known mechanisms of morphogenesis and hereditary transmission. In Piaget's view, the findings (a) that the shape of the globular variety of *L. stagnalis* was found to be genetically fixed, (b) that this fixation was encountered only in the lacustrine environments to which they were best adapted, and (c) that the same adaptation could be produced phenotypically were not easily explained by simple neo-Darwinian principles of random mutation and natural selection. And the fact that the experimentally produced phenotypic adaptations were not transmitted genetically contradicted a purely Lamarckian explanation of morphogenesis. These results led Piaget to seek a third alternative beyond Lamarckism and neo-Darwinism. Such an alternative was an intuition that he had expressed in *Recherche* before he had any facts to support it. Yet here were data that seemed to demand exactly such a third alternative. He summarized his findings as follows:

As early as the morphologico-reflex level there exist interactions between the environment and the organism which are such that the latter, without passively enduring the constraint of the former, nor limiting itself on contact with it to manifesting already preformed structures, reacts by an active differentiation of reflexes (in the particular case by a development of the reflexes of pedal adherence and of contraction) and by a correlative morphogenesis. [Piaget, 1936/1963, pp. 18–19]

This research was published in 1929 (Piaget, 1929c, 1929d) and will be considered in more detail in chapter 6. In the present context, it is important only insofar as it is relevant for his studies of sensorimotor development. As stated repeatedly in his writings, Piaget believed that definite analogies existed between functioning at the biological level and at the psychological level. Just as a third alternative between Lamarckism and neo-Darwinism was necessary to explain the facts of biological morphogenesis, so was a third alternative between empiricism and apriorism necessary to explain the facts of cognitive development.

In 1929, Piaget returned to Geneva as Professor of History of Scientific Thought and Assistant Director of the Institut J.-J. Rousseau. Three years later, he became codirector of the Institut along with Claparède and Bovet. In addition, he found time to take part in the founding of the Bureau International de l'Education, an organization later affiliated with UNESCO, and to become its director. This latter post undoubtedly appealed to the reformer in Piaget. He described in his autobiography how he saw the organization as a vehicle for contributing toward "the improvement of pedagogical methods and toward the official adoption of techniques better adapted to the mentality of the child" (Piaget, 1952a, p. 251).

Piaget described the 1930s as a period filled with teaching, research, and administrative duties. The course he taught at the University of Geneva on the history of scientific thought provided him with the historical material on which his later writings on genetic epistemology would be based. At the Institut J.-J. Rousseau he conducted his first research on concrete operations with the collaboration of A. Szeminska and B. Inhelder. At the same time, he began publishing his studies of sensorimotor development, which are the major subject of this chapter.

The origins of intelligence in children

Piaget began his first book on sensorimotor development by affirming the continuity between biology and the psychology of intelligence. This continuity consists in the fact that there exist certain hereditary factors in intellectual development. These hereditary factors are of two kinds. First, there are hereditary structures such as the nervous system, sensory organs, and so on. These structures make a substantial contribution to the development of intelligence, but are by no means sufficient to explain it in themselves. Second, in addition to these inherited structures, inherited functions also exist, including organization and adaptation. Although the respective structures change as one moves from one level to another, these basic functions remain invariant. Indeed, they are active in the formation of structures at all levels. One must therefore look to these functions in order to explain the origins of intelligence.

The function of adaptation refers to the organism's relations with its environment. Piaget had now replaced his earlier dichotomy of assimilation and imitation with the more precise terminology of assimilation and accommodation. He illustrated the operation of these functions as follows: Suppose the organism possesses an adaptive cycle consisting of the elements a, b, and c, which are adapted to accept the environmental inputs x, y, and z, respectively. Suppose further that the cycle in question is organized in the following way: Given state a of the organism, the input x produces action b, which, given input y, leads to action c, which, given input z, returns the organism to state a (Piaget, 1936/ 1963, p. 5). The "acceptance" of inputs x, y, and z by the organismic structural elements a, b, and c is what Piaget meant by the term "assimilation." The structure comprising a, b, and c *assimilates* the environmental inputs x, y, and z, and the latter are *assimilated by* the former. Now suppose that the organism in state a is confronted with the environmental input x', which differs slightly but not drastically from x. If the difference between x and x' were too great, the latter would not be capable of being assimilated by a, and the cycle a, b, $c \rightarrow a$ would not be carried out. However, if x' is sufficiently similar to x, then it will be assimilated by a, and the cycle will occur as follows: $a + x' \rightarrow b'$; $b' + y \rightarrow c$; $c + z \rightarrow a$. That is, the variation in "input" (a' instead of a) results in a compensating modification of the "output" (b' instead of b). This modification of organismic structures as a result of variation in environmental inputs is what Piaget referred to as accommodation.

The essential thing about accommodation is that the modification effected in the organism's structures compensates the corresponding variation in the environment. Piaget did not explain precisely how accommodation is able to produce compensating modifications in structure – how, in effect, it is able to discriminate between "appropriate" and "inappropriate" modifications. He took it instead as a phenomenon *sui generis*. Whereas assimilation is the recognition of functional identity (x and x' are treated as functionally the same insofar as they are assimilated to the same structure), accommodation is the recognition of functional differences (x and x' result in correspondingly different reactions on the part of the organism). Clearly, both of these functions are necessary for adaptation to occur. If the organism treated all environmental conditions as identical, it could not adapt to different circumstances; the range of inputs for each of its adaptive cycles would be much too wide. In contrast, if the organism treated all environmental conditions as different, it could not function in changing circumstances. The range of acceptable inputs would then be too narrow; a slight change in the environment would leave the organism unable to function. In short: "Adaptation is an equilibrium between assimilation and accommodation" (ibid., p. 6).

As for the function of organization, it is inseparable from adaptation. In fact, Piaget described them as complementary processes of a single mechanism. Whereas "adaptation" referred to the relations between the organism and its environment, "organization" referred to the relations among the organism's internal structures. In this context, Piaget's intuitions regarding relational totalities in organic systems reappeared. On the psychological level, the function of organization referred to the interrelations between intellectual operations:

Concerning the relationships between the parts and the whole which determine the organization, it is sufficiently well known that every intellectual operation is always related to all the others and that its own elements are controlled by the same law. Every schema is thus coördinated with all the other schemata and itself constitutes a totality with differentiated parts. [ibid., p. 7]

From the functions of adaptation and organization, Piaget went on to derive the categories of thought to be investigated by a psychology of intelligence. The adaptative function of assimilation corresponded to what Piaget in *The language and thought of the child* had called the "implicative function." It could further be divided into the logic of classes (i.e., the recognition of functional equivalence) and the logic of relations (the recognition of functional differences). Accommodation corresponded in turn to what Piaget had earlier called "the explicative function," or the "categories of reality": objects and their relations in space, and causality as it occurs in time. This scheme, incidentally, also determined the organization of his two main books on sensorimotor development. The first, *The origins of intelligence in children,* was devoted to the implicative function – that is, to the logic of classes and the logic of relations as they are manifest in sensorimotor functioning. In this sense, it covered the same ground for sensorimotor intelligence that Piaget's first two books (*The language and thought of the child* and *Judgment and reasoning in the child*) had covered for children's thinking. The second book on sensorimotor development, *The con-*

struction of reality in the child, was devoted to the explicative function – the "real categories" of object permanence, spatial relations, causality, and time. In this respect, it is analogous to what his third and fourth books (*The child's conception of the world* and *The child's conception of physical causality*) had accomplished for the investigation of children's thinking.

Corresponding to the function of organization are the categories of totality (with its correlative term, "relationship" or "reciprocity") and value (which may also be described in terms of an ideal or goal). As alluded to earlier, the category of totality/relationship refers to part–whole relations and to the reciprocal relations between the parts that together make up a whole. The category of ideality/value refers to the tendency toward ideal equilibrium. These two categories are really different aspects of the same reality, because ideals and values "are only totalities in process of formation" (ibid., p. 11). As in his previous characterizations of ideal equilibrium, Piaget sought in this way to define the directionality of intellectual development in a nonteleological manner. "Finality is thus to be conceived not as a special category, but as the subjective translation of a process of putting into equilibrium which itself does not imply finality but simply the general distinction between real equilibria and the [ideal] equilibrium" (ibid.). As an example, Piaget cited the norms of coherence and unity in logical thinking, which represent a "perpetual effort of intellectual totalities toward equilibrium" and therefore "define the ideal equilibrium never attained by intelligence" even as they regulate particular judgments (ibid.). The categories of totality/relationship and ideality/value thus constitute a "regulative function," corresponding to what he had called the "mixed" implicative-explicative function in *The language and thought of the child.*

The goal of *The origins of intelligence in children* was to discover which of the available theories of intelligence best account for the facts of sensorimotor development described in the book. Piaget stated five alternative theories at the outset, each corresponding to a different biological perspective on the relation between the organism and the environment. The first of these theories is *associationism,* the view that knowledge is acquired primarily through experience in the form of associations between habits or ideas. In biology, this view corresponds to Lamarckism, according to which the hereditary constitution of the organism itself is formed primarily through the genetic fixation of acquired habits. The second theory is *intellectualism,* which endows intelligence with an innate faculty for knowing and corresponds in biology to vitalism – the view that living beings have an innate capacity for constructing useful organs.

The third theory Piaget called *apriorism,* this being the view that innate ideas or innate structures of intelligence exist that shape experience from the beginning. In biology, apriorism corresponds to "preformism" – the view that organic structures are innate in origin and that the environment serves only to activate them. The fourth view is labeled *pragmatism,* by which Piaget means the doctrine of trial-and-error learning whereby behavior patterns are conceived of as occurring first at random and then being selected after the fact according to their instrumentality. This view corresponds to the biological theory of "mutationism," that is, to the neo-Darwinian view that variations in form first occur through random mutation and are selected according to their survival value.

The fifth theory of intelligence was Piaget's own. In contrast to the first four theories, which emphasize the role of either the organism or the environment, the fifth view implies "that the subject's activity is related to the constitution of the object, just as the latter involves the former" – in other words, that there is "an irreducible interdependence between experience and reasoning" (ibid., p. 16). Biologically, this theory corresponds to the view of organism–environment interaction that Piaget had espoused in his studies on mollusks – in effect, that "beside chance mutations there are adaptational variations simultaneously involving a structuring of the organism and an action of the environment, the two being inseparable from each other" (ibid.). To the extent that the analogy between psychological and biological theories actually holds, the reciprocal interdependence between organism and environment found in Piaget's studies of morphogenesis would suggest that a similar interdependence between subject and object might be found in the development of intelligence. Any final conclusions, however, were deferred until the evidence had been presented.

The bulk of *The origins of intelligence in children* consists of Piaget's observations of sensorimotor development in his own children during the first 2 years of life. The observed patterns of activity were classified according to six sequential stages. Although loosely correlated with age, these stages were not defined by age, but by the structure of the respective patterns of activity. In the following pages, the defining characteristics of each stage will briefly be reviewed. The reader is referred to the original for the wealth of detailed observations that Piaget provided.

Stage One: Reflexes. From birth, children already manifest organized patterns of activity in the form of reflexes. Piaget included in this category reflexes having to do with sucking, grasping, crying, vocalization, movements of limbs, and bodily movement, among others. Of these, sucking reflexes were analyzed in greatest detail. Immediately after birth, Lucienne and Laurent were observed to suck their hands or fingers. At their first meal a few hours after birth, contact between the mouth and breast sufficed for both children to initiate sucking and swallowing. Jacqueline, however, was slower to coordinate these movements, and the nipple repeatedly had to be replaced in her mouth (ibid., Obs. 1, p. 25).

Piaget followed the development of the sucking reflex in Laurent across the first 29 days after birth. Already on day 2, a kind of reflex search was observed associated with sucking; while engaged in sucking movements, Laurent moved his head back and forth as though searching for an object. On day 3, these search movements were utilized to find the breast as soon as it touched one of his cheeks. But these movements were not yet directed toward the goal from the beginning of the sequence; he hunted both on the side of his face touched by the nipple and on the other side. On day 12, however, he searched only on the side touched by the nipple. On day 20, he was observed to begin sucking the skin of the breast; apparently finding this unsatisfying, he was observed to try again 1 cm away, keeping up this "search" until the nipple was found. On the same day, Piaget offered his index finger to a hungry Laurent, who sucked it for a few seconds and then rejected it (ibid., Obs. 2–6, pp. 25–27).

These observations, together with the others provided by Piaget, sufficed for drawing some preliminary conclusions about the adaptation and organization of activity at this stage. To begin with the adaptive function of accommodation, the functioning of the reflex apparently is modified by contact with the environment. The experience of searching for the nipple makes the infant increasingly better able to find it. Similarly, the experience of sucking the nipple and other objects leads to an ability to discriminate between objects that are capable of providing nourishment and objects that are not. However, accommodation can occur only to the extent that the reflex assimilates the object to begin with. Piaget recognized three interrelated aspects of assimilation already manifest at this first stage of sensorimotor development. First, "functional assimilation" is manifest in the need for repetition. The fact that the activity of sucking is repeated even when the child is not particularly hungry indicates that the sucking reflex is not merely subordinated to the need for nourishment. In addition to the need for nourishment, a need for functioning in its own right also exists. Second, the tendency of the child to incorporate an increasing range of objects into the activity of sucking Piaget called "generalizing assimilation." Thus, he observed his children in the first weeks of life sucking their own fingers, the fingers of others, bedclothes, pillows, their coverlets, and other objects that by chance had presented themselves as objects for sucking. This kind of generalizing assimilation was observed primarily when children were not in a state of hunger. When they were hungry, they gradually became capable of discriminating between objects that would lead to satisfaction and those that would not. This ability to recognize different objects for the contributions they make to a particular aspect of the reflex (the need for satisfaction of hunger) Piaget called "recognitory assimilation." It was illustrated most vividly in Laurent's initial rejection of his father's index finger as an object for sucking, presumably because he did not "recognize" it as an object that would lead to satisfaction.

These three types of assimilation, however, are not to be thought of as radically different phenomena, but rather as different aspects of a single reality. "The reflex must be conceived as an organized totality whose nature it is to preserve itself by functioning and consequently to function sooner or later for its own sake (repetition) while incorporating into itself objects propitious to this functioning (generalized assimilation) and discerning situations necessary to certain modes of its activity (motor recognition)" (ibid., p. 38). Moreover, recognitory assimilation is not developmentally prior to generalizing assimilation in the sense that the child begins by discriminating one object (the mother's breast) and then successively applies what has been learned about this first object to a series of new ones. Instead, recognitory assimilation and generalizing assimilation develop in parallel, proceeding "from the undifferentiated schema to the individual and to the general, combined and complementary" (ibid., p. 34).

Finally, the pattern of search activity incorporated into the sucking reflex reflects the function of *organization* as defined earlier. The fact that the child searches for the breast indicates that the sucking reflex is already in some sense a directed activity. This, in turn, implies that the reflex is, in Piaget's terminology, an organized totality. "Such searching, which is the beginning of accommodation and assimilation, must be conceived, from the point of view of organization, as the first manifestation of a duality of desire and satisfaction, consequently of value and reality, of complete totality and incomplete totality, a duality which is to reappear on all planes of future activity" (ibid., p. 39).

Of the three general functions considered so far – assimilation, accommodation, and organization – Piaget concluded that assimilation is the basic fact of psychic life. Accommodation can occur only to the extent that assimilation has already occurred, and organization is simply the static fact of which assimilation constitutes the dynamic aspect. Assimilation, above all, expresses the continuity between the biological and psychological levels of reality. In Piaget's words, "The existence of an organized totality which is preserved while assimilating the external world raises, in effect, the whole problem of life itself" (ibid., p. 46). But to recognize the continuity between biological and psychological adaptation is not to reduce the one to the other. On the psychological level, the assimilation of an actual fact into a preexisting scheme presages the act of judgment and, as such, shows itself to be the basic fact on this level as well. The central role of assimilation will be manifest at all subsequent stages of sensorimotor development.

Stage Two: The first acquired adaptations. Piaget described the second stage of sensorimotor development in terms of two criteria: the "first acquired adaptations," defined as the incorporation of something into a motor scheme that was originally external to it, and the "primary circular reaction," defined as the functional repetition of an activity "for its own sake." These two criteria were not regarded as independent, inasmuch as the circular reaction could be described, following Wallon's usage, as "the functional use leading to the preservation or the rediscovery of a new result" (ibid., p. 55). The primary circular reaction is the process by which the child's first adaptations are acquired.

Given the fact that accommodation to the external environment already exists at the level of the reflex, the adaptations characteristic of the first two stages are not easily distinguished. But even though the stages merge almost imperceptibly into each other, Piaget thought it was possible to distinguish them both in theory and in practice. The difference between them is best illustrated with a concrete example. At the level of the reflex, the accommodations that occur in sucking never go beyond the activity of sucking itself. The child comes to distinguish between different objects to be sucked, but nothing external to the activity of sucking is introduced. However, as soon as children learn to suck their own fingers in a systematic way – that is, as soon as they can bring their fingers to their mouths and keep them there – then something external to the original activity of sucking has been introduced, namely, the movement of the arm and hand.

Henceforth, the movement of the arm and hand becomes subordinated to the activity of sucking. Children become capable of bringing the fingers to the mouth in order to suck them, as it were. According to Piaget, no true intentionality as yet exists in this activity, because the ends have not yet become differentiated from the means. That is, there is no goal to the activity apart from that activity itself. Only in subsequent stages, when children begin to notice the effects of their actions on the environment, does intentionality by Piaget's criterion begin to appear. In the present stage, the "goal" of activity is the activity itself, together with the immediate sensations that accompany it. Thus, action is no longer elicited in a quasi-automatic way by internal or external stimulation. Instead, it becomes forward-looking: A pattern of activity is reproduced in order to reproduce the ensemble of sensations that immediately accompany it. This is what is meant by the term "primary circular reaction."

Besides sucking, Piaget observed the development of primary circular reactions and the first acquired adaptations for seeing, hearing, phonation, and prehension. Thus, he observed his children developing beyond mere orientation reflexes to patterns of looking in order to see, listening in order to hear, grasping for the sake of grasping, and so on. Just as the activity of sucking incorporated movements of the arm and hand, these other activities began to incorporate each other into their respective patterns. Seeing incorporates hearing as children come to orient themselves visually in the direction of something heard, and so forth. In most of these examples, the first manifestations of Stage Two patterns begin to appear around the beginning of the second month.

The development of prehension as described by Piaget is more complicated than that of the other activity patterns – perhaps because it incorporates a greater number of other activities unto itself, including grasping, sucking, and vision. Five stages in the development of prehension are described that are independent of the main stages of sensorimotor development, but overlap with the first three of them. The *first stage* comprises only the grasping reflex and impulsive movements of the hand. The *second stage* is that of the first circular reactions of hand movements before these become coordinated with sucking or vision. The child is observed to grasp objects for the sake of grasping them, without looking at them or carrying them to the mouth. The *third stage* is characterized by a coordination between grasping and sucking. The hand brings to the mouth objects it has grasped at random. At the same time, vision and hand movements begin to be coordinated, insofar as the child tends to look at the hand when it enters the visual field and to keep it there in order to look at it. But only in the *fourth stage* does the child begin to grasp objects that are seen as soon as the hand and the object are seen together. Finally, in the *fifth stage,* objects can be grasped as soon as they are seen, regardless of whether or not the hand is visible at the same time. In addition, objects that are grasped are carried into the visual field in order to be looked at and are not immediately carried to the mouth. Piaget's children passed through these stages at different rates, with Jacqueline showing her first reactions belonging to this stage only in the sixth month, and Laurent already at 3.5 months.

Piaget summarized the acquisitions characteristic of Stage Two in terms of the general functions of accommodation, assimilation, and organization. The *accommodations* characteristic of this stage differ from those of the reflex stage in that they introduce modifications into the action scheme as such. In the stage of reflex activity, the child was capable of discriminating the breast from other objects to be sucked, but no major modifications were introduced into the activity of sucking itself. In the accommodations characterizing Stage Two, however, the action scheme itself becomes modified as the child learns to suck the fingers systematically. Henceforth, sucking becomes coordinated with the movements of the hand and arm, resulting in a single scheme that incorporates both activities. As for *assimilation,* Piaget found the same three forms of assimilation in this stage that he had found in Stage One, albeit at a different level of organization. Functional assimilation can be seen in the very repetitions characteristic of the primary circular reaction. Whereas reflexes were repeated because of an inherent need for functioning without regard for its consequences, the activities incorporated in the primary circular reactions are repeated in order to reproduce the immediate sensations that accompany them. Likewise, generalizing assimilation can be discerned in the extension of circular reactions to ever new objects and situations in the very process of repetition. For example, the child learns to look at new objects, persons, and events in the environment, even though these things as yet constitute only perceived phenomena and are not yet distinguished as objective occurrences independent of perception. Recognitory assimilation arises from this process of generalization, as the perceived objects, persons, or events become recognized as familiar. Piaget described, for example, how smiling can be interpreted as an affective expression accompanying recognition and how this affect directs the course of generalization: ''The subject looks neither at what is too familiar, because he is in a way surfeited with it, nor at what is too new because this does not correspond to anything in his schemata'' (ibid., p. 68).

Finally, typical forms of *organization* can also be found in Stage Two. Not only do the elementary behavior patterns characteristic of the reflex stage begin to incorporate each other in Stage Two, but in so doing they constitute a new totality. This mutual assimilation (and accommodation) of action schemes leading to the formation of greater totalities Piaget called ''reciprocal assimilation.'' One may easily see in this process a new embodiment of Piaget's familiar idea of the reciprocal relations that exist between the parts of a relational totality. In this connection, Piaget first used the phrase *structure d'ensemble* in the sense in which it would later be employed as a technical term:

Every act of prehension presupposes an organized totality in which tactile and kinesthetic sensations and arm, hand and finger movements intervene. Hence such schemata constitute "structures" of a whole [*"structures" d'ensemble*], although they were elaborated in the course of a slow evolution and over a number of attempts, gropings, and corrections. But above all these schemata are organized in coördination with schemata of another kind, chief of which are those of sucking and vision. We have seen in what this organization consists: it is a reciprocal adaptation of the schemata in view, naturally with mutual accommodation but also with collateral assimilation. Everything that is looked at or sucked tends to be grasped and everything that is grasped tends to be sucked and then to be looked at. [ibid., p. 121]

This reciprocal assimilation and accommodation of schemes distinguishes the adaptations of this stage from mere associations. Associations might explain how children learn to look at what they grasp or to grasp what they see, but it does not explain why both happen at the same time. The fact that the adaptation occurs in both directions at once indicates that the two or more schemes involved have become integrated into a single whole. "The conjunction of two cycles or of two schemata is to be conceived as a new totality, self-enclosed. There is neither association between two groups of images nor even association between two needs, but rather the formation of a new need and the organization of earlier needs as a function of this new unity" (ibid., p. 143). This concept of reciprocal assimilation would play an increasingly important role in Piaget's explanations of the behavior patterns characteristic of the higher stages of sensorimotor development.

Stage Three: Secondary circular reactions. For Piaget, intentionality was one of the central defining characteristics of intelligence. He defined intentionality in terms of the differentiation between ends and means. In general, an intelligent activity is one that is goal-directed and in which means are employed that are appropriate for the attainment of that goal. In these terms, the primary circular reactions of Stage Two are neither intentional nor truly intelligent. In looking for the sake of seeing, grasping for the sake of grasping, and so on, ends and means are not clearly differentiated from each other; the "goal" of the activity is the activity itself. Not until Stage Four do children become fully capable of performing one action as a means of accomplishing another – for example, setting aside an obstacle in order to grasp an object.

The "secondary circular reactions" characteristic of Stage Three are midway between the two extremes. Defined in terms of the attempt to recreate an effect produced on the environment by repeating the action that produced the effect, the secondary circular reaction implies an incipient differentiation between ends and means. The goal in this case is the recreation of the effect, and the means is the repetition of the corresponding action. The particular limitation of this form of intentionality is that the goal is in every case only the repetition of an event that has just occurred. The goal is set "after the fact," and for this reason the secondary circular reaction does not attain the true intentionality of Stage Four, in which the setting of a goal actually initiates a cycle of activity.

The character of the secondary circular reaction can be made clear with a few concrete examples. At 0;3(5),[1] Piaget observed Lucienne kicking her legs violently in her bassinet. This caused the cloth dolls hanging from the hood to swing back and forth. Lucienne looked at the dolls, smiled, and began to move her legs again. But it was unclear whether she kicked in order to make the dolls move or whether kicking and smiling simply constituted a total reaction expressing great pleasure. Over the next few days, Piaget continued to observe Lucienne when the dolls were suspended in front of her. At 0;3(8), a chance movement set the dolls in motion. Lucienne looked at them and shook her legs "vigorously and thoroughly" as if to make them continue. When her hands by chance passed before her eyes, she examined them briefly and then returned to the dolls. At 0;3(16), Lucienne caused the dolls to swing as soon as Piaget suspended them above her head. She shook her legs with precise and rhythmical movements, with a long pause between shakes, as if she were studying the relation between her actions and the movements of the dolls. "Success gradually causes her to smile," wrote Piaget. "This time the circular reaction is indisputable" (ibid., Obs. 94, pp. 157–158).

Piaget recounted a number of other observations having to do with secondary circular reactions arising from the spontaneous activities of his children. Thus, both Lucienne and Jacqueline learned to cause a doll hanging from the hood of the bassinet to swing back and forth by kicking it. Lucienne made the connection between the movements of her foot and the swinging of the doll, but for Jacqueline kicking was simply an incidental component of a total body movement, as indicated by the fact that she attempted to influence the doll through the same wriggling of arms, trunk, and feet, even when the doll was suspended out of range of her feet (ibid., Obs. 95–96, pp. 159–160). In a similar manner, Laurent learned to make suspended objects move or to produce audible sounds by pulling a string or a chain attached to them (ibid., Obs. 97–99, pp. 160–164). In a secondary circular reaction that would become important for its subsequent uses, all three of Piaget's children learned to set suspended objects in motion by striking them with their hands (ibid., Obs. 103, pp. 167–168).

What all of these examples of the secondary circular reaction have in common is that children's attention is focused on some event caused by one of their actions, and they attempt to reproduce that event by repeating or continuing the action. In this, their behavior may be distinguished from the patterns characteristic of Stage Two, in which attention was focused on the action itself, and from those of Stage Four, in which the goals of action are no longer limited to mere repetition. As usual, Piaget discussed his findings in terms of the adaptation and organization characteristic of the particular stage.

With respect to *accommodation,* the particular characteristics of Stage Three reveal themselves in the rediscovery of the movements that lead to the observed result. In the observation in which Jacqueline attempted to reproduce the swing-

---

1 Children's ages in years, months, and days are designated according to Piaget's abbreviated format. Thus, 0;3(5) represents 0 years, 3 months, and 5 days.

ing of a hanging doll through a total body reaction that included movements of arms and torso as well as her legs, she had not yet determined which of these movements was effective. In other observations, however, Piaget's children came to discriminate those actions that were effective from those that were not – as when Laurent learned to shake some celluloid balls by pulling a string attached first to his right hand and then to his left. According to Piaget's interpretation, such accommodations are possible only through the *reciprocal assimilation* of primary schemes. In the primary circular reaction, the child's attention was focused only on a given activity, but in the secondary circular reaction attention is extended to the external consequences of the particular activity. But this is simply to say that a reciprocal assimilation between primary schemes has occurred. In learning to set hanging dolls in motion, for example, the scheme governing leg movements is reciprocally assimilated to the scheme of looking and seeing. This reciprocal assimilation of primary schemes leads to mutual accommodation, resulting in the secondary circular reaction as such.

This pattern of reciprocal assimilation of primary schemes followed by mutual accommodation already provides a clue regarding the *organization* particular to this stage. This reciprocal adaptation results in a new totality: the secondary scheme constituted by the secondary circular reaction. Moreover, such secondary schemes embody an incipient differentiation between ends and means, the ends constituting in Piaget's terminology a value or "ideal." From Stage Three onward, children's activity begins to be goal-directed, although the goals available to them at this stage are still limited to the repetition of observed effects.

The very repetition embodied in the secondary circular reaction is an indication of the kind of functional assimilation that occurs at this stage. The basic, irreducible need for functioning manifests itself at every level of development. In the process of formation, the secondary schemes manifest this need for functioning in terms of the repetitions and reproductions that characterize them. Like the repetitions characterizing the primary circular reactions, the child's interest varies as a function of the familiarity of the situation. Children confronted by an object utilized by a thoroughly familiar secondary circular reaction often are content merely to outline the customary movements embodied in the typical reaction rather than actually to perform them. Piaget interpreted reactions of this nature as examples of recognitory assimilation.

While trying to grasp some spools hanging above her, for example, Lucienne accidentally caused them to swing. Noticing this, she broke off her attempt to reach them and shook her legs momentarily before recommencing her efforts at grasping. Based on a number of other observations of a similar nature, Piaget interpreted these outlined actions as examples of a simple form of motor recognition. Lacking language, this act of recognition is accomplished by briefly activating a motor scheme in the context of which the object is familiar. "Instead of saying: 'Oh! the spool is swinging,' or: 'There is my hand. . . . There is the parrot. . . . There is the bassinet which is moving,' the child assimilates these facts by means of motor concepts, not yet verbal, and, by shaking his own legs or hands, so indicates to himself that he understands what he perceives'' (ibid., p. 188).

According to Piaget, these recognitory assimilations indicate that there exists already at the level of sensorimotor intelligence a system of meanings or significations, implying a differentiation between signifier and signified. The signifiers characteristic of this level, however, are neither symbols, defined as an image or object chosen to represent a class of actions or images, nor signs, defined as arbitrary and collective symbols. As opposed to these more or less abstract, representational signifiers, Piaget called the concrete signifiers characteristic of sensorimotor intelligence ''indications'' and suggested that characteristic forms of such indications exist at each level of sensorimotor development. In the first two stages, elementary sensory impressions serve merely as ''signals'' that, in being assimilated to a given scheme, simply set in motion the whole cycle of activity embodied in that scheme. Thus, these elementary signals ''remain essentially functional and related to the subject's own activity'' (ibid., p. 194). The indications characterizing the third stage, however, comprise an element of foresight relating to the events that will ensue if familiar objects are acted on in certain ways. Thus, a string hanging from the hood of the bassinet is not only something to be seen, grasped, or pulled but also something that can serve to move other objects at a distance. Of course, the child is not aware at this stage of the particular causal relations that connect the objects acted on to the effects that ensue. Rather, the sight of a certain state of affairs serves as an indication of the results expected if that initial state of affairs is acted on in a certain way. The string is a signifier for the scheme of ''pulling in order to shake the hood'' (ibid., pp. 194–195). The indications characterizing subsequent stages of sensorimotor development will be described in their turn.

Finally, Piaget also found characteristic forms of generalizing assimilation at Stage Three in the form of ''procedures to make interesting spectacles last.'' Having learned to influence certain objects through the application of motor schemes in secondary circular reactions, children go on to apply these same procedures to other objects in other situations – whether or not the actions in question actually have the desired effects in those new situations. Having learned to swing hanging objects by moving her legs, for example, Lucienne applied this scheme to all sorts of new objects that happened to be outside her grasp, including a cross of Malta, a pipe, a hanging puppet, a swinging strap, and a watch (ibid., Obs. 111, pp. 198–199). This procedure, however, was also generalized beyond objects out of reach. In order to study imitation, Piaget went through a number of bodily movements in Lucienne's presence, including swinging his hands, moving his fingers, wagging his head, opening and closing his mouth. Along with intermittent efforts at imitating these movements, Lucienne also used her familiar scheme of shaking her legs in order to make her father continue these movements (ibid., Obs. 116, pp. 204–205).

These examples of ''procedures to make interesting spectacles last'' show that the child has as yet no awareness of the causal relations connecting actions with the observed effects. A functional correspondence is simply established between the action and its effect, without an awareness of the intermediaries leading from the one to the other. In another theoretical tradition, such patterns of activity might be labeled "superstitious behavior." For Piaget, they constituted a early precursor of the magico-phenomenalism characteristic of preoperational thought. His observations suggested that such patterns arise simply by extension and generalization of secondary circular reactions before children are yet capable of understanding the causal relations connecting their actions to the observed effects of those actions. This understanding develops only in the later stages of sensorimotor development.

Stage Four: Coordination of secondary schemes. Whereas the behavior patterns of Stage Three were characterized by an incipient intentionality, limited by the fact that action could at most be directed toward the goal of reproducing certain effects, the patterns characterizing Stage Four are subject to no such limitation. In the pattern that Piaget called the "application of familiar schemata to new situations," for example, one scheme is subordinated to another as means to an end. In this respect, Stage Four marks the beginning of true intentionality characterized by a real differentiation between means and ends. At the same time, this subordination of one scheme to another represents the "coordination of secondary schemes" underlying all typical Stage Four patterns.

Piaget provided a number of examples of the "application of familiar schemes to new situations." He presented Laurent at 0;6(1), for example, with a piece of paper that the child immediately attempted to grasp. But Piaget placed the paper out of reach on the hood of the bassinet and on a string connected to the hood. Laurent first applied his "procedures" for influencing inaccessible objects: shaking himself, waving his arms, and so on. When the paper was about to fall off the hood, he stopped pulling the string and reached for the paper, now within grasp. Piaget had the distinct impression that Laurent had utilized the scheme of pulling the string as a means for reaching the paper, but because the paper had been placed in the same situation in which the scheme of pulling the string was usually employed, this observation may simply have been an example of the generalization of a secondary circular reaction (ibid., Obs. 120, pp. 214–215).

A clearer example is provided by the behavior pattern of "setting aside obstacles." At 0;7(13), Laurent was presented with a box of matches placed above and behind his father's hand so that it was visible but could not be reached without setting the obstacle aside in some way. On previous days, Laurent had been unable to attain the objective blocked in this way, but now he suddenly began striking his father's hand, knocking it out of the way so as to enable him to reach the matchbox. On subsequent days, Piaget repeated the experiment with different objectives and different obstacles. Laurent clearly used the familiar scheme of striking an object as a means of attaining the end of grasping the object (ibid., Obs. 122, pp. 217–218).

Piaget also reported several examples of "setting aside obstacles" important in tracing the development of the object concept as described in *The construction of reality in the child*. At 0;8(29), Laurent found a box by removing a pillow that covered it, but it was not clear that he intended to seek the box by lifting the pillow. At 0;9(17), however, he lifted a cushion in order to find a cigar case. The fact that he lifted the cushion with one hand while reaching for the cigar case with the other indicated that the scheme of lifting was subordinated to the scheme of grasping as means to an end (ibid., Obs. 126, p. 222).

These patterns differ from those of Stage Three with respect to the intentionality involved. First, the goal is no longer limited to mere reproduction of an effect that has already occurred. The goal (e.g., grasping an object) is an action in its own right, rather than merely the repetition of an action that has already occurred. Second, the means are fully differentiated from the ends as two separate action schemes; striking, pulling, lifting, and so on, serve as means for applying the scheme of grasping. This coordination of two action schemes is accomplished through reciprocal assimilation; the schemes assimilate each other even as they both apply to a single objective:

When Laurent tries to grasp a piece of paper situated too high up and to do this, searches, then pulls a string hanging from the hood, he at first assimilates the paper to a schema of prehension (or to a more complex schema: feeling it, etc.), then, without ceasing to want to apply this first schema to it, he assimilates the same object to a very familiar schema of "pulling the string in order to shake." This second assimilation is, therefore, itself subordinated to the first; that is to say, pulling the strings in order to move the paper, he continues to desire it in the capacity of an "object to grasp" (he must at least have the impression that by shaking the objective he acquires a power over it which puts it more at his disposition). Due to this double assimilation the schema of "pulling the string" is coördinated with the schema of "grasping" and becomes a transitional schema in relation to a final schema. . . . Such a reciprocal assimilation can lead either to a symmetrical relation (pulling in order to grasp and grasping in order to pull), or to a relation of simple inclusion (pulling in order to grasp). [ibid., p. 231]

Such reciprocal assimilation of secondary schemes (together with the reciprocal accommodations that ensue) results in those schemes becoming "mobile" in the sense that they are detached from their original contents and become capable of applying to a wide range of new objects and situations. In this way, they become capable of entering into new coordinations and syntheses. "From particular schemata with special or particular contents they accordingly become generic schemata with multiple contents" (ibid., p. 238). Moreover, this newly acquired generic quality allows them to function in a manner analogous to conceptual judgments on the plane of reflective intelligence – except that children are naturally not reflectively aware of these sensorimotor "judgments," but simply carry them out in concrete actions.

Just as a logic of classes can be distinguished from a logic of relations on the level of reflective intelligence, so can analogous systems of classes and relations be distinguished in sensorimotor functioning. In assimilating any given object to a mobile secondary scheme, children effectively classify that object as belonging to the generic class of objects that can be acted on by that scheme. In reciprocally assimilating one secondary scheme to another, systems of relations are created. Relations of "appurtenance" are created in the very subordination of one scheme to another as means to ends, and spatial-temporal relations are created depending on the real relations existing among the objects and actions involved. "For example, in order to remove a cushion which is an obstacle to grasping the objective, the child does not simply class the cushion in the schema of striking and assimilate, by inclusion, this schema to that of the end of the action, but he must understand that the obstacle is 'in front of' the objective, that it must be removed 'before' trying to grasp this objective, etc." (ibid., p. 239). The very existence of an obstacle as such is a kind of practical "negation." Even rudimentary quantitive relations can be observed during this period. At 9–10 months, for example, Laurent provided evidence for a global comprehension of the number of syllables repeated by his father; he correctly imitated "pa" and "papa" and said "pa-papa" for four syllables or more. Finally, to complete the analogy, the functioning of "mobile" schemes that embody sensorimotor classes and relations is analogous to making logical judgments: "The subordination of means to ends is the equivalent, on the plane of practical intelligence, of the subordination of premises to conclusions, on the plane of logical intelligence" (ibid., p. 238).

Given the fact that accommodation can occur only to the extent that assimilation has already occurred, the forms of accommodation characteristic of Stage Four follow from the characteristic forms of assimilation. In effect, accommodation at this stage consists in the elaboration of the new relations engendered by the reciprocal assimilation of secondary schemes in the manner just described. Thus, in assimilating the scheme of striking to the scheme of grasping as means to an end, a new relation is created ("pushing back in order to"), and the striking scheme is modified accordingly. Moreover, such reciprocal assimilations make possible for the first time accommodations that reflect objective relations existing in the environment, instead of being confined to the relation between an action and its outcome, as was the case at Stage Two. Naturally, the objectivity of these relations is limited by the scope of the reciprocal assimilations possible at this stage.

The reciprocal assimilations occurring at Stage Four also define the new forms of *organization* developing at this time. First, the subordination of means to ends results in new forms of value and ideality; the means are valuable insofar as they lead to the goal, or ideal. Second, the reciprocal assimilation of secondary schemes results in new totalities containing within them the new relations that have been constructed. The mutual accommodations between schemes assimilated to each other result not only in the preservation of the relationships actually experienced but also in the construction of series of "virtual" relations resulting from the cross-products of the relations embodied in each scheme considered separately. Such construction of relations is what Piaget referred to when he wrote that "every schema, insomuch as it is a totality, is pregnant with a series of schemata virtually contained within it, each organized totality thus being, not composed of totalities of a lower grade, but a possible source of such formations" (ibid.,

p. 245). In other words, the new totalities created by the reciprocal assimilation of secondary schemes are not merely the additive sum of the elements contained in the original schemes. Instead, these elements or relations are combined through mutual accommodation in such a way that entirely new relations are produced. Because these new relations have not yet been actualized in experience, they remain, for the time being, "virtual." The construction of these virtual totalities and relations is important in Piaget's explanation of the construction of novel behavior patterns that have never before been actualized in experience and therefore cannot be explained through trial-and-error learning or through processes of association.

Finally, Piaget also described characteristic forms of recognitory and generalizing assimilation characteristic of Stage Four. In contrast to the recognition of signals or indications in the previous stages, children now become capable of recognizing "signs" independent of their own activity. For example, both Jacqueline at 0;9(15) and Lucienne at 0;10(19) were observed to begin crying as soon as the person they were with gave the impression of leaving by turning away, starting to stand up, and so on. Here the various acts generally associated with leaving became a "sign" for actual leaving. Similarly, Jacqueline at 0;9(16) was observed to accept the contents of a spoon when it came from a glass but not when it came from a bowl, because she knew that grape juice (which she liked) generally came out of the glass and soup (which she did not like) came out of the bowl. Here the glass became a "sign" for the grape juice, and the bowl a "sign" for the soup. At Stage Three, the relation between signifiers and the things signified was limited to the relations established by the child's own actions (e.g., a string that signifies action on objects at a distance), but at Stage Four the signifying relation pertains to the properties of the things themselves. The glass can signify the grape juice, and the bowl the soup, because these pairs of items in fact cooccur. Naturally, the "significations" of this stage have nothing to do with abstract representation. Rather, the signifier evokes a "concrete expectation" of the signified, and the relation between the thing evoking the expectation and the thing expected constitutes "signification" at this level of development (ibid., p. 252).

As for generalizing assimilation, Piaget described another new pattern characteristic of this stage that he called the "derived secondary circular reaction." Confronted by a new object, children apply their familiar secondary schemes to it one by one in order to "understand" it in terms of those schemes. The object, in effect, is defined in terms of its action properties. The derived secondary circular reaction arises when, in the course of such exploration of objects, children discover by chance that the object "reacts" to their manipulations in an unexpected way, and they repeat their own actions in order to reproduce the initially unexpected result. For example, at 0;10(2), Laurent was observed examining a metal case of shaving soap for the first time. Being hard and slippery, it escaped his grasp. He then went about repeating this result by intentionally letting the object slip from his grasp (ibid., Obs. 140, pp. 257–258). This pattern was classified by Piaget as a secondary circular reaction, because the child attempted to reproduce an effect by repeating an action that caused it. But it differs from the secondary circular reactions of Stage Three in that it arises not entirely by chance but in the context of the exploration of new objects. Similarly, this pattern differs from Stage Five generalizations in that the child is concerned only with the immediate effects of actions on objects, not with whatever happens to them subsequently. In the observation cited earlier, for example, Laurent was interested only in the slippery properties of the soap case that caused it to fall, not with what happened to it after it fell – as he would be in the next stage.

Stage Five: Tertiary circular reactions. The fifth stage in the development of sensorimotor intelligence is characterized by two behavior patterns, the "tertiary circular reaction" and the "discovery of new means through active experimentation." Both patterns represent a new orientation toward novelty in the child's experience. In the tertiary circular reaction, children discover some new effect that one of their actions has on the environment and go about repeating that action with variations in order to see what varied effects are produced by these variations in action. This pattern clearly resembles the "derived secondary circular reactions" of Stage Four and develops from them. The difference is that in those former circular reactions the children's attention was focused more on repeating the actions that led to a new result, whereas in the tertiary circular reactions their attention is focused on the results themselves. More precisely, it is the *variation* produced in those results as a consequence of variation in action that is of interest.

The "discovery of new means through active experimentation" also derives from and extends a Stage Four pattern, in this case, the "application of familiar schemes to new situations." In effect, the Stage Five pattern comes into being in situations in which the Stage Four pattern fails, namely, in situations in which none of the children's familiar schemes are sufficient to be used as means to a desired end. In such situations, children in Stage Five prove to be capable of a pattern of action unavailable to the Stage Four child: Different means are attempted until an effective one is discovered. In Piaget's terminology, children "grope" for the means that will enable them to attain the goal. This groping is similar to what is otherwise known in psychology as "trial-and-error learning," except that Piaget did not believe that children's successive trials are generated purely at random, but instead that their efforts are to some extent directed from the first.

A concern with the relation between variation in actions and variation in their effects is common to both the tertiary circular reaction and the "discovery of new means through active experimentation." In the former the relation between action and outcome is pursued for its own sake, but in the latter it is subordinated to the attempt to attain a goal. Actions are varied in order to find the particular variation that can serve as an appropriate means. But only those actions can be varied that the child already possesses in schematic form, and Piaget argues accordingly that the child's groping is directed from the beginning.

As an example of the tertiary circular reaction, Piaget described Laurent's behavior of letting objects fall. In the preceding description of derived secondary circular reactions, Laurent discovered the slippery properties of a soap case and repeatedly let it slide from his fingers as if to study the phenomenon. His attention in that observation remained focused on the act of letting go and letting fall, and the pattern was therefore classified as a derived secondary circular reaction. At 0;10(10), however, the pattern became tertiary. Laurent was observed playing with a piece of bread. Breaking off small pieces, he let them drop from his hand. In contrast to his behavior with the soap case, he now showed no interest in the action of letting go as such, but instead followed the trajectory of the falling object, looked at it after it had fallen, and picked it up again when he could.

On the days that followed, he applied this scheme to a number of different objects, varying both the manner in which they were dropped and the terrain onto which they fell. He was clearly interested in the outcomes of these variations; when the object fell in a new position (e.g., on a pillow), he repeated the maneuver as though studying the spatial relations involved (ibid., Obs. 141, pp. 268–269). A similar interest in the activity of letting objects fall under different conditions and following their trajectories was observed with Jacqueline (ibid., Obs. 144, pp. 270–271). Other examples of tertiary circular reactions included the following: Laurent's experiments with making a watch chain swing in different ways (ibid., Obs. 142, pp. 269–270), Jacqueline's interest in rolling different objects under different conditions (ibid., Obs. 145, pp. 271–272), her discovery that a box pressed near the edge (but not in the center) would tilt up on the opposite side (ibid., Obs. 146, pp. 272–273), and her manipulation of objects in the bathtub – letting them go under water in order to watch them rise to the surface (ibid., Obs. 147, p. 273).

With regard to the "discovery of new means through active experimentation," three main examples were provided that Piaget called the "behavior pattern of the support," the "behavior pattern of the string," and the "behavior pattern of the stick." In each case, new means for obtaining a certain objective were discovered through active experimentation, and in the process the spatial and/or causal relations between the objects involved were discovered as well. Between 0;7(29) and 0;10(16), for example, Piaget conducted a number of experiments with Laurent having to do with an object placed on top of a cushion such that the object was out of the child's reach, but could be obtained by pulling on the cushion. Although Laurent was able to reach the object in this way several times during this period, he did not yet understand the true relation between the object and the cushion, as indicated by the fact that he pulled the cushion to obtain the object even when Piaget held the object above the cushion so that there was no contact between object and cushion. Rather, Laurent, unable to grasp the objective, seemed to grasp for the nearest object, which fortuitously brought the desired object within reach.

Only at 0;10(16) did Laurent for the first time give evidence of understanding the relation "placed upon." Piaget placed his watch on a cushion as in the preceding experiments. Laurent first reached for the watch and then grabbed hold of the cushion. But instead of letting go of the cushion in order to reach for the watch again as he had previously done, he appeared to notice as if for the first time that the watch moved in a manner directly related to his own manipulation of the cushion. In this way, he was easily able to obtain the watch. As a counterproof, Piaget placed the watch on a second cushion overlapping with the first, such that the first was closer to the child and the overlap between the cushions was not too obvious. Seeing that the watch was outside his reach, Laurent began by grasping the first cushion. But he noticed right away that the watch did not move when he pulled on the first cushion. Discovering in this way the overlap between the two cushions, he grasped the second one and obtained the watch right away (ibid., Obs. 148, pp. 282–284). Similar results were obtained with Jacqueline and Lucienne (ibid., Obs. 149–151, pp. 285–287).

Jacqueline and Laurent were also observed learning to obtain distant objects by pulling a string attached to them (ibid., Obs. 153–156, pp. 290–294). Having previously understood that a distant object can be moved by shaking a string attached to that object, both children began by applying this scheme of shaking the string in order to have some effect on the desired object. Even after they discovered that the string must be pulled in order to obtain the goal, they continued to begin by shaking the string as though this were a necessary part of the whole procedure. Only gradually and after repeated attempts and self-corrections did they learn to pull the string right away. The "behavior pattern of the stick" was acquired in an analogous manner. In this case, a distant object was obtained through the intermediary of a stick rather than by a string or a support (ibid., Obs. 157–161, pp. 297–301).

With respect to the adaptive functions of assimilation and accommodation, Piaget stated that beginning with Stage Five, a new relation can be discerned between them. Not only do they become more differentiated from each other; they also become related in a more complementary manner. Previously, accommodation always followed assimilation. Schemes could accommodate to an object only to the extent that the object had already been assimilated by that scheme. Beginning with the tertiary circular reaction, however, the order between the two functions appears to be partially reversed. Accommodation is pursued for its own sake, or, expressed differently, objects are assimilated in order to explore their possibilities for accommodation. These possibilities arise, first, because the scope of assimilation has been extended; the child is now capable of assimilating the novel effects of actions, not merely the novel features of the actions themselves as in Stage Four. Second, the possibilities for accommodation are extended by the child's effort to assimilate new objects to each of its secondary schemes in turn. The child's capacity for appreciating the particularities of objects is multiplied by the possibility of assimilating an object to several schemes at once.

These new possibilities for accommodation manifest themselves in the form of groping, but this process of progressive accommodation is neither a process of chance selection (trial-and-error learning) nor an immediate structuration ("insight"). Groping cannot be interpreted as purely random trial-and-error, because the sequence of trials is directed from the first toward a goal. It is not that chance plays no part, but the range of possibilities that are selected by chance is limited by the goal-directedness of action. When the scheme of displacing a distant object by shaking a string is assimilated to the goal of grasping that object, the functioning of the shaking scheme is limited and directed accordingly. But the subsequent evolution of this directed groping is indeed shaped by success as the theory of trial-and-error would have it. Variations in the shaking scheme that bring the goal nearer are selected by success, and those that do not lead to success are gradually abandoned. These "successive approximations" are themselves evidence that groping does not occur through the sudden formation of a Gestalt-like structure. As Piaget put it: "It is by functioning that a schema structures itself and not before functioning" (ibid., p. 313).

As for the form of *organization* particular to this stage, action is organized into a totality differentiated into ends and means, just as in Stage Four. As in Stage Four, this differentiation of ends and means provides action with a directional value. The organization of action in Stage Five goes beyond that in previous stages, however, because it also makes use of one or more "auxiliary schemes." The use of such auxiliary schemes provides the principal variations leading to the discovery of new means through experimentation. In the behavior pattern of the string, for example, the goal is represented by the scheme of grasping the distant object, the initial means by the grasping of the string, and the "auxiliary" by the shaking of the string – a scheme that Piaget's children had already acquired in Stage Four as a means of influencing distant objects. This very capacity for coordinating greater numbers of schemes marks the advance of the present stage over the previous ones: "It can be said, on the whole, that an act is the more intelligent the greater the number of schemata it subsumes and the more difficulties the latter present in intercoördinating" (ibid., p. 321). But the mere capacity to "subsume" more schemes is not enough; the fact that these schemes can be coordinated into a more comprehensive totality is what makes the action more intelligent:

> It is the subordination of means to end that constitutes the intelligent act. In such behavior patterns [it is therefore always necessary to distinguish] the principal schema which, by assimilating the data, gives a purpose to the action, and the secondary schemata which constitute the means and become coördinated with the former; a certain number of auxiliary schemata can intervene besides as the search goes on; the final [i.e., principal] schema is thus called upon to systematize the ensemble of these terms in a new unit. [ibid., p. 322]

Finally, with respect to the "significations" growing out of recognitory assimilation, Stage Five extends the results of Stage Four. Children are further observed to anticipate certain properties of objects that are not immediately related to their own actions, adding to this pattern generalizations based on the behaviors characteristic of Stage Five. Thus, Jacqueline was observed at 1;2(30) touching the green wallpaper in an unfamiliar room and looking immediately at her fingers to see if the color had come off on them (ibid., Obs. 175, pp. 327–328). Piaget interpreted this observation as a generalization of previous experiences of touching substances (jam, soap lather) that left behind a colored residue. According to Piaget, these practical anticipations still do not attain the level of symbolic representation, but retain the character of generalizations based on immediate perception.

Stage Six: Invention of new means. The major characteristic of Stage Six of sensorimotor development is the "invention of new means through mental combinations." This pattern resembles the "discovery of new means through active experimentation" of Stage Five in that children are confronted with a situation in which they lack familiar means for attaining a desired goal. In Stage Five, children mastered the problem by groping, a form of active experimentation in which the adequate means are discovered through successive approximations. In other words, the solution was attained only gradually, through a series of trials and corrections. In the "invention of new means," however, no series of successive approximations is necessary; children find the correct solution almost immediately, as if they could anticipate from the beginning which actions were likely to lead to a successful result and which not. The correct solution is found before they act instead of afterward. Whereas children in Stage Five coordinated their actions after having performed them, children in Stage Six construct the equivalent coordinations before acting. According to Piaget, this construction is accomplished through "mental combination"; both children's actions and their probable consequences are represented cognitively, enabling them to select the correct action before it is actually performed. This capacity for cognitive representation is the second defining characteristic of Stage Six.

The differences between the patterns characteristic of Stage Five and Stage Six can be made clear with a few examples. Both Lucienne and Jacqueline acquired the "behavior pattern of the stick" through a gradual process of groping (ibid., Obs. 157–161, pp. 297–301). At 1;0(28), for example, Jacqueline tried to grasp a cork placed at eye level, but outside her reach. She held the stick in her hand, but did not use it. Instead, she attempted to reach the cork directly with her other hand. In an experiment in imitation, Piaget took the stick from her and showed her how to use it to knock over the cork. When the stick was handed to her, she immediately used it to make the cork fall. When the experiment was repeated with the stick lying in front of her, however, she did not use it, but again attempted to reach the cork directly. In a new attempt, Piaget handed her the stick. She took it and used it to make the cork fall. Apparently she could use the stick when it was already in her hand, but not when she had to grasp it first. Three more trials yield the same result.

When the experiment was resumed later on the same day, Jacqueline showed some progress. With the stick lying in front of her and within her visual field, she still did not grasp it in order to reach for the cork. But this time it was enough for Piaget to point to it with his finger for her to grasp it and to reach the cork. Five repetitions yielded the same result. In a final series of trials, she still reached for the cork first, but then, after a moment's disappointment, she looked for the stick herself and used it to reach the objective (ibid., Obs. 159, pp. 299–300).

In contrast to his sisters, Laurent acquired the "behavior pattern of the stick" through invention rather than groping. This was accomplished through skillful manipulation of the situation on Piaget's part. Already in Stage Three, Laurent had acquired the scheme of striking objects with a stick, but this secondary circular reaction did not suffice for using the stick to obtain objects out of reach. At 1;2(25), he used a stick to displace objects gently. He no longer merely struck objects with a stick, but as yet he did not use the stick systematically to obtain objects out of reach. Piaget had the impression that had the experiment been continued at this point, Laurent would have acquired the "behavior pattern of the stick" through groping, as his sisters had done. Therefore, he broke it off for over a month.

At 1;4(5), the experiment was resumed. With Laurent seated at a table and a stick to the right of him, Piaget placed a crust of bread just out of his reach. Without paying any attention to the stick, Laurent first tried to grasp the bread directly. Piaget then moved the stick to a position between the child and the objective. Laurent looked at the bread and the stick, then suddenly grasped the latter and directed it toward the bread. But he had grasped it in the middle, not at one of its ends, so that it was too short to reach the bread. Putting the stick down, he tried to reach the bread again directly. Then he took up the stick again at one of its ends and touched the bread with it. Displacing the bread at first gently to the right, he drew it toward him without difficulty. Two additional trials yielded the same result (ibid., Obs. 177, pp. 333–336).

In a similar fashion, Lucienne was able to bring a stick through the bars of her playpen by aligning it vertically before attempting to pull it through, and she was able to put a chain into a matchbox by rolling it up first (ibid., Obs., 178–179, pp. 356–357). Jacqueline had accomplished these tasks only through groping (ibid., Obs. 168, pp. 305–306; Obs. 173, pp. 318–320). In an extention of the experiment with the chain and the box, Piaget observed another case of invention that, because of its theoretical importance in Piaget's interpretation of the role of representation in invention, is worth quoting at length. He began by hiding the chain in the matchbox with the slit wide open. Lucienne at 1;4(0) was familiar with emptying things out of containers and easily retrieved the chain in this way. Next, Piaget hid the chain in the matchbox with the slit open only 10 mm. This space was sufficient for Lucienne to insert her index finger and retrieve the chain by pulling on one end. In the third attempt, Piaget closed the matchbox to make the slit even narrower:

Here begins the experiment which we want to emphasize. I put the chain back into the box and reduce the opening to 3 mm. It is understood that Lucienne is not aware of the functioning of the opening and closing of the matchbox and has not seen me prepare the experiment. She only possesses the two preceding schemata: turning the box over in order to empty it of its contents, and sliding her finger into the slit to make the chain come out. It is of course this last procedure that she tries first: she puts her finger inside and gropes to reach the chain, but fails completely. A pause follows during which Lucienne manifests a very curious reaction bearing witness not only to the fact that she tries to think out the situation and to represent to herself through mental combination the operations to be performed, but also to the role played by imitation in the genesis of representations. Lucienne mimics the widening of the slit.

She looks at the slit with great attention; then, several times in succession, she opens and shuts her mouth, at first slightly, then wider and wider! Apparently Lucienne understands the existence of a cavity subjacent to the slit and wishes to enlarge the cavity. The attempt at representation which she thus furnishes is expressed plastically, that is to say, due to inability to think out the situation in words or clear visual images she uses a simple motor indication as ''signifier'' or symbol. . . .

Soon after this phase of plastic reflection, Lucienne unhesitatingly puts her finger in the slit and, instead of trying as before to reach the chain, she pulls so as to enlarge the opening. She succeeds and grasps the chain. [ibid., Obs. 180, pp. 337–338]

As Piaget stated in passing, this reaction is important both as a demonstration of the role of representation in the mental combinations leading to invention and for what it reveals about the part played by imitation in the development of representation. The role of representation in invention is of primary interest in the present context. The relation between representation and imitation will be discussed later in this chapter in connection with *Play, dreams and imitation in childhood.*

In interpreting these examples of invention, Piaget extended his analogy between sensorimotor and logical operations. In these terms, the difference between groping and invention can be likened to the difference between induction and deduction. Like induction, groping is a kind of generalization based on repeated experiences. Like deduction, invention is the derivation of a new result (the conclusion) from the coordination of familiar schemes (the premises). Obviously, groping and invention differ from their logical counterparts in that they bear only on the immediate context of action. Nevertheless, this ''functional analogy'' between sensorimotor functioning and logical operations is useful in interpreting the phenomena of groping and invention and in specifying the ways in which they differ from each other. Both patterns involve the reciprocal assimilation of schemes in the pursuit of a goal. In groping, this reciprocal assimilation occurs in a cumulative, successive process. In invention, reciprocal assimilation occurs in a more sudden manner. Piaget suggested that the relative rapidity of this reciprocal assimilation may enable the necessary coordinations to occur before the child acts, rather than afterward.

In the observation involving the chain and the matchbox, for example, the scheme of the goal (grasping the chain) assimilated several schemes representing the initial means (emptying the box, sticking one's finger through the opening). When these failed, an auxiliary scheme came into play, the scheme of widening an opening. Lucienne did not possess such a scheme in a form that was immediately applicable to the matchbox, but she did possess what Piaget called a scheme of imitation. In Piaget's studies of imitation recounted in *Play, dreams and imitation*, he described how he investigated Lucienne's imitation of invisible bodily movements in the months leading up to the present observation. Among these invisible bodily movements were opening and closing the mouth and eyes. Presumably, she brought this scheme of imitation into the present situation by way of sensorimotor analogy. She could not reach the chain in the matchbox because the opening was too narrow, but she could reach it if she widened the slit just as she had previously learned to open her father's mouth with her fingers in the game of imitation (Piaget, 1945/1962, Obs. 50a, p. 59). In learning to imitate the opening and closing of her father's mouth, that spectacle became implicated in a circular reaction involving the opening and closing of her own mouth. Piaget suggested that there may have been an element of magico-phenomenalism involved. In opening her mouth, Lucienne may have expected to effect the opening of the matchbox directly. That is, she may have expected the matchbox to imitate her movements just as her father had frequently done in games of imitation. When this failed, she opened it with her fingers.

In summary, three schemes were involved in this example of invention: the scheme of grasping the chain (the goal), the scheme of emptying the box (the initial means), and the scheme of widening the opening (the auxiliary). The action as a whole was accomplished through the reciprocal assimilation of these three schemes, with the scheme of the goal taking the leading part (Piaget, 1936/1963, pp. 343–344). Moreover, this coordination had a hierarchical structure: Emptying the box was a means for grasping the chain, and opening the slit was the means for emptying the box. Thus, the auxiliary scheme of opening the slit functioned as a kind of means to the means of emptying the box. Piaget had this type of organization in mind when he likened invention to deduction. It is as if the child engaged in a practical reasoning of the following form: If the box is emptied (means), the chain can be grasped (goal); if the opening is widened (auxiliary), the box can be emptied (means); the opening is widened, the box emptied, and the chain grasped.

Invention through sensorimotor deduction is nothing other than a spontaneous reorganization of earlier schemata which are accommodated by themselves to the new situation, through reciprocal assimilation. . . . Once the goal has been set and the difficulties encountered by the use of initial means have been perceived, the schemata of the goal, those of the initial means and the auxiliary schemata (evoked by awareness of the difficulties) organize themselves into a new totality, without there being need of external groping to support their activity. [ibid., pp. 347–348]

This capacity for coordinating a third scheme (the auxiliary) with those of the goal and the initial means distinguishes invention from the Stage Four "application of familiar means." Otherwise, the child would have no further recourse following the failure of the initial means (emptying the box) in the present example. It is also interesting to note the possible relation between the coordination of these three schemes and the role of representation in invention. In general, the presence of representation in invention is indicated by the fact that the necessary schemes can be coordinated before the child acts, not afterward. In other words, children can draw the "conclusion" of their sensorimotor "reasonings" without having to carry out the deduction step by step. In contrast, the Stage Five child apparently can coordinate only two of the requisite schemes, instead of three. Thus, Jacqueline could use the stick (means) to obtain the cork (goal) as long as the stick was already in her hand. What she still could not do in the observations cited earlier was to coordinate the scheme of grasping the stick (auxiliary) with the scheme of using the stick (initial means) and with the scheme of grasping the cork (goal).

According to Piaget, the representations characteristic of Stage Six have become fully symbolic in the sense that they have become progressively detached from immediate action and accordingly "liberated from direct perception" (ibid., p. 355). But although such cognitive representation is an important element of invention, Piaget stated that it arises in the context of imitation. Further consideration of the development of cognitive representation out of sensorimotor intelligence will therefore be reserved for our review of *Play, dreams and imitation*.

Conclusion

In the final section of *The origins of intelligence*, Piaget returned to the five theories of intelligence enumerated earlier in the book and discussed them one by one in light of the evidence. The first, *associationist empiricism*, emphasizes the role of experience in the development of knowledge, and in so doing, Piaget agreed, it is undoubtedly correct. But empiricism tends to view experience imposing itself on the subject without it having to be organized through the subject's activity. In particular, there are three reasons why the associationist-empiricism hypothesis would appear to be insufficient to account for the evidence in *The origins of intelligence*: First, the extent to which the infant's knowledge of the world is affected by experience itself changes with development. In the earliest stages of sensorimotor development, children tend to assimilate the environment to their own activities, and the possibilities for accommodation to the environment are limited thereby. In the later stages, accommodation takes a leading role, and the modifications introduced into the child's schemes by experience are accordingly increased in scope. But if the capacity for experience itself changes with development, development would not appear to be explained solely through the action of experience. Second, the child's capacity for understanding objective reality similarly increases with development during the period studied. Development is not readily explained through the action of an external reality that impresses itself on the subject, if the subject is incapable of assimilating that reality. The third reason for doubting the associationist hypothesis is the assumption that complex perceptions and ideas are formed through association from elementary sense data. But the observation of sensorimotor development indicates that the mind of the child is organized from the beginning, and even sensory contact with the external world occurs only to the extent that the latter can be assimilated by the organized totalities that exist at each stage. Ultimately, the structure and complexity of these totalities change with development.

The second hypothesis, *vitalistic intellectualism,* also has certain positive features insofar as it is holistic and nonreductionistic. In insisting that intelligence is a total phenomenon that cannot be analyzed piecemeal, it renders a valuable critique of associationism and other reductionistic approaches. Nevertheless, intellectualism is also insufficient for explaining the facts of development. To begin with, it often bases its postulated irreducibility of intelligence on reflective acts of intellect. Against this, Piaget asserted a natural continuity between the mind and life itself. Intellectual reflection in itself cannot lead to knowledge about the biological bases of intellect. Another reason for rejecting intellectualism is that in considering intelligence as a phenomenon *sui generis,* it tends to neglect the adaptation to reality. If intelligence is really inexplicable in any terms other than its own, then it is essentially a faculty with the inherent capacity of adapting to reality as it is, but the facts of sensorimotor development indicate that knowledge of reality at every stage is constructed out of the interaction between the activity of the subject and the resistances of the external world. Adaptation to reality arises from the rhythm of assimilation and accommodation and is not given from the beginning.

The third hypothesis of intelligence, *apriorism,* represents Kantianism in epistemology and Gestaltism in psychology. In each case, acts of intelligence are explained through the existence of categories or forms existing prior to experience and serving to organize it. Piaget recognized that this view and his own approach have certain points in common. They are at one in postulating the existence of structured totalities that serve to organize experience, and in this respect Piaget's schemes are analogous to perceptual Gestalten. Similarly, they both agree in rejecting vitalist intellectualism as an explanation of intelligence. But here the similarity between the two viewpoints ends. The first divergence mentioned by Piaget is that, being given prior to experience, Gestalten have no history, but action schemes are shaped through the subject's experience and thus come to embody the past insofar as the subject has experienced it. The second point of divergence is that schemes become generalized in their applications as a function of experience, but the range of applicability of Gestalten must, like those forms themselves, be given from the beginning. Third, schemes consist of structured and organized activity, but Gestalten apply themselves more or less automatically to perceptual experience and accordingly are not active in themselves. Fourth, one cannot easily account for progressive corrections of action on the basis of replacing "less good" forms with "better" forms. Finally, schemes are continually being brought into relation to each other through active coordination, but Gestalten are conceived of as existing independent of each other. On each of these points, Piaget believed his observations to support his own interpretations over apriorism.

The fourth theory of intelligence is the *theory of groping.* Following Claparède, Piaget distinguished between two general types of groping. The first was the type of trial-and-error learning first proposed by Jennings and Thorndike, in which the responses of the organism are conceived as being generated purely by chance and then "selected" according to the fortuitous character of their effects. Claparède called this first type of groping "nonsystematic groping." In contrast to the random, fortuitous character of nonsystematic groping, the second type of groping was conceived of as directed from the start, not only in the context of action directed toward a goal but also directed by an awareness of relationships between actions and their probable outcomes. Claparède's term for this form of groping was "systematic groping." Piaget acknowledged that both forms of groping exist, nonsystematic groping when the subject is confronted by a problem that greatly exceeds the subject's current level of understanding, and systematic groping when the problem is commensurate with the subject's intellectual level. He rejected the notion, however, that all groping can be reduced to the nonsystematic variety. Either nonsystematic groping appears only after the subject has exhausted the familiar means available, or, even when the order of appearance is reversed, nonsystematic groping itself will be found on closer examination to have been at least minimally directed. In either case, systematic groping appears to be the rule, with nonsystematic groping appearing only in a marginal capacity.

Moreover, the relations by which systematic groping is directed are not mere chance associations between stimuli and responses. Piaget cited Claparède further to the effect that perception already involves judgments based on "implication":

If the operation which constitutes perception is identical to that which forms the backbone of reasoning, *it is because this operation is an implication.* If we notice the sweet flavor in the colored spot which the orange forms to our eye, this is not solely by virtue of association but due to implication. It is because this sweet flavor is *implied* in the other characteristics of the orange. [Claparède, cited in ibid., pp. 404–405]

One can easily see in Claparède's "implication" the same kind of sensorimotor "signification" spoken about by Piaget in his analyses of sensorimotor development. Claparède's example corresponds to the sensorimotor "signs" of Stage Five and beyond, when the child becomes able to anticipate the properties of objects and events. The color of the orange is a "sign" of the orange itself considered in its totality. This totality naturally includes the sweetness of its taste. According to Piaget, sensorimotor functioning is informed by significations and implications of this kind, and such implications make the sensorimotor "reasonings" of the higher stages possible. Thus, systematic groping is not only directed toward a goal but also directed in the choice of means by an awareness of such relationships.

So interpreted, the theory of systematic groping becomes a special case of the *theory of assimilation,* Piaget's own theory of intelligence. He summarized this theory in terms of two propositions: (a) A continuity exists between biological functioning and intellectual operations, sensorimotor activity being the bridge between the two. (b) This continuity is characterized by common laws of functioning at each level that result in a series of qualitatively different and increasingly more complex and coherent structures. These laws of functioning refer to the cycle of adaptation that comprises assimilation and accommodation. Of these, assimilation is the more fundamental, because accommodation to reality can occur only to the extent that assimilation has already taken place. In the most general sense, assimilation can be defined as "the incorporation of any external reality whatever to one part or another of the cycle of organization" (ibid., p. 408). On the biological plane, assimilation is simply the functioning of each organized system. On the rational plane, it can be likened to judgment; to judge is to assimilate a new datum to a preexisting scheme of implications. On the sensorimotor level, assimilation is "the tendency of every behavior pattern or of every psychic state to conserve itself and, toward this end, to take its functional alimentation from the external environment" (ibid., p. 411).

According to Piaget, the principal problem to be explained by this or any other theory of intelligence is how the subject comes to understand external reality as "objective." In biological functioning, the whole of reality is assimilated to the structures of the organism. In rational judgment, objective reality is already understood to exist. It is during the sensorimotor period that the understanding of objective reality first appears. According to Piaget, one might seek to explain this growing sense of reality simply as the result of progressive accommodation. But then, one could ask why those accommodations were not present from the beginning, instead of occurring in such a laborious, sequential manner. The reason for the sequential character of sensorimotor accommodations is that the progressive accommodation of schemes occurs as a function of progressively more complex and coherent coordinations and reciprocal assimilations among those schemes. We have seen how the organization characteristic of each stage depends on the coordination of schemes formed in earlier stages. Ultimately, these progressively more complex and coherent reciprocal assimilations of schemes make possible the progressively more adequate accommodations to objective reality.

This interdependence between progressive assimilation and accommodation also allows one to explain another basic problem faced by every theory of intelligence: how to explain the increasing inventiveness of the subject, together with the increasing coherence of thought. In Piaget's own terms, it is a question of explaining the "fecundity of intellectual construction" along with its "progressive rigor." One might think instead that progressive inventiveness would be correlated with subjective whimsy, rather than rigor, or that progressive rigor would be accompanied by a slavish conformity to general laws. (As we shall see in chapter 8, explaining the rigor and generativity of mathematics has been one of the basic problems in the history of mathematical epistemology.)

Piaget argued that both the rigor and fecundity of intelligence are consequences of the reciprocal assimilation of schemes. In such reciprocal assimilation, the relations embodied in each scheme considered separately become combined or multiplied with each other, and these multiplications of relations result in the creation of new interrelationships, some of which may never have been experienced by the subject as such. The subject's knowledge at each stage thus outstrips the sum of the subject's previous experiences. "Intellectual organization is fecund in itself, since the relationships engender each other, and this fecundity is one with the richness of reality, since relationships cannot be conceived independently of the terms which connect them" (ibid., p. 418).

The progressive rigor and coherence of thought also result from the multiplication of relations inherent in the reciprocal assimilation of schemes. To the extent that the relations produced in this way are reciprocal in character, an incipient reversibility is created. As we recall from the previous chapter, the reversibility of operations is Piaget's prime criterion for the rigor and coherence of intellectual functioning. "The reciprocal assimilation which accounts for the coördination of the schemata is therefore the point of departure of this reversibility of operations which, at all levels, appears as the criterion of rigor and coherence" (ibid., p. 418).

Because organization creates new relations at every stage by intercoordinating the schemes formed at previous stages, the inventions belonging to Stage Six of sensorimotor development extend and complete tendencies already present in earlier stages. This is the most likely interpretation of Piaget's rather cryptic conclusion: "In short, the problem of invention, which in many respects constitutes the central problem of intelligence, does not, in the hypothesis of the schemata, require any special solution because the organization which assimilatory activity reveals is essentially construction and so is, in fact, invention, from the outset" (ibid., p. 418). Just as the "fertility" of rational thinking had been ascribed to the logic of relations in *Judgment and reasoning in the child,* so was the inventiveness of intelligent action now attributed to an analogous "logic of relations" in sensorimotor functioning. In each case, novel adaptations were explained as the result of the new relations engendered by the cross-products of relations already understood.

OBJECTIVITY AND REPRESENTATION

The construction of reality in the child

In the companion volume to *The origins of intelligence,* Piaget extended his analysis of sensorimotor development to the "real categories" of the object concept, spatial relations, causality, and time. Because the processes involved are the same as those already described in the first volume, the present account will be limited to a brief description of the stages found for each of these four categories and to a summary of Piaget's interpretation of the behavior patterns characterizing each stage.

The object concept. Piaget's observations on the development of the conception of the permanent object focused on children's reactions to vanished objects. In the *first stage* and *second stage,* no special behavior related to vanished objects occurs. Objects are assimilated entirely to the child's action schemes, and sometimes an object that is momentarily "lost" can be recovered through repetition of the action in question. From the third day after birth, Laurent manifested a rudimentary "search" for the breast. Similarly, Jacqueline at 0;2(27) was observed to follow her mother with her eyes and to keep looking in the same direction when her mother disappeared from her visual field (Piaget, 1937/1971a, Obs. 1–2, p. 8). But Piaget could discern no indication that the object as such was as yet differentiated from the scheme of action.

In the *third stage*, the child shows a number of new behavior patterns related to objects, the most important being "the reconstruction of an invisible whole from a visible part." At 0;9(7), for example, Lucienne was able to find a plastic goose that her father had covered as long as the head or beak protruded from under the blanket. She did not merely grasp the beak, but at the same time raised the blanket to take hold of the whole animal. However, when the goose was completely covered, Lucienne behaved as if it had ceased to exist. She did not look for it under the blanket, even though she had seen it being covered and had already found it under the blanket on the previous trials when the beak had been visible. A similar pattern was observed with Jacqueline and Laurent using a variety of objects (ibid., Obs. 21–25, pp. 30–34). The progress of this stage consists in the fact that the child now shows a sense of individual objects in their concrete totality. In the terminology used in *The origins of intelligence,* the part has become an "indication" of the whole. In effect, the sight of the goose's beak evoked the whole animal. But the fact that active search for the desired object is abandoned as soon as it is completely covered indicates that the object still is not differentiated from the actions involved in recovering it. These actions (e.g., lifting the cover and grasping the object) are accommodated to the object as a concrete totality, but the sight of part of the object is still necessary to set the cycle of action in motion.

This limitation is overcome in the *fourth stage*. At 0;9(8), for example, Jacqueline found a watch hidden completely under a blanket on eight successive trials. At various ages, Laurent and Lucienne showed similar reactions (ibid., Obs. 34–38, pp. 49–53). But although a visible part is no longer necessary to motivate the search for the vanished object, the object still is not completely differentiated from the action, as indicated by the fact that the child searches for the object only in the place where it was first hidden and found. For example, after having found a doll under a cloth, Lucienne did not attempt to search for it under a blanket (ibid., Obs. 38, p. 53). Similarly, Jacqueline at 0;10(3) found a toy parrot under her father's hand in her lap. He then hid the parrot under a nearby rug and returned his hand to her lap. She searched under his hand for the parrot, not under the rug, even though she had seen it being hidden there. Thus, the general pattern was that an object once found at *A* and subsequently seen to be hidden at *B* was nevertheless sought again at *A*.

This pattern underscores the progressive character of the differentiation of the object from ongoing action. Although the act of searching no longer has to be motivated by the sight of a visible part of the object, the latter is not yet fully differentiated from the spatial location at which it was initially found. The action, as it were, becomes accommodated to the object and location together. Piaget stated that there are three possible explanations for this phenomenon. The failure to search at location *B* might first of all result from a defect in memory, in that the child does not recall the object's successive displacements. Second, the pattern might result from the lack of sufficient understanding of spatial relations, in the sense that the object's successive displacements are not coordinated with each other. Finally, the "*A, not-B* phenomenon" might be explained through the lack of a concept of a permanent object; the object is not yet differentiated from the location at which it is found. Far from trying to choose from among these explanations as mutually exclusive alternatives, Piaget stated that they mutually imply one another. Memory of successive displacements is necessary for the coordination of such displacements in space, and the coordination of displacements is necessary in order to differentiate the object from any given location.

In the *fifth stage*, the child takes account of visible, but not invisible, displacements of the object. At 1;0(20), for example, Jacqueline found a key under cushion *A* on her left, and when it was then hidden under cushion *B* on her right, she searched immediately under *B*. She did not return to *A* even when the key was buried deep under *B* and was not immediately discovered. However, she still did not follow invisible displacements. At 1;6(20), she was seated between garment *A* and cushion *B*. Piaget put the object in his hand, put his hand under *A,* and brought it out closed. Jacqueline looked first in her father's hand; not finding the object there, she looked further under *A*. He then repeated the same procedure, leaving the object this time under *B*. Jacqueline again looked unsuccessfully in his hand and then went directly back to *A*. The experiment was repeated under a variety of circumstances (ibid., Obs. 60–63, pp. 82–85). Thus, the object would appear to be differentiated from its location as long as only visible displacements are involved. With respect to invisible displacements, the object still remains dependent on the context of action.

This final limitation on the concept of the permanent object is overcome in *Stage Six*. At 1;7(20), Jacqueline found a coin that her father had hidden in his hand and then deposited under a blanket on her right. When he repeated the procedure leaving the coin under a cushion on her left, she searched immediately under the cushion. On subsequent days, she repeated her performance under a variety of conditions (ibid., Obs. 64–66, pp. 88–91). According to Piaget's interpretation, this pattern is indicative of the fact that the child has attained a cognitive representation of the object. The criterion for such an interpretation is the child's ability to reconstruct a series of invisible displacements to which the object is subjected. "True representation therefore begins only when no perceived sign commands belief in permanency, that is to say, from the moment when the vanished object is displaced according to an itinerary which the subject may deduce but not perceive" (ibid., p. 94). Further observations regarding the development of cognitive representation out of sensorimotor action will be considered later in discussing *Play, dreams and imitation in childhood*.

In interpreting his observations, Piaget argued that the sequence of stages in the development of the object concept can be accounted for neither in terms of a priori deduction nor as the result of purely empirical gropings. An a priori solution was ruled out because of the gradual and successive character of the acquisitions involved, in which each stage of development depends on the results obtained in previous stages. Nonsystematic groping could likewise be eliminated, because the child's successive efforts were always directed, not merely random. Instead, the process was characterized as a constructive deduction consisting of the reciprocal assimilation of the schemes brought into play. In particular, the finding of hidden objects consists in a reciprocal assimilation of schemes for grasping the object as a goal and lifting, emptying out, or putting aside as means. As already discussed in *The origins of intelligence,* such reciprocal assimilations result in the construction of new relations such as "above" and "below," "behind" and "in front of," "inside," and "covered by." In effect, the permanent object is a totality capable of being subject to these relations.

Spatial relations. In his analysis and interpretation of the development of children's understanding of spatial relations, Piaget introduced an idea that would play a lasting role in his theory: the idea that psychological structures can be modeled on the mathematical concept of the *group.* He apparently adopted this idea from the French mathematician, Henri Poincaré. In his book *La valeur de la science* (1914), Poincaré had pointed out that the displacement of objects in space constituted a group. That is, it constituted a system with the properties of composition under closure (any sequence of displacements results in a position also belonging to the system), associativity (any location can be reached by different routes), identity (an object that is not moved remains where it is), and inversion (the reversal of any sequence of displacement returns the object to its point of origin). Moreover, he had argued that the idea of space arises intuitively in human experience through the experience of the distinction between changes of position, which can be reversed through bodily movement, and changes of state, which cannot. In this way, the human mind comes to mirror the grouplike properties of the displacement of objects in space. For Piaget, this argument provided the framework for his discussion of the development of conceptions of spatial relations during sensorimotor development. Group structure can be identified in children's movements from the beginning, but the comprehensions of these groups differ at different stages of development.

The *first stage* and *second stage* of sensorimotor development are characterized by what Piaget called "practical groups," which are heterogeneous in character. That is, the movements comprised in different schemes possess the aforementioned properties of mathematical groups, but they are essentially independent of each other. The elementary "search" behavior embodied in the sucking reflex, for example, is reversible with respect to its right–left orientation, but these movements are not yet coordinated with grasping or other reflexes. Even after such schemes begin to be coordinated in the second stage, the groups formed thereby remain heterogeneous; no single space is yet common to all. Moreover, although the child's movements may be said to have group structure from the viewpoint of the observer, the child is not aware of this structure. That is, the child's body as such does not appear as an element or as a reference point in these practical groups. Thus, Piaget argued that Poincaré's distinction between changes of position and changes of state is not primary; as yet, the child has no overall frame of reference in which changes of position can be apprehended. In addition to the buccal space associated with sucking activity, there are visual, auditory, and tactile spaces, parallel and independent of each other.

The *third stage* is characterized by the formation of "subjective" groups through the coordination of different practical groups among themselves. With the accommodation of the primary schemes to one another, the various "spaces" that they represent coalesce in a single unity centered on the child's own activity. The development of prehension is perhaps the best example. In acquiring the ability to grasp an object and carry it to the mouth, the child in effect brings tactile-kinesthetic, buccal, and visual "spaces" in relation to each other. At the same time, the child's own body and its movements become elements in the total system; the hand that grasps and carries an object to the mouth can at the same time be seen. With regard to the positions of objects, the fact that the child does not at this stage take into account sequential displacements indicates that the space in which objects are located is wholly relative to the child's activity. Space is a container of action, not yet a container of objects that are differentiated from action. Another example of subjective groups is the system formed by the rotation of objects. Laurent, for example, was able to rotate his bottle in order to suck the nipple attached at one end. But such an action was possible only when the nipple was visible. When he was presented with the opposite end of the bottle, such that the nipple was not visible, he did not recognize it for what it was (Piaget, 1937/1971a, Obs. 78, p. 141). Several other examples were provided, including the child's ability to follow visually a rapidly moving object, the subjective groups constituted by secondary circular reactions, the child's perception of depth, and the permanence of size and form of objects. What all of these examples had in common was that the child discovered action to have certain regular and repeatable effects on the world. Space thus becomes a container not of actions alone but of actions and the transformations that they effect. Such groups of transformations are "subjective" in the sense that the relations they comprise are relations between the objects and the subject's actions. These subjective groups do not yet include relations between objects themselves, nor is the subject represented within them as an object among others.

The *fourth stage* involves a transition between subjective and objective groups and is characterized primarily by the discovery of reversible transformations. An example of the latter is the child's discovery of the reversibility of the actions of hiding and finding; an object that is hidden can be found again, and vice versa. Thus, both Lucienne and Jacqueline were observed in the 12th month to play at covering and uncovering objects repeatedly (ibid., Obs. 85, p. 172). Piaget suggested that reversibility is associated with the discovery of constancy, or invariance. The reversibility of the transformations applied to an object is what demonstrates the permanent identity of that object. The child discovers the permanency of the object by being able to return the object to its original context. Other invariances discovered by the child during this stage, according to Piaget, include the constancy of shapes and sizes across changes of position or orientation of objects in relation to the child observer, or of the child in relation to the objects. All of these invariances are established through the discovery of the reversibility of the transformations involved. Thus, Piaget observed his children studying the changing appearances of objects as they moved back and forth themselves, as the objects were moved back and forth, as they moved their heads in various ways, as objects were rotated this way and that, and so on. In each case, the reversibility of the respective actions served to establish the permanence of the object across spatial transformations.

The groups established in such a way are more "objective" than those of the previous stage because of this very discovery of the permanent identity of objects. This discovery is the beginning of the differentiation of what Poincaré had called changes of state and changes of position. In effect, the child in stage four discovers that the states of objects are not affected by changes of position. In terms of group theory, the child discovers that changes of position have the property of inversion (any change of position followed by its inverse returns the object to its starting place) and that changes of position act as identity operators with respect to state (the state of an object remains invariant across changes of position).

The chief limitation of this stage, according to Piaget, is that these reversible operations still pertain only to the spatial relations existing between the subject and the object. They do not yet extend to the relations among objects themselves. To this extent, the groups developing during this stage retain a measure of subjectivity. Having progressed beyond the purely subjective groups of stage three, they nevertheless fail to attain the true objectivity of stage five. Thus, the fourth stage remains intermediate. Even the object permanence established at this stage remains relative to the child's own reversible actions. This limitation is presumably why the child still cannot follow the successive displacements of a hidden object. Having found the object once at A, the child knows that its subsequent disappearance at this location can be reversed. So this knowledge is applied, despite the fact that the object has in the meantime been transferred to location B.

Only in the *fifth stage* do groups of displacements become truly "objective." In Piaget's terminology, this objectivity implies that in addition to the immediate spatial relations existing between subject and object, the relations between the successive displacements of the object are also considered. In respect to object permanence, for example, the child can follow the successive hidings of an object at A and B and knows that once an object has been transferred from A to B, there is no longer any reason to search for it at A. One way of interpreting these results is in terms of an extension of the field of reversibility. Whereas the child in stage four could reverse only the act of hiding itself (an object hidden at location *A* can be found at location *A*), in stage five a simple sequence of hiding plus displacement can be reversed (an object hidden at *A* and displaced from *A* to *B* can be found at *B*). The objectivity of space and the understanding of the object's permanent identity is thereby extended. Piaget observed several other examples of such reversals of simple sequences, including the throwing of objects outside the visual field and finding them by a different route than that used in hiding them, displacing objects from one place to another and back, changes in the relations (e.g., "on top of," "inside of") between one object and another, and displacements of the child's own body. As an example of the latter, Piaget described Laurent at 1;2(15) learning to walk along a garden path from point *A* to point *B*, from *B* to *P*, and back across the grass from *P* to *A* (ibid., Obs. 117, pp. 222–224). In this example, the itinerary *ABPA* forms a reversible group of displacements that can be traveled in either direction. It is not merely the reversibility of a single action (e.g., *BA* as the reversal of *AB*) that is involved, but rather the reversibility of a simple *composition* of actions (e.g., *PA* as the reversal of *AB* and *BP*).

The limitations of this stage consist in the fact that objective relations between objects are understood only insofar as they are directly perceived, and consequently children cannot apply this same understanding to relations between themselves and other objects in space. The clearest example of the dependence on direct perception is the inability to follow invisible displacements in hiding and finding. As for the problem of regarding one's own position objectively, Piaget cited examples in which his children attempted to grasp objects on which they were sitting, standing, and so on. Although they now understood themselves as existing in space, they still appeared to consider their own position as a unique center. Or, stated the other way around, they did not yet conceive of their own spatial location as equivalent to other possible locations. Indeed, they could not conceive their own location objectively as long as their understanding of spatial relations extended only to relations that were directly perceived.

This dependence on direct perception is overcome in the *sixth stage,* marked by the appearance of "representative" groups. The latter term means that the child becomes capable of representing sequences of displacements cognitively, as indicated in the ability to follow the invisible displacements of a hidden object. The capacity for spatial representation also manifests itself in the ability to understand the objectivity of one's own position. This ability, according to Piaget, requires that one view the sequence of one's own displacements as though they were seen from the outside. Such a viewpoint is impossible as long as one's understanding of spatial relations is dependent on direct perception.

The representation of one's own spatial displacements is manifest in the invention of routes or detours in moving from one point to another. For example, Laurent was observed to follow new itineraries along the intersecting paths of the garden described earlier (ibid., Obs. 125, p. 232). This pattern indicated that the space formed by the garden and its various paths had come to form a total system, allowing Laurent to generate new routes that he had never previously traveled in their entirety. Similarly, Jacqueline and Lucienne were observed to follow a variety of detours in order to circumvent obstacles in familiar spaces (ibid., Obs. 123–124, pp. 231–232). The child, in effect, was able to represent the outcomes of possible displacements before those displacements were actually realized.[2]

In concluding his discussion of the development of spatial understanding, Piaget pointed out that the psychological relevance of group theory was not limited to the case of space:

The concept of group goes far beyond the construction of space. Every self-enclosed system of operations constitutes a group, that is, it is possible to return to the point of departure through an operation which forms part of the system. In a very general sense one may say that every living or especially psychological organization contains in germ the characteristic operations of the group, since the nature of organization is precisely to constitute a totality of interdependent processes; the concept of group thus forms the principle of this system of operations which logicians have called the "logic of relations," since the product of two relations is still a relation. The logic of relations is immanent in all intellectual activity; every perception and every conception are the making of relationships. If the logic of relations is only tardily reflected as a normative system, it is virtually preformed in the functioning of every act of intelligence. We may say that the group is immanent in intelligence itself. We may even go so far as to say that every act of assimilation, that is, every relation between the organization of the subject and the external environment, presupposes a system of operations arranged in groups. In effect, assimilation is always reproduction, that is, it involves a reversibility, or a possible return to the point of departure, which precisely defines a group. [ibid., p. 236]

This is the first statement of an idea that would come to occupy a central role in Piaget's theory. With this passage he began to identify his early intuition of relational totalities with psychological structures having the formal properties of mathematical groups. The further development of this idea will be followed in chapter 4.

The immediate problem, however, is to account for the development of children's understanding of space, as described earlier. As in the case of the object concept, Piaget rejected both empiricism and apriorism as partial truths. These two points of view are both partially correct in emphasizing the role of experience and organismic structure, respectively. In fact, both experience and structure are necessary to account for development. The role of experience is reflected in the gradual and progressive character of development, according to which the constructions of each stage are based on those of the preceding stages. But the subject is open only to those experiences that correspond to the structures that

2 Piaget's observations of his children's detour behavior are highly reminiscent of the *Umweg* (detour) problems studied by Köhler (1917/1925) in *The mentality of apes*. The same can be said of the "behavior pattern of the stick," described in *The origins of intelligence*. Several passing references in the conclusion to the latter book suggest that Piaget was familiar with Köhler's work and that some of the situations in which Piaget observed his children may have been modeled directly or indirectly on Köhler's experiments with chimpanzees.

exist at that point in development. Therefore, the development of space must be described in terms of a progressive construction of ever more inclusive structures, which from this point onward begin to be identified with mathematical groups. "Space is an organization of movements such as to impress upon the perceptions shapes that are increasingly coherent. [It is] the product of an interaction between the organism and the environment in which it is impossible to dissociate the organization of the universe perceived from that of the activity itself" (ibid., p. 245).

Causality and time. Piaget's analysis of the development of causality and time in the sensorimotor period paralleled and extended his analyses of the object concept and spatial relations. Many of the same behavioral patterns that had previously been used to define the stages of development for the object concept, space, or intelligence in general were now analyzed from the point of view of causality and time. Because of this extensive overlap in empirical material, the development of causality and time will be described here only in schematic fashion.

As was the case for the development of the object and space, *stages one* and *two* in the development of causality and time remain purely practical. Although from the observer's point of view the primary circular reactions of stage two produce "effects" in the form of the immediate sensations, no reason exists to believe that the child distinguishes the sensations produced from the actions themselves. Therefore, one has no basis for assuming that the child can distinguish cause and effect. Similarly, actions can be reproduced in sequence, but one cannot assume that the child is aware of the sequence as such. In Piaget's words, "a sequence of perceptions does not necessarily entail a perception of sequence" (ibid., p. 367).

Only in *stage three* does an incipient differentiation between cause and effect appear, and this differentiation itself implies a rudimentary appreciation of temporal sequence. As in the case of spatial relations, however, the child's understanding in stage three remains purely subjective. The secondary circular reaction, for example, entails an elementary differentiation between an action and its visible effects (e.g., between kicking one's legs and the sight of swinging objects). But the child is not yet aware of the means by which the action leads to its observed effects. In this sense, Piaget referred to causality at this stage as "phenomenalistic" and "subjective." With respect to time, the elementary differentiation between action and effect implies a primitive appreciation of temporal sequence insofar as an action necessarily precedes its effect. This understanding of sequence also remains subjective, limited to actions as causes. As yet one cannot assume any appreciation of causes or of sequences in which the child's own actions are not implicated.

One important manifestation of causality at this stage is "causality by imitation": By imitating the actions of another person, the child attempts to get that person to repeat those actions. The secondary circular reaction is applied to other people instead of objects. "The only difference is that in the case of the object the child uses any means that chance reveals to him, whereas in the case of persons causality takes a precise form prescribed by the convergence of another person's body and his own – the form of imitation" (ibid., p. 286). As yet, however, children have no understanding of other persons as *independent* centers of activity; they behave as though the other person's actions were merely consequences of their own. The development of imitation is discussed later in considering *Play, dreams and imitation in childhood*.

Other persons begin to be conceived of as independent centers of action in *stage four*. But as in the case of the object and space, this stage remains intermediate between subjectivity and objectivity. The activities of other persons still are not conceived of as completely independent of children's own actions. Even while considering other persons as autonomous centers of activity, children appear to believe that their own actions are necessary to *initiate* the activity of others. A similar attitude is expressed toward physical objects. Children behave in part as though objects were capable of spontaneous activity and in part as though the latter were subordinated to their own actions. In contrast to stage three, during which they seemed oblivious of the means by which actions produced their effects, they now recognize that some spatial contact is necessary.

With respect to time, stage four also remains intermediate between subjectivity and objectivity. Children begin to comprehend simple sequences of events independent of action. In finding hidden objects, for example, they retain the sequence constituted by the object placed in a certain location followed by a screen being placed over the object. This retention of sequence, however, is limited; children still cannot reconstruct a sequence of displacements. "When the child searches in *A* for the object he has just seen disappear in *B*, the practical memory of the action linked with position *A* still prevails over all memory of the sequence of the displacements" (ibid., p. 383). This pattern thus remains intermediate between the subjectivity of purely practical sequences and the sequence of objective displacements.

In the *fifth stage*, objectivity of causality and time is finally attained. Both persons and objects are now recognized as autonomous centers of activity independent of the child's own actions. Naturally, persons differ from objects both in being more lively centers of activity and in their convergence with the child's own body, as noted earlier. But children still behave as though objects also possessed a certain spontaneity of action. The spatialization of causality also becomes more advanced in the sense that they realize that certain objects (e.g., a stick) can be used to affect other objects (e.g., an object out of reach). By virtue of its spatial properties, the one object becomes a causal intermediary between the child and another object. A corollary of this new objective causality is that children henceforth recognize their action as one cause among others. The objectivity of time in this stage is reflected in the fact that a sequential series of displacements can be reconstructed. Children no longer search at *A* for an object that has been displaced to *B*. Like the other behavior patterns characterizing this stage, this "objective" time series is still limited to events that are directly perceived.

In the *sixth stage* of sensorimotor development, causality and time begin to assume a representative character. For example, causes can be reconstructed when their effects alone have been observed, and conversely the probable effects of present causes can be foreseen and represented in advance. The time series becomes representative in the same sense. Children can now evoke memories not connected with direct perception. Alongside these new behavior patterns that define the sixth stage, Piaget also described several "residual" patterns: behaviors belonging to previous stages that nevertheless continue to occur after the new patterns have begun to manifest themselves. The most conspicuous of these residual behaviors is causality through imitation; having succeeded through imitation in getting people to repeat their actions, children apply this same strategy to certain objects (e.g., a doll). The existence of these residual patterns led Piaget to make some significant remarks regarding the nature of his developmental stages in general. The new behavior patterns characterizing each stage do not replace those of the previous stages, but are added to them: "The new stage would thus be defined by the fact that the child becomes capable of certain behavior patterns of which he was up to then incapable; it is not the fact that he renounces the behavior patterns of the preceding stages, even if they are contrary to the new ones or contradictory to them from the observer's point of view" (ibid., p. 338).

In discussing the origins of causality, Piaget returned to the five theories of intelligence enumerated earlier in *The origins of intelligence*. Each of these theories of intelligence corresponds to a different theory of causality. Associationism, for example, corresponds to Hume's theory of causality, according to which causal relations are identified as habits of the mind resulting from the constant conjunction of the events identified as cause and effect. Vitalist intellectualism corresponds to the views of Maine de Biran, for whom causality was based on the experience of effort in action. Apriorism corresponds to the Kantian theory, which traces causality back to the a priori categories of the mind. The theory of pure groping corresponds to an inductivist, or purely empirical, theory of causality. Finally, the fifth (Piagetian) theory of intelligence interprets causality as "an organization of the universe caused by the totality of relations established by action and then by representation between objects as well as between subject and object" (ibid., p. 357). As opposed to the other four theories, which emphasize either the role of experience or that of the subject in the acquisition of knowledge, Piaget argued that his observations support the view that knowledge of causal relations arises from an indissociable interaction between the subject and the objective world. From out of the interactive cycle of assimilation and accommodation, the subject constructs a knowledge of causal relations that comes to reflect reality in an increasingly more accurate manner.

In other words, knowledge begins neither with external reality nor within the subject, but at the very meeting point between the two. From this point of immediate interaction, it proceeds both outward toward knowledge of reality (space, time, causality, and the object concept) and inward toward a reflexive knowledge of reason itself (logic and mathematics). This double outward and inward movement broadly corresponds to the "explicative" and "implicative" functions already postulated by Piaget in *The language and thought of the child*.

In the conclusion of *The construction of reality*, Piaget described the transition from sensorimotor intelligence to representative and conceptual thought. But because he devoted an entire book to this topic, we proceed directly to that source.

Play, dreams and imitation in childhood

Although not published until 1945, *Play, dreams and imitation in childhood* contains a description of the transition between sensorimotor and representative intelligence and therefore provides a good bridge between his books on sensorimotor development, which appeared during the 1930s, and his studies of concrete operations, which appeared beginning in the early 1940s. Two major theses were defended in this book: that there is a "functional continuity" between sensorimotor intelligence and cognitive representation, and that the different forms of cognitive representation interact in their development (Piaget, 1945/1962, pp. 2–3). The first thesis was argued by tracing the development of imitation and play through the six stages of sensorimotor development and onto the plane of representation, and the second by following the interaction of play, imitation, and intelligent adaptation per se in subsequent development. In addition, Piaget was concerned to demonstrate that the development of representation can be completely explained neither by the action of the environment nor by preexisting structures. Like intelligence itself, representation arises from the interaction between the subject and external reality, and the cycle of assimilation and accommodation of which this interaction is composed is the basis of the distinction between the different forms of cognitive representation. Play is characterized by a predominance of assimilation over accommodation, imitation by the predominance of accommodation over assimilation, and intelligent adaptation by equal contributions of both the assimilatory and accommodatory functions.

A subsidiary issue in *Play, dreams and imitation* is the role of social life in the development of representation. Piaget defended himself against criticism by Wallon (1942/1970), who accused him of pursuing a purely individualistic psychology and of not taking collective factors sufficiently into account. Piaget replied that he by no means sought to minimize the importance of social factors in development; quite the contrary, he said, he had emphasized them in his previous works. But development cannot be explained by social factors alone, for children's understanding of social relations itself undergoes developmental change. Although the acquisition of language profoundly influences children's subsequent development, children begin to acquire language only when they are developmentally prepared for it. Part of Piaget's purpose in tracing the continuity between sensorimotor development and cognitive representation was to describe this developmental preparation for collective symbolism.

Imitation. In the first part of *Play, dreams and imitation,* Piaget followed the development of imitation through the six stages of sensorimotor development much as he had done for other areas of understanding in his previous books. In the first few days following birth, he already observed a primitive form of reflex "imitation" insofar as the crying of other babies seemed to reinforce Laurent's own crying. Only in the *second stage,* however, did imitation develop beyond the mere strengthening of an ongoing reflex activity. With respect to phonation, for example, imitation now took the form of "vocal contagion" – a kind of primary circular reaction initiated by the sound of someone else's voice. The particular limitation of imitation at this stage is that the sound of the other person's voice must be highly similar to the sounds produced by the child's own voice. In other words, the other voice must be assimilable to the existing circular reaction between the act of phonation and the sound of the child's own voice. Similar assimilations of another person's actions to primary circular reactions involving prehension and vision were also observed at this stage.

These early examples of imitation remain rather sporadic in stage two, becoming systematic only in *stage three.* In this stage, children become capable of imitating almost any sound that they can utter spontaneously and any visible movement that they can make themselves. The limitation of this stage is precisely that only actions with which children are already familiar can be imitated, and only movements that can be carried out within the field of vision.

This limitation is overcome at *stage four,* when the child becomes capable of imitating movements that are not directly visible as well as movements that are not already familiar. The most obvious example of the imitation of invisible movements involves movements of various parts of the face: opening and closing the mouth and eyes, sticking out the tongue, touching one's own nose, and so forth. Each of these examples involves a coordination of the visible images accompanying the other person's movements with the kinesthetic sensations that accompany one's own. What is especially interesting about the development of such forms of imitation is the role of transitional "indices" in establishing this coordination. In effect, the visible movements of the other person's face become coordinated with the invisible movements of one's own face through the temporary utilization of some perceptible index common to them both. For example, the imitation of certain sounds was used by Piaget's children to coordinate the movements of the other person's mouth with those of their own mouths (Piaget, 1945/1962, Obs. 19, pp. 30–31; Obs. 29–30, pp. 39–40). Similarly, the sound of blowing through the nose helped Jacqueline locate her own nose (ibid., Obs. 24, pp. 35–36). In the case of locating the mouth, the sight of the finger played the role of transitional index for Jacqueline when she assimilated the sight of her father's finger being put in his mouth to the sight of her own finger (ibid., Obs. 21, pp. 32–33). In each case, once the coordination was established, the transitional index became superfluous and dropped out altogether.

The second characteristic of stage-four imitation is that new auditory and visual models can also be imitated. For example, syllables that the child has not spontaneously uttered and that were not previously imitated now give rise to attempts at reproduction (ibid., Obs. 32a–32b, p. 46). What still remains beyond the child in stage four is the ability to combine the two characteristics of this stage: to imitate movements that are *both* new and invisible.

The latter is the defining characteristic of *stage five*. The most typical example of this stage is touching specific parts of the face in imitation of a model (ibid., Obs. 43, pp. 55–56; Obs. 45–50b, pp. 56–60). This reaction is distinguished from those involving the face in the previous stage by the fact that the movements are neither spontaneously produced nor mediated by a transitional index as they were in stage four. Rather, the correspondence established between the visually known face of the other person and the kinesthetic knowledge of the child's own face would appear to have been already sufficiently sketched out to make possible the approximate location of its various parts. Whereas the child in stage four learned to locate different parts of the face, in stage five these parts are brought into relationship with each other to form a coherent whole. But as with other stage-five behavior patterns, imitation is still limited to models that have just been perceived.

This final limitation is overcome in *stage six,* defined by the appearance of "deferred imitation." The latter is the imitation of actions that had been originally observed at some time in the past. At 1;4(4), for example, Jacqueline was observed to imitate with precision the angry behavior of a young boy that she had witnessed the previous day (ibid., Obs. 52, p. 63). For Piaget, such a pattern constituted evidence of cognitive representation, defined as "the symbolic evocation of absent realities" (ibid., p. 67). In this case, cognitive representation took the form of mental imagery. The fact that Jacqueline could imitate her young friend's behavior a day later indicated that she possessed some memorial image of his performance. But such observations raise a problem: What is the exact relation between imitation and cognitive representation? Does deferred imitation presuppose cognitive representation? Or does cognitive representation itself develop as a consequence of imitation?

Piaget's solution is significant: "May it not be that the mental image, i.e., the symbol when it is the interior copy or reproduction of the object, is merely the product of the interiorization of imitation?" (ibid., p. 70). Piaget rejected the empiricist notion that the image is simply a continuation of perception, distinguished from the latter in terms of vividness. Obviously, a sensory component exists in mental imagery. But Piaget suggested that a motor component also exists. "The ability to reproduce a tune which has been heard makes the inner hearing of it infinitely more precise, and the visual image remains vague if it cannot be drawn or mimed. The image is as it were the draft of potential imitation" (ibid., p. 70). His observations of his children imitating objects were cited in support of the idea that the mental image is a form of interiorized imitation. Both Laurent and Lucienne were observed to mimic the opening and closing of a matchbox with their mouths or hands. These observations were interpreted as attempts to understand the mechanism of the matchbox through motor analogy.

According to Piaget, such motor analogy is a simple precursor of the mental image as such. In mimicking the matchbox, Laurent and Lucienne reproduced a kinesthetic image of opening and closing. The motor component of this image was still exteriorized. Piaget suggested that the interiorization of the motor component of such images results in the mental image as such. The fact that the motor image appears in an exteriorized form before the mental image indicates that deferred imitation does not develop as the result of mental imagery being added to imitation, but that mental imagery itself develops out of imitation as the result of a progressive interiorization.

Phrased in somewhat different terms, Piaget's hypothesis would seem to be the following: Through imitation, schemes of correspondence are established between certain sensory events and the kinesthetic sensations accompanying motor activity. In his observations of the imitation of invisible movements, for example, the kinesthetically monitored movements of the mouth are brought into correspondence with the observed expressions of other persons. Later, when the motor component of this scheme of correspondence becomes sufficiently interiorized, an image of the mouth and its movements can be evoked through an interiorized activation of the motor component of this scheme.

Symbolic play and secondary symbolism. The foregoing explanation applies only to the mental image. What about other forms of cognitive representation, such as the spoken word, abstract concepts, and symbolic play? These forms of representation were discussed in the remaining parts of *Play, dreams and imitation*. Part II was devoted to the development of play. As in the case of imitation, Piaget followed the development of playful activity through the six stages of sensorimotor development. For present purposes, all that need concern us is the appearance of cognitive representation in the form of symbolic play or "make-believe" in stage six. In that stage, both Jacqueline and Lucienne were observed early in the second year pretending to go to sleep (ibid., Obs. 64a–65, pp. 96–97). For this purpose Jacqueline used various objects, including a fringed cloth, her mother's coat, and the tail of a rubber donkey, as symbolic substitutes for a pillow. Later, she also pretended that her toy animals were going to sleep.

These examples of symbolic play count as cognitive representation because they involve the evocation of absent objects. Various objects were employed by Jacqueline as props in the evocation of the pillow she usually used in going to sleep. Symbolic play differs from imitative forms of cognitive representation, however, in that children make no effort to accommodate to reality. The props used to represent absent objects need not resemble those objects in any precise manner, nor do children take part in play activities for any purpose other than the mere pleasure of doing so.

In tracing the subsequent evolution of children's play, Piaget distinguished between practice games, symbolic games, and games with rules, providing examples of each from his observations. "Practice games" consist of activities carried out for the mere pleasure of functioning and contain no symbolic elements. Such games can be found from the earliest stages of sensorimotor development in the form of the "functional assimilations" characteristic of those stages. "Symbolic games" include playful activities involving symbolic representation and are found from stage six onward. "Games with rules" may include elements from both of the other types, but have in addition a social component implied by the rules themselves. As opposed to the ritualizations found in some play activities of individuals (e.g., trying not to step on a crack in the sidewalk), rules imply an element of obligation that can come only from relations with other persons. So defined, games with rules begin to be observed in children's play only after the age of about 4 years. As described in *The moral judgment of the child*, Piaget believed that participation in games with rules was an important part of social and moral development.

After reviewing previous theories of play, Piaget gave his own explanation: Play is the pure assimilation of reality to the ego without any effort at accommodation. On the level of sensorimotor activity, it is the repetition of an activity for the sheer pleasure of acting:

After learning to grasp, swing, throw, etc., which involve both an effort of accommodation to new situations, and an effort of repetition, reproduction, and generalization, which are the elements of assimilation, the child sooner or later (often even during the learning period) grasps for the pleasure of grasping, swings for the sake of swinging, etc. In a word, he repeats his behaviour not in any further effort to learn or to investigate, but for the mere joy of mastering it and of showing off to himself his own power of subduing reality. [ibid., p. 162]

At the level of symbolic play, the situation is analogous, except that the assimilations involved are symbolic in nature. When Jacqueline assimilated various objects to the symbolic scheme of the pillow, for example, she showed little effort at accommodation, insofar as the resemblance between the "signifier" and the "signified" was minimal. It was as though the criteria for assimilation were minimal. Reality supplied just what was necessary to allow the activity to occur, and little else.

As described earlier, "symbolic play" refers only to examples of symbolism in which the child is fully conscious of the relation between the signifier and the signified. When Jacqueline assimilated the tail of a rubber donkey to the scheme of sleeping, she was fully aware of what she was doing. Such examples, however, hardly exhaust the entire field of symbolism in children's thinking. In addition to symbolic play and other forms of conscious symbolism, many examples can be found in which children (and adults) evoke absent realities in their current thought or behavior without themselves being aware of the connection. In one of the most fascinating chapters of *Play, dreams and imitation*, Piaget attempted an explanation of such "secondary symbolism" in terms of his own theory of assimilation.

One of the major forms of secondary symbolism is the symbolism of the unconscious, as identified by psychoanalysis. In discussing the topic, Piaget referred back to and extended some of the ideas expressed in his early paper "La pensée symbolique et la pensée de l'enfant" (Piaget, 1923a), which he had presented in 1922 at the International Conference on Psychoanalysis in Berlin. In that paper, he had argued that children's thinking in general offers many analogies with the unconscious symbolism uncovered by psychoanalysis. In *Play, dreams and imitation,* he focused on two areas in particular: symbolic play and children's dreams.

As examples of secondary symbolism in play, Piaget described a number of "Freudian" themes in his children's symbolic play involving excremental functions, anatomical differences between the sexes, rivalries with their parents, and birth fantasies (Piaget, 1945/1962, Obs. 95–97, pp. 173–174). In each case, the symbolism appeared to involve feelings of which the children were not completely aware. In her sixth year, for example, one of Piaget's daughters (Jacqueline) was temporarily on bad terms with her father and avenged herself vicariously by having an imaginary playmate decapitate her own father: *"Zoubab cut off her daddy's head. But she has some very strong glue and partly stuck it on again. But it's not very firm now"* (ibid., Obs. 96, p. 174). Piaget observed no indication that Jacqueline was aware of any relation between her own situation and the actions of her imaginary friend.

Many of these same themes return in the examples Piaget provided of his children's first dreams (ibid., Obs. 98–100, pp. 177–179). As with symbolic play, dreams involving wish-fulfillment, symbolic recall of difficult situations, and substitutions involving family members were described. A month or so after Jacqueline's symbolic decapitation of her father, she finished him off again in a dream: *" 'I dreamt that Dr. M. fired a gun at a man who was high up in the air. The man was very ill and was going to die so he killed him. He was very small, and then when he fell he was big: he got bigger and bigger; he had a fat tummy like you; he was just like you!'* (she laughed)." Two days later, she dreamt she was being chased by a fox, and she went inside her mother to hide (ibid., Obs. 98, p. 178).

In contrast to play, in which difficult situations symbolically recalled usually are mastered through symbolic means, some dreams involve unresolved anxiety. According to Piaget, this reflects the fact that the ego exercises less control in dreaming than in playing. Both nightmares and dreams of punishment belong in this category. In dreaming, the dreamer believes what is dreamed, or, more precisely, there is little possibility of doubting what is experienced. In playing, however, children are always more or less aware of the make-believe quality of their activity. In the general category of anxiety dreams, Piaget cited examples of both nightmares and dreams of punishment. The question to be answered with respect to both play and dreams is how the symbolism involved in each case can be explained.

In reviewing the Freudian explanation for unconscious symbolism of this nature, Piaget described the experience of psychoanalysis from the point of view of the analysand with such vividness and detail that the reader cannot help but conclude that he must have been psychoanalyzed once himself.[3] The classical Freudian interpretation of unconscious symbolism in play and dreams is that such symbolism results from repressed wishes or desires. Repressed because of their incompatibility with the ego, these desires form the latent content of the dream. They can reach consciousness only in a disguised or distorted form. Symbolism is the mechanism of this disguise. The repressed wishes in their symbolic disguise form the manifest content of the dream. The work of repression is carried out, according to this theory, by a mechanism Freud called the "censor." Like the censors of an authoritarian regime, this psychic mechanism was believed to suppress material inconsistent with the "official policy" of the superego. And as with state-sponsored censorship, repressed material can sometimes slip past the censor if it is sufficiently disguised. Such disguises constitute a kind of compromise in which the interests of both the repressed material and the superego are partially fulfilled: The repressed material is permitted to reach consciousness, but only in a symbolically distorted form. Moreover, the same conditions that allow the repressed material to reach consciousness are sufficient to ensure that its original meaning will not be understood by the ego. The goal of psychoanalysis, as conceived by Freud, was to decode the manifest content of dreams and other symbolic behavior in order to uncover the latent content and to allow the latter to enter consciousness in its original, undisguised form. In helping the symbolically encoded "messages" of the unconscious to get through to the ego, the psychoanalyst played the part of a conspirator siding with the ego against the censorship imposed by the superego.

Piaget criticized this interpretation on two grounds. First, he believed it was not sufficiently developmental in orientation and conflicted on several points with the facts of child development as revealed in his own observations of sensorimotor development. Second, the theory of a psychic censor either leads to contradictions or implies a doubling of consciousness. With respect to child development, Piaget argued that Freud ascribed feats of memory and understanding to infants and young children that his own observations rendered highly improbable. Freud assumed that we have no memories of the first 1.5 years of life because those memories are repressed ("infantile amnesia"). Piaget replied that his observations indicated that children were in any case incapable of evocative memory before the sixth stage of sensorimotor development; so repression is unnecessary as an explanation for infantile amnesia at this early age.

Similarly, Freud believed that young children formed internalized and affec-

3 This impression is confirmed by Piaget's admission in the conversations with Bringuier (1977/ 1980, p. 123) that he had once undertaken a brief "training analysis." The analysis was conducted by Sabine Spielrein, a member of the International Psycho-analytic Association who was associated personally and professionally with both Freud and Jung (Sandler, 1975; Vidal, 1986); on Spielrein's relations with Freud and Jung, see Bettelheim (1983) and Carotenuto (1982). According to Vidal (1986b), Piaget even conducted several analyses of his own, including one of his own mother (until she rebelled against his interpretations)!

tive "images" of their parents and that other personages encountered later in life were "identified" with these early images. Piaget argued that this view is not only insufficiently informed about developmental changes in children's imagery but also implies a doubling of consciousness in terms of unconscious memory and a preservation of feeling in its original form. Instead, he proposed to distinguish between feelings as they are consciously experienced and the *affective schemes* corresponding to those feelings. Such schemes are not the feelings themselves, but rather the *carriers* of the feelings. The phenomena of "identification" and "transference" were thus explained by the hypothesis of complexes of affective schemes formed in children's early interaction with their parents, which schemes are later generalized to other relationships minimally resembling the originals. Thus, one need assume neither unconscious memory nor a preservation of feeling. The original feelings associated with the parental figures are not preserved as *feelings* in the unconscious, for feeling as such implies consciousness. Rather, the schemes of those feelings are preserved, and the feelings themselves are consciously experienced when the respective schemes are applied in a new situation. The connection between such feelings and their origins in the past remains unconscious, not because it is repressed by an unseen censor, but because the schemes themselves do not carry memories of their origins. Psychoanalysis is therefore less a process of *uncovering* connections that have been preserved in the unconscious than of *reconstructing* the connections between present feelings and their origins in the past.

Piaget's criticism of the psychoanalytic theory of the censor is much the same as that advanced by Sartre (1943/1953) in *Being and nothingness:* The censor is supposed to be responsible for determining what enters consciousness and what remains repressed. In order to know what it is repressing, the censor must be conscious of it. But the ego is neither conscious of the repressed material nor conscious of the act of repression. In order to avoid a contradiction (the repressed material being both conscious and unconscious), Freudian theory must deny the unity of consciousness (between the ego and the censor). Piaget, like Sartre, found this argument unconvincing.

Another reason for doubting the psychoanalytic account of symbolism as a form of censorship is that dreams exist in which the meaning of the symbolism is obvious. Piaget cited a few examples, most likely from his own experience. In one of them, "a student of philosophy" dreamt that his professor introduced an elderly man who resembled the author of a certain textbook on logic. The latter began to lecture, but digressed so much that he was booed by all the students and finally left the lecture hall. The professor then admitted that they were right; what the lecturer had been saying was worthless. The meaning of the dream consisted in the fact that the dreamer intended to hand in a critical review of the textbook in question the following day and hoped to convince his professor of his point of view. The dream can thus be interpreted as wish-fulfillment. But if the purpose of dream symbolism is to disguise the wish that it expresses, why is this wish expressed in symbolic form at all? Or, to put it the other way around, how can the meaning of this dream symbolism be so obvious, even to the dreamer himself, if the function of symbolism is to disguise the wishes expressed in dreams?

Piaget did not doubt the importance of repression or the unconscious in mental life, but he offered an alternative theory of repression and the origins of unconscious symbolism. According to this view, the unconscious quality of secondary symbolism results not from censorship but from the fact that certain affective schemes are unable to enter into reciprocal assimilations with schemes associated with the conscious ego. Such blocking of reciprocal assimilation results from the fact that the schemes involved are affectively incompatible with each other. Repression is "the blocking [or] inhibition for a tendency incompatible with others stronger than itself because they are organised in stable assimilating schemas" (Piaget, 1945/1962, p. 204n). Thus, no agency apart from the affective schemes themselves must be postulated in order to explain repression. The latter arises instead from the intrinsic incapacity of schemes for reciprocal assimilation under conditions of mutual incompatibility. Schemes that are incompatible with the stable groups of schemes giving rise to consciousness are "repressed" in the sense that they are simply unable to reach consciousness. Instead, they perpetuate themselves only by assimilating isolated images taken from the person's experience. Dream symbolism, for example, results when affective schemes assimilate images from the dreamer's waking life – what Freud called "day residues." In general, "the unconscious symbol is an image whose content is assimilated to the desires or impressions of the subject, and whose meaning he fails to understand" (ibid., p. 205).

In this sense, unconscious symbolism does express affective relations belonging to the past. Affective schemes arise, for example, from children's early relations with their parents. In this respect, "actions related to others [i.e., other persons] are like other actions. They tend to be reproduced (reproductive assimilation), to find nutriment to sustain them (recognitory assimilation), and to discover new ones (generalising assimilation), whether it be a case of an affection, an aggressive tendency, or any other" (ibid., p. 207). In adult life, however, the infantile situations that gave rise to such schemes will no longer exist in their original forms. Instead, these affective schemes will tend to assimilate whatever images or situations in the individual's life most nearly resemble the circumstances from which they originated – a radical form of generalizing assimilation. Certain situations will be reacted to in an infantile manner despite the fact that the reactions are inappropriate to the current context.

Repression thus constitutes another example of the kind of unstable equilibrium in which the whole (the complex of mutually compatible schemes that together compose the conscious ego) is in conflict with the parts (the "repressed" affective schemes incompatible with the ego). The individual's affective equilibrium is what is now in question. Split off from the complex of schemes composing the ego, isolated affective schemes are unable to accommodate themselves to reality by means of reciprocal assimilations with the schemes of consciousness. Such isolated schemes are thus reduced to perpetuating themselves as they are by assimilating what they can. The role of psychoanalysis implied by this view is to provide a "bridge" between these isolated schemes and the ego, thus allowing an integration of the two. Only through such an integration is it possible for the previously isolated schemes to accommodate to reality, and only through such integration and accommodation can a stable affective equilibrium be achieved. This stable equilibrium will represent a stable balance not only between the parts and the whole but also, given the origins of the respective schemes, between past and present. "Equilibrium consists in preserving the living aspects of the past by continual accommodation to the manifold and irreducible present" (ibid., p. 208).

So conceived, secondary symbolism offers a number of analogies with the thought of young children. Unconscious symbolism is a form of "radical egocentrism" in which the subject is unaware of itself at the center of its own activity. Moreover, the kinds of symbolic transformations (e.g., displacement and condensation) that Freud described as characteristic of unconscious thought can be compared to certain pre-logical characteristics of child thought. Thus, the "displacements," "condensations," "projections," and "identifications" that characterize dream symbolism bear certain resemblances to the syncretism, transduction, and participations of children's thinking as described by Piaget. This comparison is consistent with his earlier contention that the egocentrism of children's thinking is midway between the "autism" of unconscious thought and directed, conceptual thought (Piaget, 1923/1955). The last part of *Play, dreams and imitation* was in fact devoted to the egocentrism of representational thinking viewed as a transition between sensorimotor intelligence and conceptual thought.

Cognitive representation. Piaget began this section of the book by describing his children's first verbal schemes – that is, their first words. For example, Jacqueline at 1;1(0) used the sound "tch tch" in imitation of a train passing by the window. On the following days, this sound was generalized to any vehicle seen out of a window, or any noise heard in the street. At about 1;1(20) she said "bow-wow" to indicate dogs. This vocalization subsequently became generalized to anything seen from her balcony, until at 1;4 it became reserved for dogs. Similar generalizations were observed in the use of "papa" and "maman"; both were applied for some weeks to persons other than her father and mother. After 1;6, she used the word "panana" not only for her grandfather but also in general to indicate that she wanted something. This latter usage probably was a reflection of the fact that her grandfather was accommodating to her wishes. Laurent was observed to use the word "maman" in a similar manner (ibid., Obs. 101a–102, pp. 216–218).

Probably the most interesting thing about these observations is their transitional character between practical activity and representation as such. Verbalization begins as an action like any other, but is especially adapted to representation by virtue of the range and variety of the human vocal capacities. Thus, Jacqueline's verbalizations "tch tch" and "bow-wow" began in pure imitation, but evolved into simple verbal representations. And names like "panana" or "maman" were used not only in a denotive fashion but also as means to the attainment of desired ends. Speech thus reveals itself as a particular form of action. The denotive character of language arises from the fact that one action can be used as a substitute for, or as a means for, another. "The act of giving a name to an object is not merely that and nothing more, but the statement of a possible action" (ibid., p. 222).

But despite the incipient generalization found in some of the foregoing examples, such early verbalizations cannot be said to represent true concepts. For one thing, they do not yet have a fixed definition; they are generalized from one instance to another in terms of the resemblances between their referents. Moreover, the relation between the word and the thing denoted is not yet arbitrary and conventional; it is still the product of direct imitation, either of the object denoted (onomatopoeia) or of words used by adults. The generalization by resemblance of these early words reflects their sensorimotor origins, for such "generalizing assimilation" is also characteristic of sensorimotor schemes. "These first verbal schemas are merely sensory-motor schemas in process of becoming concepts" (ibid., p. 219).

Between the ages of approximately 2 and 4 years, verbal schemes evolve into what Piaget called "preconcepts." Words come to denote loose proto-classes of individuals distinguished by their resemblance to each other. These preconcepts differ from true concepts, however, in that the individual and the general are not perfectly differentiated. At the age of 2.5 years, for example, Jacqueline used the term "the slug" to refer to every slug encountered on successive morning walks.

At 2;7(2) she cried: *"There it is!"* on seeing one, and when we saw another then yards further on she said: *"There's the slug again."* I answered: "But isn't it another one?" J. then went back to see the first one. "Is it the same one? – *Yes* – another slug? – *Yes.* – Another or the same? – . . ." The question obviously had no meaning for J. [ibid., Obs. 107, p. 225]

In an anticipation of later psychological theories of natural classification (Rosch, 1987), Piaget suggested that such preconcepts are organized around a prototypical individual that acts as a symbol for the class as a whole. "Thus, 'the slug' is the prototype or representative of all slugs while in a general concept all slugs are equivalent through their common abstract characteristics" (ibid., p. 228). For Piaget, the inability of children at this stage to form true concepts is an expression of their relative inability to coordinate parts and wholes. "As it is still half-way between the individual and the general, the child's preconcept constitutes a kind of 'participation' (in the sense of Lévy-Bruhl), this relationship being defined as follows: absence of inclusion of the elements in a whole, and direct identification of the partial elements one with another, without the inter-mediary of the whole" (ibid., pp. 226–227). As opposed to the more abstract character of the general class defined in terms of the common characteristics of its members, the preconcept remains bound to the concrete image of the proto-type as a typical representative.

In the remaining sections of *Play, dreams and imitation,* Piaget described the further evolution of representational thought in terms of the categories investi-gated in his first four books. For example, the preconceptual reasoning of his children was described in terms of transduction as originally discussed in *Judg-ment and reasoning in the child.* Observations of their conceptions of reality were recounted, including examples of artificialism, animism, intellectual real-ism, and magico-phenomenalism. Because these examples recall the findings of *The child's conception of the world* and *The child's conception of physical cau-sality,* they will not be reviewed again here.

In the final chapter, Piaget summarized and integrated his work on sensori-motor and representative intelligence in a new stage-developmental scheme. The first period is constituted by sensorimotor development, the second by egocentric representative activity, which includes two substages. The stage of "preconcep-tual thought" lasts from about age two to four, and the stage of "intuitive thought" from age four or five to about seven. The third period begins at roughly age seven or eight and comprises "operational representative activity." In this pe-riod, the irreversible character of egocentric representative activity becomes re-placed by reversible operations coordinated in logical structures that Piaget had in the meantime come to call "groupings." The theory of groupings was an attempt to apply group theory to logical thinking and also represented the mature form of his early theory of part–whole structures. The development of this theory is the central topic of chapter 4.

CONCLUSION

Piaget's studies of sensorimotor development played a critical role in his own intellectual evolution. In the first place, they provided data to support his "neo-pragmatic" intuition that an essential continuity exists between action and thought and that before the logic of thought there is a logic of action. In *Play, dreams and imitation,* he showed how cognitive representation arises from the interiori-zation of imitative action, and in *The origins of intelligence* he demonstrated that a practical logic of classes and relations exists at the level of sensorimotor intel-ligence and is analogous to the representational logic of classes and relations at the level of operational thought.

Second, his observations of sensorimotor development provided him with his first suggestions of the psychological relevance of group theory. Building on Poincaré's remarks on "the group of displacements," Piaget reasoned that chil-dren's conception of space was constructed from the coordination of action schemes. In coming to reflect the whole system of possible displacements in space, these coordinations acquired the formal properties of group structure. This insight was the cornerstone of his later theory of groupings.

Finally, the study of sensorimotor development also provided him with the opportunity for developing his theory of equilibrium in a more concrete fashion. On the one hand, a tendency toward equilibrium operates in the child's interaction with the environment. On the other hand, this tendency is reflected in an internal equilibrium among the child's own action schemes. Assimilation and accommodation are the adaptive functions by which the order existing in the environment becomes increasingly reflected in the organization of action schemes. But the interaction with the environment is not a one-way process. By acting on the environment, the internal order existing at any given stage of development is also reflected outward. The tendency toward equilibrium in this interaction between internal and external order constitutes the motor of development.

The two-way exchange with the environment is most obvious in the case of the child's relations with other persons. Imitation, as described by Piaget, is above all a social interactive process and the child's earliest form of intentional communication with others. In this respect, Piaget's self-defense against Wallon in *Play, dreams and imitation* may have created in some readers the mistaken impression that he minimized the importance of social factors in early development. Nothing could be further from the truth. He chided Wallon for bringing in social factors in the form of language as an explanation for the development of cognitive representation. Far from wishing to minimize the importance of social life, he argued simply that the existence of individual forms of symbolism – in play, dreams, and mental imagery, for example – indicates that language as a system of collective signs is not the only factor involved. Before children can appreciate such collective symbols, they must already have reached a stage of development in which symbolic representation in general has become possible. Thus, "the social fact is for us a fact to be explained, not to be invoked as an extra-psychological factor" (ibid., p. 4).

Stating the argument in this way was potentially misleading. Piaget meant that children's understanding of collective signs must be explained by the development of symbolism in general, not the reverse. He did not mean to deny that the infant is implicated in social relations of various kinds from birth onward. His own observations of the development of imitation demonstrate to what extent this is in fact the case. Once imitation is recognized for what it is – the child's earliest form of intentional communication – Piaget's theory that mental imagery originated from the interiorization of imitation appears more radically social in its orientation than is generally recognized. It implies that even the "private" symbolism of children has its origins in the interiorization of a communicative relation, namely, imitation. Piaget's observations of his children's imitation of physical objects were important to him because they demonstrated the intermediate step in the development of representation before the image is completely interiorized. But because of the correspondence between the child's body and movements and those of other persons and because of the capacity of others for reciprocal imitation, people provide the child with infinitely more opportunities for imitation than any physical object. For this reason, one can doubt that Piaget's examples of his children's imitation of objects represent a distinct phenomenon, rather than generalizations of schemes already acquired in imitative social interactions.

4

Concrete operations and structures-of-the-whole

In the late 1930s, even as his books on sensorimotor development began to appear in print, Piaget took a decisive step in his thinking about psychological structure. With the collaboration of A. Szeminska and B. Inhelder, he began to study the development of children's conceptions of number and physical quantities. In contrast to the early research on children's verbal reasoning in his first four books, the studies to be discussed in this chapter concentrated on children's reasoning about concrete problems. To be sure, a verbal interview method was still employed, and the data consisted mainly of children's verbal expressions of their reasoning processes. But the problems children were asked to solve were no longer purely verbal. Instead, children were asked about the properties and relations of concrete objects – flowers, dolls, pieces of clay, and so on. In short, this research focused on logical operations as applied to real objects and situations, on what Piaget came to call *concrete operations*.

The decisive step was taken when Piaget asked himself whether or not the organization of concrete operations could be described in terms of mathematical groups, as the infant's understanding of space had been described in terms of groups of displacements in *The construction of reality in the child*. The fact that arithmetical operations possessed the formal properties of group structure was well known. The system formed by the addition of whole numbers, for example, has all the formal properties of a group, including composition under closure, associativity, identity, and inversion. But what about logical operations involving classes and relations? Could such systems of logical operations also be described in terms of group structure? And what was the psychological reality underlying such systems?

With respect to the question of psychological reality, the parallel with groups of displacements is clear. In the latter case, the "operations" composing the group are real actions (i.e., displacements), and space is the whole system formed by the sum total of possible displacements. This system forms a group by virtue of the fact that the actions involved considered as a whole possess the formal properties of group structure. Thus, any two successive displacements yield a result contained within the system (composition under closure), the order in which a sequence of displacements is carried out is unimportant (associativity), the actions involved are reversible (inversion), and an object that is not displaced remains where it is (identity of position). The psychological reality corresponding to the group of displacements is simply the manner in which the actions belonging to the system are organized among themselves.

Roughly the same is true for the additive system of whole numbers, except that the operations belonging to this system (i.e., addition and subtraction) are actions that have become interiorized. The evidence for this hypothesis may be found in the facts of development, in the gradual interiorization of the respective operations as revealed in Piaget's research. The organization of these actions, once interiorized, has the formal properties of a group: Any two numbers added together yield another number within the system, and so on. But the kind of reversibility involved in each case varies as a function of interiorization: Whereas overt actions are reversible only successively in time, interiorized operations are "simultaneously" reversible (Piaget, 1941). That is, a child who has interiorized a reversible operation such as $2 + 2 = 4$ understands that it "simultaneously" implies its inverse, $4 - 2 = 2$, without having to carry out the respective overt actions (i.e., manipulating real objects). Piaget's argument for the psychological reality of concrete operational structures such as the additive system of whole numbers is based on the claim that the operations belonging to those structures derive from interiorized actions.

With respect to logical (as opposed to arithmetical) structures, Piaget concluded that the logic of classification and seriation indeed possesses the four properties of group structure. In addition, they have certain other properties not possessed by groups in general. These additional properties have to do with the noniterative character of logical operations. In arithmetic, the addition of any given number to itself yields a new number twice as great as the first ($n + n = 2n$). Indeed, the addition of any two nonzero numbers yields a third number different from the first two ($x + y = z$). This is what is meant in speaking of the iterative character of arithmetical addition. Logical addition, however, is not iterative in this sense. For example, any class added to itself yields only itself ($A + A = A$). And if one class is added to another class that contains it, the first class is absorbed by the second ($A + B = B$). In general, class addition yields a new result only when two mutually exclusive classes are added together to form a new totality ($A + A' = B$). The same noniterative properties belonging to the addition of classes are found in the addition of relations. In summary, logical operations have group-like properties as well as special properties reflecting their noniterative character.

As in the case of arithmetical structures, Piaget's argument for the psychological reality of logical structures rests on the claim that the operations involved consist of interiorized actions. The operation of class addition, for example, is an interiorization of the action of combining classes of concrete objects to form larger classes. The point of calling attention to the group-like character of such psychological structures is simply to provide a means of describing the formal properties of the total system in which the respective operations function.

Piaget first presented these conclusions in a paper entitled "La réversibilité des opérations et l'importance de la notion de 'groupe' pour la psychologie de la pensée" ("The reversibility of operations and the importance of the notion of a 'group' for the psychology of thinking"), delivered at the International Congress of Psychology in Paris in 1937 (Piaget, 1938). In this brief paper, he described succinctly why the notion of group structure is relevant to the psychology of intelligence. The properties of such structures were now cited in explaining the "fecundity" and "rigor" of reason in general. The possibility of composition under closure constitutes the constructive character of reason (in the sense that the composition of two operations can yield a new result), and the reversibility of rational operations constitutes their rigor (in the sense that reversibility guarantees noncontradiction). In another paper from this period, entitled "Les relations d'égalité résultant de l'addition et de la soustraction logiques constituents-elles un groupe?" ("Do the relations of equality resulting from logical addition and subtraction constitute a group?"), Piaget (1937) described in brief the formal properties of logical structures, both those that they shared with mathematical groups and those that they did not. Like groups, logical structures are characterized by composition under closure, associativity, identity, and inversion. As opposed to groups, logical structures were further characterized by the special properties of what he called "tautology" ($A + A = A$) and "resorption" ($A + B = B$). That is, a class (or relation) acts as an identity operator with respect to itself or with respect to a second class (or relation) that subsumes the first. Thus, the class of all mammals added to itself yields only the class of mammals, and the class of all mammals added to the class of vertebrates yields only the latter. A further implication of these special properties (which Piaget came to call "special identities") is that the property of associativity applies only to the equations taken as a whole, not to the classes or relations themselves. With respect to the addition of a class to itself, for example, associativity does not hold: $(A + A) - A \neq A + (A - A)$. These properties all reflect the "noniterativity" of logical operations as described earlier.

These ideas were further developed in a book-length treatise written in 1939 and published 3 years later. In this work, entitled *Classes, relations et nombres: Essai sur les groupements de la logistique et sur la réversibilité de la pensée* (1942), Piaget for the first time used the word *groupement* ("grouping") to distinguish logical structures from group structures in general. In the foreword, he stated the purpose of the book in terms of developing a logic conforming to, instead of diverging from, the psychological structures (or *systèmes d'ensemble*) that characterize actual mental life. The grouping is one such psycho-logical structure and was defined as follows: "A grouping is a system fulfilling the conditions of composition, associativity, and reversibility belonging to groups, but such that each element plays the role of identity operator with respect to itself" (ibid., p. 11). The book is a detailed description of the groupings identified by Piaget and their relation to the groups of elementary arithmetic. It is at the same time an exposition of Piaget's theory of the origins of numbers. According to this theory, number results from a "fusion" of the logic of classes and the logic of relations. More precisely, elementary arithmetical groups arise from the fusion of groupings involving classification and seriation. In contrast to the logicists Russell and Whitehead, who had attempted to reduce mathematics to logic and to derive number from set theory, Piaget envisioned the relation between mathematics and logic somewhat differently. In effect, mathematics emerges as something new from the synthesis of the logic of classes and the logic of relations and is not reducible to either one of them.

This theory of groupings provided the inspiration for the research on number and physical quantity that Piaget began to publish in the early 1940s. In his autobiography, he described the significance of this theory for the development of his early ideas regarding part–whole organization in relational totalities:

The study of concrete operations finally enabled me to discover the operative structures-of-the-whole that I had been seeking so long. I analyzed in children four to seven or eight years of age the relationship of part and whole (by asking them to add pearls to a group of predetermined magnitude), the sequences of asymmetrical relationships (by letting them construct series of prescribed order), and the correspondences, item by item (by making them build two or more corresponding rows), etc. These studies led me to understand why logical and mathematical operations cannot be formed independently: The child can grasp a certain operation only if he is capable, at the same time, of correlating operations by modifying them in different, well-determined ways – for instance, by inverting them. These operations presuppose, as does any primary intelligent conduct, the possibility of making detours (which corresponds to what logicians call ''associativity'') and returns (''reversibility''). Thus the operations always represent reversible structures which depend on a total system that, in itself, may be entirely additive. Certain of these more complex structures-of-the-whole have been studied in mathematics under the name of ''groups'' and ''lattices''; operative systems of this sort are indeed of importance for the development of equilibria of thought. I sought for the most elementary operative structures-of-the-whole, and I finally found them in the mental processes underlying the formation of the idea of preservation or constancy. Simpler than the ''groups'' and the ''lattices,'' such structures represent the most primitive parts of a part–whole organization: I have called them ''groupings.'' For example, a classification (whereby the classes of the same rank order are always discrete and separate) is a grouping. [Piaget, 1952a, p. 252]

In this passage, Piaget used the term ''structures-of-the-whole'' (*structures d'ensemble*) to refer both to his early notions of part–whole organization and to the concrete operational groupings, thus underscoring the essential continuity between these concepts in the development of his own thought.

In 1939, two events occurred that were to have a significant effect on the research carried out by Piaget during the following decade. The first was his appointment as Professor of Sociology at the University of Geneva. In this context, he produced several essays on sociology that significantly extended his earlier ideas on social organization and its relation to psychology. The second event was the fatal illness of Claparède, which resulted in Piaget being appointed the following year to the Chair of Experimental Psychology and being made the Director of the Psychology Laboratory. In the latter capacity, he undertook a long-range study of the development of perception, in collaboration with M. Lambercier and others. The goal of this research was to understand the relationships between perception and intelligence, to compare the properties of perceptual as opposed to logical structures, and thereby to test the claims of Gestalt psychology with respect to perception.

Piaget's work in sociology and in the psychology of perception did not prevent him from pursuing his research in concrete operations. During the 1940s, he published studies on number (Piaget & Szeminska, 1941/1964), on physical quantity (Piaget & Inhelder, 1941/1974), on time (Piaget, 1946/1971b), on movement and speed (Piaget, 1946/1970a), on space (Piaget & Inhelder, 1948/ 1967), and on geometry (Piaget, Inhelder, & Szeminska, 1948/1960). In addition, the first of several summary volumes, *The psychology of intelligence* (Piaget, 1947/1950b), appeared in 1947. In all of these works, the theory of groupings occupied a central position.

In the remainder of this chapter, Piaget's theory of structures-of-the-whole and the research on concrete operations that he carried out during the decade stretching from the late 1930s to the late 1940s are reviewed. In succeeding decades, he would make additions and corrections to the ideas developed at this time, but the fundamental concepts would remain. In the following section, the theory of groupings and the research on concrete operations are described in more detail. Then his sociological writings (Piaget, 1965/1977a) are also summarized. The research on perception that he initiated during this period is reviewed in chapter 5.

THE THEORY OF GROUPINGS AND
CONCRETE OPERATIONS

Classes, relations, and numbers

Piaget's first detailed treatment of grouping structures was in the book *Classes, relations et nombres* (1942). In all, nine groupings were described, first the "preliminary grouping of pure equivalences," followed by eight groupings of logical operations. In addition, two elementary arithmetical groups, defined by the operations of numerical addition and multiplication, were also described. Only the briefest summaries of these descriptions can be given here, and the reader is referred to the original for more detailed characterizations of each type of structure (Flavell, 1963; Piaget, 1949/1972a, 1957a).

To begin with the "preliminary grouping of pure equivalences," this grouping was defined by the following formal composition (Piaget, 1942, p. 3):

$$(A = B)(B = C) = (A = B).$$

The propositional analogue of this formalism may be verbally expressed as follows: If A equals B, and B equals C, then A equals C. As in the case of all the other groupings to follow, Piaget demonstrated the formal properties that constitute this structure as a grouping, including composition under closure, associativity, inversion, identity, and special identity. Psychologically, Piaget originally

Table 4.1. *Classification of concrete operational groupings*[a]

		Classes		Relations
Addition				
Asymmetrical	I.	Simple addition of classes	V.	Addition of asymmetrical relations
Symmetrical	II.	Secondary addition of classes	VI.	Addition of symmetrical relations
Multiplication				
Bi-univocal (one-to-one)	III.	Bi-univocal multiplication of classes	VII.	Bi-univocal multiplication of relations
Co-univocal (many-to-one)	IV.	Co-univocal multiplication of classes	VIII.	Co-univocal multiplication of relations

[a]Note that in Piaget (1949/1972a), the numbering of Groupings III and IV is reversed, as is that for Groupings VII and VIII.

believed that this structure corresponded to the conservation of quantity and number. Later, he developed other models of conservation based on commutability (Piaget, 1977b; Piaget & Inhelder, 1941/1974). With respect to the other groupings, the "preliminary grouping of pure equivalences" could be said to be implied in all of them. Alternatively, if equivalence were considered as a symmetrical relation, then this "preliminary grouping" would reduce to the "addition of asymmetrical relations," as described later.

As opposed to the "preliminary grouping of pure equivalences," the remaining eight groupings are based on operations involving classes and relations. The classification of these groupings according to classes or relations, symmetrical or asymmetrical addition, and bi-univocal (one-to-one) versus co-univocal (many-to-one) multiplication is given in Table 4.1. The following descriptions of these groupings will be limited to general remarks on the formal compositions that define them and the kinds of psychological performances to which they correspond in Piaget's research on concrete operations.

Grouping I, the "simple addition of classes," was defined by the following composition:

$$A + A' = B.$$

This formula means, in effect, that a class A combined with a complementary class A' results in a supraordinate class B that includes them both (Figure 4.1). This grouping thus corresponds to class inclusion; it is formed by the direct operation of combining two subclasses having some common property to form a single class defined by that property (a class of red squares combined with a class

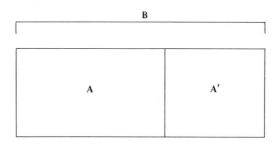

Figure 4.1. Grouping I, the simple addition of classes. (Adapted from Piaget, 1949/ 1972a.)

of red triangles yields a class of red forms). As with all the other groupings, the direct composition defining this grouping can be inverted or reversed: If subclass A is subtracted from the supraordinate class B, the complement A' is left ($B - A = A'$). This grouping forms a linear series in the sense that ever more inclusive classes can be formed through repeated inclusions: $A + B' = B; B + B' = C;$ and so on.

Grouping II was called the "secondary addition of classes" and was defined by the composition

$$A_1 + A_1' = A_2 + A_2' (= B).$$

In other words, A_1 and A_2 represent two nonoverlapping subclasses of the supraordinate class B, such that A_1 is included in A_2', and A_2 in A_1' (Figure 4.2). The supraordinate class B is in effect partitioned into three independent subclasses, defined by the intersections of the two subclasses and their complements: $A_1 \cap A_2'$, $A_2 \cap A_1'$, and $A_1 \cap A_2$ (where the symbol $\cap$ represents the intersection of classes). The grouping states, in effect, that the two subclasses together with their respective complements add up to the same whole. It is reversible in the sense that any one of the four terms can be derived from the other three (e.g., $A_1 = A_2 + A_2' - A_1'$). An example of this grouping in Piaget's research is the understanding of the distinction between one's countrymen and "foreigners" (e.g., see the paper entitled "Le développement, chez l'enfant, de l'idée de patrie et de relations avec l'étranger" in Piaget, 1965/1977a). All the people in the world (B) may be divided into those who live in France (A_1) versus all those living outside France (A_1'), and at the same time into those living in China (A_2) versus all those living outside China (A_2'). As opposed to Grouping I, which relates a given subclass to the next highest level of classification, Grouping II relates subclasses at the same level of classification. Piaget called this "horizontal" relation between subclasses *vicariance*.

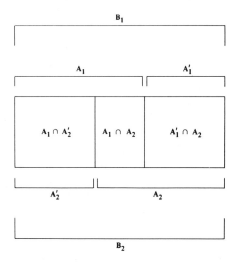

Figure 4.2. Grouping II, the secondary addition of classes (where the sign ∩ represents class intersection). (Adapted from Piaget, 1949/1972a.)

Grouping III was called "bi-univocal (one-to-one) multiplication of classes" and referred to the crossing of the subclasses formed by two different classifications of the same elements. The simplest case is when each supraordinate class (B_i) is partitioned into two subclasses ($A_i + A_i'$), such that the cross-classification results in a 2 × 2 table:

$$B_1 \times B_2 = A_1A_2 + A_1'A_2 + A_1A_2' + A_1'A_2'.$$

In other words, this grouping represents the crossing of two class inclusions ($B_1 = A_1 + A_1'$ and $B_2 = A_2 + A_2'$), such that all the possible pairings of the subclasses A_1, A_1', A_2, and A_2' are generated (Figure 4.3). Piaget was fond of providing zoological examples for cross-classifications such as this. Suppose A_1 and A_1' represent mammals and nonmammals, respectively, and A_2 and A_2' aquatic and land animals, respectively. Then the grouping will yield a cross-classification including the subcategories of aquatic mammals (A_1A_2), aquatic nonmammals ($A_1'A_2$), mammals living on land (A_1A_2'), and nonmammals living on land ($A_1'A_2'$). The operation is reversible in the sense that the subordinate categories can be derived from the supraordinate classes, as well as the reverse. This grouping was investigated by having children generate cross-classifications or parallel seriations (Inhelder & Piaget, 1959/1969; Piaget & Szeminska, 1941/1964).

Whereas Grouping III had to do with the cross-classification of two linear series (because each of the supraordinate classes B_1 and B_2 in the foregoing example may in turn be included in classes of an even higher order), *Grouping*

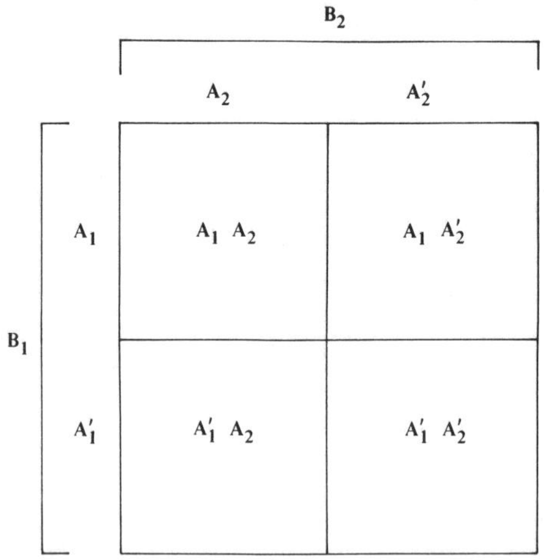

Figure 4.3. Grouping III, the bi-univocal (one-to-one) multiplication of classes. (Adapted from Piaget, 1949/1972a.)

IV consisted in a cross-classification of a linear series with a "vicariant," or same-level series, as described earlier under Grouping II. Piaget's favorite example for this grouping was the hierarchy of kinship classes that results from a genealogy. In this case, the linear series is a sequence of successive generations, and the vicariant series consists of the kinship classes existing within each generation. In the simplest two-generation case, suppose B_1 is the class of all the descendants of a single person X after two generations. This class is composed of two subclasses representing each of the two generations, the subclass A_1 being composed of X's children, and the subclass A_1' of X's grandchildren. Suppose further that B_2 is the class of kinship classes existing at each generation, consisting (after two generations) of two subclasses, the siblings in a given family (A_2) and their first cousins (A_2'). The crossing or multiplication of these two series thus yields the following grouping:

$$B_1 \times B_2 = A_1A_2 + A_1'A_2 + A_1'A_2'.$$

In other words, three kinship classes exist among the descendants of X after two generations: the children of X who are by definition siblings (A_1A_2), the grandchildren of X in one line who are siblings ($A_1'A_2$), and the other grandchildren of X who are first cousins ($A_1'A_2'$) of $A_1'A_2$ (Figure 4.4). Note that the combination A_1A_2' (first cousins in the first generation) is not included, because they would not be descendants of X. Thus, whereas the cross-classification produced by Grouping III yields a square matrix, that yielded by Grouping IV has a triangular one. Grouping IV was not actively investigated by Piaget, but given his exam-

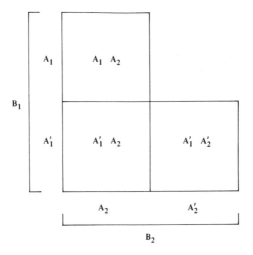

Figure 4.4. Grouping IV, the co-univocal (many-to-one) multiplication of classes. (Adapted from Piaget, 1949/1972a.)

ples, the study of children's understanding of kinship relations across generations would be an obvious possibility.

Groupings V–VIII parallel Groupings I–IV in form, but deal with relations rather than classes. Thus, *Grouping V* has to do with the addition of asymmetrical relations forming a linear series and is defined by the composition

$$(A \to B) + (B \to C) = (A \to C),$$

where the arrow is Piaget's symbol for an asymmetrical relation. This grouping in effect represents the transitivity of the respective relation (Figure 4.5). For the relation "larger than," for example, the grouping represents the fact that if A is larger than B, and B is larger than C, then A is larger than C. The grouping can be extended in a linear series of even larger objects, D being larger than C, E larger than D, and so on. The grouping is reversible, first, in the sense that the relation has a reciprocal ("A is larger than B" implies "B is smaller than A"), and, second, in the sense that $(A \to B)$ can be derived from $(A \to C)$ and $(B \to C)$, given the fact that B by definition lies "between" A and C (Beth & Piaget, 1961/1966). Psychologically, this grouping was investigated by Piaget in the form of transitive reasoning.

Like Grouping V, *Grouping VI* has to do with the transitivity of relations, this time of symmetrical relations. The composition involved is the following:

$$(A \leftrightarrow B) + (B \leftrightarrow C) = (A \leftrightarrow C),$$

where the double arrow represents a symmetrical relation (Figure 4.6). Piaget's favorite examples were again drawn from kinship relations. The relation "the

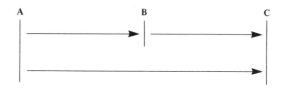

Figure 4.5. Grouping V, the addition of asymmetrical relations. (Adapted from Piaget, 1949/1972a.)

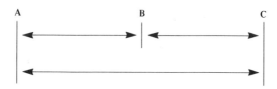

Figure 4.6. Grouping VI, the addition of symmetrical relations. (Adapted from Piaget, 1949/1972a.)

brother of,'' for example, is symmetrical in the sense that if A is the brother of B, then B is also the brother of A. In other words, the direct relation is identical with its reciprocal. The grouping represents the transitivity of the relation: If A is the brother of B, and B is the brother of C, then A is the brother of C. Children's comprehension of symmetrical relations was investigated in the story of the three brothers in *Judgment and reasoning in the child* (Piaget, 1924/1928b), although this research was in fact conducted before the theory of groupings had been developed. A special case of symmetrical relations is the relation of equality or equivalence, and in this case, the "preliminary grouping of pure equivalences" reduces to the addition of asymmetrical relations. Like Grouping II, this grouping has to do with "vicariant" relationships, or relations among elements at the same level in a hierarchy. The relation "being the brother of," for example, expresses a relation among individuals within a single generation.

To continue the analogy between the logic of classes and relations, *Grouping VII* (the "bi-univocal multiplication of relations") resembles Grouping III (the "bi-univocal multiplication of classes") in that both involve the crossing of two linear series. But where the multiplication of classes gave rise to a cross-classification, the multiplication of relations results in combinations of the two relations. The basic operation constituting this grouping may be expressed as follows:

$$(A_i \rightarrow B_j) \times (X_1 \rightarrow X_2) = (A_1 \rightarrow B_1) + (A_1 \rightarrow A_2) + (A_2 \rightarrow B_2) + (B_1 \rightarrow B_2).$$

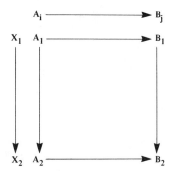

Figure 4.7. Grouping VII, the bi-univocal (one-to-one) multiplication of relations. (Adapted from Piaget, 1949/1972a.)

In plain English, the crossing of two relations – say, "longer than" ($A_i \rightarrow B_j$) and "thicker than" ($X_1 \rightarrow X_2$) – results in the following relational combinations: things that are equal in thickness but differ in length ($A_1 \rightarrow B_1$ and $A_2 \rightarrow B_2$), and things that are equal in length but differ in thickness ($A_1 \rightarrow A_2$ and $B_1 \rightarrow B_2$). Composition of these initial combinations results further in things that differ in both dimensions ($A_1 \rightarrow B_2$ and $A_2 \leftrightarrow B_1$). As in the case of the multiplication of classes, the multiplication of relations can also be represented in the form of an $n \times m$ matrix, where n and m are the numbers of elements in the respective series. In its simplest form, this grouping can be graphically portrayed by a 2×2 matrix (Figure 4.7). It was later investigated by having children complete matrices of this form (Inhelder & Piaget, 1959/1969).

Finally, *Grouping VIII*, the "co-univocal multiplication of relations," parallels Grouping IV in that both of them involve the crossing of a linear series with a vicariant series. Thus, both of them describe a hierarchical organization in which linear relations between one level and another are crossed with vicariant relations within each level. Again, Piaget illustrated this grouping with kinship relations. But where Grouping IV has to do with the classes of relatives produced by a genealogy, Grouping VIII involves the relations themselves. In the simplest case of two generations, the between-generational relation "being the child of" is crossed with the within-generational relation "being the sibling of," resulting in a triangular matrix in which the parent shares the first type of relation with each of the members of the second generation, and the members of the second generation share the second type of relation with each other. If the parent–child relation is represented as ($A \rightarrow B_i$) and the sibling relation as ($X_1 \leftrightarrow X_2$), then the composition defining this grouping is given as follows:

$$(A \rightarrow B_i) \times (X_1 \leftrightarrow X_2) = (A \rightarrow B_1) + (A \rightarrow B_2) + (B_1 \leftrightarrow B_2),$$

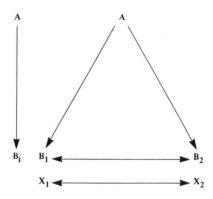

Figure 4.8. Grouping VIII, the co-univocal (many-to-one) multiplication of relations. (Adapted from Piaget, 1949/1972a.)

meaning that A is the parent of B_1, A is the parent of B_2, and B_1 and B_2 are siblings of each other (Figure 4.8). As this example (hopefully) makes clear, this grouping consists in the crossing of an asymmetrical relation ("being the parent of") with a symmetrical one ("being the sibling of"). The reversibility of the grouping consists in the fact that each of the relations involved has a reciprocal: "Being the parent of" is the reciprocal of "being the child of," but the symmetry of the relation "being the sibling of" implies that its reciprocal is identical with its direct form. As in the case of the co-univocal multiplication of classes, this grouping was not prominently represented in Piaget's research, but the understanding of kinship relations would constitute an obvious possibility for investigation.

Origins of number

As previously noted, Piaget believed that the understanding of number resulted from a "fusion" or "synthesis" of groupings involving classification and seriation. This synthesis involved a transition from purely qualitative to quantitative operations – that is, from noniterative to iterative operations in the sense described earlier. The problem is therefore one of explaining how iterative operations develop from noniterative operations.

According to Piaget, the decisive step occurs when a class A is equated with its complement A', such that the operation of inclusion $A + A' = B$ becomes iterative: $A + A = 2A$. This iterativity is possible only to the extent that the first A is distinguished from the second; otherwise this composition would revert to its noniterative form: $A + A = A$. To distinguish between one A and the next is to order them according to an asymmetrical relation "to be followed by." Thus, the first A "is followed by" another, or $A \xrightarrow{s} A$. Like other asymmetrical relations, this one can be extended into a series of A's, each distinguished from the preceding one by the relation "to be followed by."

According to Piaget, this series of iterative relations develops into a numerical series when one *iteration* is distinguished from another by a parallel series of inclusions:

$$A = A,$$
$$B = A + A,$$
$$C = A + A + A,$$

This series of inclusions is possible only to the extent that the various A's are distinguished from each other according to the iterative relation "to be followed by," as described earlier. At the same time, this series of inclusions makes it possible to keep track of the series of iterations.

$$A = 0 \overset{a}{\rightarrow} A,$$
$$B = 0 \overset{a}{\rightarrow} A \overset{b}{\rightarrow} A,$$
$$C = 0 \overset{a}{\rightarrow} A \overset{b}{\rightarrow} A \overset{c}{\rightarrow} A,$$

where 0 is the starting point, "a" marks the first instance of A, "b" the second, and so on.

Taken together, these two series constitute the number series, the series of inclusions representing its cardinal aspect (A, B, C, . . . , corresponding to 1, 2, 3, . . .) and the series of iterations representing its ordinal aspect (a, b, c, . . . , corresponding to 1st, 2nd, 3rd, . . .). Piaget demonstrated that this series with its property of iteration constitutes a group that he called the "additive group of whole numbers." In a similar fashion, the synthesis of the bi-univocal multiplication of classes and relations leads to the formation of the "multiplicative group of positive numbers." The fact that only Groupings I, III, V, and VII are involved in the construction of number no doubt explains why Piaget once called them the "principal" groupings (Inhelder & Piaget, 1959/1969, p. 279), devoting considerably more attention to them than to the other groupings.

In the final chapters of *Classes, relations et nombres,* Piaget compared his theory of the origins of number with other theories, most notably with Whitehead and Russell's (1910–1913) attempt to deduce mathematics entirely from logic. This discussion is important for the interpretation of Piaget's work, for it illustrates once again his central preoccupation with questions of epistemology and his recourse to psychology as an attempt to solve those questions:

Ever since the founding of the science of logic, the question of knowing whether mathematics is reducible to logic has been much debated. The logicians believe themselves to have effected this reduction in defining cardinal number with the notion of class, ordinal number with relations, and the essential notions of order, function, set, group, and so forth, with diverse combinations of logical operations. The adversaries of the reduction oppose it with a series of arguments founded on the special character of numerical synthesis, of mathematical reasoning, and on the irreducibility of intuitive elements.

Do the reflections contained in the preceding chapter, according to which number may be explained by a system of classes and of relations founded on a single operatory totality, tend to reduce number to logic, or to consider the latter as an incomplete mathematics due to the dissociation of the numerical components? The enunciation of such a question suffices to do it justice. If ''logic'' is taken in the narrow sense, the logic of classes defined as concepts and of qualitative relations, then number is not at all reducible to logic. These classes and qualitative relations appear on the contrary as two instruments necessarily disjoined from each other on the qualitative plane and which number alone comes to reunite in a veritable whole. [Piaget, 1942, p. 256]

Piaget went on to discuss how this operatory theory of the origins of number answers some of the other classic questions of mathematical epistemology. For example:

Mathematical reasoning is at once rigorous and generative [*fécond*]. The syllogism is rigorous, but we learn nothing more than what was already contained in the premises. Experimental induction is generative, since it doesn't even constitute a logical argument properly speaking. How does one thus explain the fact that mathematical deduction engenders conclusions which are novel, that is, not contained analytically in the premises, but nevertheless necessary, that is, connected after the fact with the premises by a connection the rigor of which gives an illusion of being analytic? [ibid., p. 266]

According to Piaget's explanation, both the generativity and rigor of mathematics can be explained by its group structure. As compared with the logic of classes, the iterative character of mathematical operations accounts for the fact that they can arrive at new conclusions, and the reversibility of those operations accounts for their rigor. With respect to generativity, the logic of relations lies somewhere between the logic of classes and mathematics. Although operations involving the multiplication of classes never result in anything that is not already contained in the original classes, operations involving relations (especially the multiplication of relations) result in a total system that is not entirely contained in the original relations. Because the operations characteristic of logic of relations are noniterative, they remain less generative than those of mathematics. The logic of classes and the logic of relations are both as rigorous as mathematics, however, and for the same reason: Their operations are likewise reversible. As Piaget had frequently maintained in his previous works, the reversibility of logical and mathematical operations accounts for their property of noncontradiction.

Furthermore, the operatory character of Piaget's theory of number resolves certain other problems in mathematical epistemology: the problem of the nature and reality of mathematical entities (in particular, of infinite classes) and the paradoxes or antinomies of set theory:

How to avoid the difficulties of actual infinity and of the class of ''all'' classes? If one admits the constructive reality of operations, it is comprehensible that the constructions effected by them are never completed and that infinity is thus the very expression of the operation iterated indefinitely. But if one denies the reality of operations, it is then quite necessary to situate infinity somewhere, in physical, logico-linguistic, or logico-ideal reality, and the antinomies reappear. [ibid., p. 267]

In a sense, Piaget carried a constructivist epistemology of mathematics to its logical conclusion in psychology. The reality of mathematical entities was derived from the constructions of the subject, conceived in this case in terms of operations as interiorized action. But important differences also exist between Piaget's theory and those of the classical constructionists and intuitionists. For one thing, he made no attempt to define the boundary limits of "valid" mathematical entities and procedures. Other differences are discussed in his later works on the epistemology of mathematics (Piaget, 1950/1973a; Beth & Piaget, 1961/ 1966), to be reviewed in the next chapter.

The attempt to found logic and mathematics on psychology presupposes that the formal systems of groups and groupings that describe the organization of mathematical and logical operations, respectively, are based on some psychological reality. The final pages of *Classes, relations et nombres* were devoted to this problem. But the same problem was discussed more thoroughly in a paper published in 1941, and we therefore proceed directly to the latter.

The mechanism of mental development

The reality of logico-mathematical structures. Although most of Piaget's descriptions of the eight groupings and other logico-mathematical structures focused on their formal aspects, he also recognized their functional reality. One of the most detailed treatments of this topic is found in an essay entitled "Le mécanisme du développement mental et les lois du groupement des opérations: Esquisse d'une théorie opératoire de l'intelligence" ("The mechanism of mental development and the laws of the grouping of operations: Sketch of an operatory theory of intelligence") (Piaget, 1941). The fact that this paper is not available in an English translation is perhaps one reason (among others) why psychologists in the English-speaking world have continued to wonder about the intended ontological status of Piaget's groupings.

From the opening pages of this paper, Piaget made it clear that he considered the groupings not merely as formalisms but also as possessing some psychological reality. One might say they have both a formal and a functional aspect. In their formal aspect, they exist in the minds of psychologists, and in their functional aspect they exist in the minds of the subjects being examined:

In order to analyze physical transformations, the mathematician expresses them in the form of "groups," but then the groups are in his mind and the physical transformations in the things. Now in the case of psychological development, the "groupings" are in the mind of the thinking subjects that are examined, and in order to retrace their formation, would one appeal precisely to the deductive theory of groupings? In reality, there is no circle involved, for the groupings that are in the mind of the subjects studied are living and causally active organizations, while the groupings that the psychologist employs to translate, analyze, and explain these organizations are formal notions, analogous to the numbers and spaces permitting the physicist to describe and explain material transformations. [Piaget, 1941, p. 217]

Here Piaget apparently drew a radical distinction between the physicist's use of the concept of group structure and the psychologist's use of grouping structure. Actually, the difference is only that the group of physical transformations has a material referent, but groupings of operations have a psychological referent. As a formalism, the group of physical transformations exists in the minds of mathematicians or physicists and represents the formal properties of transformations occurring in nature. Similarly, the formal aspect of operatory groupings exists in the minds of psychologists and represents the formal properties of actions or operations carried out by the subjects of investigation.

Piaget used the word "organization" in referring to the formal properties of psychological or biological functions. Thus, groupings were described in the preceding passage as "living organizations" that are "causally active." But to call them "causally active" does not imply that they are functionally distinct from the content of which they constitute the organization. As Piaget stated in another work contemporaneous with the 1941 essay, the form and content of psychological operations are "inseparable" (Piaget & Inhelder, 1941/1974, p. 180). In its formal aspect, a grouping is a set of formal properties. In its functional aspect, these properties are *immanent* in a living organization. Moreover, the causal activity involved is of a particular character. The grouping in its functional aspect does not determine *which* action or operation will be manifest at any given time; it determines only the ways in which certain actions can be coordinated or related to each other. In parallel fashion, a group of physical transformations does not determine which transformation will occur at a given moment, but only how those transformations will be related to each other when they do occur.

The formal or organizational aspect of groupings is also implied in the definition provided by Piaget on the following page: "A 'grouping' is a structure, at once mobile and closed, linking operations to each other according to a principle of reversible composition" (Piaget, 1941, p. 218). According to this definition, groupings are composed of logical operations like classification and seriation. Not only are particular acts of classification, seriation, and so on, linked to other operations of the same type (other classifications, seriations, etc.) through a common organization, but each particular operation is linked to an inverse operation that compensates it. The fact that operations are related to each other in this way implies further that the functional units of thought are not concepts and judgments considered in isolation, but the total systems formed by the respective operations. These total systems are the groupings as such and constitute the true psychological units of logical and mathematical thought.

Reversibility. Of the various formal properties that define grouping structure, the property of reversibility is perhaps the most important. This characteristic, above all, is what constitutes the *equilibrium* of the grouping. Elsewhere in the same paper, Piaget likened a grouping to a balance scale in which the two sides of a logical equation (e.g., $A + A' = B$) represent two weights in equilibrium (ibid., p. 283). The reversibility of the grouping ensures that the scale remains in equilibrium: What is added to (or removed from) one side of the scale is immediately compensated by an equivalent operation on the other side of the scale. To characterize the grouping as a form of equilibrium in this way, however, raises the question of how such forms of equilibrium change with development.

The main part of the paper was devoted to answering this question. Briefly, Piaget described how the forms of equilibrium change across six general levels of development from birth to adolescence. These six levels include the following: reflex activity, perception and habit, sensorimotor intelligence, intuitive intelligence, concrete operations, and formal operations. The equilibrium characteristic of each of these levels of development can be described in terms of the kinds of reversibility that are possible at each level. For present purposes, the progression from sensorimotor intelligence to concrete operations is of greatest interest.

At the level of sensorimotor intelligence, reversibility is possible only with respect to the coordination of *successive* actions. For example, after Stage Four in the development of the object concept, the action of hiding an object becomes reversible; an object that has been hidden under a cover is covered and can also be uncovered. It is not that children were previously incapable of performing the separate actions of covering an object or lifting a cover, but these separate actions were not coordinated with each other in a single reversible system. Once this coordination has been effected, children know that an object that has been covered can also be uncovered. Similarly, reversibility in space is accomplished when the action of displacement in any direction is coordinated with displacement in the opposite direction such that any displaced object can be returned to its point of origin. In each case, reversibility consists in the coordination of overt actions performed successively in time.

As these examples illustrate, groups and groupings can already be identified at the level of sensorimotor intelligence. In *The construction of reality in the child,* Piaget had already identified groups of spatial displacements. He had not identified groupings of sensorimotor actions, because the theory of groupings had not yet been developed. In retrospect, groupings of actions could also have been identified, differing from groups only in the fact that the actions involved are noniterative. For example, uncovering an object is a noniterative action. Having uncovered an object, one cannot immediately uncover it again without first hiding it a second time. The reversible coordination between hiding and finding therefore constitutes a grouping. In contrast, taking a step or displacing an object is an iterative action. One can immediately take another step or displace the object further. The coordination of actions that involve the displacement of one's own body or other objects in space therefore constitutes a group.

The difference between sensorimotor and intuitive intelligence, according to Piaget, is that actions have now become interiorized. The child can now represent the results of certain actions in a cognitive manner. However, the form of reversibility remains successive in character, and this limitation prevents the child in the intuitive stage from attaining operational thought. For example, the child can imagine the act of collecting objects together according to a common property, and also the act of separating them according to their differences. What still eludes the child at this stage, however, is thinking of the respective objects *at the same time* belonging to a common whole and to diverse subgroups. The reversibility involved remains successive rather than becoming simultaneous (ibid., pp. 228ff.). Although children at the intuitive stage often are capable of finding the correct solutions to concrete operational tasks, such solutions generally are accomplished through a process of successive grouping rather than through an immediate understanding of the necessity involved in the reversibility of operations. This observation underscores a fact often to be emphasized in this book, that Piaget defined his stages according to the means by which an answer was obtained rather than simply by the fact of a correct answer – by the organization of the observed performance rather than merely by its outcome.

The stage of concrete operations is therefore defined not by the fact that the child becomes capable of answering certain of the examiner's questions correctly but by the fact that reversibility becomes simultaneous rather than successive. The child comes to understand that a given operation simultaneously (and necessarily) implies its inverse – for example, that a collection of objects can be thought of as a whole in itself and at the same time as part of a larger whole (ibid., p. 220). Piaget called this form of reversibility "true reversibility" as opposed to the "empirical return" characterizing sensorimotor and intuitive intelligence (ibid., p. 234). By virtue of being organized in a structure characterized by such simultaneous reversibility, an interiorized action becomes an operation as such.

As the foregoing examples suggest, the kinds of "elements" incorporated into a reversible structure also change from one level to another. Piaget defined this "field of equilibrium" as "the domain of activity within which equilibrium is possible" and noted that "the extent of this field expands at each new level of development" (ibid., p. 235). At the sensorimotor level, the field of equilibrium includes only overt, successive actions; at the intuitive level, it includes successive actions interiorized in the form of cognitive anticipations; and at the concrete operational level, it includes simultaneously reversible operations.

As for the type of operations to be found at the level of concrete operations, Piaget provided the following taxonomy: (a) *Logico-arithmetical operations* include operations involving classes, relations, and numbers bearing on objects independent of the position occupied by those objects in space and time. (b)

Infralogical operations include operations bearing on the states or parts of objects insofar as they are located in space and time. (c) *Practical operations* include the coordination of means and ends. In this category belong operations involving social and moral reasoning and the coordination of individual and collective values. This classification apparently represents the latest incarnation of the earlier distinction between implicative, explicative, and mixed functions as first described in *The language and thought of the child*. The term "infralogical" should not be misconstrued. In the general sense of the word, these operations are no less "logical" than the others; they simply bear on spatial-temporal realities rather than on classes or relations as such.

Decalages. The fact that groups and groupings can be found at different levels of development was referred to by Piaget under the rubric of "vertical decalages." The latter may be opposed to "horizontal decalages," referring to the fact that within a given structurally defined level, the same structure may appear at different ages with respect to different contents. For example, Piaget and Inhelder (1941/1974) found a decalage consisting in the fact that the same operations bearing on quantity, weight, and volume developed in that order. This finding is discussed in more detail later in this chapter. What is of interest in the present context is that in seeking an explanation for horizontal decalages, Piaget first considered the possibility that they result from decalages among the groupings themselves. This possibility was rejected, based on his first researches into concrete operations (Piaget & Szeminska, 1941/1964; Piaget & Inhelder, 1941/ 1974). "At the same level and for the same notion [i.e., for the same empirical content], the different possible groupings appear to be constituted roughly [*à peu prés*] synchronously, none being thus, as an operative mechanism, more difficult to acquire and to manipulate than the others" (Piaget, 1941, p. 264). As an example, he cited the fact that conservation, seriation, and co-univocal multiplication of relations as applied to weight all appear to emerge around 9 years of age (Piaget & Inhelder, 1941/1974). He concluded as follows: "Thus, one cannot say that a grouping, in itself and by its own form, is more difficult to constitute than another" (Piaget, 1941, p. 264).

Thus, Piaget apparently believed the various groupings characterizing the stage of concrete operations to develop "roughly" in synchrony. But this conclusion clearly followed as an empirical generation from his research findings up to that time – not as a prediction of the theory. Contrary to subsequent interpretations of his theory, he did not argue that the groupings *should* develop in synchrony because they are all bound up in a single structure-of-the-whole that unites all the structural manifestations of each stage. At the time Piaget wrote this passage, he had not yet begun to use the term *structure d'ensemble* as a technical term. But as we have seen from his autobiography and from subsequent writings, this term applied to the groupings and other logico-mathematical structures taken individually. Each grouping as it functions in a given area of content was considered a structure-of-the-whole, the "whole" being in each

case the ensemble of operations that are organized together in a single structure.

Piaget was more explicit in the 1941 essay than in most of his writings about
the criteria defining the functional boundaries of individual structures. To begin
with, their functional unity is manifest to the extent that all actions of the same
kind bearing on the same object are coordinated with each other:

> We say first of all that two classifications, series, etc., are "identical" if their elements
> (classes, relations, parts or placement) A, B, C, . . . , etc. are mutually substitutable
> without conditions, with order being equal. This notion of identity permits one to make a
> preliminary psychological observation, which is moreover quite natural: that the same
> classifications, partitions, etc., are constituted at the same time. For example, if a child
> of 7 years knows that a ball of clay conserves its substance with one deformation, he will
> admit it as well for a second alteration in form. And if he contests it the second time
> (because it is more considerable than the first), then there was not yet an operational, but
> only an intuitive grouping. The generalization of the operations thus attests simply to the
> existence of the grouping, and it is precisely because all the operations of the same type
> bearing upon the same object are immediately interdependent that one can consider this
> grouping as an essential psychological reality, as an intelligent "totality" comparable to
> perceptual "Gestalten," and not only as an axiomatic structure. [ibid., p. 265]

In the second case considered by Piaget, the "same" grouping may also bear
on different objects. If the quantity of one ball of clay is recognized as being
conserved across changes in shape, then this recognition should also be extended
to a second ball. Because both balls could conceivably be joined together in a
single ball, he called the relation between them "vicariant" – using his term for
the relation between two parts of a single whole.

In a third case, the "same" grouping may bear on different objects within the
same general area of content even if they cannot be joined together in a single
whole, assuming that a relevant "correspondence" can be established between
them. For example, such a correspondence might exist between the respective
fractional parts of a ball of clay and a lump of sugar, the two halves of the ball
of clay corresponding to the two halves of the sugar, and so on. This correspondence enables the child who conserves the quantity of a ball of clay to extend
this grouping to the case of sugar dissolving in water. Such correspondences
may involve decalages – Piaget cited the case of the conservation of weight for
sugar dissolving in water developing somewhat later than the conservation of
weight for balls of clay (Piaget & Inhelder, 1941/1974). But this decalage results
from differences in perceptual information (e.g., because the dissolved particles
of sugar are invisible, in contrast to the balls of clay), rather than from differences between the groupings involved.

The fourth case is the horizontal decalage as such. With respect to logical
form, the groupings involved are the same, but they apply to qualitatively different areas of content (e.g., substance and weight). Piaget called the relation between two such applications of the "same" grouping to different areas of content
a relation of "analogy" and added that only in this case, as opposed to the other
three, are horizontal decalages regularly to be expected.

In describing the conditions under which horizontal decalages are to be expected, Piaget had not yet explained *why* they occur. His explanation for the decalage between substance, weight, and volume is discussed later in this chapter. Without such an explanation, cases of "analogous" applications of individual groupings leading to horizontal decalages could not be identified in advance. The horizontal decalages described by Piaget were identified only after the fact. But implied in Piaget's distinction between "identical," "vicariant," "correspondent," and "analogous" applications of the "same" grouping is a more general distinction between form and function. In all four cases, the groupings involved may be *formally* the same. In addition, the first three cases involve groupings that are *functionally* identical. In effect, the relations of identity, vicariance, and correspondence allow the same functional grouping to generalize immediately to new applications. In the case of qualitatively different content areas ("analogy"), however, the groupings bearing on the different contents can be considered functionally distinct, although they possess the same formal properties. The existence of horizontal decalages is the outward manifestation of this difference in functional identity.

However, the existence of a decalage is a fallible criterion for differences in functional identity. Decalages can occur for other reasons, as indicated in Piaget's example of the decalage between conservation of weight for clay and that for sugar, which results from "perceptual factors." Moreover, functional differences can exist without necessarily resulting in decalages. The eight groupings, for example, are by definition functionally distinct insofar as they represent groupings of different operations. According to Piaget, they develop at the same time because they are of roughly equivalent difficulty. Therefore, one cannot expect that the distinction between "identical," "vicariant," "correspondent," and "analogous" applications of groupings that are formally the same would be an infallible guide for predicting the occurrence or nonoccurrence of horizontal decalages.

The foregoing discussion is useful, however, in that it constitutes one of the most explicit statements in all of Piaget's works on the relations between his theory of structures and synchrony in development. This issue is important because more than any other it has figured in assessments of his theory in relation to empirical research findings. In brief, his thinking on the relation between structure and synchrony in the development of concrete operations as expressed in this paper can be summarized as follows:

1. The various groupings appear to develop about the same time, suggesting that none of them is more difficult to form than any other (but this apparent synchrony is not a necessary consequence of any alleged structure-of-the-whole underlying all structures characteristic of a given stage).

2. Horizontal decalages are frequently (but not inevitably) to be expected when formally equivalent groupings are applied to qualitatively different areas of content, such as quantity, weight, and volume. In contrast, synchrony can be ex-

pected when the same groupings are applied to different objects within the same content area.

3. A general synchrony can further be expected in some special cases. For example, Piaget's theory of the origins of number would seem to imply that arithmetical addition should appear at roughly the same time as (or at least not before) the addition of classes and the addition of relations.[1]

Piaget concluded "Le mécanisme du développement mental" with a comparison between the application of the concept of equilibrium in physics and that in psychology. Although physical systems are characterized by an irreversible increase in entropy, resulting in increasing disorder, psychological structures are characterized by an increase in the scope of reversibility, resulting in increasing order. In this respect, the complete reversibility characterizing *ideal* physical systems appears to constitute the *reality* of the structures of intelligence. In the concluding paragraph, however, he suggested that the reversibility of intellectual structures may coexist with perceptual structures that are inherently irreversible. The relation between these two types of structures he proposed to investigate in his studies of perception.

In the remainder of this chapter, the writings published by Piaget during the 1940s are reviewed in brief, including his studies of concrete operations and his papers on sociology. According to Piaget's terminology, the work on concrete operations may be divided between "logico-mathematical" thinking (logic and number), on the one hand, and the "infralogical" categories of thought (space and time), on the other. As in previous chapters, most attention will be given here to the research on logic and mathematics.

STUDIES OF CONCRETE OPERATIONS I:
NUMBER AND QUANTITY

his section reviews Piaget's studies of "logico-arithmetical" operations in *The child's conception of number* and *The child's construction of quantities,* both appearing originally in 1941. The studies of "infralogical" operations in the areas of space and time that appeared during the course of the 1940s will be treated in the next section. With respect to the first of these topics, one should note that the English version of *The child's conception of number* (Piaget, 1941/ 1952c) is an extensively abridged translation of the original *La genèse du nombre chez l'enfant* (Piaget & Szeminska, 1941/1964). Not only is Szeminska's name unaccountably missing from the translation, but the text has been cut by 15–

---

1 Piaget (1960a) once wrote that his theory of number was compatible with certain possibilities of asynchrony between classes, relations, and number. Classes and relations might develop separately before their synthesis into number occurs. Less likely, but still possible, number might develop first, followed by a "dissociation" into classes and relations. The a priori most likely possibility, however, was synchrony between the three. Piaget's theory of number is discussed more thoroughly in relation to issues of developmental synchrony in chapter 7.

20%. Moreover, some of the passages of greatest interest to the present inquiry – namely, those dealing with the theory of groupings – are missing.[2] Therefore, the present account will follow the original French text.

La genèse du nombre

This book was a milestone of sorts in Piaget's development. Not only did it represent (along with *The child's construction of quantities*) his first empirical studies of concrete operations and the theory of groupings, but it also contained some of the first examples of the tasks that would come to be known as typically "Piagetian." Three of these tasks, conservation, seriation, and class inclusion, will be described in this section. Of particular interest is Piaget's formal analyses of these tasks in terms of his theory of groupings.

Conservation. The first chapter was devoted to the conservation of continuous quantity. The procedure employed was the following: The child was shown two cylindrical containers, A_1 and A_2, having the same shape and containing the same amounts of liquid. Then the liquid in A_2 was poured into two smaller containers, B_1 and B_2, and the child was asked if the amount of liquid now contained in these two containers remained the same as that contained in A_1. In variations on this procedure, the liquid in B_1 and/or B_2 was poured into even smaller containers or into a long thin tube, and the same question was asked again. Three stages in the development of conservation were found, characterized by nonconservation, certain intermediate reactions, and (beginning about 6.5–7 years) an operational understanding of conservation. Piaget summarized the answers characteristic of the *first stage* as follows:

According to the children of the first stage, the quantity of liquid poured from one container into others increases or diminishes as a function of the shape or number of the containers. The reasons invoked in favor of non-conservation (difference of level, of width, number of containers, etc.) vary from one subject to another or from one moment to another, but every perceived change is considered as bringing about a modification in the total amount of liquid. [Piaget & Szeminska, 1941/1964, pp. 19–20]

For example, children sometimes said there was more liquid in A_1 "because it is bigger [i.e., wider]," or that there was more in the long thin tube "because it is higher," or that there was more in B_1 and B_2 "because there are more of them" (ibid., pp. 20–22). Sometimes the same child would give two or even three different reasons for different versions of the task. Thus, children at this stage often gave contradictory answers without being aware of any contradiction.

The *second stage* was characterized by certain intermediate reactions between conservation and nonconservation. For example, the child was capable of con-

2 According to Piaget (1964/1967a, p. 83), these passages were deleted because the English mathematician who translated the book found them "shocking."

serving when A_1 was compared with B_1 and B_2, but not when more than two containers were compared with A_1. Or conservation was possible when only small differences in width or level were involved, but not when large differences existed. For Piaget, these intermediate reactions were of some theoretical importance, for they suggested that the failure to conserve is not merely due to a misunderstanding of the question: Children referred to the height or width of the liquid in the containers, not merely because they thought the examiner was asking about these dimensions, but because they really believed that the quantity of liquid varied as a function of one or the other of these dimensions. This conclusion followed from the fact that the children in the second stage often began with conservation, even though the levels and widths of the liquids were not equal. Only when the discrepancy along one or the other of these two dimensions became too great did these children revert to nonconservation. Although they recognized that quantity was not identical with height, width, and number of containers, they did not yet completely understand the compensatory relations among these dimensions – that an increase in height was exactly compensated by a decrease in width, and so on.

In an interesting variation on the procedure, children were asked to fill up the long thin container until it contained the same amount of liquid as the standard A_1. Some children simply filled it until it attained the same level as A_1, disregarding the difference in widths – a reaction Piaget classified in the first stage. Other children seemed to oscillate indefinitely between equalizing levels and attempting to compensate for the difference in widths. The long thin container (L) was filled to the same level as A_1; then, having noticed that A_1 was wider, children poured more liquid into L in order to compensate this difference. But they noticed the difference in levels once again and hastened to equalize them. Because this reaction was intermediate between complete compensation between the two dimensions and no compensation at all, Piaget classified it at the second stage.

Finally, in the *third stage,* children consistently gave conservation responses, despite changes in the various dimensions involved. Piaget pointed to two types of justifications for conservation among those cited. The first type included an explicit reference to one or the other dimensions involved, along with the assertion that quantity was not a simple function of just one of them: *"It's the same amount. It appears that there is less, because it's bigger* (= wider) *but it's the same"* (ibid., p. 33). The second type of answer included no explicit reference to the height, width, or number of containers, but simply voiced the recognition that the amounts *must* be equal, because whatever was subtracted from one container was immediately added to the other. "You empty (the one) in refilling the others!" "It's always the same amount, because it always comes from the same bottle" (ibid., p. 34). In comparing A_1 and L, children recognized the compensatory relations between height and width. "Is it the same amount? – *Yes, it's the same height. . . . Oh, no!*

That one (L) *is thinner and that one* (A) *wider* (he adds more liquid to L)"
(ibid., p. 35).

In his analysis of the operatory logic involved in such examples of conservation, Piaget first pointed out that conservation cannot be attained through the
multiplication of relations alone. From the multiplication of the relations of higher
and wider, one can at most conclude the following: (a) that more liquid is in
A than in B, given that A is both higher and wider than B; (b) that A contains
more than B, given that A is higher (or wider) than B and that the widths
(heights) are equal; (c) that A contains the same as B, given that the heights
and widths are both equal. But one cannot conclude that A and B are equal,
given *only* that A is higher and narrower (or lower and wider) than B, because
these comparative relations are not fully quantified. Such quantification can
occur only if *differences are equalized* – that is, if one recognizes that the
amount gained by A in being higher is equal to the amount that it at the same
time loses by being narrower. This equalization of differences is precisely the
decisive step in the development of number, according to Piaget. In the case
of cardinal number, the differences between successive numbers are equalized,
and in the conservation of quantity, the differences along two dimensions are
equalized.

In the second chapter of *La genèse du nombre,* the conservation experiment
was repeated with discontinuous quantities; the containers used in the first experiment were filled with beads rather than with liquid. This difference in material did not affect the results; the same three stages were found, based on the
same kinds of responses. According to one child at the third stage, *"If I empty
that one* (P) *into that one* (L) *or that one* (L) *into that one* (P) *it will be the same"*
(ibid., p. 53). Piaget interpreted this as an expression of "the reversibility belonging to every logical and mathematical operation" (ibid., p. 56). Another
child remarks, *"I fill it up in my mind [en pensée], and I see where it comes"*
(ibid., p. 54).

In the chapters that followed, the development of children's understanding of
one-to-one correspondence and seriation was investigated. In one experiment,
for example, children were asked to construct a row of objects (beans, coins,
candies, etc.) containing an amount equal to that contained in a comparison row
provided. The stages obtained and the kinds of reasoning involved were similar
to those of the conservation problems involving amounts of liquid and beads.
Thus, children in the *first stage* tended to focus on the lengths of the respective
rows (or, alternatively, their densities) rather than on the numbers they contained. The two rows were judged to have the same numbers of objects when
they were the same length (or, more rarely, when they had the same density). In
a *second stage,* children constructed a row corresponding exactly to that of the
model in both spacing and number. But if the spacing of the standard was then
altered, they no longer maintained their belief in the numerical equality of the
two rows. Finally, in a *third stage,* the numbers contained in the two rows were
understood to be independent of the dimensions of length or density. In subse-

quent research, this task has come to be known as the "conservation of number" (Gelman & Baillargeon, 1983). Piaget and Szeminska, however, considered it under the aspect of one-to-one correspondence.

Seriation and number. In one of the experiments most directly related to Piaget's theory of number as a synthesis of classes and relations, children were presented with a series of pieces of cardboard $A, B, C, \ldots, K$, of equal widths but different lengths, such that $B = 2A$, $C = 3A$, and so on. First, children were asked to construct the series and to count the number of pieces from 1 ($= A$) to 10 ($= K$). Then they were asked, "How many pieces like A could one make with X ($= B, C$, etc.)." Given the materials described, the latter question was intended to probe children's understanding of the relation between ordinal number (the place of X in the series from A to K) and cardinal number (the number of pieces like A that could be obtained from X).

In the *first stage,* order and quantity were not coordinated with each other. Even if children arranged the series and counted the number of pieces correctly, their judgments of the relation between A and X depended on a global comparison between the two, or on an attempt to count the imagined divisions of X on X alone. Thus: "So how many small pieces of cardboard can one make with this one (A)? – *1.* – With this one (B)? – *2.* – With this one (C)? – *3.* – With this one (D)? – *5*" (Piaget & Szeminska, 1941/1964, p. 177).

In the *second stage,* children were able to use the series as long as they ascended step by step. But the relation between order and quantity was lost track of as soon as they began to descend the series or to jump from one piece to another. Thus, one child followed the ascending series correctly all the way to $K = 10$, but in descending he gave $J = 9$, $H = 10$, $G = 11$, and so on, until he arrived at $B = 16$! Other children completed the ascending series successfully, but when the experimenter no longer proceeded in sequential order, they reverted to the method of counting the supposed divisions on X.

At the *third stage,* children consistently determined the numerical relation between A and X by counting up the series until X (or by counting backward from K to X). Even when the cardboard pieces were mixed up, they could use this method to evaluate an X picked at random – by reconstructing the series up to X. Thus, they gave evidence of their understanding of the relationship between ordinality and cardinality. One child who began by counting the imaginary divisions on X suddenly realized he could find the answer without counting in this way, *"because I know how the numbers go"* (ibid., p. 181).

In analyzing this task, Piaget saw the same operatory processes at work as go into the construction of number itself. Each X is in effect a class containing a different number of equalized parts, each part being equal to A. At the same time, each X occupies a particular place in the series $A, B, C, \ldots$, which is characterized by an equality of differences between adjacent terms, each difference being equal to A. Finally, the number of equalized parts contained in X corresponds to the rank of X in the series, or, more precisely, the equalized parts of X can be ordered in this way because they can be distinguished from each other and thus enumerated. In Piaget's words:

A cardinal number is a class of which the elements are conceived as "unities," equivalent to each other and nevertheless distinct, their differences then consisting only in the fact that they can be arranged, and thus ordered in a series. Conversely, ordinal numbers are a series of which the terms, while succeeding each other according to the relations of order by which they are assigned to their respective ranks, are also unities equivalent to each other and consequently capable of being cardinally reunited. The finite numbers are thus necessarily at the same time cardinal and ordinal and that results from the very nature of number which is to be a system of classes and asymmetrical relations fused together in the same operatory whole. [ibid., p. 204]

Given Piaget's theory of number as the synthesis of classes and relations, one might ask why he did not examine the degree of synchrony in the attainment of concrete operations in these three areas. It would seem to follow from his theory that individual children should not develop an operatory understanding of arithmetical operations until they have already developed an understanding of the corresponding logical operations and that the development of ordination and cardination should be highly correlated. In an important passage, Piaget anticipated future critics by replying that a comparison between the development of logical and arithmetical operations would not be meaningful unless all the other relevant factors bearing on children's performances could be controlled:

It is thus easy to rediscover in the steps of ordination the same processes and the same levels as in the development of cardination. But it goes without saying that before seeking to translate the matter into a statistical form and to apply to these tests the diverse formulas of correlation from the calculation of probabilities, it would first be necessary to resolve some questions for which we admittedly have no interest whatsoever: Is such-and-such a problem of ordination which we employ of exactly the same difficulty as another or as such-and-such a problem of cardination, independently of ordination and cardination themselves? In fact it is clear that in each task there intervenes a multitude of heterogeneous factors, such as the words employed, the length of the instructions, its more or less concrete character, its relation to the individual experience of the subject, the number of objects considered, the extent to which the number system has been learned, etc., etc. Thus in the various tasks of cardinal correspondence, we were able to observe very clear decalages between the results of some of these tasks and others, of such a kind that one never attains a measure of the comprehension of this cardinal correspondence in a pure state, but always comprehension relative to a given problem and a given material. That is why the calculation of the correlation between the levels of cardination and those of ordination can only give misleading results if it is not accompanied by a very extensive qualitative analysis – unless one transforms the tasks into "tests" in which a statistical precision can no doubt be obtained without much difficulty, but at the expense of no longer knowing exactly what one is measuring. [ibid., p. 193]

The foregoing is one of the rare passages in Piaget's works in which he addressed directly some of the matters for which he is often criticized: his failure to use sophisticated statistical techniques, his supposed failure to take into consideration the multifarious factors affecting performance, and so on. This passage suggests that his neglect of these matters was a considered neglect. His remarks belie later attempts to characterize his approach as a naive "competence theory.'' He did not claim that his methods measured children's understanding (or ''competencies'') ''in a pure state.'' His recognition of other factors in development no doubt accounts in part for his lack of interest in questions of synchrony or asynchrony in development. The fact that success and failure on the tasks in question are attributable to so many different factors makes the occurrence or nonoccurrence of synchrony in development very difficult to interpret, as Brainerd (1978a), Flavell (1977), Wohlwill (1973), and others have subsequently pointed out.

The existence of such factors does not rule out the possibility that the ''very extensive qualitative analysis'' of which Piaget wrote might still be accomplished. In that case, the multitude of heterogeneous performance factors might possibly be controlled. But Piaget did not claim to be able to perform such an analysis, and he therefore abandoned for the time being the attempt to correlate development in different areas of knowledge and to predict synchrony in development. Instead, he limited himself to tracing developmental parallels in the form and sequence of stages in different areas.

Developmental synchrony. In fact, *La genèse du nombre* is one of the few books by Piaget in which one can follow the answers of the same children questioned in different areas of different content. Only once did Piaget attempt to compare the performances of children in the different areas in any systematic way. This was done in connection with the relation between children's understanding of one-to-one correspondence and the composition of relations of equivalence. In chapter 3 of that book, children's performances on a correspondence task had been described. Shown a certain number of vases and a number of flowers, they were asked to take just enough flowers from the pile so that each vase could be filled with one flower each. As with most of the other tasks in this volume, three stages were found: In the first, children were unable to effect a one-to-one correspondence between flowers and vases. In the second, they were able to do this, but when the vases (or flowers) were spaced differently, they no longer believed in the equivalence of vases and flowers. In the third stage, children's belief in the equivalence of vases and flowers was independent of their spatial arrangement.

In chapter 9, children's performances on this correspondence task were compared to their performances on another task involving the composition of relations of equivalence. Having established a one-to-one correspondence between *n* vases and a group of pink flowers, and between the same *n* vases and a group of blue flowers, children were then asked if there were the same numbers of blue and pink flowers. Piaget had originally expected that the latter task involving the composition of equivalence relations would be solved well after the establishment of equivalence relations (one-to-one correspondence), because tasks involving three terms (e.g., vases, pink flowers, and blue flowers) should be more difficult to solve than tasks involving only two terms (e.g., vases and flowers) (ibid., p. 267).

Instead of the expected decalage, performance on the two tasks was found to be closely correlated. From their performances on both tasks, four groups of children could be distinguished: (a) children who failed both tasks, (b) children who were intermediate on both tasks, (c) children who failed on the correspondence task but passed the composition task, and (d) children who passed both tasks. No child was found who passed the correspondence task and failed the composition task. Thus, if anything, the composition task involving three terms appeared to be the easier, because some children passed this task while failing the two-term correspondence task! As is often the case in Piaget's books, he did not report the number of children in each group, the total number of children tested, and other procedural information (e.g., whether or not the two tasks were presented in a single sitting, etc.). So it is difficult to know how much weight should be placed on the fact that some children (group c) failed the correspondence task while passing the composition task. In any case, he thought that the absence of the expected decalage between the two-term correspondence task and the three-term composition task needed to be explained.

Piaget's explanation was that the second part of the correspondence task was in fact a three-term task as well, even if that did not appear to be the case at first. In the second part of this task, the flowers were spaced differently in relation to the vases, and children were asked if they were still equivalent in number. According to Piaget's analysis, answering this question involved not merely a comparison between vases and flowers, but between vases, the flowers as they were originally spaced (the same as the vases), and the flowers spaced differently. If the vases are represented by V_1, the flowers spaced the same as F_1, and the flowers spaced differently as F_2, then the solution to the problem can be represented as:

$$(V_1 \leftrightarrow F_1) + (F_1 \leftrightarrow F_2) = (V_1 \leftrightarrow F_2),$$

where the double arrow represents the (symmetrical) relation of equivalence. In other words, if the number of vases is equal to the number of flowers to begin with $(V_1 \leftrightarrow F_1)$, and the number of flowers does not change when they are spaced differently $(F_1 \leftrightarrow F_2)$, then the number of vases is equal to the number of flowers, even when the latter are spaced differently $(V_1 \leftrightarrow F_2)$. Thus, this task has the same form as the composition task, which may be rendered as follows:

$$(V \leftrightarrow F_b) + (V \leftrightarrow F_r) = (F_b \leftrightarrow F_r).$$

If the number of vases (V) is equal to the number of blue flowers (F_b) and also to the number of red flowers (F_r), then the numbers of red and blue flowers are equal to each other. Both tasks are examples of the addition of asymmetrical relations (Grouping VI) and involve the same number of terms; therefore, it is not surprising that the correspondence task was not solved before the composition task.

This exception to Piaget's usual neglect of questions regarding developmental synchrony is an exception that proves the rule. Despite the similarity in form of the correspondence and composition tasks, a "mini-decalage" was found, as indicated by the third group (c) of children, who failed correspondence but passed composition. Without the kind of qualitative analysis that Piaget referred to in the passage cited earlier, this finding can be attributed only to one of the many unexplained heterogeneous performance factors acknowledged in the same passage. One has the impression that Piaget mentioned this finding only to provide an occasion for the formal analysis showing that the correspondence task really involves three terms after all.

Class inclusion. The final chapters of *La genèse du nombre* were devoted to studies of additive and multiplicative compositions of classes, relations, and numbers. The task involving the composition of equivalence relations just discussed provided an example of a study of the composition of symmetrical relations. But any review of *La genèse du nombre* would not be complete without a brief consideration of class inclusion, another of the concrete operational tasks in this book that would become identified as typically "Piagetian" and would be studied again and again by subsequent generations of psychologists.

The class-inclusion task was meant to investigate children's understanding of the relations between a certain class of objects and the superordinate class to which it belongs. Briefly, the technique was the following: Children were shown a number of wooden beads, of which the greatest part were brown and the rest white. Then they were asked if there were more brown beads or more wooden ones. In order to make sure children had understood the question, it was sometimes rephrased in a more intuitive fashion (e.g., "If you made a necklace from the wooden ones and another from the brown ones, which would be longer?"). And to make sure that the results were not solely a function of the particular objects used, the experiment was repeated with different objects (square and round beads, flowers of different colors, etc.).

Three stages were found. In the *first stage,* children replied that there were more brown beads than wooden ones, and they persisted in this belief even while recognizing that all the beads were made of wood: "Are there more wooden beads or more brown beads? – *More brown ones, because there are two white ones.* – Are the white ones made of wood? – *Yes.* – And the brown ones? – *Also.* – Then are there more brown ones or more wooden beads? – *More brown ones.*" (ibid., p. 210). Similar answers were obtained under the various task conditions. In the *second stage,* children began by giving the same kind of answer, but under repeated questioning arrived at a recognition that there were more wooden beads, *"because there are also two white ones"* (ibid., p. 224). In the *third stage,* children recognized from the beginning that there were more wooden beads than brown ones because the white beads were also made of wood.

According to Piaget's analysis, the failure of the younger children to answer this question correctly stemmed from their inability to think of the part and the whole at the same time. In effect, they were as yet unable (in this situation) to reverse the operation of inclusion. In order to recognize that there are more wooden beads than brown ones because both the brown ones and the white ones are wooden, the child has to keep three things in mind: the property of being brown, the property of being white, and the property of being wooden. The child, in effect, has to remember that the brown beads are both brown and wooden and that the white beads are both white and wooden. But this is precisely what children in the first stage seemed unable to do. Instead, the brown beads were thought of only as brown, and the white ones only as wooden (ibid., p. 219). Therefore, the child replied that there were more brown ones than wooden ones. It is as though children in this stage were able to think of only two terms at once, rather than three. In terms of the formula for Grouping I, the primary addition of classes, the three terms involved are A, A', and B, representing the brown beads, the white beads, and the wooden beads, respectively. In replying that there were more wooden beads than brown ones, "because they are all wooden," children in effect performed the composition $B = A + A'$. And in replying that there were more wooden ones, "because there are some white ones left over," they effectively performed the subtraction $B - A = A'$.

Piaget concluded the chapter on class inclusion by describing the relation between logical and arithmetical addition. In particular, he attacked Russell's (1919/1960) theory of number, according to which a given number is the "class of all classes" having exactly that number of elements. According to Piaget, this theory presupposes the very quantification that it is meant to explain, for the logic of classes recognizes no quantification beyond "none," "one," "some," and "all." In order to get from class inclusion to arithmetical addition, one must be able to distinguish the elements of a class from each other, and this is nothing more nor less than to seriate them. In this sense, number is a "synthesis" of classes and relations. Under this hypothesis, one can understand why the comparable operations for classes, relations, and numbers should appear at roughly the same time in development:

In short, one thus understands why the additive hierarchy of classes, the seriation of relations, and the operatory generalization of number (i.e., the construction of numbers beyond the intuitive wholes 1, 2 to 4 or 5) are constituted in an approximately synchronous manner, around 6–7 years, at the moment at which the child's reasoning begins to surpass the initial prelogical level: it is because the class, the asymmetrical relation, and number are the three complementary manifestations of the same operatory construction applied to equivalences, differences, and the union of equivalences and differences, respectively. [ibid., p. 235]

Thus, Piaget's theory of number represents a real exception to the rule that he was generally uninterested in questions of developmental synchrony. Although there is nothing in this theory of number that demands that operations involving classes, relations, and number should develop at exactly the same time, the assumption that number should not appear until operations involving classes and relations have both developed seems to follow from the theory (Piaget, 1960a). As a matter of fact, they all developed "approximately" in synchrony, at least according to the kinds of tasks that Piaget used to assess them.

The child's construction of quantities

Although *La genèse du nombre* and *The child's construction of quantities* were both published in the same year, the book on number was apparently written earlier, for the second book often makes reference to the first. Like its predecessor, *The child's construction of quantities* (Piaget & Inhelder, 1941/1974) begins with a series of studies on conservation, in this case having to do with the amount, weight, and volume of balls of clay that are subjected to various transformations in shape. Briefly, the method employed was the following: Children were shown two balls of clay having the same size and shape, and the experimenter then transformed one of the balls by rolling it into a coil, or flattening it into a pancake, or cutting it into pieces. Then children were asked if the two pieces of clay still contained the same amount. The experiment was further varied by asking the children if the two balls also continued to weigh the same after one was deformed, or to possess the same volume (defined operationally in terms of the amount of water displaced when immersed).

With respect to the quantity of clay, Piaget and Inhelder obtained the same results as those reported in *La genèse du nombre* in regard to liquid. Three stages were obtained, defined in terms of nonconservation, intermediate reactions, and conservation of quantity, the latter stage being reached at roughly the age of 7–8 years. Interestingly enough, children did not show conservation of substance, weight, and volume at the same ages. Instead, the same three stages repeated themselves for each separate content, with gaps of about 2 years, conservation of weight being attained about the age of 9–10, and conservation of volume at roughly 11–12. This horizontal decalage among substance, weight, and volume was perhaps the most important single finding of this study. Not only were children's justifications given for conservation the same as in the previous book, but the same justifications repeated themselves for each separate content.

With respect to quantity, for example, children justified their judgment of nonconservation by appealing to one or another of the dimensions of the transformed piece of clay. It was said to contain more clay because it was "longer" or "thicker," or less clay because it was "shorter" or "thinner," than before it had been transformed. Judgments of conservation, however, tended to be based either on identification ("There is always the same clay, so there can't be more or less") or revertibility ("It's the same thing. If we [re-]made it into a ball it would use up as much clay"). In contrast to the nonconservers, children now realized that changes in length were compensated by changes in thickness, and vice versa ("It's longer, but it's thinner: it's still the same") (ibid., pp. 12–13).

Paradoxically, many of the same children who demonstrated conservation of quantity reverted to nonconservation when it came to weight, justifying their judgments with the same kinds of arguments used to justify nonconservation of quantity. Even while agreeing that the two pieces of clay contained the same *amount,* children believed that the one was lighter because it was "thinner" or because it had been "pulled out." Thus: "Do they have as much clay as each other? – *Yes, because you didn't take any off.* – Are they as heavy as each other? – *No, because this one* (the coil) *is smaller"* (ibid., pp. 23–25). Some answers seemed to suggest that children believed that changes in shape affected the density of the clay and that weight was a function of density: *"When it's long like that, a bit of the weight gets taken away. It's more spread out, but when it's in a ball the clay is all squashed together"* (ibid., pp. 23–25). In any case, children who succeeded in conserving weight justified their judgments with the same kinds of arguments used in justifying the conservation of quantity. Thus, conservation of weight was also justified by appeal to identification (*"First it was round and now it's long, but it's the same clay; you didn't take any away"*), reversibility (*"It weighs the same, because if you put those little bits together you'll get the same ball as before"*), and composition of compensatory relations (*"This one* [the coil] *is thinner and longer and that one* [the ball] *is bigger and higher, so they're the same"*) (ibid., p. 43). Because these justifications are the same as those used in the conservation of quantity, the question naturally arises why children who used these arguments in justifying the conservation of quantity were not able to extend them immediately to the conservation of weight.

Piaget and Inhelder's attempt to answer this question will be described after the conservation of volume has also been considered, for the decalage between quantity and weight repeated itself when it came to volume. The conservation of volume was assessed by showing that two balls of the same size and shape displaced the same amount of liquid when immersed in water. The question was whether or not they would still displace the same amount when the shape of one of the balls was transformed. Remarkably, some children who had successfully conserved both quantity and weight nevertheless did not recognize that the same amount of water would be displaced, and they justified these judgments in the same way children had justified judgments of nonconservation of quantity or weight: "Is there as much clay in the one as in the other? – *It's absolutely the same.* – Why are you so sure? – *It's the same weight because you've taken none of the clay away and you can always turn it back into a ball.* – And if I put it in the water? – *The ball will make it come up more; it's bigger and takes up more room than its weight* (= it is bigger but of equal weight). *That one* (the ball) *is large and this one* (the coil) *is thin, so it'll make the water rise less"* (ibid., p. 50).

Not only were justifications of nonconservation of volume the same as those for quantity and weight, but justifications of conservation were also the same. Thus, the same appeals to identification, reversibility, and compensatory relations were also found for volume: *"It's still the same as the ball, so the water must rise the same as before"; "You can cut it up as much as you like, but when you put them together again it comes to the same as the ball"; "It's longer, but it's thinner";* and so on (ibid., p. 56).

In analyzing the operative structure of conservation, Piaget and Inhelder pointed out that neither identification nor empirical revertibility alone is sufficient for conservation. In the transitional stages leading to the conservation of each type of content, examples could be found in which children appealed to identification or revertibility in justifying momentary judgments of conservation, but such justifications did not lead to lasting conviction. One transitional response regarding quantity, for example, was the following: "One of the small balls is cut up into five little balls: 'Is there as much clay in all these together as in the big one? – *No, there is less over here* (the five balls) *because it isn't so big. –* Can we turn them back into a large ball? – *Yes, then it'll be the same again'* " (ibid., p. 10). For Piaget and Inhelder, such responses illustrated the difference between "the empirical return" (revertibility) and true (i.e., operational) reversibility. Although children in the transitional (intuitive) stage could follow a sequential return to the starting point in thought (which might be accompanied by sequential changes in the quantity of matter), operational reversibility involved the understanding that any operation is exactly and simultaneously compensated by an inverse operation, whether or not that inverse operation is actually performed. To say that this form of reversibility is "simultaneous" rather than "successive" is only to say that the operational child is capable of thinking of the direct operation and its inverse at the same time, not only in succession (e.g., a piece of clay is made thinner at the same time it is made longer).

In fact, Piaget and Inhelder (ibid., pp. 18–19, 26, 57–58) argued that there are four methods by which children can attain conservation for each type of content: (a) They can think of changes in shape as the rearrangement of parts. If a ball of clay B_1 is thought of as composed of parts A and A', and if the change in shape is thought of as a rearrangement of these parts, then the equality of the transformed ball B_2 and the original follows from the commutability of the addition of classes: $B_1 = A + A' = A' + A = B_2$. (b) Same as (a), except that the ball is thought of as composed of a number of equal units. (c) B_1 is thought of as having a height b_1 and a width consisting of $b + b'$, and B_2 is thought of as having height $b_1 + b'$ and width b. In this case, children understand that what has been lost in height is immediately gained in width. (d) Both height and width are quantified, such that children recognize the ratio between the heights of the ball before and after transformation to be the exact inverse of the respective widths. One does not always know from children's responses which of these strategies they are following. For example, even when children clearly refer to the dimensions of height and width, it is not always clear whether or not these dimensions are fully quantified.

The attempt to specify the operations involved in conservation raises the question of the decalages once again. The operations are formally the same whether quantity, weight, or volume is involved, but these three types of content in fact begin to be conserved at different points in development, separated by about 2 years on the average. The answer provided by Piaget and Inhelder is that the conservation of weight and volume involves additional coordinations in comparison with quantity. This conclusion follows from the fact that different physical operations are grouped in each case. With respect to weight, a spherical ball of clay may actually feel heavier than the same amount of clay rolled out or flattened into a pancake, because the weight is more concentrated in the first case as compared with the second. The conservation of weight therefore requires that children overcome this misleading impression. In effect, children must come to base their judgments on cognitive operations rather than on perception. In addition to the recognition that the quantity of clay is independent of shape, the conservation of weight involves the understanding that equal amounts of clay also weigh the same. Because of this additional coordination, the conservation of weight develops later than that of quantity.

With respect to the conservation of volume, children must come to understand that the density of the clay remains constant, along with its weight and quantity. Even if children know that quantity and weight have been conserved, they may continue to believe that the parts of which it is composed have somehow been squeezed together more compactly so that they occupy less space. Such compression is in fact possible for some kinds of elastic materials (e.g., sponge rubber). The conservation of volume thus involves the recognition that clay does not behave like this, that equal amounts of clay occupy equal amounts of space, or, in other words, that the density of the material remains constant.

Now this solution to the problem of the horizontal decalage may or may not be satisfying. It is clearly ex post facto, and one wonders if decalages involving other types of content could be predicted from such analyses or if they could be discovered only empirically. Moreover, Piaget and Inhelder's explanation, at most, explains why conservation appears successively with respect to quantity, weight, and volume, not why they appear at 2-year intervals beginning around 7–8 years. Perhaps Piaget would reply as he did in the passage from *La genèse du nombre* cited earlier: that he had "no interest" in trying to identify all the "heterogeneous factors" that affect children's performances, among which the effects of particular contents must be included.

But the main point is not that Piaget did or did not explain the causes of particular horizontal decalages satisfactorily; the point is rather that horizontal decalages in general may be expected when formally analogous operations are applied to different physical contents, even if the particular decalages cannot be predicted in advance. Contrary to many subsequent interpretations of Piagetian theory, the existence of horizontal decalages does not contradict the theory, because Piaget never claimed that the same groupings of operations should develop simultaneously across different areas of content. In fact, when he said anything about the issue of synchrony in development, he stated the reverse: that decalages are to be expected across different areas of content because the operations involved may be functionally distinct even if they are formally analogous. This conclusion follows from the very definition of groupings as a system of organized operations. Different areas of content can involve different physical operations, and there is no a priori reason why these different physical operations should be grouped at the same time, even though the groupings may be formally analogous once they have been formed. In short, Piaget did not make a radical ontological distinction between form and content as has sometimes been claimed.

This conclusion becomes evident in subsequent sections of *The child's construction of quantities*. Having discovered the decalage involving the conservation of quantity, weight, and volume in the opening chapters, Piaget and Inhelder asked whether or not the same decalage would be found when it came to logical compositions involving these different contents. They noted that this question involved the further problem of the relation between logical form and physical content:

If the logical form is independent of the physical context, it follows that such purely formal operations with the weight and volume must appear at the same time as those bearing on the quantity in general (substance), i.e., in advance of all physical operations. If, on the contrary, the content constitutes the true principle of development, the order of appearance of the physical operations will be determined exclusively by experience. If finally, as we believe, form and content are inseparable, the order of appearance of the logico-arithmetical operations will be linked to that of the physical operations, each giving rise simultaneously to a new type of logic and a new type of physics, and this according to the law of succession we have established. [ibid., pp. 179–180]

Far from being merely an anomalous finding in Piagetian theory, the horizontal decalage involving substance, weight, and volume was described in this passage as a "law of succession"! The same decalage was expected in the development of logical compositions involving these areas of content because of the inseparability of form and content. The logical forms (i.e., the groupings) are forms of organization among the content-bound physical operations. This organization cannot exist apart from the respective contents, because without the latter there is nothing to be organized. As Piaget and Inhelder put it in another place, "formal relations as such cannot be constructed until their content is available for composition" (ibid., p. 131).

In fact, the same decalage was found for logical compositions as for conservation. Composition of asymmetrical relations (seriation) of weights was studied in chapter 10, the composition of equivalence relations for weight in chapter 11, and equivalence relations for volume in chapter 12. The decalage between weight or volume and quantity was established by comparing these results with those reported for quantity in *La genèse du nombre*. The presence of the decalage in the development of compositions pertaining to quantity, weight, and volume indicated further that form is not independent of content:

If we look at the time lags between the compositions of substance, weight, and volume respectively we cannot but conclude that the deductive or formal factors and the (perceptive and experimental) content develop as one inseparable whole. Why, in fact, does the child fail to compose weights until after he has composed quantities of matter? The reason is that weight (or the conservation of weight) presupposes the existence of matter (or the conservation of matter), but not *vice versa*. Similarly, compositions of volumes lag behind those of weights because their conservation depends on the consistent behavior of matter, and according to the child, the latter, i.e., the incompressibility or "hardness" of objects rests on the conservation of weight. [ibid., pp. 262–263]

If this affirmation of the inseparability of form and content remains somewhat vague, perhaps it can be clarified by a brief passage from *La genèse du nombre*.

In discussing the composition of equivalence relations (between vases and red and blue flowers), Piaget and Szeminska also discussed the relation between form and content in these terms:

In our hypothesis, according to which logic is constructed, it remains to be proved that a formal mechanism like the composition of two relations can be elaborated independently of the contents to which this coordination is applied. Conversely . . . one can expect that the formal structure $(X = Y; Y = Z$ therefore $X = Z)$ is not acquired all at once independently of its content, but requires as many distinct and repeated acquisitions as there are different contents to which it is applied. What is more, the formal structure $(X = Y; Y = Z$ therefore $X = Z)$, like all formal structures, is only a coordination of a particular grade, capable of being carried out only as a function of the comprehension (structuration) of the terms or relations coordinated and consequently having to be reconstituted in the form of a new coordination every time it is applied to a new class of objects of thought. [Piaget & Szeminska, 1941/1964, p. 263]

This point of view might be summarized by saying that Piaget acknowledged both formal and functional aspects of logico-mathematical structures, but he was more interested in analyzing their form than the conditions affecting their functioning. The formal properties of these structures can be described independent of their contents. For example, the formal structure of the composition of equivalence relations $(X = Y; Y = Z;$ therefore, $X = Z)$ remains the same whether relations of quantity, weight, volume, or anything else are being composed. Similarly, the "laws of the groupings" in general – their defining properties of composition, associativity, identity, and inversion – can be enumerated and described apart from any reference to specific content. Piaget's exclusive focus on the formal aspects of these structures easily gives rise to the mistaken impression (a) that he also believed them to *function* in a content-free manner or (b) that he recognized no functional aspect of these structures at all. The first of these two possible misinterpretations – that the structures are functionally content-free – leads to a further misunderstanding: that a given structure is acquired all at once and then is "applied" to different areas of content. If this were true, then a fairly high degree of synchrony in development across different areas of content would be expected, and the occurrence of horizontal decalages would indeed be an embarrassment to the theory. But Piaget explicitly rejected this whole chain of reasoning, as indicated in the passages quoted earlier.

These misconceptions can be avoided if only the original definition of structures as the forms of organization (or "forms of equilibrium") characterizing different operations is kept in mind. So defined, these structures cannot exist apart from the operations of which they constitute the organization. As internalized actions, these operations are necessarily content-specific. Functionally speaking, there are as many different logical "groupings" as there are different content-specific operations to be grouped together, although in formal terms there are only eight of them. In the words of Piaget and Szeminska quoted earlier, a given formal structure must be reconstructed or reacquired for each new content to which it is applied. Thus, the groupings of operations in different content areas can be formally "analogous" even though they are functionally distinct.

Because the operations characterizing different content areas may present different kinds of difficulties with respect to their organization, they are not expected to develop in synchrony. With respect to the operation of class partition, for example, Piaget wrote: "It is precisely in the case of the 'analogy' that there is 'horizontal decalage': in general, two 'analogous' partitions are not contemporaneous, but one appears in psychological development as more difficult than the other" (Piaget, 1941, p. 267). It follows that a child does not pass from one stage to another all at once, but can be at different stages with respect to different areas of content at the same time. "It can thus be maintained that a notion [i.e., a content] of which the grouping is in horizontal decalage with respect to another simply attains a given level later than the first: for example, weight remains intuitive longer than the quantity of matter and reaches level V [concrete operations] only with delay" (ibid., p. 270).

Once again one may observe that the child as an individual is generally not the unit of analysis in Piaget's research. Instead, different performances are classified at different stages according to the structures or "forms of equilibrium" that they exemplify. The fact that individual children can be "operational" in some areas and "preoperational" in others, far from calling the structuralist assumptions of Piagetian theory into question (Bruner, 1983; Fischer, 1980), is fully consistent with that theory. The problem with the theory lies not in any supposed contradiction between its structuralist assumptions and the facts of child development but in its rather one-sided focus on the formal aspect of cognitive structures to the exclusion of their functional aspect. Putting the formal and functional aspects of cognitive development together, as Piaget remarked in his introduction to Flavell's (1963) book, is a matter for "interdisciplinary endeavor."

STUDIES OF CONCRETE OPERATIONS II: TIME AND SPACE

In contrast to the books on number and quantity, Piaget's subsequent research on concrete operations focused on the "real categories" of time and space. As before, Piaget and his collaborators described the formal properties of operational thought in terms of groupings of operations analogous to the groups and groupings of arithmetic and logic, but precisely because different areas of content were involved, the specific operations differed in each case. In Piaget's terminology, the groupings involved in the construction of number and quantity were *logico-mathematical* in character – that is, they pertained to classes and relations among objects. In contrast, the groupings involved in the construction of time and space were called *infralogical*. This terminology did not imply that the latter types of groupings were in any way less rigorous than logico-mathematical structures, only that they pertained to the relations involved in the construction *of* objects (or configurations of objects), rather than to the relations *among* objects. Thus, relations of infralogical inclusion refer not to class membership, but to part–whole relations in which the contiguity or proximity of the parts also plays a role in the constitution of the whole. Piaget's descriptions of infralogical groupings thus included both formal analogies with groupings in other areas and characteristics specific to infralogical operations.

The child's conception of time (Piaget, 1946/1971b) and *The child's conception of movement and speed* (Piaget, 1946/1970a) both appeared in 1946, each volume dealing with a different aspect of children's construction of time and movement. These books were followed two years later by *The child's conception of space* (Piaget & Inhelder, 1948/1967) and *The child's conception of geometry* (Piaget, Inhelder, & Szeminska, 1948/1960), which dealt with the development of spatial operations. In this section, the conclusions of these works will be summarized only in the briefest manner, skipping over the wealth of detail they contain on children's responses to particular tasks and focusing instead on the descriptions of the structures involved.

The child's conception of time

In the foreword to this book, Piaget stated that his work on the epistemology of time was inspired by Albert Einstein at an international conference on philosophy and psychology that took place in Davos in 1931. Apparently, Einstein had wondered if the study of children's conceptions of time could cast light on the question whether time was a primitive concept or was derived from more primitive intuitions of velocity. Piaget wrote that he was unable to make much progress with these questions until he had developed his theory of the groupings of concrete operations. In addition to casting light on the origins of scientific conceptions of time, his investigations were relevant for conceptions of an intuitive sense of inner "duration," such as motivated much of Bergson's philosophy.

According to the theory of groupings, a mature understanding of time has two operational components. The first is the (multiple) seriation of successive events, and the second is the "colligation" or addition of successive durations. Formally, these groupings correspond to the one-to-one multiplication of relations and to the addition of asymmetrical relations. In the course of development, each of these groupings may be derived from the other. Some children attain to the order of successions by way of the colligation of durations, but others follow the reverse path. In either case, the quantification or measurement of time follows from the "fusion" of the two groupings, much as number is constructed from the fusion of class inclusion and asymmetrical relations.

As far as succession is concerned, even young children have no trouble ordering the events in any single series of successions. The difficulty comes in recognizing the simultaneity of parallel series. In a series of experiments, Piaget demonstrated that preoperational children have difficulty understanding that two or more series of events belong to a unitary time series. In one experiment, for example, one bottle was emptied by degrees into another one placed beneath it. The sequential series of states formed by the emptying of the first bottle thus corresponded to the sequence of states formed by the filling of the second bottle.

At each stage in the process, children were asked to draw the respective levels on a picture of both bottles. Then the pictures were shuffled, and children were asked to reproduce the series as it had occurred – first with the pictures showing both bottles together, and then again after the pictures had been cut in two – so that the levels of the two bottles would correspond to each other as they had done originally.

Three stages in the performance of this task were found. In the *first stage*, children were unable to reproduce the series, even with the intact pictures. In the *second stage*, they were able to reproduce the sequence with the intact pictures, but not with the pictures cut in half. Finally, in the *third stage*, they were able to reproduce both series correctly. According to Piaget's analysis, the reconstruction of simultaneous series such as this involves the bi-univocal multiplication of relations. The asymmetrical relations of succession within each series must be crossed with relations of simultaneity existing between the two series, each event depicted in the one series corresponding to a simultaneous event in the other.

Children's understanding of durations was assessed by asking them how long it took the water to fall from one level to another in the one bottle, as compared with the time it took to rise from one level to another in the other bottle. In the *first stage*, children did not recognize that the time it took for the water to fall from level I_1 to level I_2 in the first bottle was equivalent to the time it took for the water to rise from level II_1 to level II_2 in the second bottle (where I_1 was simultaneous with II_1, and I_2 with II_2). Instead, they thought that the interval I_1–I_2 was longer than II_1–II_2, because the water appeared to drop faster from I_1 to I_2 than to rise from II_1 to II_2 (a result of differences in shape). In other words, they apparently thought time was a direct function of speed. In the *second stage*, children overcame this error, but now believed that time was inversely related to speed. Thus, II_1–II_2 was longer than I_1–I_2, and durations still had not been co-ordinated. Finally, in the *third stage*, children recognized not only that I_1–I_2 was equal to II_1–II_2 but also that I_1–I_3 was necessarily longer than II_1–II_2, and so on. In other words, they understood both the unity of the time series (such that it comprises both I_1, I_2, . . . , and II_1, II_2, . . .) and the colligation of durations (such that I_1–I_2 is included in I_1–I_3, etc.). Moreover, as soon as they had recognized that the intervals involved were all equal (i.e., that I_1–I_3 equals I_2–I_3, etc.), they also became capable of quantifying time. Then intervals could be compared not only in terms of equalities and inclusions but also in terms of the number of units they contained.

Piaget interpreted the colligation of durations as involving relations of inclusion, but this inclusion is infralogical rather than logical (i.e., class inclusion). Qualitatively, duration is more like a symmetrical relation obtaining between two events. In these terms, the colligation of durations is a form of addition of symmetrical relations (Grouping VI). If *A, B,* and *C* are three successive events, then the colligation of the durations between them can be expressed as:

$$(A \leftrightarrow B) + (B \leftrightarrow C) = (A \leftrightarrow C),$$

where the duration between successive events is represented by the double arrow. The understanding of duration according to this grouping is still qualitative in character. It becomes quantitative, according to Piaget, when some uniform, repeatable duration is taken as a standard unit such that successive durations are seen to be equal: $(A \leftrightarrow B) = (B \leftrightarrow C)$. Under these conditions, time can be quantified and measured:

$$(A \leftrightarrow B) + (B \leftrightarrow C) = 2 \times (A \leftrightarrow B).$$

The analogy with the formation of number is obvious:

Quantitative time, like number, results from qualitative groupings, but with this difference: in the case of time the groupings are infralogical, and the colligation of durations (addition of the parts of a single object) takes the place of the colligation of classes (or sets of objects); the displacement of durations, which is an operation generating time, replaces logical seriation (which is independent of the space-time order), and the operational synthesis of partitive addition and displacement is a measurement and no longer a system of abstract numbers. [Piaget, 1946/1971b, p. 189]

Other chapters in *The child's conception of time* deal with the perception (as opposed to the reconstruction) of succession and simultaneity, the equalization of synchronous durations, the transitivity of unequal time relations, the additive and associative composition of durations, the measurement of time, the concept of age, and the relation between action and "inner duration." Among the other conclusions reached in this book was that speed is a more "primitive" intuition than time, that time is in fact derived from intuitions regarding speed (or the rapidity of an action) and distance (or amount of work accomplished), and that the sense of "inner duration" therefore develops in parallel with the understanding of physical time. According to Piaget, Kant was right to insist that time was not a concept, but a "schema" or formal structure; he was mistaken, however, in concluding that time must therefore be a form of intuition, an "a priori form of sensibility." Instead, "genetic analysis has led us to a quite different conclusion, namely that time must be *constructed* into a unique scheme by operations and, moreover, by the same groupings and groups as go into the construction of logical and arithmetical forms" (ibid., p. 301). By referring to the "same" groupings and groups, Piaget meant only that they are formally analogous, not that they are functionally identical. This conclusion follows from the fact that infralogical structures are involved in the one case and logico-mathematical structures in the other.

The child's conception of movement and speed

Having concluded in *The child's conception of time* that the intuition of speed was more primitive than the intuition of time, Piaget set out in the companion volume to investigate the former. The first half of *The child's conception of movement and speed* (Piaget, 1946/1970a) was devoted to experiments on movements, including successive order (or what Piaget called "placements") and changes of location (or "displacements"). The second half was focused on speed and included experiments on both qualitative and quantitative relations of speed. In his conclusion, Piaget summarized the development of conceptions of movement and speed in terms of six operational systems, illustrated by the different experiments included in the book.

The first operational system Piaget called *placement,* and it consists in the operation of placing a series of objects in a spatial sequence or succession such that A "comes before" B, B "comes before" C, and so on. So defined, placement is clearly an infralogical analogue to the logical operation of seriation. The development of placement as an operational system was illustrated in an experiment in which three (or more) balls were placed in a tube in a certain order $(A, B, C$, etc.) and subjected to one or more 180° rotations, and the child was asked to predict in what order they would reemerge. Of major interest in this task was the development of the reversibility of this operation, that is, the ability to predict that the order would be exactly reversed after an odd number of 180° rotations, and would remain the same after an even number of rotations.

The second operational system described by Piaget has to do with operations of *displacement,* that is, with movements as such. Briefly, such operations are concerned with changes of position with respect to a preexisting series of positions that remains constant as a frame of reference. This preexisting series of positions is constructed as a series of placements $(A_0, B_0, C_0$, etc.) as described earlier, and "displacement" can be defined as an operation in which an object A originally occupying position A_0 is moved to one of the other positions in the series. Such displacements constitute an operational system when displacements can be composed with each other (the displacement A_0-B_0 plus the displacement B_0-C_0 is equivalent to the displacement A_0-C_0) and when a series of displacements is understood to be reversible (the distance covered by the displacement A_0-C_0 is equivalent to that of C_0-A_0). One can easily verify the fact that such an operational system has all the formal properties of a grouping, or of a group under the condition that one displacement (e.g., A_0-B_0) can be used as an iterative unit such that $A_0-N_0 = n \times (A_0-B_0)$. This group of displacements is closely related (formally analogous) to the group of displacements studied by Piaget (1937/1971a) in sensorimotor development, the difference being that the latter is a system of actions actually carried out by the child, whereas the former is a system of cognitive operations. The relation between the two groups thus constitutes an example of vertical decalage.

This operational grouping of displacements was studied by showing children a model of a cable car that could be moved up and down the side of a mountain along various trajectories. All of the children studied were familiar with such a mechanism at the Salève – the mountain near Geneva that played a prominent role in many of Piaget's experiments and observations. The basic question of interest was whether or not children realized that the distance from the bottom to the top of the mountain was the same as the distance from the top to the bottom. Interestingly enough, young children before the age of about 7–8 years tended to believe that the distance going up was greater than that going down, a belief Piaget attributed to children's experience that uphill journeys tend to take longer or require more effort than downhill journeys. After roughly 7–8 years, children began to understand that the way up is necessarily the same distance as the way down, an indication that the system of displacements had become reversible and therefore operational.

The third system of operations Piaget called *co-displacements,* and it has to do with the relative speeds of moving objects. Briefly, operations of co-displacements are composed of the movements of two objects through series of corresponding positions from an initial state to an end state. In fact, co-displacements may be said to involve four different types of operations: (a) Operations of relative *speed* develop from intuitions of overtaking. Such overtaking occurs when one object ends up being farther along in the series of positions than the second object after having begun at a position behind or alongside the latter. (b) The series of states intervening between the initial state and the end state constitutes a *temporal order* that is the same for the two moving objects. (c) In the interval between one state and the next, each object will have traveled a certain *distance.* In the case of overtaking, the distance traveled by one object in the respective interval is necessarily greater than that for the other. (d) Given the fact that the series of states occurs simultaneously for both moving objects, the temporal *duration* between successive states will also be the same for both objects. In short, these four types of operations involve operations of relative order with respect to space (overtaking) and time (succession), as well as operations of relative separation, again with respect to both space (distance) and time (duration).

The development of these operations was studied in a series of experiments in which children were questioned about the relative speeds of moving objects under conditions in which (a) only the starting and stopping points were visible, (b) movements were visible, but distances and durations were unequal, (c) movements were circular, (d) durations were equal, but distances unequal, and (e) distances were equal, but durations unequal. In brief, Piaget found that the youngest children judged speed primarily on the basis of visible overtaking, without taking the starting points into consideration. In a second stage, children began to take the starting points as well as the finishing points into consideration, allowing them to judge relative speeds even when overtaking was not visible, or when durations were equal but distances unequal. Finally, judgments of speed became operational around the age of 7–8 years, when children became capable of correlating the distances and durations of simultaneous movements.

The remaining three systems of operations represent further elaborations of the preceding systems of placements and displacement. The system of *relative displacements and co-displacements,* for example, has to do with the movement of an object in relation to a series of positions that itself is moving in relation to a second series. The operation involved consists in determining the displacement of the object in relation to the second series. This question was studied by showing children a snail shell on a piece of cardboard, a configuration that represented a snail moving along a board that was in turn being moved in relation to the ground. The question was how much the snail would have moved in relation to the ground given knowledge about how the snail moved in relation to the board and how the board moved in relation to the ground. Significantly, this problem was not completely solved until the stage of formal operations (in this case, around the age of 11 years), although children at the stage of concrete operations could solve the problem under certain restricted conditions (if movements are in the same direction, or in opposite directions but of equal distances). *The child's conception of movement and speed* was the first of Piaget's books following the formulation of the grouping theory in which the development of formal operations was described for a number of different tasks.

Although all the foregoing systems of operations are purely qualitative (i.e., involving comparisons of "more" or "less"), the last two systems involve quantification. The first of these, the system of *extensive* operations, is a system of quantitative relations that falls short of full measurement. In judging the speeds of successive movements when both distances and durations are unequal, children in a stage of advanced concrete operations were observed to compare the relative differences in distances and durations without using metrical proportions. Under conditions in which one object traveled 4 cm in 2 sec and the other 7 cm in 3 sec, children might reason according to this system that the difference in distance (3 cm) in relation to the distance traveled by the first object (4 cm) was greater than was the difference in durations (1 sec) in relation to the duration of the movement of that same object (2 sec). One might say that this comparison is both qualitative and quantitative at the same time. It involves quantitative ratios (3 : 4 cm, and 1 : 2 sec), but these ratios are themselves compared only qualitatively (as being "more" or "less").

Finally, *metrical* operations involve the use of units of measurement for both time and space. As described in Piaget's other books on the development of conceptions of time and space, measurement develops through the fusion of operations of inclusion and seriation. That is, a given distance or duration is taken as a unit capable of being iterated in a series. For example, in some of the simpler problems involving judgments of speed, children were able to use metrical operations involving space and time to arrive at relative judgments of speed. In the more complex tasks, such as those involving proportions, however, metrical operations were not employed until the stage of formal operations. To return to the example cited earlier in which one object traveled 3 cm in 1 sec, and another 4 cm in 2 sec, the system of metrical proportions could be employed to determine that the speed of the first object was exactly 1.5 times that of the second. In his later work on formal operations, Piaget would rank proportionality, and especially metrical proportionality, as a characteristic formal operational scheme (Inhelder & Piaget, 1955/1958).

The child's conception of space

The questions that motivated Piaget's studies of space were much the same as those pursued in the studies of time, movement, and speed. The main problem in each case was to trace the origins of the concepts involved and, in particular, to clarify the role of intuition. In the case of space, the role of intuition in geometry was one of the central questions debated in the 20th-century epistemology of mathematics (see chapter 8). The questions that motivated Piaget's work on children's understanding of space and geometry can thus be viewed in the context of contemporary discussion in epistemology.

According to Piaget, neither time nor space results from "primitive" intuitions. Instead, both are described as operationally constructed. In contrast to logico-mathematical operations, the operations involved in the construction of space and time are infralogical in the sense that they involve part–whole relations rather than class membership. Despite this fundamental difference, infralogical operations are also grouped into groupings formally analogous to the logico-mathematical groupings. Temporal groupings have to do with the ordering of successions and the colligation of durations, and spatial groupings with relations of proximity, separation, order, enclosure, and continuity (Piaget & Inhelder, 1948/1967, pp. 6ff.). In contrast to Kant, who had characterized both time and space as "forms of sensibility," Piaget derived the "intuition" of space and time from interiorized action. Spatial imagery, for example, was described as originating in the interiorization of imitation (ibid., pp. 40–41, 294–296, 452–457).

The child's conception of space is divided into three parts, dealing with topological, projective, and Euclidean space, respectively. Topological space involves only relations of enclosure and seriation, but projective space also takes into account the shapes, positions, and relative distances of geometric figures. Euclidean space further involves the conservation of distances, straight lines, parallels, and angles. Each part of the book describes a number of experiments investigating the development of different aspects of the respective spatial systems. Part 1 is devoted to topological space and contains chapters on the tactile recognition of geometric shapes, the drawing of geometric figures, linear and circular order, the notion of surrounding or enclosure, and the idea of points and continuity. Part 2 focuses on projective space and includes experiments on perspective, the projection of shadows, the coordination of perspectives, geometrical sections, and the rotation and unfolding of surfaces. In Part 3, different aspects of the transition from projective to Euclidean space are described, including the conservation of parallels, similarities and proportions, systems of reference, and simple maps.

All of the experiments in *The child's conception of space* will not be summarized here. For present purposes, the study of the coordination of perspectives (ibid., chap. 7) is perhaps most relevant, because it has given rise to a number of subsequent studies that have figured significantly in the evaluation of Piaget's theory in psychology. Therefore, it is the only task from *The child's conception of space* that will be described in any detail.

The method employed was the following: Children were shown a 1-m^2 pasteboard model of three mountains differing in height (tallest, intermediate, shortest) and color (gray, brown, green), and with different distinguishing features at their summits (snow, a cross, a little house). A doll was positioned at different points around the display (90°, 180°, or 270° in relation to the position of the child). For these different positions of the doll, children were then asked to reconstruct the doll's perspective of the display with three pieces of cardboard each shaped and colored like each of the three mountains. In alternative versions of the task, children were asked to indicate the doll's perspective by choosing from among 10 pictures representing the model as seen from different viewpoints, or, conversely, to place the doll in the position indicated in one of the pictures.

This procedure was administered to 100 children between the ages of 4 and 12 years. The very youngest children (*Stage I*) did not seem to understand the meaning of the experimenter's questions. Stages II and III were divided into two substages each. At *Stage IIA,* children consistently reproduced (or chose) their own perspectives when asked to reproduce that of the doll. At Stage IIB, children made some attempt to reproduce a perspective different from their own, but they were unsuccessful in doing so and often ended up reproducing their own perspective after all. At *Stage IIIA* (reached at roughly 7–8 years on the average), children successfully transformed certain relations (e.g., before–behind) in reproducing the doll's perspective, but other relations (e.g., right–left) were not transformed. Thus, the incipient coordination of perspectives remained incomplete. Finally, in *Stage IIIB* (after about 9–10 years), a complete relativity of perspectives was found: Children were successful in transforming both before–behind and right–left relations. Piaget discussed these results in terms of young children's "egocentrism" (even while apologizing for the inadequacy of this term) in regard to their inability to distinguish between their own perspective and that of another person in this task. The acquisition of the coordination of perspective was thus described as a gradual process of "decentration" relative to their own perspective.

In the final chapter, Piaget summarized the general conclusions to be drawn from the various experiments. To begin with, he asserted his belief that the axiomization of geometry has never been completely severed from geometric intuition and that such a complete separation is impossible in principle. His investigations reveal, however, that spatial "intuition" is no mere interiorization of perception, but an interiorization of action in the form of operations. Spatial imagery in fact originates in the interiorization of imitation, not merely in the continuation of perception. In contrast to logico-mathematical operations, spatial operations are infralogical (or "sublogical," as the term is translated in that volume). These infralogical operations are nevertheless grouped into groupings that are formally analogous to the eight logical groupings. In the better part of his final chapter, Piaget gave the analogues of the eight groupings for each of the three types of space investigated. To consider only the analogues for Grouping I: (a) In topological space, the grouping $A + A' = B$ expresses the joining of neighboring areas to form a continuous whole. (b) In projective space, this grouping refers to the joining of the neighboring parts of an object or configuration as seen from a particular point of view. In the three-mountain task, for example, A and A' might represent two mountains next to each other. (c) In Euclidean space, the operation $A + A' = B$ represents the linking of associated parts of a given geometrical figure (lines, angles, distances, etc.). Similar analogues were given for the other groupings. In the same sense, the development of quantitative geometrical relations is analogous to the development of number. The development of spatial quantification occurs through the equalization of neighboring distances, which is in turn accomplished through the fusion of groupings involving inclusion and seriation. That is, the grouping $A + A' = B$ becomes $A + A = B$, where the first A is distinguished from the second by their respective positions adjacent to each other.

Because of their specific features, the grouping of spatial operations does not necessarily occur at the same time as the grouping of logico-mathematical operations. As Piaget had previously stated in ''The mechanism of mental development'' (Piaget, 1941), horizontal decalages are to be expected in the formation of ''analogous'' groupings in different areas of content:

An operational system derives its content from a series of abstractions of the subject's actions, and not from particular features or properties of objects. But this process of abstraction may be encouraged or obstructed by the material conditions in which the various groups of objects are encountered. Thus we find number understood before spatial measurement because the discontinuity of separate aggregates suggests the repetition of a unit more readily than a linear continuity in one or two dimensions. Alternatively, a squared pattern will facilitate understanding of spatial measurement more easily than a heap of beads which cannot be estimated numerically but only as a rough ''more or less''. Thus tests and experiments of the kind used here always yield results which depend in part upon the experimental conditions and this fact tends to complicate the task of analysing them. [Piaget & Inhelder, 1948/1967, pp. 484–485]

The child's conception of geometry

Whereas *The child's conception of space* included sections on topological, projective, and Euclidean space, *The child's conception of geometry* was entirely devoted to various facets of Euclidean geometry. According to the authors, the transition from topological to Euclidean space is characterized by the elaboration of operations involving changes of position and the subdivision of lengths (Piaget, et al., 1948/1960, p. 392). As already described in the book on space, the measurement of distances in Euclidean geometry is an operatory fusion of these operations, much as number is a fusion of class inclusion and seriation. The decisive step is the division of a given length into two or more equal subsections, $A + A = B$, where the first A is distinguished from the second by their relative positions. The second A is laid next to the first, as it were, and the total length is equal to the number of successive positions occupied by the unit length: $B = A + A = 2A, C = A + A + A = 3A,$ and so on. In effect, the operational structure of geometric measurement in general is much like measuring the width of a room with a yardstick.

The roles of changes of position and subdivision of length in children's spontaneous measurement were studied in a preliminary manner in chapter 2. Children were shown a tower 80 cm high built out of blocks of various kinds on a table. They were then asked to build another tower the same height on another table nearby. Children's performances of this task could be divided into three major stages, with various substages. In *Stage I* (up to about 4 1/2 years), children relied only on approximate perceptual comparisons in judging comparative heights. During *Stage II* (about 4.5–7 years), some changes of position were involved in children's comparisons. Either the towers were simply brought closer together to facilitate perceptual comparison (Substage IIA), or children used parts of their own bodies as standards for comparison (Substage IIB). In one type of response classified as intermediate between Stages II and III, children used some third object exactly as tall as the first tower as a standard for measuring the second. Finally, in *Stage III* (beginning about 7–8 years), comparison objects no longer had to be exactly the same length as the two towers to be compared. At Substage IIIA, children limited themselves to a standard that was taller than the towers, but at Substage IIIB they recognized that they could also carry out the measurement with a standard smaller than either of the two towers through iteration of the standard used as a unit.

Subsequent chapters were devoted to studies of the conservation and measurement of length, area, and volume. The results of these studies were summarized in terms of three levels of achievement in the construction of Euclidean space (ibid., p. 389). The first of these levels, corresponding to Stage IIIA (the first substage of concrete operations), was characterized by the conservation of length, area, and volume. This accomplishment was followed at Stage IIIB by the development of simple metrical operations, including the measurement of length in one, two, or three dimensions, and the beginning of measurement of areas and angles. The third and final level was *Stage IV,* the stage of formal operations, at which the calculation of areas and volumes became possible.

As in the first book on space, both the formal analogies between spatial and logico-mathematical operations and their specific differences were described. Although both number and spatial measurement originate from the "fusion" of qualitative (logical or infralogical) operations, they differ in the manner in which this fusion occurs. Number apparently develops as soon as class inclusion and seriation have appeared, but measurement emerges somewhat later than the constituent operations of subdivision of distance and change of position (Substage IIIB as compared with Substage IIIA). Moreover, the measurement of area and of volume does not develop concurrently with that of length. Only at Stage IV (formal operations) does the measurement of area and volume become fully operational. These findings are thus consistent with Piaget's (1941) expectation that the development of analogous groupings in different areas of content should be characterized by horizontal decalages. A good part of the authors' concluding remarks was devoted to an explanation of why these particular decalages were found.

The decalage between measurement and number was explained as a result of the fact that a unit is more difficult to abstract out of continuous length than out of a collection of discontinuous objects. In the case of measurement, the unit results only from an arbitrary subdivision of the length to be measured, but in the case of number the objects to be counted are already divided into potential units. In effect, the decalage results from the fact that measurement involves an additional operation, the subdivision that constitutes the unit.

The decalage between the measurement of length and that of area and volume was explained in a similar manner. The measurement of area is more difficult than the measurement of length, because an additional operation is involved: the construction of a unit of area from the cross-product of units of length. Psychologically, the operation $3 \times 3 = 9$ is much different than the operation $3 \text{ cm} \times 3 \text{ cm} = 9 \text{ cm}^2$. The multiplication of two numbers yields a product that is also a number, but the multiplication of two lengths yields a product that is no longer a length, but an area, composed of different units entirely. For this reason, children cannot immediately apply their knowledge of arithmetical multiplication to certain problems involving the construction of areas from lengths, or vice versa.[3]

SOCIOLOGICAL ESSAYS

Although Piaget's empirical research during the 1940s focused on cognitive and perceptual development, he did not neglect the social side of his theory. In his capacity as Professor of Sociology at the University of Geneva, he wrote three essays on sociological theory during this period. These essays, entitled "Essai sur la théorie des valeurs qualitatives en sociologie statique" (1940), "Les opérations logiques de la vie sociale" (1945), and "Les relations entre la morale et la droit" (1944), originally appeared in the *Publications de la Faculté des Sciences économique et sociales de l'Université de Genéve*. They were reprinted in 1965 along with the sociological part of *Introduction à l'épistémologie génétique* (Piaget, 1950a) in a volume entitled *Etudes sociologiques*. In the third edition of this collection (Piaget, 1965/1977a), five additional "Ecrits sociologiques" spanning the years from 1928 to 1963 were added in an appendix.

All in all, these essays on sociology leave no doubt of Piaget's continued interest in problems of social organization. At the same time, they underscore the continuity between his early efforts to explain cognitive development as the

---

3 Note that the problem used by Piaget for studying the relation between length and area was the same as that used by Plato in the latter's interview of the slave boy in the *Meno*. The child in each case was asked to find the length of the side of a square that was twice the area of a given square (see chapter 8).

result of children's increasing coordination of others' points of view and his later emphasis on formal structure following the elaboration of the grouping theory in the early forties. In addition, they provide evidence against frequently repeated charges that Piagetian theory is inherently individualistic, asocial, or ahistorical (Broughton, 1981; Vygotsky, 1962; Wallon, 1947). In fact, Piaget continued to believe that analogous forms of organization could be found at "every level" of reality. The same (i.e., formally analogous) groupings could be identified at the level of social structure as had been identified at the level of individual cognition. Individual cognition was further recognized as imbued with social meanings. Piaget never claimed, as he has sometimes been accused, that the cognitive development of individuals occurs in a social vacuum. On the contrary, according to Piaget's sociological theory, the person as an individual is essentially a social construction; see especially "L'individualité en histoire: L'individu et la formation de la raison" (Piaget, 1965/1977a). Piaget's theory is in fact more thoroughly social in character than many other theories of human development.

The perception that Piaget neglected social factors in development probably arose from misapprehensions of three very real characteristics of his approach to development. First, it is certainly true that Piaget wrote relatively little about sociology or social development after about 1950. One can read many of his major works on cognitive development without running across more than token acknowledgments of the importance of social factors in development. Thus, one can easily arrive at the conclusion that he did not consider those factors at all. This impression can be corrected by a wider familiarity with the whole drift of Piaget's thought and especially with his sociological essays.

Second, Piaget on occasion (e.g., in his replies to Wallon in the introduction to *Play, dreams and imitation*) spoke out against what he considered to be overly simplistic forms of social empiricism: the idea that cognitive development can be wholly explained as a process of acquiring knowledge from the social environment. Piaget believed that this view begged the question: How do children develop to a point at which they are capable of assimilating the knowledge available in the social environment? To ask this question is not to imply that individual development is more fundamental than the social environment. Piaget's point was rather that one need not (and cannot) choose between these two factors. His theory of adaptation as a cycle of assimilation and accommodation implies an openness to the influences of the social and physical environment. But children can accommodate only to that which they are capable of assimilating at any given time. Alongside environmental influences, an internal process of equilibration produces new structures that extend the range of information children are capable of assimilating. In arguing that social or other environmental factors are insufficient for explaining development, Piaget sought to emphasize the importance of this equilibration process *in addition* to environmental influences (Piaget, 1960b). The relation between social influences and other necessary factors in development, according to Piaget, is discussed at greater length in chapter 7.

A third reason why the social dimension in Piaget's thinking has been consistently underestimated is his tendency toward formalist explanation. Given his biological background, it is perhaps surprising that he was not more interested in interindividual or cross-cultural variation in the phenomena under investigation. As indicated in the passage from *The child's conception of number* quoted earlier in this chapter, Piaget admitted to disinterest with respect to questions of interindividual differences and the "multitude of heterogeneous factors" influencing task performance. Given his predilection for drawing parallels at different levels of reality, one might expect to find a similar disinterest in the variety and particularity of phenomena at the sociological level as well. How this disinterest should be interpreted is not immediately apparent. Does it reflect an inherent failing of Piaget's theory? Or is it merely an expression of his own personal priorities?

According to the present interpretation, Piaget's relative neglect of the heterogeneity of phenomena can be traced to two considerations. First, most of his research can be described as taxonomic in character. That is, it was aimed at the identification, description, and classification of certain phenomena (e.g., children's forms of reasoning) according to their formal properties and at an ordering of these phenomena with respect to development. Second, he understood this taxonomic stage of scientific investigation to be a necessary preliminary to causal or functional explanation. The theory of groupings, for example, represented an effort to specify the formal organizational properties of concrete operational thinking in general. Identifying the factors determining particular performances was left to a later stage of inquiry. Similarly, Piaget's theory of social exchange represented an attempt to identify the forms of equilibrium in social exchange, not the factors that determine particular social outcomes. Neither of these considerations entails an *inherent* limitation in the theory. If Piaget himself remained mostly at the taxonomic stage of scientific investigation, the extension of the theory in the direction of functionalist explanation would seem to be a logical next step. This possibility is further discussed in chapter 7.

The remainder of this section is devoted to a brief review of the theory of social exchange as expounded in the sociological essays from the 1940s. Particular emphasis will be given to the essay entitled "Les opérations logiques et la vie sociale" ("Logical operations and social life"), because it is more closely related to Piaget's psychological theories than the other sociological essays from this period. Not only is the sociological theory presented in these papers of interest in its own right, but it also opens up a new perspective on the psychological theory. (For more extended commentaries on Piaget's sociological theory, see Chapman, 1986; Kitchener, 1981; Mays, 1982; Moessinger, 1979.)

A theory of social exchange

At the heart of the sociological essays is a structural theory of social exchange as applied to a variety of social phenomena, such as interpersonal relations, morality, law, and even logic. The goal of the theory is the description of the forms of equilibrium that regulate the exchange of social values in these areas. Piaget assumed that social agents share scales of social values by virtue of living in a common culture. Even if these values cannot be quantified in any precise manner, there is general agreement on their qualitative order. Many different types of social interactions can be characterized in terms of the exchange of such values.

A cycle of exchange is initiated by a transfer of value from one agent to another. This typically occurs when agent a renders a service to agent b, a service that generally entails some loss or cost to a and some satisfaction to b.[4] This transfer of value has the further consequence that b becomes indebted to a with respect to future exchanges. But this is not the end of the matter. By virtue of the debt owed by b to a, a acquires a certain social valuation for b. This valuation may take different forms, depending on the circumstances and the kinds of values that are exchanged. According to Piaget, it distinguishes social exchange from quid pro quo reciprocity. As opposed to mere economic exchanges, the social valuation arising from social exchange leads to the establishment of relationships based on mutual valuation and respect. The qualitative, imprecise character of this social valuation implies that it cannot be linked to discrete acts of exchange nor to debts that are expected to be repaid within definite periods of time. By compensating for momentary inequalities arising from discrete transactions, this social valuation contributes to the overall equilibrium of the system. Social relationships resulting from social exchanges are thus based on long-term expectations of reciprocity. For the very reason that they are not tied to specific exchanges, they can endure deviations from reciprocity as long as these deviations can be viewed as temporary.

Piaget's major interest was in describing the forms of equilibrium in such exchange systems. If the system is in equilibrium, the value of a's losses (r_a) will be recognized by the participants as equal to b's satisfaction (s_b); this satisfaction will in turn be recognized as equal to the debt incurred by b (t_b), and the latter will be further recognized as equal to the social valuation accorded to a (v_a). Taken together, these equivalences imply that a's losses (r_a) in rendering a service to b are equal in value to the social valuation (v_a) that a receives in return. In terms of the formalism employed by Piaget, this accumulation of social value can be expressed as follows:

$$(r_a = s_b) + (s_b = t_b) + (t_b = v_a) = (v_a = r_a). \tag{4.1}$$

This formula simply expresses the fact that the first three equalities on the left together imply the final equality on the right. As such, it represents the form of the system in equilibrium. If any of the first three equalities do not hold, such that v_a does not equal r_a, then the system is in disequilibrium.

Equation (4.1) represents only the first phase in the cycle of exchange in which

---

4 For simplicity, the partners to exchange are designated as a and b, instead of a and a', as in Piaget (1965/1977a).

social value is accumulated. In the second phase, the accumulated social value is realized:

$$(v_a = t_b) + (t_b = r_b) + (r_b = s_a) = (s_a = v_a). \tag{4.2}$$

Reading from left to right, b recognizes a debt equal to a's social valuation ($v_a = t_b$), b returns a service equal to this debt ($t_b = r_b$), and a recognizes a satisfaction equal to this service ($r_b = s_a$). In other words, a receives satisfaction equal to a's social valuation ($s_a = v_a$). Once again, this equation represents the equilibrium form of this phase of the exchange cycle. If any of the first three equalities do not hold, such that s_a is not equal to v_a, the system is in disequilibrium. For example, if b renders a service of less value than the debt owed (i.e., if $t_b > r_b$) and the other equalities on the left hold, then the satisfaction received by a will be less than a's original social credit ($s_a < v_a$).

Equations (4.1) and (4.2) may be said to represent the equilibrium conditions for two-party transactions, whether the parties involved are individuals or social groups of some kind. In either case, the parties involved may at the same time be participants in a larger social system, and it is of interest to consider the equilibrium conditions of the system as a whole. According to Piaget, three general forms of equilibrium can be identified at the system level, resulting from the sum total of the values exchanged within the system.

The first of these forms of equilibrium at the level of the total system Piaget called *reciprocal beneficence*. This form of equilibrium results when the total satisfaction resulting from value exchanges is greater than the total costs. With r_A representing the total costs engendered by value exchanges within a given system A, s_A the total satisfaction produced by these exchanges, and so on, the equilibrium condition of reciprocal beneficence is represented in Piaget's model as follows:

$$(r_A < s_A) + (s_A = t_A) + (t_A = v_A) = (v_A > r_A).$$

The fact that the total costs of exchanges within the system are less than the total satisfactions produced by those exchanges ($r_A < s_A$) results in a valuation of the system that more than compensates for the costs of participating in it ($v_A > r_A$). Piaget called this surplus valuation of the system a form of mutual ''sympathy.'' The form taken by this mutual ''sympathy'' depends on the nature of the system. In a system constituted by an interpersonal relationship, this ''sympathy'' would be expressed in a mutual evaluation of the relationship as an end in itself. In the case of collective exchange, the social system as a whole acquires a positive valuation for the individuals or groups of which it is composed. In either case, the surplus valuation accorded to the system invests it with a high degree of stability, providing it with a cushion of tolerance capable of absorbing momentary fluctuations in the losses incurred by social agents engaging in value exchanges.

The second form of system equilibrium is the opposite of the first and occurs when total collective satisfactions are less than the total costs. Piaget called this condition *reciprocal devaluation* and represented it in his notation in the following manner:

$$(r_A > s_A) + (s_A = t_A) + (t_A = v_A) = (v_A < r_A).$$

The fact that the costs of participating in the system are greater than its satisfactions ($r_A > s_A$) results in a devaluation of the system and mutual antipathy among the participants ($v_A < r_A$). In contrast to the condition of mutual beneficence, reciprocal devaluation is naturally unstable and, left to itself, leads to the disintegration of the system. The integrity of the system can be maintained only by forces from without. Piaget illustrated this condition with the example of a marriage or a political alliance that is no longer satisfactory to the respective partners, but continues to exist because of external legal or political sanctions.

The third form of system equilibrium is midway between the first two. If collective satisfactions are equal to the collective costs, then the systems functions in a condition of *exact equilibrium*:

$$(r_A = s_A) + (s_A = t_A) + (t_A = v_A) = (v_A = r_A).$$

The partners to exchange recognize that their satisfactions are equal to their losses ($r_A = s_A$), and accordingly their valuation of the system is just sufficient to compensate the costs of participating in it ($v_A = r_A$). This form of equilibrium is stable as long as the various equalities are maintained. But because no surplus valuation of the system exists to absorb momentary fluctuations, the system is vulnerable to competing values that can result in momentary imbalances between losses and satisfactions.

Unless the integrity of the system is secured from without, instability or disequilibrium leads inevitably to a crisis of the system. In the case of society at large, Piaget described three types of social crises corresponding to three types of disequilibrium in relations of exchange between social classes. The first type of crisis results from an inequality in the satisfactions and losses incurred in exchanges between social classes. In effect, this inequality represents the exploitation of one class by another. The second type of crisis results from an inequality between the social valuation or status accorded to a given social class and the value of that class's actions for the society as a whole. The legitimacy of the social order and the hierarchy of values that it implies is called into question. The third type of social crisis is a combination of the first two and arises from both forms of disequilibrium at once. It is therefore most likely to lead to social and political revolution, characterized by a rupture in the existing scale of values.

Despite the formalism of this model, it does not presuppose a rational accounting of gains and losses by the participants involved. What Piaget apparently had in mind was that participants would have some general sense of the fairness of the overall system of exchange and would value the system accordingly. This sense of the fairness of the system would be based on their cumulative experience of exchange relations, but not on an exact accounting. According to Piaget, exact reciprocity is to be expected only in the case of certain purely economic transactions or in social exchanges governed by formal etiquette and ceremonial protocol. In general:

One never claims all of one's credit, nor pays all of one's debts. Instead, the circulation of social values rests on a vast credit, perpetually maintained, or rather constantly eroded by usury and neglect but constantly reconstituted, a credit that disappears only in the case of revolution or of grave social crisis, that is, in the case of the total devaluation of values recognized until then. [Piaget, 1965/1977a, p. 110]

Parent–child relations. Most of the examples with which Piaget illustrated this model are rather general and abstract, but two of them are of particular interest for showing how this model of social exchange is related to the rest of his work. The first example to be considered is the distinction between *unilateral* respect and *mutual* respect as described in *The moral judgment of the child.* In terms of parent–child relations, for example, unilateral respect is represented by a pair of equations expressing the child's relative overvaluation of the parent and the parent's relative undervaluation of the child with respect to their respective capacities for practical and moral judgment. The child's overvaluation of the parent is expressed as:

$$(r_a < s_b) + (s_b = t_b) + (t_b = v_a) = (r_a < v_a),$$

signifying, in effect, that a parental action (r_a) that is relatively inconsequential from an adult point of view may have great significance for the child (s_b). In the child's eyes, the parent thus acquires an authoritative value (v_a) greater than that actually merited by the original action. The parent's undervaluation of the child has just the opposite form:

$$(r_b > s_a) + (s_a = t_a) + (t_a = v_a) = (r_b > v_b),$$

meaning that a child's actions may have greater significance for the child than for the parent $(r_b > s_a)$ and that the parent therefore accords the child less authoritative value than the child's original action was actually worth in the general scale of values. To say that the parent undervalues the child of course refers only to relations of authority or respect (in Piaget's sense of the word) and does not imply that the child does not have great affective value for the parent.

Logical operations. The second application of Piaget's model of exchange is taken from the short essay entitled "Les opérations logiques et la vie sociale" from 1945. This paper is significant for what it implies about the relation between social exchange and individual cognition. It reveals unequivocally Piaget's belief in the irreducibly social origins of individual thought and provides a link between his earlier explanations of cognitive development in terms of the decline of egocentrism and his later emphasis on cognitive structures. What emerges from this essay is the essential continuity of the earlier and later work. Individual cognition is described as originating from out of the exchange of ideas.

Piaget began this paper by stating the problem in terms of a dialectical opposition. On the one hand, some sociologists like Durkheim have argued that society as a whole constitutes a more fundamental reality than its individual members. On the other side, Tarde and others have argued that society is only the sum of the actions and interactions of individuals. Piaget sought to transcend this opposition with a third point of view: "The primitive fact, according to this third point of view, is neither the individual, nor the group of individuals, but the relationship between individuals" (ibid., p. 146). Two extreme types of relationships between individuals can be identified, corresponding to reciprocity and constraint. The latter tends to reinforce the egocentrism of the individual and the "sociocentrism" of the group. As an example of this tendency, he cited Lévy-Bruhl's account of the "participations" and "prelogic" of the "primitive" mentality.

After a brief review of the course of individual cognitive development from the sensorimotor stage to formal operations, Piaget rephrased the question about the relationship between individual cognition and social interaction in the following manner: "If logic consists in an organization of operations, which are by definition interiorized actions that have become reversible, can one conceive that individuals come to such an organization by themselves? Or is the intervention of inter-individual factors necessary in order to explain the development we have just described?" (ibid., p. 155). In order to answer this question, Piaget first discussed the close correlation between the development of logical and social understanding. For every stage in the development of logic there is a corresponding advance in the child's capacity for understanding and cooperating with others. Moreover, this correlation would appear to be a necessary one, because the cognitive structures characteristic of concrete and formal operations do not consist merely of a grouping of physical actions, but also of possible viewpoints. "A 'grouping' is a system of concepts (classes or relations) implying a coordination of viewpoints and a sharing of thought" (ibid., p. 158). But this close correlation between logical thinking and social understanding does not yet clarify the direction of influence. Does logical development enable the child better to understand the viewpoints of others? Or does social development make some intrinsic contribution to the development of logic?

Once again, Piaget argued that phrasing the question in this way poses a false antithesis. In fact, logical and social development constitute "two indissociable aspects of one and the same reality, at the same time social and individual" (ibid.). This conclusion follows, first, because the coordination of actions between individuals (cooperation) has the same formal properties as the grouping of operations within the individual. "In sum, the social relations equilibrated in cooperation thus constitute 'groupings' of operations, just as all the logical actions exercised by the individual on the external world do, and the laws of groupings define the form of ideal equilibrium common to both of them" (ibid., p. 159). Second, the organization of operations on both the individual and collective planes involve the same reality, because individual cognition originates in the context of intellectual exchange. What Piaget apparently meant by this statement was that logical operations are structured in the same way *no matter who performs them;* the whole is the sum of the parts, whether the parts are added up by you or by me or by both of us together. For Piaget, cooperation is always co-operation.

Piaget spelled out the implications of this view of cognition as intellectual exchange in terms of his general model of social exchange as previously described in equations (4.1) and (4.2):

> In the case of exchanges of thought, which is all that interests us at the moment, the various terms and relations take the following signification: (1) The individual *a* states a proposition r_a (true or false in varying degrees); (2) the partner *b* assents (or dissents in varying degrees), this assent being represented by s_b; (3) the assent (or dissent) of *b* engages him for the succession of exchanges between *a* and *b*; (4) this engagement of *b* (t_b) confers a value or validity v_a (positive or negative) on the proposition r_a, that is, it renders it valid (or not) with respect to future exchanges between the same individuals. [ibid., p. 160]

The use of this model enabled Piaget to describe the equilibrium and disequilibrium forms of the exchange in a more precise form. In brief, disequilibrium may arise either from egocentrism or from constraint. In egocentrism, a failure in the coordination of viewpoints occurs. In effect, the participants to intellectual exchange do not agree on the values to be accorded to their respective propositions. In constraint, the obligations engendered by the process of exchange are unequal. One of the partners is held more accountable than the other.

In contrast, the equilibrium form of intellectual exchange is given in equations (4.1) and (4.2). Taken together, the equivalence between the statement of a proposition by agent *a* and the way it is understood by agent *b* ($r_a = s_b$), the equivalence between this understanding and *b*'s engagement ($s_b = t_b$), and the equivalence between this engagement and the enduring value attributed to the original proposition ($t_b = v_a$) imply the equivalence between the enduring value of that proposition and its meaning as originally intended ($v_a = r_a$). One can easily recognize in these equations an example of Grouping VI, the "addition of symmetrical relations." This formal analogy is the basis for Piaget's claim that the structure of social cooperation, like that of logical operations in general, has the formal properties of a grouping. For example, one of the chief properties of groupings is their reversibility. On the social level, such reversibility is represented in the reciprocity between the viewpoints of different individuals. In order to participate fully in social cooperation, individuals must be capable of coordinating the viewpoints of others with their own. But individual cognition also involves the coordination of different viewpoints. Solving class-inclusion problems, for example, involves seeing a certain collection of objects from one point of view as a single class and from another point of view as a totality of one or more subclasses.

In concluding the paper, Piaget returned to the original question: "Would an individual left to himself come to an equilibrium assuming the form of the grouping? Or is a cooperation with others necessary to this end?" Could the individual, in effect, "construct for himself a system of stable definitions, constituting what one might call a set of autoconventions?'' (ibid., p. 169). These questions were answered in the negative. The very construction of such a set of auto-conventions requires that the individual is to some extent able to coordinate different points of view. At the very least, one must be able to ''agree'' with oneself on the definitions to be employed. But such an agreement is only a form of interiorized social interaction. ''In short, in order to render the individual capable of constructing 'groupings,' it is necessary from the beginning to attribute to him all the qualities of the socialized person'' (ibid., p. 170).

The relation between social cooperation and logical thinking is not one-way. Cooperation itself presupposes a certain level of cognitive organization among the participants. In order to play an organized game, the players must know and understand the rules. In this sense, Piaget referred to the individual cognition and social organization as partaking of ''one and the same reality.''

CONCLUSION

In 1942, during the German occupation of France, Piaget was invited to give a series of lectures in the Collège de France in Paris. It was apparently a moving experience for him. He never referred to this occasion without a certain fervor. It was a time when ''university men felt the need to show their solidarity in the face of violence, and their fidelity to permanent values'' (Piaget, 1947/1950b, p. v). For him personally, it was an opportunity ''to bring to our French colleagues . . . testimony of the unshakable affection of their friends from outside'' (Piaget, 1952a, p. 254). In a preface to the text of these lectures published after the war, he avowed, ''It is difficult for me, as I rewrite these pages, to forget the welcome given by my audience, as well as the contact which I had at that time with my friends'' (Piaget, 1947/1950b, p. v). Although World War I had caused Piaget to question the values he had professed up until then, World War II was an occasion for reaffirming his faith in higher values. Characteristically, Piaget located these values in the domain of scientific research, of collaboration and solidarity with friends and colleagues.

The revised text of these lectures was published in 1947 under the title *The psychology of intelligence* (Piaget, 1947/1950b). This book was a summary and interpretation of his research and theory up to that point. But it was also something more. In this book more than in any of his previous works, he took the time to describe some of the questions that his theory was meant to answer and to compare his theory to other approaches in psychology and epistemology. In the process of reflecting on his work, he developed it further. In this book, for example, he began to use the phrase *structure d'ensemble* as a generic term referring to relational totalities in cognitive development. For this reason, it is fitting to conclude this chapter on structures-of-the-whole with a brief reference to this work.

As mentioned in chapter 3, the term *structure d'ensemble* was used in an incidental manner already in *The origins of intelligence*. The reader of *The psy-*

chology of intelligence, however, can almost perceive this term coming to be used in a technical sense in the course of the book. Piaget began this work much as he did *The origins of intelligence,* by describing intelligence as a form of adaptation of the individual to the environment. Theories of adaptation may be divided into two general classes: those that take the possibility of evolution into account and those that do not. Within each of these general classes, three sub-classes may be distinguished: (a) theories that emphasize factors external to the individual, (b) theories that emphasize innate or internal factors, and (c) theories that insist on the indissoluble interaction between internal and external factors. Piaget gave examples of each type of theory. Among "fixist" theories, (a) Platonic realism (like the early epistemology of B. Russell) emphasizes external factors in the form of eternal "Ideas" or universals existing outside the mind, (b) apriorism (like that of Kant) emphasizes the inherent organizing factors within the mind, and (c) "emergence" theories (like modern phenomenology or Gestalt psychology) argue for the "emergence" of new structures out of the interaction between internal and external influences. In this context, the notion of *structures d'ensemble* first appears in the book. According to Piaget, such "emergence" theories attribute adaptation to "the 'emergence' of complete structures [*structures d'ensemble*], irreducible to elements and determined simultaneously from within and from without" (ibid., p. 12). He described the structures of Gestalt psychology as *formes d'ensemble,* defined in terms of perceptual totalities irreducible to their respective elements.

With respect to "genetic" theories, (a) empiricism (like most theories of learning) emphasizes the role of external reality in the formation of knowledge, (b) the theory of groping (like that elaborated by Claparède) emphasizes the internal factors in the form of hypotheses generated by the individual and selected after the fact by the occurrence of success or failure, and (c) Piaget's own theory of operatory intelligence emphasizes the indissociable interaction of internal and external factors in the form of assimilation and accommodation. Like Gestalt theory, Piagetian theory postulates the existence of organized totalities that are irreducible to the elements of which they are composed. But while the *formes d'ensemble* of Gestalt theory are essentially static and based on perception, the structures of Piagetian theory are based on actions that have become interiorized and grouped into "complex systems" (*systèmes d'ensemble*) (ibid., p. 17). These systems are composed of operations, but they are not reducible to individual operations. Operations as such do not exist in isolation, but only as a part of such total systems:

Psychological reality consists of complex operational systems [*systèmes opératoire d'ensemble*] and not of isolated operations conceived as elements prior to these systems; thus, only in so far as actions or intuitive representations organise themselves in such systems do they acquire the nature of "operations" (and they acquire it by this very fact). [ibid., p. 36]

The foremost examples of such systems in Piagetian theory are the groupings of concrete operations. These groupings consist of various operations (classifications, seriations, etc.) that have been "grouped" together into total systems. Much of Piaget's theorizing with respect to concrete operations was devoted to descriptions of the formal properties of these groupings. As formal systems, these groupings are abstractions based on the concrete performances of the children observed by Piaget and his colleagues. But they correspond to a certain psychological reality, and this reality is what he now designated by the term *structures d'ensemble*:

> In the case of the qualitative systems peculiar to thought that is purely logical, such as simple classifications, matrices, series based on relations, family trees, etc., we shall call the corresponding complex systems [*systèmes d'ensemble*] "groupings." Psychologically, a "grouping" consists of a certain form of equilibrium of operations, i.e. of actions which are internalised and organised in complex structures [*structures d'ensemble*], and the problem is to describe this equilibrium both in relation to the various genetic levels which lead up to it and in contrast to forms of equilibrium characteristic of functions other than intelligence (perceptual or motor "structures", etc.). [ibid., pp. 36–37]

This double formal and functional character of *structures d'ensemble* has led to certain misunderstandings about their nature. Piaget considered his major task to lie in characterizing the *forms* of organization that these structures represent, and for the most part this task could be accomplished without reference to their specific content. This relative neglect of content has led to a widespread but mistaken assumption that he also believed operational structures to *function* in a content-free manner. As we have already seen in this chapter, he asserted form and content to be "inseparable" (at least at the level of concrete operations). *Structures d'ensemble* were viewed as the forms of organization particular to groupings of operations that were themselves imbued with specific content. Piaget's preoccupation with formal description followed from the questions he set out to answer, not from any radical ontological distinction between form and content.

One of the most explicit statements of Piaget's aims and methods relevant to this question comes toward the end of the first part of *The psychology of intelligence*. This passage is important not only as a statement of what Piaget seeks to explain but also as a description of the kind of explanation that is to be sought:

> The psychological explanation of intelligence consists in tracing its development and showing how the latter necessarily leads to the equilibrium we have described. From this point of view, the work of psychology is comparable to that of embryology, i.e. a work which, in the first instance, is descriptive and which consists in analysing the phases and periods of morphogenesis up to the final equilibrium constituted by adult morphology, but this study becomes "causal" once the factors which ensure the transition from one stage to the next have been demonstrated. [ibid., pp. 48–49]

Functionalist-minded psychologists would later reproach Piaget for being merely "descriptive" (Brainerd, 1978b), and indeed, most of his published research was devoted to a descriptive taxonomy and developmental ordering of children's forms of reasoning. But following the simile with embryology, one can argue that such descriptive classification and formal explanation is precisely what is called for at a preliminary stage of research. Later, Piaget would attempt to move to the stage of causal explanation in his theory of equilibration, to be discussed in chapter 6.

Subsequent chapters of *The psychology of intelligence* review Piaget's research on perception, sensorimotor development, and concrete operations. The book thus brings the story of his intellectual development up to the point reached at the end of the 1940s. The notion of *structures d'ensemble* had now become the central theoretic concept embodying the three basic ideas that he had pursued ever since *Recherche*: (a) His early *neo-pragmatism* was expressed in the idea that *structures d'ensemble* are formed from actions that have become interiorized as operations and grouped together. (b) The idea of *part–whole interaction* was reflected in the relation between a given operation and the total structure of which it is a part. (c) These structures were further characterized as forms of *equilibrium* among the constituent operations and the tendency toward ever greater forms of equilibrium as a factor contributing to development from one stage or level to another.

Piaget himself underscored the continuity between the concept of *structures d'ensemble* as it developed during the late 1940s and his earlier philosophical ideas. In the conclusion to his 1952 autobiography, he answered the question he had posed in the opening paragraphs. There, referring to the rediscovery of his adolescent philosophical writings, he had cited Bergson to the effect that "a philosophical mind is generally dominated by a single personal idea which he strives to express in many ways in the course of his life," adding that even if an autobiography does not succeed in conveying that idea to the reader, "it will at least have helped the author to understand it better himself" (Piaget, 1952a, p. 237). After having described his professional development up to that point, he was in a better position to articulate the "single idea" that had dominated his own intellectual development:

My one idea, developed under various aspects in (alas!) twenty-two volumes, has been that intellectual operations proceed in terms of structures-of-the-whole [*structures d'ensemble*]. These structures denote the kinds of equilibrium toward which evolution in its entirety is striving; at once organic, psychological and social, their roots reach down as far as biological morphogenesis itself. [ibid., p. 256]

In a few words, Piaget reaffirmed the centrality and continuity of the concept of structural wholes from his early philosophical speculations to his mature psychological theory. Equally significant is his statement that these structural totalities represent the forms of equilibrium toward which evolution tends in its entirety ("les types de l'equilibre vers lequel tend l'évolution tout entière" – Piaget, 1976a, p. 23). At one level, this phrase may simply be regarded as a restatement of his long-standing belief in equilibrium as a process capable of providing evolution and development with a nonteleological directionality. But the phrase "evolution in its entirety" suggests further that he had not abandoned his earlier belief in the continuity of life "at all levels" of organization and in the power of science to illuminate the great chain of becoming that links each level to the next.

5

The new science

In the preceding chapters of this book, Piaget's 1952 autobiography has served as a guide to his understanding of himself. This autobiography and the autobiographical narrative of *Recherche* have made it possible to trace the "inner development" of his ideas. The remaining chapters will follow this same strategy, drawing on Piaget's additions to his autobiography from 1966 and 1976 (Piaget, 1976a). These additions enable us to follow the development of his thought from his own point of view into the final decade of his life. The present chapter covers the period from about 1950 to 1966, and chapter 6 the years from 1967 onward.

In the autobiographical segment covering the years from 1950 to 1966, Piaget disposed of the external events occurring in his life in summary fashion. Between 1952 and 1963, he had taught developmental psychology at the Sorbonne, commuting back and forth between Paris and Geneva. He had been forced to give up this post eventually because of his increasing duties at the International Center for Genetic Epistemology, established at the University of Geneva in 1956 with support from the Rockefeller Foundation. His work at the center had involved him in numerous collaborative research projects and publications. At the same time, he had continued his active involvement in international and professional organizations such as UNESCO and the International Bureau of Education and served from 1954 to 1957 as the second president of the Union Internationale de Psychologie Scientifique.

Two themes dominated Piaget's account of these years. The first was his awareness of the criticisms raised from various quarters against his theories and interpretations. The second was his growing involvement in collaborative research at the Center for Genetic Epistemology.

Criticism was nothing new for Piaget. From the publication of his first books, his ideas had been the cause of controversy. For the most part, he believed that his early critics missed the point more or less entirely, and usually he had not bothered to reply in print in the belief that he would be justified by subsequent research. His more recent critics, however, generally did not dispute the facts reported in his books so much as his interpretations of those facts. In particular, his theory of *structures d'ensemble* had come under attack, along with the idea that such structures are progressively constructed at a pace that cannot be indefinitely accelerated.

One of Piaget's preferred methods of dealing with critics was to engage them in dialogue and thereby reach some mutual understanding. He cited his experiences with the French experimental psychologist P. Fraisse and the Dutch logician E. W. Beth as following this pattern. Such a method, however, had an obvious limitation: One can enter into direct dialogue only with so many critics at once. As a result, many criticisms had gone unanswered, especially those raised by geographically more distant commentators:

This leads us back to the problem of structures, the subject of the most frequent and most central of contemporary criticism, emanating, however, from authors in the U.S.A. and the U.S.S.R. whom I have had little occasion to see on a continued basis. The theses with which they oppose me are simple, and to my taste, much too simple: that thought consists in constructing images of objects and in directing or organizing these images according to verbal signs, language itself constituting an adequate description of things; that the activity of the subject thus amounts only to constructing faithful representations of reality; and consequently that nothing prevents one from accelerating at will this development by learning and social transmission to the point of skipping stages or of telescoping them into immediate acquisitions. From the pedagogical point of view, one will then call "optimistic" the perspective according to which the child can be taught anything at any stage, and I am considered a "pessimist" for maintaining that the child has need of structures that he constructs by his own activity in order to assimilate what one teaches him. [Piaget, 1976a, p. 27]

Citing Bruner as one of the few such critics with whom he actually had contact, Piaget expressed his surprise that the representatives of great countries such as the United States and the Soviet Union, each of which proposed to change the world, having constructed sputniks and planned voyages to the moon, should have such passive representations of the knowing subject. He would not have been surprised if an old-fashioned schoolmaster had considered "optimistic" the ideal of teaching students as much as possible in the shortest amount of time, but he could not understand how creative minds could be disquieted by the idea of attributing to each child the capacity for invention:

In short, taking operations and operatory structures seriously consists in believing that the subject can transform reality, whereas the primacy of images and language leads to a fundamentally conservative model of human intelligence. Is intelligence essentially invention or representation? Such is the problem: one cannot explain invention by the simple play of representations, when in fact these already imply an important part of active structuration. [ibid., p. 28]

According to Piaget, he had frequently been reproached for straying too frequently outside the bounds of psychology into the fields of logic and epistemology. On this point, he broached no compromise: "The decisive experience which I had had during the last decade, essentially in our Center for Genetic Epistemology, on the contrary convinced me of the necessity for interdisciplinary investigations and of their fruitfulness [*fécondité*] in solving problems which are specifically and authentically psychological" (ibid.). On the one hand, any psychological theory carried far enough would tend to overstep the boundaries of psychology as such. Bruner's approach, for example, opposed Piaget's structural hypotheses with an appeal to imagery, language, and communication among individuals, an approach that implied an eventual collaboration with neurology, linguistics, and sociology. On the other hand, Piaget wondered how a psychology of cognitive functions was at all possible without specific recourse to logical models and constant epistemological analysis. To argue that number is socially transmitted, for example, explained little: neither how children develop to the point at which they are capable of assimilating such social transmissions nor how number developed in the first place. But these were the very questions that interested Piaget. His view was that it had to be invented by someone before it could be socially transmitted and that every child's acquisition of number contains an element of invention or reinvention, even with all the social support provided by present-day education.

Interdisciplinary collaboration, however, does not imply that psychology should become reabsorbed by philosophy. In this connection, Piaget referred to his book *Insights and illusions of philosophy* (Piaget, 1965/1972b), in which he had attempted to define the boundaries separating philosophy from science. According to his view, the quest for objective *knowledge* belongs exclusively to science. The attempt to derive psychological knowledge from philosophical reflection is an illusion. To philosophy belongs instead the quest for *wisdom*, defined as the coordination of values.

This unremitting emphasis on interdisciplinary cooperation was embodied in the Center for Genetic Epistemology. In most research institutes, Piaget wrote, each investigator was specialized in a particular domain and pursued a line of research more or less independently:

The research organization that we have sought to attain consists on the contrary in choosing some common task before engaging the research staff for several years at a time. Each week, the investigators are brought together by B. Inhelder and myself for the clarification of techniques and results, with preliminary drafts of manuscripts for which I am generally responsible. The critique of these drafts by everyone is of use in additional controls and new projects. This procedure is repeated until the point at which one has the feeling that there is no longer anything new to be gained. [Piaget, 1976a, p. 33]

To judge from this autobiography, the establishment of the Center for Genetic Epistemology and the collaborative research that it engendered were the most important events in Piaget's professional life in the years from 1950 to 1966. In effect, they represented the fulfillment of a lifelong dream. In *Recherche,* Piaget had already forecast his plan for establishing a ''new science of genera'' aimed at pursuing the origins of knowledge through scientific methods. In fact, the new science of genetic epistemology as practiced at the center in Geneva was the concrete realization of this goal.

Piaget's praise of collaboration in this autobiographical essay might also be interpreted in this vein. In his early writings on religion (Piaget, 1928a, 1930), he came close to equating cooperation and collaboration with the Divine. From this perspective, his collaboration with colleagues from many disciplines at the Center for Genetic Epistemology could have taken on connotations of self-transcendence in the sense of feeling oneself to be a part of a greater totality. One can understand, from this point of view, the obvious care with which he undertook the otherwise tedious task of compiling and editing the discussions that took place at the weekly center meetings for publication in the early volumes of *Etudes d'épistémologie génétique* series. At one point in the autobiographical segment from 1950–1966, he suggested that his autobiography would better be termed a "symbiography" of all the persons who had been engaged in the work described (Piaget, 1976a, p. 26).

The final paragraphs of this autobiographical segment were devoted to an enumeration of some of the research projects carried out under the auspices of the center. Included among these were the studies of mental imagery (Piaget & Inhelder, 1966/1971), of learning and logical structures (Inhelder, Sinclair, & Bovet, 1974), of language and thought (Sinclair, 1967), and memory (Piaget & Inhelder, 1968/1973). He concluded by expressing the hope for a return to the study of causality in the near future.

In fact, the research mentioned by Piaget represented only a fraction of the work carried out at the Center for Genetic Epistemology during the years in question. Other research in addition to that mentioned in his autobiography is also discussed in this chapter, organized around the theme of genetic epistemology as a new science. The focus of attention will be Piaget's epistemological writings, especially the three-volume *Introduction à l'épistémologie génétique* (Piaget, 1950/1973a, 1950/1974a, 1950a) that in many ways could be considered his magnum opus. Piaget would revise and extend many of his basic epistemological ideas during the last three decades of his life, but he would never produce a more comprehensive exposition of those ideas than in this *Introduction*. The contents of these three volumes provide a constant background for his later works, and one could argue that his subsequent publications cannot be fully understood without some familiarity with the epistemology they presuppose. The fact that the *Introduction* has not been widely read is an important factor contributing to some widespread misconceptions of his epistemological theories (see chapter 8).

Among the epistemological works Piaget produced during this period were also some of his contributions to the first 20 volumes of the *Etudes d'épistémologie génétique*. Begun in 1957, this series of publications embodied the work conducted at the Center for Genetic Epistemology. Typically, each of these volumes was devoted to a particular theme and contained contributions by the various participants in the seminars at the center. These contributions included theoretical statements as well as reports of empirical studies. In addition, Piaget's own contributions to this series often included detailed accounts of arguments and comments voiced by the participants in the seminars during a given year. If the *Introduction* provides a broad background for all of his subsequent work, his contributions to the *Etudes*, at least during the first decade of publication, tended to be concerned with more detailed treatments of particular topics within the general framework of the theory as a whole. Accordingly, only those contributions that provided substantial comments on the major themes discussed in this book are reviewed in any detail.

Despite the centrality of the "new science" of genetic epistemology, Piaget did not limit himself to epistemological topics during the period in question. In addition, he wrote several theoretical works on operatory logic (Piaget, 1949/1972a, 1952b, 1957a) and together with B. Inhelder published several important books on the development of logical and mathematical thought in childhood and adolescence (Inhelder & Piaget, 1955/1958, 1959/1969; Piaget & Inhelder, 1951/1975). At the same time, research on other psychological topics was also pursued. In 1961, a summary volume entitled *The mechanisms of perception* (Piaget, 1961/1969) was published, drawing on the research in perception that he had pursued since the 1940s, and in 1966 *Mental imagery in the child* (Piaget & Inhelder, 1966/1971) appeared, bringing together a series of studies on mental images that he had conducted in collaboration with Inhelder. Following a review of these developments, this chapter closes with a glance at *Insights and illusions of philosophy* (1965/1972b), Piaget's most thorough statement of the boundaries between science and philosophy and his views of the tasks particular to each.

INTRODUCTION TO GENETIC EPISTEMOLOGY

Piaget's *Introduction à l'épistémologie génétique* was published in three volumes. The first (Piaget, 1950/1973a) was devoted to mathematical knowledge, the second (Piaget, 1950/1974a) to physical knowledge, and the third (Piaget, 1950a) to biological, psychological, and sociological knowledge. The first two volumes were reprinted in a second edition in 1973 and 1974, respectively, and the material contained in the third volume was extensively revised by Piaget and published separately. His mature thoughts on the epistemology of biology appeared in *Biology and knowledge* (Piaget, 1967/1971c), and his later ideas on the epistemology of psychology in *Main trends in psychology* (1972/1973c). His chapter on sociology from the third volume of the *Introduction* was reprinted unchanged in *Etudes sociologiques* (Piaget, 1965/1977a).

Despite the fact that Piaget revised some of the ideas expressed in the third volume of the *Introduction,* all three volumes of the original edition are of interest in tracing the development of his ideas. In the present section, the contents of the original work are reviewed, chapter by chapter. Emphasis will be placed on the new developments in Piaget's thinking rather than on restatements of theories or ideas already presented in his previous works.

Aims and methods of genetic epistemology

Piaget began the first volume of the *Introduction à l'épistémologie génétique* (Piaget, 1950/1973a) with a general introduction to the object and methods of genetic epistemology that is valuable for understanding Piaget's conception of both the aims and goals of genetic epistemology, as well as the means to be used in attaining those goals. This introduction opened with a discussion of the relation between philosophy and science. Traditionally, philosophy has taken as its object the whole of reality, including the reality of the mind, the reality outside the mind, and the relation between the two. In contrast, the sciences tend to address particular aspects of reality as represented by particular disciplines. This is not to say that the boundary between philosophy and science is completely fixed; on the contrary, Piaget repeated his previous statement that some of the greatest advances in the history of philosophy have resulted from reflection on developments in the sciences.

But the increasing specialization of the sciences has had the "catastrophic" effect that philosophy has come to be thought of as one kind of specialized knowledge among others. Thus, professional philosophers have tended to "reflect" on the nature of reality without having conducted any relevant research and without even having taken the empirical evidence into consideration. For example, the relevance of empirical research in psychology has often been overlooked or even denied in philosophical theories of perception.

In contrast to such pure speculation, Piaget argued that another tradition in philosophy must be considered: that of professional scientists who have reflected on the nature of knowledge in their own particular disciplines. He cited the debate in the early 20th century regarding the foundations of mathematics as a chief example of this latter tradition. The debate on mathematical epistemology was carried out for the most part by mathematicians themselves. Piaget pointed out that many of the greatest names in the history of philosophy either were scientists themselves (Leibniz, Descartes) or were directly affected by the science of their time (Plato, Kant). Descartes, who not only is known as the father of modern philosophy but was also the founder of analytic geometry, even went so far as to limit himself to 1 day per month for philosophical speculation. Genetic epistemology resembles this latter approach in its attempt to trace the development of the mind and its relation to reality in the context of specific areas of science.

Piaget argued further that every attempt to discern the nature of the mind or of reality presupposes a theory of the relation between them: a theory of how the mind can come to know reality. This problem is complicated by the fact that there are many forms of knowing, represented by the various sciences. The problem of knowledge can be solved only by examining particular forms of knowing. Genetic epistemology proposes to examine these forms of knowing from the perspective of their development in time. The question to be addressed is the following: "How did the scientific thought at work in the cases to be considered . . . proceed from a state of lesser knowledge to a state of knowledge judged to be superior?" (ibid., p. 18).

Implied in this question are two assumptions fundamental to the notion of genetic epistemology. The first is the idea of a sequence of states or levels of knowledge, each one successively more adequate than the one that preceded it. The second is that one must begin by considering each science as a specific case. It may happen that there are certain formal analogies among the levels of knowledge to be found in different sciences or that the processes leading from one level to another are also similar in each case. But one has no way of knowing

Table 5.1. *Classification of theories of knowledge*

Relation between subject and object	Nongenetic theories	Genetic theories
Primacy of the object	Realism	Empiricism
Primacy of the subject	Apriorism	Pragmatism and conventionalism
Indissociability between subject and object	Phenomenology	Relativism

Source: Piaget (1950/1973a, p. 31).

this before the different sciences themselves are examined. The attempt to investigate the actual development of scientific knowledge makes genetic epistemology itself a science with its own distinctive subject matter. It may be thought of as a science of a second order in the sense that its subject matter is scientific knowledge itself.

The development of scientific knowledge may be traced either in history (the historico-critical method) or in the lives of individuals (the psychogenetic method). Piaget described these two methods as complementary. On the one hand, the development of scientific knowledge in the lives of individuals is influenced by the historical conditions under which they live. On the other hand, the psychogenetic method may provide information about certain elementary levels of knowing that are inaccessible to the historico-critical method, and for this very reason the processes leading from one level of knowing to another may be more apparent in psychogenesis than in history. Moreover, the way in which individuals can be influenced by the historical conditions in which they find themselves is itself a function of the developmental level they have attained at the time. Although the genetic method may take both historical development and psychological development as its subject matter, the primary innovation of genetic epistemology is its use of psychogenesis as a key to the development of knowledge.

One might think that the methods of genetic epistemology are theoretically prejudiced insofar as they assume from the start that knowledge does in fact develop. Piaget took pains to argue that that was not the case. In fact, even nongenetic theories of knowledge could be verified by the genetic method if they were true. By cross-classifying genetic versus nongenetic theories of knowledge with theories that emphasized the primacy of the object, the subject, or the indissociability of the two, Piaget arrived at the types of epistemologies shown in Table 5.1. This classification corresponds to the six possible views of the relation between the organism and the environment as described in *The psychology* of *intelligence,* reviewed in chapter 4. This time, these six possible views are presented exclusively in their epistemological aspect, rather than in biological or psychological terms. Among the nongenetic theories, *realism* is the view that "universals" exist outside the mind in the form of transcendent ideas (Platonic realism) or immanent within things themselves (Aristotelian realism). Knowledge originates from the direct intuition of these universals. In the 20th century this theory has been represented by mathematical "Platonism," the view that mathematical entities exist independent of the human mind and that new mathematical truths are discovered through the direct intuition of these entities rather than through invention or construction. The second nongenetic theory is Kantian *apriorism,* according to which experience is conceived as being organized in particular ways by the structure of the mind itself. In contrast to realism, apriorism finds the basis of knowledge within the mind rather than outside it. This theory is considered nongenetic, because the organizing structure of the mind is conceived of as fixed, rather than as having a developmental history. The third nongenetic theory is represented by Husserl's *phenomenology,* according to which knowledge is the result of intentional acts of the mind that are necessarily and essentially directed toward an object. Thus, neither the subject nor the object is given predominance over the other, but neither does development have any intrinsic role in the act of knowing.

Piaget argued that only the study of development can determine if knowledge can arise *without* development according to one or the other of these three nongenetic theories. For example, if the intuition of mathematical truths were found to occur without reference to or dependence on the subject's previous constructions, then this would constitute evidence for a nongenetic theory of mathematical knowledge. Such evidence, however, could be generated only if the constructions of the subject were actually studied.

For the genetic theories of knowledge listed in Table 5.1, genetic methods are obviously appropriate. Only the study of the relations between subject and object over time can determine whether knowledge of the object originates from the imprint of the object on a passive subject according to *empiricism,* whether the subject models reality as a function of its own activity according to *pragmatism* (or as a function of pure intellectual construction according to *conventionalism*), or whether such knowledge arises from the indissociable interaction between subject and object across time, as argued by *relativism.* Piaget's own theory of intellectual development is clearly a form of "relativism" in this sense (Brunschvicg's historico-critical relativism being another exemplar of this category). But he took pains to show that the result of applying the genetic method was not prejudiced by the method itself. The very fact that the genetic method seeks to explain the nature of knowledge by observing its formation confronts it with the problem of the relation between the possible and the real. Normative knowledge, whether in the field of mathematics, logic, or the empirical sciences, appears to comprehend more possibilities than have been realized up to that time. According to Piaget, this problem is not confined to epistemology, but is also found in biology:

Embryological development today appears as a choice among an ensemble of potential forms infinitely richer than the forms effectively produced. Likewise, every mental equilibrium (perceptual, operatory, etc.) rests upon a play of possibilities which surpasses, to a greater and greater extent in the course of development, real actions or movements. [ibid., p. 36]

Nongenetic theories of knowledge tend to explain the real in terms of the possible. That is, the subject's existing knowledge is explained in terms of the intuition of preexisting forms, categories, universals, or "essences" that contain in themselves all the known possibilities. Indeed, the fact that knowledge often appears to extend beyond what has previously been experienced is one of the arguments advanced in favor of realist and apriorist epistemologies. For methodological reasons, however, the genetic approach is constrained from explaining the real in terms of preexisting possibilities – unless it can be shown through independent evidence that the subject reflexively situates the present reality within a preexisting system of possibilities. If such a system cannot be shown to precede the subject's past actions, then it must be concluded that the system was constructed from those actions (ibid., p. 40). In this context, the concept of equilibrium may take on an important explanatory function.

As understood by Piaget, any equilibrium is based on a certain form of reversibility in the sense that any deviation from equilibrium will tend to be compensated by an equal and opposite reaction returning the system in question to its equilibrium state. One cannot assume that all possible reactions are preprogrammed into the system; this would imply that the system could anticipate all the possible deviations in equilibrium that could possibly occur, in effect, that it had perfect knowledge of its environment and all the possible disturbances of equilibrium that the latter might incur. But such perfect preknowledge is impossible. At least in the case of biological systems, one can never assume that organisms possess perfect knowledge of their environments from the beginning, nor that they are preprogrammed to react in particular ways to all of the environmental disturbances that could possibly arise. Rather, the equilibrium of the system functions as an "attractor"; deviations from equilibrium are relatively unstable and tend to revert of themselves to the equilibrium state. Thus, one may argue that a system in equilibrium comprehends many more possible actions or reactions than will ever be realized in the actual history of that system.

Piaget further recognized the stability of equilibria as a relative term. Some forms of equilibrium are more stable than others. Development is in fact characterized by a succession of forms of equilibrium, each more stable or reversible than the last. To say that a system has become more reversible or more stable is to say that the range of possibilities that it comprehends has increased. Moreover, the actions of some systems can engender new possibilities beyond those actions that have hitherto been realized in fact. Such creation of new possibilites occurs, for example, in systems consisting of reversible compositions. In such systems, for any two actions A and B there exists a third action C' capable of reversing A and B taken together and thereby returning the system to its starting point before A and B were performed. Thus, the action C' is a possibility belonging to the system, even when only A and B have in fact been realized. C' is a possibility constructed from the composition of A and B. In general, to any set

X of realized actions there corresponds a set Y of possible actions resulting from the total possible compositions among the actions of X. In this sense, new possibilities are constructed from the actions that have already been realized at any given moment.

The business of genetic epistemology is in fact to identify the series of states characterizing the development of a given science and to establish the law of succession between them. But this raises a problem: Genetic epistemology is itself a science in development. From what privileged point of view is the genetic epistemologist to study the evolution of other sciences?

In effect, the geneticist or the historian studies a series of stages A, B, C, . . . , X, of which he establishes the law of evolution and the eventual limit. But in order to do this, he is obliged to choose a system of reference, which will be constituted by reality such as it is given in the state of scientific knowledge considered at the moment of his analysis and by the instruments of rationality such as they are given in the state in which logic and mathematics are elaborated at the same moment in history. But this system of reference is itself in motion. [ibid., p. 44]

The genetic epistemologist traces the development of a given science up to its current point of development from the point of view of the researcher's own knowledge at *its* current point in development. Future developments in both are, of course, possible.

This relativity of perspective does not solve the whole problem of the frame of reference. Genetic epistemology uses psychology, among other tools, in reconstructing the developmental history of a particular science. But psychology is a science among others. Psychological knowledge might itself be viewed from the standpoint of that other science. Which point of view takes precedence?

In answering this question, Piaget introduced a notion to which he would repeatedly return in his epistemological writings: the idea of the "circle of sciences." Psychology sooner or later must base itself on the findings of biology. Biological explanation, in turn, tends to be completed in explanations based on physics and chemistry. But physical theory is based on mathematical explanation, which in turn rests once again (by way of genetic epistemology) on psychology. Thus, the different forms of scientific explanation compose a closed circle. Progress in each domain sooner or later affects all the others. The sciences evolve together, and no final level in the description of reality exists that is fundamental.

From this point of view, one may distinguish between "restricted" and "generalized" approaches to genetic epistemology. In the restricted approach, the evolution of a particular science is traced independent of the others up to its current stage of development. The frame of reference is given; it is the state of scientific knowledge existing at the moment. The development of one science can be traced from the viewpoint of each of the others. In the generalized approach, the evolution of the circle of sciences is considered as a whole. But the circle of sciences encompasses the frame of reference; the latter can no longer be distinguished from the object of investigation. The frame of reference is itself viewed as evolving and as "open" toward the future. The question is how to maintain the objectivity of the genetic method under these conditions.

Piaget answered this question by describing two "precautions" for a generalized genetic epistemology. First, one cannot assume that the direction of development of the sciences is determined in advance. The results of epistemological investigation may suggest some directionality in development, but such directionality cannot be assumed a priori. Second, the evolution of the sciences as investigated by a generalized genetic epistemology cannot be projected into the future. Genetic epistemology is essentially a reflection on scientific progress; it is descriptive, rather than prescriptive or predictive. Its descriptive character does not preclude the finding of some "orthogenetic" principle underlying the development of scientific knowledge, but the manifest results of such a principle can be known only after the fact.

The image of the circle of sciences suggests the immediate tasks faced by genetic epistemology. Because psychology is the principal tool of the genetic method, the relations between psychology and its neighboring disciplines in the circle (i.e., mathematics and biology) are especially problematic. With respect to mathematics, the question is how the *contingent* facts of psychological development are related to the *necessary* facts of logic and mathematics. Psychological development and psychological processes all occur in time, whereas mathematical and logical truths are atemporal. Yet insofar as logico-mathematical operations are carried out in the minds of psychological subjects, some relation between the two must exist. With respect to biology, the question is how the mental phenomena studied by psychology are related to biological processes. Again, two dissimilar levels of description are apparently involved, but the two levels are necessarily related insofar as thinking beings are also biological organisms. In one form or another, Piaget continued to pursue these two questions in his epistemological writings throughout the rest of his life.

Mathematical knowledge

Having addressed the general question of the aims and methods of genetic epistemology, Piaget continued the first volume of *Introduction à l'épistémologie génétique* with chapters on the construction of number, the construction of space, and the relation between mathematics and reality. In a brief introduction to this section of the book, he stated the main problems to be considered in the genetic approach to mathematical knowledge as follows: How does one explain the generativity [*fécondité*] of mathematics and at the same time its manifest correspondence with reality? On the one hand, mathematical activity leads to new results that continually surpass experience, even if they were originally based on experience (e.g., experiences of counting, measuring, etc.). On the other hand, even the new results that surpass experience often later turn out to conform to or to predict certain aspects of the physical universe. Piaget cited the "discoveries" of non-Euclidean geometries or imaginary numbers as examples.

These questions are the classical questions of mathematical epistemology. They are also among the questions that Piaget had pursued in his studies of the development of mathematical concepts. But although such questions had remained in the background in his psychological studies, they now became the main focus of attention.

The construction of number. Piaget began the chapter on number with a brief review of some empiricist theories of number. According to Mach, number results from a prolongation of the activity of counting into a "mental experience." According to Rignano, mathematical reasoning is a sequence of operations or experiences carried out in thought. According to Helmholtz, the knowledge of number can be traced to an intuition of the order of succession of the subject's own states of consciousness. Against these theories, Piaget asserted that two types of "mental experience" can be distinguished, corresponding to two different types of abstraction. The first type of mental experience consists simply of imagining some aspects of external reality as it exists outside the subject. This sort of mental imagery is analogous to perception, except that it is initiated by the subject instead of by the action of reality on the sensory organs. Corresponding to this type of experience is what Piaget called *physical abstraction,* which is little more than a simple generalization. By virtue of some physical quality perceived in the object (e.g., its whiteness), the latter is recognized as belonging to a particular class (the class of white objects). The second type of mental experience consists of imagining actions carried out by the subject with respect to physical objects. This is also a form of mental imagery, but it is analogous to reflection on the subject's own activity rather than to perception. Corresponding to this latter type of experience is *reflective abstraction,* another concept that would occupy an increasingly important place in Piaget's epistemology. In contrast to physical abstraction, reflective abstraction is no mere generalization, but a new construction on a higher developmental level. To reflect on one's own activity is to represent that activity to oneself. Such cognitive representation is also an action of sorts, but of a different kind than the action represented. In fact, as Piaget's psychological research showed, cognitive representation belongs to a higher developmental level than action or sensorimotor activity as such. Through a process of reflective abstraction, concrete operations are derived from reflection on cognitive representations, formal operations from reflection on concrete operations, and so on.

Piaget argued that number cannot be derived through a process of physical abstraction from the experience of objects, real or imagined, because number is not a property of physical objects. Number can result only from reflection on the operations that the subject is capable of performing on physical objects. In this sense, Piaget argued for an *operatory* theory of number. This theory has been presented in chapter 4 and need not be reviewed again here. What is significant in the present context is how Piaget contrasted and compared his own theory of number with the classical theories of mathematical epistemology. Following his typical dialectic expository style, he presented his own theory as a *tertium* between the logicism of Russell and Whitehead and the intuitionism of Brouwer and Poincaré.

Piaget's criticism of Russell's attempt to define the cardinal and ordinal aspects of number in terms of the logic of classes and the logic of relations, respectively, was also touched on in chapter 4. The attempt to define a given number *n* as the class of all classes having exactly *n* members presupposes what it attempts to explain. A class is properly defined in terms of the quality or qualities that the members of that class have in common. The problem in determining the relation between mathematics and logic is to specify the nature of the relation between quantity and quality. But in Russell's approach, quantity already enters into the definition of the "class of all classes having a given number of members" from which number (quantity) is supposed to be derived.

Against the intuitionist view that number is derived from the pure intuition that a unity can be added to a collection of unities (Poincaré), Piaget argued that this view adds nothing to the operatory theory of number. The intuition described still presupposes the operations of reunion and seriation. Adding a unity to a collection presupposes the operation of reunion, and distinguishing the various unities from each other presupposes the operation of ordering or seriation. Piaget cited his developmental data to the effect that number develops in children only when they have also developed the requisite logical structures.

Thus, Piaget advanced his own operatory theory of number against both logicist and intuitionist theories. Number results from an operatory synthesis of the logic of classes and the logic of relations, that is, of groupings involving classification and seriation. Number is found to be closely related to logic without being reducible to it. Both the cardinal and ordinal aspects of number depend on this synthesis of classes and relations. The difference between cardinality and ordinality is a difference of perspective; they reflect the synthesis, as it were, from different perspectives. At the same time, number is not derived from an irreducible intuition. Rather, the intuition of number is possible only after the synthesis of classes and relations has occurred.

This synthesis or "fusion" of classes and relations as thus far described leads only to the series of whole numbers. The rest of the chapter on number was devoted to a demonstration of how negative numbers, fractions, and irrational and imaginary numbers developed according to the operatory theory. For Piaget, these further developments in number theory made it even clearer that number originates in abstraction from the subject's operations rather than from abstraction from objects. Neither zero nor the negative numbers would have been recognized as numbers if number were abstracted from objects. As long as only discontinuous objects are counted, the number series can only be positive and can begin only with 1. Once the operations of addition and subtraction are interpreted as movements in different directions, and numbers as points on a line, then the positive and negative numbers may be intuitively understood as series extending in opposite directions from a given point of origin.

Piaget showed how the development of ever more powerful or inclusive conceptions of number derives from the generalization of operations that were limited or constrained in the previous conceptions. Their intuitive representations (such as the positive and negative numbers as points on a line) come later, almost as rationalizations after the fact. In the series of positive whole numbers, for example, the operation of subtraction is the inverse of addition. Although addition has unlimited application, certain cases of subtraction are ruled out: No number can be subtracted from a number smaller than itself. The construction of the series of positive and negative numbers removes the limitation on subtraction by generalizing the operations of addition and subtraction, and the symmetry or equilibrium between them is thereby restored. Within the series of whole numbers, the operation of division is similarly constrained: No number can be divided by another number unless the first is a whole multiple of the second. In the series of real numbers, this limitation is overcome by a generalization of the operations of multiplication and division. This generalization is intuitively grasped by representing the series of real numbers as points on a line.

This process of operatory generalization followed by intuitive representation is even more obvious for irrational and imaginary numbers. In both cases, a limitation on the operation of taking the square root is involved, and in both cases the intuitive representation remained problematic long after the operatory generalization was made. In the series of rational numbers (all numbers that can be expressed as a ratio of two whole numbers), the operation of taking the square root has no solution when applied to certain integers, for example, $\sqrt{2}$. This limitation was overcome by recognizing the existence of irrational numbers that cannot be expressed as a ratio of whole numbers. But the question remained how to represent such numbers intuitively in terms of the real-number line, given that every point on that line is a rational number. This question persisted long after the existence of irrational numbers was recognized. One answer was provided by Dedekind, who suggested that irrational numbers could be defined in terms of "cuts" between points on the real-number line. This solution is still controversial (Kline, 1972).

Another limitation on square roots in the real-number system is that they cannot be applied to negative numbers. Within the limits of this system, the expression $\sqrt{-1}$ has no meaning. This limitation was overcome by postulating the existence of *imaginary numbers* – numbers that, when squared, yielded negative numbers. These numbers were called "imaginary" because, as Euler put it, "they exist only in the imagination" (Kline, 1972, p. 594). Some steps toward an intuitive definition of imaginary numbers were taken already in the 17th century by Wallis, who proposed that such numbers could be represented on an axis that runs perpendicular to the real-number line. The operation of multiplying a number by $\sqrt{-1}$ thus took on the meaning of a 90° rotation in the plane so formed.

These operatory generalizations in number theory provide a good example of what Piaget meant by the term "reflective abstraction." As opposed to physical abstraction, which involves the mere classification of an object in a more general class based on one (or more) of its properties, the generalization characteristic of reflective abstraction is *constructive*. In generalizing the operation of subtraction beyond the whole numbers, for example, a whole new class of numbers (i.e., the negative numbers) was constructed. This capacity for generalizing one's own operations is the basis for the generativity of mathematics.

Such an explanation of the generativity of mathematics still leaves open the second central question of mathematical epistemology – the question of the relation between mathematics and reality. If mathematics develops through the constructive activity of the subject, why should the products of this construction tend to agree with reality? Piaget's answer was that operations are derived from actions, and therefore the generalization of operations can lead only to ever greater sets of possible actions. Some of these possible actions, though perhaps not all, will be capable of realization in the appropriate physical context. Thus, even such abstract mathematical entities as imaginary numbers have found physical applications in the theory of relativity, some hundreds of years after their adoption in mathematics. According to Piaget, this capacity of mathematics to ''anticipate'' reality is possible because mathematics is derived from generalizations of operations conceived as interiorized actions accommodated to reality, rather than from the particular properties of physical objects.

The construction of space. Piaget began the chapter on space with a brief review of previous theories of the origins of the understanding of space and geometry. Once again he found that these previous theories could be classified according to the sixfold scheme shown in Table 5.1. Among those advocating nongenetic theories, for example, the early Russell had argued that the truths of geometry represent an analytic a priori and as such are comparable to the universals of logical thought. Because this theory leaves no room for the constructions of the subject, it is used in Piaget's scheme as an example of a nongenetic theory that asserts the primacy of the object. In contrast, Hilbert characterized axiomatic geometry as the result of the free construction of the subject, relying on a ''preestablished harmony'' to explain the congruence between this free construction and physical space. The nongenetic interactionist position is represented by phenomenological interpretations of geometric construction as the expression of rational intuition.

With respect to genetic theories, the empiricist approach is represented by a number of authors who sought to explain geometry in terms of progressive abstraction from physical experience, especially of a sensory or perceptual nature. The primacy of the subject is represented by Poincaré's ''conventionalism'' and the nominalism of the logical positivists. Finally, the genetic interactionist approach is represented in a partial form by Enriques and Gonseth and is developed fully in Piaget's own operatory theory.

In the rest of the chapter, Piaget considered these various positions in the context of outlining the ontogenesis of space from pure perception to formal operations. He began by showing how the controversy between ''nativism'' and ''empiricism'' arose when psychologists like Müller, Helmholtz, Hering, Wundt, and others sought to decide between classical empiricism and Kantian apriorism by appeal to the facts of psychology. Whereas nativists explained the intuition of space in terms of hereditary perceptual structures, empiricists sought an explanation in terms of abstractions from perceptual experience. Piaget argued that any attempt to explain geometric knowledge by appeal to perception, whether in the form of inherited perceptual structures or by abstraction from perceptual experience, founders on the fact that perceived space differs in fundamental ways from space as conceived in geometry.

These differences may be summarized by saying that perceptual space and geometric space are characterized by different forms of equilibrium. Perceptual structures are only partially reversible, but the operations characterizing geometry as a science achieve complete reversibility. For example, two lengths A and B may be perceived as equal, and B may further be perceived as equal to C. However, A and C may be perceived as unequal. In other words, the differences between A and B and B and C are subliminal, whereas the difference between A and C is not. At an operational level, however, the two ''premises'' $A = B$ and $B = C$ *necessarily* imply that $A = C$. In Piaget's words, perception involves ''noncompensated transformations,'' but geometric operations are fully compensated. The compositions characteristic of perception are nonadditive, but those characterizing geometric operations are completely additive.

A further consequence of this difference involves the relations between parts and wholes at the two levels. ''The rule in the domain of perceptual organization is . . . the deformation of the parts as a function of the totality'' (Piaget, 1950/1973a, p. 166). Perceptual illusions, for example, result from deformations of this kind. Certain lengths are overestimated or underestimated because of their relations to other lengths within a total configuration. At the operatory level, however, there exists ''an interdependence between the parts and the whole, that is, the fact that the element could not exist without the totality as well as the reverse'' (ibid., p. 169). This latter type of totality is characteristic of group and grouping structures. ''In the 'group' of displacements, for example, a particular displacement could only be defined as a function of the ensemble'' (ibid.). This ''interdependence'' between an operatory structure and its component parts is another echo of the forms of equilibrium between the parts and the whole in *Recherche*.

These two types of part–whole equilibrium, however, tend to be confused by theorists attempting to trace geometry back to perceptual experience. Gestalt psychology, for example, attempts to explain both the ''good forms'' of geometry and perceptual illusions with the same set of principles. In fact, the first involves additive compositions, and the second nonadditive. This fundamental difference between the two levels renders any purely empiricist theory of geometry highly problematic. The appeal to perceptual experience cannot explain how structures characterized by additive composition derive from structures that are nonadditive. In fact, perceptual information is meaningful to the subject only in terms of the latter's real or possible actions, and for this reason conceptions of space in geometry cannot be derived simply from perceptual experience. "Far from being more real than intellectual space, sensory space rests only on indices of reality and not upon its immediate expression, and these indices are translated into knowledge – even a simply perceptual knowledge – only by the intermediary of a sensorimotor activity that passes straightaway beyond what is perceived and has recourse to the motor functions" (ibid., p. 181).

This line of thinking led Piaget to a consideration of sensorimotor space. Perceptual space is limited to the relations existing among elements perceived within each successive centration without any general coordination between these successive fields, but sensorimotor space allows some general coordination between the fields perceived in these successive centrations. For example, an object may be followed through successive displacements. In this connection, Piaget acknowledged his debt to Poincaré for the latter's insight that the spatial displacements that an individual is capable of carrying out in action have the structure of a mathematical group. That is, each individual displacement is part of a total structure that is the group of displacements taken as a whole. But Poincaré was criticized for his belief that the general concept of a group "pre-exists" in our minds as a potential reality (ibid., p. 184). Piaget cited his own research on sensorimotor development as evidence both for the essential role attributed by Poincaré to the group of displacements and against the alleged innateness of the group concept. The facts of development as described in *The construction of reality in the child* suggest that, far from being innate, the group of displacements is constructed only gradually by the infant. According to Piaget, the development of the understanding of space is thus to be explained neither through abstraction from perception nor by appeal to innate structures of action. Like number, space is progressively constructed.

But what is the relation of this sensorimotor space to the abstract space defined by the axioms of geometry? For Poincaré, axiomatic space was a "conventional" construction that originated in the practical space of sensorimotor activity but subsequently freed itself from these humble origins. The overall agreement between axiomatic space and physical space was the result of a progressive adjustment between the intuitions of the mind and the facts of experience (ibid., pp. 194–195). For Hilbert, on the other hand, axiomatic geometry was a purely logical and a priori construction, and the agreement between axiomatic and physical space could be explained only through a "pre-established harmony" between human intuitions and reality (ibid., pp. 195ff.).

Again, the results of the genetic method provide an alternative solution. Piaget's research on the development of the understanding of space revealed three general stages between sensorimotor space and axiomatic space. First, an *intuitive* stage results from the interiorization of imitative action. The fact that these actions are not yet composable among themselves gives this stage a decidedly static character. In the stage of *concrete operations,* these interiorized actions become subject to reversible compositions. That is, they become operations as such, but they as yet apply only to concrete, manipulable objects. At the level of *formal operations,* geometric space is expressible in terms of propositions, the content of which is still imagined. According to Piaget, the geometry of Euclid's *Elements* belongs to this stage (ibid., p. 198). Moreover, *all* of these three stages would be considered "intuitive" in the sense in which mathematicians use the term, in contrast to axiomatic geometry. The latter thus represents a level of reflective abstraction *beyond* formal operations. "In effect, one could say that axiomatic schemas are to formal schemes what the latter are to concrete operations" (ibid., p. 226). Unlike the "pseudo-axiomatics" of Euclid and classical geometry, according to which axioms were understood as intuitively self-evident propositions, the axioms of contemporary geometry are severed from any intuitive justifications and are chosen for their deductive consequences.

Piaget concluded the chapter on space with a discussion of the relations between the knowledge of number, knowledge of physical reality, and knowledge of space. This discussion is of interest for Piaget's thinking about the specificity of development in these three areas. The difference between number and physics reduces to the distinction between the two types of abstraction described earlier, the one proceeding from the coordinations among actions as such (reflective abstraction), and the other from the objects that are acted on (physical abstraction).

In brief, logic and number are due to coordinations of the subject's actions as such and are not extracted from the object, even if it is only upon the occasion of acting upon objects that these coordinations become manifest. . . . In contrast to this general coordination of actions, physical knowledge is due to differentiated and particular actions: actions of weighing in one's hand, of pushing, of accelerating, of slowing down, etc. And the elements of knowledge are abstracted from the objects upon which these actions bear (it being understood that these objects are known only by means of their assimilation to these actions). [ibid., p. 253]

Both logico-mathematical and physical abstractions occur in the context of acting on objects, and this fact ensures that they remain closely related. Nevertheless, they should not be confounded with each other, for reflective abstractions originating from the general coordination of actions are not based on specific accommodations to the properties of objects acted on, but physical abstractions originating from particular actions (e.g., weighing) are necessarily based on accommodations to the properties of objects relevant to those actions (e.g., weight).

Since action always bears upon objects, the most general coordinations of actions, once they have become susceptible to reversible compositions, result in a permanent accommodation to a generalized object [*l'objet quelconque*]. This stable accommodation is distinguished from particular accommodations, insofar as the coordinations among actions differ from those actions considered in their diversity. [ibid., p. 255]

The question remains how geometric knowledge is related to logico-arithmetical and physical knowledge. According to Piaget, the knowledge of space, like that of number, is derived from the general coordination of actions, with this difference: Logico-mathematical operations of inclusion and ordering are based

on the similarities and differences among objects, but spatial inclusions and ordering are based on proximity between the parts of a single "object," or configuration (ibid., p. 255). Such relations of proximity (in space or in time) form the
basis of Piaget's distinction between logical and infralogical operations. Certain
physical operations (e.g., movements, displacements) also involve relations of
spatial proximity. Physical space can be distinguished from mathematical space,
depending on whether it pertains to physical operations involving spatial proximity or to the general coordinations among such operations.

> Alongside mathematical space due to the coordinations of the subject himself, there arises
> a physical space or experiential space bearing upon objects differentiated by their distinc-
> tive characteristics. In other words, among several forms elaborated thanks to the activity
> of the subject, some can be more suitable than others for such a system of specific objects
> determined by their physical properties, that is, by the particular actions applied to those
> objects (as opposed to the general coordinations of actions). [ibid., p. 256]

This brings us back to the question of the *relation* between mathematical space
and physical space. According to Piaget, these two systems converge insofar as
they both originate by abstraction from physical actions involving spatial proximity, even though two different types of abstraction are involved that proceed
in different directions. "This convergence is obvious, since we only know physical objects by means of the particular actions exerted upon them . . . and since
the general coordinations of action which engender mathematical space will always be in accord with these particular actions, even in surpassing them" (ibid.,
p. 258). As in the case of number, the agreement between geometry and reality
is guaranteed by the fact that both mathematical knowledge and physical knowledge have a common origin in actions exerted on physical objects.

Mathematics and reality. In the last chapter of the first volume of the *Introduction,* Piaget returned to the question of the agreement between mathematics and
reality. How can mathematics, apparently proceeding from the imaginative constructions of the subject, lead to new results that are nevertheless found after the
fact to agree with objective reality? His approach in this chapter was to follow
the historical evolution of mathematics from the age of classical Greece to the
present. His aim was to show that this evolution can be characterized as a growing awareness (*prise de conscience*) of the essential role of operations in mathematical constructions.

Greek mathematics distinguished itself from earlier mathematical thinking by
its formal character. Egyptian science was essentially "empirical" or "utilitar-
ian," but that of the Greeks was based on deductive reasoning. The emergence
of Greek mathematics was equivalent to a historical transition from concrete to
formal operations. The inherent limitation of Greek mathematics, however, was
its nonrecognition of the operatory nature of these formal operations. With their
essentially contemplative orientation, the Greeks located the reality of logical
and mathematical entities outside the subject. Thus, Pythagoras taught that num-

ber was to be found in things, and Plato that logical forms existed in a transcendent world of universals.

This realism was gradually overcome in the subsequent development of mathematics. The invention of algebra implied a growing awareness of numerical operations, because algebraic operations applied not to specific numbers but to *generalized* numbers in the form of *variables* defined by the operations themselves. The subsequent discovery of analytic geometry by Descartes extended this generalization to geometry. The theory of functions reflected a recognition of operations as such, and the theory of groups implied the recognition of the *systems d'ensemble* uniting these operations to one another.

But this historical *prise de conscience* of mathematical operations led to an epistemological dilemma. If operations are at the basis of mathematics, then mathematical knowledge is the result of subjective constructions carried out by the application of the operations in question. But mathematical truths are not arbitrary. Mathematicians are in some sense constrained in their constructions; otherwise the notion of mathematical truth would be meaningless, and mathematics would be reduced to subjective fantasy. The question regarding the source of this "intrinsic objectivity" of mathematical operations is the origin of the controversy between empiricism and apriorism. The empiricists attempted to trace the "intrinsic objectivity" of mathematics back to external reality, but the apriorists explained it in terms of preexisting structures in the mind of the subject.

The latter question above all is what genetic epistemology seeks to answer. After reviewing the solutions of other contemporary epistemologists of mathematics (Poincaré, Goblot, E. Meyerson, Russell, and Hilbert, among others), Piaget presented his own views. Both the generative character of mathematics and its "intrinsic objectivity" can be traced to the fact that mathematics is based on operations rooted in action. Thus, mathematics is generative for the same reason that action itself is generative; new actions or operations can be constructed through the composition of two or more existing actions or operations.

Mathematical thought is generative [*féconde*] because, as an assimilation of reality to the general coordination of action, it is essentially operatory. It is generative first of all because the compositions of operations constitute new operations and because these compositions, from which mathematical reason extracts structures, merge at their source with the very coordination of actions. [ibid., p. 324]

The "intrinsic objectivity" of mathematics also results from the fact that mathematical operations originate in action, for these actions at their source are accommodated to reality. As the products of coordinations among actions, operations preserve these original accommodations even while generalizing them.

One thus understands why logico-mathematical operations are accommodated in a permanent manner to objects at the same time they assimilate them to the subject. It is because the cycle of assimilation constituted by the initial coordinations from which these operations originate is at the meeting point between the most general functional laws of the organism and the most general characteristics of objects. One's own body is, in effect, simultaneously an object among others, determined by the laws of reality, and the center of an assimilation of other objects to its own activity. Consequently, to the extent to which it acts according to the most elementary forms of composition (inclusions, order, etc.) its actions express both the exigencies of the universe which determine it from within by its constitution as a living being, and the organization imposed by action and thought on the universe that they assimilate. Whereas this operatory organization is applied to the external universe in the course of actions bearing upon it, the general laws of the universe of which these actions are in other respects the product are analyzed from within by the very coordination of acts and not from without by the pressure of objects. . . . In sum, the problem of the contact between mathematics and reality is thus susceptible to a solution which links its "intrinsic objectivity" to physical or extrinsic objectivity but by the intermediary of psychophysical coordinations within the subject. [ibid., p. 338–339]

This argument provides one of the clearest examples of why epistemology and biology, such seemingly disparate disciplines, were intrinsically linked in Piaget's mind. In effect, this link explains the mysterious relation between mathematics and reality. It is not, however, a reductive link. Operations derive from actions that are themselves constrained by biological and physiological realities. But operations can be reduced neither to action nor to physiology, because they possess their own intrinsic properties. Unlike actions, operations are both interiorized and reversible. As interiorized actions, operations are subject to some of the same forms of organization as actions and accordingly display some of the same generalized adaptations to objects. Ultimately, this parallel in the forms of organization characterizing actions and operations explains the agreement between mathematics and reality.

This comparison between actions and operations also illustrates why the drawing of formal parallels between developmentally linked levels of reality is so important for Piaget. This practice will become particularly evident when we consider his biological writings. What at first may appear to be merely a series of formal analogies between biology and psychology takes on the character of evidence in the context of his theory as a whole.

Physical knowledge

The second volume of *Introduction à l'épistémologie génétique* (Piaget, 1950/ 1974a) was devoted to the physical sciences and included chapters on kinetics and mechanics (time, speed, and force), on conservation and atomism, on chance, irreversibility, and induction, on the epistemological implications of microphysics, and on causality. Whereas mathematical knowledge originates in the general coordinations of action, physical knowledge develops by abstraction from the accommodation of particular actions to the specific properties of physical objects. But the boundary between mathematics and physics is not absolute. The dual character of the notion of space, for example, has already been touched on in our review of the first volume of the *Introduction*: Space has a mathematical character to the extent that it is oriented to the operations of the subject, and it has a physical character to the extent that it is oriented to objects.

Physics, too, has a dual character. On the one hand, it consists in an assimilation of reality to the operatory schemes belonging to the subject. In this respect, it resembles (and makes use of) mathematics. On the other hand, it accommodates itself to the particular properties of reality, and in this respect it is distinguished from mathematics (ibid., pp. 8–9). This dual character of physical knowledge was illustrated in the first chapter of the second volume of the *Introduction* in regard to the kinetic notions of time and speed and the mechanics of physical force.

Time, speed, and force. Piaget began this chapter by tracing the possible explanations for the knowledge of time, speed, and force. According to the first explanation, physical knowledge is derived from the external experience of the senses. According to the second, physical knowledge is derived instead from "interior experience," the knowledge of time from the immediate intuition of duration, the knowledge of force from sensations of effort, and so on. Piaget argued that genetic research provides support for neither of these solutions and instead suggested a third: that physical knowledge arises from "a necessary union between logico-mathematical structures born of the coordination of actions and the facts of experience assimilated to these structures" (ibid., p. 17). The notions of time, speed, and force, for example, are found to derive from such a union of operatory structures and the facts of experience.

With respect to time, in particular, Piaget acknowledged that Bergson had been correct in seeking the origins of psychological time in action. Insofar as actions must be carried out in sequence and with a certain rhythm, those actions can be said to be ordered already in time. Bergson had taken duration to be an irreducible psychological intuition, but Piaget's research on the development of sensorimotor development had demonstrated that the understanding of temporal order and duration in action develops only gradually during the first year of life.

As for the operational understanding of time, Piaget's account of its development has already been considered in chapter 4. Temporal order is constructed through the operation of seriating a succession of events, and duration through the addition of the intervals between events. Time becomes objective when events occurring in different temporal sequences are linked through relations of simultaneity, and it acquires a metrical character when the durations separating successive events in the time series are equalized into units. Physical time results from the assimilation of external events to these operatory structures, psychological time from reflection on these operations themselves.

Thus, time is not a "primitive" intuition. It is constructed from perceptions of speed and amount of work accomplished (distance traveled, number of repetitions of an action, etc.). The intuition of duration results from an internal metric constructed by the repetition of an interiorized action at a constant speed. Because of this derived character of time, Piaget classified it as a form of physical knowledge. Unlike space, which could be constructed by the operations of the subject apart from any specific objects to be located in it, time is constructed from operations that must be accommodated to the specific properties of the events occurring within it – namely, the speed with which those events succeed one another.

In the 20th century, our conception of time has been further affected by the theory of relativity. In a remarkable passage, Piaget showed how the results of this theory could be explained in terms of genetic epistemology. We have seen how objective time is constructed from relations of simultaneity that link different sequences of events into a single time series characterized by units of equal duration. But given the fact that light travels at a constant speed (i.e., that communication across vast distances is not instantaneous), the very notion of simultaneity breaks down on a cosmic scale. More precisely, the notion of simultaneity is relative to the perspective of the observer; it is no longer possible to link different sequences of events occurring at great distances into a unitary time scale. Described in this way, the theory of relativity provides a good example of the thesis that time is operationally constructed. The relativity of time on a cosmic scale results from the fact that certain physical laws (such as the constant speed of light) constrain the operations by which time is constructed.

In the rest of the chapter on time, speed, and force, the development of the notion of force was traced, both in history and in psychogenesis. This survey led to the following conclusions: First, a general parallel exists between the development of the idea of force in history and the development of the individual. They follow similar sequences of stages and are characterized by a progressive decentration. Prescientific conceptions of force, for example, were characterized by a confusion of objective and subjective elements. This confusion can also be discerned in the physics of Aristotle. It was overcome only in classical mechanics, although the latter was still limited to events occurring on a human scale. Finally, in relativity theory, the laws governing events occurring on the scale of human action were found to have only local validity with respect to events occurring on a cosmic scale. This progressive decentration is also found in the psychogenesis of physical knowledge. In either case, it is characterized by a double movement: by a progressive "grouping" or coordination of the subject's operations, and at the same time by progressive accommodation to the specific properties of physical reality.

Conservation and atomism. In any system of transformations, there is a corresponding invariant: something that retains its identity even while its properties are transformed. In medieval philosophy, this relation was conceived in terms of substance and accident. In physics, invariance has been considered in terms of conservation of various quantities (mass, energy, etc.). The epistemology of E. Meyerson in particular was based on the rational recognition of identity in nature. For Piaget, the essential question was where these various forms of conservation originate. As usual, he presented three possible solutions: They can stem directly from experience, from rational deduction, or from a progressive construction involving elements of both reality and rationality (ibid., p. 109).

The most fundamental of these physical invariants is the very concept of the physical object. Piaget referred to his own research on the development of the object concept in infancy as evidence that the object concept is not a prior form imposed on the data of sensory experience. Psychological investigation reveals, instead, that the concept of the object is laboriously constructed. "In fact, the object is not merely a bundle of qualities rendered constant thanks to perceptual-motor regulations: It is above all the substrate of these qualities, that is a 'substance' conceived as continuing to exist even apart from every perceptual field" (ibid., p. 115). The object is in fact the identity element in the system of transformations constituted by the coordination of actions by which the subject manipulates and displaces things. "This coordination is nothing more than the practical 'group' of displacements, whereas the actions so coordinated are precisely the actions accommodated to the physical qualities of color, weight, etc., characteristic of each particular object" (ibid.).

Thus, the concept of the physical object represents a union of "specialized actions" and general coordinations among actions (ibid., p. 118). As emphasized throughout the first volume of the *Introduction,* these general coordinations of action are not derived by abstraction from particular objects, but from the subject's actions on objects in general. "Instead of abstracting their structure from the object, these most general actions on the contrary return to *add* characteristics issuing from the activity of the subject" (ibid.; emphasis added). The substantiality or continuous identity of the object is one such characteristic added to the object by virtue of the coordinated actions to which it is subject.

But what is the relation between these general characteristics added to objects by the coordination of actions and the specific characteristics inherent in the objects themselves? In other words, what is the relation between the general coordinations of actions leading to logico-mathematical knowledge and the specific accommodations to reality leading to physical knowledge? According to Piaget, the relation is asymmetric. The general coordinations of actions presuppose that objects exist, but they do not presuppose any of their particular properties. In contrast, the specific accommodations that constitute physical knowledge presuppose the coordination of actions and the general properties that these coordinations confer on physical objects as such. An object can acquire specific properties or "accidents" only insofar as it is conceived of as a substantial object in general. "In other words, from the most elementary sensorimotor action a logic and a geometry is necessary in order to attain physical qualities, whereas even if the general coordination of actions presupposes the existence of particular actions to coordinate, these can be any actions whatsoever and do not enter into the mechanism of coordination by way of their specificity" (ibid., p. 119).

This dual character of physical knowledge is a theme that returns again and again, not only in this chapter on conservation but also through the entire volume. In respect to the conservations characterizing the stage of concrete operations, for example, the same theme appears in the form of a discussion on the relation between form and content in physical knowledge. This discussion is also important for what it reveals about Piaget's thinking on the content specificity of cognitive structures.

The experiments carried out by Piaget and Inhelder on the conservation of physical quantity were described in chapter 4 of this book. In a typical experiment, children were shown two equal balls of clay. One of them was flattened into a pancake or rolled out into a sausage-shaped coil, after which the children were asked if they thought the two pieces of clay still contained equal amounts. Before the age of roughly 7–8 years, children tended to believe that the piece of clay that had been modified in shape contained more or less clay than the unmodified piece, depending on the spatial dimension cited in evidence. Only after approximately 7–8 years did they recognize that the two pieces of clay *necessarily* contained the same amounts of matter, because nothing had been added, because the modified ball could be returned to its original shape, or because one dimension (e.g., length) had been exactly compensated by an opposite change in another dimension (e.g., width).

The same sequence of development was observed in experiments involving the conservation of weight and volume, with the difference that the average age at which conservation was first observed varied among cases. In contrast to the conservation of quantity, the conservation of weight was not observed until about 9–10 years, and the conservation of volume not until about 11–12 years. This horizontal decalage was found despite the fact that the very same arguments were used to justify judgments of conservation for each of the three types of content. Thus, the discussion of the content specificity of cognitive structures in the *Introduction* bears not only on the relation between logico-mathematical knowledge and physical knowledge but also on the horizontal decalage involving quantity, weight, and volume.

According to Piaget, cognitive structures develop "in parallel" within different areas of content. By this, he meant that they progress through the same sequences of development and are analogous in form. However, they involve groupings of different actions and are therefore functionally distinct. *Logico-mathematical* structures involve the grouping of actions such as reunion and seriation that are not accommodated to the specific properties of objects. In this sense they are not content-specific. The generality of logico-mathematical structures implies not only that they may assimilate any objects whatsoever but also that they carry no information regarding the specific properties of the objects that they assimilate. *Spatial* operatory structures also involve the grouping of actions that are not accommodated to the specific properties of objects, but they differ from logico-mathematical structures insofar as they are based on relations of proximity. For example, spatial inclusions are based on relations between contiguous parts and wholes rather than on relations between discrete elements and classes. In contrast to both logico-mathematical and spatial structures, *physical* operatory structures involve actions (pushing, weighing, etc.) that are in fact accommodated to specific properties of physical objects. Because of this content specificity, they are restricted with respect to the objects (or the properties of objects) that they can assimilate.

From the point of view of the relations between the logico-mathematical coordination (that is, the grouping of operations or the relations engendered by them) and physical or experiential content (that is, the particular actions bearing upon the object and which are transformed into operations only by their grouping), it is thus completely clear in the case of this first representational invariant [i.e., conservation] as well as in that of the permanent sensorimotor object that the two sorts of elements are indissociable. On the one hand, there could hardly be coordinations without actions to coordinate. On the other hand, these actions are never given in an isolated state, but are from the first linked by coordinations susceptible to diverse regulations which are led by progressive equilibration to reversible composition. Now as this structural coordination progresses, the actions themselves are reciprocally transformed in an organization in which form and content are narrowly correlated. [ibid., pp. 127–128]

One might suppose that because logico-mathematical structures are generalized to assimilate any objects whatsoever, conservation and other examples of physical knowledge simply result from the application of these general logico-mathematical structures to specific contents. This assumption indeed forms the basis of a popular interpretation of Piagetian structuralism, leading to the erroneous conclusion that the theory implies synchrony in development across different content areas: If formally analogous performances in different domains resulted from the application of a single general structure to different areas of content, then one might reasonably assume that an individual would manifest the same developmental level of performance in all those domains at once. As soon as a higher-level structure appeared, the corresponding level of performance would be apparent in all its specific domains of application. According to this interpretation, the structure not only would be general in *form,* but also would *function* in a generalized manner, being immediately applicable to any domain of content.

Despite the intuitive appeal of this interpretation, Piaget indicated quite clearly that it was not what he had in mind:

In the particular case [of conservation], the operatory groupings at work consist in logical additions of parts and in logical multiplications of relations (without mathematical quantification intervening from the first). One could thus suppose these are the corresponding logical groupings bearing upon classes and relations of any kind or the infralogical groupings of a spatial order . . . which, on the basis of their preliminary forms, come to be applied to the physical problem of the conservation of matter. . . . However, such an interpretation would be erroneous, for there is no ''application'' whatsoever of anterior groupings, logical or infralogical, to the new problem of the physical conservation of matter, but rather parallel and convergent organization of actions bearing upon ensembles of discontinuous objects (classes and relations), on the spatial properties of the object, and on its physical properties, and it will later be the reflexive interrelation of all these structures that will constitute formal logic. To be sure, the coordination of physical actions that engenders the invariance of quantity of matter is a logical coordination (subsequently to be mathematized), but it does not result from an application of other logical coordinations and simply constitutes a structuration parallel to that of other domains. [ibid., p. 128]

To say that logico-mathematical, infralogical, and physical structures develop in ''parallel'' from groupings of different actions means that these different types of structures are formed independent of each other, even though they may be analogous in form. Therefore, no reason exists to assume that they should develop in synchrony within individuals.

This parallel and independent formation of structures occurs not only between the general domains of logico-mathematical, infralogical, and physical coordinations but also between different areas of content *within* the general domain of physical knowledge. Although these structures are all formed by the grouping of content-specific actions, the particular actions and contents differ in each case. As evidence for this argument, Piaget cited the example of the decalage involving substance, weight, and volume. Far from constituting an anomaly in Piaget's theory, such a decalage in the development of the same operations within three different areas of physical content provides evidence for the hypothesis that the structures pertaining to each area develop independently insofar as they are constituted by the grouping of different actions. In Piaget's words, these structures ''are not yet formal in the sense that they cannot immediately be generalized from one domain to another'' (ibid., pp. 129–130).

The fact that this decalage develops in a particular order can also be explained in terms of the characteristics of the actions involved in each case. The actions pertaining to the conservation of substance (rejoining pieces of matter that have been separated or deformed) are simply easier to coordinate than the actions involved in the conservation of weight (weighing).

To begin with, the action of weighing implies that of union while the reverse is not the case. To acknowledge that the quantity of matter is the same in a coil as in the ball from which it came is to reunite in thought the parts of this whole which have simply been displaced. This implies no act of weighing whatsoever, whereas to reunite in thought the weight of the same parts in order to equalize their sum to the initial whole is already to reunite the pieces. From the point of view of action, the invariance of weight presupposes that of substance, without the reverse being the case. As for the considerable time which elapses between the constitution of the two systems of operations relating to matter and to weight, the reason is equally simple: it is much more difficult to coordinate (directly) successive actions of weighing among themselves than to group actions of reuniting. The latter only require spatial displacements and reunions coordinating actions of seeing, grasping or touching, etc., thus physical actions that are little specialized, which make their decentration and coordination easy. Weighing, however, is a specialized action that requires a relatively precise estimation and the awareness of which thus for a long time favors subjective egocentric evaluation, antagonistic to grouping. [ibid., p. 138]

The important thing about this passage is not the adequacy or inadequacy of Piaget's explanation of horizontal decalage, but the conception of cognitive structure that it implies. Cognitive structures were described as coordinations or groupings of particular actions that have become cognitive operations by virtue of the very fact that they have been interiorized and grouped together. With respect to knowledge of the physical world, these actions are accommodated to specific contents, that is, to the specific properties of physical objects. It follows that different structures formed from the grouping of different actions will be content-specific (even if these structures are analogous in form) and need not develop at the same time. In Piaget's words, ''the coordination of actions of the type (A =

B; B = C, therefore A = C) is in fact a different operation in the case of weight than in that of substance, since, while the coordination ends in the same form, the actions to be coordinated are different'' (ibid., p. 139). Only at the level of formal operations does form become (more or less) dissociated from content.

The remainder of the chapter on conservation and atomism was devoted to an interpretation of various kinds of invariants in science in terms of systems of operatory transformations. Conservation may be interpreted in each case as the manifestation of the identity operator in the respective system of transformations. Something remains the same even as it is transformed. In atomistic theories, for example, matter is recognized as capable of being transformed in a number of ways (divided, compressed, etc.), but remaining invariant across these transformations with respect to the number of particles that it contains. This principle is not violated by the finding of modern physics that even ''elementary'' particles are capable of division; only the conception of what remains the same across these transformations has changed. ''Whatever variation the experiment manages to introduce into the characteristics of matter, we will always find another invariant capable of assuring the material existence of 'something constant' '' (ibid., p. 149).

Chance, irreversibility, and induction. As we have seen, Piaget characterized the development of physical knowledge in terms of a double movement. Like logico-mathematical knowledge, physical knowledge consists in a grouping or coordination of actions into cognitive structures. Unlike logico-mathematical structures, however, the structures that constitute physical knowledge are composed of actions accommodated to specific properties of physical objects. This dual character of physical knowledge results in the close ''correlation'' between form and content observed in the conservations characterizing the stage of concrete operations.

In some respects, these two characteristics of physical knowledge appear to conflict with each other, especially as development proceeds beyond concrete operations. Cognitive structures form the basis of the sense of necessity, but many physical processes are governed purely by chance. Cognitive structures evolve toward ever greater reversibility, but some physical processes (e.g., the steady increase of entropy) are characterized by irreversibility. Finally, cognitive structures tend to develop into closed deductive systems, but physical reality can never be determined purely by deduction and is instead approached through experimental induction.

Piaget argued that these discrepancies are only apparent, and his explanation is of interest for the epistemology of science. According to his research on the development of the understanding of chance in children (to be described in more detail later in this chapter), the idea of randomness in nature is fully understood only at the level of formal operations when children have developed the capacity for combinatorial thought. This combinatorial system implies notions of necessity and possibility. Each operation of combination (or permutation) necessarily results in a complete range of possible outcomes. To the extent that children have mastered the system, all the possible outcomes can be generated from any given combinatory operation. For example, exactly six possible combinations can be generated from the elements A, B, C, and D, taken two at a time. In a random process of physical combination, however, all the possible combinations will not necessarily be represented at once. Nor will they necessarily be represented in equal numbers during any finite number of trials. Only as the number of trials approaches infinity will the different combinations tend to appear with equal frequencies – the so-called law of large numbers.

Thus, although the system of combinations taken as a whole necessarily implies all of its parts (i.e., all the individual combinations), the system is never represented as a whole in reality. What actually occurs is only a selection from among the total possibilities. Even if enough trials are conducted so that all the possible combinations are realized at least once, the particular sequence of outcomes is only one among a number of possible sequences that could have been generated in that number of trials. In this sense, Piaget spoke of random combinations as an incomplete realization of a total structure. The necessity embodied in this structure is never completely realized in physical reality, but only approximated ''at the limit,'' that is, as the number of trials approaches infinity. Ultimately, no contradiction exists between the necessity of cognitive structures bearing on physical reality and the contingency of physical reality itself. It is just that the one can be only incompletely assimilated to the other.

Because the necessity embodied in a cognitive structure is ultimately based on its reversibility, the same argument holds for the apparent discrepancy between the reversibility of structures and the irreversibility of nature. The second law of thermodynamics states, in effect, that physical reality tends to evolve toward its most probable state. This process is unidirectional and irreversible. The very understanding of probability, however, is based on a reversible combinatory structure. This structure is reversible in the sense that, given any subset of possible outcomes, the whole set of possible outcomes can be generated, and vice versa. This sort of reversibility, unlike the irreversible growth of entropy, is not a temporal process. In Piaget's terminology, cognitive structures are ''simultaneously'' reversible, but temporal processes can at most be ''successively'' reversed. The apparent conflict between the reversibility of cognitive structure and the irreversibility of nature thus reduces to the fact that two kinds of reversibility are at play. The combinatory cognitive structure encompasses all the possible outcomes at once, but nature is limited to the realization of only one combination at a time. In this sense, random processes understood in terms of probability represent an incomplete assimilation of an irreversible reality to a reversible structure: ''Operations are reversible because they embrace all the possibilities, while reality is irreversible to the extent that it is only a chance drawing from among these possibilities'' (ibid., p. 178).

This thought raises the further question whether the incomplete assimilation of reality to cognitive structures is in any sense inevitable or only represents a contingent limitation on knowledge. In other words, is the probabilistic understanding of natural processes only an approximation to unknown deterministic laws? Or is nature in some sense inherently probabilistic, and hence indeterminate? The advances of 20th-century physics have given this classical epistemological question a new urgency. Piaget's operatory theory provides the following answer: On the scale appropriate to human action, the probabilistic understanding of nature can be said only to approximate a deterministic understanding. Probabilistic interpretations of reality constitute an incomplete assimilation, and deterministic interpretations a complete assimilation, of reality to reversible operatory structures. However, on a cosmic or subatomic scale, where events transcend the limits of our possibilities for acting on distinct physical objects, no deterministic understanding of nature is possible, and nature cannot be interpreted in a deterministic manner. In this case, physical reality must be said to behave in a probabilistic manner insofar as we can know it at all (ibid., p. 178).

This idea of the incomplete assimilation of reality to operatory structures is also useful for understanding the problem of induction. Science begins with particular facts determined through experiment or observation and proceeds to universal laws that govern a range of physical possibilities, many of which may never have been observed. The question is how this movement from the particular to the universal is accomplished. This is one of the central questions addressed in epistemology under the general heading of the problem of universals, to be discussed in chapter 8.

According to Piaget, induction consists of an operatory structure in the process of formation. That is, the particular actions that gave rise to the particular facts begin to be grouped together in a total structure. In Piaget's theory, an operatory structure of this kind encompasses a range of possible actions that extend beyond those that originally went into its construction. The question is whether or not the realization of these possible actions will also give rise to facts consistent with the system as a whole. To the extent that it does, the structure becomes completed, and one can reason deductively (from the general to the particular) with some confidence. If, however, the realization of these actions gives rise to facts contrary to the system, then the structure will remain incomplete. Reality will remain for the time being only partially comprehended, although these new actions and the new facts that they have generated may be grouped into a more inclusive structure, and the cycle will be repeated.

On the one hand, induction is not composed of closed and completed operatory systems-of-the-whole comparable to those which permit the exercise of deduction. On the other hand, induction is only possible when such deductive models already exist and can serve as guides to research. Induction is thus the ensemble of the thought processes which tend to organize the facts of observation or experience, that is, to class them in the form of concepts capable of hierarchical inclusions and to bring them into logical or mathematical relations capable of constituting systems which are entirely composable. Either induction then succeeds in these attempts and progressively yields to deduction, or it fails because of an inability to dissociate the invariant from the fortuitous, and it remains in quasi-deductive but incomplete systems because of incomplete composition. [ibid., p. 186]

To the extent that induction succeeds in forming reversible structures that remain in accord with experience, it passes over into theories from which natural events can be predicted from a few basic principles after the manner of Newton's *Principia*. But to the extent that reality remains unassimilable to a reversible structure, events can be predicted only according to their probability of occurrence.

The epistemology of microphysics. The advances in atomic and subatomic physics in this century have changed our way of thinking about reality and the world. At the subatomic level, many of the familiar features of our everyday world seem to vanish. Intuitive notions of space, time, causality, and even the substantiality of physical objects take on entirely new meanings, defined entirely in terms of abstract mathematical symbolism. For Piaget, these facts were of great significance for epistemology. In the first place, they demonstrate that science cannot take epistemology for granted. At the very frontiers of contemporary physics, questions of the nature and limits of our knowledge about the external world are found to be directly implicated in questions about the nature of the world itself. In the second place, the epistemological paradoxes of modern physics provide a kind of test case for genetic epistemology. Can a science that traces the development of our notions of space, time, causality, and the object concept explain why physical science appears to have developed beyond these concepts?

Piaget's answer was unequivocal: Not only can genetic epistemology explain why the paradoxes of microphysics have arisen, but these paradoxes are found to be a natural consequence of the way that our knowledge of the world is acquired in the first place. As described repeatedly in the second volume of the *Introduction*, knowledge of the physical world arises from the coordination of actions accommodated to the specific properties of physical objects. In contrast, logico-mathematical knowledge arises from the coordinations among actions that are accommodated only to objects in general, not to any of their specific properties. This difference might also be stated by saying that logico-mathematical structures consist of *logically* possible actions on objects, but physical operatory structures are limited to coordinations among *physically* possible actions on objects.

This distinction, in turn, presupposes that the actions themselves can be differentiated from the objects on which they are brought to bear. But this differentiation between actions and objects breaks down at the subatomic level, at which the means used by physicists to act on the objects of interest themselves affect the facts observed. Because of this impossibility of completely differentiating the action from the object acted on, the very permanence and individuality of objects break down, and with them our usual notions of space, time, and causality. "When the action of following an individualized particle is not possible," wrote Piaget, "the notion of an individual object loses its sense" (ibid., p. 222). But our everyday notions of time, space, and causality are also constructed from coordinations of actions bearing on physical objects. "Localization in space or the temporal instant, trajectories or durations, sizes and measures, in brief all the usual notions are subjected to a profound modification by the very fact of the limits of experimental action on physical objects and by the desire not to exceed these limits by an illegitimate extrapolation of thought'' (ibid., p. 223).

Like the infant in the early stages of sensorimotor development, the contemporary microphysicist must do without the usual concept of object permanence. The contemporary microphysicist "devotes himself like the very young infant to believing in objects only to the extent that he can locate them and to know space and time only insofar as he can construct them, reconstructing one by one the elementary relations of position, of displacement, of form, and so on'' (ibid., p. 226). The difference between the infant and the physicist is, of course, that the infant has not yet acquired our everyday notions of space, time, causality, and the object concept, but the physicist, having already acquired these notions, deliberately refrains from applying them in contexts in which they are no longer operable. Instead, ''he constructs a whole system of intellectual and mathematical operations in order to translate deductively this disappearance of the object on the plane of experimental action'' (ibid., p. 222). Thus, on the microphysical scale, as on the familiar scale of everyday action, knowledge of space, time, causality, and the object concept forms an interrelated system of concepts arising from the coordinations of the actions possible on each level. The actions possible on each level differ in the extent to which they are composable:

On our scale, these actions are directly and completely composable among themselves by the fact that they are developed as a function of immediately accessible objects. As a result, space and time appear to constitute contexts independent of their content, because they form the context of every action bearing upon reality. . . . In contrast, at the upper or lower limits of our activity, the dissociation between the context and its content is no longer possible because the compositions of our actions are no longer direct nor complete. At the upper limits [i.e., on a cosmic scale], as we have seen, the subject is included in the phenomena to be measured and consequently his measuring sticks and clocks are bound up with the transformations to be detected instead of remaining outside them. . . . At the lower limits [i.e., on a subatomic scale], the opposite occurs. It is the phenomenon that is included in the action of the subject, since objects remain relative to the action which locates them. [ibid., p. 235]

One consequence of this relativity of action and object on the microphysical scale is that certain phenomena can appear to take on different qualities depending on the method by which the physicist observes them. For example, light appears as a particle under certain conditions and as a wave under other conditions. This characteristic of reality to take on apparently contradictory properties was called "complementarity" by Niels Bohr. For Piaget, the possibility of attributing contradictory predicates to the same reality in turn (but not at once) was of great epistemological significance, because it seemed to herald a new principle of logic. In terms of purely formal logic, this possibility of affirming contradictory judgments of the same reality has a paradoxical character. In terms of Piaget's operatory logic, however, it can be explained in a fairly natural fashion. Two judgments can be contradictory only to the extent that they occur within a single operatory system. The contrary judgments that light is a wave and a particle occur, however, within two *different* operatory systems, corresponding to the differing observational procedures employed in each case. The "principle of complementarity" is in fact an attempt to coordinate the two operatory systems in a more comprehensive structure. This coordination is possible only by weakening the principle of noncontradiction – by allowing the same reality to take on contradictory properties as it is assimilated to different operatory systems in turn.

"Complementarity" consists in a relation, not between isolable terms, but between operatory totalities themselves. The fact that a micro-object is sometimes a wave and sometimes a particle means that it can be inserted sometimes in one system of relations and sometimes in another, but not in the two at once. [ibid., p. 245]

Piaget added that the principle of complementarity so understood is not necessarily limited to microphysics, but is potentially applicable to other domains as well.

In sum, the lesson of microphysics for epistemology consists in the fact that it makes obvious what is in fact true at every level of human action: that knowledge results from the interaction of subject and object. On the scale of everyday human action, the modifications introduced into the object by the subject (through assimilation) and into the subject by the object (through accommodation) can conveniently be ignored so that the subject can have the illusion of knowing reality in itself, independent of action, and of existing as a subject, independent of objects (ibid., p. 250). But on the subatomic scale of microphysics, as on the cosmic scale of relativity theory, these illusions can no longer be sustained. Subject and object are found to be indissolubly linked by their interactions, such that knowledge of the subject and knowledge of objects are interdependent. Genetic epistemology is well equipped to illuminate the epistemological significance of contemporary physics, for one of the main conclusions that Piaget drew from his psychogenetic research is that knowledge arises from the interaction of subject and object.

Reality and causality. Like other forms of knowledge about the physical world, knowledge of causality involves a coordination among actions that are accommodated to the specific properties of physical objects. What distinguishes causality from other forms of knowledge is that the capacity of the subject to act on objects is projected on the relations among objects themselves. Thus, objects are conceived of as acting on each other in a manner analogous to the way in which objects are acted on by the subject. In short, causality develops by abstraction and generalization of human agency. The transformations that can be brought about in physical objects by means of human action are viewed as leading to further transformations among objects:

Logico-mathematical operations consist in actions exercised by the subject on objects, while causality adds to these (which it also includes) analogous actions ascribed to the object as such. In causality, it is thus the transformations of the object which become operations, as they are incorporated in the composition of the very operations of the subject. [ibid., p. 267]

As evidence for this interpretation, Piaget reviewed his own research on the development of causal thinking in childhood. The surest indication that causality proceeds from agency is the fact that causality and agency are initially not distinguished from each other. Thus, young children tend to give magico-phenomenalist, animist, or artificialist explanations for natural phenomena – all forms of explanation in which human agency and natural causality are imperfectly differentiated. Similar trends in the historical evolution of causal thinking can be found. For example, the magical thinking characteristic of precausal thought resembles the phenomenalism of preoperational thinking. In each case, human actions are believed to affect natural processes.

Piaget went on to review theories of reality and causality in modern epistemology, including those of Comte, Duhem, Poincaré, Frank, E. Meyerson, Brunschvicg, Bachelard, and Juvet. Of particular interest from the standpoint of Piaget's own development are the theories of Brunschvicg, whose historico-critical review of the development of conceptions of causality in history paralleled in many ways Piaget's investigations of the development of causal thinking in the life of the individual, as well as the theories of Juvet, who like Piaget saw group structure as the key for understanding our knowledge of both mathematics and the external world. According to Juvet (as paraphrased by Piaget), group structure plays much the same role in the generation of knowledge as Platonic ideas or universals: It is a structure "that we discover in ourselves without having created, and that we locate in things without having abstracted it from them" (ibid., p. 322).

Like other forms of physical knowledge, causal thinking involves the insertion (or assimilation) of an observed datum into an operatory system. This system defines a universe of possibilities of which the observed datum constitutes a specific example. In the case of causality, the observables consist in the dynamic relations between objects or events. If the assimilation of such observed relations to the operatory system is complete, those relations take on the character of necessity. That is, the observed outcome is completely determined within the system; only one possibility can follow from the antecedents given. This exclusion of all but one possibility is the origin of the notion of causal necessity. The character of necessity is added to the mere temporal contiguity of events by the assimilation of those events to an operatory system that defines the outcomes recognized as physically possible. In contrast, if the assimilation of the observed relations between objects or events to the operatory system is incomplete – if the observed outcome is not completely determined within the system – then the relation between events can be described only as more or less probable, not as necessary.

This dual character of physical knowledge, both empirical and operatory at once, raises the question of the nature of the reality known by physics. The observed datum taken by itself cannot be equated with the "true" reality, for (as Hume pointed out) necessary laws cannot be extracted from isolated observations. But neither can the operatory system taken by itself be identified only as the true reality, for considered in isolation this system is a pure construction. Piaget implied that the reality known by physics can be identified only with the *assimilation* of observations to an operatory system, which by virtue of such assimilations becomes accommodated to reality. "The 'true' reality is thus that which situates the datum in the ensemble of realizable, but not simultaneously realized possibilities, whereas the 'apparent' is reduced to the existing reality alone in contrast to the possible" (ibid., p. 335). According to this account, physics hovers between realism and idealism. By the very nature of their research, physicists are committed to a reality existing outside the activity of their own minds. However, the reality that is known, insofar as it is recognized as a system of possibilities that exceed the data observed at any one time, depends on operatory construction.

Piaget concluded the second volume of the *Introduction* with a suggestive passage in which he intimated that the distinction between the real and the possible, because of its operatory character, can be sustained only on the scale of human action. To the extent that microphysics and astrophysics approach the limits of this scale, the distinction tends to break down. "On scales characterized by the limits of human action, the opposition of the real and the possible becomes more and more blurred in a mixed region which is that of the probable in various degrees" (ibid., p. 336). At the limits of human action, the causal operations attributed to the object become indistinguishable from the operations by which the subject can act on those objects. Physics tends to become idealized as reality more and more becomes describable only in mathematical terms, and "the common margin between subject and object tends to grow" (ibid.).

Biological knowledge

The third volume of *Introduction à l'épistémologie génétique* contains chapters on the nature of biological, psychological, and sociological knowledge. Because Piaget extensively revised the material on biology and published it in 1967 in *Biology and knowledge* (to be reviewed in chapter 6), only the major trends of thought on the epistemology of biology in the *Introduction* will be touched on here. Even though this material was subsequently superseded, it is useful for understanding the development of his thinking in this area. Many of the themes fundamental in Piaget's intellectual development are especially apparent in his writings on biology.

Piaget began his remarks on the epistemology of biology with the observation that the classification of organisms into genera and species follows the laws of "groupings" of classes and relations. Such classification can already be observed in the writings of Aristotle:

If the relationship between this inclusion of logical classes and the hierarchy of zoological classes were doubted, it would be sufficiently attested to by the fact that, according to Aristotle, the theory of genera attained by logic rules the physical universe in its totality. The biomorphic character of Aristotle's physics and of his whole ontology is sufficiently clear that this extension of the system of classes demonstrates the connection of such a logic with the biological preoccupations of its author. [Piaget, 1950a, pp. 14–15]

Piaget shared with Aristotle both a preoccupation with biology and a sense of the connection between biology and logic. Indeed, we may recall from chapter 1 that Piagetian structuralism originated in part from the insight, appropriated from Bergson, that the theory of genera might profitably be reintroduced into modern science. But the connection between biology and logic was much different for Piaget than for Aristotle. The latter understood genera and species as fundamental categories of the natural world, but Piaget saw them instead as the result of assimilating biological reality to operatory structures (i.e., the groupings).

This idea is illustrated by several examples taken from the history of modern biology, including the issue of defining biological species and the distinction between phenotype and genotype. With regard to the latter distinction, Piaget showed how the notions of genotype, phenotype, and environment are related through an operation of logical multiplication. In effect, phenotypes result from the crossing of genotypes and environments (ibid., pp. 26ff.). In contrast, the genotype, which can never be observed directly, is derived from the phenotype by abstracting the effects of different environments – a reversal of the operation of logical multiplication. This account has the virtue of demonstrating why the notion of genotype is not absolute, but is relative to the range of environments (and corresponding phenotypes) considered.

With the advent of Mendelian laws of inheritance, biology ceased to be solely qualitative and began to take on a certain quantitative character. The possibilities for mathematizing biology are constrained, however, by the fact that genera and species have an irreversible evolutionary history. That is, they are determined by certain contingent relationships existing in the environment during their periods of formation. For this reason, they cannot be completely assimilated to a reversible mathematical structure; at best, they can be treated only in terms of probability. To be sure, some subdisciplines in biology, such as physiology or physio-chemistry, can be mathematized much more than biology conducted on the level of organisms.

The acknowledgment of irreversible evolutionary processes in biology, however, raises two further questions: the question of finality and that of entropy. Piaget argued that equilibrium processes operating in evolution provide it with a certain directionality, without implying that it has any final destination.

Objectively or biologically, that which is called finality thus corresponds to a march toward equilibrium. This march is oriented to be sure, but by the very laws of this equilibrium, and this orientation does not imply any more finality in the causal process as such than the compensations or "moderations" expressed in the principle of Le Châtelier constitute a system of final causes [in physio-chemistry]. [ibid., p. 69]

But one might ask further how the "march toward equilibrium" in biology results in the evolution of ever more ordered forms, although the tendency toward equilibrium in thermodynamics results in a continual increase in disorder?

Piaget reviewed previous attempts to answer this question by Helmholtz and C. E. Guye, but did not attempt to provide any definitive answer himself. Instead, he intimated that future research at the boundary line between chemistry and physiology would result in discoveries capable of reconciling the theory of evolution and the second law of thermodynamics.

Piaget's remaining remarks on the epistemology of biology consisted in an extended comparison between theories of evolution and theories of cognitive adaptation. These comparisons are essentially the same as those contained in *The origins of intelligence* and *The psychology of intelligence,* as reviewed in previous chapters, and they will not be described in detail here. Thus, vitalist fixism in biology corresponds in epistemology to faculty theories of intelligence, preformist biological theories correspond to apriorist epistemologies, "emergence" theories of evolution correspond to phenomenology and Gestalt psychology, Lamarckism corresponds to empiricism, mutationism to "conventionalist pragmatism," and biological interactionism to epistemological interactionism. More important than the details of these comparisons is their raison d'être. These correspondences apparently had great significance for Piaget; otherwise he would not have repeated them so frequently in his various works. But are they only analogies and nothing more? Or did he believe that they contain something of substance?

Piaget wrote that there are in fact two lessons to be drawn from such comparisons (ibid., pp. 126–127). First, similarity of explanations in biology and epistemology results from the fact that the problems investigated also have certain similarities. "In the case of the sciences of life, organic or mental, the common element is the history of forms, since in each of the domains of life or knowledge, one finds oneself in the presence of forms that evolve according to a real historical process, and of forms that perpetuate themselves by assimilating the environment, even as they accommodate themselves to it" (ibid., p. 127). The second lesson is that there is a developmental continuity between organic reality and knowledge, reflecting the fact that the knower is also a living organism. Between physiological processes and the higher forms of cognition, a continuous chain exists, with links formed by sensation, perception, reflex activity, and sensorimotor intelligence. One of the major goals of Piaget's theory was to trace this continuity between life and knowledge in some detail. As we shall see in chapter 6, Piaget's penchant for formal analogies reflected his conviction that certain "laws of form" operate in similar ways at different levels of reality. Tracing such analogies was thus more than an expository device. It was in fact an attempt to call attention to these laws of form as they apply at different levels.

Psychological knowledge

Like physics, psychology has a dual character, according to Piaget. Whereas physics oscillates between mathematical idealizations and experimental realism, psychology hovers between physiology and logic – or, in Piaget's terminology, between *causality* and *implication*. Physiology is an endeavor to explain human behavior in terms of causal dynamics, but logic is a search for explanations in terms of meaningful implication. The independence of these two types of explanation can be illustrated by the fact that although physiology conceivably could explain the utterance "two plus two equals four" in terms of its neurological antecedents, it cannot explain why this utterance expresses a *necessary truth*. The necessity of such a proposition is a matter of implication (the province of logic), not of causality (the province of physiology). These two forms of explanation are not reducible one to the other. "Material or physical causality and logical or mathematical implication are, in the last analysis, the two irreducible terms of the relation that exists between physiological explication and at least certain aspects of what one sometimes calls somewhat loosely the 'phenomenology' of psychology" (ibid., p. 141).

Although "implication" in its most highly developed form may be found in logic and mathematics, it is in fact much broader in scope. In Piaget's usage, "implication" coincides with "meaning" or "signification" in the broadest sense, and as we have seen in Piaget's writings on infancy, he believed that the roots of signification could be traced back into the beginnings of the sensorimotor period. Thus, a certain perceptual configuration can "imply" the presence of a physical object to a child at a certain stage of development. Similarly, a symbol can "imply" the thing symbolized, and so on. As these examples suggest, action itself is imbued with meanings and implications. Thus, psychology as the science of action or behavior hovers between causality and implication, for action can be explained in terms of both its causes and its implications. "The role of psychological explication, in contrast to logic or pure axiology, is thus to integrate the series of implications in the context of 'behaviors' [*des 'conduites'*] themselves, each of which has a causal aspect" (ibid., p. 152). As Piaget pointed out, the distinction between causal and implicatory explanation corresponds to the German distinction between *erklärende* and *verstehende* social science, between a science that seeks to "explain" and one that seeks to "understand." From his point of view, psychology need not and should not have to choose between these two points of view.

The attempt to retain two forms of explanation that are irreducible to each other naturally raises the further question as to how they are related. Piaget's answer to this question was rather involved. To begin with, if explanation by causality and explanation by implication are really irreducible one to the other, then no causal force may be attributed to the mind, which is exclusively involved with relations of implication. Theories that do attribute an illegitimate causal character to mental entities Piaget called "substantialist." In contrast, an operatory psychology views the relation between causality and implication in genetic (i.e., developmental) terms. According to operatory theory, the necessary implications of logical operations originate in actions that have become interiorized. Action itself develops from reflex and physiological mechanisms in which the role of implication can hardly be discerned independent of causality. Thus, psychic development may be described as a gradual differentiation of implication and causality in which the relative importance of implication becomes progressively greater. This differentiation occurs by virtue of the fact that the equilibria characteristic of each stage of development become less and less restricted to reactions based on existing states of affairs and more and more extended to include anticipations of possible states of affairs.

As the domain of equilibrium becomes enlarged from stage to stage, . . . that is linked to more extended anticipations, it is thus clear that this aspect of implication becomes augmented in importance with the development of behavior, while the strictly causal aspect (i.e., the real as opposed to the possible) diminishes correlatively. This is why the psychology of behavior, which utilizes explications based at once on causality and on implication as far as elementary behaviors are concerned, becomes less and less causal and more and more operatory or implicative to the extent that it moves away from the primitive forms and approaches the final equilibrium. [ibid., p. 166]

Piaget took care to assure the reader that this developmental linkage between physiological causality and mental implication does not imply a reduction of the one to the other. At most one can say that a certain isomorphism or "parallelism" exists between them once they have become differentiated. These considerations are of course closely related to the mind–body problem in philosophy. Piaget argued that the commitment to the scientific method itself prohibits psychologists from choosing among the classical metaphysical solutions to this problem (interactionism, epiphenomenalism, idealism, and monism). Instead, one can only assert a principle of "parallelism": that every mental or implicative connection has a corresponding physiological (or causal) connection (although the reverse is not necessarily the case), and that this correspondence cannot itself be interpreted in terms of causality (i.e., interactions or epiphenomena) or implication (i.e., idealism or identity).

As a form of explanation, causality does not assume a fundamentally different role in psychology as compared with the other sciences. Explaining relations of implication in psychology, however, calls for a new form of logic. Although formal or axiomatic logic is concerned with logical truth and necessity as such, this new logic is concerned with logical truth and necessity only as they are understood by the subject. It is, in fact, a logic of implicative relations as they actually occur in thought and action. This new logic of thought is, of course, what Piaget's own operatory logic was meant to be, and we may recall that he also believed sensorimotor intelligence to be governed by a "logic of action" that he summarily described in his books on sensorimotor development. But however much operatory logic differs from formal logic and mathematics, the two are related by the fact that both are the products of human thought. Therefore, even formal logic and mathematics derive from operatory logic. For this reason, operatory logic as a form of psychological explanation can have an important role to play in the solution to a basic problem in contemporary epistemology of logic and mathematics, namely, the problem of foundations:

We have seen in fact that mathematicians today seek the solution of the problem of foundations in two essential directions. . . . Some seek to explain mathematical notions by psychology, as Poincaré interprets space and the group of displacements by means of the effective motricity of the organism. Others base mathematical notions on the elementary notions of logic and appeal to logistics. Now if logic itself proceeds from psychology as we would now suppose, these two solutions eventually reduce to a single one, and this is what we will seek to maintain. [ibid., p. 182]

The relation between Piaget's epistemology and the problem of foundations in mathematics will be further discussed in chapter 8.

Sociological knowledge

The chapter on sociology from the third volume of the *Introduction* represents Piaget's last major treatment of problems of sociology. Only the brief and rather more specialized essay "Problèmes de la psychosociologie de l'enfance," originally published in 1963 and reprinted in Piaget (1965/1977a), was later. It is therefore of interest to review these last published thoughts on the general problems of sociological knowledge.

To begin with, Piaget recognized a close parallel between the epistemological problems of sociology and those of psychology, with the obvious difference that the collective dimension is more strongly emphasized in the first as compared with the second:

Each of the problems raised by psychological explanation is thus found with respect to sociological explanation, apart from the fact alone that the "I" is now replaced by the "we" and that actions and "operations," once supplemented by a collective dimension, become interactions (i.e., behaviors modifying each other according to all the steps intervening between conflict and synergy) or forms of cooperation (i.e., operations effected in common or in reciprocal correspondence). [Piaget, 1950a, p. 191]

The same duality between implication and causality found in psychology may also be found in sociology. In the case of sociology, "implication" refers to the norms and representations shared by a given society, and "causality" to the objective factors that intervene in the history of that society.

Moreover, the psychological study of the child cannot really be separated from sociology, for children grow up only within a particular social context. Insofar as child psychology studies the progressive socialization of the child, it must indeed be considered a part of sociology:

Child psychology would surely explain the mode of formation of concepts or operations, one should say, if the child could be studied in himself, independently of all adult influences and if he would thus construct his thought without drawing elements essential for it from the social milieu. But what is the child in himself? And do not children exist only in relation to certain well determined collective environments? That is perfectly obvious, and if it is agreed to call "child psychology" the study of individual mental development, this is simply by reference to the experimental methods utilized by this discipline. In fact, both in regard to the explanatory notions of which it makes use and in regard to its own object of investigation, child psychology constitutes a sector of sociology devoted to the study of the socialization of the individual as well as a sector of psychology itself. [ibid., pp. 194–195]

This passage serves to correct widespread misinterpretations of Piaget's theory as the same kind of narrow, "individualistic" approach to child development that he here rejected.

One reason why Piaget has been misunderstood on this point is that he used the word "socialization" in a slightly different sense than it is commonly used in psychology. In many learning-theoretical approaches to child development, "socialization" includes nearly all influences exerted on children that tend to make them conform with social norms and practices. In contrast, Piaget used this word in a more restricted sense to refer to the process by which children come to consider such social norms and the viewpoints of other persons *in their own thinking*. In the learning-theoretical usage, one can say that much "socialization" occurs even during the first 2 years of life. In Piaget's usage, children's thinking remains "unsocialized" during sensorimotor development, because they are as yet incapable of forming truly cognitive representations of other persons or their needs. In this latter sense, the degree to which children's thinking becomes "socialized" increases with cognitive development.

Social factors intervene before language in the form of sensorimotor training, imitation, etc., but without essential modification of preverbal intelligence. With language its role increases considerably, since it gives rise to exchanges of thought from the latter's very formation. The progressive construction of intellectual operations presupposes a growing interdependence between mental factors and interindividual interactions. . . . Once operations are constituted, an equilibrium is finally established between the mental and the social in the sense that the individual who has become an adult member of society can hardly think outside of this completed socialization. [ibid., p. 197]

Despite these parallels between sociology and psychology, however, sociological knowledge poses some unique problems. Chief among these is the question of the nature of social totalities. Piaget reviewed the classic debate between Tarde, who explained society as the sum of the interactions among individuals, and Durkheim, who believed that society has a reality in itself over and above the individuals of which it is composed. As we have already seen with respect to another of Piaget's sociological writings reviewed in chapter 4, he himself advocated a third alternative.

Each social relation constitutes . . . a totality in itself producing new characteristics and transforming the individual in his mental structure. Already from the interaction between two individuals to the totality constituted by the ensemble of the relations between the individuals of the same society, there is thus continuity, and in the last analysis, the reality thus conceived would appear to consist, neither in a sum of individuals nor in a reality superimposed on individuals, but in a system of interactions modifying these individuals in their very structure. [ibid., p. 203]

Moreover, society in this sense may be said to oscillate between two kinds of totalities. At one extreme, certain social exchanges are integrated into equilibrated structures that may be compared on the collective plane with the operatory groupings of individual thought. Piaget cited his general model of social exchange (reviewed in chapter 4) as an example of such a collective "grouping" of interactions. At the other extreme are interactions that interfere with each other to a greater or lesser degree and that, to the extent that they are integrated into overall systems of exchange, are not entirely reversible. Society is, in effect, a compromise between these two types of totalities (ibid., p. 210). On the one hand, it is subject to forces of equilibration in many areas, such as law, morality, and so on. On the other hand, it is also affected by history and by many contingent and irreversible factors belonging to and determining that history (ibid., pp. 210ff.).

One example of such imperfectly equilibrated social factors is ideology. Piaget described ideology as "socio-centric" by analogy to the egocentrism of preoperatory thought in individual development (ibid., p. 241). He compared this description of ideology to that of Marx. "The merit of K. Marx is indeed to have distinguished in social phenomena an effective infrastructure and a superstructure oscillating between symbolism and an adequate awareness [*prise de conscience*] in the same sense (and Marx himself states it explicitly) that psychology is obliged to distinguish between real behavior and consciousness" (ibid., p. 249). In Piaget's terms, the social superstructure oscillates between science and ideology. Ideally, science reflects the material relations that constitute the infrastructure onto the plane of collective consciousness, but ideology is a sociocentric symbolism centered on the interests of a particular social class rather than on the society as a whole (ibid., pp. 249–250).

Piaget ended this chapter on sociology by addressing the same question that motivated "Logical operations and social life," reviewed in chapter 4: "Do logical operations . . . constitute individual actions, actions of a social nature, or both at once?" (ibid., p. 255). The answer is unequivocal:

The individual left to himself would never be capable of complete conservation and reversibility, and it is the exigencies of reciprocity that permit him this double conquest by the intermediary of a common language and a common scale of definitions. But at the same time, reciprocity is only possible among individual subjects capable of equilibrated thought, that is, capable of that conservation and reversibility imposed by exchange. [ibid., p. 271]

Conclusion

In the general conclusion to the *Introduction,* Piaget returned to the image of the "circle of sciences." This image implies that there is no level of description in science that is more fundamental than all the others. Rather, psychology and sociology, biology, physics, and mathematics all represent different perspectives bounded by their different methods and subject matter. To be sure, certain "reductions" are possible: Psychology and sociology could conceivably be "reduced" to biology, biology to physics, physics to mathematics. But mathematics could in the same sense be "reduced" to psycho-sociology in the form of a psychologically informed epistemology of mathematics. Thus, the "reduction" of one science to another reveals itself to be a change of perspective, rather than a move to an essentially more fundamental level of description.

Although all scientific knowledge is based on the interaction between subject and object, the balance between them is somewhat different from one science to another. Because mathematics and logic are based on coordinations among operations as such, the emphasis is on the activity of the subject. In physics, knowledge develops from coordinations among actions that are accommodated to particular properties of objects; therefore, physical knowledge involves a balance (or oscillation) between subject and object. In biology, the relation between subject and object is different. On the one hand, the activity of the subject is less emphasized, because mathematization has proceeded less far in biology than in physics, much of biological science having been concerned with classification. On the other hand, another kind of relation between subject and object is opened up in biology, based on the fact that the subject of knowledge is also a living being, one of the organisms that constitute the object of biological science. Finally, in psychology and sociology the relation between subject and object becomes even more complex, because the ''object'' of psycho-sociological knowledge is in fact another subject. By the same token, the subject can become an ''object'' of the subject's own self-knowledge.

According to this scheme, the boundaries between the sciences become ''frontiers'' of knowledge, where a coordination of perspectives becomes possible. Piaget intimated that new discoveries are likely to be made in the future along these frontiers. In this context, one can understand some of Piaget's own preoccupations, for his operatory theories of logic and mathematics deal with the frontier between mathematics and psychology, and his penchant for drawing parallels between psychology and biology has to do with the frontier between those two disciplines.

The growth of scientific knowledge, according to Piaget, involves both the construction of novelties and a reflective establishment of continuity with the past. This view may be illustrated in the history of number theory. Thus, $\sqrt{-1}$ can be explained as a generalization of operations of the type $\sqrt{+n}$; $\sqrt{-1}$ was not contained or even implied in the number series before the adoption of imaginary numbers. As a number, it is a new construction, but not a construction *ex nihilo*. As an operatory generalization or ''reflective abstraction,'' it maintains a necessary continuity with the number series as the latter had previously been conceived. Both novelty and continuity have their places in Piaget's operatory theory: ''If abstraction from previous actions or operations explains the continuity between the old and the new, the composition of several abstractions in a single operatory totality in which it had not participated until then accounts for the novelty of construction'' (ibid., p. 303).

Does this mode of progress imply that the growth of scientific knowledge has a direction? In one sense, yes. The growth of knowledge, according to Piaget, is no mere accumulation of facts, but a progressive re-equilibration. Science progresses toward more and more equilibrated forms – just as the number system was more equilibrated following the adoption of $\sqrt{-1}$ as a number than it was before, when the operations of negation and taking the square root were not intercoordinated, and $\sqrt{-1}$ was merely an anomaly. Another example of such re-equilibrations in science cited by Piaget is the overtaking of Newtonian physics by relativity and quantum theory in the 20th century. The fact that the growth of scientific knowledge possesses a certain directionality, however, does not imply that it has a final destination.

STUDIES OF LOGIC

Operatory psycho-logic

In 1949, Piaget published *Traité de logique,* a rather voluminous exposition of his system of operatory logic. In the introduction to the second edition of this work, retitled *Essai de logique opératoire* and published in 1972, Piaget stated the goal of the book as follows: ''The problem from which this essay originates is to understand how the elementary structures of classes, relations, numbers, propositions, etc., formalized in complete autonomy and independence by the logician, are constituted and to find out what kinds of relations they have with the weaker and nonformalized 'operations' of 'natural' thought'' (Piaget, 1949/1972a, p. xi). This *Essai* thus picked up where the earlier book *Classes, relations et nombres* left off. Not only did Piaget in this work go beyond the ''groupings'' of classes and relations to consider the operatory structures of propositional logic, he also went further in discussing the relation between his operatory theory and the problems of modern logic.

As the study of the operations of natural thought, operatory logic constitutes a kind of bridge between psychology and formal logic: *''Logic is the axiomatics of operatory structures, the real functioning of which is studied by the psychology and sociology of thought''* (ibid., p. 15). As a bridge between logic and mathematics, on the one hand, and social science, on the other, operatory logic occupies one of the ''frontiers'' of knowledge described in the *Introduction à l'épistémologie génétique.* At the same time, operatory logic may be distinguished from genetic epistemology, the latter having to do with the relations between subject and object in the development of knowledge, and the former having to do with the formal analysis of that knowledge (ibid., p. 4).

Piaget began his analysis by defining propositions as statements that can be either true or false, going on to distinguish between ''interpropositional'' and ''intrapropositional'' operations. Interpropositional operations allow one to determine the truth value of compositions among other propositions whose truth values are known, regardless of their contents. Intrapropositional operations are transformations of the elements of propositions such that the truth values of the resulting propositions depend on the combinations of those elements. Given this distinction, Piaget identified interpropositional operations with formal logic, and intrapropositional operations with the logic of classes and the logic of relations (i.e., with concrete operations). Given a propositional function xa, defined as a statement that in itself is neither true nor false but that can acquire a truth value when the variable x is identified, a class may be defined as a collection of terms capable of giving the propositional function xa a truth value when substituted for the variable x. A relation can then be defined as the intermediary between two terms. Neither classes nor relations can be considered apart from the operations by which they are constituted, and every operation is part of a total structure. In Piaget's words: "Every class is in fact bound up with a classification" (ibid., p. 81). The question is how to characterize the systems of which operations of classification and ordering are parts. Piaget demonstrated that classification does not have the structure of a group, because (among other reasons) the compositions of a group always yield a new result, although those of a classification do not (a class A united with itself or with another class B that includes it yields only A or B, respectively). Likewise, classification cannot be considered as having a lattice structure, because the compositions of a lattice are not completely reversible.

Piaget continued with a formal exposition of the grouping structure in general as well as the eight particular groupings of classes and relations. Because these groupings have already been described in chapter 4, they will not be further pursued here. Instead, we move directly to the major innovation of the *Essai*: Piaget's characterization of the structure of propositional logic.

Propositional logic

As opposed to the intrapropositional operations of the logic of classes and relations, propositional logic has to do with interpropositional operations, operations that serve to link propositions together. The truth value of the product of such an interpropositional operation depends on the truth values of the original propositions that are linked together by the operation in question. In the simplest case of two original propositions (conventionally labeled p and q), four combinations of truth values are possible (both p and q can be true, both false, p true and q false, or p false and q true). Thus, the product of any operation linking p and q will have a truth value that may change, depending on which combination of truth values of p and q is the case. In other words, each bi-propositional operation will have a distinctive "profile" of possible truth values corresponding to the four possible combinations of truth values of p and q. This being so, 16 distinctive profiles (and therefore 16 possible binary operations) are possible. These operations and their respective profiles are shown in Table 5.2. Elsewhere, Piaget acknowledged the fact that these profiles are "isomorphic" to the method of truth tables introduced by Wittgenstein (1922/1961) in the *Tractatus* (Piaget, 1952b, p. 145n).

It is unnecessary to examine each of these operations in detail. An example will suffice. The disjunction of two propositions p and q (operation 3 in Table 5.2) is itself a proposition that is true when either p or q is true, but not when they are both false. In contrast, the conjunction of p and q is true only when both p and q are true, and so on. Some of the operations in Table 5.2 (like conjunction

Table 5.2. *Truth table for the system of 16 binary operations*

	Binary operations	Truth values of p and q			
		T, T	T, F	F, T	F, F
1. $p*q$	(complete affirmation)	T	T	T	T
2. $\circ$	(complete negation)	F	F	F	F
3. $p \vee q$	(disjunction)	T	T	T	F
4. $\overline{p \cdot q}$	(conjoint negation)	F	F	F	T
5. $p \mid q$	(incompatibility)	F	T	T	T
6. $p \cdot q$	(conjunction)	T	F	F	F
7. $p \supset q$	(conditional)	T	F	T	T
8. $\overline{p \supset q}$	(nonconditional)	F	T	F	F
9. $q \supset p$	(inverse conditional)	T	T	F	T
10. $\overline{q \supset p}$	(inverse nonconditional)	F	F	T	F
11. $p \equiv q$	(biconditional)	T	F	F	T
12. $p \, \mathbf{W} \, q$	(exclusion)	F	T	T	F
13. $p[q]$	(affirmation of p)	T	T	F	F
14. $\overline{p}[q]$	(negation of p)	F	F	T	T
15. $q[p]$	(affirmation of q)	T	F	T	F
16. $\overline{q}[p]$	(negation of q)	F	T	F	T

Source: Piaget (1949/1972a, p. 213).

and disjunction) are familiar operations in formal logic. Others (like complete affirmation and complete negation) are less familiar. According to Piaget, they are all part of the total system generated by considering all the possible combinations of truth values for the four combinations of truth values that can be jointly assumed by p and q.

Piaget argued that although intrapropositional and interpropositional operations are fundamentally different by their very definition, they are nevertheless filiated with each other developmentally. That is, the 16 binary operations are derived from concrete operations by a kind of recursive application of concrete operations on concrete operations. Such recursive operations can be illustrated as follows: The four possible combinations of truth values of p and q are obtained through a simple operation of logical multiplication in which the two possible truth values (true, T, or false, F) for p and q are crossed with each other to yield the four pairings TT, TF, FT, and FF. This operation is isomorphic to the grouping of bi-univocal multiplication of classes as described in chapter 4 of this book. In this application of the grouping, the propositions p and q assume the roles of "classes" of possible statements, each of which may be divided into "subclasses" of true and false statements.

From the product of this first logical multiplication, the profiles of the 16 binary operations can be derived through a recursive logical multiplication in which the four pairings obtained in the first operation are crossed with themselves, yielding the 16 profiles shown in Table 5.2. This recursive operation of

Table 5.3. *Disjunctive forms of the 16 binary operations*

Binary operations		Disjunctive forms			
1. $p*q$	(complete affirmation)	$(p \cdot q)$ V	$(p \cdot \bar{q})$ V	$(\bar{p} \cdot q)$ V	$(\bar{p} \cdot \bar{q})$
2. $\circ$	(complete negation)		$(\circ)$		
3. $p \vee q$	(disjunction)	$(p \cdot q)$ V	$(p \cdot \bar{q})$ V	$(\bar{p} \cdot q)$	
4. $\bar{p} \cdot \bar{q}$	(conjoint negation)				$(\bar{p} \cdot \bar{q})$
5. $p \mid q$	(incompatibility)		$(p \cdot \bar{q})$ V	$(\bar{p} \cdot q)$ V	$(\bar{p} \cdot \bar{q})$
6. $p \cdot q$	(conjunction)	$(p \cdot q)$			
7. $p \supset q$	(conditional)	$(p \cdot q)$	V	$(\bar{p} \cdot q)$ V	$(\bar{p} \cdot \bar{q})$
8. $\overline{p \supset q}$	(nonconditional)		$(p \cdot \bar{q})$		
9. $q \supset p$	(inverse conditional)	$(p \cdot q)$ V	$(p \cdot \bar{q})$	V	$(\bar{p} \cdot \bar{q})$
10. $\overline{q \supset p}$	(inverse nonconditional)			$(\bar{p} \cdot q)$	
11. $p \equiv q$	(biconditional)	$(p \cdot q)$	V		$(\bar{p} \cdot \bar{q})$
12. $p \mathbf{W} q$	(exclusion)		$(p \cdot \bar{q})$ V	$(\bar{p} \cdot q)$	
13. $p[q]$	(affirmation of p)	$(p \cdot q)$ V	$(p \cdot \bar{q})$		
14. $\bar{p}[q]$	(negation of p)			$(\bar{p} \cdot q)$ V	$(\bar{p} \cdot \bar{q})$
15. $q[p]$	(affirmation of q)	$(p \cdot q)$	V	$(\bar{p} \cdot q)$	
16. $\bar{q}[p]$	(negation of q)		$(p \cdot \bar{q})$	V	$(\bar{p} \cdot \bar{q})$

Source: Piaget (1949/1972a, p. 254).

logical multiplication forms the basis for what Piaget called a *combinatorial system.* Such a system has the structure that he labeled *l'ensemble des parties,* or "the set of all sub-sets." This system not only forms the basis of propositional logic but also is found to underlie the understanding of probability and combinatory thinking. The fact that both propositional logic and combinatorial thinking are based on the same *structure d'ensemble* is the reason, according to Piaget (1957a, p. xviii), that they are found to develop roughly at the same time in the stage of formal operations – an example that indicates that Piaget was not above interpreting instances of developmental synchrony when they occurred, even if he declined to predict them in advance.

The 16 binary operations link the two elementary propositions p and q together, and they are also linked formally to one another. In fact, one can express any one of the 16 binary operations in terms of any of the others. For Piaget, such transformations reflected the fact that all 16 operations are embedded in a total system, as illustrated in the following example.

Piaget often expressed the binary operations in the form of disjunctions. These disjunctive forms are given in Table 5.3 for all the 16 binary operations. In this table, the symbol p refers to the affirmation of the respective proposition, $\bar{p}$ refers to the negation of that proposition, and so on. Thus, the operation of disjunction (operation 3 in Table 5.3) can be expressed as $(p \cdot q)$ V $(p \cdot \bar{q})$ V $(\bar{p} \cdot q)$. That is, the operation of disjunction is equivalent to the affirmation of p and q, the affirmation of p and the negation of q, or the negation of p and the affirmation of q. It is incompatible, however, with the negation of both p and q, and this is why the expression $\bar{p} \cdot \bar{q}$ is not included in the disjunctive form of this operation.

The isomorphism between the disjunctive forms of the binary operations (Table 5.3) and their truth-table forms (Table 5.2) is obvious. The disjunctive form may be derived from the truth-table form by substituting an appropriate conjunction of p, q, $\bar{p}$, or $\bar{q}$ for each T in the truth-table profile. The generation of the disjunctive forms through recursive logical multiplication was described by Piaget as follows: First, the total set of combinations of affirmations or negations of p and q is generated according to the operation $(p \vee \bar{p}) \cdot (q \vee \bar{q}) = (p \cdot q) \vee (p \cdot \bar{q}) \vee (\bar{p} \cdot q) \vee (\bar{p} \cdot \bar{q})$. This operation (equivalent to "complete affirmation" in Table 5.3) is isomorphic to the bi-univocal multiplication of classes as given in chapter 4: $(A_1 + A_1') \times (A_2 + A_2') = A_1A_2 + A_1A_2' + A_1'A_2 + A_1'A_2'$. Then the set of all subsets of this primary set of combinations is generated, the result being the 16 disjunctive forms shown in Table 5.3 (Piaget, 1957a, pp. 29–30). Elsewhere in the *Essai*, Piaget (1949/1972a, pp. 217–226) expressed the disjunctive forms of all 16 binary propositional operations in terms of class intersections. Thus, operation 3 in Table 5.3 can be expressed alternatively in propositional form as $(p \cdot q) \vee (p \cdot \bar{q}) \vee (\bar{p} \cdot q)$ or in terms of class unions as $PQ \cup P\bar{Q} \cup \bar{P}Q$.[1]

Certain of the 16 binary operations may also be transformed from one to another in terms of inversion (or negation), reciprocity, and correlation. Formally, these transformations may be defined as follows: The *inverse* (negation) is the complement of an operation with respect to complete affirmation. Thus, disjunction is the inverse of conjoint negation, incompatibility the inverse of conjunction, and so on (Table 5.3). The *reciprocal* of an operation is the same operation, but with the signs reversed. Thus, disjunction is the reciprocal of incompatibility, conjoint negation the reciprocal of conjunction, and so on. The *correlative* can then be defined as the inverse of the reciprocal. Thus, disjunction is the correlative of conjunction, and conjoint negation the correlative of incompatibility. Not all the 16 binary operations are related to each other by these transformations. Rather, they divide into six subgroups, each closed on itself with respect to the operations of inversion, reciprocity, and correlation. These subgroups are also shown in Table 5.4.

In fact, each of these subgroups may be said to have group structure in the

---

1 Piaget's account of propositional logic was challenged by Parsons (1960) and Ennis (1975) as contradictory and inconsistent with standard logic. In reply, Leiser (1982) argued that these problems vanish if Piaget's formalism is interpreted as a logic of possibilities. In solving the kinds of formal operational tasks posed by Inhelder and Piaget (1955/1958), children must determine which of a range of logical possibilities are also physically possible. Apostel (1982) argued that Piaget's account of propositional logic in terms of truth functions is inconsistent with his description of propositional operations in terms of class union and intersection. In Apostel's view, only the latter is original with Piaget and of theoretical interest. Piaget and Garcia (1987) admitted, in effect, the justice of this point and proposed a revision of Piaget's (1949/1972a) account of the logical structure of formal operations. This revision would be based on intensional logic rather than extensional logic and would conform to Piaget's (1949/1972a) interpretation of propositional operations in terms of class unions and intersections rather than to the truth-functional interpretation. Criticisms of Piagetian logic will be considered in greater detail in chapter 8.

Table 5.4. *Subgroups of the 16 binary operations formed by the operations of inversion, reciprocity, and correlation*

Identity	Negation	Reciprocal	Correlative
1. $p*q$	(o)	$p*q$	(o)
2. (o)	$p*q$	(o)	$p*q$
3. $p \vee q$	$\bar{p} \cdot \bar{q}$	$p \mid q$	$p \cdot q$
4. $\bar{p} \cdot \bar{q}$	$p \vee q$	$p \cdot q$	$\underline{p \mid q}$
5. $p \mid q$	$p \cdot q$	$\underline{p \vee q}$	$\bar{p} \cdot \bar{q}$
6. $p \cdot q$	$p \mid q$	$\bar{p} \cdot \bar{q}$	$p \vee q$
7. $p \supset q$	$p \cdot \bar{q}$	$q \supset p$	$\bar{p} \cdot q$
8. $p \cdot \bar{q}$	$p \supset q$	$\bar{p} \cdot q$	$q \supset p$
9. $q \supset p$	$\bar{p} \cdot q$	$p \supset q$	$p \cdot \bar{q}$
10. $\bar{p} \cdot q$	$q \supset p$	$p \cdot \bar{q}$	$p \supset q$
11. $p \equiv q$	$p \mathsf{W} q$	$p \equiv q$	$p \mathsf{W} q$
12. $p \mathsf{W} q$	$p \equiv q$	$p \mathsf{W} q$	$p \equiv q$
13. $p[q]$	$\bar{p}[q]$	$\bar{p}[q]$	$\underline{p[q]}$
14. $\bar{p}[q]$	$p[q]$	$p[q]$	$\bar{p}[q]$
15. $q[p]$	$\bar{q}[p]$	$\bar{q}[p]$	$q[p]$
16. $\bar{q}[p]$	$q[p]$	$q[p]$	$\bar{q}[p]$

Source: Piaget (1949/1972a, p. 258).

formal sense, because they are characterized by composition under closure, associativity, inversion, and identity. If the letters I, N, R, and C are taken to represent the operations of identity, negation, reciprocity, and correlativity, respectively, then the compositions characterizing these groups may be given as follows: I = NRC, N = IRC, R = INC, and C = IRN. In contrast to these INRC groups, the system of 16 binary operations taken as a whole is a grouping, characterized by the special identities of grouping structures (e.g., $p \vee p = p$, $p \cdot p = p$, etc.).

This analysis of the relations among the 16 binary operations was extended to the system of 256 ternary operations (i.e., interpropositional operations linking three propositions, p, q, and r) in *Essai sur les transformations des opérations logiques* (Piaget, 1952b). By virtue of the number of combinations possible in this system, the analysis of families of operations existing in this system and of the possible transformations among families was exceedingly complex. The psychological implications of operatory logic, however, were clearly and concisely presented in *Logic and psychology* (Piaget, 1957a), perhaps the best introduction to Piagetian operatory logic in English. Here Piaget explicitly referred to operatory logic as a "psycho-logic," forming a third term between axiomatic logic and psychology.

The psychological applications of the interpropositional operations analyzed by Piaget were discussed more thoroughly in *The origin of the idea of chance in children* (Piaget & Inhelder, 1951/1975) and *The growth of logical thinking from childhood to adolescence* (Inhelder & Piaget, 1955/1958). The method behind these applications can be illustrated with a few examples from each book without attempting to review their contents in detail.

Chance and necessity

Probability. Discussing chance and logic together might seem strange, because they might appear to be totally antithetical on the surface. Although logic is marked by the construction of necessary relations, relations governed by chance are by definition fortuitous. However, in a variety of experiments involving random mixtures, probabilistic distributions, games of chance, and random drawings, Piaget and Inhelder (1951/1975) found that the idea of chance developed roughly at the same time as the idea of necessity in the context of concrete operations. In general, three stages were found in the development of the idea of chance across all of the experiments. Before the age of about 7–8 years, children did not distinguish between what can be predicted from logical necessity and what is merely possible (i.e., that which is essentially unpredictable). Instead, they predicted outcomes for "capricious" reasons (e.g., a counter drawn at random was predicted to be red, because the child liked red, or because it went with a color previously drawn). Sometimes they evinced an "intuitive" understanding of probability, as when a child predicted a counter of a certain color would be drawn because there were "more of them," but this reasoning was neither consistent nor systematic.

Only around the age of 7–8 years did children begin to acquire a sense of logical necessity as a consequence of the development of concrete operations. Chance outcomes came to be understood as those that could *not* be explained in terms of logical necessity. What occurred by chance was one possible outcome among a range of alternative possibilities. What was still missing at this stage was a complete and systematic delineation of the range of possibilities. For example, in drawing differently colored counters without replacement, children correctly estimated the initial probabilities by the initial distribution of colors, but they did not recognize that the distribution (hence the probabilities) changed as counters were drawn and not replaced.

This limitation was overcome in the third stage, beginning at about the age of 11–12 years. Children were now able to reconstruct the complete range of possibilities governing a particular situation and therefore became capable of specifying relative probabilities in terms of the relative proportions of the total possibilities. For example, the probability of drawing a counter of a certain color was seen to change as one made successive drawings without replacement. Similarly, the relative probability of drawing a counter of a certain type out of two bags was judged to be a function of the proportions in each bag; it is more likely that a counter marked by a cross will be drawn from bag *A* as compared with bag *B* if the proportion of counters with crosses is greater in bag *A* than in bag *B*. Only in this stage did children come to understand the law of large numbers: that although single outcomes cannot be predicted with certainty from a knowledge of the probabilities involved, the actual distribution of outcomes will approach that predicted by chance as the number of trials increases.

Piaget and Inhelder argued that the ability to construct the entire range of possibilities in a situation governed by chance reflects the development of a combinatorial system. As evidence, they cited the results of experiments in which they asked children directly to construct all the possible combinations or permutations of objects of different colors. Briefly, they found the same three stages in the development of the construction of combinations and permutations as they had found for the development of the understanding of probability. Only after the age of about 11–12 years were children systematically able to construct all the possible combinations of a certain number of elements (e.g., the four elements A, B, C, and D taken two at a time can be combined in six possible ways: AB, AC, AD, BC, BD, and CD). Somewhat later, at about 14–15 years, children learned to construct systematically all possible permutations (e.g., the 12 possible permutations of 4 elements taken 2 at a time).

Formal operations. This development of combinatorial systems links the understanding of probability to propositional logic as common aspects of formal operations. In *The growth of logical thinking from childhood to adolescence,* Inhelder and Piaget (1955/1958) illustrated the 16 binary operations in terms of one of the tasks they had previously used in *The origin of the idea of chance.* In this task, children were shown a kind of roulette wheel consisting of a metal pointer attached to a rotating disk surrounded by a ring of eight boxes. Children were asked to predict where the pointer would stop when the wheel was spun. In one version of the task, magnets were attached to one pair of boxes opposite each other so that the pointer always stopped in one place, and children had to discover why this occurred. The boxes varied in weight, providing an additional, irrelevant variable. In the book on chance, this task had been used to study the conflict between chance (the behavior of the wheel when the magnets were not present) and causal determination (when the magnets were present). In the book on logic, the 16 binary operations were illustrated in examples from the protocol of a single Stage III child.

For example, the operation of disjunction ($p \lor q$) was illustrated by the child's comment that "it's either the distance or content" of the boxes that influenced the wheel (where p is the assertion that distance is effective, and q the assertion that content is effective). Conjunction ($p \cdot q$) was illustrated by the finding that both distance and content were in fact effective. In determining that neither weight (p) nor color (q) was effective, the child provided an example of conjunctive negation ($\bar{p} \cdot \bar{q}$), and so on through the list.

Most of the tasks described in *The growth of logical thinking* involved some particular subfamily of operations from the full set of 16 binary operations. Children's solutions to the problems were followed from the preoperational period to formal operations. This procedure allows the reader to observe the limitations of preoperational and concrete operational thinking and the distinct advances made by formal operational thought. For example, in the chapter entitled "Equilibrium in the balance," the problem was to discover the inverse relation between weight and distance for varying weights placed along the arms of the balance at varying distances from the center (or, alternatively, the relation involving weight, distance, and the height of the arms).

In the *preoperational stage,* no systematic coordination of weight and distance was observed. Between the ages of roughly 3 and 5 years, children tended to confuse the action of the apparatus with their actions *on* the apparatus. That is, children asserted that they could bring the balance into the horizontal position, but they did so only by moving it with their hands. From about 5 to 7 years, children attempted to right the balance using the weights, but they accomplished this only through successive approximations; they exhibited no systematic effort to equalize either weights or distances.

In the stage of *concrete operations,* weights and distances began to be equalized. At first, this equalization was symmetric; equal weights were placed at equal distances from the center. At a later substage, children realized that changes in distance could compensate for inequalities of weight, and vice versa. According to Inhelder and Piaget's analysis, this realization involved the grouping of bi-univocal multiplication of relations. As applied to the present problem, however, that grouping had several limitations. For one thing, it was not yet quantified; children reasoning according to this substage could not predict what would happen when both weight and distance were varied – that is, when one of the weights was made lighter and at the same time moved away from the center (or made heavier and simultaneously moved toward the center), these operations could result in either an increase or decrease in height, depending on the exact proportions involved.

The discovery of this proportionality was the chief feature of the stage of *formal operations.* Inhelder and Piaget stated that quantitative proportions are acquired by way of logical proportions with the discovery that simultaneously increasing the weight and the distance on one arm of the balance is equivalent to decreasing the weight and increasing the distance on the other arm. This equivalence can be expressed symbolically as

$$\bar{p} \cdot q = R(p \cdot \bar{q}), \qquad (5.1)$$

where $\bar{p}$ is a statement of the decrease in weight, q is a statement of the increase in distance, R represents the reciprocity between the two arms of the balance, and so on. The equivalence may also be represented in terms of the proportion

$$\frac{p}{q} = \frac{\bar{p}}{\bar{q}}, \qquad (5.2)$$

meaning that an increase in weight on one arm is to an increase in distance on the other as a decrease in weight on the second arm is to a decrease in distance on the first. This equation is in turn isomorphic to the quantitative proportion relating changes in weight to changes in distance:

$$\frac{nW}{nL'} = \frac{W'/n}{L/n}.$$

(5.3)

In other words, increasing the weight (W) on the first arm by a factor of n may be balanced by increasing the distance (L') on the opposite arm by the same factor, just as dividing the weight (W') by a factor of n on the second arm can be balanced by dividing the distance (L) by the same factor on the first.

In fact, Inhelder and Piaget argued that the inverse proportional relation between weight and distance can be expressed in terms of the INRC group. The following equation, for example, expresses the additional fact that a change in weight *or* distance on one side of the scale can be used to balance simultaneous changes in weight *and* distance on the other side:

$$\frac{p \cdot q}{\overline{p} \cdot \overline{q}} = \frac{p \vee q}{\overline{p} \vee \overline{q}},$$

(5.4)

which can be rewritten as

$$\frac{I}{R} = \frac{C}{N},$$

(5.5)

where $I = p \cdot q,$ and so on (Table 5.4).

Inhelder and Piaget analyzed the formal structures that presumably underlay the reasoning of children on a number of such tasks, including discovering the equality between angles of incidence of a rebounding billiard ball, finding the rule that determines whether material bodies will float or sink in water, discovering the factors that determine the flexibility of rods, finding the rules governing the oscillation of a pendulum, discovering which combinations of several liquids will change color and which combinations will remain colorless, determining the factors governing the sizes of shadows projected on a board, among other problems. In each case, children's thinking at the stage of formal operations was found to involve combinatorial operations, the system of binary operations, or a subfamily of this system such as the INRC group.

Although these analyses demonstrated that children's reasoning *could* be interpreted in this way, one wonders what alternative interpretations might also be possible and how one would decide between them. This problem of uniqueness raises a question about the relation between the data and the system of logic by which they are interpreted. Evidently, the logic was not derived solely from the data. Rather, examples of children's reasoning were used to illustrate the logical system. A further question has to do with the ontological status of the operatory structures involved. In what sense can such structures be said to determine children's reasoning? Or to what extent do they exist only as interpretative schemes applied by the psychologist after the fact?

Reality and possibility. Inhelder and Piaget addressed some of these questions in the concluding chapters of the book. Formal thinking may be characterized by a general subordination of reality to possibility in the sense that what is real at any given moment is recognized as only one manifestation of a wider range of possibilities. The possible, however, can be divided into two types: those operations or relations that children themselves recognize as possible even without actually performing or constructing them, and those possibilities recognized by an observer, but not by the children themselves. Inhelder and Piaget (1955/1958, pp. 259–260) called these two types of possibility *instrumental possibility* and *structural possibility,* respectively. However, structural possibility does not exist only with reference to the observer. Instead, the authors argued, "we must exclude the notion of not attributing the structurally possible to the subject as such" (ibid., p. 263). Instrumental possibilities of which the subject is aware are not the only active causes in determining children's reasoning; some causal determination must be attributed to structural possibilities as well. But what sort of causality can be attributed to the merely possible?

In answering this question, Inhelder and Piaget made what appears to be at first a somewhat puzzling reference to the maturation of the nervous system: "If, in psychology, we accept the view that the development of mental functions is linked to the maturation of the nervous system . . . it follows as a matter of course that a coordination could appear in a potentially general form although it would first give rise to certain specific applications only" (ibid., p. 264). The authors continued by speculating that "without committing ourselves to such hypotheses," the latter could nevertheless be useful in explaining the synchronisms that are frequently observed in development. Thus, certain coordinations or operations appear more or less synchronously in analogous problems, because the different coordinations or operations become structurally possible at the same point in development (ibid., pp. 264–265).

This rather ambiguous passage is easily misunderstood if it is not viewed in the context of Piaget's work as a whole. It was not meant to imply that cognitive structures develop as a direct consequence of maturation. Piaget was not abandoning his long-standing position that cognitive structures are constructed by the subject in interaction with the environment. Expressed in more contemporaneous terminology, Inhelder and Piaget were saying something like the following: that the development of structures at a given level of operative complexity may require certain organismic resources, which in turn develop through maturation. These resources are necessary but not sufficient for the construction of the respective structures; they make this construction possible, but they are not sufficient for realizing it. If the other conditions for the construction of structures (e.g., familiarity with the specific content, opportunities for constructive activity) are already fulfilled in different domains, then the maturation of the necessary resources can lead to the synchronous emergence of analogous structures across those domains. If these other conditions are not fulfilled, however, then the development of the necessary resources will not result in the simultaneous appearance of similar structures in different domains.

Inhelder and Piaget argued, for example, that the linkage between the development of formal operational structures and the maturation of the nervous system "is far from simple, since the organization of formal structures must depend on the social milieu as well" (ibid., p. 337). In other words, the social environment constitutes one of the additional necessary conditions for the development of cognitive structures. "Far from being a source of fully elaborated 'innate ideas,' the maturation of the nervous system can do no more than determine the totality of possibilities and impossibilities at a given stage. A particular social environment remains indispensable for the realization of these possibilities" (ibid.). In this way, Inhelder and Piaget avoid the extremes of both maturationism and environmentalism, consistent with the whole thrust of Piaget's thought.

The formal structures are neither innate *a priori* forms of intelligence which are inscribed in advance in the nervous system, nor are they collective representations which exist ready-made outside and above the individual. Instead, they are forms of equilibrium which gradually settle on the system of exchanges between individuals and the physical milieu and on the system of exchanges between individuals themselves. Moreover, in the final analysis the two systems can be reduced to a single system seen from two different perspectives. And this comes back to what we have said many times before. [ibid., p. 338]

Of course, one can always explain the real in terms of the possible after the fact. Inhelder and Piaget argued that the postulated causal role of structural possibility is saved from this kind of vacuity by the fact that "there are algebraic instruments which enable us to uncover the role of general structures and to calculate their extension as well as their elements" (ibid., p. 266). In other words, if children manifest certain aspects of a given formal operational structure (e.g., the 16 binary operations), they should be capable of manifesting the remaining aspects, at least with respect to the same problem or content.

This argument may or may not be convincing. At the very least, it would seem to be incomplete as long as the conditions under which the merely possible can be expected to be realized are not specified, or until the cognitive resources that determine structural possibility as such are identified. Because this chapter is devoted exclusively to the exposition of Piaget's ideas, not to their evaluation, further consideration of these questions will be deferred until chapter 7.

Inhelder and Piaget concluded *The growth of logical thinking* with a chapter on adolescent thinking in which some typical characteristics of adolescent thought were related to the development of formal operations. For example, the idealism, Messianism, and reformism often considered typical of adolescents can be traced to the subordination of the real to the possible characteristic of formal operational thought – that is, to the discovery that things could be other than they are. As described in chapter 1, several of the examples cited in this connection recall episodes in Piaget's own adolescence.

Classification and seriation. Inhelder and Piaget's book on formal operations was followed 4 years later by *The early growth of logic in the child* (Inhelder & Piaget, 1959/1969), devoted to the study of classification and seriation. Previously, the logical groupings of classification and seriation had been studied primarily in terms of their role in the development of number, quantity, space, and measurement. Now they were investigated for their own sake. In addition, Piaget had completed a major series of studies on perception; so he was also in a better position to consider perceptual contributions to the solution of logical problems.

In general, Inhelder and Piaget found that classifications and seriations based on perceptual configurations were gradually superseded by operations based on logical criteria. For example, young children between the ages of 2.5 and 5 years tended to classify colored geometric shapes and letters into "graphic collections" based on successively perceived similarities between objects. However, the basis for the similarity could change from one comparison to the next, such that children produced spatial arrangements of objects based on alternating criteria (e.g., form, then color, then form again) instead of logical classes as such. Sometimes the objects were only partially classified, leaving a number of them unclassified. According to Inhelder and Piaget, young children are unable to form logical classifications because they do not distinguish "similarity," from "belonging" (i.e., relations based on common properties from relations based on spatial configurations).

During a second stage between the ages of approximately 4.5 and 7 years, children were found to classify the same objects in terms of "non-graphic collections." In other words, children eliminated the inconsistencies in classificatory criteria characterizing graphic collections through successive approximations, but remained dependent on spatial proximity for establishing that several objects belong together (and this is why such nongraphic collections were still considered "collections" rather than classes as such).

Finally, beginning at about 7–8 years, children began to classify the objects into classes and subclasses based on consistent and exhaustive criteria. For example, one subject was reported to divide the objects into geometrical shapes and letters, both of these general classes being subdivided into shapes and letters having common forms. One characteristic of these logical classifications was that they were no longer dependent on spatial proximity, but only on the possession of a common quality (e.g., shape).

Also characteristic of this stage was children's acquisition of the understanding that one class may be included in another. This understanding involves the coordination between "all" and "some" – the recognition that *all* the members of the subordinate class are members of the supraordinate class, but that only *some* of the members of the supraordinate class are members of the subordinate class.

As an example of such hierarchical classification, Inhelder and Piaget asked children to classify species of plants and animals, recalling Piaget's (1950a) remarks to the effect that biological classification exhibited the structure of concrete operational groupings. Unexpectedly, a horizontal decalage was found between the classification of flowers and animals, with 60% of children passing inclusion problems at 8 years for plants, but only at 12–13 years for animals. This finding led Inhelder and Piaget to remark: "We have here a remarkable instance of the way in which the emergence of concrete operational reasoning depends very closely on the intuitive character of its content. . . . That different results are obtained when animals are used must be due to the fact that these classes are more remote from everyday experience and therefore more abstract'' (Inhelder & Piaget, 1959/1969, p. 110). An alternative explanation might be that the respective series of inclusions used by Inhelder and Piaget differed in the relative levels of abstraction involved, rather than just in the degree of familiarity; the series "ducks, birds, animals" apparently involves a higher level of abstraction than "yellow primulas, primulas, flowers."

In addition to this decalage between different areas of content, Inhelder and Piaget found a developmental lag between different groupings as applied to the same type of content. The simple multiplication of classes (intersection) was passed by 75% of children only at the age of 9–10 years, but the complete multiplication of classes (matrix cross-classification) was passed by 75% of children already at 7–8 years of age. This decalage was explained by the assumption that "simple multiplication means abstracting a portion of the total system of complete multiplication" (ibid., p. 177). Again, other explanations are possible in terms of the specific procedures employed.

These decalages are of interest not so much for the question whether or not Inhelder and Piaget explained them adequately but rather for the authors' views on the relation between such decalages and the theory of operational structures. Neither the decalage between different areas of content nor that between groupings within a single area of content was viewed as contrary to expectation. Indeed, the explanation of the decalage between simple and complete multiplication was stated in the form of a prediction. These remarks thus constitute additional evidence that developmental synchrony, either between or within content domains, was not intended to follow as a necessary consequence of Piaget's theory of structure.

The fact that developmental synchrony was not predicted did not mean that it could not be interpreted after the fact. In summarizing their findings, Inhelder and Piaget remarked that despite certain differences in the extent to which perception intervenes, it was a "remarkable fact" that the four principal groupings in the logic of classes and relations (i.e., the addition and multiplication of classes and relations, respectively) were found to appear in development "at roughly the same period" (ibid., p. 279). But this "rough" developmental synchrony was not cited as evidence for the functional unity of all four groupings. Instead, the authors argued as follows: Several considerations suggest that these groupings would be differentially affected by language and perception; therefore, the fact that they develop roughly in synchrony suggests that language and perception cannot be the major determining factors in their development:

From a theoretical point of view, the parallelism [in the development of classification and seriation] is most important because it constitutes the strongest argument possible in favour of the thesis that the development of operational behaviour is an autonomous process rather than a secondary consequence, depending on the development of perception or of language. [ibid., p. 290]

This is not to say that the factors of language, perception, maturation, and learning are not necessary for the development of operations, only that they are not in themselves sufficient. In addition to such factors, one must consider the factor of equilibrium. In the case of classification, for example, the decisive characteristic of the transition between preoperational and operational classification is the recognition that the "ascending method" (building ever more general classes out of more specific classes) is exactly compensated by the "descending method" (building more specific classes out of more general ones). Similarly for seriation: A series can be constructed by beginning at either end. The simultaneous coordination of these two procedures, pursued alternately and successively rather than simultaneously at the preoperational level, constitutes the reversibility characterizing the form of equilibrium at the level of concrete operations.

FIGURATIVE VERSUS OPERATIVE THOUGHT

In 1961, Piaget published *The mechanisms of perception* (Piaget, 1961/1969), a summary and interpretation of the research on perception that he had conducted since the early forties. That book was followed by *Mental imagery in the child* (Piaget & Inhelder, 1966/1971) and *Memory and intelligence* (Piaget & Inhelder, 1968/1973). Each of these works focused on what Piaget came to call the *figurative* aspect of intelligence: forms of cognition that involve the construction of more or less accurate "copies" of reality and include perception, imitation, and mental imagery. In contrast, the *operative* aspect of intelligence involves forms of knowing having to do with the modification or transformation of reality, including sensorimotor actions, interiorized actions, and cognitive operations (Piaget distinguished between the adjectives "operative" [*opératif*], referring to the active aspect of intelligence in general, and "operational" [*opératoire*], referring to logico-mathematical operations in the strict sense) (Piaget, 1961/1969, p. 283n).

So defined, the figurative and operative aspects of intelligence were viewed as complementary functions. Figurative structures, in effect, provide the data on which operative structures can act, and operative structures link figurative states to one another. As Piaget put it: "Operative structures supply knowledge of transformations from one configuration to another, and figurative structures supply knowledge of states which are linked by transformations" (ibid., p. 284n). The relation between the two types of knowledge, however complementary, is not symmetrical. Piaget often spoke of a "primacy" of transformations over configurations in the sense that the significance of a particular configuration for the subject depends on the system of operational transformations into which it is inserted (ibid., p. 357). In his research on both perception and mental imagery,

Piaget was concerned to emphasize that knowledge cannot be explained in terms of the figurative aspect alone, either in the form of abstractions from perception or in terms of associations among mental representations. Not only is the operative aspect of intelligence necessary to explain the development of knowledge, it is the dominant member of the pair.

In the following section, Piaget's work on perception, mental imagery, and memory will be briefly reviewed. As elsewhere, the emphasis will be on theory and epistemology, although a few examples from the actual experiments will be given. This summary cannot substitute for reading the original works. Instead, it serves the function of providing the overall context within which the individual studies can be more easily understood.

Perception

In this section, Piaget's theory of perception as presented in *The mechanisms of perception* (Piaget, 1961/1969) is reviewed, along with a few illustrative studies. Then the epistemological implications of this research are summarized.

The basic data of perception, according to the theory, result from "encounters" between certain aspects of the object perceived and the sensory apparatus of the subject. Piaget did not attempt to specify exactly what aspects of physical reality and what aspects of the nervous system are involved in such encounters. In order to explain the phenomena of interest to him, the existence of such encounters could simply be postulated. The theory is open with respect to the physical or neurological nature of the postulated processes. Retinal, cortical, neuronal, or ocular activities were all mentioned as possible physiological processes compatible with the theory (ibid., p. 83). In any case, the object perceived (e.g., a line) was conceived of as consisting of a certain number n of encounterable elements, and the sensory apparatus was assumed to sample these elements in a stochastic fashion without replacement. Once a given stimulus element has been encountered, it is no longer "encounterable" a second time. Moreover, this sampling activity is a temporal process, such that the perceived object is built up from a quickly accumulating number of encounters that approaches an asymptote as the number of elements encountered approaches the maximum possible. The estimated size of the object perceived, one of the main phenomena that Piaget sought to explain with his theory, depends on the total number of elements encountered and tends to increase during the interval, however short, in which the number of encounters is rapidly increasing. This temporal process of increasing perceived size Piaget called "over-estimation." In effect, the object is repeatedly overestimated with respect to the previous estimated size during the period of accumulating encounters. The perception of size as a function of the number of accumulated encounters was called "elementary error I." It leads to the following prediction: Given two lines of equal length, the one that is fixated (or "centrated") more will be relatively overestimated in relation to the other, because the number of encounters varies as a function of centration – the so-called error of the standard.

The situation becomes more complicated when two lines of unequal length capable of being perceived in a single centration are compared with each other. Under these conditions, the longer of the two lines is relatively overestimated with respect to the shorter. That is, the difference between the two lines is perceived as being relatively greater than it is in fact. Piaget called this "elementary error II" and explained it in the following manner: In order to be perceived as a single configuration, the encounter with the elements of one line must be brought into relation with those on the other. The relations among encounters Piaget called "couplings." The overestimation of one line relative to another results when these couplings are incomplete, that is, when the density of encounters on one line is greater than that on the other. In the case of lines of unequal length, the longer one attracts a greater density of encounters by the fact that it subtends a greater angle in the visual field (ibid., pp. 96, 99). Two kinds of predictions follow from these assumptions: First, the degree of overestimation should be calculable as a function of the relative lengths of the lines to be compared. Second, the encounters belonging to the two lines should accumulate at different rates, so that a moment should exist between the beginning of this process (at which time the densities of encounters on the two lines have not yet greatly diverged from each other) and the end (at which time the number of accumulated encounters approaches the asymptote for both lines) when the illusion is at its maximum. Many of the experiments reported in the first part of the book were meant to test these hypotheses under varying conditions.

The degree of overestimation in a given perceptual illusion is calculable according to a formula derived from the model of encounters and couplings. Piaget called this formula the *law of relative centrations*:

$$P = \frac{(L_1 - L_2)L_2}{S} \times \frac{nL}{L_{\max}}, \tag{5.6}$$

where P is the proportion by which the longer line (L_1) is overestimated relative to the shorter line (L_2). In interpreting this formula, one may divide it into the two parts that are multiplied together. Theoretically, the first part is the more important. In the simplest case of two parallel lines of unequal length, the quantity $(L_1 - L_2)L_2$ represents the number of possible couplings between the shorter line (L_2) and the difference between L_1 and L_2 (i.e., the part of L_1 that extends beyond L_2). For this reason, Piaget called these couplings "difference couplings." The number of difference couplings is obtained by multiplying L_2 and $(L_1 - L_2)$, because each encounter on L_2 can potentially be "coupled" with each encounter on the part of L_1 that extends beyond L_2 (i.e., on the length $L_1 - L_2$). These difference couplings are represented as a proportion of S, the total number of couplings possible between the two lines in question. In the present example of two parallel lines, S is equal to $(L_1)^2$.

The second part of the formula is a corrective factor for cases in which there are also other lines in the figure. The quantity n refers to the total number of comparisons to be made. In the case of two parallel lines, there is only one such comparison: L_1 is compared to L_2. L refers to the reference length, which in this example is L_1, and L_{max} is the longest length in the entire figure, in the present case also L_1. Thus, in the example of two parallel unequal lines, the second part of equation (5.6) drops out altogether, and the degree of deformation in the illusion is given entirely by the ratio of difference couplings to the total possible.

In the first part of *The mechanisms of perception,* the predictions generated by the law of relative centrations were tested against actual estimates for a number of illusions, including illusions of rectangles, the horizontal–vertical illusion, illusions of parallelograms, the Müller-Lyer illusion, the Delboeuf illusion, the Oppel-Kundt illusion of divided spaces, and several others. In each case, the dimensions of the figures were varied, and the predictions generated by equation (5.6) for these varying dimensions were compared with the relative estimates of actual subjects. In general, the obtained results conformed to those predicted, although as Vurpillot (1959) noted in her early review of these experiments, the data are not above criticism. Most serious is the lack of information on the variability of subjects' estimates. Without such information, the significance of deviations from the predicted values is difficult to assess.

The second general type of prediction derived from the model of encounters and couplings is the pattern of temporal growth of perceptual illusions. The model predicts that the illusion will be minimal at both extremely short and relatively long (i.e., more than 1 sec) exposures. The maximum effect will be found at exposures of intermediate durations. The *form* of temporal change in illusions, rather than the exact point of maximum effect, is what is predicted. This hypothesis was tested with tachistoscopic viewings of various illusions at different exposures from a few hundredths of a second to 1 sec or more. Again, the results were generally in conformity with prediction: The illusions tended to demonstrate temporal maxima at intermediate exposures. The exact points at which the maximum effects were observed varied from one illusion to another.

The kinds of illusions discussed so far were called *primary illusions* by Piaget. Functionally, they result from "field effects" involving the configural relations among stimulus elements within a single centration. Developmentally, they demonstrate a typical pattern: Although the quantitative magnitude of the illusion decreases with age, its qualitative form (i.e., the magnitude of the illusion as a function of the relative dimensions according to the law of relative centrations) remains the same. In contrast, *secondary illusions* result from "perceptual activities" that link successive centrations together. Because these perceptual activities are schematized through active experience, their quantitative magnitude tends to increase with age, and their qualitative form also tends to show developmental changes. Piaget described a number of different types of perceptual activities and illustrated them with experiments that demonstrated their development across several age groups. Included among the perceptual activities discussed were exploratory activity (directing one's centrations so as to obtain the maximum relevant information), effects of practice or repetition, so-called polarized explorations (asymmetrical distribution of centrations as a function of direction), effects of frames of reference, spatial transports (comparing a point on one stimulus element with a point on another), dimensional transpositions (comparing sets of relations), temporal transports (effects of dimensional estimates of one element with estimates of the next), perceptual anticipations, and schematizations (generalizations occurring through the repeated applications of common schemes to new situations). The effects of such perceptual activities on perceptual constancies and the perception of causality, movement, speed, and time were also discussed. In each case, Piaget argued that development in the respective concepts by way of progressive coordinations and interiorizations of actions reflects back on perceptual activities and thereby influences the ways in which the corresponding phenomena are in fact perceived.

With regard to the relation between perceptual and cognitive structures, Piaget was primarily concerned to refute forms of classical empiricism according to which higher forms of knowledge are derived from perception by a process of progressive abstraction. Such forms of knowledge cannot originate in perception, he argued, because there are certain differences between the mechanisms of perception and cognition besides their relative abstractness. Chief among these differences is the fact that perceptual compositions, unlike operative compositions, are nonadditive and irreversible. This difference can be illustrated by comparing the infralogical operations of plane geometry with the mechanisms of perception as applied to the same figure.

Consider a line B divided into two unequal parts, A and A'. According to the operation of infralogical inclusion, the whole is equal to the sum of the parts: $B = A + A'$. This operation is also reversible: $A = B - A'$. In general, these relations do not hold for direct perception. As documented in the experiments on perceptual illusions, a longer line is relatively overestimated when viewed in relation to a shorter one. In Piaget's symbolism: $A(A') > A$. As a consequence, $A + A' > B$. If the overestimation is represented by the "noncompensated transformation" P, then: $B = A + A' + P$. But P intervenes only when A and A' are viewed together; thus, P represents "a measure of perceptual irreversibility" (Piaget, 1961/1969, p. 292).

Another reason for doubting that cognitive structures develop directly from perceptual structures is that the two can manifest different developmental trajectories. In the extreme case, they can develop in opposite directions. For example, Piaget et al. (1948/1960) found that children began to conserve length only with the onset of concrete operations at approximately 7–8 years. When presented with two lines of the same length, one of which was advanced slightly beyond the other, younger children tended to assert that the advanced line was longer because it projected beyond the other line. Older children, however, recognized that this projection of the one line was compensated by a projection of the other at the opposite end. When it came to perceptual estimates of the lengths involved in this configuration, 5-year-olds actually did considerably better than 8-year-olds, even while maintaining that one line was longer than the other (Piaget, 1961/1969, pp. 315–316). Piaget interpreted these results by saying that the *conception* of length develops differently than does its *perception*. The conceptual conservation of length results from the development of concrete operations. In contrast, the perceptual estimation of length deteriorates among older children, according to Piaget, because they have begun to structure their perceptual space into coordinate axes, making the oblique comparison of parallel lines more difficult.

Thus, operative structures cannot be said to derive from perception. If anything, the influence runs in the opposite direction. Once operative structures have been elaborated, they "enrich" the corresponding perceptual structures by guiding the relevant perceptual activities. In this way, perceptual structures may come to "prefigure" cognitive structures to the extent that operative transformations are anticipated in perception. Thus, the perception of constant size across varying depths appears to prefigure the operational coordination of size and depth as abstract dimensions. Because of this remarkable prefiguration of operations by perception, empiricists have been led to postulate the perceptual origins of knowledge. For Piaget, however, the "enrichment" of perceptual structures by operational structures testified to the subordinate role of the figurative aspect of knowledge with respect to the operative aspect (ibid., pp. 356ff.).

Mental imagery

The relation between the figurative and operative aspects of intelligence was also the central topic of Piaget and Inhelder's *Mental imagery in the child* (1966/1971). As in the case of perception, the major question revolved around the relative dominance of the figurative or operative aspects of intelligence. A second important question concerned the developmental course of mental images themselves.

With respect to this second question, Piaget and Inhelder found that the images of children younger than about 7–8 years tended to be relatively static and that only later did they become capable of representing or anticipating movements and transformations. When asked to draw or otherwise indicate the movement of a rod around one of its ends, for example, the younger children tended to represent only the beginning and end states; only after about 7–8 years of age did children also become capable of representing the intermediate stages of this movement. Among 7-year-olds, these intermediate stages were somewhat easier to represent by an imitative gesture or by choosing a correct drawing than by actively drawing it, suggesting that drawing was a more difficult form of representation than the other response alternatives. This developmental sequence from static to "kinetic" imagery was found in a number of other tasks as well.

The fact that the capacity to represent movements and transformations develops around the same age as concrete operations does not indicate what the relation between imagery and operations might be. This latter question was addressed by asking children to anticipate the results of the transformations occurring in some concrete operational tasks. For example, in a modified version of a typical conservation-of-quantity task, children were shown two glasses of liquid A_1 and A_2 of the same size and shape and filled to the same level. First, they were asked to anticipate the level that would be reached by the liquid in A_1 if it were to be poured into another glass wider (B) or narrower (C) than A_1. Then this transformation was actually effected, and they were asked the typical conservation question: whether or not the amount contained in B or C was equal to that remaining in A_2. Briefly, they found that the capacity for anticipating the correct levels developed somewhat earlier than conservation: 30% of children between the ages of 4 and 8 years failed both to anticipate the levels and to conserve; 23% anticipated the levels, but failed to conserve; 5% demonstrated conservation, but were unable to anticipate the levels; 42% answered both questions correctly ($N = 74$) (Piaget & Inhelder, 1966/1971, pp. 260ff.; Piaget & Inhelder, 1963/1977, p. 680).

The establishment of a developmental decalage between anticipatory imagery and conservation, however, does not explain the relation between them. Piaget and Inhelder were aided in the interpretation of this decalage by an additional finding: When asked to fill B or C until it contained the same amount as A_1, the 23% who had demonstrated correct anticipation, but not conservation, tended to fill B or C until a level was reached that was equal to that of A_1. In other words, even though they had been able to anticipate the levels attained when the liquid was poured from A_1 to B or C, this transformation was not reversible; when asked to fill B or C with the same amount as A_1, they equated the same *amount* with the same *level*. For Piaget and Inhelder, this finding signified that anticipating the effects of a transformation through mental imagery is insufficient to bring about an understanding of the compensatory relations involved in the operational solution (same amount = wider glass × higher level). Correct anticipation may simply result from past experience, under the assumption that children had previously poured liquids from one glass to another. But the memory of the outcome of such an action does not guarantee an understanding of operational reversibility. In contrast, the comprehension of the operation guarantees that the results of the transformation will also be correctly anticipated by the imagination. In this sense, operations play the dominant role in the relation with figural representations. "The conclusions to be drawn from this type of experiment . . . are therefore first that operations transcend images, while making use of them; and second that, once brought into play, operations direct images and even determine them almost entirely in some cases" (Piaget & Inhelder, 1963/1977, p. 681).

In the conclusion to *Mental imagery in the child,* Piaget and Inhelder considered the epistemological implications of their research. Following Piaget's previous conclusions in *Play, dreams and imitation,* they argued that mental images, like verbal signs, are cognitive representations or signifiers. They differ from verbal signs, however, in two ways: First, images are "motivated" symbols in the sense that they resemble the things they signify, but verbal signs

Table 5.5. *The symbolic function in its figural and*
general aspects

	Signified	Signifier
Figural	Objects	Images
General	Concepts	Verbal signs

Source: Piaget and Inhelder (1966/1971, p. 383).

represent the things they signify only through arbitrary convention. Second, images also differ from verbal signs with respect to the kinds of things that they signify: Words represent the "conceptual articulations" (classes or relations) in terms of which the object is interpreted, but "the image designates the object itself with its particular perceptual details and its concrete figural characteristics" (Piaget & Inhelder, 1966/1971, p. 383). The relations among objects, images, concepts, and verbal signs are summarized in Table 5.5.

One of the most interesting things about Table 5.5 is that it reflects an implicit orientation to the problem of universals in its epistemological aspect (see chapter 8 of this book). Piaget and Inhelder made an oblique nod toward this problem in a brief reference to Wallon's (1942/1970) comparison between the Platonic forms and mental images, adding: "In a mode of thought so astonishingly static as that of the Greeks the lack of reflexive awareness of the operational processes and their intrinsic dynamism would indeed lead to over-estimation of the image's role, and to undifferentiation of the image and the concept" (Piaget & Inhelder, 1966/1971, p. 384). Platonic idealism resulted from an overestimation of the reality of the image in relation to the object and a confusion between the particular character of the image and the general character of the concept.

Table 5.5 also contains an implicit critique of nominalism as the view that the generic character of classes and relations can be reduced to the conventional use of words and names. Piaget and Inhelder's schema implies that nominalism results from an overvaluation of verbal signs with respect to concepts (just as Platonic realism overvalued images with respect to objects). Like the early conceptualists, Piaget and Inhelder argued, in effect, that verbal signs are to be distinguished from concepts and that the former represent the latter. But Piaget and Inhelder's position must be distinguished from that of conceptualists such as Locke, whose conception of "ideas" did not sufficiently distinguish between images and concepts. Indeed, an awareness of this confusion was what led Berkeley to reject the Lockian notion of "general ideas" (see chapter 8).

Piaget's epistemology implies a radical distinction between images and concepts. Because conceptual thought, according to Piaget, results from the development of operations, this distinction reduces to that between the figurative and operative aspects of knowledge. The fault of empiricist epistemologies is that in interpreting knowledge as a "copy" of reality, they have overvalued the figurative aspect and undervalued the operative aspect of knowing. In Piaget's theory, objects acquire generic properties *through the operations of the subject* – by being grouped into classes, related to each other, and so on. Piaget thus differed from earlier conceptualists in his emphasis on the role of the subject's operations in conceptual knowledge. The operative aspect of intelligence is what is responsible for knowledge of the general properties of objects, and the figurative aspect involves the representation of their particular properties.

Memory

The relation between the operative and figurative aspects of intelligence was also the main theme of *Memory and intelligence* (Piaget & Inhelder, 1968/1973; see also Piaget, 1968a). The language of this book was influenced by the terminology of information theory, perhaps more so than any other of Piaget's works. Memory phenomena, for example, were described in terms of the encoding and decoding of information. But this model was given a characteristically Piagetian twist. Most previous information theories of memory development had assumed that observed age-related differences in memory performance could be explained in terms of the development of children's skills in encoding and/or decoding information. The code itself was implicitly assumed to remain more or less constant. But if the subject's operations were at all involved in the memory code, then one might expect that the memory code itself would change with the development of the operations. Not only would the processes of encoding and decoding be dependent on the subject's operational schemes, but during periods of rapid development the organization of those schemes might itself change in the interval between encoding and decoding.

This hypothesis was tested in a series of experiments in which Piaget and Inhelder studied memory in relation to children's levels of understanding after various periods of delay. In one experiment, for example, children were shown an array of sticks arranged in order of increasing size. They were then asked to draw or describe what they had seen after a week, and again 8 months later. Following the memory test in the second session, children's operational levels for seriation were also assessed according to methods previously employed (Inhelder & Piaget, 1959/1969).

To begin, memory for the series after 1 week was found to be highly correlated with children's operational levels. Children capable of operational seriation were considerably more likely than those incapable of seriation to remember the original series correctly, and children in a transitional stage of seriation through trial and error fell in between the other two groups in memory performance. This result is consistent with the general assumption that children's operational schemes are indeed involved in the memory code.

More interesting were the results from the third session. Children were able to recall what they had seen 8 months before, and their memory performance tended to *improve* over that of the second session. Of the 30 children retested in the third session, not a single one showed deterioration of memory as might be expected from a simple decay model. In fact, 24 of them remembered better after 8 months than they had after 1 week. Piaget and Inhelder interpreted this result as an indication that the memory code (i.e., the children's operational schemes) had undergone development between the second and third sessions, allowing them to decode the relevant information more accurately at the later session. This interpretation was suggested by the fact that most of children's improvements in memory performance consisted of movement from one stage or substage to the next.

This experiment was repeated with a variety of different materials involving memory for other additive or multiplicative logical structures, as well as causal and spatial structures. These experiments tended to support the hypothesis that the memory code is operative in character and that this code changes with the development of operations. As in the experiment on memory for series, operative development frequently led to improved memory performance after longer, as opposed to shorter, intervals. This was not universally the case, but even these exceptions were illuminating for what they revealed about the relation between memory and operations.

In one experiment, for example, children were shown eight matches, four of them laid end-to-end (row A), and the other four arranged parallel to the first, but in a flattened-W pattern (row A'). The particular difficulty of this configuration consisted in the fact that although both rows contained the same number of matches, A was longer than A'. This constituted a contradiction for younger children, who viewed the length of a row as a function of the number of elements. Moreover, the results of this experiment suggested that this contradiction tended to become suppressed in children's memory performance after 1 week. Either the lengths of the elements of A' were increased so that its total length was equal to that of A, or the actual number of elements in A' was increased to the same effect. Although some children in all ages from 5 to 9 years correctly reproduced the configuration after 1 week, the tendency to suppress the contradiction between equal numbers and unequal lengths was found to decrease with age. After 6 months, the memory performance of 5- and 6-year-olds tended to deteriorate; none of them correctly produced the configuration this time, and the tendency to eliminate the contradiction between number and length was even greater than before. Correct representations were maintained only by 7–9-year-olds, that is, among children who were likely to have overcome the apparent contradiction through the development of the relevant concrete operations.

Most of these experiments dealt with recall, or what Piaget called "evocative memory." Another result of Piaget and Inhelder's research was to establish a developmental sequence between three different types of memory: recognition, reconstruction, and recall. This was accomplished by comparing memory performances in different versions of the same experiments: by letting children choose from among alternative representations of to-be-remembered configurations (recognition), by allowing them to construct what they had seen before with the same materials (reconstruction), or by requiring them to draw or describe the model (recall). Piaget and Inhelder found not only that reconstruction tended to be easier than recall but also that these two types of memory could have different developmental courses. In an experiment on memory for double classification, the recall of children between 4 and 8 years of age generally tended to regress after 6 months, as compared with 1 week following the original presentation. For reconstruction memory, however, only 4–5-year-olds tended to regress, whereas 6–8-year-olds tended to improve or remain the same.

Piaget and Inhelder concluded from these results that memory consists of two components: operative and figurative. The operative component includes action schemes or representational (operational or preoperational) transformations and has a general organizational influence on the memory code. The figurative component includes perception (in the case of recognition), imitation (in the case of reconstruction), and mental imagery (in the case of recall) and provides memory with its particular experiential content. Conceived in this way, memory is viewed as a special case of the activity of intelligence in general. The operative aspect provides the memory code with organizational structure, and the figurative aspect with the content that is structured. But operative development is what accounts for the kinds of age differences in memory performance observed by Piaget and Inhelder and for their somewhat counter-intuitive finding that memory for some kinds of content can actually improve across time during periods of rapid operational development.

CONCLUSION

In 1965, Piaget published a little book entitled *Insights and illusions of philosophy* (Piaget, 1965/1972b) that purports to be an account of his "deconversion" from philosophy. The book is in part autobiographical in character, and it affords us an additional clue to his intellectual development during the period of his life considered in this chapter.

Piaget began the book with a brief recounting of his early infatuation with philosophy, his enthusiastic discovery of Bergson's vitalism, and his subsequent decision to devote his life to philosophy, with the goal of reconciling science and religion. He recalled his first efforts to realize this goal in the form of a new science of genera, described as a kind of holistic natural philosophy. He had expressed these ideas in a student essay entitled *Réalisme et nominalisme dans les sciences de la vie,* in which the problem of universals was interpreted biologically. Unfortunately, he soon discovered that he had been anticipated in this interpretation by Aristotle, whose conception of "form" referred both to the structures of thought and to those of the organism. Henceforth, he rejected the Bergsonian antithesis between living organization and rational thought, recognizing instead a continuity between the two.

Ostensibly, Piaget recounted his early "conversion" to philosophy in order to demonstrate that he had not begun his professional life with a prejudice against it. His first academic appointment was in fact to the chair of philosophy at the University of Neuchâtel vacated by his former teacher, A. Reymond. Only gradually did he became disenchanted with philosophical methods. Most of *Insights and illusions of philosophy* was devoted to a detailed defense of the reasons for his disenchantment.

He stated three such reasons. First, he began to feel a conflict between the methods of verification proper to psychology and biology as sciences and the reflective speculation that appeared to be the preferred method of many philosophers. He stated his belief that to affirm a proposition presumably relevant to the domain of facts when this proposition cannot be verified by anyone else is a form of intellectual dishonesty.

The second reason for his disaffection was his perception to what extent philosophical opinions are affected by contemporary social and political currents. As an example, he cited the decline of liberalism and the ascent of what he called a "narrow Calvinism" among Swiss Protestants after World War I. Perhaps he spoke from personal experience here, for he recounted being invited by a Protestant student organization shortly after the war to give two or three conferences on immanentism and religious faith, adding that he would have been booed by them a few years later. (As described in chapter 2, Piaget had in fact encountered heated opposition to his ideas on immanentism – perhaps from some of the same narrow Calvinists mentioned here.) He cited similar shifts in philosophical opinion occurring as a consequence of the social and political upheavals surrounding World War II. For Piaget, this dependence of philosophy on the social and political climate cast doubt on the objectivity and universality of its conclusions and stood in marked contrast to scientific methods of verification, which are subject to the collective control of the scientific community.

Piaget's third reason for his disillusionment with philosophy was that he had been involved in a number of dialogues with philosophers across the years, and this experience had convinced him that he spoke a different language than they did. He described several of these "dialogues of the deaf" in some detail. Their cumulative effect was to make him feel even more estranged from philosophy as a discipline. His tenure at the Sorbonne would appear to have contributed to this impression; having succeeded Merleau-Ponty at the Faculté des Lettres, he felt that he had been treated as though he, too, were a philosophical psychologist, and his research in genetic epistemology received little attention. He devoted some pages to a historical account of the difficulties of establishing empirical psychology in the French academic system.

In the rest of the book, these arguments were elaborated in terms of specific examples. The philosophies of Bergson and Husserl, in particular, were criticized for their reliance on intuition as a method. Although introspective intuition can lead to interesting results when regarded as a subject of psychological investigation, it cannot be supposed to yield valid truths when employed as a method in itself. A number of philosophical approaches to psychology – those of Sartre, Maine de Biran, Bergson, and Merleau-Ponty – were also criticized in some depth. Piaget stated his belief that philosophical speculation in psychology is not only misleading but also downright harmful insofar as it impedes the progress of empirical research.

Piaget did recognize a positive role for philosophy, but it was seen to lie in the pursuit of wisdom, defined as the "coordination of values," rather than in the search for truth. Understood in these terms, philosophical intuition can lead to subjectively (or intersubjectively) valid insights without raising claims to objective universality. Different wisdoms may coexist, but there is only one objective truth, and it is the province of science. Still, the boundary between science and philosophy is not fixed, but constantly changing. Piaget concluded this essay by acknowledging that this conception of philosophy was not original with him; it had in fact been proposed by philosophers themselves, most notably Jaspers in his *Einführung in die Philosophie,* published in English under the title *Way to wisdom* (Jaspers, 1950/1954).

It was perhaps no coincidence that Piaget cut his ties with philosophy only after genetic epistemology was comfortably established at the Center for Genetic Epistemology in Geneva. Until then, he may have been reluctant to dissociate himself from the discipline in which many of his epistemological questions had originated. He devoted a number of pages in *Insights and illusions of philosophy* to a description of the center and the type of interdisciplinary collaboration on which it was based.

But because of the very interdisciplinary character of Piaget's new science, his ideas have continued to straddle traditional academic boundaries. The questions he asked and the phenomena he sought to explain lay in the interstices of the established disciplines. Only with difficulty can one approach his work solely from the perspective of any one of those disciplines taken separately. He has found greater acceptance in psychology than in philosophy or biology, but psychologists have not fully understood him either. Although he apparently spoke the same language as psychologists, a closer look suggests that he used many familiar psychology terms for unfamiliar purposes. Some of the confusion resulting from his idiosyncratic use of familiar psychological terms will be taken up in chapter 7, but first we shall complete our survey of his intellectual development by considering the period from 1965 to 1980.

6

Cognitive development and evolution

In the final segment of Piaget's autobiography covering the years from 1966 to 1976, he wrote that if one does not wish to age too quickly, it is well to think of all the work one still hopes to accomplish (Piaget, 1976a, p. 35). This may explain in part why he lived as long as he did, for in the last 15 years of his life he still had much to do. In terms of sheer volume, this period was one of the most productive of an already prodigious scientific career. Some of his most innovative and novel ideas were conceived well after the conventional "retirement age." The works that he produced after age 70 alone would have been sufficient to secure him a place in the pantheon of psychology.

Piaget was the first to acknowledge that he owed much to the team of researchers that he had assembled around him at the Center for Genetic Epistemology. In his autobiography he recounted an occasion when he had congratulated two of his collaborators for a paper they had given him only to be reminded that he was in fact the author! This anecdote was used to illustrate the fading powers of memory in old age, but it could also stand as an example of the closeness of collaboration that characterized the research carried on at the center. Piaget avowed that in writing about these years it took some effort to distinguish between himself and his colleagues. Without them, he would have remained "formal and speculative" (ibid.).

He went on to recite the list of works that appeared during the period in question. He judged the success of his "scandalous little book," *Insights and illusions of philosophy* (1965/1972b), as an indication that its theses may have been shared by a silent majority of readers. In describing some of the difficulties he had experienced in editing a volume entitled *Logique et connaissance scientifique* (Piaget, 1967b), he implied that it might have been easier to write the whole volume himself than to get all the contributors to turn in their articles on time. Piaget's contributions to another collective enterprise, the *Tendances principales de la recherche dans les sciences sociales et humaines,* sponsored by UNESCO, were published separately by Gallimard under the title *Epistémologie des sciences de l'homme* (Piaget, 1970b). A successor to parts of the third volume of *Introduction à l'épistémologie génétique,* this book represents Piaget's fullest statement of his views on the epistemology of psychology and the social sciences. Finally, the "Que sais-je?" series published by the Presses Universitaires de France gave him the opportunity to express his ideas succinctly in the three volumes he contributed to that series: *Structuralism* (Piaget, 1968/1970c), *The psychology of the child* (Piaget & Inhelder, 1966/1969), and *The principles of genetic epistemology* (Piaget, 1970/1972c). Because of the economy of expression imposed by the format, these books provide one of the best introductions to Piaget's ideas in psychology and epistemology.

Turning to the psychological research conducted during the decade preceding 1976, Piaget mentioned first the volume *Memory and intelligence* (Piaget & Inhelder, 1968/1973), which continued the work on figurative thought from *Mental imagery in the child* (Piaget & Inhelder, 1966/1971). A series of investigations on causal thinking was summarized in *Understanding causality* (Piaget, 1971/1974b), originally published as Volume 26 in *Etudes d'épistémologie génétique*. The results of some of these studies appeared in Volumes 26–30 of the series. The research on causality led to two volumes of studies on the relation between action and conceptual thought: *The grasp of consciousness* (Piaget, 1974/1976b) and *Success and understanding* (Piaget, 1974/1978b). These studies led in turn to a series of *Experiments in contradiction* (1974/1980a), originally published as Volumes 31 and 32 of the *Etudes*. Whereas the studies on contradiction focused on the specific role of contradiction in cognitive development, the processes by which such contradictions are overcome were studied in *Recherches sur l'abstraction réfléchissante* (Piaget, 1977c, *Etudes* vol. 34 and 35). Together, these investigations formed the empirical basis for *The equilibration of cognitive structures* (Piaget, 1975/1985, *Etudes* vol. 33), Piaget's most comprehensive statement of the concept of equilibrium that played such a central role in his thinking. In this book, "equilibration" was described as the process leading from one form of equilibrium to another (i.e., from one stage of development to the next).

Parallels between the equilibration of thought in ontogenetic development and in the evolution of scientific thought were investigated in what Piaget (1976a) called a "soon-to-be-completed" work by himself and R. Garcia. This book, which appeared posthumously under the title *Psychogenèse et histoire des sciences* (Piaget & Garcia, 1983), represented Piaget's most mature statement of the relations between psychogenesis and the epistemology of the sciences. Finally, Piaget's theory of structures was significantly extended in a series of studies on correspondences, published under the title *Recherches sur les correspondances* (Piaget, 1980b, the 37th and final volume of the *Etudes*). Inspired by the mathematical theory of "categories" (MacLane, 1972), these studies extended the research on functions that had appeared in *The psychology and epistemology of functions* (Piaget, Grize, Szeminska, & Vinh Bang, 1968/1977, *Etudes* vol. 20). Together, the studies of functions and correspondences provided a whole new dimension in Piaget's thinking about cognitive structures.

As if these multifarious psychological investigations were not enough to occupy his mind, Piaget also returned to another central theme in his life's work: the relation between biology and intelligence. This theme was developed in a major work, *Biology and knowledge* (Piaget, 1967/1971c), in which numerous parallels between biological and cognitive functions were spelled out in detail. The processes underlying the genesis of new forms at both levels of reality were described as formally analogous. Both were characterized as constructive processes leading from one form of equilibrium to another. In this view, trial-and-error learning is insufficient for explaining the development of cognitive structures, just as the neo-Darwinian theory of random mutations and selection after the fact is insufficient for explaining the evolution of biological forms. In two subsequent books on this topic, *Adaptation and intelligence* (1974/1980c) and *Behavior and evolution* (1976/1978c), the argument was extended with particular reference to Piaget's own investigations of biological adaptation in Alpine mollusks (Piaget, 1929c, 1929d, 1965b) and in the succulent plant genus *Sedum* (Piaget, 1966b). Piaget (1976a) recounted the bemused reactions of some of his colleagues at the center with regard to his biological theories. B. Inhelder, for example, was quoted as describing *Adaptation and intelligence* as "a novel, but a good novel" (ibid., p. 40).

Piaget concluded this final segment of his autobiography by listing some of the many awards and honors he had received over the years. None was more fondly described than the celebration of his 80th birthday. In effect, Piaget defended the theses advanced in *The equilibration of cognitive structures* before a panel of distinguished scientists, including the Belgian physicist and chemist I. Prigogine, the neurobiologist P. Weiss, epistemologist and biologist C. Nowinski, mathematician S. Papert, logician J.-B. Grize, logician L. Apostel, and psychologist P. Gréco. Piaget's colleagues apparently had proposed that Piaget (who held no advanced degrees in psychology) be granted a doctorate on the basis of this performance. University officials, however, dismissed this proposal as insufficiently serious, leading Piaget to conclude his autobiography with the words: "I will die without real diplomas, taking with me the secret of the gaps in my development" (ibid., p. 43).

This chapter attempts the difficult task of summarizing the main lines of Piaget's thinking from 1966 through the late works that appeared posthumously following his death in 1980. The major emphasis is on the process of equilibration and how it is manifest both in biological evolution and in cognitive development.

A CONSTRUCTIVIST THEORY OF EVOLUTION

In an interview conducted in the mid-1970s, Piaget was asked if he had returned to the biological preoccupations of his youth. He replied that he had never left biology (Bringuier, 1977/1980). As the study of Piaget's intellectual development makes clear, this statement was true in a double sense. In the first place, he had never left biology in his investigations of cognitive development, for he had always been convinced that there was a continuity between cognitive processes and biological functioning. This conviction was the basis of his naturalistic approach to the problems of knowledge. In the second place, biology occupied a prominent place in his epistemology of the sciences, as illustrated in the third volume of *Introduction à l'épistémologie génétique*. Insofar as he continued to pursue epistemology, his preoccupation with biology was implied if not stated explicitly.

In terms of empirical research and theory construction, however, he may indeed be said to have returned in the last 15 years of his life to the problems in biology that had occupied him as a young man. In 1965, he published a short article on mollusks, in a sense picking up where he had left off in his doctoral dissertation (Piaget, 1965b). In this article, he reported on a colony of *Limnaea stagnalis lacustris* that he had planted in a stagnant pond at 700 m altitude on the Vaudois plateau near Lausanne in July 1928. These animals possessed the typical contracted shell and enlarged opening generally found only among members of this species living in lakes where the waters are generally agitated. The fact that they had not lost this characteristic shape in 1943 when the pond dried up indicated to Piaget that this characteristic was genetically fixed and was not merely a phenotypic adaptation to the lacustrine environment. This article was followed a year later by a paper on the succulent plant genus *Sedum,* describing variations in the way in which different species of the genus can reproduce asexually by dropping branches that then take root (Piaget, 1966b). Cultivation of these plants under conditions other than those characterizing their natural habitats suggested that, as in the case of *L. stagnalis,* certain morphological variations that had originally occurred as phenotypic adaptations to new environmental conditions had become genetically fixed over the course of generations.

The attempt to explain how such phenotypic adaptations could become transformed into genotypic traits led Piaget to propose a theory of evolution that he called the "phenocopy," referring to the fact that the phenotypic adaptation is apparently "copied" by the genotype. This usage of the term "phenocopy" is somewhat idiosyncratic. Other biologists use this term to refer to the copying of a genotypic adaptation by the phenotype, and the term "genocopy" to denote the process that Piaget described (Piattelli-Palmarini, 1980, pp. 61ff.; Piaget, 1974/1980c, p. 11n). Be that as it may, Piaget's theory represented the fulfillment of the dream announced in *Recherche* – to find a "third term" between Lamarckism and neo-Darwinism. The phenomenon he sought to explain with the theory of phenocopy was no less than the process by which originally acquired characteristics may become capable of being transmitted through genetic inheritance. According to Piaget, neither Lamarckism as a theory of the direct effect of the environment on the genome nor the neo-Darwinist theory of random mutation followed by natural selection is sufficient to explain the facts. The theory of the phenocopy as a genetic response to a disequilibrium occurring at the level of phenotypic adaptation was advanced as a plausible, although admittedly speculative, solution. This theory was briefly discussed in *Biology and knowledge* (Piaget, 1967/1971c) and elaborated in more detail in *Adaptation and intelli-*

gence (Piaget, 1974/1980c) and *Behavior and evolution* (Piaget, 1974/1978c). In the following section, this theory of evolution, the evidence on which it is based, and its relation to the rest of Piaget's work are reviewed.

Biology and knowledge

So many lines of Piaget's thought came together in *Biology and knowledge* that it may be difficult to identify the major points on a first reading. They are clear enough, however, to a reader familiar with the development of Piaget's ideas. The aims of the book can be summarized under three headings: (a) an attempt to trace certain analogies or "partial isomorphisms" between biological and cognitive functioning, (b) the presentation of an epistemology of biology, and (c) a sketch of a new theory of evolution, later to be known as the theory of the "phenocopy." It is difficult at first reading to keep these themes separate, because in Piaget's view they implicated one another mutually. Both the epistemology of biology and the new theory of evolution involved comparisons between biology and cognition, and the new theory of evolution appeared as the outcome of developments that Piaget surveyed in his critico-historical approach to the epistemology of biology.

As we have seen, parallels between biological and cognitive functioning characterized Piaget's work from the beginning. In *Biology and knowledge,* they reached their apotheosis. Given the importance that Piaget obviously attached to such comparisons, one must consider just what they were intended to signify. Were they mere analogies of exposition as they might appear at first? Or were they intended to represent something more substantial?

In fact, *Biology and knowledge* was animated by much the same insight expressed some 50 years previously in *Recherche*: that there are common principles of organization operating at all levels of life, from the evolution of species in nature at large to the development of concepts in the mind of the individual. These common principles can be illuminated by comparing biological and cognitive functioning at various levels.

The method underlying this general form is to list the problems common to biological studies and psychological research into cognitive functions or scientific epistemology. Now, in any attempt to set up such a list it immediately becomes apparent that these common problems are either of an entirely local or of the most general kind – the kind, in fact, which is bound to recur at every important juncture in the study of biology. [Piaget, 1967/1971c, pp. 50–51]

Piaget's comparisons between biology and cognition were thus more than mere analogies. They were meant to reveal common forms of organization characterized by self-regulation and a tendency toward equilibrium. "Life is essentially autoregulation," wrote Piaget at one point (ibid., p. 26), or, more precisely, "Every living organization, at every level of evolution, contains autoregulations, and the same thing applies, a fortiori, I would say, in the field of behavior" (ibid., p. 34). Moreover, the concept of autoregulation is closely related to that other key concept of Piaget's thought, namely, equilibrium. Autoregulation is a process by which living forms are equilibrated. Together, autoregulation and equilibration constitute one of the three main factors governing organic growth, the others being genetic programming and environmental influences (ibid., p. 35). These three factors are independent of one another. Such independence implies that equilibration and autoregulation can be reduced neither to genetic programming nor to environmental influences, but constitute a kind of universal tendency of organic matter toward stability and the creation of new forms. Just as the second law of thermodynamics specifies a universal tendency of mechanical systems to dissipate their energy and to approach a state of thermodynamic equilibrium, so do universal laws of organic systems reflect the tendency of such systems to conserve their form even as they adapt to new conditions. Piaget's attempt to specify the "laws of form" characterizing living systems brought him into contact with the ideas of systems theorists such as Waddington, Weiss, von Bertalanffy, and Prigogine, authors whose influence became ever more pronounced in Piaget's later works.

After defining the problem to be solved and the comparative method to be followed, Piaget devoted a chapter to the epistemology of biology. Beginning with the diachronic or developmental concepts of biology, Piaget traced the development of the concept of evolution from Aristotle's hierarchy of forms through creationist notions of the timelessness of biological species to the concept of evolution as such in the work of Lamarck and Darwin. Converging research in the fields of paleontology, comparative anatomy, embryology, and genetics had made the theory of evolution increasingly acceptable to science. Indeed, the attempt to assimilate the genetic code to a combinatorial system had led to a kind of genetic preformism that interpreted all new developments in ontogenesis as realizations of the possibilities already contained in the genetic code. In contrast, Piaget argued that the trend in modern biology is toward a conception of "constructive evolution" involving a genetic system governed by systems-theoretical notions of equilibrium. According to this conception, it is unnecessary to assume that every new development is preprogrammed in the genetic code, for new possibilities can instead emerge as the system shifts from one form of equilibrium to another (ibid., p. 77). This notion of constructive development is also found in psychogenesis in terms of the progressive construction of the operatory structures of intelligence (ibid., pp. 84–85).

Turning toward synchronic or nondevelopmental concepts, Piaget drew a parallel between conceptions of the relation between the individual and the species in biology and conceptions of the relation between the individual and the social group in psychology and sociology. Aristotelian and creationist conceptions of the species were essentially realist in that they considered the species to exist in its own right above and beyond the individuals of which it is composed. Evolutionists like Lamarck, however, interpreted the notion of species in a nominalist or atomistic fashion. The very fact that species can evolve was taken as an indication that they possess no reality in themselves, but are in fact only the classes or populations of a certain number of individuals having certain characteristics in common. Both nominalist and realist conceptions of species, however, are now giving way to a conception of the species as a relational totality defined by the genetic pool of an interbreeding population (ibid., pp. 86–89). Similarly, there have been realist, nominalist, and relational conceptions of society in sociology, depending on whether society has been conceived of as something that exists in its own right, as the class of individuals that make it up, or as the totality of the relations among the individuals and social classes that it contains (ibid., pp. 97–98).

Perhaps Piaget's most important comparison between biology and cognition, however, was one involving the relations between the organism and the environment, on the one hand, and between the subject and the object, on the other (ibid., pp. 99ff.). This comparison, of course, had appeared in many of his previous works. In *Biology and knowledge* it took the form of parallels between biological theories of the organism in relation to the environment and psychological or epistemological theories of subject–object relations. Such parallels could be established for biological theories of preestablished harmony, Lamarckian mutationism, apriorism, and the search for a "third term" between the alternating emphasis on the organism versus the environment. The most notable exponent of this third way in biology was Waddington. According to Piaget's summary, Waddington's approach was characterized by two major ideas: first, the concept of a relational totality among the various subsystems of the evolutionary system considered as a whole, and second, a radical interaction between the organism and the environment. According to this view, the organism not only is influenced by the environment in its behavior and development but also modifies its environment in turn. This biological interactionism represents a close parallel to the psychological interactionism that Piaget had championed in his previous works (ibid., p. 125).

These considerations brought Piaget to the heart of his argument: Similar organizational principles apply at all levels of biological functioning, including cognition. In order to elucidate these principles, he first set out to define his terms. Most important among these were structure and function (ibid., pp. 138ff.). A structure can be defined in terms of five general characteristics. First, a structure consists of elements, but those elements cannot be isolated or defined apart from the relations that exist among them. Second, structures may be considered in formal terms apart from the particular elements that constitute their content. This is not to say, however, that they *exist* apart from their elements. Third, following B. Russell, structures may be described in terms of increasingly abstract or more general "types"; there may be structures of basic elements, structures of structures, and so on. Fourth, isomorphisms exist between structures to the extent that one-to-one correspondences can be established between the various relations among their respective elements. In this case, one may state that the same (formal) structure applies to two different sets of elements. Finally, a structure may also be characterized by substructures that constitute parts of the total organization. This hierarchy of organization should not be confused with differences in "type" as defined earlier, because both supraordinate and subordinate structures in terms of organization may bear on contents of the same logical "type."

The distinction between a total structure and its substructures formed the basis for Piaget's definition of "function." In general, "function is the action exerted by the functioning of a substructure on that of a total structure" (ibid., p. 141), provided that this action (or actions) is normal or "useful" for preserving the total structure. It follows from this definition that the function of a structure is relative to the organizational context of which it is a part. Thus, gastric juice possesses a "function" only in relation to the process of digestion as a whole. Piaget extended this definition of function, however, in a significant way: "If specialized functions consist of actions exerted by the function of a substructure on that of a total structure, then the organizational function in its turn is the action (or class of actions) exerted by the functioning of the total structure on that of the substructures contained in it" (ibid., p. 142). Thus, the action of a substructure on the whole is described as a "specialized function," and the action of the whole on the parts is the organizational function in general. The elucidation of this general organizational function was perhaps the most important topic of *Biology and knowledge*.

According to Piaget, the organizational function is characterized by three interrelated properties: conservation of form, differentiation of parts, and continuous self-renewal (ibid., pp. 148–150). Conservation of form implies that the organization in question (organ, organ system, organism) endures over time. It endures across continuous activities, transformations, and exchanges with the environment, not as a static entity. The whole that is conserved is not merely the sum of its parts, because the parts may be constantly changing. But it does not exist independent of its parts either, because without the parts that are organized, there would be no organization. Instead, the organized whole is a *relational totality*, the ensemble of its parts and the relations among those parts. This conservation of form in terms of a relational totality implies the second property of the organization function, namely, the differentiation of the parts. The fact that the parts of the whole are differentiated from each other, and as such interact with each other, constitutes the relations among those parts of which the whole is composed. This conservation of form further implies the third property of the organization function, the property of perpetual self-renewal. Neither the content nor the parts of the organized whole are conserved across time. What are conserved are the relations among the parts, which in turn constitute the form of the whole. The individual parts may be continuously replaced, but the relations among them remain the same. In other words, the form of the whole is conserved by its capacity for self-renewal.

Such *properties* of living organization, however, are not themselves conserved along with the form of the whole. They are instead the necessary *conditions* for this conservation to occur at all.

In this sense, the organization qua functioning is not transmitted by heredity as are characteristics such as shape, color, etc.; it continues and succeeds itself qua functioning as *a condition necessary to every transmission and [not] as a transmitted content.* [ibid., p. 148][1]

In short, the organizational function is not a specific property of particular organizations, but the general condition of all living organizations. Just as the second law of thermodynamics applies to all physical systems, regardless of their content, so do certain "laws of form" apply to all living systems. How these biological laws of form with their capacity for conservation and self-renewal are to be reconciled with the second law of thermodynamics is, of course, a different question, to which we shall return.

If Piaget's laws of organization are really universal, it follows that they should apply to living systems on every level and of any content. This assumption is the basis for the ubiquitous parallels between biological and cognitive functioning found in *Biology and knowledge*. Because thought is an activity of an organism, it is subject to the same laws of organization as the organism itself. Thus, the comparison between biological and cognitive organizations does not involve a reduction of the one to the other. Rather, to the extent that such parallels can be shown to exist, they provide evidence for the generality of the respective laws of organization.

In fact, the three properties of the organizational function – conservation, differentiation, and self-renewal – are also found to characterize cognitive organization (ibid., pp. 150–152). Sensorimotor schemes, for example, represent the organization of actions, the form of which is conserved over different applications. Coordinations of action schemes enable the child to recognize certain invariants in the real world, such as the permanence of objects. Similarly, perceptual schematizations result in perceptual constancies, and operatory structures in the conservation of quantity, weight, and volume – the forms of invariance that characterize physical reality. Similarly, Piaget found that cognitive organizations, from sensorimotor schemes to operatory structures, are characterized by differentiation of parts and renewal of form.

Piaget compared his idea of organizational structure with Bertalanffy's notion of an "open system," also described in terms of a totality consisting of its parts and the relations between them (ibid., p. 155). In particular, living systems are "open" with respect to exchanges with the environment. Bertalanffy had described the structure of open systems as hierarchical in character, and Piaget added that many biological functions are also organized as a temporal cycle. Thus, hunger leads to alimentation, to digestion, and once again to hunger. Some cognitive organizations are also characterized by such a cyclical organization, for example, the circular reactions of sensorimotor intelligence.

Piaget went on to describe some of the formal properties that characterize organized structures in general. These properties can be classified under two headings: inclusions and order (ibid., pp. 158ff.). Here again, certain analogies

---

1 By omitting the crucial negation, the English edition alters the sense of the passage considerably.

between cognitive and biological functioning may be found. At the level of conceptual thought, for example, structures of inclusion and order are found in the logic of classes and the logic of relations that characterize the stage of concrete operations. At quite another extreme, biological species are organized in terms of inclusions in different genera and families that in turn have evolved in a particular temporal order. The implication is that structures of inclusion and order can be found at all levels of biological functioning. Just as Piaget had once affirmed that a logic of action underlies the logic of thought, now this idea was extended to all biological functioning. Thus, there is a "logic" of the organism, of organs, of organic substances, and finally of organic evolution – all governed by the same general laws of biological organization.

The remainder of *Biology and knowledge* consisted in an attempt to trace these laws of organization as they occur at various levels of biological functioning: in the nervous system and the reflexes, in "instinctive" behavior, in perception, in learning and intelligence. Piaget concluded that three main types of knowledge exist: (a) inherited forms, of which the prototype is "instinctive" knowing, (b) logico-mathematical knowledge, a category expanded here to include all inter-coordinations among the organism's own actions, not merely the higher forms of logico-mathematical knowledge per se, and (c) acquired knowledge, including all forms of learning. Piaget devoted a whole chapter to "the biological interpretation" of these three forms of knowledge, of which only the briefest indication can be given here.

With respect to instinct, Piaget argued that this form of knowing results from transindividual genetic regulations occurring at the level of the population. That is, disequilibrium occurring in the development of individuals is reflected back to the level of the transindividual "genetic system." A re-equilibration occurring at this level is then reflected in the genetic inheritance of individuals in subsequent generations. This hypothesis is one of the most controversial theses advanced in this book, because it appears to endorse the inheritance of acquired characteristics. Piaget was careful, however, to distance himself from classical Lamarckism. He did not propose that the habits acquired by one generation are directly transmitted to subsequent generations, but rather that disequilibria occurring in the interaction between the population and its environment result in the production of directed variations, some of which are then selected, resulting in the evolution of new forms of instinctual behavior. This theory differs from classical neo-Darwinism in that variations are not explained as the result of purely chance mutation, but as directed in a general way from the outset. The theory was described at greater length in his writings on the phenocopy.

With respect to logico-mathematical knowledge, Piaget began by arguing that this form of knowledge can be explained neither as a result of learning nor as a result of heredity. Rather, it results from the organizational function itself as it is manifest on the level of cognition. As in many of his earlier writings, cognitive operations are described as internalized actions that have become coordinated among themselves in operatory structures. This intercoordination among operations occurs in conformity with the general laws of organization previously described. Logico-mathematical knowledge, as the product of these coordinated structures, can thus be characterized as the *necessary* product of such coordinations, although they are neither inherited nor developed solely as the result of maturation. The fact that Piaget sometimes referred to both maturation and the equilibrations leading to logico-mathematical knowledge as "endogenous," in contrast to the "exogenous" processes of learning and environmental acquisition, should not obscure the profound differences that he recognized between the two.

In contrast to these "endogenous" forms of knowledge, experiential knowledge is "exogenous" insofar as it results from direct adaptations to the environment. Even so, it does not operate independently of the other two forms of knowing. In their more elementary forms, experiential adaptations rely on innate forms of knowing. Conditioned reflexes, for example, depend on unconditioned reflexes that are themselves innate. In its higher forms, experiential knowledge relies in an analogous manner on logico-mathematical knowledge. For example, physical knowledge results from the same kind of coordinations among operations as logico-mathematical knowledge, with the difference that these physical operations remain adapted to the particular characteristics of physical objects, whereas the particular properties of objects play no role in logico-mathematical operations as such. In this sense, Piaget argued that acquired knowledge requires a "logico-mathematical framework" (ibid., pp. 334ff.).

In the conclusion to *Biology and knowledge,* Piaget reaffirmed his fundamental assumption that knowledge of whatever form results from an interaction between the organism and the environment. Anyone who interprets the book as advocating either one of these factors over the other, he added, has failed to understand him (ibid., p. 348). As an "open system," the organism is constantly involved in exchanges with the environment. As a finite system, it cannot be preadapted to all the environmental circumstances that might possibly occur. Therefore, the environment is constantly the source of disequilibria in the very organization of the organism. By virtue of its capacity for organization, the organism reacts to these disequilibria with re-equilibrations that either return the organism to its previous state or result in new forms of organization. Of these two outcomes, the latter is theoretically the more significant, and several of Piaget's subsequent works were devoted to explaining how equilibration processes can indeed result not merely in a return to a previous state but in the evolutionary construction of new forms of organization. The reader of *Biology and knowledge* will not be surprised to learn that the equilibration processes leading to the genesis of new forms in cognitive development have much in common with those that lead to the evolution of new biological species.

Adaptation and intelligence

Although one can easily get lost among the baroque parallels and isomorphisms of *Biology and knowledge,* the slender volume entitled *Adaptation and intelli-*

gence (Piaget, 1974/1980c) is a model of clarity and conciseness in comparison. If the earlier book suffered from the attempt to accomplish too much at once, the later one was characterized by an economy of expression unusual for Piaget. It was as though *Biology and knowledge* had satisfied his need to write an epistemology of biology, freeing him to concentrate on the essentials of his biological theories. These theories might be better understood if *Adaptation and intelligence* were as well known as its predecessor.

Concise though it may be, this book covers a lot of ground. It contains not only succinct summaries of Piaget's own extensive biological investigations and the theory of the phenocopy that these studies inspired but also one of the clearest accounts of the relation between biological and cognitive equilibration processes that he ever produced. It is one of the first of Piaget's publications in which he explicitly acknowledged the kinship between his own theory of equilibration and contemporary theories of self-organizing systems. For this reason, it is a central document for understanding the development of his ideas in the last decade of his life.

Biological research. We begin with a brief summary of Piaget's biological research, already alluded to in previous chapters. This work can be summarized under two headings: first, the research on mollusks he had conducted as a young man (Piaget, 1929c, 1929d, 1965b); second, the research on the plant species *Sedum sediforme* (Piaget, 1966b). Both series of investigations focused on the mechanisms by which the species in question adapted to the conditions of their natural environments. Both had yielded results that Piaget interpreted to be incompatible with simple neo-Darwinian interpretations to the effect that evolution results solely through a process of random mutation followed by natural selection. According to Piaget, his results could be explained only by assuming that certain acquired adaptations can under some conditions lead to genetic modifications and to the hereditary transmission of the acquired adaptation. His theory of phenocopy was an attempt to specify a possible mechanism by which this genotypic copy of a phenotypic adaptation might be explained. Because the inheritance of acquired characteristics has generally been dismissed by mainstream evolutionary biologists, it is worth considering the evidence on which Piaget's rather heretical conclusion was based.

The bulk of Piaget's work on the mollusk species *Limnaea stagnalis* was devoted to establishing the natural distribution of five varieties distinguished on the basis of relative elongation (i.e., by the ratio of the length of the shell to the diameter of its opening). The more elongated forms (varieties 1–3) were found only in aquatic environments characterized by still water: in ponds and marshes, in the placid inlets of large lakes, or along shorelines where the lake bottom drops off quickly. In contrast, the shortened varieties (4 and 5) were found exclusively on gently sloping, rocky shorelines that were exposed to wind and waves. In the intermediate zones, a mixed population was found, including both elongated forms (varieties 2 and 3) and shortened forms (varieties 4 and 5).

Piaget hypothesized that the shortened morphology of varieties 4 and 5 resulted from an adaptation to the turbulence of the water in the environments in which they lived. During the development of the organism, it anchors itself against such turbulence by attaching itself to a pebble with a powerful suction force. This behavior has the consequence of pulling on the muscle that attaches the animal to its shell, causing a ceaseless drag on the latter's growth. At the same time, the opening of the shell is pressed against the rock, causing it to widen as it grows (Piaget, 1974/1980c, pp. 29–30).

Although this shortening of the mollusk's shell through the direct action of the environment could be demonstrated by raising the animals in a controlled environment (i.e., in an aquarium with an agitator), the shortened forms exhibited by varieties 4 and 5 in nature were in fact genetically fixed. This fact was demonstrated by the finding that these varieties retained their shortened forms even when they were raised in still water (in the aquarium or in still ponds). Further evidence for the hereditary character of the shortened forms was obtained by crossing varieties 1 and 5. In conformity with Mendelian laws of inheritance, this interbreeding resulted in an intermediate form in the first generation and a segregation of forms in the second generation.

According to simple neo-Darwinian interpretations, the fact that shortened forms of *L. stagnalis* were not to be found in still-water habitats could be explained by the hypothesis that the shortened shell represented a selective disadvantage in that environment. In order to test this hypothesis, Piaget placed a number of egg sacs of variety 5 in a stagnant pond on the Vaudois plateau that had not previously contained animals of this species. From that summer in 1928, Piaget's colony survived with their shortened forms intact until 1943, when the pond dried up. Piaget concluded that no obvious reason existed to explain why the shortened varieties could not survive in still-water environments.

Such a finding raises the further question why the short forms were found only in the turbulent environments, where shortening of the shell might also be expected to occur through acquired adaptations. If the mutation responsible for the genetic fixation of this trait had occurred completely at random, one might expect the shorter forms to be found everywhere, not merely in turbulent waters. Piaget argued that the balance of fossil evidence favored the hypothesis that the phenotypic adaptation preceded the mutation in question and somehow contributed to it.

Some of Piaget's observations of the succulent plant genus *Sedum* (of which one species, *Sedum morganianum*, is commonly known as the houseplant "burro's tail") led him to the same conclusion. In the course of studying the fall of secondary branches in *Sedum,* Piaget discovered a previously unknown variety that he called *parvulum*. This variety displayed several distinctive features, including diminutive size, dark-green color, and frequent vegetative reproduction through the dropping of secondary branches. Each of these features was found to develop in some degree in well-known species of *Sedum* when the latter were exposed to marginal environmental conditions. Such phenotypic adaptations could be interpreted as having a compensatory function in those marginal habitats, the small size resulting in more efficient alimentation, the dark-green color resulting in greater photosynthesis, the vegetative reproduction compensating for reduced flowering. Although these phenotypes reverted to their usual forms when returned to their normal environments, the same characteristics turned out to be genetically fixed in *parvulum,* as demonstrated by their constancy under wide environmental variations. Piaget concluded that "the *S. sediforme-parvulum* itself constitutes a local genotype, having succeeded phenotypes with the same apparent characteristics" (Piaget, 1974/1980c, p. 42). Just as phenotypic adaptations to turbulent waters in *L. stagnalis* were replaced by genetic "phenocopies" with the same shortened form, so had *parvulum* come to replace what had orginally been acquired adaptations to marginal environmental conditions.

The theory of the phenocopy. The problem was twofold: first, how to account for the replacement of a phenotypic adaptation with genetic mutations leading to the same ultimate form, as apparently occurred in *L. stagnalis* and *S. sediforme,* according to Piaget's observations; second, and equally important, why such genetic "copies" did not occur more often. Piaget cited other examples of this phenomenon from the biological literature. But even if such genetic replacements are conceded to occur with some frequency, they are by no means universal; many phenotypic adaptations do *not* become replaced by the corresponding genotypes. With his theory of the phenocopy, Piaget set out not only to explain how the genetic replacement of a phenotypic adaptation is possible but also to specify the general conditions under which it is likely to occur.

He began by considering the existing hypotheses. The usual interpretation of the phenocopy is that the phenotypic adaptation "copies" a genotype that has not yet appeared. That is, the same environmental pressures that select a given phenotype in the course of ontogenetic development also select a genotype having the same form across many generations. Piaget considered several variations of this hypothesis and found them all wanting. In general, they all have difficulty explaining why genotypic selection should continue to occur once an adapted phenotype appears. It is a truism in evolutionary theory that genotypes can be selected by the environment only insofar as they are embodied in their respective phenotypes. But given two identical phenotypes, one resulting from an acquired adaptation and the other from genetic fixation, how can one genotype be selected over the other? Moreover, the conventional hypothesis has no differential predictive power. Even if it were accepted as an explanation of how phenocopies might possibly occur, it could not explain why they occur in some instances and not in others.

According to Piaget's own theory of the phenocopy, the genotype copies the phenotype, rather than the reverse. The process by which a new genotype comes to replace a phenotypic adaptation was explained as follows: Ontogenetic development is a series of organizational levels, beginning with the DNA and extending upward through enzyme production, cell formation, the growth of tissue, the development of organs, the organism as a whole, the organization of behavior, and, finally, cognition. Development at every level occurs in interaction with the environment, although the scale on which this interaction occurs differs from one level to another. At the higher levels, the organism (or the subject) interacts with the external environment. At the lower levels (e.g., the DNA, cell formation, tissue growth, etc.), the "environment" is internal to the organism (hence Piaget's somewhat confusing term "the internal environment").

At every one of these levels, variation can occur in the normal or typical course of development. Some of these variations may fall within the range of developmental possibilities permitted by the internal environment, but others may not. The former may then result in further variation on the next higher level, whereas the latter will be, in effect, "selected out." So far, the theory simply restates the hypothesis of "organic selection" proposed by Baldwin (1896).

The originality of Piaget's model consists in his proposal that in addition to this "ascending" effect of variations at one level of development that result in corresponding morphological variations at the next higher level, there is a "descending" effect of disequilibria at higher levels causing corresponding disequilibria at lower levels of morphogenesis. In effect, this descending feedback conveys the information that something has gone wrong in a certain area of development at a higher level. Piaget supported his argument for such a descending feedback effect by citing recent discoveries in molecular genetics that apparently indicated that information could flow not only from DNA to RNA but also, under some conditions, in the reverse direction.

The central feature in Piaget's model is the following: This descending disequilibrium has the effect of causing new variations on each lower level to which it penetrates. Moreover, the new variations that are so produced occur only in the areas of development affected by the disequilibrium. This directedness of variations is perhaps the main difference between Piaget's model and neo-Darwinian theories. For Piaget, the process leading to the production of new variations was not completely random, nor was it teleological or finalistic. Instead, the range of the variations so produced was viewed as restricted by the character of the disequilibrium involved. Within the area of disequilibrium, variations might indeed be generated at random. But the fact that the range of potential variations was restricted meant that these variations were to some extent directed.

A similar model of a restricted random process had been advanced by Piaget in *The origins of intelligence* in order to explain groping or trial-and-error learning in the fifth stage of sensorimotor development. There he had argued that groping does not occur merely through the random generation of "trials" and selection by contingent reinforcement. In this view, neither the generation of behaviors in learning nor the generation of variations in evolution is a completely random process; rather, they are both restricted or directed from the start. This view is only another statement of Piaget's oft-repeated analogy between neo-Darwinism and theories of trial-and-error learning. "Variations . . . have come to be considered as exploration or trials, according to the model of groping by trial and error" (Piaget, 1974/1980c, p. 53). The same formative processes are operative on both levels.

Returning to the theory of the phenocopy, Piaget proposed that the new variations produced by disequilibrium at any given level are then selected by the pressures of the internal environment at that same level. The variations that survive this selection process result in the genesis of new forms on the next higher level of organization through a kind of "re-ascending" process of transmission. These new forms are subject to selection on the higher level, and the surviving forms produce new forms of organization on the next highest level, and so on. Because the range of variations is already directed by the original disequilibrium, these re-ascending variations tend to result in re-equilibrations at each higher level until the original disequilibrium itself is removed. A phenocopy, in Piaget's sense, results when the original disequilibrium descends all the way to the level of the genome, and re-equilibration occurs by the re-ascent of variations occurring at that level. Piaget did not claim to know the exact mechanisms by which such disequilibria descend from one level to another, nor how they bring about genetic variations that are then passed to the offspring by way of the germ cells. He was careful not to go beyond the data available to him. He argued simply that the observed phenomena suggested that some such process must occur, whatever its ultimate character. His own theory of phenocopy was an admittedly speculative hypothesis that he believed to be more plausible than existing alternatives, given existing information.

Piaget's model had the further advantage that it provided an answer for the second problem raised by the phenomenon of the phenocopy: why phenotypic adaptations are not universally replaced by genetic modifications. Because the phenocopy presumably is produced by the disequilibria resulting from a phenotypic adaptation, no phenocopy will be expected to result from phenotypic adaptations that do *not* result in disequilibria at the level of the genome. In other words, the phenocopy does not universally occur, because disequilibrium is not a necessary consequence of acquired adaptations. "When a phenotype is sufficiently stable and does not threaten to disturb the equilibrium of the epigenetic system, then there is no reason why it should be replaced by a genotype of analogous form. . . . On the other hand, if the phenotype is the source of varying degrees of disequilibrium, then the genotype will reestablish a normal interplay of syntheses ensuring precorrection of errors rather than corrections only under constraints" (ibid., p. 63).

As in the case of cognitive development, Piaget seemed to equate disequilibrium with conflict or opposition. In the case of *Limnaea stagnalis,* the phenotypic shortening of the shell in environments characterized by agitated water conflicts with the programmed tendency of the shell to grow longer. Similarly, the increase in chlorophyll content in *Sedum sediforme* under marginal environmental conditions conflicts with the genetically programmed level (ibid., p. 69).

Piaget did not provide an a priori method for identifying disequilibria sufficient to produce phenocopies, but he did give a theoretical specification of the conditions leading to them.

He was careful to distinguish this model from Lamarckism, although the end result might appear to be the same in both cases. Unlike Lamarck, he did not propose that acquired adaptations are inherited directly nor that the environment impresses itself directly on the genotype. In Piaget's model, the acquired adaptation itself is an active response on the part of the organism to environmental conditions. Only those responses that result in functional disequilibria (i.e., that conflict in some way with other normal functions of the organism) have any effect on the genetic system. Even the latter does not respond passively to these disequilibria, but actively, by producing new variations. These variations are then selected by the internal and external environments, resulting in reequilibration. The active response of the organism to the environment at all levels constitutes the constructive aspect of evolution.

It is worth emphasizing, finally, that this interpretation of the phenocopy is basically constructivist in nature. The new genotype constitutes the ultimate result of conflicts and interactions between organism and environment, and the environment thus necessarily intervenes as one of the transforming elements in its causality. If this is so (and here lies the constructivism), then the adaptation itself has, as its producing factor, not the environment as such, but rather the constant action of the organism on the environment, which is by no means the same thing. [ibid., p. 73]

By insisting on the radical interaction between the organism and the environment, Piaget arrived at the "third term" between neo-Darwinism and Lamarckism of which he had dreamed since *Recherche*. According to the theory of the phenocopy, evolutionary change results neither from the environmental selection of random variations nor from the direct action of the environment on the organism. Instead, the organism actively constructs variations in response to environmental pressure. New forms evolve through the selection of these actively constructed variations.

Phenocopy and cognition. The second part of *Adapation and intelligence* is devoted to problems in the study of cognition and to certain parallels between biology and cognition. We have already seen how certain cognitive processes (e.g., the directed trials in trial-and-error learning) served Piaget as a model for analogous biological processes (directed variations in response to environmental pressures). Now the search for parallels ran in the opposite direction: Having framed his theory of the phenocopy in biology, Piaget looked for its cognitive equivalent.

If the phenocopy can be defined very generally as the replacement of an exogenous formation (e.g., phenotypic adaptation) by an endogenous one (e.g., genotypic adaptation), then the cognitive equivalent of this process can be found in the replacement of physical (i.e., exogenous) knowledge by a logico-mathematical (i.e., endogenous) reconstruction. Such replacement occurs when the child observes a regularity in the physical world. The recognition of such a regularity constitutes physical knowledge, in Piaget's terminology. If the child now attempts to specify the necessary and sufficient conditions for the occurrence of the regularity in question, this physical knowledge is superseded by knowledge of the *necessary* connections between the observed phenomena. The mere recognition of regularity has been replaced with a structure that explains it. Because this structure is based on and is in a sense derived from the physical observations, it may appear to be an extended copy of them, as empiricist theories have long contended. According to Piaget, the structure with its element of necessity is in fact a cognitive reconstruction and generalization of the original phenomena. This replacement of a physical generalization by logicomathematical generalization Piaget called the "cognitive phenotype" by analogy with its biological counterpart. Although he did not frame it as such, the theory of the "cognitive phenotype" has to do with what has generally been considered as the problem of induction in the epistemology of science. In Piaget's view, scientific laws are not arrived at by an "inductive leap" from the observed phenomena. Instead, the law is a cognitive reconstruction of the phenomena that serves to explain them.

Despite the fact that exogenous influences are replaced by endogenous constructions on both the biological and cognitive levels, important differences also exist between the ways in which this replacement occurs in various cases. The most important difference is that cognitive reconstructions do not involve genetic adaptations. The disequilibria that occur at the cognitive level, unlike those occurring at the morphological level, do not "descend" level by level back to the level of the genome. Cognitive disequilibria are compensated at the same level at which they occur, or at most at adjacent levels. Another important difference is that organic forms cannot be dissociated from their content, but a progressive dissociation between form and content occurs in cognitive development. "In the organic sphere, no form can ever be dissociated from its content, whereas the proper function of cognitive processes, on the contrary, is to construct forms, then forms of forms, and so on. These constructs will be ever more abstract, and freer or more detachable from all content" (ibid., p. 99).

These differences should not obscure the fundamental fact that both biological evolution and cognitive development were described by Piaget as constructive processes that are directed without being teleological. This directedness is a result of the tendency of organic systems to seek equilibrium. We have seen that this general tendency toward equilibrium played a central role in Piaget's thinking ever since *Recherche*. His most mature statement of this theory (Piaget, 1975/1985) is reviewed later. In the present context, we shall limit ourselves to two observations. The first is that Piaget introduced here for the first time the term "optimizing equilibration" (*l'équilibration majorante*), which would play such an important role in his later thought. Although the process of equilibration had frequently been described as a compensation of a disturbance leading to the reinstatement of a previous condition, the "optimizing equilibration" is a process of compensation that results in a new condition entirely. Rather than reinstating a previous form of organization, it raises the system to a higher and inherently *better* level of organization (hence the term, "optimizing equilibration").[2] Henceforth, this type of equilibration was invoked by Piaget as the process responsible for transitions from one stage or level of development to another. "In cognitive terms, this type of equilibration comes about as a response to disturbance, which may be positive (contradiction, etc.) or negative (blanks or gaps in data). The ensuing compensation tends not simply to return to the former state, but to go beyond it in the direction of the best possible equilibrium compatible with the situation" (Piaget, 1974/1980c, p. 111).

The second observation is that Piaget linked the process of equilibration (and especially "optimizing equilibration") for the first time to contemporary theories of self-organizing systems. He cited Atlan (1972) to the effect that self-organizing systems in biology not only resist disorder but also are capable of transforming random processes into ordered structures (ibid., p. 110). Piaget compared such self-organization to the equilibrating process by which an external perturbation is compensated so that a whole new dimension is added to the functioning of the system. In this way, the level of organization can be "optimized." This connection between equilibration and self-organization became increasingly important in Piaget's subsequent theorizing.

EQUILIBRATION AND THE GENESIS OF STRUCTURES

The connection between equilibration and self-organization was stated most comprehensively in *The equilibration of cognitive structures* (Piaget, 1975/1985), a book that provides a kind of "general conclusion" to all of his previous psychological theorizing. Having elaborated a constructive theory of the origins of organic structures inspired in part by his psychological observations, Piaget returned from these biological speculations to create a a new theory of the genesis of cognitive structures.

We have had ample occasion in this book to see how Piaget's view on the parallels and isomorphisms between biology and psychology came to influence his research method. As in the case of biology, the first task of a psychologically oriented genetic epistemology was seen to consist in description and classification. Only on the basis of a developmentally ordered taxonomy of structures would an explanatory account of morphogenesis be possible. In this sense,

---

2 The verb *majorer* literally means "raising" or "increasing." The image Piaget apparently had in mind was that of an equilibrium that is "raised" from a lower to a higher level of organization. Because this higher level of organization was conceived to be inherently more adequate, I have followed previous practice in translating *l'équilibration majorante* as "optimizing equilibration"; see T. Brown and K. J. Thampy's comments on their translation of this term in Piaget (1975/1985, p. xviii). However, the term "optimizing" should not be understood as implying that every *équilibration majorante* results in an "optimal" equilibrium. Rather, as Piaget (1974/1980c, p. 111) wrote, it is in the *direction* of the best possible equilibrium.

Piaget's method can be described as a classification and developmental ordering of forms of cognition in the process of becoming. This task could be compared to that of the embryologist or paleontologist who seeks to identify successive forms in a process of morphogenesis. To be sure, Piaget was not content to wait until the job of classification and ordering was complete before attempting an explanation; rather, he sought to explain the sequence of forms that he found in each domain investigated as he went along. Each subsequent investigation, however, added to the evidence contributing to the explanation. In this sense, the theory of equilibration presented in *The equilibration of cognitive structures* was based on the accumulated evidence of his life's work.

As we have seen in chapter 1, Piaget had regarded the tendency toward equilibrium as a principal explanatory concept in psychology already in his adolescent philosophical period, even before he had conducted the observations that this concept would later serve to explain. Along with his ideas of action and structure, it remained one of his "core" concepts throughout his scientific career (cf. Beilin, 1985). Together with maturation, physical experience, and social influences, equilibration was viewed as one of the four major factors contributing to psychological development (Piaget, 1952d, 1960b). Each of these factors was seen to be necessary for cognitive development; only the four factors taken together were considered to be sufficient. In making this argument, Piaget did not wish to minimize the importance of the other factors, only to emphasize the importance of equilibration.[3]

Throughout the first half of Piaget's professional life (i.e., before 1950), the concept of equilibrium was constantly evoked as an explanatory principle, but he provided no major statements on the nature of equilibration as a process in its own right. After 1950, however, Piaget published a series of attempts to clarify his ideas about the tendency toward equilibrium in psychological life. In his inaugural lecture at the Sorbonne, for example, he characterized *structures d'ensemble* as "forms of equilibrium," and stages of cognitive development as "levels of equilibrium" (Piaget, 1952d). The second volume of the *Etudes d'épistémologie génétique* was devoted to the topic of logic and equilibrium, and in Piaget's (1957b) contributions to the volume he presented a new probabilistic theory of equilibration. According to this theory (influenced by his probabilistic approach to perception), the probability of attending to two dimensions of a problem at once is the product of the probabilities of attending to each dimension separately. The theory was presented in an abbreviated form in an essay on equilibrium as an explanatory concept in psychology, published in English translation as one of *Six psychological studies* (Piaget, 1964/1967a). The relation between equilibration and other factors in development formed the main topic of Piaget's (1960b) contribution to a "Research Study Group on the Psychological Development of the Child," sponsored by the World Health Organization. This

---

3 Piaget (1966c) listed the four factors somewhat differently, as follows: (a) biological factors, (b) the equilibration of actions, (c) interindividual coordinations, (d) educational and cultural transmission.

paper was published along with the discussions it engendered among the other members of the study group (Tanner & Inhelder, 1960). In this book, the reader has the rare opportunity to see how a panel of distinguished scientists (including Konrad Lorenz, John Bowlby, Margaret Mead, Grey Walter, J. M. Tanner, Réné Zazzo, and Ludwig von Bartalanffy, among others) reacted to Piaget's ideas on equilibrium and stages of cognitive development and, even more interesting, how he replied to their comments and criticisms.

The early attempt to state a specific theory of equilibration in probabilistic terms was eventually rejected by Piaget as inadequate, and he described *The equilibration of cognitive structures* (Piaget, 1975/1985) in its preface as an attempt to reexamine the whole problem. The new theory of equilibration was decisively influenced by the psychological research conducted between 1965 and 1975, and it is therefore useful to review this research however briefly before examining the theory.

Causality, action, and contradiction

Causal explanation. In the late 1960s, the Center for Genetic Epistemology was engaged in a series of studies on causality. One hundred studies on different aspects of causal knowledge were conducted. These studies, summarized in Volume 26 of the *Etudes* (translated into English under the title *Understanding causality* – Piaget, 1971/1974b), included investigations of transmissions of movements, changes in states of matter, the concepts of force and work, the compositions of forces, and the concepts of energy, light, and heat, among other topics. Some individual studies of causality were published in Volumes 27–30 of the *Etudes* (Piaget, 1972d, 1972e, 1973d, 1973e).

No dramatically new conception of causality emerges from this research. Piaget adhered throughout to the idea, already enunciated in *Introduction à l'épistémologie génétique,* that causal knowledge results from the attribution of operations to objects considered in themselves. But the individual studies described in *Understanding causality* provide a wealth of detail on the development of causal understanding with respect to specific problem areas. Unlike logico-mathematical reasoning, in which most of the specific properties of the objects that are counted, sorted, or ordered are ignored in carrying out the respective operations, causal understanding necessarily has to do with the specific properties of physical objects. It follows that causal knowledge is more content-specific than logico-mathematical knowledge. Children must consider the physical properties of different kinds of objects in attributing to those objects the formal properties of operations. Causal knowledge thus represents an exceedingly diverse field of study in comparison with logico-mathematical knowledge.

The concept of weight, for example, had been symbolic of the problems posed by the understanding of physical content ever since Piaget and Inhelder (1941/1974) had found a horizontal decalage between operations applied to physical quantity and the same operations applied to weight. Previously, Piaget (1941) had generally been content to explain this decalage in terms of the particular difficulties posed by the understanding of weight in comparison with mere quantity. From the studies reported in *Understanding causality,* however, Piaget gained a more detailed understanding of the development of the concept of weight in its own right. The particular difficulty of weight consists in the fact that it subsumes two somewhat different concepts that he called weight-quantity and weight-action (Piaget, 1971/1974b, p. 86). Weight-quantity is equivalent to what is known in physics as the *mass* of an object, and weight-action refers to the *force* of attraction between the mass of an object and that of the earth (i.e., gravity). In ordinary language, both concepts are subsumed under the single term "weight." The development of the concept of weight during childhood can be described as the progressive differentiation and intercoordination of the two subconcepts (ibid., pp. 91ff.).

In the preoperational stage, weight-quantity and weight-action are undifferentiated, and weight is understood as a function of size, or "bigness." In the first substage of concrete operations, weight-quantity is conserved as long as the shapes of the objects in question remain constant. Weight-action is understood as a force that is generally exerted in a downward direction, but not necessarily vertically; if a ruler is held and let go in an inclined position, children believe that it will fall according to its angle of inclination. Only in the second substage of concrete operations is weight-quantity conserved despite changes in size or shape, and weight-action understood as acting only in a vertical direction. At this stage, weight-quantity and weight-action are still uncoordinated with each other. Children still believe that the amount of liquid displaced by an immersed object is a function of its weight rather than its volume and that objects weigh more when they are closer to the ground than when they are higher up.

The two aspects of weight become intercoordinated only at the level of formal operations. This intercoordination seems to be possible only to the extent that weight-quantity becomes distinguished from other spatial intuitions of quantity, such as volume. Thus, the concept of density that appears at this stage is the product of an operational composition involving the quantity of space subsumed by an object (volume) and its weight as a quantified force. In addition, the weight of an object is understood as remaining constant despite its position along the vertical axis.

The particular difficulties presented by the concept of weight in comparison with other quantitative properties of physical objects consist in the fact that, unlike its spatial properties (e.g., size), weight as quantity is not immediately visible and must be operationally constructed. Before this operational construction occurs, weight tends to be confused with other quantitative dimensions (weight as a function of "bigness"). This confusion also accounts for the developmental decalage that separates the development of concrete operations involving weight and operations involving other quantitative dimensions of physical objects. Because weight as a concept must be operationally constructed, the application of concrete operations to weight involves a second-order application of operations on the product of other operations.

Just as the concept of weight-quantity comes to be differentiated from (and coordinated with) other quantitative physical dimensions, so the concept of weight-action comes to be understood in relation to other dynamic concepts. Only at the stage of formal operations is the force exerted by a weight on a balance scale understood to be exactly proportional to its distance from the fulcrum. Thus, a 3-kg weight placed 10 cm from the center exerts the same force as a 1-kg weight placed 30 cm from the center. Obviously, the weight of the object as such does not change by changing its position along the horizontal axis. Rather, the force that it exerts changes as a product of the weight of the object and its distance from the fulcrum. As this example indicates, the development of different physical concepts must be traced independently, insofar as they involve accommodations to the specific properties of physical objects. At the higher levels of development, these concepts become intercoordinated in operational compositions (e.g., force = weight × distance). Such operations, however, are attributed to the objects themselves rather than to the actions of the subject, and this attribution is what distinguishes causal knowledge from logico-mathematical knowledge.

Action and consciousness. The study of causality led Piaget to the study of the conceptualization of action. In acting, children themselves become sources of causal influence, and as we have seen, Piaget believed that action was the original source of both causal and logico-mathematical knowledge. But the knowledge of one's own actions poses certain problems not present in the knowledge of causality or logico-mathematical operations. First, one might suppose that although children must construct the knowledge of causal relations in general, they have immediate reflexive knowledge of their own actions. Second, both causal knowledge and logico-mathematical knowledge are oriented to understanding (i.e., to the truth or falsehood of propositions regarding objects in the world), but knowledge of action is oriented instead toward the success or failure in attaining a desired goal. These two aspects of the problem are reflected in the titles of the two books that Piaget published on this topic: *The grasp of consciousness* (Piaget, 1974/1976b) was devoted to the study of children's awareness of the means by which they attain the goals of successful actions, and *Success and understanding* (Piaget, 1974/1978b) to the relation between action and conceptualization in situations in which success depends on understanding.

One of the conclusions to emerge from the first of those books was that children appear to be aware of the mechanisms of their own actions only to the extent that they are able to conceptualize them. As Piaget put it at one point, awareness of one's own action *is* the assimilation of the action to a conceptual scheme (Piaget, 1974/1976b, p. 336). Moreover, such conceptualizations do not result from immediate intuitions of one's own actions, but from reconstructions involving inferential coordinations (ibid., p. 348).

These conclusions were derived from observations indicating that children often are unaware of how they have executed an action even when it has been successfully performed. In one of Piaget's simplest and most telling examples, children of various ages were asked to crawl on all fours along the floor. Then they were asked how they had done it. Nothing would appear to be simpler to determine if the theory of immediate intuition were correct. Yet children's awareness of even this most elementary and familiar physical action was dependent on their conceptualizations of it. Before roughly 7–8 years of age, children replied that they had moved either both their arms and then both of their legs (in the pattern of a Z) or the right arm and leg together and then the left arm and leg together (in the pattern of an N). In fact, they all had moved the right arm and left leg together and the left arm and right leg together (in the pattern of an X). The latter is the natural and automatic way of walking on all fours for both human beings and animals. Nevertheless, only at about 7–8 years did children begin to be aware of how they had executed this simple movement.

In an amusing (but instructive) extension of this experiment, the distinguished invited guests participating in one of the annual symposia at the Center in Geneva were asked to perform the same action and to describe how they had done it. The physicists and psychologists in the group described the X pattern correctly, but the logicians and mathematicians described themselves (wrongly) as having executed the N pattern. Piaget attributed this result to the fact that physicists and psychologists were in the habit of observing facts outside of themselves, but the logicians and mathematicians gave the explanation that seemed to them to be the simplest and most logical (Piaget in Bringuier, 1977/1980).

In this example, children's awareness of their own actions appeared to result from a conceptual reconstruction rather than from an immediate reflexive intuition. In other experiments, children's conceptualizations of their own movements appeared to "repress" a nascent awareness of their own actions when their conceptions and intuitions were in conflict. For example, children were asked to sling a wooden ball attached to a cord into a box placed in front of them. Even the youngest of the children tested were able to accomplish this with practice. When they were asked how they did it, however, their answers again appeared to conform to the developmental course of their conceptualization of this action. Before the age of 7–8 years, children invariably said they let go of the cord directly in front of the box (i.e., at 12 o'clock), although in order to reach the goal they had in fact let go 90° to the right or left (at either 9 o'clock or 3 o'clock), depending on which direction they were swinging the sling. Between the ages of 7–8 and 11–12, children demonstrated a progressive decentration during the course of the experiment, sometimes arriving at the correct answer, sometimes at a "compromise" between the correct answer and the tendency to say that they let go of the sling right in front of the box. For example, some children said they let go of the sling between 11 and 12 o'clock when swinging the ball in one direction, and between 12 and 1 o'clock when swinging in the other direction. In fact, they had let go at 9 and 3 o'clock, respectively. Only after the age of about 11–12 (with several precocious exceptions already at 9–10 years) did children begin to give the correct answer from the beginning.

The "compromise" solutions found in the intermediate stages in this experiment suggested that children were at least partially aware of the action of letting go of the ball to one side. This nascent awareness, however, conflicted with their more primitive conceptualization of the action, resulting in the compromise solution. According to Piaget, contradictions of this kind can lead to a kind of cognitive "repression," in which the (veridical) perceptual knowledge is more or less successfully "repressed" by the (in this case, nonveridical) conceptual scheme. Piaget explicitly compared this kind of cognitive "repression" to the affective repression described by Freud (Piaget, 1974/1976b, pp. 339f.).

One of the clearest examples of such cognitive repression was presented in *Success and understanding*. Children were shown an N-shaped pulley arrangement consisting of a string, which was free to pull at the lower left end (*A*), glided around a nail at the upper left corner (*B*), was retained by the child's finger placed at the lower right corner (*C*), and was fixed in place at the upper right end (*D*). The question was the following: If the string is pulled a certain distance (from *A* to *A'*), how far upward (from *C* to point *X*) will one's finger be displaced? With this arrangement, the distance *AA'* was always greater than the distance *CX*. Moreover, the difference was perceptible and was accurately reported by children below the age of 7–8 years. Beginning at about 7 years, however, children began to report that the distance *AA'* *must* be the same as *CX*, because the string conserves its length. In other words, the clearly perceptible difference between *AA'* and *CX* came into conflict with children's conceptualization of the situation, and the former was "repressed" by the latter. Only at the age of 9–10 years did children begin to notice the contradiction, and only at 11–12 years could they also explain it: *AA'* is greater than *CX* because in pulling at *A*, one takes up length from both segments *BC* and *CD*.

This experiment reversed the usual outcome of Piaget's studies. Ordinarily, children's increasing logical competence enabled them to make progressively more veridical judgments. In this case, however, the judgments of preoperational children were more veridical than those of children in the initial substage of concrete operations. The latter children had come to comprehend the necessity involved in the conservation of length, but they were not yet able to take all the relevant factors into consideration. These results also provided Piaget with a strong counterexample for classical empiricist theories of knowledge. If conceptual knowledge is derived primarily from sense experience, how could younger children accurately report on the evidence of their senses and older children could not? Indeed, how could the conceptual understanding of the older children bring them to *ignore* the evidence of their senses? Piaget's answer was that conceptual knowledge is by no means derived only from sensory experience, but from the active constructions of the subject. Under certain circumstances, these constructions can lead even to nonveridical judgments and contradictions, but these errors are temporary and are overcome at higher stages of development.

In summing up the evidence of these two books, Piaget argued that in addition to forming the basis for the development of both logico-mathematical and causal knowledge, action constitutes a domain of knowing in its own right. But the knowledge of action differs from the other two types of knowledge in being oriented toward success rather than toward understanding. As such, it constitutes a *savoir-faire,* a technique rather than a science. Further, the knowledge of action begins at the "periphery" – that is, at the point of contact between the acting subject and the object acted on. From there it proceeds toward the "center" – toward the subject on the one hand and the object on the other. The knowledge of action is thus derived neither directly from the object through perception nor directly from the subject through intuition, but indirectly through interaction between subject and object.

Because children's knowledge of themselves originates in this way from the knowledge of action, Piaget's experiments are relevant for understanding the nature of "reflective consciousness" (*la prise de conscience*). Piaget interpreted the results of his experiments to imply that reflective consciousness is not simply a matter of throwing light on one's own actions (or thoughts) and passively viewing what is thereby revealed. Rather, it involves active conceptualization from the beginning (Piaget, 1974/1976b, pp. 338ff.). This conclusion follows from the fact that children do not grasp what is observable in their own actions if it conflicts with their conceptualization. In the experiment with the sling, for example, young children quickly learned to let the ball go at a tangent in order to hit a target in front of them. Although this fact was clearly observable, they were not aware of it. It appeared to be "repressed" from consciousness. But one need not appeal to a "censor" in order to explain this cognitive "repression." Piaget argued instead that children are consciously aware only of what they are able to represent to themselves in cognition. According to this view, the contents of consciousness are no more and no less than those facts that can be cognitively represented. Cognitive representation is further viewed as an active process, and children's conceptualizations are the forms by which these active representations are constructed. Instead of being "censored," the facts that are "repressed" from consciousness are simply those that have no place in children's cognitive constructions.

The experiment with the sling also suggests that consciousness is not an all-or-nothing process. The fact that children in an intermediate stage professed to let go of the sling somewhat to the right or left of the target rather than directly in front of it or 90° to one side suggests that degrees of integration are involved in the construction of a veridical conceptualization. According to Piaget, one can distinguish several general levels in the development of reflective consciousness. The first is material action itself. The fact that material action can already involve complex coordinations is indicated both in children's precocious successes in the experiments described in this section and in Piaget's previous work on the development of sensorimotor intelligence. The second level is that of conceptualization, which proceeds by way of abstraction from the coordinations among actions. On the one hand, empirical abstraction involves knowledge of the properties of objects considered in themselves. On the other hand, "reflective abstraction" (*l'abstraction réfléchissante*) involves the cognitive reconstruction of the coordinations of material actions. In being reconstructed on a cognitive level, actions become transformed into operations, and the intercoordinations among actions into "inferential coordinations." The process of reflective abstraction thus results in the development of concrete operations.

At the third level in the development of reflective consciousness, children become aware of the mechanisms of the inferential coordinations of the previous stage as well as of the products of those coordinations. This awareness comes about through a further process of abstraction in which children constructively represent the communalities among different applications of the same operations. This form of abstraction Piaget called "reflected abstraction" (*l'abstraction réfléchie*). In his words, it involves the application of operations on operations, or the reflection of thought on itself, and leads to the development of formal operations (ibid., p. 352). Each of these successive levels of abstraction represents a further step from the periphery to the center and therefore a deepening of children's reflective awareness.

On contradiction. The occurrence of contradictions in children's thinking about action led Piaget to study the phenomenon of contradiction in its own right. This research was published in Volumes 31 and 32 of the *Etudes* and appeared in English under the title *Experiments in contradiction* (Piaget, 1974/1980a). Four general questions were addressed in this work: (a) What is the nature of the contradictions found in children's thinking? (b) How are these contradictions overcome? (c) What is the relation between contradiction and the process of equilibration? (d) How are contradictions related to the successive stages of cognitive development?

From 15 different experiments, Piaget concluded that the common characteristic of contradictions in children's thinking is that they consist of incomplete compensations between affirmations and negations. An "affirmation" is understood here in a general sense as the attribution of a property a to a given class A, and "negation" is the attribution of the property not-a to the complementary class A'. An incomplete compensation is thus an incomplete coordination between intension (attribution of a or not-a) and extension (separation of A and A'), such that some elements end up being attributed both properties a and not-a at the same time.

To consider only one example, children were shown a series of seven disks A through G in order of increasing size. The difference in size between successive disks was so small (0.2 mm) as to be imperceptible, but the difference between the first disk and the last disk was clearly visible. The apparent contradiction therefore consisted in the fact that the disks appeared to be equal in size when compared successively, but unequal when the end points were compared with each other. In the preoperational stage (5–7 years), children gave contradictory explanations for this fact without realizing that a contradiction was involved. One 6-year-old, for example, asserted that disk *A* was equal to *BCDEF*, that *G* was also equal to *BCDEF*, but that *A* was nevertheless smaller than *G*, with no recognition that these statements conflicted with each other (ibid., p. 6). With the development of concrete operations (beginning at 7–8 years), however, children began to understand that the pairwise equivalence of *ABCDEFG* implied that *A must* equal *G*. The observation that *G* was in fact bigger that *A* was thus experienced as a real contradiction. Children of 7–8 years tended to resolve the contradiction by dichotomizing the series into "little ones" (e.g., *ABC*) and "big ones" (e.g., *DEFG*). They ran into problems, however, if they went on to compare the neighboring elements (*C* and *D*) of the two classes, for this dichotomy implies that *C* < *D,* and inspection revealed that *C* = *D*. This discovery tended to lead children to adjust their dichotomy (e.g., *ABCD* as "small" and *EFG* as "large"). But this dichotomy was subject to the same problems as the first. Some children even asserted that the disks appeared to be changing in size, because they were sometimes "small" and sometimes "large"! In other words, they could recognize the contradiction at this stage, but were unable to resolve it.

Between 9 and 10 years approximately, children tended to group the disks into multiple equivalence classes (instead of mere dichotomies) and sometimes suggested the possibility that neighboring disks might indeed be different in size even if this difference was not visible. But the possibility that these invisible differences might be added together across the series to produce a visible difference still eluded them. This solution was found only by children at an average age of 11–12.

If the contradiction involved in this problem can be characterized in terms of an incomplete compensation between affirmation (that some elements are "equal") and negation (that others are "smaller" or "larger"), how can the transcendence of this contradiction be described? According to Piaget, the transcendence of contradictions occurs through two complementary processes: On the one hand, the system of reference is broadened, and on the other hand, concepts are relativized. Children become capable of seriating perceptible differences already at the age of 7–8 years on the average. The contradiction involved in the preceding problem is overcome when the system of reference of this operation is extended to include the seriation of imperceptible differences. At the same time, a relativizing of the concepts "big" and "little" occurs. Instead of dichotomizing the elements (or even dividing them into multiple equivalence classes, such as "little," "middle-sized," and "big"), the disks are recognized as being "bigger" or "littler" *in relation to* other elements. In this case, the concepts of "the same" versus "bigger" or "littler" are relativized insofar as the disks are recognized as being perceptibly the same size, but imperceptibly different.

This brings us to what Piaget called the "central problem" of this book: the relations between contradiction and equilibration. First, he argued that the main factor leading to disequilibrium is the primacy of affirmation over negation. Especially in the preoperatory stages, children do not realize that every affirmation is compensated by a corresponding negation. The younger children in the experiment described earlier, for example, did not understand that the affirmation of equality among "the big ones" implied that all the members of this class were not equal to all the members of the class of "small ones." Otherwise, they could not have asserted that "the big ones" and "the small ones" could have members in common. Equilibration is the process by which each affirmation comes to be balanced by a corresponding negation that compensates it exactly. Such compensation is only another aspect of operatory reversibility, by which every direct operation is brought into correspondence with its reverse operation. According to Piaget, "the use of negation makes progress only with the gradual construction of whole structures [*structures d'ensemble*], and does not become systematic until the latter attain operatory status" (ibid., p. 296).

This balance of affirmation and negation in the development of operatory structures provides the key to the relation between contradiction and the stages of cognitive development. Piaget in fact distinguished between three types of contradictions corresponding to the two preoperatory substages and the emergence of operations. The first type of contradiction involves a total centration on affirmations and a corresponding neglect of negation. This type of contradiction is shown by preoperatory children who successively affirm contradictory properties of objects without noticing that each affirmation in fact excludes the other (e.g., certain elements are classified alternately among "the big ones" and "the small ones").

The second type of contradiction similarly involves successive contradictory affirmations, but there is a rudimentary attempt to coordinate each affirmation with its negation and hence to explain the change from one affirmation to the next. The older preoperational children investigated by Piaget, for example, also assigned certain elements alternately to classes of "big" and "little" objects, but they explained the difference by asserting that the objects had "changed" in size.

Finally, children at the level of operations realize that affirmations and negations are compensated exactly. Contradictions are therefore understood to be only momentary errors of observation or reasoning. Piaget's concrete operational subjects, for example, recognized that a logical contradiction was involved in assigning the same objects alternately to two different equivalence classes and that therefore some error of judgment had been made (even if the youngest of these subjects were unable to figure out where the error lay). Piaget compared contradictions at this level with those arising in the history of science when new observations appear to contradict established theories. It may not be immediately clear whether the contradiction results from an error of observation or an error in theoretical reasoning. In any case, the contradiction must be removed by a reestablishment of the equilibrium between affirmation and negation. "In such cases," wrote Piaget, "it is clear how the equilibration of affirmations and negations remains a general problem for all developing thought from its first tentative steps through to the level of early childhood, and right on up to the transformations and hesitations that may characterize the phases of transition and invention proper to the highest scientific advances in periods of crisis or renewal'' (ibid., p. 305).

The theory of equilibration

On the first page of *The equilibration of cognitive structures,* Piaget defined equilibration as ''a process that leads from a state near equilibrium to a qualitatively different state at equilibrium by way of multiple disequilibria and reequilibrations'' (Piaget, 1975/1985, p. 3). This definition already determined most of the questions raised in this book: how to describe the different forms of equilibrium that characterize cognitive development, how to explain the disequilibria and re-equilibrations that lead from one form to another, and, above all, how to account for the fact that the most important re-equilibrations in cognitive development lead not just to different forms of equilibrium, but to *better* forms. As we have already seen in reviewing Piaget's evolutionary theory, he referred to re-equilibrations of the latter type as ''optimizing equilibrations'' (*les équilibrations majorantes*). One of the major tasks of the book on equilibration was to explain how such optimizing equilibrations occur and how they are even possible.

The general model. Piaget began by stating that cognitive equilibria are much different from mechanical or thermodynamic equilibria, resembling instead the equilibria of biological systems. Like organisms, cognitive systems involve closed cycles of activity that are nevertheless ''open'' to exchanges with the environment. This openness to the environment involves the fundamental processes of assimilation and accommodation: As a cognitive system, an assimilatory scheme ''tends to incorporate external elements that are compatible with it'' and at the same time is ''accommodated to the elements it assimilates'' (ibid., p. 6). The scheme endures to the extent that assimilation and accommodation are in equilibrium, that is, to the extent that the modifications introduced into the scheme through accommodation are effected without loss of continuity in functioning.

Although Piaget defined equilibration generally in terms of ''mutual conservation between a system as a whole and its parts'' (ibid., p. 7), he distinguished between three different forms of equilibration. First, equilibration occurs between action schemes and external objects by means of assimilation and accommodation. Second, equilibration occurs among the various subsystems of a total system through the *reciprocal* assimilation and accommodation of the respective schemes to one another. Third, equilibration occurs between subsystems and the total system of which they are a part through a simultaneous differentiation of the parts and their integration into the whole. In cognitive systems, this third form of equilibrium can be defined in terms of the laws of composition by which the subsystems (e.g., operations) are integrated with each other to form a total system (the *structure d'ensemble*).

Interestingly, these three forms of equilibration correspond exactly to the forms of equilibrium described by Piaget in *Recherche* some 57 years previously. In that early work, he had already described equilibrium in terms of the relations between the parts and the whole, among the parts themselves, and between those parts and external influences. This parallel underscores once again the continuity of Piaget's thinking across the decades of his professional life. (Inhelder et al., 1977, also noted the connection with *Recherche* in their introduction to a discussion of equilibration on the occasion of Piaget's 80th birthday.)

The three forms of equilibrium also parallel the three types of contradictions described in the conclusion to *Experiments on contradiction*. Each form of equilibrium involves a balancing of affirmations and negations of different types. In assimilating an object to a scheme, the subject must distinguish between those characteristics (a) of the object by virtue of which it is assimilated and the other characteristics of the object (not-a), as well as between the scheme that assimilates them (A) and other schemes (not-A). Similarly, when schemes assimilate each other reciprocally, those qualities that they have in common (and by virtue of which they can assimilate each other) must be distinguished from those qualities that they do not have in common. Finally, the integration of subsystems into a totality involves a differentiation between the properties particular to each subsystem and those that it excludes. Regardless of which form of equilibration is considered, "only exact correspondence between affirmation and negation can ensure equilibrium" (Piaget, 1975/1985, p. 10).

This latter requirement provides a clue to how cognitive disequilibria arise. Disequilibrium must be reckoned an important factor in cognitive development, for, as Piaget noted, "it is obvious that one of the sources of progress in the development of knowledge must be sought in disequilibria as such." This conclusion follows because "disequilibria alone force the subject to go beyond his current state and strike out in new directions" (ibid.). Although disequilibria may be necessary for development, they are not sufficient. They lead to progress only when the subject is able to surpass them through a process of re-equilibration. Such re-equilibration necessarily leads to a new form of equilibrium, for the way back to the former equilibrium is blocked by the very contradictions that resulted in disequilibrium in the first place. Moreover, the new form of equilibrium is "better" than the previous one precisely because it transcends contradictions that could not be reconciled according to the previous form.

The connection between disequilibrium and contradiction provides a clue regarding the origins of disequilibrium. Contradictions arise out of an imbalance between affirmation and negation. This imbalance, which always consists in an initial primacy of affirmation over negation, may even be taken as constitutive of disequilibrium. The reason for this primacy of affirmation is relatively straightforward: The positive characters of an action or an object are precisely those that are perceived directly, but its negative characters must be constructed.

Such construction is a laborious process, and cognizance of the positive characters will therefore always precede that of the negative ones. Especially during
the earlier stages of cognitive development, young children do not possess the
operative structures that would enable them to balance each positive character
with its negation. But disequilibrium can arise at all levels of cognitive development, leading to a re-equilibration involving the construction of new negations
and resulting in development toward a new level of cognitive activity.

According to Piaget, such re-equilibration occurs through regulations that
compensate the perturbations that originally led to disequilibrium. Two types of
regulations may be distinguished, corresponding to the two general types of perturbations against which they are directed. Negative feedback is a type of regulation that tends to correct for perturbations caused by obstacles or resistances to
assimilation, and positive feedback (or reinforcement) is a regulation that pro-
longs assimilation by filling in gaps or lacunae in the conditions necessary to
attain some goal. The two are not mutually exclusive, for corrections may also
be involved in the prolongation of assimilation due to reinforcement. Negations
are constructed through the compensation of perturbations by regulations. Compensation through negative feedback is a negation of an obstacle or resistance,
and compensation through positive reinforcement is the negation of something
missing. For this reason, Piaget called the latter a negation of a negation. Because of this constructive activity, such compensatory regulations do not return
a system in disequilibrium to the same form of equilibrium that characterized it
previously. The new equilibrium is more stable than it was previously, because
it encompasses more compensations. A new form of equilibrium has evolved.
Compensatory regulation is thus the very mechanism of "optimizing equilibration."

A system that acquires a more stable form of equilibrium through compensatory regulation may be enriched in several ways. First, the field of content to
which it applies may become extended. For example, a child begins to consider
the positions as well as the heaviness of weights on a balance scale. Second, the
system may become more integrated and differentiated at the same time. Compensatory regulations result in new subschemes that allow the assimilation of
previously unassimilable external elements, and as these more differentiated subschemes reciprocally accommodate to one another, the total structure becomes
more integrated. Third, the reciprocal accommodation of a greater number of
subschemes within a total system means that the *assimilation norms* (i.e., the
class of assimilable elements) of each scheme will be expanded. Such reciprocal
accommodation increases the probability that new subsystems will be formed
through the reciprocal assimilation of schemes.

The construction of negations through compensatory regulations means that
the system involved begins to function on a new level. For example, the compensation of positive actions by their respective negations results in the construction of operatory structures. The system no longer functions solely on a practical
level, but begins to function on a conceptual level as well. This projection of

something originating on one level onto another is what Piaget elsewhere called "reflective abstraction." On the one hand, a certain feature of the lower level is "reflected" on the higher level (e.g., the negations of positive actions become the inverses of direct operations). On the other hand, the subject becomes aware of what has been "reflected" in this way. Henceforth, the higher-level system functions as a regulator of the lower-level system (e.g., action becomes regulated by conceptualization), such that second-order regulations of regulations come into being (e.g., the regulations of action regulations themselves become regulated by conceptualizations).

Equilibration in action. Having outlined his general model of equilibration in the first chapter of *The equilibration of cognitive structures,* Piaget went on in chapter 2 to describe how it functions. This description was based on a distinction between what he called *observables* and *coordinations.* In brief, "an observable is anything that can be established by immediate experience of the facts themselves. In contrast to this, coordinations involve inferences and go beyond what is observable" (ibid., p. 37). The distinction is not absolute; what is observable at any one level of development is dependent on coordinations from the preceding level. Thus, observables cannot simply be identified with perceptions. Depending on the coordinations that have already been established, subjects may believe they perceive what in fact they have not perceived, or they may not notice what is in fact perceptible.

Piaget defined *coordinations* in terms of inferences that go beyond the observables of that level. Thus, coordinations cannot simply be identified with subjects' expectations that a certain event will occur as the result of a preceding event (e.g., a ball will move as the result of being hit by another ball). However, the explanation of this sequence of events may well involve a coordination to the extent that this explanation relies on entities that are not directly observable (e.g., the first ball transmits energy or force to the second ball).

Observables and coordinations can be further differentiated into those pertaining to the actions of the subject and those relative to objects. In rolling a ball of clay into a sausage shape, for example, the act of rolling something out is an observable relating to the subject's action, and the elongation of the lump of clay is an observable relating to the object. An example of coordinations relating to the subject's action is the transitivity of relations established between objects by the actions of the subject, and an example of coordination pertaining to objects is the transmission of kinetic energy from one object to another. Again, the distinction between coordinations of actions and of objects is not absolute, for in cases in which the operations of the subject are directly applied to objects (as when two rows of objects are arranged in one-to-one correspondence), the momentary coordinations thereby imposed on the objects directly reflect the coordinations of the subject's actions.

Given these distinctions, Piaget represented the relations among the observables and coordinations pertaining to subject and object as shown in Figure 6.1.

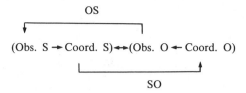

Figure 6.1. Relations between observables pertaining to the subject's actions (Obs. S), inferential coordinations of the subject's actions or operations (Coord. S), observables pertaining to the objects (Obs. O), and inferential coordinations among objects (Coord. O) in Piaget'ss model of equilibration. (Adapted from Piaget, 1975/1985, p. 45.)

The abbreviations "Obs. S," "Coord. S," "Obs. O," and "Coord. O" refer to subject observables, subject coordinations, object observables, and object coordinations, respectively. The exact interpretation of these terms depends on whether the interaction involves causal or logico-mathematical knowledge. In the case of logico-mathematical knowledge, Obs. S refers to the subject's awareness of his or her own "operatory intentions" (ibid., p. 50). Piaget did not elaborate, but one can perhaps assume that these "operatory intentions" refer both to projected actions that the subject can observe as they are carried out and to interiorized operations of which the subject can be reflexively aware. Coord. S refers to compositions of actions or operations that constitute, in effect, the means by which these "operatory intentions" are realized. Such compositions vary according to the subject's level of development; an example would be compositions effected according to the laws of the concrete operational groupings. When these coordinations are applied to the objects in question, they result in Obs. O, that is, in modifications introduced into the objects as a result of the subject's actions or operations. For example, the objects might be ordered in a series, grouped into classes, or arranged in correspondence with each other. By comparing Obs. O with Obs. S, subjects determine whether or not their operatory intentions have been realized. This comparison is indicated in Figure 6.1 by the arrow labeled OS. Finally, Coord. O refers, in the case of logico-mathematical knowledge, to the coordinations among objects introduced by the application of Coord. S to the objects in question. This application is indicated in Figure 6.1 by the arrow labeled SO. (In the case of causal knowledge, SO refers to an *attribution* rather than to an application of Coord. S to the objects, and the correspondence between Coord. S and Coord. O is never so exact as in the case of logico-mathematical interactions.)

Figure 6.1 shows how equilibration functions only at a given level of development. It remains to be explained how transitions from one level to another occur. Such transitions are shown in Figure 6.2 for the case of logico-mathematical development. As indicated in this figure, development from

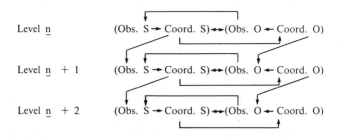

Figure 6.2. Relations between coordinations and observables in the development of logico-mathematical knowledge from one level to the next. (Adapted from Piaget, 1975/1985, p. 47.)

one level to another occurs when the coordinations of one level become treated as the observables of the next. This process Piaget referred to as "reflective abstraction," represented in Figure 6.2 by the arrows linking Coord. S and Coord. O at one level with Obs. S and Obs. O at the next. In effect, development is a succession of forms; what is a form at one level becomes content at the next. "At level *n*, objects are the content of the form that is applied to them; at level *n* + 1, the form of level *n* becomes the content and objects only constitute a content of content. At level *n* + 2, the form *n* + 1 becomes a content of the new form while at the same time being a form of forms" (ibid., p. 51). This characterization of development as a succession of forms was nothing new for Piaget. In his books on operatory logic (Piaget, 1942, 1949/1972a), he even described the succession of forms as the psychological equivalent of Russell's "theory of types." At one level, a class is a set of concrete objects, but at the next higher level, classes themselves become the elements of more abstract sets, and so on. Similarly for number: At one level, number is a form of which objects are the content, but at higher levels, number itself becomes a content for more abstract mathematical operations.

The development of causal knowledge is somewhat more complicated; it does not progress simply by means of reflective abstractions based on the subject's operations, but must also take the specific properties of objects into consideration. Therefore, the diagram in Figure 6.2 would have to be modified by adding arrows leading from Obs. S and Obs. O at one level to Obs. S and Obs. O, respectively, at the next level (Piaget, 1975/1985, p. 47). In this case, the observables at one level are not simply derived from the coordinations of the previous level; rather, the observables and coordinations of one level lead to the discovery of new observables at the next highest level. In other words, when the subject begins to understand certain aspects of a causal relationship (e.g., the fact that when one ball strikes a second one off center, the second does not continue in the same trajectory as the first was traveling before collision), then previously neglected aspects or dimensions of the situation (e.g., the directions traveled by the balls before and after collision, the point of impact, etc.) may become relevant. The new observables cannot be derived simply from the coordinations of the subject's actions, but must also include the particular properties of the objects in the situations in which they are observed.

For both logico-mathematical knowledge and causal knowledge, the succession of forms that constitutes development is also characterized by a progression in the development of compensations. In this connection, Piaget distinguished between three types of reactions to perturbations, characterized by increasing degrees of regulatory compensation. *Alpha reactions* are characterized by the absence of any attempt to integrate the perturbations into the system in question. Instead, the perturbations are simply ignored or actively removed. For example, children may classify objects together based on some shared property without taking account of their differences, or if those differences are noticed, they will simply remove the discrepancy by forming a new collection without taking their previous classification into consideration. As this example illustrates, alpha reactions involve a total centration on the affirmations (the properties the objects have in common) and a corresponding neglect of negations (the differences between those objects).

In contrast, *beta reactions* involve a modification of the system in order to accommodate an external perturbation. For example, children's classificatory schemes may be modified so as to take previously unacknowledged differences among objects into consideration. Instead of distinguishing between only objects having a certain property (e.g., "the big ones") and objects lacking that property (e.g., "the little ones"), they may recognize an intermediate group as well. Thus, beta reactions involve partial compensations based on the construction of partial negations.

These partial compensations are completed at the level of *gamma reactions*. In contrast to alpha and beta reactions, gamma reactions involve the anticipation of possible perturbations. Insofar as these possible variations are fully integrated into the system, they lose their character of perturbations and simply become potential transformations of the system. In effect, every possible transformation is fully compensated by an inverse transformation, and every possible affirmation by a corresponding negation. Thus, objects are recognized as the "same" with respect to some properties and "different" with respect to others, and these similarities and differences are coordinated with each other. Categorical affirmations (e.g., "big" or "little") may become relativized, such that every direct relation (*A* is "bigger than" *B*) is compensated by its reciprocal (*B* is "littler than" *A*).

The resemblance between the complete compensations of gamma reactions and operational reversibility is obvious. The development from the earliest reactions characteristic of the preoperational stage through certain intermediate reactions to the appearance of concrete operations is one example of the progression from alpha to beta to gamma reactions. But the three stages in the construction of compensations are not to be identified with any single set of stages in cognitive development, for they recur at different levels of development, from the sensorimotor stage to the development of operations. Although there is a ''systematic progress'' from alpha to gamma reactions, ''this is not to say that it is a matter of three general stages. Rather, it is a matter of phases that are quite regularly found according to the area studied or the problem posed in the course of the sensorimotor period, then from two years up to the age of ten or eleven, and finally up to the level of formal operations'' (ibid., p. 58).

As this statement suggests, the nature of the compensations developing out of the progression from alpha to gamma reactions varies according to the global level of cognitive development and to the particular problem area. The second part of *The equilibration of cognitive structures* is devoted to the application of this model to a number of different problem areas, including sensorimotor, perceptual, and spatial regulations, as well as the construction of logico-mathematical structures in the development of conservation, classification, and seriation. For simplicity, we limit ourselves here to a consideration of one of these applications, namely, the conservation of quantity.

Equilibration and conservation. Piaget followed the equilibration process through four levels in the development of the conservation of quantity. As described in *The child's construction of quantities* and *Mental imagery in the child,* children were shown little balls of clay that were subsequently rolled out into sausage-shaped cylinders. They were then asked, in effect, if the quantity of the clay was the same as it had been before. Four levels in the development of conservation could be discerned.

At *level I,* children's attention is centered on the length of the clay cylinder. In the terms of Piaget's model (Figure 6.1), Obs. S corresponds to the intended action of making the clay longer, and Obs. O refers to its perceived lengthening. Coord. S and Coord. O both refer to children's belief that the action of rolling out results in a lengthening of the clay. Because other dimensions of the clay cylinder are ignored, this example refers to an alpha reaction.

At *level II,* Obs. S remains centered on the action of lengthening the clay, but at some point children also begin to notice that the clay cylinder has become thinner in the process. In other words, Obs. O now includes two sorts of observations, that the clay becomes longer and that it becomes thinner, but the two are not yet coordinated with each other. Coord. S and Coord. O thus remain in an ''unstable equilibrium.'' That is, when children center on the length of the cylinder, they reason that the act of rolling out leads to an increase in length, and when they center on its thickness, they reason that rolling out leads to its becoming thinner. But insofar as these two outcomes are not coordinated with each other in a single centration, this level of thinking is still characterized by an alpha reaction; when one dimension is centered, the other is simply ignored.

At *level III,* Obs. S becomes more differentiated in the sense that the action of lengthening the clay is now seen to involve making it longer and thinner at the same time. Piaget believed that this differentiation was a result of feedback from Obs. O. Already at the previous level, Obs. O included alternating observations regarding length and width. These observations now affect Obs. S by way of the feedback loop OS shown in Figure 6.1. By extension, Coord. S and Coord. O are also affected. The subject now understands that the action of rolling out a piece of clay makes it *simultaneously* longer and thinner. At level II, children could center either on changes in length or on changes in thickness, but now both are combined in a single centration.

Level III still stops short of complete conservation. Although children understand that changes in length and thickness occur at the same time, they do not yet understand that the changes in the two dimensions compensate each other exactly. Similarly, children at this stage become capable of comprehending what Piaget calls "the empirical return" – the fact that a ball of clay once rolled out can be returned to a spherical form – but they do not yet comprehend the principle of operational reversibility in terms of the compensatory relations between transformations of length and width.[4] This reversibility, once it is acquired, implies conservation as such. Because the type of thinking characterizing this stage involves the integration of what was formerly an external perturbation (the observation that a change in width accompanied intended changes in length) into the cognitive system, a beta reaction is involved with respect to the development of compensation.

The significant development at *level IV* is that children now become capable of predicting in advance that rolling out the clay involves changes in both length and thickness that are compensatory in nature. Piaget interpreted this development as an effect of Coord. S and Coord. O from the previous level on Obs. S and Obs. O of the present level by means of reflective abstraction (represented by the oblique lines in Figure 6.2). The fact that changes in length and thickness are conceived to be compensatory means that every affirmation (increase in one dimension) is matched with its corresponding negation (decrease in the other dimension). What was previously a perturbation (intended changes in one dimension accompanied by unintended changes in another) is now fully integrated within the system in the manner of a gamma reaction.

The compensatory character of transformations of length and width at level IV results in a sense of necessity, reflected by the fact that children recognize that

4 This distinction between "the empirical return" and operational reversibility is another example of Piaget's fundamental contrast between *successive* and *simultaneous* coordinations (see "The mechanism of mental development and the laws of the grouping of operations" – Piaget, 1941). "The empirical return" is a coordination of representations that succeed one another in time, and operational reversibility is the simultaneous representation of compensatory transformations. In his later works, Piaget used the term *renversabilité* (variously translated as "revertibility" or "empirical reversibility" – Vuyk, 1980, p. 264) to refer to the empirical return, and *réversibilité* to refer to operational reversibility as such. Similarly, he sometimes used the terms "temporal" and "nontemporal" in referring to successive and simultaneous coordinations, respectively (Piaget, 1977c, vol. 2, p. 324).

transformations of length must be accompanied by corresponding changes in thickness without having to verify their judgments through actual measurements. The appearance of such a sense of necessity may seem to raise more questions than it answers. For Piaget, this development was understood in terms of the construction of a grouping structure:

> Let us begin with two facts. First, inferential necessity is an index of the closure of an operatory structure. Second, the first such structures are the *groupements*. It will also be helpful to recall that conservation on the whole is the thing all *groupement* structures have in common and that the operations essential to such structures specifically include identity (plus or minus 0) and reversibility $(T \cdot T^{-1} = 0)$. In other words, *groupements* involve complete compensation of affirmations by negations. [ibid., p. 99]

Thus, the reflective abstraction leading from one level to another involves the compensation of affirmations through the construction of negations and at the same time the closure of a new structure, in this case, a grouping of concrete operations. The sense of necessity results from this closure of an operational structure.[5]

But what did Piaget mean when he wrote of "the closure of an operatory structure"? And why should this "closure" result in the sense of necessity? What he probably had in mind can be summarized as follows: First, children center on one dimension (usually length) as a criterion of quantity. In Piaget's terminology, making the clay longer without noticing that at the same time it becomes thinner is a noncompensated affirmation. Next, children notice that rolling out the clay also results in making it thinner, but they still do not recognize that it gets longer and thinner at the same time. Instead, they alternately center on length and thickness. The change in thickness is not yet conceived of as a negation that compensates the change in length, nor are changes in length understood as compensations with respect to changes of thickness. The alternating centrations on length and thickness constitute successive affirmations, as yet uncoordinated with each other.

Only at the third level described by Piaget do negations as such appear in the form of the "empirical return" or "revertibility" of transformations involving length and thickness. That is, a clay cylinder that is lengthened by rolling out can be "returned" to its original state. Similarly, a cylinder that is made thinner can also be made thicker again. Further, children realize that rolling out the clay makes it both longer and thinner at the same time. What is still missing is the understanding that these simultaneous transformations (longer and thinner) compensate each other exactly. In other words, each type of affirmation (making

---

5 To say that the closure of a structure results in a sense of necessity does not imply that this sense of necessity is always justified. Recall the experiment with the pulleys in *Success and understanding* (Piaget, 1974/1978b) summarized earlier. There the closure of an operational structure resulted in a false judgment of conservation that was (erroneously) accompanied by a sense of necessity. As Piaget (1981a, 1983) described in his two books on the possible and the necessary, the closure of an operational structure results in the recognition that some of the compositions it comprehends are possible, others impossible, and still others *necessary*. Whether or not this structure leads to a veridical judgment in a given situation is another question.

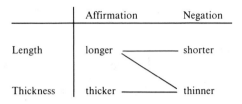

Figure 6.3. Incomplete compensation of affirmations (longer, thinner) and negations (shorter, thicker).

longer and making thinner) is compensated separately by its respective negation (making shorter and making thicker). Further, affirmations (becoming longer and thinner at the same time) are composed with each other, but there is as yet no composition of negations to compensate this composition of affirmations. The actions of making longer and making thinner are not yet combined, *together with their respective negations,* in a single structure. Instead, the affirmative poles of each dimension (making longer and making thicker) are compensated separately by their respective negations (making shorter and making thinner). At most, affirmations belonging to the more salient dimension are composed with negations of the other dimension (making longer and thinner at the same time). These relations are represented in Figure 6.3.

What is still missing at this level is the simultaneous recognition (a) that making thicker and making longer considered separately (i.e., with the other dimension held constant) both increase the total quantity, (b) that making shorter and making thinner considered separately both have the opposite effect, and (c) that making longer coincides with making thinner even as making thicker coincides with making shorter. In other words, each transformation coincides with another transformation that is equivalent to its own negation with respect to the total quantity. The compensatory relations that result constitute a new form of negation: operational reversibility. These new relations are represented in Figure 6.4.

According to this interpretation, the movement from Figure 6.3 to Figure 6.4 symbolizes in a general way what Piaget meant in referring to the "closure" of an operatory structure. Quantity is no longer identified in terms of one dimension only, but is seen to be the joint product of both length and thickness. Considered separately, the affirmations and negations of both dimensions have similar effects on the total quantity. Increases or decreases in either dimension (with the other dimension held constant) result in respective increases or decreases in quantity. In rolling out a ball of clay, an increase in length coincides with a decrease in thickness. Moreover, the decrease in thickness is exactly equivalent to the negation of the increase in length, so that the total quantity is conserved. Because these relations apply to all possible applications

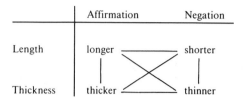

Figure 6.4. Complete compensation of affirmations (longer, thinner) and negations (shorter, thicker).

of the actions in question (manipulations of length and thickness by rolling out or other deformations of shape), quantity is understood as being conserved *by necessity*.

Description versus explanation. In the Appendix to *The equilibration of cognitive structures*, Piaget replied to certain criticisms from his colleagues. Foremost among these was the objection that he had only *described* the process of equilibration in this book, but had not *explained* it. In reply, Piaget wrote that if explanation consists in inserting the facts within a deductive system capable of providing reasons why those facts should be as they are, then he had indeed provided at least the beginnings of an explanation for the phenomena in question. He divided the reasons provided into two types: functional and structural. Both types of reasons were discussed at various points throughout the book; so the following account is limited to an attempt to summarize the most important of them.

In terms of function, the perturbations constituted by contradictions and lacunae in cognitive systems give rise to certain "needs." In effect, the organism is motivated to maintain the coherence of the cognitive system by transcending these perturbations in some way. In this sense, the contradictions and lacunae that produce disequilibrium constitute the motivating force behind cognitive development.

But contradictions and lacunae can produce disequilibrium only in the context of an existing system and its previous form of equilibrium. This consideration leads to some of the structural reasons in Piaget's explanations. His general argument was that disequilibria are produced through noncompensated transformations, an initial imbalance between affirmations and negations. In the initial phase (alpha reactions), children's attention is centered on affirmations, and negations are ignored. Only through a fairly laborious process are negations constructed for every affirmation. But what is implied by the fact that negations are initially ignored? Are they simply not perceived? Or are they perceived, and then put aside? If they are not perceived, then one is obliged to explain how they become perceived in the course of development. And if they are perceived, but actively "repressed," then one must explain not only how this occurs but also why it ceases to be the case with further development.

Piaget wrote that the centration on certain properties or dimensions to the exclusion of others has two fundamental characteristics: "On the one hand, it is characterized by the impossibility of dealing with everything at once, owing to the limitations of the field of visual fixation or of attention. On the other hand, it is characterized by systematic deformation based on overestimating what is centered on the field and underestimating what remains at the periphery" (ibid., p. 114). In the case of the development of operations, the centrations involved are cognitive-representational, not merely perceptual. Still, one may speak of the overestimation of the elements centered as compared with those that are not. Children cannot focus on all the relevant dimensions from the beginning because of limitations in what Piaget called their "span of assimilation": "Not succeeding in widening an initially too restricted field or 'span' of assimilation, the subject is able to proceed only by making pairs or juxtaposition, temporarily leaving aside other elements or their properties" (ibid.). In addition to this quantitative limitation in the scope of children's centrations, a structural factor exists as well: "Naturally, to go beyond simple metaphorical analogies it is necessary to specify the dynamics of such processes in terms of interactions between the conceptual form adopted and the perceptual or perceptible content derived from objects assimilated. In effect, the extension of a conceptual field, as is partly the case with perceptual fields as well, depends on its structure" (ibid.).

In short, Piaget distinguished between two different processes. On the one hand, children appear to be unable to center on all the relevant factors to begin with because their "span of assimilation" or "conceptual field" is too narrow to permit it. On the other hand, to the extent that they become able to perceive some of the factors initially ignored, the conceptual structure they bring to bear on the situation continues to resist assimilating the neglected contents. As he put it a few pages later, "the form rejects certain elements of the content, in which case a force belonging to the rejected content opposes the force exerted by the form" (ibid., p. 119). This opposition constitutes an unstable equilibrium between the structure or form and the rejected content that is eventually superseded by a more stable equilibrium in which the structure or form accommodates to the previously rejected content.

But why should an accommodation to a previously rejected content result in the construction of the particular kinds of structures that Piaget described? In the case of concrete operations, for example, why should equilibration result in structures that have the form of groupings? Recall that the two basic properties of groupings are composition and reversibility, where reversibility implies the existence of both inverse operations and an identity operator defined in terms of the composition of a direct operation and its inverse. One interpretation of Piaget's brief remarks is that the property of composition arises directly from the expansion of the subject's "conceptual field" and from an accommodation to the previously neglected contents. The subject is able to combine or compose two operations to the extent that they are both centered simultaneously.

As for reversibility, Piaget's remarks suggest that it develops from a deep-seated tendency toward symmetry in the development of organic forms. At one point, Piaget referred to the Prägnanz or "good form" of cognitive structures (ibid., p. 10). Of course, Piaget's usage of this term differs from that of the Gestalt psychologists. The latter were primarily interested in the "good form" of perceptual structures involving certain spatial symmetries, but Piaget was concerned with the "good form" of operatory structures possessing certain symmetries of transformation. This tendency toward transformational symmetry is expressed in the development of operatory structures insofar as every direct operation comes to be compensated by its inverse operation. The main point of this argument is that one has no need to postulate any particular mechanism in accounting for the development of such symmetries in cognitive structures, because the occurrence of symmetry is a characteristic of organic growth and development in general. In any event, the symmetry (reversibility) of cognitive forms, together with their capacity for composition, results in the development of grouping structures as such.

Whether or not Piaget's functional and structural explanations are satisfactory is an open question. The answer probably depends to a great extent on the questions that one seeks to answer in constructing a theory of cognitive development. Perhaps what Piaget's critics had in mind was not that he had not provided any explanations, but that the explanations he did provide were largely of a post hoc character. One is hard-pressed to specify the empirical predictions that could be derived from his explanations that would enable one to test his theory empirically. We shall return to this question in chapter 7.

LAST WRITINGS

In the years remaining to Piaget after the publication of *The equilibration of cognitive structures,* he published several important volumes of psychological research, including studies of reflective abstraction (Piaget, 1977c), generalization (Piaget, 1978d), correspondences (Piaget, 1980b), and dialectic (Piaget, 1980d). Still other works have appeared posthumously, including two volumes on possibility and necessity (Piaget, 1981a, 1983), a comprehensive treatment of the relation between psychogenesis and the history of the sciences (Piaget & Garcia, 1983), and a volume (described by the publisher as "Piaget's last book") on the logic of significations (Piaget & Garcia, 1987). Taken together, these works not only represent Piaget's most mature thought on several topics of central importance to his theory but also contain a number of new ideas that develop the theory in substantial ways.

These characteristically voluminous works present all the usual difficulties for summarization. No brief review can hope to convey the detail on which their conclusions are based. A good summary, however, can serve the useful purpose of placing each individual work in the context of Piaget's theory as a whole. Thus, we shall continue the strategy used throughout this book in summarizing the main conclusions of each volume, giving particular emphasis to the development of themes running through the corpus of Piaget's life work.

Reflective abstraction and generalization

Reflective abstraction. Following *The equilibration of cognitive structures,* the next two volumes to appear in the *Etudes d'épistémologie génétique* were both devoted to studies of reflective abstraction (Piaget, 1977c). The first volume of these *Recherches sur l'abstraction réfléchissante* contained studies of abstractions pertaining to logico-arithmetical relations and included chapters on elementary arithmetical operations, the construction of common multiples, the inversion of arithmetical operations, transfers of unities, problems of inclusion and inference, the understanding of correlation, and concrete forms of the INRC and Klein groups. The second volume focused on abstractions involving order and spatial relations, with chapters on additive series, the order of practical actions, relations between the surfaces and perimeters of rectangles, diagonals, and the rotation of a rod at the sensorimotor level, among other topics.

A common feature of these studies involved presenting children with two or more tasks sharing certain formal properties and examining development not only in the performance of each task taken separately but also in children's understanding of how the two tasks resembled each other. For example, in the study of common multiples, children were first shown two piles of differently colored counters and asked to form two new collections having equal numbers, but formed, in one case, by taking counters two-by-two from the first pile, and in the other case, by taking them three-by-three from the other pile. Then they were shown two piles of wooden blocks, the two differing in color and block size, and asked to build two towers of equal height such that each tower was constructed from blocks of only one color. With regard to both tasks, children were asked how they would proceed if the numbers were changed. Finally, they were also asked what the two tasks had in common. (For simplicity, the two colors employed in each case will be called red and blue. Note also that the red blocks were two-thirds the height of the blue ones.)

At *stage I* (under 7–8 years of age), children were unable to foresee how one could arrive at equal numbers of counters unless one took equal numbers from the two piles each time, and they were astonished when they did obtain equal numbers by trial and error. Even when they solved the task in this way, they were unable to say how they had done it or how one might do it again. Similar reactions were observed in the case of the blocks, but children did not see any similarity between the two tasks because they tended to compare only the physical properties of the objects involved (the counters were square, but the blocks were round; or the counters were flat, but the blocks tall; etc.).

At *stage IIA* (beginning at age 7–8), children understood that they should be able to achieve equality of numbers in the two collections by taking more frequently from the pile from which they took only two at a time, as compared with the pile from which they took three at a time. In other words, they began to understand the compensatory relations between the number of counters taken each time and the number of times they drew from the pile. But they did not yet arrive at the exact numbers involved (2-at-a-time $\times$ 3 times = 3-at-a-time $\times$ 2 times) and succeeded in solving the problem only by trial and error. Their reactions were similar with the blocks. As for the comparison between the two tasks, children at this stage focused on the actions involved rather than merely on the properties of the objects, but only the goals of the actions employed were viewed as similar, not their structures. Thus, the tasks were said to resemble each other only insofar as they tried to achieve the "same" in each case (i.e., the same number of counters, and towers of the same height).

At *stage IIB* (age 9–10), children solved the problem with the counters more or less immediately (i.e., they foresaw that 2 times 3 would equal 3 times 2), but they still continued to have some difficulty with the towers, reaching a solution only after some experimentation. With respect to the comparison between tasks, they now understood that both involved correspondences between three units from one category of objects and two units from the other.

At *stage III* (11–12 years), the problem of the towers was also solved immediately. Given the fact that three red blocks reached the same height as two blue ones, children recognized that the red blocks were two-thirds the height of the blue ones.

In the conclusion to that chapter, Piaget wrote that this study had to do with the development of the operation of multiplication from the operation of addition. Of the two, addition is developmentally the more primitive; Piaget called it "the most elementary of constructive actions" (Piaget, 1977c, p. 42). Multiplication is a second-order operation insofar as it consists in applying the operation of addition to itself – in effect, adding the number of times that one has added a certain number. This "reflection" of an action or operation onto a higher level Piaget called "reflective abstraction." Through reflective abstraction, an action or operation that previously was merely *carried out* now becomes the *object* of some higher-order operation.

Such reflective abstraction is lacking at the preoperational level. At stage I, Piaget's subjects simply carried out the action of adding by 2's or by 3's without taking account of how many times they did so. At stage IIA, the beginning of such a reflective abstraction could be observed, but it remained only qualitative in nature. That is, children recognized that they must add two objects more times than they added three objects in order to achieve the same result, but the number of times was not yet quantified. At stage IIB, the reflective abstraction was complete, at least with respect to the first task. Children could now keep track of the number of times they added a given number of counters to the pile.

As for the decalage between the two tasks, Piaget did not attempt to explain it there. But based on previous interpretations of similar decalages (Piaget & Inhelder, 1948/1967), one may surmise that it may have been attributable to the differences between number and spatial measurement. In the counter task, the ratio between the numbers of counters taken from the two piles is clear from the beginning, but in the tower task the ratio of lengths becomes clear only after the child has built two towers of equal heights and counted the number of blocks in each.

In the general conclusion to the two volumes on reflective abstraction, Piaget distinguished between three different types of abstractions. *Empirical abstractions* are drawn from observables, either those pertaining to objects or those pertaining to the material aspects of the subject's own actions. As such, they contribute to the development of physical knowledge. In contrast, *reflective abstractions* are drawn from the coordinations among actions and form the basis of the development of logico-mathematical knowledge. A third type, *pseudo-empirical abstraction,* is drawn from momentary properties of objects that stem from the coordinations of the subject's actions. At the stage of concrete operations, for example, the child becomes aware of operatory compositions (classifications, seriations, etc.) to the extent that objects are actually classified, ordered, and so forth. Thus, pseudo-empirical abstractions really constitute a special case of reflective abstractions and are not, as they might appear at first, derived from empirical abstractions.

In terms of development, empirical abstractions are dependent on reflective abstractions. At every level, empirical abstraction begins by assimilating physical contents to a form (structure) already elaborated by reflective abstraction. The form is then accommodated to the specific contents. In contrast, reflective abstraction begins by supporting itself on pseudo-empirical abstractions. Structures having the form of functions or operations are formed by reflection on the properties that objects have acquired by virtue of being subject to the coordinated actions of the subject. At the next higher level, however, these structures themselves become the objects of further reflective abstraction, and higher-order structures (e.g., formal operational structures) are formed that take the lower-order structures as their content. What was a form on the lower level becomes a content on the next higher level, and so on. "The functions of form and content are relative, every form becoming content for those which encompass it" (Piaget, 1977c, p. 319).

Thus, the successive development of empirical abstraction from level to level results in forms that are progressively more adequately adapted to physical content, and the development of reflective abstraction from one level to the next results in forms that are progressively more removed from physical reality. In effect, they become progressively more "formal" in character. This progressive formalization occurs not only in psychogenesis but also in the history of thought. Physics has progressed by applying forms developed in mathematics to the understanding of physical reality. Mathematics itself has developed in the direction of increasing formality. Although physics develops in a series of revolutions in which old models of reality are replaced by new ones, mathematics develops through ever increasing generalizations in which old theorems are recognized as special cases of new theorems, but are not replaced by them. Accordingly, relativity replaces Newtonian physics (even if the latter is recognized as approximately correct within a limited sphere of application), but non-Euclidean geometries only relativize Euclidean geometry (the latter being recognized as completely valid, within its own sphere, that sphere, however, representing only one of many possibilities).

Generalization. The next volume in the *Etudes* series, *Recherches sur la généralisation* (Piaget, 1978d), represented a closer investigation of themes that had occupied Piaget all his life, what he called "the two great mysteries of knowledge": the fact that new structures are continually constructed and the fact that these structures nevertheless appear to be necessary after the fact (ibid., p. 5). These themes were a direct continuation of his studies on abstraction, for the processes of abstraction and generalization were intimately connected in Piaget's thinking. In parallel with the distinction between empirical and reflective abstraction, Piaget distinguished between two forms of generalization. *Inductive generalization* represents the extension of the field of application of an existing form or structure and, like empirical abstraction, takes observables as its point of departure. In contrast, *constructive generalization* involves the generation of new forms (and contents) and, like reflective abstraction, is drawn from the coordinations among the subject's actions or operations. *Recherches sur la généralisation* is essentially a study of the processes involved in this latter type of generalization. The manner in which these processes were studied will be illustrated with an example involving the addition of lengths.

In this study, children were given 24 solid rectangles varying in length and width by unit increments. Using these figures, they were asked to build alignments reaching from a fixed notch running right to left in front of them forward to a "goal line" marked by an elastic band, the point being to choose the rectangles so that the far end of the alignment would exactly reach the goal line without going over. Thus, the main task involved the addition of lengths and/or widths. In a variation on this procedure, children were shown two different goal lines and asked to choose rectangles so that both lines could be reached with alignments built from the same rectangles (i.e., by rotating one or more of them so that the length of the alignment as a whole would be appropriately altered). In a further variation on this double-goal procedure, the goal lines were set so that it was impossible to reach both with the same rectangles, given a restricted set of rectangles to choose from. (The goal lines were set two units apart, but all the rectangles had lengths that were three units greater than their widths.)

In *stage IA* (5 years), children were able to reach the goal by adding lengths in a trial-and-error process. There was no spontaneous use of rotations. If children wanted to make the alignment longer or shorter, they would exchange one of the rectangles for a different one, rather than rotating one of the rectangles they already had. Even when this strategy was demonstrated to them, they did not continue to use it on their own. Thus, they did not believe one could reach two goals with the same elements. At *stage IB* (6 years), children discovered the use of rotation and were subsequently able to solve some of the double-goal problems, but such solutions were accomplished only through trial and error, not by deduction. According to Piaget, these stages are dominated by purely inductive generalizations involving the application of an existing scheme (addition of lengths) to a new situation. At stage IB, the beginning of a constructive generalization in the coordination of addition and rotation could be observed, but it remained rudimentary because the results of any particular rotation were noted after the fact and were not foreseen in advance.

At *stage IIA* (7–8 years), children began to predict the effects of rotating individual rectangles on the total length of the alignment in advance. Thus, they began to understand the "point" of the two-goal task in terms of choosing rectangles with appropriate differences between their lengths and widths, but despite the fact that these tasks were generally solved successfully, the solution involved much trial and error. As for the impossible solutions, children did not comprehend the general reason why they could not be solved. This reason was discovered at *stage IIB* (9–10 years), although in other respects children's performances continued to be characterized by trial and error. When asked about the total number of possible combinations, children replied that there were two possibilities (corresponding to length and width) for each rectangle in the alignment: two possibilities for one rectangle, four for two rectangles, six for three, and so on. According to Piaget, constructive generalization progessed during these stages insofar as the coordination of addition and rotation involves the construction of a new scheme.

At *stage III* (11–12 years), children discovered a systematic method for solving the two-goal task (e.g., choosing rectangles such that the differences between their lengths and widths add up to the distance between the two goal lines). Further, they now understood that the total number of possibilities inherent in any alignment of n rectangles was equal to $2n$: two possibilities for one rectangle, four for two, eight for three, and so on. Piaget described this development as an almost "pure" example of constructive generalization. Once children discovered that there were four possibilities in an alignment of two rectangles, this solution was immediately extended to three and more rectangles, without any confusion regarding false additive solutions.

In his concluding remarks, Piaget returned to the "two great mysteries of knowledge" mentioned in his introduction:

The central question of the development of constructive generalizations is that of explaining their powers, in other words, the mechanism of the very construction of novelties. In this regard, we rediscover our permanent problem, recalled in the introduction: If these novelties consist only in the actualization of preexisting virtualities in the manner of Aristotle's potential and act, they are not new. But if they really are novel, how does one explain why they appear to be necessary after the fact and have effectively become so? [ibid., p. 237]

Previously, Piaget had explained the generativity of mathematical thought by its capacity for constructing new operations on existing operations. This recursive construction is the very mechanism of constructive generalization. But identifying this mechanism only displaces the problem, for one can still ask whether or not those higher-order operations were already potentially contained in the existing operations.

Either the operations exist from all time in a "universe of possibilities" independent of the epistemological subject and are discovered by the latter in the course of trial and error by individual subjects, or this universe is itself in motion, consisting by this fact in a series of openings onto new possibilities. . . . Now the second interpretation seems to be necessary for two reasons: On the one hand, the subject exists as a source of cognitive activities and of novel connections, and on the other hand, the "set of all possibilities" is an antinomical notion, the logical existence of this "all" being itself only a possibility and one which transcends the limits of combinatorial predictability.

If these remarks are justified, it is hard to see how a static once-and-for-all character can be conferred on a set of possibilities, while the peculiarity of operatory construction is not only to engender existing relations, but to "make possible" from them a series of others, the determination of which is still in question. [ibid., p. 239]

Thus, the generativity of logico-mathematical thought can be explained by the recursive character of operations such that a whole new realm of possibilities is opened up in the process of constructing higher-level operations that act on existing operations. However, it remains to be explained how such constructions come to be thought of as necessary after the fact. According to Piaget, this result follows from the compensatory relations inherent in the process of equilibration. The balancing of affirmations by their respective negations leads to the formation of closed structures in which *all the possibilities are accounted for*.

In this regard, the peculiarity of the optimizing equilibration that characterizes every successful constructive generalization is the increase of the internal necessity of the system. In general, this necessity depends upon the degree of closure of structures and results precisely from this equilibrium of negations and affirmations: to derive the necessity of *a* is to establish the impossibility of *not-a*. Closure can thus be conceived of as the ensemble of possibilities and impossibilities inherent in the system. [ibid., p. 246]

The evolution of closed structures in which all possibilities are accounted for does not exclude an openness toward new possibilities of an entirely different kind. The possibilities accounted for within a closed structure are defined *as possibilities* by that very structure. To the extent that such a structure becomes an element in a higher-order totality, a new realm of possibilities is created. "The closures obtained never exclude the opening on new totalizations" (ibid., p. 247). This never-ending process of openings on new levels of generality, followed by the evolution of closed structures through progressive equilibrations, ensures that the "proactive generativity" of the subject's constructions will not contradict their "retroactive rigor" (ibid.).

Functions and correspondences

The 37th and last volume of the *Etudes d'épistémologie génétique* (now called *Etudes d'épistémologie et psychologie génétiques*) appeared in 1980, the year of

Piaget's death. Entitled *Recherches sur les correspondances* (Piaget, 1980b), this final volume continued the work on the development of functions begun nearly 20 years previously. In order to understand the later research, a brief look at the earlier work is necessary.

The epistemology of functions. During the years 1961–1963, discussion at the Center for Genetic Epistemology centered around the problems of time and of functions. These discussions are recounted by Piaget in Volume 20 of the *Etudes*, entitled *L'épistémologie du temps* (Grize et al., 1966). The resulting studies on time were published in this same volume, and the work on functions in Volume 23 of the *Etudes*, translated into English under the title *Epistemology and psychology of functions* (Piaget et al., 1968/1977). In the conclusion to this latter book, Piaget described the purpose of investigating functions in children's thinking in terms of isolating a logic (or a relatively coherent pre-logic) of preoperatory structures (Piaget et al., 1968/1977, p. 192). Previously, preoperational thought had been defined only negatively, as a type of thinking that lacked operational structures. Now, however, this stage came to be seen as having its own characteristic structures in the form of functions and correspondences.

Piaget was influenced in his decision to study such structures by a new development in mathematical theory called *category theory* (MacLane, 1972). In the terminology of this theory, a "category" is a type of structure defined by the composition of one-way functional mappings of certain variables on other variables. In his studies of the development of functions in children's thinking, Piaget accordingly concentrated on the development of the composition of functions. Of particular interest was the demonstration that certain such compositions resulted in the formation of operational structures. In effect, concrete operational structures develop out of preoperational functions. Piaget distinguished further between (a) preoperatory or "constitutive" functions, which he described as being essentially qualitative insofar as they are mappings of one logical variable (class or relation) onto another, and (b) quantified or "constituted" functions that he believed to develop as a consequence of operations. The developmental link between functions and operations can best be illustrated with one of the studies from the book on functions.

In a chapter entitled "From constitutive functions to equivalence classes," Piaget described the development of classification from preoperational mappings to operational inclusion in the context of a particular problem. Children were first shown a series of four *fixed* base cards, A, B, C, D, divided into red and white regions as shown in Figure 6.5a. In addition, they were shown 12 *movable* cards, A_1, A_2, A_3, B_1, B_2, B_3, and so on, all red in color and having an irregular shape as shown in Figure 6.5b. (Only 3 of the 12 movable cards, C_1, C_2, and C_3, are shown in the figure.) The task was to choose those movable red cards that when placed on top of each of the fixed red-and-white cards would result in a completely red square. The cards were so constructed that 3 of the 12 movable cards would cover each fixed card in this way. Because of the similar placements of the vertical elements of the movable cards, A_1, A_2, and A_3 would cover the

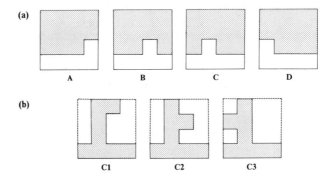

Figure 6.5. Fixed base cards (a) and movable cover cards (b) used in the experiment on constitutive functions and equivalence classes. (Adapted from Piaget et al., 1968/1977, p. 17.)

base card A, and B_1, B_2, and B_3 would cover the base card B, and so on. Children were further asked whether or not and in what ways the 12 movable cards were similar to each other.

Three stages in the development of equivalence tasks were found with respect to this problem. In *stage I* (5–6 years), children discovered the many-to-one mapping between the movable cards and their corresponding fixed cards only through trial and error. Thus, children divided the movable cover cards into subclasses solely on the basis of their empirical ''suitability'' for fulfilling the action of covering the white regions on the base cards and did not provide a reason for this suitability in terms of the positions of the vertical elements on the respective cards. Instead, two cover cards were recognized as more or less similar depending on how easily the one could be transformed into the other (e.g., by moving the vertical elements, changing the right–left orientation, etc.). Piaget compared this way of thinking to that of a boy who thought a small gray cat was like a large brown dog ''because I can make him larger, cut his whiskers, and paint him brown'' (Piaget et al., 1968/1977, p. 23). In effect, the properties of the objects were not completely differentiated from the transformations that could be applied to them.

At *stage II* (7–8 years), children began to recognize that certain of the movable cards were similar because they all covered the same base card. But this similarity was only one among other recognized similarities, such as orientation and shape, and children still did not recognize the position of the vertical elements as the common property that enabled different movable cards to cover the same base card. Nor did children recognize the different properties of the different base cards as determining the classification. In Piaget's words, this classification as yet had no hierarchical structure.

At *stage III* (9–10 years), this hierarchical structure was attained. Not only did children group the 12 movable cards into four subclasses of three each based on their ability to cover the respective base cards, but they explicitly mentioned the common positions of the vertical elements in both sets of cards as the basis for this correspondence. In addition to the many-to-one mapping of cover cards to base cards, they also understood the one-to-many mapping of the base cards to their respective cover cards. In other words, the one-way functional relation characterizing the earlier stages had been replaced by a reversible (two-way) operational classification.

Other chapters in *Epistemology and psychology of functions* had to do with the coordination of pairings, proportionality, causal and spatial functions, covariation, the composition of differences, variations of variations, and quantified or "constituted" functions. The volume concluded with theoretical essays by J.-B. Grize and Piaget. In his conclusion, Piaget wrote that three types of functional dependencies may be distinguished: (a) a "notional" dependence, such that the knowledge of *y* depends on the knowledge of *x;* (b) a "physical" dependence, such that an event *y* depends on a prior occurrence *x;* (c) a dependence relative to an action of the subject, such that an action *x* produces a certain outcome *y.* Consistent with his action-oriented epistemology, he argued that the first two types of dependencies result from the third. Moreover, the first type of dependency eventually results in the development of operations (as exemplified in the study of equivalence classes described earlier), and the second type in the development of causal thinking. In other words, the functional dependencies inherent in action constitute the common source of both logico-mathematical operations and causality. Once differentiated, these two types of knowledge develop in "parallel," but this parallelism (consistent with Piaget's other writings on the relation between logical operations and causality) is largely formal in character and implies neither developmental synchrony nor any systematic decalage: "Operations can precede and give rise to causality even prior to any experimentation and observation of laws, . . . but a hypothetical causal model can also impose itself on operations and compel them to imitate it in the same manner" (ibid., p. 180).

Thus, preoperational thinking was characterized by a logic of functions. The major limitation of this logic was that it consisted in only one-way applications and lacked the reversibility of operations. The one-way character of functional thinking led Piaget to describe it somewhat facetiously as "only half a logic." Operations as such develop when the logic of constitutive functions finds its "second half" in the form of reciprocal mappings in both directions (ibid., p. 193).

Correspondences. In *Recherches sur les correspondances,* Piaget (1980b) carried this research on preoperational thinking to even more fundamental structures. Both functions and operations involve transformations. For example, the functional relation $y = f(x)$ relates an initial state *x* to the state *y* that results when *x* is modified or transformed by a particular action (represented by the function f itself). In contrast, a correspondence is merely a comparison involving two or more states that are not modified in the process. Piaget and his collaborators argued that correspondences precede the development of transformations, that transformations develop from correspondences, and that correspondences become subordinated to transformations once the latter have appeared.

The development of correspondences was studied in a number of experimental situations, including children's drawings, correspondences among objects, the transformations involved in the rotation of a disk, and the correspondences among the elements of a series, among other situations. Some of these studies involved children as young as 2–3 years, and one study (on the transformations relating to the rotation of a disk) included children in the second year of life. Thus, these investigations help to provide the "missing link" in Piaget's account of children's cognitive development, between the end of the sensorimotor period in the second year and the earliest preoperational period (4–5 years) studied in his research on concrete operations.

As an illustrative example of this research, the chapter "Correspondences and transformations in the case of intersection" will be reviewed. Although this study involved older children between 7 and 10 years of age, it is chosen for consideration because it is easy to compare with Piaget's previous work on class inclusion. Children were shown several sets of objects involving an intersection of subclasses. For example, one set included three ducks that were not blue, three blue ducks, and two blue animals that were not ducks. Then the children were asked questions of the following form: "Are there more blue animals or more ducks?" This question differs from the typical class-inclusion problem in that it does not merely involve the inclusion of a subclass in a supraordinate class (as in the question "Are there more animals or more ducks?"). Instead, it has to do with the relations between two partially overlapping subclasses. In a second problem, children were asked to count the ducks and the blue animals in turn, writing their answers down on a piece of paper. Then the objects were covered, and children were asked how many animals there were altogether.

Three "steps" were identified in the development of the understanding of class intersection with respect to this problem. In *step I* (7–8 years), children replied to the first question by including the blue ducks either among the blue animals or among the ducks, but without acknowledging the fact that they belonged to both subclasses at once. Their answers were either of the form "There are more ducks than blue animals, because there are six ducks and only two blue animals" or of the form "More blue animals than ducks, because there are five blue animals and three ducks." Interestingly, children gave answers of this kind even though they were able to answer the typical class-inclusion task ("There are more animals than ducks, because there are eight animals and only six ducks"). In the second procedure, they added the number of ducks to the number of blue animals to obtain the total number of animals. In terms of the present example, they would have predicted that there were 11 animals (6 ducks plus 5 blue animals) altogether.

In *step II* (8–9 years), children recognized that there were "more ducks than blue animals," because there were six of the former and only five of the latter. That is, they counted the blue ducks among both subclasses from the beginning. Having succeeded on this problem, they still failed the second procedure; with the objects covered, they declared that there were 11 animals altogether, and they were surprised to find only 8 animals when the latter were uncovered. After the fact, they realized that they were mistaken to have counted the blue ducks both among the ducks and among the blue animals.

In *step III* (9–10 years), children solved both problems from the beginning. They recognized not only that there were six ducks and five blue animals but also (even with the objects covered) that there were only eight animals altogether, because three animals were both ducks and blue.

According to Piaget's analysis, these three steps represented children's understanding of this task, from the establishment of mere correspondences between objects and their properties to the construction of an operational classification as such. In step I, children established a many-to-one mapping between the individual objects and one or the other of their properties (being a duck or being blue). As yet, there was no reciprocal one-to-many mapping of some objects (e.g., the blue ducks) onto more than one property (being a duck *and* being blue). Children at step I recognized such objects as partaking in one or the other property alternately and successively, but they did not recognize them as partaking in both properties simultaneously. This succession was expressed directly in some of these children's language: "Sometimes you can count it among the ducks, then other times among the blue animals" (ibid., p. 123).

By step III, however, the many-to-one mapping of objects onto a single property was balanced by one-to-many mapping of objects onto multiple properties. Instead of recognizing certain objects as having one or the other of two properties in succession, these objects were recognized as partaking of both properties simultaneously. This recognition was expressed by the children themselves: "It goes with both of them because it is both white and a duck at the same time," "It's white and at the same time it's a duck," and so on (ibid., pp. 128–129). Thus, the passage from correspondences to operations was at the same time a passage from successive to simultaneous coordinations.

One other aspect of this task deserves to be pointed out, although it was not explicitly mentioned by Piaget. This task was one of the few concrete examples in all of his research of the grouping called the "secondary addition of classes" (Grouping II in Table 4.1). As opposed to the "primary addition of classes," which has the form $Y = X + X'$ and constitutes the basis of the class-inclusion problem, the "secondary addition of classes" has the form $Y = X_1X_2' + X_1X_2 + X_1'X_2$ and can be translated into the terms of the present example as follows: The total number of animals (Y) is equal to the sum of the blue animals that are not ducks (X_1X_2'), the blue ducks (X_1X_2), and the ducks that are not blue ($X_1'X_2$).

Further, the examples given by Piaget suggest that a systematic decalage occurs between the primary and secondary addition of classes as applied to the same content featured in this task; the children cited earlier as examples of step

I were described as capable of solving the class-inclusion problem based on the "primary addition of classes," but they were not able to solve the problem of intersection based on the "secondary addition of classes." The fact that Piaget acknowledged this decalage without further comment indicates that he recognized no contradiction in the existence of developmental decalages between different concrete operational groupings as applied to the same physical content. This question will be taken up in greater detail in chapter 7.

In the conclusion to *Recherches sur les correspondances,* Piaget wrote that whereas transformations (functions or operations) involve the application of a general form or structure to a particular content, "the distinguishing feature of correspondences, and that which makes them indispensable in cognitive development, is in fact to furnish a knowledge of *contents as such*" (ibid., p. 189; emphasis added). Transformations act to modify the contents to which they are applied and bear on only those properties that are relevant to the modifications. In contrast, correspondences do not modify the contents to which they are applied, but enrich the subject's knowledge of those contents by drawing comparisons among their particular features.

This statement of the nature of correspondences suggests that they might be related to the figurative aspect of knowing, for the latter also involves knowledge of the particularities of content without transformation. The fact that Piaget devoted a whole chapter to the study of correspondences in the development of children's drawings, together with the fact that he described correspondences as the developmental precursors of operations, raises the question whether or not correspondences compose the common source of both operative knowledge and figurative knowledge. Any answer to this question must remain speculative. Curiously, Piaget did not even mention the figurative–operative distinction in that volume.

The possible and the necessary

The publication of two volumes by Piaget on the development of the possible and the necessary in children's thinking followed within a few years of his death. Piaget had edited the manuscript of the first volume (Piaget, 1981a) himself, but the editing of the second volume (Piaget, 1983) was completed by B. Inhelder. In these two books, Piaget described development from one stage to another as involving the generation of new possibilities, and the formation of closed structures as resulting in a feeling of necessity. He had previously considered the development of the possible and the necessary only in connection with the development of operatory structures, but now he investigated them for their own sake. Just as his studies of operations had been concerned with both logico-mathematical knowledge and physical knowledge, so was his current investigation directed toward the possible and the necessary as they pertained to both logico-mathematical reasoning and reasoning about physical reality. (For a summary in English of Piaget's theory about the possible and the necessary, see Piaget, 1986, or Piaget & Voyat, 1979.)

Possibility. The study of the possible and the necessary in children's thinking was also intimately connected with Piaget's constructivist epistemology. As he wrote in the introduction to *L'évolution des possibles chez l'enfant* (Piaget, 1981a), the first of the two volumes on these topics, the demonstration that all new knowledge results from a regulatory process of equilibration is not sufficient for defending a constructivist epistemology against innatism or empiricism. One could always argue that this regulatory mechanism itself is either hereditary or acquired. The study of the development of the possible would seem to provide another approach to this problem. Against empiricism, one can argue that the possible as such is not an observable, but the product of an interaction between the activities and operations of the subject and certain of the properties of the object. The possible transcends the real; therefore, its development cannot be explained solely with reference to the experience of reality.

But constructivism is not the only alternative to empiricism. One might also argue that the possible preexists in the mind. Against this, Piaget reasoned that the idea of "the set of all possibilities" is meaningful only in relation to a deductive system in which all the possibilities may be deduced. The study of children's thinking shows that the development of the possible goes hand in hand with the progressive development of such deductive systems. These considerations imply that the "set of all possibilities" is never definitively and absolutely closed; it is always open to further development that results in ever new possibilities. Even the "set of all possibilities" attributed to the mind in preformist theories is itself only a hypothetical construction that loses its specific meaning if it is used in an absolute manner. Piaget had expressed a similar idea in the conclusion to *Recherches sur la généralisation* when he had called the "set of all possibilities" an antinomical notion.

The two specific goals pursued in the study of the possible in children's thinking were described as follows: first, to discover how the understanding of the possible develops with age, and second, to determine how the development of the possible is related to the development of operatory structures. Does the development of such structures engender the understanding of possibilities? Or, on the contrary, does the development of the possible prepare the development of operations? Piaget believed that the bulk of the evidence supported the latter hypothesis. Briefly, an initial understanding of possibilities develops from the use of successive means in actions directed toward the attainment of a goal, but operatory structures develop only when children realize that a number of possibilities coexist in a systematic relation. One can easily see in this formulation another manifestation of Piaget's basic distinction between successive (or temporal) and simultaneous (or atemporal) coordinations in thought or action.

These considerations led Piaget to state a new taxonomy of schemes. *Presentational schemes* bear on the simultaneous properties of objects and conserve their particular character even when they are incorporated into more general schemes. They are called "presentational" rather than "representational" because they can include sensorimotor as well as cognitive-representational schemes. In contrast, *procedural schemes* consist in means oriented toward a goal. In any succession of means employed in the pursuit of a particular goal, those employed initially are not necessarily conserved. Moreover, procedural schemes are fairly context-specific: In order to be successful in goal attainment, a procedural scheme must be well accommodated to the contingencies of the particular situation. It follows that they are not as easily generalized from one context to another as are presentational schemes. Finally, *operational schemes* constitute a kind of synthesis of the other two types of schemes. Insofar as an operation is carried out in time, it has the character of a procedure, but the relations among the possible compositions of operations share with presentational schemes the character of simultaneity or atemporality. The simultaneity of operational schemes differs from that of presentational schemes in that the former have to do with simultaneous coordinations among the operations of the subject, but the latter assimilate the simultaneous properties of objects. One can see in this taxonomy of schemes a further evolution of Piaget's previous distinction between the figurative and operative aspects of intelligence. The features of figurative thought are by and large incorporated into the category of presentational schemes, and operative thinking is now differentiated into the procedural and the operational as such.

The format of *L'évolution des possibles* followed that of Piaget's previous books. The development of the possible in children's thinking was traced in a number of different situations, and certain general conclusions were drawn from the total results. The third chapter, devoted to "the possible forms of a partially concealed reality," provides a representative example of the situations studied. Not only is this study remarkably simple in conception, but the results obtained reflect many of the basic features that Piaget found characteristic of other tasks as well. Briefly, children were shown a number of objects (triangles, irregular shapes, or recognizable and structured objects such as a crystal or a shell), parts of which were hidden under cotton wadding, and they were asked questions of the following kinds: what they thought was under the wadding, how the object continued beyond the parts that were visible, how it ended, whether or not other shapes were also possible, and how many different shapes were possible in all. Three levels in the development of children's thinking about these possible shapes were found, roughly coinciding with the stages in the development of operations reported in his previous works.

In *stage I* (5–6 years), children began by recognizing only a single possibility: that the hidden parts of the objects presented were essentially the same as the visible parts. According to Piaget, children at this level did not clearly differentiate among reality, possibility, and necessity. Because the only possibility recognized was derived immediately from perceptible reality, it was viewed as essentially inevitable. For example, one of the children at this stage stated that the hidden part of a triangle could not be different than he had indicated, "because it's a triangle and a triangle always has three sides." Similarly, when asked about the color of the hidden side of a cardboard box, he asserted that it must be the same color as the visible side, "because the box is all white, so the back side cannot be a different color" (Piaget, 1981a, p. 41). Piaget believed that this kind of thinking represented a kind of "pseudo-necessity," because only one possibility was recognized as valid. In contrast to true necessity, according to which many possibilities are recognized and all but one of them are excluded, only one possibility was even acknowledged at this level. In a second substage belonging to this level, children began to recognize at least one other possibility and were therefore no longer certain of their initial attempt to describe the hidden part of the object in terms of its visible features.

At *stage II* (7–10 years), children recognized multiple possibilities in this situation, but the possibilities recognized were still limited to those that were concretely imaginable. Thus, one child at this stage admitted that the hidden part of the object might have "7, 8 or even 9, 10, 11, 12" possible shapes. Another child acknowledged as many as 200. A third asserted that the hidden face of the cardboard box might be "green, violet, blue, white, yellow," but added, "That's all" (ibid., p. 44). In contrast to stage I, children at this level had begun to differentiate the real and the possible, recognizing the real as only one of many possibilities. In contrast to the next higher level, the possibilities recognized were still limited to a finite number that might be concretely imagined.

At *stage III* (11–12 years), this limitation was overcome. Children now recognized that the number of possible shapes was effectively unlimited: "It could be any shape whatsoever," "One can imagine all possible shapes" (ibid., p. 48).

In his general conclusions to this volume, Piaget returned to the two questions that he had enunciated in the introduction: How does the idea of the possible develop in children's thinking? How is this development related to the development of operational structures? With respect to the development of the possible, the studies included in this book generally conformed to the sequence found in the example described earlier. A first stage was characterized by the recognition of successive possibilities, one at a time. In the second stage, this limitation was superseded by the recognition of a range of simultaneous "co-possibilities," which may be more or less concrete or abstract. In the third stage, an unlimited number of possibilities was acknowledged. The close correspondence between these stages and the stages of operational development, both with respect to form and to age, raises the question of the relation between the two.

According to Piaget, it is difficult to imagine how the understanding of the possible could develop out of operations, for the latter are characterized by necessity, and the range of the necessary is much more restricted than that of the possible. More likely, the reverse is the case. From the broad (even infinite) range of possibilities, the relations among some of them form closed structures.

This closure of structures gives rise to the sense of necessity; if a certain number of the possibilities in a closed structure are given, then the remaining possibilities are determined.

Piaget argued that three conditions must be fulfilled in order for operational structures to develop from the field of possibilities. First, the consideration of successive possibilities must be superseded by a consideration of a simultaneous field of co-possibilities. Second, consistent with his previous theorizing on the compensatory processes of equilibration, affirmations must be coordinated with negations. That is, children must recognize that certain possibilities exclude others. Finally, the connection between the possible and the necessary must be realized: The necessity of a given possibility consists in the exclusion of its negation. In other words, the necessity of x consists in the impossibility of not-x.

Necessity. The development of the sense of necessity as such and its relation to the development of possibilities and operations were investigated in the second volume in the series, *L'évolution du nécessaire chez l'enfant* (Piaget, 1983). One of the clearest examples of the relations between the development of the possible and the necessary in this book was inspired by the game "Mastermind." The exact technique employed was the following: Three animals, a sheep (S), a rabbit (R), and a chicken (C), were arranged in order from left to right behind a screen so that children could not see them. They were then asked to try and arrange three identical animals in the same order. After each attempt, they were told only how many of the animals had been placed in the correct positions, but not which ones were correct. The task was to find the correct order in as few trials as possible.

The way in which this task can be solved is evident. There are only six possible orders in which three objects can be arranged (in this case, SRC, SCR, RSC, RCS, CSR, and CRS). By being told after each trial how many positions have been correctly guessed, the subject can successively eliminate certain of these possibilities until only one is left. This remaining possibility is then "necessarily" correct. Three general stages were found in the development of children's solutions of this task.

Stage I (5–7 years) was characterized by the lack of a cumulative accounting of the possibilities excluded on successive trials. In a first substage, no continuity between trials was observed; but in a second substage, children utilized simple procedures that, although insufficient for solving the problem, nevertheless linked one trial to the next. For example, one child followed the rule of "doing the opposite," and another based the positions of animals on the frequencies with which those animals had appeared in particular positions on previous trials.

Stage II (7–8 to 10–11 years) was marked by a recognition of a field of co-possibilities and some systematic exclusion of those possibilities that had proved to be false in previous trials. For example, several children at this stage realized that after two trials in which none of the animals were placed correctly, all possibilities except one had thereby been eliminated. If the child had tried the orders RCS and CSR and none of the positions were correct in either case, then the only possibility that remained was that S should be in the first position, R in the second, and C in the third. In other respects, the exclusion of possibilities at this stage was not completely systematic, in that children sometimes forgot exactly which possibilities had been excluded over an extended series of trials, a tendency that was more pronounced when four animals instead of three were used. Further, none of the children appeared to recognize the fact that it was impossible to get only two of three (or three of four) positions correct, for if $n - 1$ positions are correct, the nth position must also be correct.

At *stage III* (10–11 years), the exclusion of possibilities was systematic even with four animals, and children realized immediately the impossibility of getting two of three or three of four positions correct. After obtaining a correct solution by chance, they further recognized that another series of trials would have been possible, leading (inevitably) to the correct solution by the progressive elimination of possibilities. According to Piaget, the main interest of this study lay in showing the essentially negative character of necessity and its relation to possibility: The necessary is the one possibility that remains when all others have been excluded.

In summarizing all the studies included in this volume, Piaget concluded that the development of the understanding of necessity runs parallel to that of possibility. First, a stage of "pre-necessity" or "pseudo-necessity" occurs, consisting in the fact that children recognize only a single possibility as valid. A stage of "limited co-necessities" follows, meaning that certain necessities are seen to entail others, although the possibilities recognized at this stage are limited to some concrete subset of all hypothetical possibilities. The final stage is that of "unlimited co-necessities," so called because all possibilities are recognized as necessary, the negation of which results in contradiction.

This sequence also explains how the possible, the necessary, and the real gradually come to be differentiated from each other. At first, the real is the only possibility recognized as valid and is therefore considered "necessary." But as soon as the real is recognized as only one possibility among others, then it cannot be considered necessary unless all the other possibilities have been excluded. It follows that necessity is not something that is extracted from reality, but arises from the subject's construction of possibilities and an accounting of their interrelations.

Piaget denied that this subordination of the real to subjects' cognitive constructions results in either idealism or a Kantian dualism of phenomena and noumena. Idealism is not implied, because the subject of knowledge is recognized as part of reality even as that reality is known only in terms of the subject's constructions. In a passage that summarizes his whole biological approach to the problem of knowing, Piaget wrote that "the real learns to know itself only in engendering . . . living beings and, through them, the subject himself to which we return by an unavoidable circle (or spiral . . .)" (ibid., p. 41).

As for the Kantian distinction between the object as it is known in appearance and the (unknowable) object in itself, such a dualism is ruled out precisely because of the facts of cognitive development, for in the successive approximations constituted by the subject's cognitive constructions, the object in itself becomes known increasingly *better,* even if it is never known *completely.* Thus, the object in itself, viewed as a "limit" to knowledge that is ever approached but never reached, replaces the Kantian notion of the essentially unknowable noumenon.

Dialectic, psychogenesis, and the history of science

Although Piaget had not been directly influenced by the dialectical tradition stemming from Hegel and Marx, his theory can nevertheless be considered dialectical in the fundamental sense that it implies an interdependence of contraries in development. Like Marx and Hegel, Piaget described development as a process that proceeded from opposition and progressed by transcending oppositions. The dialectical character of Piaget's theory had been pointed out years previously by Goldmann (1959), a Marxist sociologist and a long-standing friend and colleague (Piaget, 1973f; see also Meacham & Riegel, 1978). But only in the two books now to be considered did Piaget himself explicitly deal with the relation between his own theory of cognitive development and the dialectical tradition. In *Les formes élémentaires de la dialectique* (Piaget, 1980d), he investigated dialectical processes in children's thinking, and in *Psychogenèse et histoire des sciences* (Piaget & Garcia, 1983), similar processes were traced in selected examples from the history of science. In the first of these two books, Piaget approached many of his previously elaborated ideas from the new perspective of dialectic, and in the second he returned to one of the fundamental themes of his life's work: the attempt to understand the principles governing the development of scientific knowledge by investigating the development of children's thinking. Indeed, *Psychogenèse et histoire des sciences* was his final and most advanced statement of the implications of the developmental approach for the epistemology of science. The two books are closely related, both in their reference to dialectic and in the contributions of R. Garcia, a physicist and epistemologist with whom Piaget had also collaborated in *Understanding causality* (Piaget, 1971/ 1974b).

The development of dialectic. Piaget described the purpose of *Les formes élémentaires de la dialectique* in terms of two primary goals: to show that dialectical processes are active at every level of development and to "demystify" the concept of dialectic in some of its current interpretations. In contrast to certain unnamed authors who assumed that all forms of thought are constantly dialectical in character, Piaget argued that development alternates between a phase of dialectical construction in which new structures and relations are created and a phase of purely discursive or deductive thinking in which the implications of those new structures and relations are spelled out. Piaget saw in this alternation of dialectic and deduction the solution to the problem of how certain forms of thought can be acknowledged as necessary once they develop, without having to assume that they were predetermined. As we have just seen in his work on the possible and the necessary, necessity is meaningful only in a defined context of possibilities. In the phase of dialectical construction, new contexts of possibilities are acknowledged, and in the phase of deduction the necessary interrelations among these new possibilities are comprehended. These necessary interrelations cannot be said to have predated the constructive process, for only through that process were the contexts created in which those interrelations could be affirmed as necessary.

Piaget's investigation of dialectical processes in concrete problems can be illustrated by the first chapter, on "the dialectical circularity of logical connections." This example is also of interest because it treats of several other long-standing themes in Piaget's work, including children's understanding of concepts and classification, the development of possibility and necessity, and the relation between form and content. The technique employed was exceedingly simple: Children were given 20 pictures of animals representing different families, genera, and species, such that some animals in one genus shared some characteristics (having four legs, the ability to fly) with some animals of other genera. The experimenter also had pictures of the same 20 animals. From that pile, the experimenter would choose one of the animals without the children being able to see which one. The task consisted in trying to guess which animal the experimenter had chosen by asking the fewest possible questions.

Three stages in the performance of this task were found. In *stage I* (4–6 years), children simply asked about the individual animals: "Is it the tiger?" "Is it the snail?" This form of questioning allowed them to eliminate only one possibility at a time. In *stage II* (7–11 years), children asked about certain generic characteristics: "Does it fly?" "Does it have four legs?" This form of questioning was superior in that it allowed for the elimination of several possibilities at once, but children's inclusions at this stage were not exhaustive, and they consequently did not use this form of questioning consistently. Having eliminated several possibilities through a generic question, they would revert to asking about individual animals, or they would ask questions resulting in redundant information. Only in *stage III* (11–12 years) were children's classifications characterized by exhaustive hierarchical inclusions, and they were accordingly able to draw inferences regarding the possibilities that necessarily remained after each of their questions had been answered. These references were reflected in their use of terms such as "since" and "then" (e.g., "since it doesn't have wings and does have antenna, then it can't be A, B, or C"). Similar results were obtained using geometric shapes instead of animals.

According to Piaget's brief analysis, this simple task involved a dialectical circle of predicates, concepts, judgments, and inferences. At stage I, children's questions bore on single "conceptual objects" (e.g., an animal species), each of which was recognized as being composed of a number of predicates. In stage II, children judged objects to fall under certain concepts by virtue of sharing certain predicates with other objects. In stage III, children drew inferences based on their previous judgments.

Further, the series uniting predicates, concepts, judgments, and inferences in all reasoning is developed in two opposing directions at the same time. In the ascending series, predicates are composed in the single object, objects are composed under concepts, concepts are composed in making judgments, and judgments are composed in drawing inferences. In contrast, the descending series consists in the progressive differentiation of possibilities: An inference is based on a range of possible judgments, each judgment on a range of possible concepts, and each concept on objects defined in terms of their possible predicates. These opposing series are nevertheless interdependent. The ascending movement of composing different objects under a single concept corresponds to a descending movement of acknowledging in those objects the properties by which the concept is defined (and which enables those objects to be assumed under that concept). For Piaget, this interdependence of opposing series exemplified the fundamental interaction of subject and object in all knowing and corresponded to the ''identity of opposites'' of traditional dialectic. He argued, however, that this interdependence of opposites does not entail their identity. Against Hegel (who was frequently referred to in this book), Piaget argued that a concept does not ''contain'' its contrary, but *implies* it in the same sense that each direct operation implies the possibility of its inverse. ''For us, the idea that every concept 'contains' its opposite signifies dialectically that the construction of each concept implies that of its contrary, or at least its possibility'' (Piaget, 1980d, p. 224).

In the postface to that book, R. Garcia compared genetic epistemology to traditional dialectic as exemplified in the works of Hegel, Marx, and Lenin. He concluded that whatever other differences exist between the two approaches, genetic epistemology falls under traditional definitions of dialectic. He went on to introduce some of the basic themes to be developed in their joint work, *Psychogenèse et histoire des sciences* (Piaget & Garcia, 1983). The basic idea is that certain parallels can be drawn between psychogenesis and the history of sciences, not so much with respect to the particular forms of knowledge pertaining to each as with respect to the general characteristics of the processes of development leading from one form of knowledge to another. One of the most important of these processes is the sequence *intra-, inter-,* and *trans-,* a dialectical triad that for Piaget and Garcia replaces the thesis, antithesis, and synthesis of traditional dialectical theory. This sequence was drawn from the analysis of psychogenesis: ''The three notions intra-, inter-, and trans- correspond to certain constants extracted from psychogenetic analysis: centration on the elements, then on their transformation and only finally on their mode of production within a total system [*système d'ensemble*]'' (Garcia in Piaget, 1980d, p. 241). The same general sequence can be found in the history of particular sciences, consisting in ''knowing the interrelationship of states before understanding them as results of local transformations, and the discovery of transformations before conceiving them as manifestations of a total structure [*structure totale*] of which they result as intrinsic variations" (ibid., pp. 241–242).

Psychogenesis and the history of science. One of the main tasks of *Psychogenèse et histoire des sciences* was to trace the sequence intra-inter-trans in the history of several domains of science, including the theories of mechanics, geometry, and algebra. Euclidean geometry, for example, can be considered intrafigural in that it is primarily concerned with the internal relations among geometric figures. Geometry became interfigural with the ascendance of analytic and projective geometry, because the properties of figures came to be viewed as connected by potential transformations. Finally, the transfigural period was inaugurated by Klein and the "Program of Erlangen," in which all geometries characterized by systems of transformations were subsumed under group structure. Similarly, algebra originated in an intraoperational stage, characterized by the search for solutions to specific equations. This stage was superseded in the 18th century by an interoperational period, exemplified by the discovery that equations of one form could be transformed into another form so that solutions could be found that would otherwise have been impossible. These transformations were themselves systematized in the transoperational period with the discovery of groups and other algebraic structures.

For each of these domains of science, parallels from Piaget's study of cognitive development were described. For example, the sequence from intraoperational to transoperational in the history of algebra can also be discerned in the development of logico-mathematical thinking from the preoperational to the formal operational stages. The preoperational stage can also be called "intraoperational" insofar as it is characterized by a centration on single operations. By this same reasoning, concrete operational thought can be considered "interoperational," because it involves the establishment of systematic interrelations among operations of the same kind in the form of grouping structures. Finally, formal operational thinking can be considered "transoperational" in that it is characterized by the integration of operations of different kinds in systems of transformations (e.g., the integration of negation and reciprocity in the INRC group).

Psychogenèse et histoire des sciences would be considerably less interesting if it were concerned only with establishing such parallels between stages of psychogenesis and stages in the history of scientific thought. Instead, as the authors repeatedly proclaim, "the goal is in no way to establish a correspondence between sequences of a historical nature and those revealed by psychogenetic analysis with an accent on content, but something quite different: to show that the mechanisms of transition from one historical period to the next are analogous to those of transition between one psychogenetic stage and that which follows" (Piaget & Garcia, 1983, p. 41). In an important passage, Piaget and Garcia compared their own approach to those of some recent philosophers of science, including Popper, Kuhn, Feyerabend, and Lakatos. They argued that these thinkers have debated the question to what extent the replacement of one theory by another is (or can be) rationally justified to the neglect of the specifically epistemological problem of how the transition from one theory to another in fact occurs. In contrast to the views of Popper and Lakatos, this transition is not viewed as a consequence of refutation or falsification. Instead, one theory is *surpassed* by another in such a way that the theory surpassed is integrated in the theory that surpasses it (*Le dépassé est toujours intégré dans le dépassant*) (ibid., p. 303).

The manner in which this surpassing occurs was described in the following manner: A theory is intended to explain certain phenomena within a given domain of experience in terms of a certain repertoire of concepts. Among these concepts are some that may be described as *observables* and others that can be called *theoretical constructions*. The observables correspond to the properties of reality that are directly measured or otherwise observed in methodical experiment. Such observation involves a process of empirical abstraction; certain aspects of experience relevant to the observables of the theory are noted, and other aspects are ignored as irrelevant. The theoretical constructions are concepts involving certain coordinations or interrelations among observables, but that themselves do not correspond to properties of reality recognized as observable within the theory. In classical mechanics, for example, the observables would include such concepts as distance, speed, mass, and duration, and space and time as such would be theoretical constructions. In Piagetian terminology, the theoretical constructions are derived from the observables through a process of reflective abstraction in which the coordinations among observables are themselves conceptualized.

This distinction between observables and theoretical constructions is relative to the particular theory in question. The decisive step in the surpassing of one theory by another occurs when *the theoretical constructions of the theory surpassed become conceived as observables by the surpassing theory*. Space and time, which were theoretical constructions in classical mechanics, become "observables" for the theory of relativity. In the context of relativity, space and time themselves acquire measurable properties. Space can be more or less curved; time can have different speeds. These properties of space and time can be determined through coordinated observations. On the one hand, this movement from theoretical constructions to observables describes the process by which one theory is surpassed by another. On the other hand, this same process constitutes the "superiority" of the surpassing theory. The surpassing theory is more general, not merely in the sense that it includes a greater range of observables, but by the fact that its observables are qualitatively different and more encompassing. At the same time, the surpassed theory is preserved as a special case. Note the resemblance between this account of scientific progress and the equilibration theory as described earlier in this chapter: The theoretical constructions of one theory became the observables of a succeeding theory just as the coordinations characterizing one stage of development became the observables of the next stage (Figure 6.2).

The foregoing account of scientific progress differs in several ways from those of the other philosophers of science mentioned by Piaget and Garcia. In contrast to Kuhn, who emphasized the discontinuity between successive theories, Piaget and Garcia affirmed that both continuity and discontinuity may be observed. The theories are discontinuous with respect to their differences in what is considered observable. But because of the *developmental* continuity from the observables of the surpassed theory to the observables of the surpassing theory (by way of the former's theoretical constructions), this discontinuity of level is not absolute. The observables of the lower-level theory are in fact integrated in and presupposed by those of the higher-level theory.

Against Popper, Piaget and Garcia viewed scientific progress not as a sequence of conjectures and refutations but as a process of theoretical construction and surpassing. And against Feyerabend, they did not view the process of surpassing as inherently irrational, although they recognized that the rational development of science is constrained in a nonrational manner by an "epistemic frame" (*cadre épistémique*) that derives from the particular social and historical contexts in which scientific thought develops.

For us, at each historical moment and in each society, there predominates a certain epistemic frame, which is a product of social paradigms and the source of a new epistemic paradigm. Once a certain epistemic frame is constituted, it becomes impossible to dissociate the contribution stemming from the social component from that intrinsic to the cognitive system. So constituted, the epistemic frame begins to act as an ideology which conditions the subsequent development of science. This ideology functions as an epistemological obstacle that permits no development outside the accepted conceptual frame. It is only in moments of crisis, of scientific revolutions, that there is a rupture with the dominant scientific ideology and one passes to a different state with a new epistemic frame, distinct from that which went before. [ibid., pp. 282–283]

This concept of an epistemic frame is illustrated with a few comparisons between the development of Chinese science and Western science. The Chinese view of the world in a constant state of flux facilitated the understanding of the principle of inertia in physics as early as the sixth century B.C. In contrast, the static view of the world characteristic of Greek thought hindered the understanding of the same principle in the West until nearly 2,000 years later.

Although Piaget and Garcia traced the sequence intra-inter-trans in detail with respect to both psychogenesis and the history of science, their theory of scientific progress as the surpassing of one theory by another was unfortunately sketched only very schematically and abstractly. Few examples were provided, and only with difficulty can the reader imagine how the theory would apply in particular cases. The question thus remains how well this model of scientific progress, drawn from the investigation of cognitive development in children, adequately describes the process of historical scientific revolutions.

In spite of this limitation, *Psychogenèse et histoire des sciences* provided a fitting statement of Piaget's last thoughts on the epistemology of science. Together with his other epistemological works (Beth & Piaget, 1961/1966; Piaget, 1950/1973a, 1950/1974a), this book described the end to which all his years of studying cognitive development in children were only a means. In attempting to understand and evaluate Piaget's grand enterprise, one must keep in mind that, as he put it, "the goal of genetic epistemology is not to explain the psychogenesis of knowledge by the history of science, but insofar as it is possible, the reverse" (Piaget, 1983, p. 104). Stated in these terms, *Psychogenèse et histoire des sciences* provided a clear statement of what may be the major conclusion to be drawn from Piaget's work: that scientific progress, like psychogenesis, is a process of constructive evolution.

A *logic of significations*

In distinguishing between the dispensable and core elements of Piaget's research program, Beilin (1985) argued that Piaget was not committed to any particular set of logico-mathematical models. As evidence he cited Piaget's constant adoption of new models, from the theory of groupings to category theory and the theory of correspondences. Most intriguing in this connection was Piaget's apparent conversion, toward the end of his life, to a logic of "meanings," or "significations" (Piaget, 1980e). In effect, he proposed to recast his system of operatory logic, originally based on extensional logic (in which implication is defined in terms of truth tables as described in chapter 5), in terms of an intensional logic (in which implication would be based on the meanings of the concepts involved). Beilin noted that such a radical revision would make all textbook accounts of Piagetian logic obsolete. In magnitude, it could only be likened to the revolution that occurred in Wittgenstein's thought between the positivism of the *Tractatus* and the language-game philosophy of the *Philosophical investigations*.

Against this background, the publication of "Piaget's last book" (Piaget & Garcia, 1987) was of particular interest. Entitled *Vers une logique des significations* (Toward a logic of significations), this book was devoted to the revision of Piagetian logic that Piaget (1980e) had signaled earlier. The question was whether Piaget and Garcia had succeeded in effecting the radical revision that Beilin had foreseen.

The book is divided into two parts, the first written by Piaget and the second by Garcia. Piaget's contribution was a typical collection of studies carried out with the help of a number of collaborators. The topic in this case was the logic of significations as it develops in children's thought and action. The cornerstone of this logic is what Piaget called "signifying implication," or what one might otherwise refer to as "implication by meaning." In this view, one proposition (or concept) implies another if the meaning of the second is contained in the first. But such signifying implications are not limited to conceptual thinking and propositional logic. According to Piaget, relations of implication also exist among actions. For example, the action of turning right implies that one does not turn left, and so on. The logic of significations is thus the fulfillment of an idea that can be traced back to Piaget's earliest philosophical speculations: that there is a logic of actions as well as a logic of thought (see chapter 1). This idea had been rather vaguely and metaphorically treated in *The origins of intelligence,* but in this last book it acquired a more definite and specific form.

For example, in one study (Piaget & Garcia, 1987, chap. 2) children were shown a toy car in a ramp that split into two, then into four, then into eight branches. At the end of each of these eight branches was a garage where the car could come to rest. The path followed by the car was traced with a ribbon, but the branching ramps and the garages were covered so that children could see where the car had traveled only by opening windows at various points. Children were asked which windows must be opened in order to find out the exact route taken by the car.

In *stage I* (4–6 years of age), children were generally unable to foresee the entire range of possibilities implied by the fact that the car had traveled down a given branch. For example, from the fact that the car had traveled down one of the two main branches, they inferred that it would arrive at a particular garage instead of realizing that four different destinations were possible. Such anticipations of possibilities appeared in *stage II* (7–8 years), along with the realization that if one begins with the main branch, one can always trace the complete path of the car by opening only three windows (corresponding to the three successive branchings). Finally, in *stage III,* children understood that because each branching was composed of only two alternatives, opening a window on a ramp and seeing nothing was just as informative as opening a window and seeing the ribbon. In other words, the absence of the ribbon in one branch implied its presence in the other.

In discussing these results, Piaget pointed out that children's understanding of the implications involved in this task can be modeled on some of the 16 binary operations of propositional logic. For example, the fact that the car takes one branch ($= p$) implies that it must arrive in one of the garages ($= q$) to which that branch eventually leads (thus, $p \supset q$). These binary operations, however, are not yet coordinated into a total system, nor are they at first understood independent of their particular content. These two conditions are met only later in the stage of formal operations.

Garcia returned to this point in the second half of the book, which is a theoretical excursus on the place of logic in genetic epistemology and on the move from extensional to intensional logic. According to Garcia, logical operations develop neither in isolation nor simultaneously. Instead, they first appear in the form of "fragments of structures" that gradually become coordinated into total structures through self-organizational processes similar to those described by Prigogine (e.g., 1980). For this reason, a given stage of cognitive development is not defined by any single structure, but is distinguished instead by certain characteristic structures (Piaget & Garcia, 1987, pp. 157, 168).

Garcia went on to sketch an intensional reinterpretation of Piagetian logic based on Anderson and Belnap's (1975) logic of entailment. One of the main problems of extensional logic modeled on truth tables is that certain paradoxes arise with regard to the relation of implication when certain propositions are involved. According to the truth-table account, for example, the implication $p \supset q$ is true if q is true, even if p is false (see Table 5.2). Literally, that means that the following conditional statement should be true: "If all Germans are theosophists, then Canadians are North Americans." In fact, these two propositions have nothing to do with each other. In basing propositional logic on truth tables, Piaget inherited the paradoxes associated with extensional logic.

Garcia argues, however, that Piaget's (1949/1972a) alternative interpretation of propositional logic in terms of class inclusions is free of such paradoxes. According to this interpretation, a conjunction of properties implies each property separately. The fact that a group of cows are black and sleeping implies both that they are black and that they are sleeping. From this perspective, there is simply no relation between the propositions, "All Germans are theosophists," and "Canadians are North Americans," consistent with our intuitions. This interpretation of propositional logic not only avoids the paradoxes of extensional logic but also bears a natural affinity to Anderson and Belnap's logic of entailment. According to Garcia, Piaget's (1949/1972a) account of propositional logic needs to be renewed along the lines of such a logic of significations (Piaget & Garcia, 1987, p. 184). Garcia described the intensional interpretations of some of the 16 binary propositional operations, but added that the work of such a "renewal" of Piagetian logic still needs to be done (ibid.).

Thus, the revolution that Beilin (1985) foresaw is not quite accomplished in *Vers une logique des significations*. However, Piaget and Garcia confirmed Beilin's larger point: that particular logical models are not part of the core elements of Piagetian theory. The main idea is to find models that characterize the forms of reasoning actually used by children in different stages of their development. The importance of Piaget's last book thus lies in the authors' indication of one direction in which the theory might be further developed. In this way, they demonstrate that the theory is not a finished product, but a research program capable of constructive progress.

7

The psychological theory

In the first six chapters of this book, the development of Piaget's basic ideas was traced from their inception to their full fruition in the final decades of his life. In the two remaining chapters, his theory is evaluated in the light of its development. Its psychological aspects are considered in chapter 7, and its implications for a theory of knowledge in chapter 8.

The psychological and epistemological aspects of his theory are evaluated separately because of the way that Piaget used psychology as a means for addressing epistemological questions. As described in chapter 1, he originally set out as an adolescent to reconcile science and religion or, as he viewed it, the conflict between truth and value. Implicit in this goal was the assumption that human beings need values by which to live. Truth itself is such a value. But what happens if the search for truth in the form of science undermines the other values that make life meaningful? This was the dilemma that confronted the young Piaget. In his eyes, it was the major intellectual and spiritual crisis faced by Western civilization in the years preceding World War I. Epistemology was a means of approaching this problem. If a method could be found of distinguishing superior from inferior forms of knowledge – and, by implication, superior from inferior forms of judgment – then this method could be applied to questions of value as well as matters of fact. Epistemology cannot tell us which values are right nor which theories are true, but it might possibly aid us in choosing among different ways of *judging* among values or theories (Piaget, 1922a).

This particular goal determined the nature of Piaget's epistemological questions. Traditional epistemology had been concerned with how knowledge in general can be justified and with giving an account of how knowledge is at all possible, but Piaget sought criteria whereby more adequate forms of knowing and judging could be distinguished from less adequate forms. In this connection, his evolutionary-developmental perspective was of crucial importance. One way of determining what distinguished inferior from superior forms of knowing was to look at how the latter developed from the former. Both the history of science and the cognitive development of children provided examples of successively more adequate forms of knowing developing from out of relatively less adequate forms. An examination of this process could provide clues for determining what distinguishes the one from the other. Implicit in this approach was the idea, repeatedly affirmed by Piaget (1927/1966a, pp. 239–240, 1950/1973a, p. 44), that the present state of knowledge and present forms of knowing are not final. One cannot extrapolate beyond the present, but one can learn about the developmental processes leading from one form of knowledge to another.

Thus, Piaget did not propose to answer traditional epistemological questions with naturalistic methods. Rather, he posed new questions, together with new methods for answering those questions. Developmental psychology and the history of science were not new ways of solving old problems, but new ways of solving new problems. As the history of science itself has illustrated, progress is sometimes attained not by finding different answers for the same questions but by asking new questions.

If epistemology had been a means to an end for Piaget, psychology was a means to a further means. The study of children's cognitive development was a way of answering certain questions regarding the evolution of knowledge that in turn would provide criteria for deciding among different forms of judgment involving questions of truth and value. In this connection, the developmental perspective on Piaget's own ideas in this book can be of value. In such a developmental perspective, Piaget's original questions can be reconstructed, and in the light of these questions, his answers can be understood in their own terms. Many misunderstandings in regard to Piaget's theory have resulted from the mistaken assumption that he was trying to answer the same questions as other psychologists and epistemologists. This is an understandable mistake. Piaget's better-known works contain few hints regarding the problems by which he was originally motivated. Even though psychologists frequently acknowledge Piaget's epistemological interests, the *specific* ways in which these interests influenced his psychological theory have not generally been recognized. In viewing Piaget's theory in the light of the same kinds of problems addressed by other psychological theories, many otherwise astute commentators have interpreted certain "biases" in the theory as essential limitations. In fact, they are better understood as selective emphases resulting from the use of psychology as a means for answering particular epistemological questions. Viewing the theory in the perspective of the questions it was intended to address can help to distinguish between such selective emphases and essential shortcomings.

The appeal to Piaget's epistemological priorities, however, is not intended as an apology for real limitations in the psychological theory. As he pointed out himself (Piaget, 1950/1973a, pp. 23ff.), previous attempts to use psychology in answering epistemological questions had not always been based on a psychological theory adequately grounded in empirical investigations. If psychology is to provide a basis for answering epistemological questions, it must be adequate in its own terms – as a psychological theory. This same prescription can be applied to Piaget's own theory. In any evaluation of the theory in purely psychological terms, the gaps resulting from his use of psychology for epistemological ends must be recognized, and an attempt must be made to fill them in. Certain suggestions for how this might be done may be found in Piaget's writings themselves, but the actual process of completion will necessarily involve some constructive development of theory beyond the state in which Piaget left it. Like any other theory, Piaget's theory deserves to be evaluated not only in terms of its existing state but also in terms of its possibilities for further development. In this chapter, Piaget's psychological theory is evaluated on the basis of an assessment of its future possibilities.

A comprehensive summary of research relevant to the theory is not attempted. Rather, representative studies are considered with respect to their particular relevance for the theory, for in many cases the relevance of existing research for Piaget's theory is precisely what needs to be reconsidered. Hopefully, the discussion of representative studies will be generalizable to the vast body of empirical investigations on various aspects of Piagetian theory accumulated over the years (for useful summaries of this research, see Brainerd, 1978a; Cohen, 1983; Gelman & Baillargeon, 1983; Vuyk, 1980).

Nor does this chapter include a summary of all the various criticisms of Piagetian theory that have accumulated along with the empirical research literature (Vuyk, 1980). A piecemeal discussion of these criticisms might prove enlightening, but it might not be possible to draw any coherent conclusion from such a discussion. Instead, the following approach is taken: Some of the major criticisms of Piagetian theory that have repeatedly been advanced over the years are discussed in the light of Piaget's intellectual development as described in the preceding chapters of this book. Three such criticisms will be considered: (a) the question whether Piaget's approach is more descriptive than explanatory, (b) the charge that his theory is contradicted by evidence of asynchrony in development, and (c) the argument that his theory neglects certain important factors in development, such as social relations, affectivity, and figurative thought. In general, the argument is that most of these criticisms have been based on real limitations in the theory, but the nature of those limitations must be rightly understood if the theory is to be adequately assessed.

DESCRIPTION VERSUS EXPLANATION

One of the most frequent criticisms raised against Piagetian theory has been that it is concerned only with description, not with explanation. This point was raised in one form or another by several of the commentators on the theory of equilibration in the discussions held in celebration of Piaget's 80th birthday (Inhelder et al., 1977). Piaget took these questions seriously enough to include a reply in an appendix to his book on equilibration (Piaget, 1975/1985). A similar point was made by Brainerd (1978b) in an oft-cited paper on Piagetian stage theory. Brainerd's article is also of interest because it contains an explicit description of what he considers to be the necessary conditions for adequate psychological explanation. Piaget also contributed several essays on the nature of psychological explanation (Piaget, 1950a, 1963/1968b, 1970/1973c). These essays reveal that Piaget differed from many of his critics not only in regard to substantive questions but also in regard to the very terms of discourse. He did not simply offer different explanations for the same phenomena, but different conceptions of the phenomena to be explained and of the nature of psychological explanation itself. In order to evaluate the claim that Piaget provided only descriptions of psychological phenomena, not adequate explanations, one must therefore consider his conception of psychological explanation.

Explanation in psychology

According to Brainerd (1978b), "legitimate explanatory constructs" must satisfy the following three criteria: First, the phenomena to be explained must be specified and described. In the case of stage theory, certain "target behaviors" that undergo age change must be specified. Second, certain "antecedent variables" must be posited that are believed to be responsible for the phenomena to be explained. With regard to stages, for example, certain experiential and maturational variables believed to produce stage-like developmental changes in behavior have been posited by various investigators. The third requirement of a legitimate explanation is that the antecedent variables should be measurable independent of the phenomena to be explained. The experiential, maturational, and/or other factors that produce stage-like developmental changes must be measurable independent of the changes that are so produced.

The form of explanation described by Brainerd is shared by many contemporary Anglo-American psychologists, as evidenced by the types of theories and models pursued in current research programs. Overton (1985) has called it "contingent explanation," insofar as it attempts to specify the contingencies that result in the appearance of a given phenomenon. It further resembles what Beilin (1983) has called "functionalist" (or "neofunctionalist") explanation, according to which certain outcome variables are explained "as a function" of certain antecedent variables. This kind of "functional" explanation resembles the Aristotelian concept of "efficient causality," insofar as efficient causes can be construed as antecedent variables with respect to the effects produced (Overton & Reese, 1973; Reese & Overton, 1970). However, more is implied by a causal relation between cause and effect than by a functional relation between antecedent and consequent. Part of the meaning of the causal relation is that causes in some sense *produce* their effects (Bunge, 1963, 1971), but such productive effects are not necessarily implied in functional relations. Many examples of functional relationships that are not strictly causal may be found in psychology. Buss (1978) has argued, for example, that attribution theory has tended to confuse *causes* and *reasons*. Although a certain antecedent–consequent relation exists between an agent's reasons for acting a certain way and the actions that are performed for those reasons, this relation cannot properly be called causal in character. From a much different perspective, Skinner (1953) sought to characterize the relations between behavior and the contingencies of reinforcement in terms of functional rather than causal relations because of the presumed anthropomorphic character of the concept of causality.

With respect to Piaget's theory, Brainerd (1978b) argued that it falls somewhere between pure description and true explanation. He did not dispute that Piaget provided an adequate description of stage-like developmental changes in children's thinking (or behavior). The question was whether or not Piaget's theory satisfied the other two requirements for "legitimate explanation." Although Piaget (1960b) specified several antecedent variables (including maturation, experience, and equilibration) by which transitions from one stage to another can be explained, he did not provide, in Brainerd's judgment, a sufficiently fine-grained analysis that connects specific variations in these factors to specific stage transitions. With respect to the third requirement of "legitimate explanation," Piaget's theory is particularly deficient. Piaget's research was largely confined to the observation and analysis of age-related changes in behavior; it is not clear how the antecedent variables that he described are to be measured independent of the age-related changes to be explained.

In the commentary published along with Brainerd's (1978b) article, a number of authors objected that his concept of legitimate explanation was too narrow. For example, Olson (1978) and Fischer (1978) suggested that Piaget subscribed to a different form of explanation than that prescribed by Brainerd. In contrast to Brainerd's antecedent–consequent scheme, Piaget attempted to explain cognitive development in terms of its structure. Such structural explanation is characterized by its emphasis on wholeness, transformation, and self-regulation. Observed behavior is not explained merely as the outcome of a particular antecedent, but as an exemplar of a total system of elements related to each other in specific ways. A structural theory of this kind defines an entire range of possibilities and their interconnections, such that certain possibilities taken singly or in combination are seen to engender others in a lawful manner. Instead of explaining a given phenomenon in terms of any single set of antecedent conditions, the phenomenon is explained in terms of whole families of possible "antecedents" consisting of the transformations permissible within the system. Olson related Piagetian structuralist explanation to structuralist traditions in anthropology and linguistics, but as both Olson and Fischer noted, structuralist explanation is also to be found in mathematics, physics, biology. In atomic physics, for example, the properties of different elements were explained in terms of the structural system that defined the ways in which electrons, neutrons, and protons could combine with each other (Harré, 1985). According to Olson and Fischer, Piaget attempted to approximate this kind of structural explanation with his theory of structures.

In Brainerd's reply, he argued (a) that it is not clear that Piaget really meant to offer the kind of structuralist explanations that Olson and Fischer described, (b) that Piaget's structures are really only descriptions of tasks or behavior, (c) that structuralist explanation consequently reduces to abstract descriptions, and (d) that structuralist explanation is probably an attempt to rationalize bad theory after the fact (Brainerd, 1978b, p. 211). Curiously, neither Brainerd nor his critics cited Piaget's own discussions of the nature of explanation in psychology (Piaget, 1950a, 1963/1968b, 1970/1973c), although in some of these writings he explicitly evaluated the explanatory status of his own theory.

In fact, the charge that Piaget's theory is more descriptive than explanatory involves at least three different questions: (a) What was Piaget trying to explain with his theory? (b) What were the explanatory mechanisms proposed? (c) What was the form of explanation employed? Once these preliminary questions have been answered, one can further ask to what extent the theory succeeded in its own terms, and, indeed, what terms are appropriate for evaluating the theory.

What Piaget sought to explain

In fact, Piaget already differed from many of his critics (and from some of his supporters) with respect to the phenomena he wished to explain. Above all, he sought an answer to the question of how new forms of knowledge and reasoning come into being. This search for the origins of the new might be called the basic problem of genetic epistemology, and it differs in significant ways from many of the questions typically pursued in developmental psychology. Within the prevailing "neofunctionalist" perspective described by Beilin (1983), for example, developmental outcomes are explained in terms of their causal or functional antecedents. Explanation consists in showing how particular changes or transitions are affected by (or at least associated with) particular antecedent conditions. In a sense, what is actually explained in this approach is the variation that occurs in the particular outcomes of interest. In contrast, Piaget sought to explain how developmental change is even possible, insofar as it results in adaptations that are new and (in some sense) better than those that went before. His pursuit of epistemological questions regarding the very possibility of novelty and progress in development accounts for his preoccupation with the more general features of development and his relative lack of interest in particular variations. The types of questions that he asked determined the kinds of explanations that he provided.

Piaget's approach to the role of the environment as an explanatory factor can be taken as an illustrative example. Psychologists who seek to specify the environmental antecedents of behavior will generally be content to show that certain classes of behaviors occur as a function of certain specifiable antecedents – for example, that certain variations or changes in environmental conditions result in corresponding variations or changes in behavior. For Piaget, the issues were somewhat different. The particular antecedent–consequent relations between environmental conditions and behavioral outcomes do not provide a direct answer to the question of how essentially new forms of knowledge originate. Instead, the issue is whether or not the environment constitutes a *sufficient* condition for the generation of new forms of knowledge. In Piaget's constructivist theory, the answer is clearly negative. If the environment were the only source of knowledge available to individuals, one could never explain how some individuals generate knowledge that goes beyond what has been communicated by their immediate environment. One might be able to explain how children come to learn what is known by the community in which they grow up, but one could not explain how the total knowledge of the community itself increases.

The claim that Piaget did not sufficiently take the environment into consideration (Fischer, 1980) must be evaluated in this light. Such criticism is generally based on the observation that Piaget did not state (or attempt to state) the functional relations uniting specific environmental conditions to specific behavioral or psychological outcomes. This charge is certainly true. But the "sufficiency" or "insufficiency" of a theory is relative to the problems it is intended to solve (Laudan, 1977; Popper, 1979). Piaget (1960b) certainly acknowledged that the environment could affect behavior and even that certain environmental conditions were necessary for cognitive development, but the explanation of behavior in terms of its functional antecedents (environmental or otherwise) simply was not the problem that the theory was intended to solve.

The stage question, too, must be viewed in the light of these considerations. Significantly, Piaget himself considered his stage theory to be primarily descriptive: "Description attains a certain number of general facts *such as stages of development,* the directions development follows, the relation between one characteristic and another, and the factors involved in formative processes" (Piaget, 1975/1985, p. 147; emphasis added). From this passage alone, one might conclude that Piaget had agreed with Brainerd's (1978b) criticism of him before the fact. But matters are not that simple. For Piaget, stages of cognitive development represented successive forms of knowledge observed in psychogenesis. As he wrote in *The psychology of intelligence* (Piaget, 1947/1950b, pp. 48–49) and elsewhere, he believed that an epistemologically oriented developmental psychology, like embryology, must begin with the classification and ordering of developmental stages. Only when this purely taxonomic phase of research is accomplished can one begin to search for an explanation of the passage from one stage to another. If the developmental classification of forms of thinking and reasoning can be compared to the classification of biological species, then the attempt to explain the mechanisms of transition from one stage to another can be likened to the attempt to explain the origins and evolution of species. (On the importance of taxonomy in organismic accounts of development, see Langer, 1969.)

From this perspective, cognitive structures were described by Piaget in terms of the formal properties of thinking at each level of development, much as plant or animal species were distinguished by naturalists in terms of their morphological characteristics. The question of the "reality" of the stages thus defined has a historical parallel in the question of the "reality" of biological species that so fascinated the young Piaget (Vidal, 1984). Many interpreters have mistakenly considered Piaget's structurally defined stages as functional explanatory constructs in themselves. Otherwise, Brainerd's (1978b) claim that the stages were more descriptive than explanatory in character would have been noncontroversial. But the structures characteristic of a given stage were not intended as functional antecedents of the particular behaviors found at that stage. The relation between structures and their corresponding stage-related behaviors is formal and taxonomic. Far from being explanatory constructs in the functionalist sense, structures serve to identify and distinguish morphologically the phenomena to be explained. (The relation between structures and observed behavior is examined in greater detail in chapter 8.)

Explanatory factors

With respect to developmental transitions from one form of knowledge to another, Piaget (1952d, 1960b) recognized four explanatory factors: the physical environment, the social environment, maturation, and equilibration. His treatment of these factors, however, must be understood in the context of his primary question of how new forms of knowledge come into being. From this point of view, the essential problem was not to show how variations in any one or more of these factors lead to corresponding variations in development, but to specify the necessary and sufficient conditions for the emergence of new forms of knowledge. His argument was that neither the physical nor social environments, nor the maturation of the nervous system, nor any combination of these three factors was sufficient. In other words, Piaget's attempt to explain the emergence of new forms of knowing centered on the demonstration that in addition to the effects of the environment and maturation, the factor of equilibration is also necessary. This demonstration proceeded through a process of elimination. At most, the effects of the environment can explain only how existing forms of knowledge become acquired by the individual, not how new forms emerge. Similarly, maturation can explain new forms of knowledge only by assuming that they were somehow preprogrammed – in effect, by denying their essential novelty. To the extent that these solutions can be ruled out, some additional factor must be posited as necessary. For Piaget, this additional factor was equilibration.

In summary, the process of equilibration was invoked (along with maturation and experience) as an essential explanatory factor in answering the question of how new and better forms of knowing can possibly develop from existing forms. The fact that Piaget did not attempt to specify how maturation or the environment affects particular behaviors does not mean that he overlooked the importance of these factors, only that variation in particular behaviors was not the phenomenon he sought to explain. Anyone who approaches Piaget's theory with such problems in mind is bound to be disappointed, not because they could not possibly be pursued with the theory, but because the theory was originally intended to solve problems of a quite different character.

The nature of psychological explanation

Given an understanding of what Piaget wanted to explain and what he invoked as explanatory mechanisms, one may still ask if his explanations were satisfactory in their own terms. Thus, some critics familiar with the aims of genetic epistemology have also questioned whether or not the theory of equilibration rises above description (e.g., Nowinski in Inhelder et al., 1977). In order to understand Piaget's reply to this criticism, one must consider his own views on the nature of explanation in psychology. These views are contained in his various writings on the epistemology of psychology (Piaget, 1950a, 1963/1968b, 1970/1973c).

Characteristically, Piaget approached this problem by positing three stages in psychological research. The first he considered purely descriptive, consisting in the establishment of facts and general laws. This stage is not yet explanatory, because it is concerned only with the generality of observed ''facts.'' Significantly, Piaget (1970/1973c) recognized the establishment of functional relations to be an intermediate step between pure description and explanation as such. The establishment of functional relations is the beginning of a coordination between facts. Explanation as such, however, is attained only in the second stage of psychological research, when the coordination among facts is carried further in the form of a deductive system. ''Explanation . . . presupposes a system of laws among which one can be constructed or reconstructed deductively from the others, and *there* is the first specific characteristic of explanation as opposed to simple generalization'' (Piaget, 1963/1968b, p. 160). Explanation in this sense involves an element of necessity – not that facts themselves can be considered necessary, but certain coordinations among general laws based on the facts have necessary consequences.

However, even such deductive explanations do not yet attain the status of true ''causal'' explanations. This status is achieved only at the third stage of psychological research, when a deductive system of laws is embodied in a ''model'' of reality. In addition to explaining that certain outcomes occur as a necessary consequence of a system of general laws, true ''causal'' explanations also attempt to explain how such outcomes are generated in terms of a model of the processes involved. In the Piagetian vocabulary, this kind of causal model involves an ''accommodation'' of the deductive system of laws to reality and an ''attribution'' of the deductive relations of this system to reality itself. It is interesting to note that these three ''stages'' of psychological research generally correspond to the intrafactual, interfactual, and transfactual stages in the development of a science, as described by Piaget and Garcia (1983).

Given this conception of psychological explanation, Piaget could have said of the ''functionalist'' form of explanation described by Brainerd (1978b) what Brainerd said of Piagetian stage theory: that it falls ''somewhere between pure description and true explanation'' (Brainerd, 1978b, p. 175; cf. Piaget, 1970b, p. 111). More to the point is the question of how Piaget rated his own theory in these terms. This question can be answered with reference to Appendix 1 in *The equilibration of cognitive structures,* where Piaget wrote: ''We can boast neither of a highly developed deductive theory nor of agreement with verified facts except for certain intersections among the results of various investigations. Nevertheless, we believe that we have gone beyond the level of description on a certain number of points and that it has become possible to invoke 'reasons' in those areas'' (Piaget, 1975/1985, p. 148). Thus, Piaget placed his theory of equilibration in the second stage of psychological research, although admitting that it was not "highly developed'' as a deductive theory. Elsewhere, he made it clear that the form of structuralist explanation he employed was based on "abstract models'' (Piaget, 1963/1968b). That is, it went beyond the "simple'' deduction of everyday language to model psychological phenomena on logical or mathematical systems. Although he assumed that such abstract models correspond to real causal mechanisms of some kind, he did not attempt for the time being to specify the nature of those mechanisms.

Such abstractness may be precisely what many commentators have objected to in Piaget's theory of equilibration. Although the latter attains a certain level of explanation in terms of an abstract model based on some general "facts'' of observation, it is unclear to what mechanisms of reality this model corresponds. Still, the possibility remains that Piaget's theory of equilibration could be further extended in the direction of a truly causal model. The kinship between Piaget's theory of equilibration and contemporary theories of self-organizing systems is particularly promising in this regard. This theme is discussed at greater length in chapter 8.

Even if one admits that Piaget's theory attains a certain level of explanation, a more serious charge is that it is contradicted by the facts of child development. In Fischer's words: "The problem with Piaget's theory is not that it fails to explain. The problem is that some of its explanations are apparently false'' (1978, p. 186). In particular, Fischer argued that certain developmental sequences and synchronies predicted by Piaget's structural analyses are not in accord with observed facts. In order to evaluate this claim, one must consider exactly what is and is not predicted by Piaget's structuralist theory.

STAGES, STRUCTURES, AND
DEVELOPMENTAL SYNCHRONY

One of the most widespread criticisms of Piaget's theory of stages is that it is contradicted by the existence of asynchronous development among tasks presumably belonging to the same stage. Thus, Fischer (1980) wrote that the concept of *structures d'ensemble* implies a high degree of synchrony in stage development, but that the evidence indicates asynchrony rather than synchrony to be the rule. In the same vein, Bruner (1983) argued that evidence of asynchrony in stage development calls the structuralist basis of Piaget's theory into question, likening such horizontal decalages to the epicycles of pre-Copernican astronomy.

In fact, the issue of synchrony versus asynchrony in development subsumes several different cases, and the evaluation of claims that Piaget's theory is contradicted by developmental asynchrony requires a consideration of each case individually. The first case includes what might be called *content decalages*:

developmental lags between the ages at which a given structure emerges with respect to different areas or domains of content. The classical example of this kind of asynchrony in development is the horizontal decalage involving physical quantity, weight, and volume first reported by Piaget and Inhelder (1941/1974). Another example is the decalage reported to exist between analogous operations applying to logico-mathematical content versus infralogical content (Piaget & Inhelder, 1948/1967; Piaget et al., 1948/1960). Although Piaget (1941, 1950/1974a) tried to explain the occurrence of such decalages within his theory, some interpreters have argued that the existence of asynchrony across domains of content cannot be reconciled with a concept of structure that unites the domains in question.

A second case involves developmental synchrony among groupings within, but not necessarily between, domains of content. Following Piaget's (1941) most explicit statement on horizontal decalage, Pinard and Laurendeau (1969) pointed out that, far from predicting developmental synchrony across domains, Piaget actually stated that the same groupings applied to different contents should not be expected to emerge at the same point in development. This expectation followed from the fact that the actions (or operations) grouped in each case were adapted to different contents, and the relative ease of grouping those operations may vary from one content to another. Pinard and Laurendeau argued further that instead of predicting synchrony across areas of content, Piaget's theory actually predicts synchrony within areas of content among the structures (e.g., groupings) characteristic of a given stage. According to Brainerd (1978a), research findings appear to contradict this interpretation of Piagetian theory as well: Rather than synchrony, replicable within-content decalages have been found among tasks (such as conservation and transitivity) representing different concrete operational structures.

A third form of asynchrony in development will here be called *procedural decalages,* referring to frequently reported findings that different versions of the same task are nevertheless solved by children at different ages. Because the tasks in question bear on the same physical content and presumably involve the same operational structures, they appear to contradict even the most liberal interpretation of Piaget's structural-stage theory: that developmental synchrony is expected only in regard to a given grouping (Flavell & Wohlwill, 1969; Jamison, 1973). Research on such procedural decalages has often been discussed in terms of the ''competence–performance distinction.'' The logic of this distinction as applied to Piaget's theory can be traced back to Braine's (1959) influential monograph on the study of the development of certain logical operations by means of nonverbal methods.

Braine argued that Piaget generally overestimated the age at which certain logical operations appear in children's thinking, because he ''fails to eliminate important variables which are not involved in the definition of the processes he sets out to investigate'' (Braine, 1959, p. 16). Although Piaget meant to assess the development of the formal reasoning used in particular cognitive tasks, his clinical interview method was more likely to assess the development of certain linguistic skills or children's familiarity with and interest in the particular materials employed. In order to assess the development of children's reasoning more accurately, one should use procedures in which the possible effects of such extrinsic factors are eliminated. In the case of transitivity, for example, Braine employed nonverbal methods in order to eliminate the possible effects of purely linguistic skills and found evidence of transitive reasoning in children 2 years younger, on the average, than in Piaget's studies. This result was interpreted as evidence that Piaget's methods depended too much on cognitive abilities unrelated to those meant to be assessed and that his estimates of the ages at which certain forms of reasoning develop were accordingly inflated.

This argument was subsequently rephrased in the vocabulary of competence versus performance (Brainerd, 1978a) and applied to a great many other Piagetian tasks, including conservation, transitivity, and class inclusion, as reviewed by Gelman and Baillargeon (1983). The general strategy followed in studies of this nature has been to simplify tasks by eliminating certain "performance factors" presumably unrelated to the "competencies" being assessed. This simplification strategy is intended to reduce false negative error (Brainerd, 1973a, 1977) and thereby to develop more valid measurement procedures. With these procedures, children are generally found to solve the tasks in question at an earlier age than that reported by Piaget. This result is interpreted as demonstrating that his methods were "too conservative" and that he therefore "underestimated" children's true abilities. A further argument is that a "competence theory" such as that of Piaget, based on the logical structure shared by different tasks, needs to be replaced by a "performance theory" built on a consideration of the performance factors mediating the expression of children's logical competencies (Brainerd, 1978a; Broughton, 1981; Overton, 1985).

A fourth case in which issues of developmental synchrony or asynchrony are relevant to Piaget's theory has to do with some of his specific hypotheses regarding the relationships among particular structures. For example, he believed that number develops from an operatory "synthesis" or "fusion" of groupings involving ordering and classification (see chapter 4). Thus, some degree of synchrony might be expected in the development of children's understanding of number and of the logic of classes and relations. In reviewing research bearing on this hypothesis, Brainerd (1978a) concluded that it was not supported by the evidence. Instead of synchrony among tasks used to assess the understanding of classes, relations, and number, a replicable sequence had been found, with relations appearing first, followed by number and classes. Another example of a specific hypothesis regarding developmental synchrony is Piaget's (1957a) statement that combinatorial reasoning and propositional logic both develop around the age of 11–12, because both are based on a combinatorial system.

In each of these four cases, synchrony in development was expected as a consequence of an assumption that different performances share a common underlying structure. The problem is in determining the functional extension of the structures in question – the class of performances subsumed under a given structure. The evaluation of different interpretations regarding the developmental synchrony predicted by Piaget's theory thus necessitates an examination of his concept of structures and their functional extension. Only then can one decide among these different interpretations and evaluate the relevance of the evidence for the theory accordingly.

Piaget's concept of structure

Piaget's use of the term "structure" is characterized by a certain ambiguity. On the one hand, "structure" may refer to the formal properties of a certain type of thinking. In this sense, concrete operational thinking is said to be characterized by the grouping structure. On the other hand, Piaget believed that cognitive structures of this kind possess a functional reality. They do not exist merely as a formal description in the mind of the observer, but, as he once put it, they are "causally active" in the mind of the subject (Piaget, 1941, p. 217). Thus, when Piaget described two different performances as examples of the "same" structure, he could have been saying merely that they have the same formal properties, or he could have been making the stronger statement that they are the observable manifestations of the same functional organization (Chapman, 1987a).

The difference between these two usages was explicitly discussed in "The mechanism of mental development and the laws of the grouping of operations" (Piaget, 1941), summarized in chapter 4. There Piaget described how formally "analogous" groupings could be expected to appear at different points in development with respect to different contents. Such an expectation implies that groupings of operations in different areas of content do not constitute a *functional totality* merely by virtue of their *formal analogy*. The reason why this should be the case is not difficult to understand if Piaget's account of the origins of such structures is kept in mind: At the level of concrete operations, grouping structures consist of actions that have become interiorized, reversible, and "grouped" together. In this process, they become "operations" in the logical or mathematical sense. Two or more groupings can have the same formal structure and still be functionally distinct, because the operations of which they are formed stem from different actions. For example, the operations utilized in the conservation of physical quantity derive from actions of dividing objects, putting them back together, changing their shape, and so on. The operations used in the conservation of weight, however, stem from the actions involved in weighing. Clearly, the actions involved are adapted to their respective contents. The action of weighing refers to weight as its content, and this reference distinguishes it from actions referring to other contents. When content-specific actions are interiorized and grouped together as operations, the resulting structures accordingly retain the content specificity of the operations of which they are composed.

Horizontal decalages result because the grouping of certain actions is more difficult than the grouping of others. Such differential difficulty is what Piaget

(1971d) referred to when he spoke of the "resistance" of certain contents. This appeal to the "resistance" of different contents to the grouping of operations does not yet explain why groupings bearing on different contents should vary in difficulty, but it does provide a rationale for the general expectation that analogous structures need not appear in different areas of content at the same time. Although the structures in question may have the same formal properties, different kinds of actions do not necessarily acquire these properties all at once.

Piaget's elusive concept of *structures d'ensemble* must be understood in this context. This concept has generally been understood to refer to the functional unity of behaviors characterizing a given stage. Thus, Kohlberg wrote, "In addition to sequence, stages must meet the criterion of consistency implied by the notion of a 'structural whole' " (Kohlberg, 1969, p. 388), and Fischer (1980) appealed to *structures d'ensemble* in arguing that Piaget's theory predicts a high degree of synchrony in development. Corrigan captured this interpretation succinctly: "The structuralist position taken by Piaget and his followers is that synchrony between task domains is a fundamental developmental principle because overall structures [i.e., *structures d'ensemble*] explain functioning in many different areas" (1979, p. 620).

In fact, Piaget had nothing of the sort in mind. Although the concept of *structures d'ensemble* was closely related to his stage theory insofar as different stages are characterized by different types of structures, he never implied that all behaviors belonging to a given stage are bound up in a single functional unity, regardless of content. As we have seen from the evidence in "The mechanism of mental development and the laws of the grouping of operations" (Piaget, 1941), he explicitly rejected this view. But if *structures d'ensemble* do not represent the functional unity of all behaviors belonging to a given stage, what were they intended to represent?

As described in the review of the development of Piaget's basic ideas in the previous chapters of this book, the term *structure d'ensemble* was used by Piaget to refer to relational totalities arising out of the interactions and compositions of certain component operations. As expressed already in *Recherche* (Piaget, 1918) and most clearly in his autobiography (Piaget, 1952a), the interactions among "parts" of various kinds give rise to a new "whole" that possesses certain formal or relational properties not contained in those elements taken individually. Beginning in *The psychology of intelligence* (Piaget, 1947/1950b), he began to call these relational totalities *structures* (or *systèmes*) *d'ensemble*.

In defining the functional extension of such relational totalities, the "elements" that interact with each other to give rise to the *structures d'ensemble* characterizing a given stage of development must be specified. The nature of these "elements" should be clear from previous chapters. At the sensorimotor level, actions carried out successively in time become integrated into the higher-order schemes that Piaget (1947/1950b) referred to as the structures of sensorimotor intelligence. The most completely analyzed example of such a scheme was the group of displacements involved in the development of the infant's understanding of physical space (Piaget, 1937/1971a). At the preoperational level, new structures having the form of morphisms, correspondences, and functions develop (Piaget, 1980b; Piaget et al., 1968/1977). These structures are formed from coordinations of actions that have become interiorized, but are not yet reversible (in the precise sense in which Piaget used this term). Only at the level of concrete operations do the compositions of interiorized actions become reversible, and these reversible compositions constitute the groupings characteristic of this stage (Piaget, 1941, 1942, 1947/1950b, 1957a, 1949/1972a). In acquiring the property of reversibility and being "grouped" into the structures Piaget called "groupings," these interiorized actions become operations in the strict sense. Because such operations retain a very definite content specificity at this stage, the totalities formed by their "grouping" are likewise differentiated from each other according to physical content. Finally, at the stage of formal operations, new totalities emerge in the form of structures such as INRC groups that link certain propositional operations together (Piaget, 1957a, 1949/1972a; Inhelder & Piaget, 1955/1958). Piaget believed that the sequence of stages was hierarchical in form, that the totalities characterizing one stage became the "elements" of the new highest stage. Thus, the functions and correspondences of the preoperational stage become integrated into the groupings of concrete operations, and these groupings are in turn integrated into the formal operational structures. (See Piaget, 1971d, for a brief account of the structures characteristic of each stage of cognitive development.)

Given the frequent vagueness and ambiguity of Piaget's writing style, one can easily see how this conception of structure could be misinterpreted to imply the functional unity of all behaviors belonging to a given stage. Such interpretations result from misunderstanding the extension of the "elements" united by particular *structures d'ensemble*. Instead of viewing the elements as operations that are grouped together, the "elements" of the totality are understood as referring literally to all the behaviors belonging to a given stage. For example, the following passage from Piaget is cited by one interpreter in support of the view that *structures d'ensemble* underlie cognitive functioning across domains of content: "We are looking for total structures or systems with their own laws, systems which incorporate all their elements and whose laws cover the entire set of elements in the system. It would be these structures which become integrated with development" (Piaget, 1971d, p. 3; quoted in Corrigan, 1979, pp. 620–621). This passage supports the intended interpretation only under the assumption that the "elements" mentioned refer to cognitive functioning in many different areas of content. This interpretation misses the specificity of Piaget's terminology. As we have seen, the hierarchical and recursive character of Piaget's structurally defined stages implies that the "elements" differ from stage to stage and in any case do not embrace all behaviors belonging to that stage, regardless of content.

This conclusion follows unmistakably from many passages in Piaget's works reviewed in previous chapters. In *The child's conception of number*, for example, he wrote that a formal structure is not acquired all at once regardless of its content, but must be reacquired or reconstructed as a new coordination with respect to each new area of content (Piaget, 1941/1952c, p. 204). The content specificity of structures was referred to by Piaget and Inhelder (1941/1974) in terms of the "inseparability" of form and content and was invoked to explain why the same operations appear at different points in development with respect to quantity, weight, and volume. In a functional sense, the structure (i.e., form) does not exist apart from its content. The structure is immanent in the content structured. The structures (groupings) that characterize the stage of concrete operations are composed of operations adapted to specific contents. It follows that these structures do not embrace behaviors from all content areas in a single functional totality. The idea that the concept of *structures d'ensemble* implies developmental synchrony across content areas is based on a confusion between *formal analogies* and *functional totalities*. The fact that Piaget recognized the same formal structure (e.g., one of the eight groupings) to characterize thinking in different areas of content does not imply that these areas are united in any single functional totality.

In another passage frequently cited in support of the interpretation that *structures d'ensemble* imply global synchrony in development, Piaget wrote: "We advance further towards the *maximum* programme of criteria of stages if we then say that it is justifiable to ascribe all the preparations leading to a stage and all the achievements characterizing this stage, to the existence of a *general* (or total) *structure* in the sense defined above [i.e., to a *structure d'ensemble* defined as a form of equilibrium]" (Piaget, 1960b, p. 14). But only by reading these remarks out of context can the phrase "all the achievements characterizing this stage" be interpreted to mean all the behaviors belonging to a given stage of development, regardless of content. Two paragraphs later, Piaget continued as follows:

This leads to a still more fundamental problem: do *general* stages exist, i.e. stages including at the same time, for a given level, the totality of organic, mental and social aspects of development? I would like to submit to the Study Group the following hypotheses, which seem to be the most cautious expression of the degree of synthesis which we may hope to attain.

1. There are no general stages. Just as, in connexion with physical growth, Tanner showed us that there was an absence of close relationship between the skeletal age, the dental age, etc., similarly, in the various neurological, mental and social fields, we see an intermingling of processes of development which are evidently interrelated, but to different extents or according to multiple temporal rhythms, there being no reason why these processes should constitute a unique structural whole at each level. [ibid., pp. 14–15]

In a discussion among the contributors to a 1955 symposium in Geneva on the problem of stages in child development, Piaget justified his lack of belief in general stages by denying what he called the "structural unity of the person." The latter phrase was his term for the idea that all behaviors of an individual of a given stage are manifestations of a single structure. "Nowhere have I seen structural unity, at no stage in the development of the child. . . . And if there is no structural unity, there are no general stages that permit fixed correspondences, verifiable in all domains and between all functions'' (Piaget in Osterrieth et al., 1956, p. 58). In short, contrary to widely accepted interpretations of his theory, Piaget did not believe in general stages of development characterized by developmental synchrony across domains of content, and such an interpretation of stage development cannot be derived from the concept of *structures d'ensemble*. The idea that *structures d'ensemble* imply developmental synchrony results from a confusion of Piaget's specific concept of *structures d'ensemble* as relational totalities with the notion of "structural unity" across domains of content. This latter notion he specifically denied.

Synchrony within areas of content

The fact that Piaget's structural-stage theory does not imply developmental synchrony across areas of content was pointed out by previous interpreters, including Pinard and Laurendeau (1969), Brainerd (1978a), Longeot (1978), and Gelman and Baillargeon (1983), among others. But what about Pinard and Laurendeau's argument that *structures d'ensemble* imply synchrony among the various groupings within, rather than between, areas of content. This interpretation was based on two rather obscure passages from the paper "The mechanism of mental development and the laws of the grouping of operations" (Piaget, 1941). In the first of these passages, Piaget wrote, "Let us note that at the age at which grouping thus becomes possible on the deductive or logical plane, all forms of grouping appear at the same time, and the constitution of those distinguishable by psychological or logical analysis cannot be ordered into stages" (Piaget, 1941, p. 246). And in the second: "At the same level and for the same notion [i.e., content], the different possible groupings appear to be constituted roughly [à peu près] in synchrony, such that none of them, as an operatory mechanism, is more difficult to acquire and to master than the others" (ibid., p. 264; quoted in Pinard & Laurendeau, 1969, p. 38).

Nowhere did Piaget imply, in these passages or elsewhere in that article, that this apparent synchrony among the groupings within a given area of content follows necessarily from the concept of *structures d'ensemble*. The language used and the context in which these passages occur indicate instead that the synchrony between groupings referred to is noted as an empirical generalization rather than as a theoretical deduction. On the basis of the evidence available to him, Piaget was simply unable to order the groupings into a developmental sequence; they "appear" to develop "roughly" in synchrony and therefore to be equally difficult to acquire. These are descriptive statements, not predictions. A similar interpretation of these passages was made by Flavell (1971).

Indeed, the same argument against the view that *structures d'ensemble* refer to functional unities embracing different areas of content applies to the interpretation that they are functional unities embracing different groupings within areas of content. Because the groupings are groupings of operations, the grouping of different operations within a given area of content results in functionally distinct totalities. Accordingly, one would not expect different groupings to develop in synchrony even within content areas. The fact that this view was shared by Piaget was indicated in Inhelder and Piaget's (1959/1969) conclusions in *The early growth of logic in the child*. There they expressed some surprise that classification and seriation applied to similar contents were found to develop at roughly the same time. Instead, they suggested that these two operations from different concrete operational groupings might have been expected to follow different developmental courses, classification being more closely related to language, and seriation to perception. Clearly, different groupings could not follow different developmental paths unless they were functionally distinct. If Inhelder and Piaget had shared Pinard and Laurendeau's interpretation regarding developmental synchrony among groupings, they could not possibly have expressed surprise in finding that seriation and classification in fact developed at the same age. (Their surprise was noted as "paradoxical" by Pinard & Laurendeau, 1969, p. 139n.)

In summary, the *structure d'ensemble* is neither a functional totality uniting manifestations of the "same" structures in different areas of content nor a unity of different groupings within a single area of content. Each individual grouping is a relational totality resulting from a grouping of particular operations and as such is differentiated from other groupings according to both content (e.g., quantity, weight, and volume) and type of operation (e.g., classification, seriation, multiplication of classes, and multiplication of relations).[1] The same general argument applies for other stages of development as well. Piaget's writings contain no suggestion that all structures belonging to any developmental stage are united in a single functional totality and must therefore develop in synchrony.

Procedural decalages between different versions of a single task

Even if Piaget's theory allows developmental decalages between areas of content and between different groupings within areas of content, the third case of decalages involving differences in the administration procedures used in different versions of the "same" task remains to be explained. In this case, one is apparently confronted with decalages that occur both within one area of content and with respect to the same operatory structure. On the surface, such decalages would appear to raise real problems for Piaget's structural-stage theory.

Many examples of such "procedural decalages" could be enumerated. Following the strategy of eliminating extrinsic "performance factors," many researchers have demonstrated that children can solve typical Piagetian tasks at a significantly earlier age if the procedures are simplified so as to reduce their "performance demands." To mention only a few of the many studies following this pattern: Borke (1975) argued that Piaget and Inhelder's (1948/1967) three-

---

1 Flavell and Wohlwill (1969) and Jamison (1973) suggested that the individual groupings should be considered functionally distinct, but, curiously, this interpretation was proposed as an alternative to Piaget's presumed claims of synchrony among the groupings.

mountain task required too much of children's cognitive skills in requiring them to reconstruct the perspective of another observer with pictures, and she found that even 3- and 4-year-olds could represent the observer's perspective if they were required only to rotate a moving display to a position that would recreate the observer's perspective at the position occupied by the child. Similarly, Gelman (1972) reported that even 4- and 5-year-olds were capable of conserving number if only two or three objects were used in each of the two arrays to be compared. Further, Bryant and Trabasso (1971) argued that some children might fail typical transitive reasoning tasks not because they lack transitivity but because they forget one or more of the premise relations before they can deduce the correct answer. In an experiment that sparked much controversy, they found that even 4- and 5-year-olds could solve the transitivity task if they were trained for memory on the premise relationships. Finally, Braine's (1959) study of transitivity in children's measurement set the pattern followed in much research of this nature. In an effort to eliminate extraneous effects of children's verbal skills, children were trained to find candy under the longer of two uprights. In the test phase of the experiment, the difference in heights of the two uprights was not perceptible, and children had to determine which was longer through the use of a measuring stick intermediate in length. Using this method, Braine found that even children as young as 4 and 5 years of age apparently exhibited transitivity in measurement.

The results of such studies have generally been interpreted (implicitly or explicitly) in terms of a measurement model. Because Piaget's methods depended on one or more extraneous "performance factors," his results were characterized by a certain amount of false negative measurement error. Younger children tended to fail his tasks not because they lacked the competence in question but because they lacked one or another of the extraneous performance factors. Simplifying tasks so as to eliminate those performance factors thus led to a reduction of false negative measurement error and to the finding that children could solve the tasks in question at earlier ages. (For the rationale behind this measurement model, see Brainerd, 1973a, 1977, and Flavell, 1977.) Further, the finding that Piagetian tasks can be solved by younger children following slight procedural modifications has been widely interpreted as contradicting predictions of developmental synchrony among tasks having the same logical structure according to Piaget's structural analyses.

The foregoing conclusion (as well as the measurement-model analogy) rests on the assumption that the performances of both the original and simplified versions of the tasks in question really do have the same "logical structure" – that the same competence is being measured in each case. In fact, the truth of this assumption is by no means obvious. According to the argument, the "logical structure" of a task is an abstract feature of that task that remains invariant across variations in administration procedures. Thus, Braine (1959) considers the structure of the transitivity task to be of the form "If A is longer than B, and B is longer than C, then A is longer than C," both in the original version used by Piaget and in his own version of the task. If this were not the case, the results obtained by the two different versions would not be directly comparable.

But operatory logic as conceived by Piaget differs from standard formal logic precisely in the effort to capture the formal properties of the subject's actual reasoning, rather than an abstract norm of inference. The "logical structure" of a task in operatory terms thus refers to the manner in which the subject actually goes about solving the task, not to any abstract feature of the task that remains invariant regardless of how it is administered. If a modification in administration procedures allows the subject to solve the task with a different form of reasoning, then the "logical structure" of the modified task accordingly differs from that of the original. In this case, developmental decalages between the tasks in question cannot be considered true *horizontal decalages*, because the latter are defined as tasks solved by children at different points in development through the use of the same structures. (A similar distinction between "legitimate" and "nonlegitimate" horizontal decalages was made by Longeot, 1978.)

Some evidence indeed exists to suggest that many procedural decalages may be of this nature. For example, Cooper (1984) argued that the apparent horizontal decalage in number conservation reported by Gelman (1972) actually resulted from the fact that young children can "subitize" or count small numbers of objects and thereby produce a conservation-like response without considering the transformations in the spatial arrangement of the objects in question. When more than two or three objects are involved, as was the case in Piaget and Szeminska's (1941/1964) original studies, this method does not suffice, and children must consider the compensatory relations between the total length of an array of objects and the distance between them. The different procedures used by Gelman (1972) and Piaget and Szeminska (1941/1964) thus appear to involve two structurally distinct abilities, and the decalage between them is therefore not strictly horizontal.

A similar argument was made by Chapman (1987a) with respect to two different versions of the transitivity task. In a typical Piagetian version of this task, comparison objects are presented only two at a time (e.g., sticks A and B, then B and C), and the transitivity question refers to the relative lengths of the two objects (A and C) that have not yet been seen together. In a widely used variation on this procedure, however, all comparison objects are present at once, arranged from left to right in order of increasing (or decreasing) length. Differences in length between adjacent objects are too small to be perceived directly, and "premise" comparisons are made by moving the adjacent objects (A and B, B and C) close together so that the difference in lengths can be seen. The "transitivity" question refers in this case to the relative lengths of the nonadjacent objects (A and C).

From the standpoint of standard formal logic, both of these versions of "the transitivity task" would appear to have the same logical structure: the relation between A and C is inferred from a composition of the premise relationships between *A* and *B* and between *B* and *C*. In the terminology of Piagetian operatory logic, this form of inference is an example of the grouping called ''the addition of asymmetrical relations.'' The fact that the two versions of the transitivity task are solved by children at different ages therefore appears to pose serious problems for Piagetian theory. Although children solve the first version only around the age of 7–8 years, the second version is easily solved by 5-year-olds (Brainerd & Kingma, 1984). The fact that children who should be in the preoperational stage according to Piaget's age norms nevertheless appear to be capable of transitive reasoning on this task would appear to contradict his stage theory, or at least to demonstrate the insufficiency of his methods.

However, Chapman (1987a) argued that whereas the ''standard'' Piagetian version of this task (in which comparison objects are visible only two at a time) ensures that a transitive inference can be drawn only from an *operational* composition of premise relationships, the ''alternate'' version (in which comparison objects are all simultaneously visible and arranged from right to left according to length) allows children to make a correct inference through the use of *functional* reasoning: When children are presented the ''premise'' relationships among adjacent objects in the latter version, they learn in effect that the longer of the two objects is always on the right (or left). The ''transitivity'' question regarding the relation in length between nonadjacent objects can be inferred as a function of their (right–left) relation in space, and the individual ''premise'' relationships need not be considered at all. Because one version of this task requires the composition of relations and the other does not, they reflect two different structural competencies: operational and functional reasoning, respectively. (Children's use of right–left position cues was interpreted in terms of a ''fuzzy trace'' theory by Brainerd & Kingma, 1984.)

In a study in which children were given both versions of this task, Chapman and Lindenberger (1988) found that in the ''alternate'' version, children invariably justified their correct judgments through the use of functional reasoning: Relations in length were inferred from relations in space. On the ''standard'' version, however, a correct answer could be validly justified only through the use of an operational composition of premise relationships, because the procedures did not allow for the use of spatial cues. Therefore, the developmental decalage that was found between the two tasks could not be considered a true horizontal decalage. It was not a case of a given structure appearing at two different ages depending on the procedure used, for the structures of children's reasoning actually differed under the two procedures. Instead, the observed decalage was an example of a stage-developmental difference between the use of a preoperational function and the use of a concrete operation involving composition of relations.

These findings suggest that the results of studies of transitive reasoning that have used procedures analogous to the ''alternate'' transitivity task, as described earlier, may need to be reinterpreted, and the relevance of those studies for Piagetian theory reassessed. Bryant and Trabasso's (1971) study of the role of memory in transitive inference is a case in point. Children were trained to remember the relative lengths of the adjacent members in a series of cylinders. "Transitivity questions" had to do with the relative lengths of nonadjacent cylinders. The procedures were analogous to the "alternate" version of the transitivity task described earlier insofar as the cylinders in question were arranged in order of increasing length from left to right. These cylinders stood in holes bored in a wooden block, such that differences in the lengths of the cylinders were compensated by differences in the depths of the holes. Thus, the relative lengths of the cylinders could not be perceived directly so long as the cylinders remained in their holes. The relative lengths of adjacent cylinders were demonstrated by removing them from their holes, so that the difference in length became apparent.

Because the comparison objects in Bryant and Trabasso's study were arranged in order of increasing length from left to right, children could have used these spatial cues in seriating the cylinders. As in the Chapman and Lindenberger study, children then could have answered questions about nonadjacent objects by inferring the relative lengths of the cylinders from their relative positions in the series, rather than by composing all the intermediary adjacent relationships. The difference between the two studies was that the series of comparison objects was perceptually present in the Chapman and Lindenberger study, but it would have been interiorized through training in the Bryant and Trabasso study. Thus, Bryant and Trabasso may have found children to solve "the transitivity task" at an early age not because training on the premise relationships helped them remember those premises in making a transitive inference but because the procedures used did not require memory for those particular premises in the first place. This conclusion is consistent with the results of a study by Brainerd and Kingma (1984) in which children's memory for adjacent comparisons was found to be stochastically independent of their generation of correct answers in a task in which length was similarly correlated with spatial position.[2]

This general line of reasoning can easily be extended to other examples of procedural decalages. In Borke's (1975) modified version of the three-mountain task, for example, young children rotated a moving display in order to recreate the perspective of an observer occupying another position. A plausible explanation of this result is that children were able to solve this task simply by noting which object was closest to the observer and rotating the display until that object was closest to themselves. The relations between objects in the display were held constant by the physical structure of the display itself. In contrast, Piaget and

2 Brainerd and Kingma (1984) argued that children solve the transitivity task with a "fuzzy memory trace" having the form "big things begin on the right." From the statistical independence between memory for premises and the generation of correct answers, they further inferred a functional independence between short-term and working memory (Brainerd & Kingma, 1985). In Piagetian terminology, their "fuzzy trace" is structurally identical with a constitutive function linking relations in length to relations in space. In this view, the reason why memory for the "premises" $A > B$ and $B > C$ was independent of the conclusion that $A > C$ was because these particular premises simply were not required in the derivation of the conclusion. Instead, $A > C$ could be derived from the spatial relations between A and C by means of the said function.

Inhelder's (1948/1967) original version of the three-mountain task required children to reconstruct the relations between objects in the display as seen by the observer. This reconstruction involved transforming or reversing right–left and before–behind relations, depending on the position of the observer relative to themselves. In terms of the inferences children must make in generating a correct answer, the two versions of this task cannot be said to have the same structure. For this reason, the differences in ages at which children were observed to solve these two tasks cannot be considered to constitute a horizontal decalage. More likely, a stage-related change was involved, with children in Borke's version being able to rotate the display to the correct position as a function of the position of one object in the display, and children in Piaget and Inhelder's version solving the task only through operational transformations of relations. (Piaget's, 1980b, account of young children's use of correspondences in understanding the rotation of a disk would appear to approximate Borke's version of the three-mountain task.)

In some ways, this line of reasoning resembles the criticism raised by Smedslund (1963) against Braine's (1959) study of transitivity in measurement. Briefly, Smedslund argued that the children in Braine's study might possibly have inferred a correct answer through the use of "nontransitive hypotheses." For example, instead of inferring that object A was longer than object C through a composition of relations between A and B and between B and C, they may have inferred that A was longer than C from the mere observation that A was longer than B. Alternatively, they may have inferred that C was shorter than A from the observation that C was shorter than B. This criticism led to an exchange of views (Braine, 1964; Smedslund, 1965) that resulted in both participants agreeing that, for lack of appropriate experimental controls, neither of them had succeeded in demonstrating one way or the other whether or not such nontransitive hypotheses provided an alternative explanation for Braine's original results. Brainerd (1973a, 1973b) summarized this controversy by saying that the existence of nontransitive hypotheses as described by Smedslund had never been demonstrated in any strict sense; studies designed specifically to eliminate such nontransitive hypotheses through the use of a mixed series of equalities and inequalities (Murray & Youniss, 1968; Youniss & Murray, 1970) may have harbored additional sources of difficulty involving children's understanding of mixed series in their own right.

In contrast, Chapman (1987a) argued that although one has no reason to expect Smedslund's nontransitive hypotheses to be found in most studies of transitive reasoning, such nontransitive inferences may well have resulted as an incidental by-product of Braine's (1959) training procedures. In that study, children were trained to find candy under the taller of two uprights. In the test phase of the experiment, the difference between the two uprights was not great enough to be perceived directly, and children had to determine which was longer through the use of a movable measuring stick intermediate in length. Thus, the fact that upright A was longer than upright C presumably could be inferred from the fact that A was longer than the measuring stick B, and B was longer than C.

Chapman argued, however, that through repeated trials with the measuring stick, children could have acquired an expectation that the measuring stick would always be longer than one upright *and* shorter than the other. Under these circumstances, the information provided by comparing the measuring stick to one upright would have been redundant with that provided by comparing it to the other upright. Thus, children would not have had to consider both comparisons between A and B and between B and C in drawing an inference regarding the relation between A and C. Instead, the conclusion $A > C$ could have been inferred either from the observation that $A > B$ or from the observation that $B > C$. Because these "premises" were redundant in the particular task situation, no composition of premise relations would have been necessary; a correct answer could have been be inferred from either one of them. Because the redundancy of the premises depended on the fact that one of the comparison objects (the measurement stick) could be identified as the "intermediary" in advance of actual measurement, such "single-premise inferences" would not be a factor in studies in which such prior identification was not possible. In the "standard" version of the transitivity task used by Chapman and Lindenberger (1988), for example, the initial comparison of sticks A and B gave no clue as to which of them would function as an intermediary. Only when the relation $A > B$ was composed with $B > C$ could B be identified as intermediate in length between A and C. Thus, children had to consider both premises in concluding that $A > C$.

In this view, the reason why Braine (1959) found children to exhibit "transitivity" at an earlier age than in studies using typical Piagetian methods was not because he succeeded in eliminating the extraneous effects of their verbal skills but because his training procedure incidentally allowed children to generate a correct answer through single-premise inferences. Because no composition of relations was necessary, this form of inference can be said to have been preoperational in character. Again, tasks presumed to have the same logical structure may be found to differ when judged in terms of the means by which children actually inferred their answers in the respective task situations. The decalage between Braine's results and those obtained by Piagetian methods cannot be called a true horizontal decalage if different competencies were in fact assessed in the two cases.

In summary, procedural decalages do not represent true horizontal decalages if differences in the procedures employed allow children to solve the tasks in question with different forms of reasoning. Instead, the observed age differences between tasks may be interpretable as stage differences rather than as true horizontal decalages. The generality of this interpretation of procedural decalages has yet to be determined. The problem has been complicated by the lack of agreed-upon criteria for determining when researchers using different methods are assessing the "same" competency with different degrees of measurement error and when they are instead assessing quite different structurally defined competencies altogether. Much research showing that concrete operational tasks can be solved by children much younger than Piaget imagined has been carried out in ignorance of his work on preoperational structures (functions, correspondences, and morphisms) that theoretically could allow preoperational children to generate correct answers under certain task conditions. The modifications introduced into some typical Piagetian procedures may have resulted not in measurement of the "same" (concrete operational) competency with less measurement error but in measurement of different competencies altogether (e.g., the use of preoperational structures).

One reason why different logical competencies have not been clearly distinguished in much previous research is that many investigators have defined their dependent variables solely with respect to the correctness of children's judgments rather than in terms of the forms of reasoning by which those judgments were inferred. This practice has been justified with the argument that the use of judgments plus explanations as criteria for logical competence involves more measurement error than the use of judgments alone (Brainerd, 1973a, 1977). But judgments alone are quite insufficient for distinguishing among different forms of reasoning for the simple reason that a correct judgment can sometimes be inferred alternatively by different forms of reasoning. In Piaget's studies of concrete operations, for example, children classified at an intermediate stage between preoperational and concrete operational thinking often were capable of making correct judgments, as were children classified at the stage of concrete operations (Piaget & Inhelder, 1941/1974; Piaget & Szeminska, 1941/1964). Clearly, these two stages could not have been distinguished on the basis of judgments alone. By definition, they were distinguished in terms of the forms of reasoning by which correct judgments in each case were inferred. Children's explanations were necessary in making this distinction, for a form of reasoning is a form of explanation or justification. In a similar manner, Chapman and Lindenberger (1987) found that one frequently used version of the transitivity task could be solved by either operational or functional reasoning. Again, children's explanations were necessary for distinguishing between these two forms of reasoning. Nor do more advanced forms of reasoning always lead to more veridical judgments, as the example of the pulley task in *Success and understanding* (Piaget, 1974/1978b, chap. 10) makes clear. This example illustrates the fact that stage progression was defined by Piaget in terms of the structure of children's reasoning (i.e., the formal relations among premises and conclusions as manifest in children's explanations and judgments), not in terms of the mere correctness of their judgments. The tendency of researchers to focus on judgments alone has simply obscured the fact that different forms of reasoning can sometimes lead to the same judgments. (The issue of judgments alone versus judgments plus explanations is discussed at greater length by Chapman, 1987a, 1987b.)

The existence of procedural decalages therefore cannot be interpreted as contradicting the structural aspects of Piagetian theory unless one can demonstrate that variations in procedures indeed produce tasks that are solved at different ages *with the same form of reasoning*. Typically, researchers have simply assumed that "the logical structure" of a given task remains invariant across variations in administration procedures. However, Piagetian operatory logic differs from standard logic precisely in the endeavor to represent the forms of reasoning actually used by the subjects involved. From this point of view, the "weakness" of Piaget's theory consists not in being contradicted by the facts but in lacking a means of specifying the task conditions that allow structures belonging to different levels (e.g., preoperational versus operational) to be used successfully. In contrast, the weakness in the arguments of many of his critics consists in the fact that they did not have adequate structural criteria for determining when they were dealing with the "same" competency and when they were not. The results generated by the strategy of eliminating presumably extraneous performance factors will therefore remain ambiguous as long as it is unclear when the elimination of a given "performance factor" results in the measurement of the same competency and when it allows children to generate correct answers using different competencies.

The first step in resolving this problem would seem to be that already initiated by Piaget – attempting to identify the formal properties of children's thinking at different points in their development. For this purpose, logical and mathematical structures can be useful, although one cannot assume that such structures will serve as adequate models for natural reasoning without modifications. As Brainerd (1978b) rightly argued, this step is descriptive, not explanatory in a functional sense. Nor was it meant to be anything else. The structures identified by Piaget provide a developmental *taxonomy* of phenomena that *remain to be explained*. Functional explanation begins in a second step when the situational, experiential, or organismic conditions that allow children to use one structure rather than another are identified. Both steps are recognized in what Chapman (1987a) has called a "structural-functional" theory of cognitive development. In such a theory, children's forms of reasoning are identified in terms of their formal structure, and only then can the functional antecedents of these forms of reasoning be determined. This topic is discussed in more detail later in this chapter.

The theory of number

As described in chapter 4, Piaget believed that the understanding of number developed as a "synthesis" or "fusion" of operations involving classification and seriation. From this theory, Brainerd (1978a) derived two empirical predictions regarding developmental synchrony in these areas: that children's understanding of classes, relations, and number should develop in close synchrony, as should the understanding of ordinal, cardinal, and natural numbers. In reviewing a number of "replication studies" of relevant tasks, he found that these predictions were not supported by the evidence. Instead of synchrony involving classes, relations, and numbers, a developmental sequence running from transitivity to the conservation of number to class inclusion had been reported in several independent studies. Instead of synchrony involving cardinal, ordinal, and natural numbers, the replication studies provided evidence for a sequence parallel to that found for classes, relations, and number: The understanding of ordinal number tended to develop first, followed by basic arithmetical computations and cardinal number, in that order. From these results, Brainerd concluded that the evidence did not support the hypothesis that classes, relations, and number (or the ordinal, cardinal, and natural aspects of number) developed in synchrony and that the developmental sequence found among these competencies contradicted Piaget's theory of number as the operational synthesis of the logic of classes and the logic of relations.

In evaluating this claim, one must consider what Piaget himself wrote about the predictions to be derived from his theory of number, as well as the validity of the tasks used to test these predictions. To begin with, the theory of number as the operatory synthesis of the logic of classes and the logic of relations does not necessarily imply that they should all develop at the same time. One might suppose, instead, that the understanding of classes and relations should develop first, followed by their eventual synthesis in number. In fact, in his opening contribution to Volume 11 of the *Etudes, Problèmes de la construction du nombre* (Gréco, Grize, Papert, & Piaget, 1960), Piaget described three different patterns of development that he believed to be compatible with his theory of number. First, the understanding of classes and relations might develop first, with their synthesis in the form of number to follow only subsequently. The second possibility was that number might develop first as an initial synthesis of classes and relations, and the understanding of classes and relations considered separately would develop only subsequently by dissociation or differentiation. Although compatible with the theory, this possibility was considered by Piaget to be the least likely of the three. The third and a priori most likely possibility, in his view, was that classes, relations, and number would indeed develop simultaneously. Thus, developmental synchrony was only one of several developmental patterns consistent with the theory, albeit the most likely. What was definitely ruled out by the theory was the absence of any interactions between the three areas.

This passage is of interest for what it suggests about the functional implications of structural analysis. The analysis of number was first carried out on a formal level. The formal properties of number were seen to be composed of a synthesis of the formal properties of the logic of classes and the logic of relations (see chapter 4). But the essence of Piaget's operatory theory is that the structures revealed through structural analysis should possess a functional reality. They exist in some sense in the mind of the subject, not merely in the mind of the psychologist-observer (Piaget, 1941). The question is how the formal properties of the structures described by the observer are mapped onto the functional properties of the structures active in the mind of the subject. The relations among structures determined at the formal level must in some way be reflected on the functional level, but the manner in which formal structures are reflected on the functional level is not clear from the beginning. The formal analysis is only the first step; the second step is to clarify the nature of the mapping between form and function.

The process by which this mapping is clarified is a process of accommodating formal analysis to functional reality. As in the case of mathematical physics, in which the mathematical models employed by physicists are progressively accommodated to the physical reality they are intended to represent, the logical models employed by the psychologist must be progressively accommodated to the psychological reality that they are intended to represent. As this process becomes more advanced, the predictions derived from formal analysis will become progressively more precise. At the beginning of this process, however, the functional implications of formal analysis will be considerably more equivocal.

Piaget's remarks in *Problèmes de la construction du nombre* indicate that he was more cautious and equivocal in this regard than some of his interpreters. However, these remarks do not rescue his theory from the evidence cited by Brainerd, because that evidence suggests a sequence (from transitivity to the conservation of number to class inclusion) that is incompatible with any of the three possibilities mentioned by Piaget. This brings us to the second general problem in evaluating the relevance of this evidence for the theory: the validity of the tasks used to test the prediction.

In this connection, Piaget's own thoughts on the subject are again relevant. In an important passage from *La genèse du nombre* referred to in chapter 4 in connection with the problem of form and content in concrete operations, Piaget and Szeminska (1941/1964) discussed the relation between ordinal number and cardinal number and their development. From the hypothesis that both ordinal and cardinal numbers reflect a single underlying structure, one might predict that tests of children's understanding of these two aspects of number would show a close correlation in development. Such correlation was in fact attempted in the studies summarized by Brainerd (1978a).

Piaget and Szeminska, however, cautioned against such a procedure. Although their findings suggested that ordination and cardination develop through steps that are *formally* parallel, the attempt to "correlate" their development in terms of relative synchrony or asynchrony presupposes that the tests employed either measure children's understanding in a pure state or are at least equated in terms of their dependence on extrinsic factors. Without further analysis, neither of these conditions can be assumed to obtain, and the results of such studies are therefore inherently ambiguous.

Thus in the various tasks of cardinal correspondence, we were able to observe very clear decalages between the results of some of these tasks and others, of such a kind that one never attains a measure of the comprehension of this cardinal correspondence in a pure state, but always comprehension relative to a given problem and a given material. That is why the calculation of the correlation between the levels of cardination and those of ordination can only give misleading results if it is not accompanied by a very extensive qualitative analysis – unless one transforms the tasks into "tests" in which a statistical precision can no doubt be obtained without much difficulty, but at the expense of no longer knowing exactly what one is measuring. [Piaget & Szeminska, 1941/1964, p. 193]

One encounters in this passage something similar to the competence–performance distinction before the fact. Because individual tasks assess the understanding of ordination and cardination only with respect to a given problem and material, they cannot be assumed to measure understanding in a "pure" state. Without extensive "qualitative analyses" of possible extraneous factors, one cannot assume that such factors have been equated in the tasks to be compared. The appeal to further qualitative analysis can be interpreted in terms of the progressive accommodation of formal analysis to psychological functioning, as described earlier. Clearly, Piaget did not believe that such qualitative analysis was sufficiently advanced at the time of writing to derive unequivocal predictions regarding developmental synchrony from his structural theory of number. Several considerations suggest that it still may not be sufficiently advanced to accept the evidence reviewed by Brainerd (1978a) as an unequivocal test of Piaget's number theory.

In a previous section of this chapter, evidence was described to the effect that certain versions of "the transitivity task" permit children to generate correct answers through the use of functional reasoning rather than through the operational composition of relations. In particular, the spatial arrangement of comparison objects in order of increasing or decreasing values on the relevant dimension (e.g., length or weight) allowed children to infer relations in this dimension from the spatial relations between the comparison objects. Significantly, a number of the studies cited by Brainerd (1978a) in his review of the evidence pertaining to the development of classes, relations, and number employed procedures of this nature (Brainerd, 1973b, 1973c, 1974, 1979; Brainerd & Fraser, 1975; Hooper, Toniolo, & Sipple, 1978).

Each of these studies assessed transitivity by showing children a series of comparison objects *A, B,* and *C,* arranged from right to left in order of length or weight. First, *A* was compared to *B,* and *B* to *C;* then the children were asked about the relation between *A* and *C.* According to the argument summarized earlier, a significant feature of this procedure is that the objects are *already arranged in order.* In order to answer the question about *A* and *C,* children have to know only *in which direction* (right or left) objects increase in size or weight. This information can be determined by attending to either one of the adjacent comparisons; one need not take them both into consideration. Tasks using this procedure thus do not necessarily measure the operational composition of relations that Piaget believed to enter into the understanding of number. The evidence of several studies (Brainerd & Kingma, 1984, 1985; Chapman & Lindenberger, 1988) suggests instead that they measure something developmentally more primitive: in Piagetian terms, the use of constitutive functions. The preoperational character of such functions would explain children's precocity in solving these tasks.

The evidence is similarly equivocal with respect to the reported sequence between the conservation of number and class inclusion. In an extensive review of research on studies of class inclusion, Winer (1980) found a wide range in the reported ages at which class-inclusion tasks were successfully performed in different studies. In the majority of the studies reviewed, children were found to solve class-inclusion problems at a later age than that originally reported by Piaget (i.e., around 7–8 years). However, the results of a number of studies agreed with Piaget's age norms. A few studies, most notably Smedslund's (1964) extensive study of concrete operations, even found class inclusion to develop somewhat precociously, in advance of conservation. In this connection, one should recall that Inhelder and Piaget (1959/1969) themselves found an appreciable decalage between the class inclusion for flowers and that for animals, a decalage the authors tentatively attributed to possible differences in children's familiarity with the superordinate classes involved (see chapter 5). In view of these findings, Piaget's own age norms for the development of class inclusion cannot be taken as unequivocal.

Winer (1980) further reviewed a number of experimental studies showing that perceptual variables, linguistic factors, and the specific content of the classes employed can all make a difference in class-inclusion performance, but these factors taken singly or in combination were not sufficient to explain the age differences among the studies reviewed. He concluded by saying that different processes are likely to be operating in the class-inclusion performances observed in children of different ages – or, to put it the other way around, successful class-inclusion performances as observed at different ages are likely to represent different psychological processes. The obvious next step would be to try to identify those processes.

The immediate conclusion to be drawn, however, is that until one knows why children do not solve different versions of the class-inclusion task synchronously, the interpretation of synchrony or asynchrony between one or another version of ''class inclusion'' and some other task (such as the conservation of number) will be inherently ambiguous. Pending more detailed analysis, it is unclear which class inclusion task is most appropriate for use in such comparisons. The problem is not that Piaget's theory of number has been contradicted by the evidence; rather, the problem is to determine in an unequivocal way what empirical evidence the theory in fact predicts.

Stage and structure reconsidered

A similar conclusion can be drawn with regard to research on the other three kinds of developmental synchrony already discussed. Developmental decalages (a) among different areas of content, (b) among different same-stage structures within a given area of content, or (c) among versions of the ''same'' task do not in themselves contradict Piaget's theory; they only contradict simplistic interpretations of that theory. As we have had ample occasion to see in the course of this book, Piaget was more cautious than many of his interpreters and explicitly declined to predict developmental synchrony across areas of content, across groupings within areas of content, or across tasks varying in administration procedures. Even in the specific case of his theory of number, he acknowledged that developmental synchrony was only one of several possible patterns of development compatible with the theory.

But without developmental synchrony, one is tempted to ask: What is left of the concepts of stage and structure? What empirical content do they have? The present interpretation of Piaget's ideas would appear to rescue his theory from apparently contradictory evidence only at the expense of exposing it as an untestable formalism that makes no unequivocal empirical predictions.

In order to answer such questions, one must reconsider the context in which the concepts of stage and structure developed in Piaget's thinking. Piaget's conception of developmental stages was largely determined by questions of the following form: How does a particular type of knowledge (mathematical, physical, logical, etc.) develop? His stages of development were developmentally ordered classifications of the intermediate forms of knowing leading to the mature forms. Three points may be noted: First, the very form of such questions is domain-specific. The answer to the question of how knowledge develops in domains such as mathematics, logic, and physics is necessarily domain-specific as well. The second point is that "structure" appears in this classificatory-descriptive phase of investigation as a summary description of the formal properties of the successive forms of knowing in a given domain-specific stage sequence. The relation between the "structure" and the observed performance is morphological and taxonomic. One stage is differentiated from another in terms of their respective formal properties.

The third point is that the unit of analysis in such structural-morphological classification is what Piaget called the "epistemological subject," not the concrete individual (Piaget, 1981a, p. 188). In effect, the "epistemological subject" is an abstraction from the population studied, much as a biological "species" for the naturalist is an abstraction from a population of individuals. Thus, "the preoperational child" refers not to an individual child (still less to an individual child who is preoperational in every aspect) but to a "species" of thought, defined in terms of certain morphological properties distributed to a greater or lesser extent among the population of individuals studied.[3] If Piaget is more concerned with the commonalities among individuals than with the differences between them, it is because in the taxonomic-descriptive phase of investigation he was more interested in developmental differences between "species" of thought than in variation among individuals. The move to systematic explanation no doubt

3 On the taxonomic character of developmental stages, Piaget stated: "Genetic psychology seeks to envisage mental functions in their construction, and stages are the preliminary instrument for the analysis of these formative processes. But it is necessary to insist vigorously on the fact that stages do not constitute an end in themselves. I compare them to zoological and botanical classification in biology, which is preliminary to analysis" (Piaget in Osterrieth et al., 1956, pp. 56–57).

involves a greater consideration of variation within and between populations. But unless this move toward explanation is prepared by a taxonomy sufficient for distinguishing among the various phenomena of interest, theorists will never be clear about what it is they are trying to explain. For example, if functional and operational reasoning cannot be distinguished, one cannot even begin to ask about the conditions that determine which of them is likely to be used in a particular case (cf. Chapman & Lindenberger, 1988). Typically, Piaget is blamed both for remaining at the level of description and for the problems arising from premature attempts to translate his taxonomic structural analyses into explanatory predictions.

These three points make it easier to understand the role of developmental synchrony in Piaget's conception of stages. Having analyzed the development of forms of knowing in different domains, Piaget found that certain stages defined in terms of analogous formal descriptions developed at roughly the same average ages across domains in the populations studied. The fact that the analogous stages possessed the same formally defined properties only served to identify those stages as being structurally analogous. It did not yet explain anything. The finding that certain formally analogous stages developed at the same average ages in different domains *remained to be explained*. Because only population averages were involved, this finding did not even translate into a prediction that the structurally analogous stages should develop at the same time in every individual. Piaget was quite explicit on the relativity of his findings with respect to the populations studied:

One can characterize stages in a given population by a chronology, but this chronology is extremely variable. It depends on the previous experience of the individuals and not only upon their maturation, and it depends above all on the social milieu which can accelerate or retard the appearance of a stage, or even prevent its manifestation. Here we find ourselves in the presence of a considerable complexity and I wouldn't know how to judge the value of the average ages of our stages with respect to any population whatever. I consider the ages only relative to the populations with which we have worked; they are thus essentially relative. [Piaget in Osterrieth et al., 1956, p. 34]

Piaget's epistemologically oriented conception of stages differs in important respects from that to which most developmental psychologists are accustomed. The object of psychological investigation is generally the individual. Historically, stages have been conceived of in developmental psychology as age-related phases through which individuals develop (Gesell & Ilg, 1943, 1946). From this point of view, the very coherence of the stage concept depends on its generality as a description of the behaviors presumed to define the age period in question. In contrast to Piaget's structural classification of different forms of knowledge in terms of their formal properties, psychological stage theories generally have involved the classification of behaviors in functional units belonging to different age periods. Whereas the explanation of Piagetian stages involves the identification of functional constraints on structurally defined forms of knowing, the explanation of age-related stages in psychology tends to focus on the identification of the factors underlying and uniting different age-specific behaviors. For Piaget, the sequence of forms of knowing was what required an explanation; but for most developmental psychologists, the age-related generality of stages has been identified as the phenomenon to be explained.

Inevitably, perhaps, developmental psychologists assimilated Piaget's structural-stage theory to their own functionalist approach. Thus, Piaget's observation of rough developmental synchrony at the population level was interpreted as implying synchrony at the individual level, and his "structures" were understood as functional constructs intended to explain this synchrony. Instead of being seen as morphological criteria for classifying forms of knowing and reasoning, structures were viewed as the *functional antecedents* of age-related behaviors. This assimilation represented one possible interpretation of Piaget's stage theory, but it was widely taken for the theory itself. The observation of asynchrony in development thus came to be understood not as evidence for the failure of a particular functionalist interpretation of Piagetian theory but as evidence that contradicted the structuralist approach in general.

The beginnings of such an interpretation of Piaget's theory can be seen in Braine's (1959) monograph referred to earlier. In attempting to derive empirical predictions from Piaget's structural analysis, Braine reasoned as follows:

Piaget adopts the following research method. He sets children problems whose solution requires a certain line of logical reasoning. He then observes how children at various ages solve these problems, and he tries to observe the method of solution. Consideration of the ages of the children who solve the problem leads Piaget to specify the age at which the reasoning process involved in the problem develops.

He finds that certain types of problems are solved at the same age. Although he never explores the intercorrelations between success and failure on different problems, he concludes that reasoning processes develop in groups at particular ages. . . .

It can be seen, therefore, that Piaget's notion that reasoning processes develop in groups clearly implies the postulate that where operations, inferences, etc., are mutually interdependent (i.e., the logical definition of the one involves the reference to the other, or that both derive from the same interpretation of a logical calculus), then the corresponding reasoning processes develop in association in children's thinking. . . . As an illustration of how Piaget's theory might operate, this postulate will be used to predict a high correlation between success in the tasks described in the two previous sections. [Braine, 1959, p. 29]

The assimilation of Piaget's theory to a functionalist psychological framework is neatly described in this passage. From the fact that Piaget found logically interdependent reasoning processes to develop at roughly the same average ages in populations of children, Braine derived the prediction that they should develop in association with each other among individual children. Braine carefully phrased his interpretation "as an illustration of how Piaget's theory *might* operate," but the distinction between the theory and its interpretation was not always maintained by subsequent commentators. What was assumed in this interpretation was that the logical connections revealed by formal structural analysis parallel psychological connections on the functional level. Although Piaget's operatory theory indeed implies that some such correspondence should exist between formally defined structures and psychological functioning, this correspondence need not be a direct one-to-one or point-for-point correspondence. The move toward explanation in Piagetian theory is a move toward the specification of this correspondence. As previously discussed, this move is likely to involve both an identification of functional constraints on different forms of thought and a progressive accommodation of formal analysis to these functional constraints. In this way, "cognitive structures" would cease to be merely summary descriptions of the morphological properties of different forms of thinking and would be gradually transformed into structural-functional models of the psychological processes corresponding to those different forms of thinking.

Structural-functional theory

The attempt to specify the functional antecedents of structurally defined forms of thinking was previously described as a *structural-functional theory* of cognitive development (Chapman, 1987a). So defined, structural-functional theory unites a structuralist taxonomy of forms of thinking and reasoning with functionalist forms of explanation. It therefore represents one way of extending Piagetian structuralism in a direction compatible with contemporary functionalist psychology. Before describing some examples of structural-functional research, the role of structural analysis in this theory is briefly examined.

Structural analysis. According to the view expounded so far in this chapter, the first and fundamental purpose of the kind of structural analysis practiced by Piaget was to identify forms of thinking and reasoning and to specify the criteria by which they can be identified. In Brainerd's (1978b) terms, this phase of analysis is primarily descriptive, but it is also something more insofar as it involves a taxonomic classification and ordering of the phenomena described. This taxonomic phase of investigation is a necessary preliminary to any attempt at "explanation," for it serves to identify what is to be explained. Many controversies in psychology have resulted from attempts to apply antecedent–consequent explanatory schemes before any general agreement has been reached about the nature of the consequents for which antecedents are sought. The historical dispute between behaviorism and cognition, for example, has centered around the nature of the phenomena appropriate for psychological investigation.

Toulmin wrote of this problem as follows: "In the behavioral field, no generally agreed criteria yet exist for deciding when a human action is intelligible or unintelligible, or what types of conduct constitute genuine 'phenomena', and so pose theoretical problems for psychology or sociology at all" (Toulmin, 1972, p. 382). This statement does not imply that different research traditions in psychology do not identify the phenomena investigated in a consistent manner. The point is rather that research traditions differ not only in the explanations they provide but also in their understanding of the phenomena to be explained. Some philosophers of science (Feyerabend, 1975; Kuhn, 1965) have argued that such conceptual differences imply that different "paradigms" in science are *incommensurable* with each other. This argument and the issues it has raised are discussed in more detail in chapter 8 (Overton & Reese, 1973; Reese & Overton, 1970).

When such conceptual differences are not recognized as such, "conceptual confusion" may result. Conceptual issues are confused with theoretical and methodological issues. Although the representatives of different research traditions may use the same terms, these terms are used in different ways. The result is that, without being aware of it, they are not even talking about the same things. Examples of such conceptual confusion in psychology were analyzed by Chapman (1987b) from a Wittgensteinian perspective. The general argument was that different investigators who "operationalize" a given construct in different ways go on, as a result, to investigate qualitatively different phenomena. However, this difference in the phenomena investigated often is obscured by the fact that different operationalizations can be subsumed under a single "family-resemblance" concept, drawn either from ordinary language or from a more technical vocabulary. As described by Wittgenstein (1958), such family-resemblance concepts can cover a variety of cases that resemble each other in different ways, but need not have any common defining characteristics. Because of the family-resemblance character of the concepts subsuming different operationalizations, the investigators involved may have the illusion of studying "the same thing" rather than phenomena that differ in significant ways. Such confusions are frequent in discussions of research on Piagetian topics.

With respect to "perspective taking," for example, Piaget and Inhelder (1948/1967) required children to reconstruct the perspective of another person with pictures representing the objects seen. This method followed from their concern with the development of operations and the operational transformations of relations involved in the coordination of perspectives. The phenomenon of interest was a particular (operational) form of reasoning. In contrast, Borke (1975) required children only to rotate a moving display so as to reproduce the perspective of an observer. In following this procedure, she was motivated by different concerns than were Piaget and Inhelder. In effect, the phenomenon investigated was children's success or failure solving the task, not the form of reasoning by which they tried to solve it (successfully or not). With Piaget and Inhelder's methods, children succeeded in "taking the other's perspective" only at 9–10 years of age; with Borke's methods, even 3- and 4-year-olds were found capable of "perspective taking." That different methods should lead to different results is not surprising. The problem is to know what to conclude from these results. Do they imply that Piaget and Inhelder's methods were "too conservative"? Or that they "underestimated" children's "perspective-taking abilities"? Or do the different results follow from the fact that the respective investigators were studying qualitatively different phenomena?

Borke's results demonstrate at least that one case subsumed by the general concept of "perspective taking" develops at an early age. Piaget and Inhelder's results indicate that another case develops later. Only at the general level of the family-resemblance concept can the respective investigators be said to have studied the same phenomenon. At this level of generality, nothing can be concluded about the relative validity of the two methods, for quite different competencies might be subsumed under "perspective taking" as a family-resemblance concept. If, in contrast, children's performances in these two tasks are defined in structural terms, then one can argue that two different competencies could well be involved. Piaget and Inhelder's task requires the operational transformation of relations among objects in the display, but Borke's version could perhaps be solved by noting the spatial correspondences between the observer and one of the objects in the display, as argued earlier in this chapter. In this case, one could not argue that Piaget's methods were "too conservative" and subject to false negative measurement error. Such a conclusion would follow only if one could further demonstrate that children in Borke's study demonstrated "perspective taking" in the same structurally defined sense as in Inhelder and Piaget's investigations (i.e., through the transformation of relations among objects). Instead, the general level of the family-resemblance concept (e.g., "perspective taking" versus "egocentrism") has typically been conflated with the more specific structurally defined level of conceptualization (e.g., preoperational versus operational thought) in interpreting the differences in obtained results. Thus, different methods generally have been assumed to measure the same structurally defined phenomenon, when in fact they arguably involve different structural competencies subsumed under one family-resemblance concept.

To be sure, other examples might exist in which Piaget's methods really did "underestimate" children's abilities as defined in structural terms. The point is that two different possibilities have not been clearly distinguished in research of this kind: (a) the possibility that different methods result in the assessment of the same structurally defined competency, with different degrees of measurement error, and (b) the possibility that different methods result in the assessment of different structurally defined competencies altogether. This confusion has led many researchers to abandon the very kind of structural analysis that possibly could clear up the confusion in question. What is needed is more structural analysis, not less. Without such analysis, investigators focusing only on performance outcomes (e.g., correct or incorrect answers) will continue to confound different forms of reasoning that might lead to the same performance outcome.

Functional explanations of cognitive development require adequate structural analysis in order to determine whether different theorists are explaining the same phenomena in different ways or are explaining different phenomena. The mere fact that certain kinds of training can bring about correct responses on various Piagetian tasks, for example, does not imply that the development of the forms of thinking studied by Piaget has been "explained" in terms of the kinds of experience provided by training. An alternative explanation is that some incidental aspect of training has altered the form of reasoning leading to a correct answer – as argued earlier in this chapter with respect to the training procedure used by

Braine (1959). The main point is that functional explanations of cognitive development depend on an adequate taxonomy of what develops, and the latter is what Piaget's structural theory is intended to provide.

Functional explanations. Given such a structural taxonomy, the functional explanation of children's forms of reasoning (and their development) will consist in specifying the antecedent conditions of these structurally defined phenomena. Such antecedent conditions might include situational, experiential, or organismic factors, among others.

With respect to the situational antecedents of children's forms of reasoning, the vast research literature on procedural decalages is directly relevant. However, a reinterpretation of this literature is necessary. Although many studies of procedural decalages have been interpreted as contradicting Piagetian structuralism, one might argue instead that such studies actually demonstrate the fact that different cognitive structures have different situational antecedents. In Chapman and Lindenberger's (1988) study of transitivity, for example, a situation in which comparison objects were simultaneously perceptible and arranged in order from left to right allowed children to derive a correct answer through the use of a preoperational function. In contrast, a situation in which comparison objects were presented only two at a time (and relations in length or weight were uncorrelated with right–left spatial relations) allowed a solution only through the use of operational composition. In short, research on procedural decalages provides raw data for a structural-functional theory of the situational antecedents of different forms of reasoning. Obviously, the search for situational conditions leading to one form of reasoning rather than another presupposes structural criteria for distinguishing among those forms of reasoning.

Similarly, training studies of performance on Piagetian-type tasks provide raw data for a structural-functional theory of the experiential conditions of different forms of reasoning. Such a theory would involve the analysis of task-specific structures formed through training, in comparison with structures employed by children in solving the same tasks without training. The formulation of such a theory, however, presupposes a greater sophistication in structural analysis than has generally been the case. Instead of assuming that successful training necessarily allows children to employ the "same" form of reasoning at an earlier age, the possibility must also be recognized that training may allow children to solve the "same" task with a different form of reasoning than is possible without training. Once again, an adequate taxonomy of forms of reasoning is necessary as a precondition of explanation.

With respect to the organismic antecedents of forms of reasoning, several theorists (Case, 1985; Halford, 1982; McLaughlin, 1963; Pascual-Leone, 1970, 1984; summarized by Chapman, 1987a) have attempted to specify the attentional-capacity requirements of structurally defined stages of cognitive development. These theorists have differed among themselves with respect to the precise relevance of Piagetian operatory logic for task analysis. However, to the extent that development through Piaget's stages is what capacity theorists seek to explain, they must at some point confront the taxonomic problem of identifying those stages. At this point, in the present view, Piaget's operatory logic becomes unavoidably relevant, for it is by means of characteristic logical structures that one stage of development is distinguished from the next.

An elaboration of a full-fledged structural-functional theory of children's cognitive development is beyond the scope of this chapter. The intended goal is considerably more modest: to argue for the possibility of such a theory and to give some brief indication regarding the general direction in which such a theory might be developed. In this context, Piagetian structural analysis assumes the taxonomic function of identifying the phenomena to be explained. Ultimately, Piaget's particular system of operatory logic may not prove to be the most useful system of structural analysis for this purpose.[4] Some other system may prove to be more desirable. But in order to choose between alternative systems of analysis, one must first be clear about the purposes for which they are intended.

Questions regarding the formal and empirical adequacy of the specific structures proposed by Piaget are deferred until chapter 8. Here, discussion has been limited to a consideration of the relation between Piaget's concept of structure and the issue of synchrony in development. For many interpreters, the presumed link between *structures d'ensemble* and developmental synchrony was the major empirical prediction to be derived from Piaget's structural analyses. Findings of asynchrony in development thus led them to reject the structural approach in general, rather than the link between structure and synchrony. Instead, I have argued that Piaget's concept of *structures d'ensemble* did not imply a *structural unity* of functioning in different areas of content, nor among different structures belonging to a given stage. Although questions of synchrony or asynchrony in development may be interesting and important in their own right, they are not directly relevant for testing the empirical implications of Piaget's theory. His structural analyses are better understood as part of a taxonomic effort to identify the forms of reasoning that succeed one another in cognitive development. The subsequent phase of explanation consists in identifying the functional antecedents of different forms of reasoning in terms of the situational, experiential, or organismic conditions that allow children to use one form of reasoning rather than another.

NEGLECTED FACTORS IN DEVELOPMENT

Another family of criticisms frequently directed against Piaget concerns allegations that he neglected one or more important factors in cognitive development.

---

4 Beilin (1985) argued that the specific logico-mathematical models posited by Piaget need not be considered a core element of his theory, because his ideas on this score were constantly changing. In his later works, for example, he turned away from traditional extensional logic toward an intensional "logic of meanings" (Piaget, 1980e; Piaget & Garcia, 1987). A critical assessment of possibilities for the future development of Piagetian logic is given by Apostel (1982), as summarized in chapter 8.

Included among these neglected factors have been the environment in general (Beilin, 1980; Fischer, 1980; Smedslund, 1977), the social environment in particular (Apostel, 1986; Atkinson, 1983; Broughton, 1981; Buck-Morss, 1975; Cohen, 1983; Hamlyn, 1978; Rotman, 1977; J. Russell, 1978; Sigel, 1981; Toulmin, 1972; Vygotsky, 1962; Wallon, 1947), affects and emotions (Cowan, 1978; Gruber, 1982), and figurative knowing (Bryant, 1974; Bruner, 1964). The relation between each of these factors and Piaget's theory is briefly considered in this section. Although the claim that Piaget neglected these factors can certainly be justified, one should consider the reasons for this neglect. In particular, one should consider how his theory was "biased" by the particular questions he sought to answer and to what extent the factors he thereby neglected could be integrated into the theory without changing its basic assumptions.

The fact that Piaget was primarily motivated by epistemological questions and that developmental psychology was largely a means to this end has been sufficiently documented in previous chapters of this book. Here it is a question of how this interest affected the weighting of different factors in his psychological theory. Above all, Piaget was interested in explaining how new knowledge was generated, not only by individuals in their own development but also by scientists and mathematicians in the history of their respective disciplines. In order to answer this question, showing how knowledge is transmitted from one generation to the next is not enough, for such explanations explain neither how knowledge is generated in the first place nor how individuals can go beyond what they acquire from others. In arguing that Piaget neglected the environment or other important factors in development, many of his critics have meant that he did not demonstrate how development is *affected* by these factors. This claim is certainly justified; one finds very little in Piaget's writings about how variations in environmental, social, or other conditions result in corresponding variations in the course of development. For many developmental psychologists, the latter question is of greatest interest.

Piaget, however, was primarily interested in specifying the necessary and sufficient conditions for the generation of new knowledge. He viewed the factors influencing development almost exclusively in this light. In several writings (Piaget, 1952d, 1960b) he acknowledged four major factors influencing development, including maturation, the material environment, the social environment, and equilibration. In enumerating these factors, he was concerned to demonstrate that the first three are necessary, but not sufficient, for the generation of new knowledge. Maturation is not sufficient, because much new knowledge involves specific properties of the specific environment, and one cannot assume that knowledge of all possible environmental contingencies is preprogrammed in the nervous system. The material environment cannot be a sufficient explanation for the generation of new knowledge either, because (among other reasons) it cannot account for the sense of necessity. Of course, individuals can acquire knowledge through social transmission. But before such knowledge could be transmitted, it had to exist already. Social transmission cannot explain how the total knowledge available to the group can increase over time.

In order to explain the generation of new knowledge, according to Piaget, one must appeal to an additional factor: equilibration. In effect, equilibration is a process by which knowledge is self-generated, given certain necessary preconditions. The theory of equilibration is thus the psychological (and epistemological) equivalent of theories of self-organization in other areas of science (see chapter 8). Piaget's insistence that maturation, the material environment, and social factors are not sufficient in explaining the generation of new knowledge did not mean that he believed them to be unimportant or that they have no place in his theory. The fact that he was personally not interested in specifying the effects on development of variation in various antecedent factors does not prevent the theory from being extended in this direction. His "neglect" of antecedent factors in development resulted from his interest in other questions, rather than from an essential limitation in the theory.

Social factors

The social character of individual thought. In connection with "social factors," Piaget has frequently been reproached for his "individualism," for portraying the individual as inherently self-contained and for overlooking the essentially social nature of human beings. This, for example, was one of the criticisms leveled at him by Wallon (1947). Like many other criticisms of Piaget, it is justified in one sense, but not necessarily in the sense that it was originally intended. No one familiar with Piaget's sociological theory could conceivably refer to him as an "individualist" in any meaningful sense. In the essay, "Logical operations and social life" (Piaget, 1965/1977a) discussed in chapter 4, for example, he asserted that the primary reality is neither the individual nor the collective, but the *relations* among individuals. With this remark, he tried to steer a difficult passage between individualism and collectivism toward a kind of interpersonal relationalism. In the same essay, he denied that logical operations could be conceived in purely individualist terms as a system of auto-conventions, explicitly repudiating the view frequently attributed to him that logical structures develop within the individual acting alone. Far from being a merely individual acquisition, the grouping of operations is at once individual and social in nature:

The "grouping" is only a system of possible substitutions, whether within the thought of an individual (operations of intelligence) or from one individual to another (cooperation). These two kinds of substitutions constitute a general logic, at once individual and collective, that characterizes the form of equilibrium common to cooperative as well as individualized actions. [Piaget, 1965/1977a, p. 170; see also p. 92]

Nor was this social-relational view of development limited to his sociological writings; it permeated the book on moral development as well (Piaget, 1932/1965a). In fact, this view followed inevitably from his germinal concept of relational totalities stated in *Recherche* (Piaget, 1918). Just as the "reciprocal assimilation" among schemes leads to higher-order structures in the course of cognitive development, so do the interactions among individuals lead to higher-order social totalities (Piaget, 1965/1977a, pp. 26ff.). In this view, the logic of individual thought and the logic of social exchange are totally interdependent:

The individual can only achieve his inventions and intellectual constructions insofar as he is the seat of collective interactions that are naturally dependent, in level and value, on society as a whole. [Piaget, 1967/1971c, p. 368; see also Piaget, 1947/1950b, chap. 6]

The social character of Piaget's psychology and epistemology is further discussed by Apostel (1986), Chapman (1986), and Smith (1982).

The view of Piaget as individualist stems largely from interpretations of his two books on sensorimotor development (Piaget, 1936/1963, 1937/1971a) and from the fact that he wrote little on social topics after 1950, devoting himself instead to the development of logico-mathematical and causal knowledge. Because of his prodigious output, one can read many of his writings without encountering a discussion of social topics. But the centrality of the social dimension is revealed by a more thorough reading. Indeed, the essentially social character of human development follows directly from Piaget's constructivism, and one of the goals of the present developmental survey of his ideas is to show why this is the case.

In the books on sensorimotor development, children appear to develop in interaction with the physical environment, but more or less in isolation from other persons. In fact, the mind of the young child as it emerges from the sensorimotor period is more radically social, according to Piaget, than has generally been realized. The relevant account is found in *Play, dreams and imitation* (Piaget, 1945/1962), rather than in the earlier books on sensorimotor development. In his description of the development of imitation, Piaget argued that it is one of the main sources of cognitive representation as such.[5] But imitation is a thoroughly social activity. As described by Piaget, imitation is possible because of the perceived similarity between the child's own bodily movements and those of others. Because of this similarity, infants can assimilate the movements of other persons to their own movements from Stage Two of sensorimotor development onward as long as these movements are visible to them (see chapter 3). Even in Stage Four, when they begin to imitate movements that they cannot see themselves making (e.g., opening and closing the eyes and mouth), such imitation is at first accomplished by means of sensory "indices" that provide a kind of common denominator for the visible movement of the other person and the child's own invisible movement. Piaget's children, for example, used certain reproducible sounds as indices for the imitation of invisible movements of the mouth. The other person's audible vocalization was assimilated to the sight of the movements of that person's mouth, and the same sound as uttered by the child was assimilated to the movement of the child's own mouth (Piaget, 1945/1962, Obs. 19ff.).

---

5 As a matter of historical accuracy, one should note that Wallon (1942/1970) described the connection between imitation and representation several years before Piaget (1945/1962) took up the same theme in *Play, dreams and imitation*. See Piaget (1962/1972–1973).

One cannot assume that children at these early stages distinguish between themselves and other persons as independent agents; rather, the movements (or vocalizations) of the model evoke the same movements by the child through direct assimilations (cf. Chapman, 1987c).

Even the imitation of objects can be seen to have developmental antecedents in the imitation of other persons. For example, Piaget's observation of Lucienne imitating the opening of a matchbox by opening her own mouth is frequently cited by him as an intermediary step in the transition between sensorimotor intelligence and mental representation. What is missing in the account of this incident in *The origins of intelligence* (Piaget, 1936/1963, Obs. 180), however, is the information that Piaget had experimented with Lucienne's ability to imitate the opening and closing of his mouth and eyes for months previous to this observation. In *Play, dreams and imitation,* we learn that Lucienne began to imitate movements of the mouth between 0;9 and 0;10 (Piaget, 1945/1962, Obs. 18) and that at 1;0(16) she responded to Piaget's opening and closing his eyes by opening and closing her mouth (ibid., Obs. 29). These performances were observed approximately 2.5 months before Lucienne reacted in a similar manner to the matchbox (ibid., Obs. 57). Thus, her imitation of the matchbox was well prepared by interpersonal imitation. Possibly, she was able to imitate the opening of the matchbox only by assimilating it to a circular reaction involving the sight of another person's mouth, although this interpretation cannot be definitively established from the information provided.

Piaget himself did not emphasize the radical social character of cognitive representation as it develops from imitation. In the course of the debate with Chomsky in 1975, he cited the observation with Lucienne as an example of the relation between imitation and the development of the "symbolic or semiotic function":

Imitation appears to me to play a very large role in the formation of the semiotic function. I mean by imitation not the imitation of a person – the child may not imitate someone's gesture – but the imitation of an object, that is, the copying by gestures of the characteristics of that object (for example, the object has a hole that must be enlarged, and this enlargement is imitated by the motion of opening and closing the mouth). [Piaget in Piattelli-Palmarini, 1980, p. 166]

Perhaps Piaget himself did not recognize any connection between the imitation of persons and the imitation of objects. Or perhaps he believed the imitation of objects was significant because it revealed the extent to which schemes of imitation could be generalized beyond their original interpersonal context.

In any case, "the symbolic function" as described by Piaget includes a variety of phenomena, from the "secondary symbolism" of unconscious processes to the conventional signs of linguistic communication. These phenomena differ with respect to their origins in "individual" versus "social" processes. At one extreme, "secondary" symbols depend on a resemblance of some kind with the thing symbolized and originate more in individual processes, rather than social processes. Piaget might have said that social influences are not necessary prerequisites for secondary symbolism, although they surely affect it by providing much of its content. Many of the examples of secondary symbolism provided by Piaget in *Play, dreams and imitation* involve relations with other persons, especially family members. At the other extreme, linguistic signs are related to their referents through mainly arbitrary conventions. These conventions are thoroughly social in origin, although an element of individual creativity or invention is possible here as well. For example, Piaget (1945/1962) described Lucienne at 4 years of age as stating that she once looked at the Salève mountain outside Geneva and saw that it was really called "Solève," and she continued to call it that even though no one else did.

According to the present interpretation of Piaget's theory about imitation and representation, secondary symbolism and linguistic convention have a common origin in the fact that both develop out of perceived resemblances between children's own actions and those of other persons. In the case of language, resemblances between children's own vocalizations and the utterances of those around them are involved. The continuity between interpersonal imitation and language thus becomes clear: Imitation is the first form of intentional *communication* of which children are capable. As Piaget's examples indicate, these early forms of communication are sensorimotor before they take on a representative character as such. In this sense, language can be said to develop from sensorimotor intelligence. According to this view, language and representational thought in general have sensorimotor precursors in the form of interpersonal imitation, not (merely) in interaction with physical objects. Therefore, the question whether or not paraplegic children develop language normally has no direct bearing on the theory (cf. Monod in Piattelli-Palmarini, 1980, pp. 140–141); what is essential is that children be capable of imitating other persons, especially (but perhaps not exclusively) by vocal means. Obviously, the human vocal apparatus provides the developing infant with an especially wide range of possibilities for such interpersonal imitation.

In the last analysis, Piaget's personal biases are less important than the distinction between what is essential and what is merely incidental to the theory. His lack of interest in the diverse effects of "social factors" can be explained by the fact that the true object of his investigations was the development of new forms of knowing. Even when all effects of social factors on individual development are accounted for, some degree of individual innovation remains, and this creative activity is what he sought to explain. The effects of social factors can be studied within the theory without requiring essential modifications. As we have seen, the charge that Piagetian psychology is inherently "individualist" is incorrect. From the very beginnings of cognitive representation to the higher efflorescences of logical thinking, individual cognition possesses an essential social character as a node in a network of intellectual exchanges. Piaget's portrayal of children's thinking as developing from "egocentricism" toward a more socialized decentration does not imply that thought begins with the isolated individual and only gradually acquires a social character. Instead, it reflects the view that children's thinking begins as *syncretically social* and develops toward greater differentiation and coordination of perspectives. Although frequently overlooked, the social dimension in Piaget's theory has been recognized by an increasing number of interpreters (Apostel, 1986; Edelstein, 1983; Furth, 1980, 1986; Murray, 1983; Smith, 1982; Youniss, 1980).

Cultural bias. Another criticism frequently leveled at Piaget in regard to social factors is that he described development only as it occurs in children growing up in a Western industrialized society and did not take into consideration the variety of developmental paths and end points that might exist under differing cultural conditions. In other words, Piaget's account of human development is culturally biased (Buck-Morss, 1975; Schöfthaler & Goldschmidt, 1984). This criticism is valid to the extent that Piaget's goal is interpreted to be the description (or explanation) of universal features of human development. But again, in evaluating this charge, one must carefully consider Piaget's use of developmental psychology as a means to answer specific epistemological questions.

Piaget's original goal was to illuminate the processes involved in the development of scientific thought, including logic and mathematics. The study of the development of thought would provide criteria for distinguishing superior forms of judgment from inferior forms. The development of children's thinking provided him with a concrete field of investigation. Children's development from one form of thinking to another was seen to embody in an elementary form the same constructive processes active in the development of scientific knowledge as a whole. His goal of explaining the development of scientific thought delimited the range of psychological processes he considered relevant for his purposes. In fact, he did not set out to provide a truly universal account of human development; in terms of its subject matter, his psychological theory was limited from the start by the questions he sought to answer.

Moreover, "science," for Piaget, was predominantly Western science. The fact that other cultures in the world developed other forms of knowledge or other forms of cognition was, for a first approximation, not immediately relevant to his project of investigating the development of scientific knowledge as it had occurred in Western culture. In effect, he pursued the question of how we in Western industrialized countries arrived at where we now are. One may object that this separation of scientific forms of knowing from other forms of knowing cannot be maintained indefinitely, especially in the light of Piaget's (1950/1973a) own argument that a psychologically based epistemology must begin with an adequate psychological theory. In this connection, research on cross-cultural variations in human development becomes relevant to the Piagetian enterprise, besides being a worthwhile subject of investigation in its own right.

On a different level, one could argue that Piaget's theory was culturally biased *as an epistemology of science* insofar as he did not consider the development of science in non-Western contexts. This criticism is implicitly acknowledged by Piaget and Garcia (1983, pp. 280ff.) in their remarks on the different developmental courses taken by the sciences in China and in the West. One can only speculate what a cross-cultural genetic epistemology of science would be like. At the very least, it would have to admit the possibility of variation in developmental pathways between different scientific traditions, while retaining the idea of developmental progress within traditions. Such a cross-cultural genetic epistemology would be a legitimate, logical, and perhaps an inevitable extension of Piaget's original project. It would further presuppose the study of cross-cultural variation in psychogenetic pathways among individuals growing up in different social contexts. Piaget himself may have recognized the inevitability of such an extension:

I got interested in Chinese science because of the book we're doing with Garcia. The problem was whether there is only one possible line of evolution in the development of knowledge or whether there may be different routes, which, of course, will lead to common points sooner or later. Well, Garcia, who is quite familiar with Chinese science, thinks they have traveled a route very different from our own. So I decided to see whether it is possible to imagine a psychogenesis different from our own, which would be that of the Chinese child during the greatest period of Chinese science, and I think that it is possible. [Piaget in Bringuier, 1977/1980, p. 100]

Figurative and affective knowing

The possibility of variation in developmental pathways raises the further question along what dimensions such variation might be ordered. For Piaget, two dimensions are of interest: the vertical and the horizontal. The vertical dimension is development itself, conceived of as the progression toward ever more stable forms of equilibrium. The horizontal dimension refers to the different contents in which these progressively more stable forms of equilibrium are manifest. Piaget's discussions of cross-cultural variation as well as interindividual variation generally were limited to a consideration of these two dimensions. Cultures may differ in the degree to which they hinder or facilitate the vertical movement toward higher forms of equilibrium (Piaget & Garcia, 1983, chap. 9). Even within a given culture, individuals can vary in terms of the speed with which they develop within different domains of content with which they are more or less familiar (Piaget, 1972f).

Figurative knowing. One wonders, however, if the only two dimensions of variation in cross-cultural and interindividual development are the vertical and the horizontal. Piaget's theory often opens new vistas for exploration even in those directions in which his own perspective remained quite limited. His distinction between figurative and operative knowing is a case in point. One cannot argue that Piaget overlooked figurative knowledge entirely. After all, he devoted two important books to the subject (Piaget, 1961/1969; Piaget & Inhelder, 1966/1971). But he clearly considered operative knowing to be considerably more important. Not only did he expend more effort in studying operative knowledge, as opposed to figurative knowledge, but even in the books on perception and mental imagery, the development of figurative knowing was invariably described as a progressive subordination to operative knowing. In general, figurative knowing was described as providing the material contents on which operative transformations could act, not as being particularly important in its own right.

Again, this operative "bias" in Piaget's theory is a function of his particular research goals. In the preface to *Mental imagery in the child*, Piaget and Inhelder (1966/1971) admitted to a "considerable omission" in their work on this topic. They were not concerned in that book with children's creative imagination, described as a "splendid subject," but only with the role of mental imagery in problem solving as such. Specifically, they wished to determine the extent to which mental images are the source of operative thinking, and in what ways they might hinder or facilitate the development of operations. In other words, the true subject of the research on figurative thinking was operative thinking; mental imagery (or perception) was primarily of interest in its relation to the development of operations. Once again, the biases in Piaget's psychological research can be traced to his particular epistemological questions. In this case, empirical data are brought to bear on the problem of empiricism – to what extent operative knowledge is a product of experience, either through the direct perception of reality or through its "internalization" in mental imagery. From this perspective, the fact that figurative knowledge becomes subordinated to operative knowledge in the course of development constitutes evidence that the latter does not originate from the former.

Significantly, Piaget and Inhelder traced stages in the development of mental imagery that to some extent ran parallel to stages in the development of operations. The fact that this development was found to culminate in a subordination of mental imagery to concrete operations resulted in part from the kind of problem-solving situations studied. This finding does not exclude the possibility that other areas of figurative thinking may exist that continue to develop independent of operational thought. Such areas might include the "creative imagination" that Piaget and Inhelder reluctantly eliminated from consideration. The relative emphasis on figurative versus operative knowing might even be viewed as an important dimension of individual differences in cognition.

In this connection, Piaget (Bringuier, 1977/1980) once described himself as having an "abstract mind," a remark intended to explain a self-confessed lack of visual imagery.[6] His lack of interest in figurative thinking might therefore be traced to his own lack of aptitude for it. At the very least, this remark indicates that he implicitly recognized an aptitude for figurative thinking as a possible dimension of individual differences. Such a possibility raises the obvious question of how the balance between figurative and operative thinking in an individual would affect development in different areas.

Another way in which Piaget's theory might be further developed to take fig-

---

6 As an example of the nonvisual character of his thinking, Piaget recounted that if he merely looked at his watch to see what time it was, he forgot a moment later. But if he looked at his watch and at the same time *said* what time it was, he remembered much better (Piaget in Bringuier, 1977/ 1980, p. 5).

urative thinking into account is suggested by the late work on correspondences (Piaget, 1979, 1980b). As mentioned in chapter 6, this research seems to imply that correspondences are a *common* source of figurative and operative thinking. Correspondences were studied both in the context of children's imitative drawings and in the context of steps leading to the development of operations. Characteristically, Piaget was primarily concerned with the developmental path leading from correspondences to operations, but one can easily imagine a parallel path leading from correspondences to developmentally more advanced forms of figurative knowing. Whether or not such steps in the development of figurative knowledge can be identified and how they might be characterized are obvious questions for further research.

Although Piaget's interest in the epistemology of science might explain and (to some extent) excuse his relative neglect of figurative knowing in psychology, one might argue further that figurative factors play an important role in the evolution of scientific thought as well, especially in relation to the role of intuition in the generation of new models (Medawar, 1969). One need only think of Kekulé's celebrated dream of the benzene ring or Einstein's attempt to imagine himself traveling alongside a beam of light at the same speed. Figurative knowing might even provide an alternative mode of understanding certain natural phenomena. For example, Steiner (1897/1963) interpreted Goethe's approach to natural science as an attempt to obtain an intuitive understanding of organic processes, rather than as an attempt to frame theoretical models. In short, one should not be too hasty in eliminating figurative thinking from the epistemology of science.

Affectivity. The relation between epistemology and affective factors in development is perhaps more distant. Significantly, Piaget once disclaimed any interest in affectivity, because he considered himself an epistemologist, not a psychologist (Piaget in Bringuier, 1977/1980, p. 49). This remark is consistent with the interpretation advanced in the present book that many of the "biases" in Piaget's psychology result from his specific use of psychology to answer epistemological questions. The argument has been that such biases might be correctable within the broader scope of a Piagetian psychology. In the case of affectivity, a preliminary indication of how that might be accomplished already exists in the form of Piaget's Sorbonne lecture notes from 1953–1954, published in English under the title *Intelligence and affectivity* (Piaget, 1954/1981b). These notes are suggestive, both in regard to the role of affectivity in Piaget's theory and with respect to the reasons why he did not devote more time to the study of feelings and emotion.

He began these lectures by denying any radical dichotomy between affect and cognition. Instead, affectivity refers to the energetic aspect of action, including all cognitive activity. In general, the affectivity involved in cognition takes the form of interest. As such, it can influence both the vertical and horizontal dimensions of cognitive development. The speed with which individuals develop vertically from one stage of cognitive development to another depends in part on the extent of their interest in the cognitive activities in question. Similarly, the extent to which individuals' cognitive development is focused on one content area rather than another depends on their relative degrees of interest in those different areas. The fact that affectivity can influence cognitive development, however, does not imply that it is the cause of cognition. To consider affect as the cause of cognition (or the reverse) is to presuppose the very dichotomy that Piaget sought to deny.

In Piaget's view, cognitive psychology is the study of intellectual structure. It cannot claim to account for all aspects of behavior. This focus on structure is the major reason that affectivity was not considered more thoroughly in his research on cognitive development. However, this choice of subject matter did not imply any denial of the importance of affectivity in development. As Cowan pointed out in the preface to *Intelligence and affectivity*, Piaget's focus on cognitive structure was another consequence of his concern for regularities rather than individual differences in cognitive development.[7] Although differences in interest can determine differences in the content of cognitive structures or in the speed with which they are formed, they do not determine the formal laws by which the structures themselves are governed. Affects may influence the extent to which individual children engage in classification and seriation, as well as the objects classified or seriated, but they do not affect the rules of classification or seriation. If affective reactions are reflected on intellectually, *affective structures* may develop. The latter are structures that have affective reactions as their particular content. An example would be a hierarchical ordering of values.

According to Piaget, the distinction between cognition and affect is less meaningful than that between interactions with objects and interactions with other persons. Both types of interactions have cognitive (structural) and affective (energetic) aspects. Given this functional indissociability between cognition and affect, one can describe affective development in terms of the development of parallel structures relating to the understanding of objects and other persons. For example, a parallel can be drawn between the stages of sensorimotor development and the development of what Piaget called "intraindividual feelings." To the *hereditary organizations* (sensorimotor Stage One), correspond instinctual drives and other inborn affective reactions. To the *first acquired schemes* (sensorimotor Stages Two and Three) correspond the first positive and negative affective reactions linked to particular actions and perceptions. To *sensorimotor intelligence* as such (Stages Four through Six) correspond feelings related to the activation and inhibition of actions, as well as "terminal reactions" such as feelings of success or failure.

Similar parallels can be drawn with respect to the preoperational, concrete operational, and formal operational stages of cognitive development. Corre-

---

7 Elsewhere Piaget confessed: "I have no interest whatsoever in the individual. I am very interested in general mechanisms, intelligence and cognitive functions, but what makes one individual different from another seems to me – and I am speaking personally and to my great regret – far less instructive as regards the study of the human mind in general" (Piaget in Green, 1971, p. 211).

sponding to the *preoperational stage* are intuitive feelings regarding interpersonal relations and moral sentiments. To the *concrete operational stage* correspond autonomous moral feelings that no longer depend on obedience to a rule. And in the *formal operational stage,* interpersonal feelings for other persons as individuals are overlaid with feelings inspired by collective ideals. Much of *Intelligence and affectivity* is devoted to an elucidation of these developmental parallels. At most, these lecture notes can be considered only an outline sketch of a structural-developmental theory of affectivity. But they provide an important source of information on how Piaget conceived of the roles of affects and emotions in individual psychology. They further dispel the notion that affectivity and emotion have no place in Piagetian theory and that his theory cannot distinguish between interactions with objects and interactions with other persons (Suarez, 1980). Piaget's attempts to show how feelings of self-esteem, of moral norms, and of respect develop out of interpersonal interactions in fact foreshadow more recent interpersonal theories of emotion (Kemper, 1978; De Rivera, 1976), but these theories lack the explicit developmental dimension of Piaget's approach. A Piagetian approach to a theory of emotion is described by Brown and Weiss (1987).

Whether or not Piaget's particular ideas on affectivity do justice to the subject is another question. The main point of the present section has been that, contrary to some critical interpretations of Piaget's theory, it does have a place for affect and emotion. His neglect of affect in most of his work, like his neglect of social factors in development, resulted primarily from his exclusive epistemological interests.[8] For this purpose, some aspects of psychological development were more relevant than others. Piaget's personal bias, however, does not prevent other researchers from using his psychological theory for other purposes. Such use would necessarily involve creative extensions of the psychological aspects of his theory beyond the state in which he left it. This would be entirely in keeping with his own understanding of his work. In a postface to *Hommage à Jean Piaget* published in honor of his 80th birthday (Piaget, 1976c), he wrote of his conviction that he had drawn a very general theoretical framework containing many gaps. He foresaw that these gaps could be closed through a process of differentiation, resulting in new interpretations of the theory as a whole, without, however, contradicting it. Much of the subsequent psychological research of the Piagetian "school" has been conducted in this spirit (Bullinger & Chatillon, 1983; Murray, 1979; Schulman, Restaino-Baumann, & Butler, 1985).

CONCLUSION

In any evaluation of a theory as a whole, one must be able to distinguish between limitations that are intrinsic and those that are merely circumstantial. The major

8 If one accepts Feyerabend's (1975, 1978) views on the role of nonrational factors in scientific revolutions, then one might argue that an adequate epistemology of science cannot neglect affective factors any more than an adequate psychology of development can do so (see chapter 8).

goal of this chapter has been to provide evidence useful for distinguishing between the accidents of Piaget's own interests and the essence of his theory. Many of the limitations of his psychological theory have been argued to result from the fact that psychology, for him, was a means to further ends. As such, these limitations are not intrinsic and conceivably can be overcome through creative extensions. The value of the theory should be determined not merely by the number of facts that it predicts in its current form but also by the new perspectives it opens up and by its usefulness as a framework for further exploration. Much recent criticism of Piaget's theory has tended to take circumstantial limitations for intrinsic shortcomings or to mistake simplistic interpretations of theory for the theory itself. Accordingly, much of the evidence frequently cited as contradicting Piaget's theory (such as findings of asynchrony in development) is based on a premature assimilation of Piaget's structuralist method to functionalist psychology, and this premature assimilation is what is in fact contradicted by the evidence. Because of the very subordination of psychology to epistemology in Piaget's theory, a more thorough evaluation of the psychological theory must await further development of some of its latent possibilities. This limitation, however, need not prevent us from proceeding to evaluate the theory in regard to its original epistemological questions. Some preliminary steps toward such an evaluation are attempted in chapter 8.

8

The theory of knowledge

In chapter 7, the evaluation of Piaget's psychological theory was argued to present certain difficulties, because the problems addressed in that theory were not those of most psychologists. For Piaget, psychology was primarily a means of answering epistemological questions. But the evaluation of his epistemology presents similar difficulties, for his epistemological questions also differed from those traditionally addressed by the theory of knowledge (Hamlyn, 1978). Rather than trying to justify knowledge or to answer skeptical doubts, Piaget sought instead to discover the ways in which superior forms of knowledge succeed relatively inferior forms. In doing so, he hoped to discover a criterion for determining what is "better" about more advanced forms of knowing. In effect, Piaget proposed to make progress in epistemology not by providing better answers to the traditional questions but by pursuing different questions that potentially could be answered through empirical investigation.

The task of this chapter is therefore more difficult and at the same time more modest than that of chapter 7. In evaluating the psychological theory, the primary problem was to understand the theory correctly so that the relevance of a vast body of empirical research could be judged appropriately. In attempting to evaluate Piaget's genetic epistemology, one must first determine in what respects this approach is at all relevant for traditional issues of epistemology. Only then can one ask to what extent this new approach represents an advance in understanding. Although the originality of Piaget's approach consisted in posing new epistemological questions, many points of contact exist between his results and traditional epistemology. These points of contact are especially apparent with respect to contemporary debate regarding the nature of scientific change. Only in the posthumous *Psychogenèse et histoire des sciences* (Piaget & Garcia, 1983) was the connection between Piaget's theory and contemporary debate on the dynamics of theories explicitly discussed. One has the impression that the specific epistemological import of Piaget's work would have been considerably better understood if he had more frequently described the relations between his work and contemporary debate in the philosophy of science. (For a comprehensive treatment of Piaget's epistemology, see Kitchener, 1986.)

In attempting to specify the relevance of Piaget's theories for epistemology, one faces the further difficulty that philosophical approaches to the epistemology of the sciences are divided among the epistemologies of mathematics, of logic, of the empirical sciences, and so on. The issues are somewhat different in each case. For this reason, a common area of inquiry pursued both by Piaget and by traditional approaches to the philosophy of the various sciences, if such exists, would be useful as a focus of discussion.

In this connection, Piaget's autobiography once again provides a clue. As described in chapter 1, Piaget (1952a) related in his autobiography how he had conceived his ideas on relational totalities as a consequence of his encounter with the age-old problem of universals. Like Aristotle, Piaget saw a connection between the genera of nature and the universals of human knowledge. Unlike Aristotle, however, he recognized an evolutionary continuity between the forms of nature and the forms of knowledge and described both in terms of the same laws governing relational totalities. As related in chapter 1, these laws were first given a preliminary expression in *Recherche* (Piaget, 1918), but remained central to his thinking throughout his scientific career. They were clearly apparent, for example, in his theory of equilibration (see chapter 6).

The problem of universals therefore provides us with a focus for tracing the relationship between Piaget's thinking and traditional epistemological problems. Not only was this problem germinal in Piaget's own intellectual development, it has also been (and continues to be) one of the central problems of philosophical epistemology. One need not go as far as Staniland (1972) in asserting that almost any philosophical problem, if pursued far enough, leads to the problem of universals. It is sufficient for our purposes that the problem arises in one form or another in the various areas of the epistemology of the sciences.

Because every reader of this book cannot be assumed to be familiar with the problem of universals, this chapter begins with a brief review of the history of the problem in philosophy, including its relevance for contemporary issues in the epistemology of science and mathematics. This review provides the background for understanding Piaget's particular "solution" to the problem and, more generally, the relation of his theory to contemporary issues in epistemology and the philosophy of science. The chapter continues with a consideration of his contributions to biology and logic and concludes with a discussion of the question that he set out to answer as a young man: the relation between truth and value. Providing a definitive evaluation of Piaget's contributions to these issues is beyond the scope of this book. Instead, an attempt is made to specify the context within which such an evaluation would be possible.

THE PROBLEM OF UNIVERSALS

The problem of universals as it has traditionally been treated in philosophy has been described by Ewing as follows:

It is strange and significant that hardly any of the words we use with the exception of those called "proper names" stand for particular things. They stand for kinds of things, or for qualities, relations or actions, which do not exist by themselves at all. But, while one sees plenty of particular tables or particular men, one never sees a table in general or a man in general. For what then do such universal terms stand; and if they do not stand for anything in the world, what is the point of using them? This is the problem of universals. [Ewing, 1952, p. 212]

One obvious solution is to assume that the individual things subsumed under a general name possess a common, essential nature and that the latter is the proper referent of the general name. Because this essential nature is presumed to be universally present in each individual subsumed under the respective general name, it has traditionally been called a "universal," and the view that such universals exist in reality has been called *realism*. The opposite view, that universals do not really exist and that general names are "only names" that refer to many individuals severally, has been known as *nominalism*. A third position, that universals exist only in the mind in the form of general concepts and that these concepts are the referents of general names, has been called *conceptualism*.

The problem of general names is only one aspect of the problem of universals. Behind this semantic problem of reference lurks an epistemological problem: How, and on what grounds, do we recognize one thing as being *of the same kind* as another? The fact that we have relatively little trouble recognizing new exemplars of known categories suggests that our knowledge of those categories is truly general and that the respective categories or concepts are no mere collections of the exemplars we have previously encountered. Still, our knowledge of concepts is somehow derived from the experience of particulars; without some acquaintance with particular things, we do not arrive at general concepts. How, then, do we proceed from the experience of particulars to the knowledge of concepts as such? Related to this epistemological problem is an ontological problem: To what extent is the objective world really divided into natural categories (genera and species)? Realists can explain our conceptualization of the world as a reflection of such real, natural categories, but nominalists tend to deny the reality of genera and species and to explain our concepts in terms of linguistic convention.

These are only some of the questions that have traditionally been associated with the problem of universals. The present section consists of a brief review of the history of the problem in philosophy and is intended to provide some background for an appreciation of Piaget's epistemology. Although Piaget did not explicitly address this problem in most of his writings, it nevertheless provides a backdrop for many of his ideas. From this point of view, Piaget's theory can be seen to provide a highly original approach to this venerable problem.

Plato and Aristotle

Many of the basic issues associated with the problem of universals were already enunciated in Plato's famous dialogue, the *Meno* (Hutchins, 1952, vol. 7). The dialogue begins with a question: Meno asks Socrates if virtue is something that can be taught, or if it is acquired through practice, natural aptitude, or in some other way. Socrates replies that he cannot speculate about how virtue is acquired without knowing what virtue is, and on this point he must confess his ignorance. Meno is incredulous. Surely there can be no difficulty about the matter, he asserts confidently, proceeding to give a wealth of examples. There is one virtue for a man, another for a woman, still another for a child, an old man, or a slave. But Socrates is not satisfied with this answer. Enumerating different kinds of virtue does not tell one what virtue is *in general*.

Meno suggests several candidates for the essence of virtue, including justice and the desire for good things. But under closer examination, these, too, turn out to be only examples of particular virtues, not the essence of virtue itself. Meno admits to being perplexed; he has frequently held forth on the subject of virtue in front of large audiences, and now he cannot even say what it is. Socrates suggests a joint inquiry into the nature of virtue. Meno objects: How is this possible? If they knew what virtue was, they would not have to search for it. And if they do not know what it is, how are they going to recognize it if they find it?

As a way out of this impasse, Socrates proposes a theory of knowing that was in fact Plato's own. The state of knowing and yet not knowing is really not so uncommon. We all experience a similar condition whenever we momentarily forget the name of someone well known to us. At that moment we cannot recall the person's name, but we *know* it nevertheless. Plato suggested that our knowledge of universals is of a similar nature. He argued that we are born with a complete knowledge of universals, but that this knowledge is latent, just like the familiar name we cannot remember. Only under propitious circumstances can this knowledge be recalled. For this reason, Meno and Socrates are able to recognize that the desire for good things is not the essence of virtue, although they cannot state exactly what this essence is. The knowledge of universals is not acquired through learning, but through *recollection*.

In order to demonstrate the validity of this theory, Socrates conducts an experiment. Much as Piaget would do more than 2,000 years later, he interviews a child – a slave boy from Meno's household.[1] He begins by drawing a square on the ground 2 ft by 2 ft so that the boy can see that it is made up of 4 ft^2. Now, Socrates asks, suppose we drew a square with an area twice as big, how long would the sides of that square be? The boy answers that they would be twice as long as those of the first square, or 4 ft. Socrates then draws a square with 4-ft sides, and the slave boy sees that its area is 16 ft^2, not 8 ft^2 as he had supposed. As for the length of the sides of the 8-ft^2 square, he now confesses he has no idea.

Socrates compares the boy's present state of confusion with the perplexity that Meno felt when he was unable to state the essence of virtue. Both believed that they knew something that on further questioning they realized they did not know

1   As noted in chapter 4, the mathematical problem posed by Plato in the *Meno* (the relation between the length of a side of a square and its area) was also studied by Piaget in children (Piaget et al., 1948/1960).

in fact. Socrates suggests that this initial perplexity is a necessary step in the process of recollection. As a result of further inquiry, the slave boy reaches an answer to the original question: An 8-ft^2 square will have sides equal to the diagonal of the square that is 2 ft by 2 ft. The boy now demonstrates knowledge he did not previously possess, but the question is where this knowledge came from. Socrates did not give him the answer, but only posed appropriate questions. Nor had the boy ever learned geometry. Therefore, he apparently possessed this knowledge from the beginning.

Plato recognized only two possibilities: Either knowledge has been learned or it has been present from the beginning. If it could not have been learned, then it must have been present from the beginning – a classic argument of all nativist theories of knowledge. Given the conclusion that the knowledge of universals is present at birth, the question naturally arises how such a state of affairs is possible. According to Plato's theory, ideal universals or *forms* exist apart from all sensible particulars. Over and above all the particular trees we may ever encounter, a supersensible form of the universal tree also exists. Our knowledge of such forms is acquired before birth when our souls are capable of apprehending the forms directly. After we are born, this knowledge is forgotten, but may be partially recovered through the process of recollection. Plato assumed, in effect, that all knowledge is the knowledge of *something*. The fact that we possess knowledge of universals therefore implies that universals exist. These universals cannot be identical with any of the particular objects that we perceive, so they must exist on an ideal plane. In holding these views, Plato became the first proponent of what later came to be known as *extreme realism* – referring to the assumption that universals exist both outside the mind and apart from particular things. For present purposes, the important point to note is that Plato adopted this ontological commitment to the reality of universals as a means of answering an epistemological question: How the knowledge of universals is at all possible.

Despite the originality of Plato's solution, it leads to certain intractable difficulties. Perhaps the most important of these involves the relationship between the ideal forms and the sensible particulars. How is any individual tree related to the form of all trees? Plato suggested two possible answers: The particular might be related to the form either as part to whole or as copy to an original. Neither of these alternatives was quite satisfactory, as Plato himself admitted in the *Parmenides* (Hutchins, 1952, vol. 7). If the particular is related to the form as part to whole, then the form must be divisible, a conclusion Plato could not admit. And if the relation is one of copy to original, then there must be a *likeness* between particulars and the respective form. But the existence of forms was postulated in the first place precisely in order to explain how different individuals of the same genus are like each other. If the individuals and the form are merely *like* each other, then we are left with the same problem with which we began: how to explain in what way different things may be alike. Plato was never able to answer such objections in a completely satisfactory way.

Already in Plato's time there were philosophers like the Cynics and the Megarians who denied the reality of universals. According to the extreme form of this argument, the only thing that the members of a given genus have in common is the name that we give them, a position that came to be known as *extreme nominalism*. Although this position avoided some of the logical problems in the assumption that universals exist outside the mind, the problem of how knowledge of genera was at all possible remained. Without a credible answer to this question, the rejection of realism tended to slide into skepticism: the denial that our presumed knowledge of genera and species is really valid.

Aristotle's writings on this subject may be viewed as an effort to give a credible account of the knowledge of universals while avoiding the more obvious difficulties of extreme realism. His position differed from that of Plato in two major respects: Like Plato, Aristotle believed that universals exist outside the mind. Unlike his teacher, however, Aristotle did not hold that universals exist apart from particulars. Instead, universals were thought of as existing *in* individual things, a position known as *moderate realism*. Thus, whiteness or roundness does not exist independently, but only as manifested in things that are white or round. The second major difference between the two thinkers lies in the importance that Aristotle attached to experience in acquiring knowledge. Prior to experience, the person possesses only a potential capacity for knowing universals. Through experience, this potential knowledge is actualized. By experiencing individual things, the person comes to know the universals that are manifest in them. Thus, Aristotle rejected Plato's nativism in favor of an *empiricist* account of the knowledge of universals. He differed from modern empiricists, however, primarily in his emphasis on the existing potential of the rational intellect for actualizing the universals encountered in experience.

In ascribing this role to experience, Aristotle set it apart from mere sense perception. All animals possess the capacity for sense perception, he argued, but only some of them possess the capacity for memory, understood as the retention of sense impressions within the soul. Of those animals possessing memory, only some possess the capacity for experience as such, described as the "systematizing" of those sense impressions that are retained. This experience, constituted by "a number of memories," is nothing more nor less than "the universal now stabilized in its entirety within the soul, the one beside the many which is a single identity within them all" (Aristotle, *Posterior analytics,* in Ross, 1955, vol. 1, 100^a). Because the knowledge of universals is actualized through experience in this way, the scientist or craftsman can acquire superior knowledge of a general nature as the result of experience.

One might still ask *how* the human mind is able to extract the knowledge of universals from the experience of particulars. Aristotle did not provide a definitive answer to this question, but he did offer an intriguing simile:

We conclude that these states of knowledge [i.e., knowledge of universals] are neither innate in a determinate form, nor developed from other higher states of knowledge, but from sense-perception. It is like a rout in battle stopped by first one man making a stand and then another, until the original formation has been restored. The soul is so constituted as to be capable of this process. . . . When one of a number of logically indiscriminable particulars has made a stand, the earliest universal is present in the soul: for though the act of sense-perception is of the particular, its content is universal – is man, for example, not the man Callias. A fresh stand is made among these rudimentary universals, and the process does not cease until the indivisible concepts, the true universals are established: e.g., such and such a species of animal is a step towards the genus of animal, which by the same process is a step towards a further generalization. [ibid., 100^a–100^b]

Aristotle likened the particulars of sense experience to individuals who make a stand in battle. Implied in this image was that each experienced particular tends to bring along some of its fellows, that is, other members of the same genus to which it belongs and from which it is "logically indiscriminable." The person's initial sensory experience is, as Aristotle wrote elsewhere, of a "confused mass" or general "whole," that gets sorted out only later (Aristotle, *Physics,* in Ross, 1955, vol. 2, 184^a–186^b). For this reason, a child begins by calling all men "father" and all women "mother," only later coming to distinguish them as individuals. Through the experience of several such confused "rudimentary universals," the whole class (i.e., the universal as such) becomes firmly established in the mind. In this way, knowledge of genera is acquired that exceeds the sum of the particulars actually experienced, even though the knowledge of universals is acquired only through the experience of particulars. In this sense, universals exist potentially in particular objects outside the mind, for such objects have the potential for actualizing knowledge of universals when they come into contact with the human mind.

By denying that universals exist apart from individual things, Aristotle avoided Plato's problem of accounting for the relation between them. But this solution poses problems of its own. In particular, it appears to exclude the possibility of universals corresponding to general terms that do not in fact stand for anything (e.g., a unicorn). If general terms can be meaningful without a referent, then at least one of the major reasons for postulating the existence of universals disappears (cf. Staniland, 1972).

The medieval debate

As defined by Plato and Aristotle, the problem of universals generated one of the most heated controversies of medieval philosophy. Platonism became a dominant influence in early Christian thought by way of Saint Augustine, who suggested that the Platonic forms could be understood as ideas or patterns in the mind of God, a doctrine known as *exemplarism.* Creation was the unfolding or development of these preexisting forms, and the individual mind could acquire knowledge of them only through divine illumination. This fusion of Platonic idealism and Christian belief gave the problem of universals a new context and a new sense of urgency. According to Augustine's doctrine of divine illumination, individuals could attain direct knowledge of the mind of God. The possibility of such direct knowledge, however, potentially conflicted with the church's claim to arbitrate the truth.

According to some accounts (Weinberg, 1964), the problem of universals in its traditional form was bequeathed to the Middle Ages in the following way. In the third century A.D., Porphyry, a student of the neo-Platonist philosopher Plotinus, wrote an *Introduction to Aristotle's categories* in which he set out to discuss the nature of "genus, species, difference, property, and accident." Porphyry explicitly refused to speculate on the nature of genera and species – whether or not they existed apart from the mind, and if so, whether they existed in or apart from individual things. Despite this reticence, his statement of the problem determined the form in which it would be debated by medieval thinkers.

Porphyry went on to define the individual thing as a unique collection of attributes, and this definition was interpreted by many medieval commentators to mean that the individual was derived from the species through the addition of a unique set of attributes or "accidents." Thus, Odo of Tournai argued in the 11th century that there is a universal human nature present in every human being and that one individual is distinguished from another only in the unique set of accidents possessed by the universal substance in each case. According to this medieval version of extreme realism, universals are prior to individuals, and the latter depend on the former for their existence. The opposite view, that universals are only names given to collections of individuals, was articulated by Roscelin, also in the 11th century. According to his extreme nominalist position, universals do not exist in reality; only individuals are real. For example, no universal human substance exists; "man" is only a name we give to the collection of all men. The knowledge of universals thus follows the knowledge of particular things.

The controversy between nominalism and realism implicitly challenged the foundations of authority on which medieval society was based (Adams, 1913/ 1959). Reason appeared to dictate a choice between the two alternative positions. In fact, either view carried to its logical conclusion ended in heresy. By denying the reality of individuals, realism tended toward pantheism. By asserting the reality of sensible individuals, nominalism tended toward materialism. The compatibility of reason and faith appeared to be in question.

In this context, Abelard advanced a preliminary solution to the problem of universals in its medieval form. Abelard studied with both the nominalist Roscelin and with William of Champeaux, a realist who, like Odo of Tournai, defended the view that an individual consists of a universal substance with a unique set of accidents. In his own solution to the problem, Abelard attempted to steer between the extremes of both positions, distinguishing carefully between the ontological and epistemological aspects of the problem. Abelard's epistemology involves an explicit psychological theory, and this feature makes his thinking relevant to later approaches to the problem.

In order for individuals to be subsumed under a single universal term, Abelard argued, they must at least resemble one another in some way. Such a resemblance does not imply a common essence existing apart from the particulars themselves. Rather, in perceiving a resemblance among particulars, the human mind abstracts a single concept that subsumes all the individual things sharing in that resemblance. In the concept, the individuals are "confused" in the sense that they are considered alike with respect to a given quality or qualities. Thus, the universal concept is not a subjective fiction (for it refers to the real qualities by which individuals resemble one another), nor is it a mere copy of those objective qualities (for it considers them not as they actually are in coexisting with other qualities in the individual thing but only as they are abstracted by the mind). The concept is the proper referent of the universal name, and the universal name indirectly represents the individual things by way of the concept. In this way, one can explain how the universal term can represent individuals and at the same time how it can remain meaningful even when no individuals actually exist. Thus, "the name of the rose" retains its significance even in winter when there are no roses. Because Abelard's definition of a universal as that *"which is formed to be predicated of many"* (Abelard in Van Iten, 1970, p. 30) extended only to words, not to things, he is generally considered to be a nominalist. But because of the centrality of the concept in his account, he can also be considered a forerunner of conceptualism. By demonstrating that no universal essence was required to explain the significance of universal names, Abelard destroyed the main argument for extreme realism and laid the foundation for later approaches to the problem.

Saint Thomas Aquinas, for example, extended the psychological theory of abstraction in his grand synthesis of Aristotelian and Christian thought. The extreme realists had claimed that universals existed prior to individual things (*universalia ante res*), the nominalists claimed that knowledge of universals followed the knowledge of individual things (*universalia post rem*), and Abelard claimed that universal names must correspond to real resemblances in the things themselves (*universalia in rebus*). In Aquinas's doctrine, each of these three conceptions had its place. As ideas in the mind of God before creation, universals existed before individual things; as abstract concepts in the minds of human beings, universals follow individuals; and as potential universal concepts, they exist in the things themselves. Although the senses have the power to perceive only particulars, the active intellect possesses the capacity to abstract universals from the perceived particulars. Because the mind contains nothing that has not come through the senses, it can have no innate ideas. Aquinas's position thus entailed a partial differentiation of the ontological and epistemological aspects of the problem. Ontologically, he can be considered a realist, for he accepted Augustine's doctrine of exemplarism. With respect to the purely epistemological aspects of the problem, however, he must be viewed as a moderate realist and empiricist in the Aristotelian mold.

Subsequent approaches to the problem focused more specifically on its epistemological aspect. Duns Scotus argued that a "formal distinction" can be made between the common nature of the things subsumed under that concept and the things taken individually. In so doing, he sought to avoid the pitfalls of nominalism and realism in their extreme forms. The nominalist denial of any objective common nature shared by individual things seemed to imply that our concepts are mere mental fictions. But if our concepts are only fictions, then all judgments based on them will necessarily be unfounded. The realist assumption of a real distinction between the common nature of things and the things taken individually led to unacceptable epistemological consequences, as demonstrated by Abelard. In particular, the assumption of a common nature among discrete things appeared to imply their numerical identity, a contradiction in terms. Scotus's idea of a "formal distinction" was meant to provide the basis for the assumption of a common nature among things that was objective, but not real. Thus, the objectivity of conceptual knowledge could be preserved while avoiding the difficulties of extreme realism.

Even this subtle form of moderate realism was rejected in the 14th century by William of Ockham. Ockham began with the premise that everything that exists must be singular. To assume the opposite leads to contradiction. Objectively, things cannot be both the same (as sharing a common nature) and different (as distinct individuals) at the same time. If individuals share a real common essence, then they cannot be created or annihilated independent of one another. Nor does Scotus's postulation of a "formal distinction" between things as individuals and their common nature escape the problem. If this distinction is objective, then it must be real. If it is real, then the argument is subject to all the same difficulties as other realist positions. Thus, Ockham rejected all arguments that universals can have any existence whatsoever outside the mind. Even Augustine's doctrine of exemplarism was not acceptable.

Ockham's uncompromising rejection of all forms of realism did not, in his own view, undermine the objective basis of human knowledge. By allowing for the existence of universals within the mind, Ockham instead became one of the first proponents of conceptualism. Like Abelard, Ockham believed that the objective basis of universal concepts consists in the resemblance of individual things to one another and that concepts come to represent particulars through a form of resemblance. In resembling things that resemble each other, the concept acts as a "natural sign" for the individuals it represents. Thus, the concept is no mere fiction, but neither does it imply any common nature in the things that it subsumes.

Ockham's conceptualism may be viewed as a transitional position between medieval and modern approaches to the problem of universals. In his rejection of universal essences existing outside the mind, he stood with the moderns, but in his view of the relation between the mind and reality, he was typically medieval. According to the medieval view, the sensed qualities of physical objects were thought to reside in the objects themselves. Greenness was in the leaf, warmth in the fire, and so forth. Nominalists and realists may have differed in characterizing these qualities as singular or universal, but they never doubted that the mind perceived those qualities as they existed in reality. This assumption was abandoned, however, in the modern era; according to new conceptions of the nature of physical reality, sensory qualities came to be regarded as having a subjective, rather than an objective, character.

The epistemological revolution in modern philosophy

The unity of the object and its perceptual qualities was destroyed by Galilean and Newtonian physics. As a result of his scientific observations on the nature of heat, Galileo concluded that matter was composed of minute particles that were imperceptible in themselves, but that had the power of producing sensory qualities when they came into contact with the sensory organs. In other words, sensory qualities were no longer located in the objects, but in the perceiving subject, the objects being only the cause or occasion of those qualities. Newton came to a similar conclusion in his work on optics; color was not a property of light itself, but a phenomenon occurring in the sensorium of the perceiver. With respect to the problem of universals, this conclusion implied, first, that the ontological aspect of the problem tended to be replaced by a psychophysical problem regarding the relation between physical states or events and subjective sensory impressions or percepts. Second, the epistemological aspect of the problem also came to be regarded in a more psychological light: How does the mind come to form universal concepts, given the particulars of sensory experience? With this realignment of the issues, many of the epistemological arguments in the medieval debate returned on a different plane.

Galileo's contemporary, Hobbes, for example, produced a totally materialistic model of the human psyche. Impressed by Galileo's discoveries regarding the motion of physical bodies, Hobbes argued that all psychological phenomena could be explained in terms of matter in motion. The motion of physical matter coming into contact with the body excites the motion of the particles composing the nervous system, and the latter in turn give rise to sensory experience. Thus, sensory qualities are located in the subject, not in the object. In regard to universals, Hobbes took an extreme nominalist position, arguing that universal names are merely names that refer to a collection of individuals. Realism is a fallacy that arises when the names of things are improperly conjoined with the names of names, as in the compound "a general thing." According to Hobbes, only names can properly be called general or universal.

Although Hobbes's psychology freed him of the medieval requirement that universal names must have objective referents in order to be meaningful, his extreme nominalism still involved insuperable epistemological problems. For example, Descartes argued that we have many ideas that could not possibly have been acquired through the senses as implied by empiricist theories like that of Hobbes. The universal concepts of mathematics are particularly of this nature. No one has ever seen a perfect triangle as it is defined in geometry. At most, we have seen more or less good approximations of this ideal triangle. Because we have never experienced a perfect triangle, such an idea could not have been derived through the senses. Instead, according to Descartes, it must be innate. At any rate, the potential for such an idea must be innate, experience serving only to awaken the potential. Because most of us have experienced neither God nor the soul, the potential for these ideas must likewise be innate. Over and against Hobbes's nominalist empiricism, Descartes represented rationalism and innatism by recognizing both the creative imagination and innate ideas as sources of knowledge, in addition to experience. Against Hobbes's materialism, Descartes postulated a dualism consisting of the extended, material world on the one hand and nonextended, immaterial mind on the other. The rationalist tradition was upheld by Spinoza, Leibniz, and other philosophers of the 17th and 18th centuries, who, like Descartes, took mathematics and logic as their model of certain knowledge, but without necessarily sharing his dualism.

Descartes's innatism was attacked by subsequent empiricists, most notably by Locke, who devoted the first book of his *Essay concerning human understanding* to a refutation of the theory of innate ideas. One of Locke's major arguments was that the ideas previously presumed to be innate, such as the idea of God or the law of contradiction, are discovered on closer examination to be acquired only gradually by children as a result of experience.

He that attentively considers the state of a child, at his first coming into the world, will have little reason to think him stored with plenty of ideas, that are to be the matter of his future knowledge. It is *by degrees* he comes to be furnished with them. And though the ideas of obvious and familiar qualities imprint themselves before the memory begins to keep a register of time or order, yet it is often so late before some unusual qualities come in the way, that there are few men that cannot recollect the beginning of their acquaintance with them. And if it were worth while, no doubt a child might be so ordered as to have but a very few, even of the ordinary ideas, till he were grown up to be a man. [Locke, *An essay concerning human understanding,* in Hutchins, 1952, vol. 35, p. 122]

Like Locke, but on a vastly different scale of empirical detail, Piaget would later point to the gradual character of children's intellectual development as one kind of evidence against innatist theories of the origins of intelligence.

Locke maintained the post-Galilean, post-Newtonian distinction between the objective qualities possessed by objects and the subjective impressions or "ideas" that those qualities arouse in the mind. Having rejected Descartes's argument for innate ideas, Locke nevertheless retained a kind of Cartesian dualism, according to which the objective qualities inhere in a physical substance, and subjective ideas in a mental substance. His broad use of the word "idea" to cover the contents of both sensation and thought already betrays the kernel of his theory of knowledge. The abstract ideas employed in thinking are only faint copies of the concrete sensory impressions that arise when mental substance comes into contact with physical substance. In fact, Locke recognized two forms of experience: sensation and reflection. Ideas may be acquired either through the perception of external objects or through the mind's perception of its own operations.

Given that experience is the only source of ideas, how is it that the mind acquires general ideas? As Descartes had pointed out, general ideas like that of a perfect triangle have never been met with in experience. Locke followed many of his predecessors in appealing to abstraction as the process by which universal ideas are derived from the data of the senses. Locke's way of posing the problem is as significant as his solution:

Since all things that exist are only particulars, how come we by general terms; or where find we those general natures they are supposed to stand for? Words become general by being made the signs of general ideas: and ideas become general, by separating from them the circumstances of time and place, and any other ideas that may determine them to this or that particular existence. By this way of abstraction they are made capable of representing more individuals than one. [ibid., p. 255]

Given the two premises (a) that ideas are acquired only through experience and (b) that all things experienced are particular, Locke was led to the unavoidable conclusion that the particular is epistemologically prior to the general. From the particulars of sense experience, the person arrives at general ideas by the process of subtracting those ideas that distinguish one thing from another. Significantly, Locke illustrated his argument once again with reference to child development:

There is nothing more evident, than that the ideas of the persons children converse with (to instance in them alone) are, like the persons themselves, only particular. The ideas of the nurse and the mother are well framed in their minds; and, like pictures of them there, represent only those individuals. The names they first gave to them are confined to these individuals; and the names of *nurse* and *mamma,* the child uses, determine themselves to those persons. Afterwards, when time and a larger acquaintance have made them observe that there are a great many other things in the world, that in some common agreements of shape, and several other qualities, resemble their father and mother, and those persons they have been used to, they frame an idea, which they find those many particulars do partake in; and to that they give, with others, the name *man,* for example. And thus they come to have a general name, and a general idea. Wherein they make nothing new; but only leave out of the complex idea they had of Peter and James, Mary and Jane, that which is peculiar to each and retain only what is common to them all. [ibid., pp. 255–256]

In a similar fashion, children arrive at the general idea of an animal by leaving out of account those properties that distinguish humans from other animals and the other animals from one another.

Although Aristotle and Locke both appealed to the facts of child development to illustrate their accounts of the origins of general concepts, the facts they cited and the conclusions they drew were quite different. Aristotle described young children as indiscriminately calling all men ''father,'' and only later learning to discriminate their fathers from other men. This experience of particulars as ''rudimentary universals'' constitutes a process of generalization that leads eventually to general concepts. In contrast, Locke described young children as calling their parents and nurses by their individual names from the beginning. Only later do they come to use and understand general names. This movement from the particular to the general is accomplished through abstraction, conceived of as the subtraction of differences. For Aristotle, the differences among particulars were at first not discriminable and became discriminated with experience, but for Locke differences existed among particulars from the start and then became subtracted. Significantly, Piaget (1945/1962) studied this same question in turn, finding that his children first used the words ''mama'' and ''papa'' in connection with several different persons and only later learned to restrict them to their mother and father, respectively (see chapter 3).

Another consequence of Locke's position is that universals exist only in the mind, not in reality. This conclusion follows from the proposition that all things are particular and that the mind arrives at universal ideas through the subtraction of properties. Thus, Locke's empiricism radically differed from that of the scholastics. For Aquinas, knowledge also had its origins in sensory experience, but sensed qualities were believed to be resident in the objects perceived. No meaningful concepts could be abstracted by the mind that were not in some sense already in the objects. Abstraction was thus the mind's ability to perceive the universal as it existed in the things themselves. Given the post-Galilean localization of sensory qualities in the perceiver, Locke was freed of this requirement. Universal names were meaningful in referring to universal ideas, themselves formed through abstraction conceived in terms of the subtraction of particular sensed qualities.

An account of Locke's approach to the problem of universals would be incomplete, however, without some mention of his theory of the association of ideas. The idea of a particular thing is a complex idea, a compound of all the simple ideas, such as size, shape, color, and location, that distinguish it from other particular things. Abstraction as the subtraction of ideas is possible only because the particular idea is complex, and complex ideas are formed from simple ones through the "association" or "connection" of ideas. Locke recognized two forms of natural connections between ideas, those that derive from the nature of the ideas themselves, and those that derive from chance or custom. The complex ideas corresponding to particular things are formed through "natural" association of those particular ideas that are always encountered together because of their inherence in a single object. Locke spent more time discussing chance associations of ideas, however, because he thought such chance associations were a major source of error and prejudice. For this reason, he believed educators should observe and prevent undesirable association of ideas in children and young people. For example, fear of the dark might result from an unnatural association between the idea of darkness and the idea of goblins in stories told by "a foolish maid." Or an aversion to reading and study might result from the chance association between children's ideas of books and the "pain" they had endured in school (Locke in Hutchins, 1952, vol. 35, pp. 249–250).

Locke's empiricism thus took on an atomistic quality. Simple ideas can be joined together through association, and they can be separated again through abstraction. Although some suggestions of a theory of association were already found in Hobbes, Locke was the first to use the term and to develop the concept systematically. Locke's immediate successors in the British empiricist tradition accepted this atomistic view of the mind, but demonstrated that it contradicted other aspects of his theory. Berkeley, for example, took issue with the doctrine of abstraction by subtraction. If the ideas of the human mind are composed of elementary sensory qualities, Berkeley argued, it follows that all ideas must be particular. In order to conceive of any determinate thing at all, it must be conceived in its particularity. Locke had maintained, for example, that the general idea of a triangle is formed from the idea of a particular triangle by abstracting from the latter all of its particular qualities. The result is a triangle that is "neither equilateral, equicrural, nor scalenon, but all and none of these at once" (ibid., p. 339). Berkeley replied that the mind cannot conceive or imagine any triangle the sides of which are both equal and unequal, or neither the one nor the other. Any triangle conceived by the mind must have some definite form. In rejecting abstract ideas, Berkeley was careful to point out that he did not deny general ideas as such, only the notion that general ideas are formed through abstraction. A particular idea becomes general by being used to represent a number of other particulars indifferently with respect to certain properties. The ideas of a particular triangle, say a right triangle, may be used to represent all triangles with respect to those properties (e.g., angles summing to 180°) unrelated to the particular property that distinguishes it from other triangles (e.g., having one 90° angle). Thus, universal words acquire their significance not by representing abstract ideas but by representing many particular ideas or, what amounts to the same thing, by representing one particular idea that in turn represents a number of other particular ideas (Berkeley, *The principles of human knowledge,* in Hutchins, 1952, vol. 35).

Berkeley's rejection of the doctrine of abstraction by subtraction, together with his empiricist epistemology, led to the idealism with which his name is usually associated. According to Berkeley, if the idea of a material substance is understood as what remains after all the particular sensory qualities are abstracted from material objects, then it can be shown to be nonsensical. For after all sensory qualities are subtracted from a physical object, nothing remains. If sensory qualities are located in the subject (as the physics of Galileo and Newton demanded) and if all our knowledge originates in sensory perception, then we can never know whether or not there exists an objective physical matter beyond our mere perceptions. Berkeley concluded that reality was fundamentally mental or spiritual in nature.

Hume took this line of reasoning even further. Accepting Berkeley's arguments against the existence of abstract ideas, Hume showed that they could also be applied to the mind itself. Not only is the idea of material substance not based in experience; the same can be said of a mental substance. According to Hume, the self as such is never grasped in experience. The self is only a bundle of particular perceptions, and these are what are encountered in the act of reflection. Hume is perhaps best remembered for his attack on rationalist conceptions of causality. If all our ideas are grounded in perceptual experience, then it is unclear how the idea of a necessary causal relation originates. All that one can ever observe is the fact that one event follows another with a certain regularity. Nothing in the perception of this constant conjunction supports the idea of a necessary connection between the two events. The causal relation is rather an example of the association of ideas or impressions. From the experience of a constant conjunction of sensory impressions the mind comes to expect that the same impressions will be similarly conjoined in the future. The causal relation is thus not a property of the events themselves, but a belief resulting from the association of ideas.

One may recognize in Hume's discussion of causality another aspect of the problem of universals. In this case, the problem does not involve genera and species, but universal relations – in Hume's terminology, *general rules*. By observing the conjunction of particular events, the mind arrives by habit or custom at the general rule that these events will always be so conjoined. "When ev'ry individual of any species of objects is found by experience to be constantly united with an individual of another species, the appearance of any new individual of either species naturally conveys the thought to its usual attendant" (Hume, 1739/ 1957, p. 143). Just as universal words denote only a collection of particular impressions or ideas that happen to resemble each other, so do general rules represent only an association originally formed between two particulars and extended to other particulars resembling the first two.

Hume's denial of any necessity in causal relations can also be viewed as an attack on inductive reasoning. According to his account, nothing in the constant conjunction of particular events supports the inference that those events will continue to be conjoined in the future. No logical justification exists for moving from the particular events to the general rule, but only an expectation born of habit. In this form, Hume's argument continues to play an important role in contemporary philosophy of science (Popper, 1979).

The Kantian synthesis

The philosophy of Kant has often been regarded as a reply to Hume. Kant related how his encounter with the works of Hume awakened him from his "dogmatic slumber," and he presented his own "critical" philosophy as a synthesis transcending the opposition between the "dogmatism" of the Wolffian school and the "skepticism" of Hume. Because Wolff's system represented Leibnizian rationalism and Hume's arguments were empiricist in origin, Kant's philosophy can also be viewed as an attempt to overcome the opposition between rationalism and empiricism. In order to achieve this synthesis, Kant had to explain how the "necessity and generality" of reason attacked by Hume were possible and justifiable after all.

Hume had argued that much of our supposed "knowledge" is not based in experience. No experience corresponds to general ideas, because all experience is particular. Nor does any experience correspond to the general rule of causal necessity; all that is experienced is the succession of particular events. Having subscribed to the empiricist premise that knowledge originates in experience, Hume was led inevitably to the conclusion that concepts not derived from experience are mere fictions or illusions of the mind. Kant replied that the creations of the mind do not invariably lead to error, so they need not be considered illusory. The problem is rather to distinguish those constructions that are valid from those that are not. Kant believed he could give clear examples in which the operations of the mind could result in new knowledge that was not immediately derived from experience.

According to Kantian terminology, a proposition that states anything new is *synthetic*. It asserts something in the predicate that is not already contained in the subject. In contrast, propositions in which the predicate merely restates what is already asserted in the subject are *analytic*. This definition implies that only synthetic propositions are capable of extending knowledge. Propositions may be further differentiated as a priori or a posteriori, that is, as preceding experience or following from it. In these terms, empiricism is committed to the thesis that all synthetic propositions are a posteriori, which is equivalent to saying that all extensions of knowledge are the result of experience. Against this, Kant cited what he considered to be clear examples of synthetic a priori propositions, the clearest cases being taken from the field of mathematics. Consider the arithmetical proposition $7 + 5 = 12$. This proposition clearly can be verified prior to experience; one need not count out 12 objects each time in order to determine its truth, assuming one knows the rules of arithmetic. But the proposition is also synthetic; the idea of 12 is not already contained in the idea of adding 7 and 5 together. In Kant's terms, it is a synthetic a priori proposition. The problem that Kant set for himself is represented in the question, How are such synthetic a priori propositions at all possible? In effect, how can knowledge be extended without reference to experience? This is one of the central questions to which Kant's *Critique of pure reason* (Hutchins, 1952, vol. 42) is addressed.

In choosing mathematical propositions to illustrate the question regarding synthetic a priori propositions, Kant was following the lead of the rationalists, who took mathematics or logic as the paradigm of knowledge. Indeed, the problem of synthetic a priori propositions can be viewed as a restatement of the problem of the generativity of intelligence that had preoccupied epistemologists since Plato. According to Kant, both rationalists and empiricists had made the mistake of not distinguishing among (a) reason as applied to possible experience, (b) reason as applied to the possibility of experience, and (c) reason as applied to matters that could not possibly be experienced. Only the first two applications, according to Kant, lay within the proper sphere of creative reason. Rationalists were led into contradiction in attempting to extend the use of reason beyond its proper boundaries, for reason can be used to support contradictory arguments in matters that transcend experience. In rejecting this illegitimate use of reason, skeptics like Hume ended by denying its legitimate uses as well. Kant's solution was to trace the boundaries of the proper uses of reason. For him, this meant delimiting the boundaries of possible experience.

The empiricists' mistake was in taking experience for granted. They overlooked the organizing activities of the mind that make experience as we know it possible. Hume, in particular, had explained general ideas in terms of their use in representing a collection of particular ideas or impressions that resemble each other. The self, for example, was not an entity in itself, but only a bundle of impressions. Such an argument implies that the mind is capable of considering a bundle of impressions or a collection of ideas as a totality. This capacity of the mind is itself prior to experience and determines the form in which experience can occur. Otherwise, we would experience only a whirl of impressions, not even a bundle, and even the *illusion* of a self would be impossible.

By calling attention to the form of experience, in addition to its content, Kant was able to point out the ways in which it is organized by the mind. The same phenomenon can be considered separately in its *unity,* diverse phenomena can be considered in their *plurality,* and the same phenomena taken together can be considered in their *totality.* These are three of the a priori "categories" by which experience is organized by the understanding. The fact that experience comes to us already ordered according to these categories indicates, according to Kant, that they are imposed on experience rather than derived from it. In addition to these three categories of *quantity* (unity, plurality, totality), Kant recognized categories of *quality* (reality, negation, limitation), of *relation* (substance and accident, cause and effect, reciprocity), and of *modality* (possibility–impossibility, existence–nonexistence, necessity–contingency). Corresponding to these 12 a priori categories are 12 a priori forms of judgment: of quantity (universal, particular, singular), of quality (affirmative, negative, infinite), of relation (categorical, hypothetical, disjunctive), and of modality (problematical, assertorical, apodictical). We shall not pursue the question of how Kant arrived at these 12 categories and forms of judgment, nor what they all mean in practice. Instead, we shall limit ourselves to the relevance of Kant's system for the problem of universals.

In Kant's view, the philosophical problem of the nature of genera and species results from the application of the categories of unity, plurality, and totality to the manifold of natural phenomena. In reality, phenomena are in some ways similar and in some ways dissimilar, but reason can focus on the homogeneity, variety, or continuity of forms. As long as these principles are recognized as regulative, as a priori organizing principles, no problem arises. But if they are recognized instead as constitutive (i.e., if one assumes that reality must correspond to the results of reasoning), then contradictions inevitably arise, for reasons may be found to support different points of view:

This reasoner has at heart the interest of *diversity* – in accordance with the principle of specification; another, the interest of *unity* – in accordance with the principle of aggregation. Each believes that his judgment rests upon a thorough insight into the subject he is examining, and yet it has been influenced solely by a greater or less degree of adherence to some one of the two principles, neither of which are objective, but originate solely from the interest of reason, and on this account to be termed *maxims* rather than *principles.* . . . So long as they are regarded as objective principles, they must occasion not only contradictions and polemic, but place hindrances in the way of the advancement of truth, until some means is discovered of reconciling these conflicting interests, and bringing reason into union and harmony with itself. [Kant, *Critique of pure reason,* in Hutchins, 1952, vol. 42, pp. 199–200]

According to Kant, the knowledge of general concepts does not follow from the knowledge of particulars by way of abstraction or any other psychological process. Rather, the capacity for organizing the objects of experience into universal and particular forms, conceived of as complementary opposites, is inherent in the mind itself. General ideas are therefore constructions of the mind, but they are not on this account mere fictions. Their validity is derived not from a correspondence with the objects of experience but from their role in the constitution of reality as it is experienced. The idea of the self, for example, is derived by considering the totality of subjective phenomena as an absolute unity. The rationalists erred in taking the unity of the self as an object of intuition. In fact, the unity of the self is a unity in *thought,* not a unity of an experienced object (ibid., pp. 126–127). The empiricists, for their part, erred in believing that if the self could not be found in experience, then it was illusory. In fact, "consciousness in itself is not so much a representation distinguishing a particular object, as a form of representation in general" (ibid., p. 122). The idea of the self is valid when understood for what it really is, as a form of experience rather than as an object in experience. By employing synthetic a priori reasoning to deduce the formal determinants of experience, Kant believed that the meaning of such transcendental ideas could be clarified.

The importance of Kant in Piaget's thinking has been asserted by a number of commentators (Hamlyn, 1978; Rotman, 1977; Toulmin, 1972). Given Kant's significance in the history of modern epistemology, one could hardly imagine that Piaget should not have been influenced by him in one way or the other. Piaget (1952a) himself testified that he had read Kant at a formative period in his own development. But this connection between Kant and Piaget should not be overemphasized. The tendency to see Piaget in terms of a "historicized Kant" can lead to serious distortions of his position (Huttner, 1982).

After Kant, the synthesis he had tried so carefully to preserve tended to come apart. Kant had recognized two legitimate applications of a priori reason: (a) to the realm of possible experience, as in the case of a science that constructs general laws to define the expected results of possible experiments, and (b) to the possibility of experience, as in his own transcendental philosophy. His successors in 19th-century philosophy tended to emphasize one or the other of these uses of reason. In Germany, the idealists Fichte, Schelling, and Hegel extended the use of reason as a means of analyzing the subjective conditions of possible experience. In France and England, the positivists carried the attack against metaphysics further than Kant himself in limiting the sphere of reason to the objective facts of positive science. These different positions regarding the proper role of reason implied very different views on the status of universals in cognition.

In the preface to *The phenomenology of mind,* for example, Hegel (1807/1967) defined the object of philosophy as the universal that contains the particular. All experience, according to Hegel, entails a relation between subject and object, but this relation is not merely between a particular subject and a particular object.

The perception of a particular object as an object already presupposes the universal concept of an object as such. Similarly, the consciousness of self as pure subjectivity presupposes the notion of universal self-consciousness, or spirit. Hegel's basic question is how this universal self-consciousness comes to know itself. It can do so only by reflecting on its own activity. Thus, philosophy acquires a necessary developmental dimension. The history of philosophy becomes a series of stages in the spirit's knowledge of itself. By absorbing the essence of previous stages of knowledge, the individual can pass beyond them, and in this way the spirit develops further. This development is dialectical; progress toward knowledge of the universal is possible only through the synthesis of particular, partial, and seemingly contradictory perspectives.

For Hegel, the universal mind or spirit was no mere abstraction. Sometimes it appears more real than the individual. "The particular individual," he wrote, "is incomplete mind, a concrete shape in whose existence, taken as a whole, one determinate characteristic predominates, while the others are found only in blurred outline." In contrast, "the general mind . . . constitutes the substance of the individual" (Hegel, 1807/1967, pp. 89—90). The particular individual becomes important in the development of the spirit when that person becomes the embodiment of general currents in the historical process. Such a person is a world-historical individual, in whom the acts of the universal spirit take on a particular form.

Just as Kant had criticized the empiricists for taking experience for granted, so Hegel criticized Kant for taking knowledge for granted. Kant's critical epistemology, he argued, requires us to know how knowledge is possible before we know anything at all. This is like wanting to swim before going into the water (Hegel, 1833/1982, p. 361). Knowledge regarding the conditions of knowing is itself a phenomenon and should therefore be subjected to the same kind of criticism as other phenomena. In particular, Kantian epistemology cuts off knowledge regarding the conditions of experience from the experience of self, obscuring the essential subject–object relation underlying all knowledge and experience.

Some distinct correspondences between Piaget's theory and Hegel's philosophy have been pointed out, especially in connection with the idea of development in forms of knowing (Fetz, 1982; Garcia, 1980; Kesselring, 1982). As described in chapter 6, Piaget (1980d) cited Hegel frequently in his book on dialectic. Because of their common emphasis on development and dialectic, one could argue that Piaget's kinship with Hegel is closer than that with Kant. Fetz (1982) went so far as to call Hegel a "precursor" of Piaget. If only because of this common kinship with Hegel, some very definite parallels exist between Piaget and Marx (Apostel, 1986; Garcia, 1980; Goldmann, 1959; Wartofsky, 1982).

In France and England, 19th-century philosophy developed in a different direction. Positivists like Comte in France and J. S. Mill in England took the empiricist epistemology and applied it to method as well. If knowledge in general is solely the product of experience, then valid scientific and philosophical knowledge can be derived only from experiment and observation. Unlike Locke,

Berkeley, and Hume, they no longer took direct perception as the model of certain knowledge, but rather systematic observation informed by inductive reasoning and scientific method. Comte, who coined the term "positivism," ordered the sciences from mathematics through astronomy, physics, chemistry, and biology to sociology according to the generality of their subject matter. Psychology, he believed, could never be a positive science because the mind as the organ of observation could never observe itself. In *A system of logic*, however, J. S. Mill (1843/1875) not only set down the principles of inductive reasoning to be used in scientific investigation but also laid the foundations for psychology as an empirical science by building on the "laws of association" already described by his father (J. Mill, 1829/1869). A number of the early empirical psychologists, including Wundt, are believed to have been directly or indirectly influenced by Mill's *Logic* (Klein, 1970). As an epistemologist, Mill carried empiricism to its logical conclusion by considering even mathematics as an empirical science. While admitting that mathematics was more general than the other sciences, he believed that mathematical knowledge was justified by its empirical applications.

The 20th century

A review of all of the arguments and counterarguments that have informed contemporary discussions of the problem of universals is beyond the limits of this chapter. Instead, this section is limited to a selective review of some of the major positions that have been advanced in this century. Also discussed are some aspects of the problem of particular interest to the present inquiry, including the foundations of mathematics, the philosophy of science, and the epistemology of psychology.

Recurrence and resemblance. The distinction between the ontological and semantic aspects of the problem of universals is useful in understanding contemporary discussions of the problem. The ontological aspect is the question whether or not universals exist, and the semantic aspect whether or not our use of general terms is purely conventional. Historically, these two aspects of the problem have not always been distinguished. Thus, realists have argued that universals exist as the referents of general terms and that our use of general terms is therefore nonarbitrary. In contrast, the exponents of extreme nominalism have denied the existence of universals, arguing instead that general terms are "only names" – that is, their use is arbitrary and conventional. According to Staniland's (1972) summary of the current debate, many different philosophers have taken as their starting point the relative merits of recurrence and resemblance theories. In both theories, extreme nominalism is rejected. That is, the proposition that our use of general terms is nonarbitrary is affirmed, but the question whether or not the nonarbitrariness of general terms entails the existence of universals is answered differently.

According to *recurrence theory,* the nonarbitrariness of general terms is explained by the fact that certain common properties and/or relations "recur" in the particular things to which general terms refer. Thus, two or more objects can be nonarbitrarily called "blue," because they share the common property of blueness. The use of general terms is explained in terms of real, existing common properties, and recurrence theory can accordingly be considered a form of moderate realism. In contrast, resemblance theorists attempt to explain how general terms can be used in a nonarbitrary manner without assuming the existence of universals as common properties. According to this view, we call two or more objects "blue" not because of any common property of "blueness" but because the particular objects involved resemble each other in a certain way. Some versions of this theory assert that all the particulars falling under a given general term are related to each other insofar as they all resemble a certain "standard particular." Thus, all blue things are related by the fact that they all resemble some standard shade of blue. There is an obvious affinity between this version of resemblance theory and "prototype" theories of classification in cognitive psychology (Rosch, 1987).

A consideration of all the many arguments that have been brought for and against recurrence and resemblance theories is beyond the scope of this brief summary. Instead, we shall limit ourselves to a few of the standard objections against them. One problem with recurrence theory is that it does not seem to admit intermediate cases: Either an object has a given property or it does not. But many cases occur in real life in which the borderline between having a certain property and not having it is not so sharp. Staniland (1972) cited the example of "off white" – cases in which objects are not definitely white, but not definitely not-white either. At what point do such objects cease being white and start becoming pale gray, for example? We are tempted to say that at some point the classification of an object as pale gray rather than as off white becomes an arbitrary decision. But recurrence theory was intended precisely to explain the nonarbitrariness of our classifications.

Resemblance theory has no difficulty in explaining borderline cases, for the admission of degrees of resemblance is not a problem. Thus, the color of an object can be more or less like a standard shade of white. Nor does it face any difficulty in imaging an object resembling two different standards at the same time. However, one can doubt that resemblance theory really succeeds in doing away with universals altogether. B. Russell (1912/1967) argued that resemblance theorists succeed in eliminating all universals except one: resemblance itself. If we call blue things "blue" by virtue of the fact that they all share a certain resemblance, then this commonly shared resemblance is a universal. Thus, resemblance theory has not succeeded in eliminating universals entirely, but only universals based on common properties.

Another attempt to demonstrate the nonarbitrary character of our use of general names without assuming the existence of either common properties or relations is based on Wittgenstein's (1958) concept of "family resemblances." In an influential article, Bambrough (1960–1961) claimed that Wittgenstein actually "solved" the problem of universals with this concept. Wittgenstein argued, in effect, that the things named by a general term may not resemble each other in any single way, but may in fact share multiple, overlapping resemblances. In Wittgenstein's paradigmatic case of "games," for example, one kind of game resembles another in one way, while the second may resemble a third in quite a different manner, and so on. Because of these multiple, overlapping resemblances, no single property, nor even any one type of resemblance, is shared by all the activities we call "games." Still, the use of the general term "game" is not completely arbitrary; the multiple resemblances shared by different games make them sufficiently "alike" that the meaning of the term can be taught to someone learning our language without crippling confusion. The influence of Wittgenstein's concept of family resemblances on psychological theories of classification was also described by Rosch (1987).

According to Bambrough (1960–1961), both nominalists and realists are right in some respects and wrong in others. The nominalist is right to deny that all the things named by a general term must possess something in common, but wrong to assert that our use of such terms is therefore arbitrary (i.e., that they are "only names"). The realist is correct in denying the arbitrariness of general names, but wrong in assuming that this nonarbitrariness entails common properties or relations. Wittgenstein solved the problem by recognizing the ways in which nominalists and realists are both right and by rejecting the ways in which they are wrong: Because of family resemblances, one can affirm that our use of general terms is nonarbitrary without thereby assuming that the things named by general terms must necessarily share common properties or relations.

Other philosophers (McCloskey, 1964) have doubted that Wittgenstein really solved the problem of universals, even while agreeing with the general thrust of his argument. For one thing, not all general terms actually refer to families of the kind that Wittgenstein described; many such terms (e.g., "triangle") really can be defined in terms of common properties ("having three angles"). This is not to say that family-resemblance concepts are anomalous, but it does imply that many of the issues associated with the problem of universals remain in the case of these "classical" concepts, based on common properties or relations.

In one respect, however, Wittgenstein may be said to have affected the form in which the problem of universals is likely to be debated in the future. By showing that general terms can be meaningfully employed without assuming any common referent among the things that it names, he effectively knocked one of the last supports out from under a traditional argument for realism: the idea that one must assume the existence of universals as the referents of general terms. This proposition has variously been called "the argument from meaning" (Armstrong, 1978a) or "the problem of naming" (McCloskey, 1964). Both Armstrong and McCloskey considered this semantic issue to have confused the traditional discussion of the problem of universals. More important to these authors was the problem of genera and species (to what extent our classifications and conceptualizations of reality can be said to reflect real categories in nature) and what might be called the problem of *scientific realism* (to what extent the natural laws discovered by science can be said to reflect universal relations among real categories of natural events). On these issues depends another: to what extent our conceptualizations and theories about reality can properly be said to constitute valid knowledge, as opposed to mere belief. Piaget's work is relevant to the problem of universals primarily with respect to issues such as these.

Induction and scientific change. According to Armstrong's (1978b) theory of universals and scientific realism, a natural law can be characterized as a relation among universals (i.e., among the real properties and relations pertaining to particular things). As such, natural laws constitute second-order universals. Armstrong's scientific realism is an argument for the existence of both first-order universals (the properties and relations of particular things) and second-order universals (the formal properties and nomic relations among the properties and relations of particular things) and for the thesis that such universals are known by science.

This conceptualization of natural laws as second-order universals raises all the epistemological problems traditionally associated with the problem of universals. Science presumably arrives at knowledge through observation and experiment. But because all observation and experiment rest on the experience of particular objects and events, one must ask how scientists can go beyond mere acquaintance with these particulars to the knowledge of universal laws. Traditionally, philosophers have tried to bridge this gap by appealing to a principle of *induction*. As formulated by B. Russell (1912/1967), for example, this principle states that if two kinds of things are found to be associated with one another a sufficient number of times, then the probability that they will be similarly associated in the future approaches certainty without limit. As opposed to this, Hume's denial of necessity in causal relations can be viewed as a denial of any logical principle of induction. According to Hume, nothing in the constant conjunction of particulars justifies the inference of a universal law. The movement from particular cases to universal laws can be explained only in terms of habit or custom – a psychological propensity to generalize from our experiences.

The more serious consequence of this view is that beliefs regarding natural ''laws'' cannot aspire to universal validity, for they have no rational justification. Yet this conclusion conflicts with certain of our intuitions; given the successes of the natural sciences in this century, we are reluctant to deny that science has attained some degree of valid knowledge. Thus, a number of philosophers of science have sought to restore to science the rationality denied by Hume.

One such philosopher was Popper (1979). In his autobiography, Popper described how (like Piaget) he had become fascinated with the problem of universals as a young man (Schlipp, 1974). For Popper, however, the problem of universals had less to do with the problem of general terms than with the problem of universal laws. Popper essentially accepted Hume's denial of induction as a means of attaining knowledge about universal laws, but he rejected Hume's psychological account. Instead, scientific progress was described in terms of a progressive process of conjecture and error elimination. In order to solve particular problems, scientists construe hypotheses in the form of conjectures ("bold guesses"). These conjectures are then subjected to criticism of various kinds, and errors are eliminated through the rejection of hypotheses that do not survive the tests of criticism. The elimination of errors through criticism leads to new problems, and the cycle is repeated. The rationality of science, according to Popper, is based on criticism rather than justification (Bartley, 1984). Although one never arrives at certain knowledge of universal laws through this process, one can be assured that scientific theories will be characterized by ever increasing "verisimilitude." That is, the progressive elimination of errors guarantees that scientific theories continually approach the truth, even if they never reach it. This kind of scientific realism has been called "convergent realism": The world is believed to have a real structure that can be progressively better known, even if it is never known in its entirety.

Despite the appeal of Popper's theory, it has itself been subject to many criticisms, only a few of which can be dealt with here. First, Popper appeared to acknowledge rationality in science only after the fact – that is, only in the criticism of theories after they have once been formulated. This position denies, in effect, that the process of scientific discovery and the formulation of theories can also have a rational character. Some philosophers (Harré, 1985) have argued that the process of discovery is also governed by certain rational principles, even if the latter are not adequately described by principles of induction. Second, one might object to the doctrine of verisimilitude combined with the theory of truth as a correspondence between theoretical statements and objective facts. The doctrine of verisimilitude is supposed to replace the assumption of knowledge of the truth with continuous progress toward the truth. But how can one know that one is approaching the truth without already knowing what the truth is? Third, the idea that two or more theories can be compared in terms of relative verisimilitude assumes that there is a common language in terms of which those theories can be compared. In order for a rational choice among theories to be made on the basis of their relative truth content, those theories must at least be commensurable in this respect. This assumption has been denied, most notably by Kuhn (1965) and Feyerabend (1975).

From historical examples of scientific change, both Kuhn and Feyerabend argued that the meanings of the terms used in different theories vary as a function of their employment in different theoretical contexts. This principle holds true for both "theoretical" and "observational" terms. Thus, no common language exists in terms of which the theories can be objectively compared. The very criterion of relevant evidence changes from one theory to another. In this respect, the theories are incommensurable. This position appears to deny the possibility of any rational comparison among rival theories, and indeed, both Kuhn and Feyerabend pointed to nonrational factors in the transition from one theory to another in moments of revolutionary change in science. Kuhn likened the "paradigm shift" that occurs in scientific revolutions to the "Gestalt shift" occurring when an ambiguous figure is suddenly perceived in a different way. Feyerabend wrote that scientific revolutions are effected as much by persuasion and propaganda as by rational argument.

However, such incommensurability among theories does not necessarily imply that theories are incomparable in all respects (as many critics of Kuhn and Feyerabend have assumed). As Feyerabend (1977) once wrote, his conception of incommensurability may imply an incomparability among theories with respect to truth content or verisimilitude, but it does not preclude other bases of comparison, such as coherence, simplicity of solutions, and predictive power. The question of how such criteria are to be defined and specified in particular cases, of course, remains. Feyerabend added that although these other criteria of comparison are "reasonable" in a general sense, they are not totally objective. For one thing, they are likely to lead to differing results. Two different theories may be equally coherent, or one theory may be at the same time more coherent and less simple than another. For this reason, the subjective preferences of individual scientists are likely to come into play alongside rational considerations. Kuhn (1976) also affirmed that his conception of incommensurability does not preclude all forms of comparison among theories, but only point-by-point comparisons in terms of a common language.

Other philosophers of science have argued that Kuhn and Feyerabend overstated the nonrationality of scientific change. For example, Shapere (1984) wrote that the differences in meaning between the same terms as employed in two different theoretical contexts are not absolute. Degrees of variance or invariance of meaning among theories and, consequently, degrees of commensurability, can be shown to exist. In many cases, such partial commensurability may be sufficient to permit rational comparisons among theories with respect to their consistency with observation. Similarly, Lakatos (1970) argued that even if theories are incommensurable to begin with, they can be made to be comparable with the help of what he called "methodological falsificationism."

Lakatos distinguished between "naive" and "sophisticated" falsificationism. According to the former, theories are falsified by facts that contradict them. The problem with this view is that theories faced with apparently contradictory evidence can always be "saved" by modifying the theory so as to account for the facts in question. Nor is this maneuver essentially irrational or intellectually dishonest; one might argue that the evidence runs counter to prediction not because it truly contradicts the theory but because of other facts consistent with the theory that were not taken into consideration in deriving the original prediction. Such a conclusion might even prove fruitful insofar as it sets off a search for the "other facts" in question. This invulnerability of theories to falsification, however, raises the question of how any theory comes to be eliminated. Sophisticated falsificationism addresses this problem by admitting that theories are never falsified merely by facts alone. Rather, a theory is falsified (i.e., considered a candidate for rejection) when (a) another theory exists that explains all the same facts as the original theory and more and (b) some of this excess content is corroborated by evidence.

One might object that this sophisticated falsificationism at most characterizes scientific change in its "normal" periods, not during periods of revolutionary change, for the comparison between theories required by sophisticated falsificationism presupposes that the theories are comparable with respect to content. According to Feyerabend and Kuhn, however, such commensurability between theories does not obtain in periods of revolutionary change. Lakatos acknowledged that "research programs," like Kuhn's "paradigms," may be in some sense incommensurable with each other, but he argued that such incommensurability need not preclude rational comparison. Even incommensurable research programs can be compared on the basis of the internal dynamics of growth within each of them, rather than on the basis of their respective contents. Other things being equal, a research program characterized by "progressive problem shifts" (a series of theories leading to new facts) is preferable to research programs characterized by "degenerating problem shifts" (a sequence of development in which no new facts are discovered).

Whether or not this approach provides a satisfactory answer to the challenge to scientific rationality posed by the hypothesis of incommensurability is an open question. Lakatos admitted, in effect, that the content of theories need not be the only basis of rational comparison between them. But his solution still assumes that the relative progressiveness of competing research programs can be unambiguously determined, and such comparison may not be possible if the research programs are indeed incommensurable. Another problem in determining relative progressiveness was pointed out by Feyerabend (1970): How long must one wait before being in a position to decide whether a given research program is progressing or degenerating? A research program that appears to be degenerating might in fact progress if allowed to continue.

In a manner reminiscent of Lakatos, Laudan (1977) argued that rational choice between incommensurable research traditions is possible, based on their adequacy and rate of progress in solving the problems they have set for themselves. Against this proposal, Feyerabend (1981) replied that what is considered to be a problem in one research tradition may not be so considered in another, and the rate of progress of a new research tradition is unlikely to be known at the time it is adopted. Thus, choosing between research traditions based on their relative adequacy and progressiveness in problem solving may be impossible in practice, and in any case the historical record indicates that choices among research traditions have not in fact been made in this fashion.

A further attempt to deal with the problems of scientific change was the "structuralist" approach of Sneed (1971) and Stegmüller (1976, 1979). This point of view departs from previous philosophies of science that have considered theories as collections of statements or propositions. In contrast to the "statement view," Sneed and Stegmüller defined theories as consisting of two basic components: a mathematical structure and an (open) set of intended applications. This definition allowed them to distinguish between "normal" and "revolutionary" scientific progress in a rigorous way. "Normal" progress consists in progressive extensions of the core-structure and/or a widening of the set of intended applications. In contrast, "revolutionary" change is the replacement of one core-structure with another. Both types of changes can be "progressive," defined, following Lakatos, as the replacement of one theory by another such that the new theory accomplishes everything the old theory accomplished and more. In the case of the revolutionary replacement of core-structures, progress can be formally defined in terms of a "reduction" relation: Generally speaking, one theory is "reducible" to another if the core-structure of the first can be reconstructed as a special case of the second.

The structuralist approach allows for certain kinds of incommensurability between theories, but denies that such incommensurabilities preclude all rational comparison leading to genuine "progress." The most extreme kind of incommensurability would appear to follow from a strong view of the theory ladenness of observation (Stegmüller, 1979). According to such a view, what counts as a fact or even a valid phenomenon can itself vary from one theory to another. Any comparison between theories in terms of the facts they can explain is precluded, because what counts as a "fact" varies in each case. In order to understand the structuralist explanation of such "empirical incommensurabilities," the structuralist conception of theory hierarchies must be understood. The structuralist approach is characterized by the fact that it rejects any absolute dichotomy between theoretical and observational terms. Instead, a theoretical term with respect to one theory may be nontheoretical with respect to another. In fact, certain theories can be said to underlie other theories in the sense that the theoretical terms of the underlying theories are nontheoretical terms in the supraordinate theories. For example, physical theories depend on theories of physical measurement, or geometries. What counts as an observation with respect to the physical theory depends on the theoretical terms in the underlying physical geometry. In the same way, topology underlies physical geometry, and mereology (the theory of objects) underlies topology, such that these various theories are related to each other in a hierarchical manner.

Stegmüller (1979) argued that "empirical incommensurabilities" can arise between theories that are based on incompatible underlying theories. Thus, certain empirical incommensurabilities exist between classical particle physics and relativistic particle physics, because they are based on incompatible physical geometries. But this very incompatibility means that the underlying theories are not incommensurable. The empirical incommensurability existing at one level in the hierarchy of theories can be resolved by descending one or more levels in the hierarchy.

In summary, contemporary discussion in the philosophy of science, as described earlier, has revolved around issues raised by the rejection of inductive reasoning. The principle of induction had been used to justify the validity of our knowledge of the world. Hume's rejection of induction accordingly appeared to cast doubt on the validity of scientific knowledge. The resulting crisis of justification can be seen to involve many of the same issues as the classical problem of universals: to what extent our existing beliefs about existing categories of natural phenomena and the causal relations among them actually reflect the structure of reality ("scientific realism"), or to what extent these beliefs are arbitrary, conventional, or subjective (a "nominalism" of sorts). Popper (1979) took an avowedly realist position, arguing that certain methodological procedures guarantee that scientific knowledge will always approach reality, even if it cannot be known in its entirety. In contrast, Kuhn's (1970) comparison between languages and scientific paradigms evokes a form of nominalism. While admitting that "nature cannot be forced into an arbitrary set of conceptual boxes" (p. 263), Kuhn also held that different conceptualizations of reality have been recognized as valid at different times. Although he admitted that later theories may in some (unspecified) sense be "better" than earlier theories, he denied that they can be characterized as better approximations of reality as such. The other authors considered in this section may also be characterized as more or less "nominalist" or "realist," depending on the extent to which they believed the progress of scientific knowledge to converge on the true structure of reality. As we shall see presently, Piaget's epistemology can also be interpreted in these terms.

The foundations of mathematics. As we have just seen, recent discussion in the philosophy of science has been concerned with the question of the extent to which the concepts and theories of the natural sciences can be said to reflect reality as such. In the case of mathematics, the relevant epistemological questions are somewhat different. One question involves the sort of reality, if any, that is denoted by mathematical terms. Any answer to this question must further be able to account for the fact that mathematics can sometimes yield valid insights about objective reality and for the fact that it can yield rigorous results even when it is not directly applied to reality.

As long as mathematics had been viewed as representing truths about the world of experience, these questions were not so urgent. The existence of mathematical entities and the applicability of mathematics could easily be understood on the assumption that mathematics was an idealization of experience. But with the discovery of non-Euclidean geometries and new algebraic systems in the 19th century, such a dependence of mathematics on reality was called into question (Kline, 1980). These systems were not simply abstractions from experience, nor did they clearly apply to physical reality. If mathematical concepts did not ultimately refer to physical realities, to what could they be said to refer? And if mathematics was not an idealization of experience, then how could it ever yield valid insights about the world?

The realization that mathematics was not simply built on reality led to a search for new foundations that would clarify the nature of mathematics and guarantee its consistency. One could no longer assume that the physical truth of mathematics guaranteed that it was free of contradictions. In fact, some of the new mathematical systems were indeed found to contain contradictions in the form of "paradoxes." Set theory, in particular, seemed prone to such paradoxes, one of the most notorious of which came to be known as "Russell's paradox."

Russell (1919/1960) noted that many of the paradoxes of set theory had to do with a set that contained itself as a member. Some sets are members of themselves, whereas others are not. For example, the class of all mathematical concepts is itself a mathematical concept and therefore a member of itself, but the class of all human beings is not a human being, and for that reason not a member of itself. Now consider the class N of all classes that are not members of themselves. Is this class a member of itself? If N is not a member of itself, then, by definition, it *is* a member of itself. And if it is a member of itself, then, by definition, it is *not* a member of itself. Either way, one encounters a logical contradiction.

The search for the foundations of mathematics was motivated by the desire to rid mathematics of such paradoxes and to guarantee its freedom from contradiction. Three major approaches to the problem were proposed. The first, represented most prominently by Frege, Russell, and Whitehead, was called *logicism* and was based on an attempt to found mathematics on logic. The second, represented by Kronecker, Brouwer, and Poincaré, founded mathematics on direct intuition and therefore came to be known as *intuitionism*. The third, represented primarily by Hilbert, was based on the argument that both mathematics and logic should be considered as purely formal systems, and it was accordingly known as *formalism*.

The problem of universals was relevant in this context in that each of these approaches to the foundations of mathematics took a different view of the nature of mathematical reality (cf. Quine, 1980). Logicists like Russell tended to acknowledge the existence of abstract entities corresponding to mathematical concepts, a view that came to be known as "Platonism" because of its resemblance to Platonic idealism. (The use of the label "Platonism" in this context does not imply acceptance of any other aspect of Plato's philosophy.) Because mathematical entities were granted an existence independent of the human mind, this view has an obvious affinity with the *realist* approach to the problem of universals. In contrast, intuitionists like Brouwer tended to admit existence only to concepts whose construction could be described in a finite number of steps. For obvious reasons, this version of intuitionism was called "constructivism." Insofar as mathematical concepts were believed to exist only as products of the human mind, this view was analogous to *conceptualist* solutions to the problem of universals. Finally, formalism denied mathematical concepts any real, independent existence whatsoever. Instead, the object of mathematics was considered simply to be the mathematical symbols themselves. Because such symbols were freed from the requirement that they should stand for anything else, formalism bore a close resemblance to *nominalism*.

The differences among these three points of view were particularly apparent with respect to the question of the existence of infinite sets (Stegmüller, 1956). Platonists have no problem in recognizing an actual, existing infinity. Constructivists, however, recognize infinity as existing only potentially, for an infinite set cannot actually be constructed. Nominalists do not recognize the existence of sets in any case, claiming that the notion of a set containing a number of elements can be completely replaced with the notion of a concrete whole and its parts. So conceived, nominalism has difficulty accepting the existence of any form of infinity (Stegmüller, 1956).

As in the case of the medieval debate about universals, the modern discussion of the foundations of mathematics has an epistemological side as well as an ontological side. In addition to questions about the existence of mathematical entities, questions about the nature of mathematical knowledge have also been raised. In particular: How do new concepts and constructs enter mathematics and become an accepted part of mathematical knowledge? How can the certainty or necessity of mathematical truths be accounted for? On the one hand, mathematics appears to be the product of human invention and intuition, but on the other hand, it is nonarbitrary and can even lead to new discoveries about physical reality. The problem is how to reconcile these two facts. If mathematical concepts are inventions of the human mind, why should they produce necessary results or yield new insights about reality? And if they are not products of the mind, then how do they become known to begin with? One is not surprised to learn that the three major approaches to the philosophy of mathematics provide very different answers to these questions.

For Platonism, the answers to these questions are straightforward. As preexisting ideal entities, mathematical concepts and relations are discovered, not invented. Their rigor and agreement with reality can be explained by a kind of preestablished harmony. The difficulty with this point of view is in explaining how the human mind acquires knowledge of such an ideal world. For intuitionism, mathematical concepts are thought of as inventions of the human mind. Mathematical certainties can be explained by the fact that they are derived from intuition, which in turn is based on real experience. But if this is so, why should mathematics yield insights about reality that frequently are counter-intuitive? To many mathematicians, constructivist versions of intuitionism further appeared to limit the scope of mathematics unduly. Formalism, like intuitionism, views mathematical concepts as products of human invention. In this case, the rigor of mathematics is explained solely by the avoidance of contradiction. But if mathematics is only the manipulation of symbols, then the question of how it can result in new insights about the nature of reality has no clear answer.

These issues continue to be debated in contemporary contributions to mathematical epistemology (Kitcher, 1984; Kline, 1980). Piaget's work on the development of mathematical concepts must also be understood in this context. Genetic epistemology was intended in part to provide a radically new approach to the search for the foundations of mathematics. The novelty of this approach consisted in the fact that it was based on developmental psychology. In effect,

Piaget founded mathematics on the operations of the subject. The kinds of answers that this approach provides for classical problems in mathematical epistemology and how it differs from other contemporary approaches are discussed in the following sections.

PIAGET AND THE PROBLEM OF UNIVERSALS

As recounted in chapter 1, Piaget encountered the problem of universals at an early age. Already as a young naturalist he had addressed the problem of genera and species in the context of biological taxonomy: Do plant and animal species exist as such? Or do they merely reflect arbitrary classificatory schemes imposed on nature by taxonomists? (See Vidal, 1984.) Piaget initially assumed a nominalist position with respect to this problem, denying that biological species were based on any objective reality. This position is reflected in a recently discovered manuscript entitled ''La vanité de la nomenclature'' (ibid.) – the text of a talk he delivered at the age of 16 before the young naturalists' club of which he was then a member. In this manuscript, he argued that the system of nomenclature in biology is ''essentially abstract,'' ''purely artificial,'' and therefore ''without any intrinsic value'' (ibid., p. 101). The same point of view was reflected in ''L'espèce mendelienne a-t-elle une valeur absolue?'' (Piaget, 1914), a short article on the classification of mollusks published 2 years later.

According to Vidal (1984) in his introduction to ''La vanité de la nomenclature,'' the manuscript was written shortly after Piaget's fateful introduction to Bergson's philosophy on the shores of Lake Annecy, as described in his autobiography. A nominalist view of genera and species was even justified in this presentation with reference to a Bergsonian intuition of the continuity of nature. Later, after Piaget had encountered the problem of universals a second time in the lessons of A. Reymond at the University of Neuchâtel, the influence of Bergson was to work in the opposite direction. As described in his autobiography (and recounted here in chapter 1), Piaget articulated his early ideas on genera as relational totalities in the general context of the problem of nominalism and realism. These views were espoused in a manuscript (now lost) entitled ''Réalisme et nominalisme dans les sciences de la vie,'' mentioned in Piaget (1965/1972b) and in *Recherche* (Piaget, 1918). They were viewed as a fulfillment of what he perceived to be a call for a resurrection of the Greek conception of genera in modern science by Bergson (1907/1944). Genera as relational totalities were now seen to possess an organizing tendency of their own, and this tendency was viewed as a possible subject of scientific investigation. His new perspective on the problem of universals can accordingly be labeled a species of scientific realism. It was in any case a rejection of nominalism; Piaget's later denials that logic could be reduced to language can be understood as an implicit denial of the extreme nominalist view that universals are only a matter of linguistic convention. At all levels of development, he believed that logical operations were based in part on the real properties and relations pertaining to the contents to which those operations were applied.

But to label Piaget's theory simply as a form of realism without further qualification is to overlook its distinctive features. For he believed that genera and species as relational totalities existed not only in the external world in the form of natural categories and laws of nature but also inside the mind in the form of cognitive structures. In terms of the traditional labels, one might thus be tempted to call Piaget's approach a realism tempered by a form of conceptualism, although this description does not grasp the essence of his views either.

A more accurate view is – as Bambrough (1960–1961) said of Wittgenstein – that Piaget preserved the insights of both nominalism and realism, while trying to avoid the difficulties of each. In agreement with nominalism, he acknowledged that the mind has a certain latitude in conceptualizing the world. In agreement with realism, he also recognized that these conceptualizations are not purely arbitrary or conventional. Reality provides certain constraints on the mind's constructions, but within these constraints a certain range of alternative possibilities remains. Piaget would perhaps have agreed with Kuhn (1970) in saying that nature cannot be forced into an arbitrary set of conventional boxes, even though different conceptualizations of nature have been accepted as valid at different times (and at different points in development). For Piaget, knowledge and experience arise from the interaction between subject and object – or, what amounts in his case to the same thing, from the interaction between the structures of the mind and the structures of reality. Because of this emphasis on the interactive relation between subject and object, Piaget described his epistemology as a species of interactionism (Piaget, 1947/1950b) or "relativism" (Piaget, 1950/1973a).

What sets Piaget's approach apart from other forms of interactionism (like that of Kant) is its constructive, developmental character. In the context of his theory, psychological investigation reveals that the human mind develops through a sequence of stages, each stage consisting of relational totalities (structures) that are constructed from the interactions among the totalities pertaining to the previous stage. Formal operational structures are constructed from concrete operational structures, which are in turn constructed from preoperational structures (representational schemes), and so on back through sensorimotor and reflex schemes to organic and even inorganic structures. Because the latter are the respective objects of the sciences of biology and physics, this "chain of becoming" connects the knowing subject with the object of knowledge. In other words, a developmental continuity exists between the structures of the mind and the structures of reality that are known by the mind.

This continuity between the knowing subject and organic reality is the essence of Piaget's biological approach to the problems of knowledge. Through the evolution of the knowing subject by way of living organisms, reality, in effect, comes to know itself (Piaget, 1983, p. 41). This curious remark may appear to commit Piaget to some form of metaphysical monism, but things are not quite that simple. In fact, his theory hangs in the space between monism and dualism (or pluralism) without committing itself to either one. For the evolutionary continuity between subject and object both unites the two terms and separates them as well. Because all knowing is an interaction between subject and object, reality must be differentiated into knower and known in order to "know itself." Thus, the evolutionary continuity between subject and object unites them without making them identical. The interaction of subject and object in the process of knowing results from a process of constructive evolution, and for this reason Piaget's epistemology can be further characterized as a species of *constructive interactionism.*[2]

This constructive interactionism can be described as a form of realism, for it presupposes the existence of an epistemological subject and an object of knowledge that in some sense exist apart from their mutual interactions. But Piaget's realism is not a form of "naive" realism; he does not assert that the object of knowledge possesses all the same properties it appears to possess, even apart from the interactions by which those properties are known to us. Instead, his "realism" is a form of "scientific" realism: The object of knowledge can be known to exist along with certain of its properties through scientific investigation. The only properties we can know it to have are those properties that are revealed to us in the course of our interactions with it. The principle is the same from the level of perception, where the subject's perceptual activities interact with external stimulation pertaining to the object, to the level of scientific experimentation, where scientists interact with the object by means of their experimental operations. The most that can be said about "reality in itself," aside from the fact that it exists, is that it possesses the capacity for being known and experienced in particular ways when we interact with it in a certain manner.

The rejection of naive realism raises certain questions regarding the "truth" of our presumed knowledge. How do we know our knowledge of the object is true if we cannot in some sense compare it with the object "as it really is"? Yet such a comparison is ruled out by Piaget's constructive interactionism. In arguing against "copy theories" of knowledge, Piaget (1970d, p. 15) stated that we cannot know if our model of reality is a true *copy* of reality unless we are able to compare it with reality itself. Such a comparison presupposes that we can know reality apart from our copy of it, but only through copying do such theories explain how our knowledge of reality originates. This same kind of objection has frequently been raised against correspondence theories of truth – theories to the effect that our knowledge can be asserted to be true only to the extent that it corresponds with the facts of reality. The problem with such theories is that they beg the question: how we know what the true facts are (Dancy, 1985).

Piaget's rejection of correspondence theories of truth (or "copy theories" of knowledge) leads neither to skepticism nor to a Kantian dualism of phenomena

2 Because Piaget believed the interactions between subject and object to be prior to the subject and object themselves, a more accurate designation of his position might be *constructive transactionalism.* (On this point, see Kitchener, 1985.) This usage has the additional advantage of conforming to Piaget and Garcia's (1983) dialectical triad, *intra-, inter-,* and *trans-.*

and noumena. In his theory, the truth of our knowledge of the world is not absolute, but relative. We cannot assert that our model of the world either does or does not correspond to reality in any straightforward way. Given two models of the world, however, we can in some cases know that one "fits" reality better than the other (cf. von Glasersfeld, 1982). Instead of an unknowable and transcendent noumenon, Piaget described the object of knowledge as a kind of "limit" that can endlessly be approached, but never reached (Piaget, 1983, p. 173). Thus, one model of reality can be known to approach the limit more closely than another.

But how are we to know that one model approximates reality better than another unless we can compare them both with the reality that they are supposed to approximate? Such comparisons are clearly ruled out by Piaget's rejection of "copy theories." His attempt to provide a standard for judging the relative adequacy of different models of reality without recourse to correspondence theories is perhaps one of the most important contributions of genetic epistemology to the general theory of knowledge. His particular solution is best understood in the context of recent discussion of the philosophy of science.

The problem of scientific progress

In the preceding discussion of induction and scientific change, the issues were described in terms of questions regarding scientific progress. For some philosophers (most notably Popper, with his doctrine of "verisimilitude"), scientific change represents real progress toward more valid knowledge of reality as it "really is." In the most general sense, this view can be called "convergent realism," for scientific knowledge is believed to "converge" on reality. In contrast, other theorists (such as Kuhn and Feyerabend) have argued that the incommensurability between "theories" or "paradigms" precludes judgments regarding their comparable validity as representations of reality. Such theorists have often been called "relativists," although both Kuhn (1970) and Feyerabend (1977) denied that they ruled out all possibility of choosing among competing theories or paradigms. The position chosen as "better" simply cannot be known to be a closer approximation of reality than its counterpart; the choice is based on other criteria. This view is best described as a kind of skepticism with regard to convergent realism. In the case of Kuhn (1970), this skepticism took on a nominalistic character.

In describing the object of knowledge as a "limit" of knowing, Piaget allied himself with convergent realism. He differed from Popper, however, in his rejection of a correspondence theory of truth. Such a rejection raises the question of how we can know whether one model of reality approaches reality "itself" more closely than another if we cannot compute the extent to which each model approaches reality.

In order to understand Piaget's particular solution to this problem, one must explore what is implied in his metaphor of reality as a "limit." This metaphor is not original with Piaget, but it has specific connotations in the context of his theory. Consider, for example, the expansion of π. Just as successive expansions of π approach its true value as a limit, so do the successive extensions of our knowledge of the world approach reality, according to Piaget. No "final" or "complete" expansion of π exists, and no final or complete model of reality can be known. Further, one cannot determine that one expansion of π is closer to the true value than another by computing the difference between each expansion and the true value, because the true value is not computable in a finite number of steps. Similarly, one cannot determine that one theory is closer to reality than another by measuring their respective distances from reality, for analogous reasons. In the case of π, however, determining which of two expansions is closer to the true value is relatively unproblematic: Certain rules exist for the expansion of π, and one knows that one approaches the true value more closely with every additional step that is carried out according to the rule.

In the present view, Piaget's solution of the problem of comparison in convergent realism is roughly analogous: One can know that a given model is closer to reality than another not *per impossibile* by comparing both models with reality itself but by gauging the distance that each model takes one *away from one's initial state of ignorance*. This method of justification is Piaget's epistemological "Copernican revolution" (cf. the "evolution from primitive beginnings" described by Kuhn, 1965, p. 169). The validity of this method presupposes criteria (a) for judging that one is traveling in a direction that leads from a state of greater ignorance to a state of lesser ignorance and (b) for comparing relative distances traveled. For Piaget, the study of child development was the means by which such criteria could be identified. By investigating clear cases of developmental progress in forms of knowing during childhood, he hoped to discover criteria for identifying stages of progress from inferior forms of knowing toward superior forms. This goal, already implicit in the program laid out in *Recherche* (Piaget, 1918), was explicitly articulated in *The child's conception of physical causality* (Piaget, 1927/1966a). There, Piaget described the purpose of investigating the development of children's thinking in terms of discovering psychological laws relating one stage of intellectual development to the next. His announced intention was then to extend these psychological laws into epistemological laws linking one stage in the development of scientific thinking to more advanced stages (ibid., pp. 239–240) (see chapter 2).

Piaget's entire opus can be viewed in part as an attempt to articulate such laws of development. For present purposes, his conclusions may be summarized as follows: One form of knowing is developmentally more advanced than another to the extent that it is more *decentered*. This principle is perhaps most intuitively explained in terms of the coordination of perspectives (Piaget, 1980d, chap. 10). One "theory" of an object can be judged as more advanced than another to the extent that it involves the coordination of a broader range of perspectives on that object. Such a theory can be known to approach more closely the object "as it really is" – that is, as it would appear under a coordination of all possible perspectives. Because the number of possible perspectives on the object is infinite, such "complete knowledge" is beyond finite comprehension (much as the "true value" of π is incalculable in a finite number of steps). Nevertheless, we can know that one model of the object approaches the limit of "complete knowledge" more closely than another if we can determine that one of them has developed farther beyond the initial centration on partial aspects and single perspectives. The idea that more advanced forms of knowledge should be characterized by greater universality is hardly original with Piaget; what is new is the attempt to make use of developmental psychology in seeking empirically based criteria for such increasing universality.

The principle of progressive decentration (and the related concept of reflective abstraction) thus plays a similar role in Piagetian epistemology as do rules of expansion in the computation of π: Both are procedures guaranteeing a progressive approximation to the "truth." In other respects, however, the analogy breaks down. Whereas a rule of expansion would appear to provide a unidirectional path toward the approximation of π, decentration allows for multiple routes away from ignorance, depending on which new perspectives, previously ignored, come to be coordinated (cf. Stegmüller's, 1979, remarks on "progress branching"). Piaget's remarks on Chinese science (Bringuier, 1977/1980; Piaget & Garcia, 1983) suggest that he recognized such multiple progressive paths, although he expressed his belief that such alternative pathways would eventually converge. This conclusion indeed follows from the decentration model. Different coordinations of perspectives will tend to converge as the number of perspectives coordinated approaches the (infinite) number possible.

Several philosophers of science have mentioned Piaget in discussions of scientific change (Churchland, 1979; Feyerabend, 1970, 1975; Kuhn, 1971).[3] In each case, Piaget the psychologist has been cited, rather than Piaget the epistemologist. For example, Piaget's observation that children's perception is affected by their conceptual schemes was referred to by Feyerabend (1970, pp. 223–224) in support of the idea that scientists' observations are similarly affected by their theoretical schemes. In effect, Piaget's research was cited in sup-

---

3 Kuhn (1971) discussed Piaget's work briefly in his contribution to *Les théories de la causalité* (Volume 25 of the *Etudes d'épistémologie génétique*). In this chapter, entitled "Les notions de causalité dans le développement de la physique," he stated that he had once told his teacher, the eminent historian of science Alexandre Koyré, that he himself had come to understand Aristotle's physics by way of the children studied by Piaget. To this, Koyré had replied that he himself had come to understand the children studied by Piaget by way of Aristotle's physics! Kuhn went on to describe four stages in the development of causal explanations from the 17th century to the present, arguing that these principles of explanation developed in symbiosis with the new physical theories that employed them. Although each new theory was clearly more powerful than its predecessors in explaining natural phenomena, each new principle of explanation was "simply different" than those that had gone before. Thus, Kuhn apparently admitted the possibility of progress with respect to theories while remaining a relativist in regard to principles of explanation. (But one might ask why principles of explanation could not be progressively ordered in terms of the power of the theories *that they made possible*.)

port of the notion of incommensurability. In fact, Piaget the epistemologist did not embrace the conception of incommensurability. Each succeeding theory was seen to extend the scope of its predecessors through a sequence of reflective abstractions (Piaget & Garcia, 1983, pp. 232–234). Even while allowing for certain discontinuities in the development of science, the basic continuity between successive theories was expressed by the formula that the surpassed theory was always integrated in that which surpassed it (ibid., p. 303).

A similar idea was expressed by Churchland in writing that "the new theory contains as a substructure an equipotent image of the old" (Churchland, 1979, p. 82). But he further pointed out that this "equipotent image" of the old theory is not *identical* with the old theory in its original form. Instead, it is a relativized reconstruction of that theory. For example, Newtonian physics is recognized in relativity theory as being valid within a restricted field of application, although no such restrictions were originally part of Newtonian physics. Thus, a certain continuity can be traced between the two theories, even if they are in some sense incommensurable. This idea of a reconstruction of an "equipotent image" of an old theory within the theory that surpasses it is close to Piaget's idea of how reflective abstraction operates in the history of science (Piaget & Garcia, 1983).

Piaget's epistemology of science is in fact closer to the structuralist view of Sneed (1971) and Stegmüller (1976, 1979) than to the views of Kuhn and Feyerabend. (On this point, see also Ascher, 1981, Fetz, 1980, and Kitchener, 1986.) The comparison is illuminating on both sides. Consider, for example, the Sneed-Stegmüller conception of a theory as consisting of a mathematical structure together with an open set of intended applications. Among other things, this conception enabled them to explain the differences between different types of progress in science. "Normal" scientific progress results when the set of intended applications is successfully broadened or when the mathematical core-structure is extended without changing its basic form. "Revolutionary" progress ensues when one core-structure is replaced by another. In the latter case, a definite reduction relation connects the original theory with the new theory that replaces it.

Each of these points has a direct counterpart in Piaget's theory. Physical knowledge was described by Piaget (1950/1974a) in terms of a logico-mathematical structure accommodated to specific areas of physical content. Here the logico-mathematical structure assumes the role of the core-structure of children's physical theories, and the specific contents to which this structure is accommodated together constitute the set of intended applications. Given this parallel in the conceptualization of theoretical knowledge, what Piaget called "horizontal decalage" can be likened to "normal scientific progress" in the Sneed-Stegmüller conception. Two types of decalages can be distinguished, corresponding to the two types of normal scientific progress: The classical horizontal decalage between different areas of content such as physical quantity, weight, and volume (Piaget & Inhelder, 1941/1974) corresponds to the broadening of the set of intended applications, and decalages based on increases in the number of elements integrated in one type of structure (e.g., between transitivity for three versus four comparison objects) correspond to extensions of the basic core-structure. And if horizontal decalages can be likened to normal scientific progress, the transition from one stage of cognitive development to another in Piaget's theory is comparable to revolutionary scientific progress as conceived by Sneed and Stegmüller. In each case, one structure is replaced by another, and the new structure in some sense incorporates the old one. Piaget and Garcia's (1983) formula that the surpassed is integrated in what surpasses it may be taken as an informal summary statement of the formal reduction relation as stated by Sneed and Stegmüller. In both cases, these ideas have the function of providing criteria for developmental "progress" without recourse to a correspondence theory of truth. (See Stegmüller, 1979, p. 69, regarding his rejection of correspondence theories.)

Whereas the "structuralist view of theories" articulated by Sneed and Stegmüller can help to explicate certain aspects of Piaget's developmental theory, the latter can also aid in concretizing the former. Sneed and Stegmüller explained the theory-ladenness of observation in terms of the existence of "theory hierarchies." Physical theories depend on geometric theories for the basis of their measurements. Similarly, geometric theories depend on underlying topologies, which in turn are based on theories of objects, or "mereologies" (Stegmüller, 1979, pp. 73–75). In Piaget's theory, such theory hierarchies can be concretely identified in the form of developmental sequences in children's thinking. Thus, the development of the "theory of the object" at the end of the sensorimotor period precedes and makes possible an understanding of basic topological relations, which in turn leads to the development of metrical geometries, which in their turn make possible the development of metrical conceptions of the physical world. This sequence does not imply that any of the underlying theories in the hierarchy cease to develop further once they have appeared. The fact that certain levels of physical knowledge presuppose certain levels of geometry does not mean that geometric thinking ceases to develop once it has made a contribution to physical knowledge. On the contrary, the development of new geometries can lead to new theories about the physical world. According to Stegmüller (1979), something similar occurred in the transition from Newtonian to relativistic mechanics: These two physical theories are based on different underlying geometries.

Both Piaget's genetic epistemology and the Sneed-Stegmüller structuralist approach to theories have the added merit that they illuminate the relation between mathematics and the empirical sciences. In effect, mathematics (and, in some cases, logic) provides the core-structures for theories of the world. In this view, the activity of the scientist consists in determining which of a number of possible logico-mathematical structures provides the best model for a particular application, and the activity of the (pure) mathematician consists in the elaboration of structures without regard to their real-world applications. In a very similar manner, Kitcher (1984, p. 159) described the division of labor between mathematics and science in the following way: Mathematics explores the possibilities of theory construction, whereas science determines which theory is correct in a particular case. These reflections bring us to a consideration of the relevance of Piaget's theory for the epistemology of mathematics.

The nature of mathematical knowledge

The simplest way to clarify the particular relevance of Piaget's theory for issues in the epistemology of mathematics is to compare his approach to a recent contribution to this field. Kitcher's (1984) book *The nature of mathematical knowledge* is excellent for this purpose. In this work, Kitcher presented an original approach to the understanding of mathematical knowledge that resembles Piaget's theory in a number of respects. These similarities are instructive for understanding the kinds of answers that Piaget provided for traditional questions in mathematical epistemology. At the same time, the differences between the two approaches point out the unique contributions that Piaget's theories potentially could make to the understanding of mathematical knowledge.

Kitcher began by arguing for a psychologistic theory of mathematical knowledge. His basic claim was that psychological accounts can provide warrants for distinguishing between knowledge and true belief. In particular, Kitcher adopted the empiricist view that mathematical knowledge can ultimately be traced back to perceptual experience. He acknowledged, however, that his basic epistemological views are compatible with other psychological explanations of the origins of knowledge. In any case, he contrasted the psychologistic approach to an "apriorist" account of mathematical knowledge: the view that mathematical knowledge is based on formal proof. Three types of apriorism can be distinguished, depending on their views of mathematical reality. *Realism* identifies mathematical reality with a Platonic world of abstract mathematical entities that exist independent of the human mind. In contrast, *constructivism* identifies mathematical reality with the constructions of the mind. Finally, *conceptualism* derives the truth of mathematics solely from our understanding of the relevant mathematical concepts. Considering each of these three approaches in turn, Kitcher argued that none of them suffices to provide a basis for an apriorist explanation of mathematical knowledge. The basic problem is explaining how the knower can have a priori access to the respective form of mathematical reality (the Platonic world of abstract entities, the constructions of the mind, or the relations among mathematical concepts).

As opposed to all three types of apriorism, Kitcher argued that mathematical knowledge must be grounded in experience. The problem with previous forms of mathematical empiricism was not that they were fundamentally mistaken but that they were based on bad psychology. The solution is not to abandon the link between mathematics and experience, but to replace the faulty psychological assumptions of previous empiricist theories with more adequate ones. The resemblance between Kitcher's solution and that of Piaget is apparent in the following passage:

> I begin with an elementary phenomenon. A young child is shuffling blocks on the floor. A group of his blocks is segregated and inspected, and then merged with a previously scrutinized group of three blocks. The event displays a small part of the mathematical structure of reality, and it may even serve for the apprehension of mathematical structure. I shall try to find a way of construing mathematical structure which will enable us to see clearly why this is so.
>
> Children come to learn the meanings of 'set,' 'number,' 'addition' and to accept basic truths of arithmetic by engaging in *activities* of collecting and segregating. Rather than interpreting these activities as an avenue to knowledge of abstract objects, we can think of the rudimentary arithmetical truths as true in virtue of the operations themselves. By having experiences like that described in the last paragraph, we learn that particular types of collective operations have particular properties: we recognize, for example, that if one performs the collective operation called 'making two,' then performs on different objects the collective operation called 'making three,' then performs the collective operation of combining, the total operation is an operation of 'making five.' Knowledge of such properties of such operations is relevant to arithmetic because arithmetic is concerned with collective operations. [Kitcher, 1984, pp. 107–108]

Like Piaget, Kitcher traced the knowledge of mathematical truths back to concrete operations, to activities involving classification and ordering. The two theories are compared in more detail later. For the moment, we continue our review of Kitcher's theory.

One potential problem with the view that mathematical truths derive from the concrete activities of the subject is that the scope of mathematical possibilities would appear to outstrip the finite set of relevant activities in which a human subject could hope to engage during the course of a limited life span. According to Kitcher, mathematics is not based merely on the operations that we actually perform, but rather on our *idealizations* of those operations: "Arithmetic owes its truth not to the actual operations of actual human agents, but to the ideal operations performed by ideal agents" (ibid., p. 109). Such ideal operations are not pure abstractions, however; they are *grounded on* the real physical operations actually performed by human subjects. "Mathematics consists in a series of specifications of the constructive powers of an ideal subject. These specifications must be well grounded, that is, they must be successful in enabling us to understand the physical operations which we can in fact perform upon nature" (ibid., p. 160).

The constructive derivation of mathematics from the operations of the subject provides at one stroke solutions to the problems of the nature of mathematical truth and the relation between mathematics and reality. In this view, mathematical terms ultimately refer not to a Platonic world of abstract "entities" but to the operations of an ideal subject. Because these ideal operations are "grounded" or based on the real operations of human subjects, mathematics comes to represent the possibilities inherent in reality. In Kitcher's words, "I propose that the view that mathematics describes the structure of reality should be articulated as the claim that mathematics describes the operational activity of an ideal subject" (ibid., p. 111). The capacity of mathematics for describing the operations of an ideal subject (i.e., the possibilities for operating on physical reality) is what distinguishes it from natural science. As Kitcher put it, mathematics explores the possibilities of theory construction, and natural science determines the correctness of particular theories.

The resemblance between these views and Piaget's mathematical epistemology hardly needs to be emphasized. Like Kitcher, Piaget claimed that the "reality" to which mathematics pertains consists in the operations of an ideal (or, in Piaget's words, an "epistemological") subject. Although these "ideal" operations are based on the natural subject's real actions, they are not merely the sum of those actions. Instead, they express a certain range of possible operations that are opened up by the subject's physical operations. The parallels between the two theorists go beyond this basic identification of mathematical reality with the operations of a knowing subject. Like Piaget, Kitcher attempted to specify the concrete operations from which an elementary understanding of mathematics derives. In Kitcher's case, they are operations of collecting and segregating and of correlating things with each other (cf. Piaget's operations of classifying and of placing things in correspondence). Both theorists, moreover, recognized that operations have a recursive character. Several discrete operations of collecting can themselves be collected together. In performing such a higher-order operation, the lower-order operation functions as a content or representation with respect to the higher one. *"To collect is to achieve a certain type of representation, and, when we perform higher-order collectings, representations achieved in previous collecting may be used as materials out of which a new representation is generated"* (ibid., p. 129). The idea of a Platonic realm of abstract entities existing independent of the mind results from a reification of the subject's recursive operations: "Statements which the Platonist construes as asserting the existence of abstract objects, sets, can be recast as statements asserting the existence of operations performed by the ideal subject" (ibid., p. 132). Kitcher even wrote of the possibility of specifying "stages" in the constructive activity of the ideal subject, a possibility that recalls Piaget's stage theory of cognitive development. More generally, both Kitcher and Piaget (in contrast to many previous mathematical epistemologists) were concerned with processes of change and evolution in mathematical thinking. At one point Kitcher referred to his approach as an evolutionary theory of mathematical knowledge (ibid., p. 92). He closed his book with several chapters on the nature of change in the history of mathematics, comparable in scope and intent to the chapters on the development of mathematical concepts in Piaget and Garcia's (1983) *Psychogenèse et histoire des sciences.*

In addition to these considerable similarities between Kitcher and Piaget, some substantial differences exist as well. Beginning with the premise that the operations of arithmetic are based on the operations of the subject, Kitcher went about demonstrating its plausibility by reconstructing arithmetic in the language of "Mill arithmetic." The primitive notions in this reconstruction are the operations of segregating a single object, of ordering operations in succession, of adding operations, and of matching operations. Beginning with the same initial premise, Piaget proceeded differently: by observing the actual concrete operations performed by real children, attempting to articulate the formal properties of these concrete operations by analogy with known logical and mathematical structures, and showing how arithmetic could be derived from these structures. Which of these approaches is more adequate to the task cannot be determined here. In effect, Piaget and Kitcher approached the boundary between psychology and mathematics from different directions: Kitcher from within mathematics, with a few borrowings from psychology, and Piaget mainly from within psychology, with borrowings from logic and mathematics.

Perhaps the greatest difference between Kitcher and Piaget, however, is in their respective conceptions of the psychology on which the epistemology is based. Kitcher's psychologistic approach to mathematical epistemology was avowedly empiricist: Mathematical knowledge is conceived of as ultimately traceable back to sensory experience. Piaget, of course, spent most of his life arguing against empiricist psychologies of this kind. Although Kitcher, like Piaget (1950/1973a), argued that a psychologistic epistemology must be based on adequate psychological theory, he did not devote much time to a defense of the particular psychology on which he based his theory. He suggested that his empiricism would be especially compatible with J. J. Gibson's (1979) "ecological realism," while recognizing that it might be compatible with other psychological theories as well. He exposed one of the main weaknesses in his empiricist epistemology in admitting the assumption that perception functions as a basic warrant for knowledge only to the extent that the acquisition of knowledge through perception is not affected by one's prior beliefs. (He suggested, however, that his basic thesis is also compatible with a more complicated view of perceptual process; see Kitcher, 1984, pp. 18–19.) Certainly this proposition would not be universally accepted in psychology, given the demonstration that perception can be influenced by the expectations of the perceiver (Bruner, 1973). Piaget's research has indicated further that perception is strongly influenced by children's cognitive development (see chapters 5 and 6), a proposition that might be interpreted to the effect that children's perceptual experience is influenced by the structure of their beliefs about the nature of the world.[4]

---

4 The claim that perceptual experience is influenced by cognitive development need not be interpreted as implying that individual subjects perceive external objects only indirectly, through the medium of phenomenal images. The difference between Piaget and J. J. Gibson (1979) *in this respect* is less than has sometimes been alleged (E. J. Gibson, 1969; J. J. Gibson, 1979). Where Gibson wrote of the "extraction" or "detection" of external information by the perceptual system, Piaget (1961/1969) referred to the "assimilation" of external reality to a perceptual scheme. Both Gibson and Piaget described perception as an active sampling process, and Piaget attempted to explain perceptual illusions in terms of the probabilistic character of much of this sampling. But although Gibson asserted that objectively existing information needs only to be attended to, not constructed by the subject from "sense data," Piaget argued that perceptual schemes as patterns of perceptual activities are indeed constructed in development. The organism's contribution to

Indeed, one might argue that Kitcher's operational constructivist epistemology would be more compatible with an operational constructivist psychology like that of Piaget than with an empiricist psychology as such. According to Piaget, mathematical knowledge (and scientific knowledge in general) cannot be ultimately derived from sensory experience, because the latter is itself a function of the subject's repertoire of schemes. Whether at a sensorimotor or operational level, these schemes are derived from action and are themselves forms of possible actions. Functionally, schemes incorporate (or assimilate) the object of knowledge as an essential part of their activity. The fundamental shortcoming of empiricism, according to Piaget, lies in neglecting the activity of the subject (see "The myth of the sensorial origin of scientific knowledge," in Piaget, 1970/1972g). Instead of deriving mathematical knowledge from sense experience, Piaget traced it back to its origins in action – or, more accurately, to the coordination of actions bearing on relevant aspects of reality.

In summary, comparing Piaget's epistemology of mathematics with that of Kitcher is instructive, because the basic epistemological issues are stated more clearly on the whole by Kitcher than by Piaget. However, the basic assumptions of their respective theories are close enough that Kitcher's arguments regarding mathematical truth and the relation between mathematics and reality are immediately relevant for Piaget's theory as well. Both Kitcher and Piaget agree in the fundamental assumption that the operations of the (ideal or epistemological) subject constitute the very "reality" to which mathematics pertains. And the fact that these operations are ultimately grounded in experience (sensory experience, according to Kitcher, and logico-mathematical experience, according to Piaget) explains how mathematics can anticipate reality. Both theorists recognize that children's operations involving concrete objects are germinal in an elementary understanding of arithmetic, and both are interested in describing and explaining the historical evolution of mathematical concepts and practices.

Piaget's logic

Any account of Piaget's mathematical epistemology would be incomplete without considering his ideas on logic, for, as we have already seen in previous chapters (especially chapters 4 and 5), he believed that an essential and nonreductive connection exists between logic and mathematics. According to Piaget, the essential difference between logical and arithmetical operations consists in the iterative or noniterative character of their respective operations: Although the adding of a given class or relation to itself does not result in anything new, the adding of a number to itself yields a new number. Piaget's theory of number was an attempt to explain this iterative character of arithmetical operations in terms

perception lies in the construction of the schemes by which the structure of reality is assimilated, not in the construction of percepts out of "raw" sensations. Piaget (1967/1971c, p. 7) was fond of quoting von Weizsäcker to the effect that to perceive a house was not to perceive something that had entered one's eye, but something into which one might enter.

of a "fusion" of the logical operations of classifying and ordering. Whatever the merits of this particular hypothesis, it underscores the nonreductive continuity between logic and mathematics in Piaget's thinking.

In attempting to evaluate Piaget's operatory logic, one must distinguish between his more general approach and his specific analyses. His general approach can be described as an attempt to represent the formal properties of the actual operations carried out by subjects in solving different kinds of problems. His specific analyses involved the particular structures (e.g., groupings, INRC group, etc.) with which he sought to represent the formal properties of his subjects' operational activities. As Apostel (1982) and Beilin (1985), among others, have pointed out, the general approach to operatory logic can be accepted without necessarily accepting all of the particular structural analyses. However, one can hardly evaluate the particular analyses unless the general project in which they are embedded is accurately understood. According to Apostel (1982), many critics of Piaget's specific structural theories (Ennis, 1975; Parsons, 1960) actually contribute to an understanding of his basic intuitions, once the specific hypotheses are differentiated from his more general goals.

Any evaluation of Piagetian logic therefore presupposes an identification of Piaget's general approach and a conception of the possibilities that it contains. His specific theses can then be seen as a materialization of one of those possibilities, not necessarily the best of them. This point of view is represented in an enlightening article, "The future of Piagetian logic," by Apostel (1982), a logician who was associated with the work carried out at the Center for Genetic Epistemology for many years. In attempting to understand the possibilities inherent in Piagetian logic, this article is a good place to begin.

According to Apostel, the major problem with Piaget's writings on logic is that he attempted to express original intuitions with the aid of existing formalisms. Sometimes the two did not go together. Sometimes they were even at cross purposes. This accounts for much of the bewilderment with which Piagetian logic has been greeted by logicians (Parsons, 1960). In such cases of conflict between Piaget's basic intuitions and his formalisms, Apostel sided with the intuitions, seeking alternative formulations that presumably express these intuitions more faithfully.

One example of such a conflict between the medium and the message is the theory of groupings. Apostel (1982, p. 606) described the true goal of Piagetian logic in terms of the development of logical activities. In this view, the theory of groupings is actually a theory (or fragments of a theory) of classifications and seriations. Piaget described it, however, as a logic of classes and relations, which is quite a different thing. Apostel attempted to spell out the rudiments of a logic of classification and seriation more in keeping with the original intentions of Piagetian logic. Such a logic "is essentially a logic of the thinking and searching subject and this subject should be present in its formalisation" (ibid., p. 576). This thinking and searching subject is, moreover, an evolving subject (and presumably the evolution of the subject should also be reflected in the formalism).

As an example of how such a logic of classification might look, Apostel presented the following hypothetical protocol:

The subject S is . . . grouping objects. Let us consider that (S) he applies a criterion K (fi: colour or volume). Let us follow the behaviour in time. Let us suppose that at a certain stage the subject S either cannot make up his mind, or that he leaves certain things out of the classification, stating that they cannot be classified. Let us now endow the subject S with a growth rule: after n uncertainties and r unclassifieds, use another criterion of classification L (for instance weight or odour), but create a copy of the result of your first classification at the moment when you end applying it. Then continue classifying according to L. Again after f(d) uncertainties and g(r) unclassifieds, abandon the second criterion, create a copy of the result, and try classifying combining K and L together. [ibid., p. 606]

Similar growth rules could be specified for orderings. The similarity between this hypothetical analysis and task analyses in the information-processing approach to cognitive development (Siegler, 1983) is apparent. The major difference – not particularly clear in Apostel's example – is that the application of a rule or an operation, in Piaget's view, never occurs in isolation, but always as part of a total structure. The structure is a simultaneous (or "atemporal") coordination introduced at the appropriate moment into the sequential (or real-time) procedure by which the subject goes about solving the problem in question. Although most of Piaget's work had focused on analyzing the formal properties of such cognitive structures, Apostel (like many information-processing theorists) focused on the temporally ordered organization of procedures. Piaget's later distinction between procedures and structures pointed the way toward an integration of these two approaches (Inhelder & Piaget, 1979; Piaget, 1981a).

Another example of a contradiction between Piaget's intuitions and their expression was his account of the propositional logic characterizing formal operational thinking. According to Apostel, Piaget constantly wavered between two interpretations. The first was the interpretation of propositional logic as the theory of truth functions. The second was the interpretation of propositional logic as the theory of statements about classes and relations. Apostel argued that only the second of these interpretations is original, corresponds to Piaget's valid intuitions, and is of any theoretical interest.[5] In his major work on operatory logic, for example, Piaget (1949/1972a) expressed the 16 binary propositional operations both in terms of truth tables and in terms of intersections between classes (see chapter 5). According to this latter interpretation, the proposition "p implies q" can be represented as the statement that the intersection between class P and the complement of Q (i.e., $\overline{Q}$) is empty, but that the three other possible intersections between P, Q, and their complements (i.e., $P \cap Q$, $\overline{P} \cap \overline{Q}$, $\overline{P} \cap \overline{Q}$) are occupied.

According to Apostel, this interpretation of propositions in terms of classes was Piaget's "major inspiration" with respect to propositional logic, because it

5 According to Osherson (1974), the natural logic of adolescents is unlikely to be based on truth functions because the difficulty of making logical inferences does not appear to be correlated with the number of entries in the corresponding "truth table."

corresponds to his intuition that formal operational thinking develops out of concrete operational thought. "Piaget's intuition demands that our propositions are operations. This means: actions on classifications and networks [i.e., orderings]" (Apostel, 1982, p. 597). But Piaget overlooked both the fact that this interpretation is incompatible with the theory of propositional logic as truth functions and the fact that if propositions are operations on concrete operations, they can be operations on orderings as well as on classifications. In this view, a great deal of work remains to be done in spelling out a "full propositional logic" corresponding to Piaget's original intuitions. Apostel made some suggestions in regard to the direction that such work might take. In particular, he stressed that Piagetian logic must at some point incorporate functional and/or modal logic. Apostel stated that he was led to this conclusion by consideration of the remarks of certain critics of Piagetian logic, especially Ennis (1975) and Parsons (1960). Reading these criticisms with Piaget's basic insights in mind can provide a better understanding of Piagetian logic and how it might be further developed.[6] As noted in chapter 6, Piaget and Garcia (1987) also recognized the necessity for revising Piaget's (1949/1972a) account of propositional logic and offered their own suggestions for such a revision.

The insight that interpropositional operations must be understood in terms of intrapropositional operations (i.e., classifications and orderings) has certain immediate consequences for Piagetian theory as a whole. To begin with, it means that there can be no purely formal stage of development. The "differentiation of form and content" at the level of formal operations is only relative: The contents to which formal operations apply and to which they are adapted are simply more abstract than the contents of concrete operations. Further, the stage of formal operations cannot be considered the "final" stage of cognitive development in Piagetian theory. Indeed, there can be no final stage in Piagetian theory; from the operations at any level of development, higher-order operations can be formed by reflective abstraction. Apostel added that category theory (MacLane, 1972) has a unique capacity for representing such reflexive operations on operations. Piaget's interest in category theory was therefore no mere aberration, but fol-

---

6 Leiser (1982) has shown that the difficulties found by Ennis and Parsons in Inhelder and Piaget's (1955/1958) account of formal operational logic disappear if that account is interpreted according to a particular modal logic. By this interpretation, the task faced by children in Inhelder and Piaget's experiments on formal operational reasoning is generally to determine which of a total set of logical (combinatorial) possibilities are also physically possible (and which are physically impossible). In the process of arriving at a solution, each of the logical possibilities gets assigned a value of physically possible or impossible. Apparently contradictory interpretations of Inhelder and Piaget's formalism in different passages of their book are found to be noncontradictory if they are taken to refer to different states of knowledge: (a) a state of incomplete knowledge in which only some of the logical possibilities are known to be physically possible or impossible; (b) a state of complete knowledge in which all of the logical possibilities have been assigned values as physically possible or impossible. This interpretation conforms very nicely to Piaget's (1981a, 1986) late work on development in children's understanding of possibility and to his insistence on an intimate connection between combinatorial reasoning and propositional logic at the stage of formal operations (Piaget, 1957a).

lowed logically from the recursive character of his theory. (See Wittman's, 1973, 1982, formalization of grouping structure in category theoretical terms.)

The interdependence of form and content at all levels of development further implies that what Apostel (1982, p. 603) called "the myth of global stages" must be abandoned once and for all. If the structures pertaining to any given level of development are adapted to their specific contents (and contexts), then no reason exists to believe that the structures defining a given stage of cognitive development should be applicable to all contents and contexts at once. Properly understood, Piaget's theory in fact *rules out* such lockstep synchrony in stage development across areas of content and contexts. (Thus, Apostel arrived at the same conclusion stated earlier in chapter 7.)

The interdependence of form and content is itself a consequence of the fact that the structures characterizing every level of development were conceived of by Piaget as arising from the interactions of the structures pertaining to the preceding level of development. This constructive character of development is the reason why the structures of thought are developmentally related to the structures of action, and the latter are rooted in still more elementary biological structures. In short, a continuity exists between biology and logic. According to Apostel, this continuity is the core-hypothesis of Piagetian logic: *"Logic and mathematics simply reproduce on the functional level of the interaction of advanced organisms with their environment the self organising properties of life"* (Apostel, 1982, p. 577). In this view, the "fertility" or generativity of mathematics (and of the mind in general) requires no special explanation; it is simply the self-organizing properties of life itself manifest at the level of thought. Piaget's comparisons between cognitive development and biological processes such as morphogenesis and evolution are thus more than metaphors; they are the expression of similar underlying principles of self-organization functioning at different levels of reality: "A generalisation of Piaget's work in the direction of a dynamic theory of self organising systems is an evident prerequisite for the final evaluation of his proposals" (ibid., p. 578). This brings us to a consideration of Piaget's biological ideas.

Evolution, equilibration, and entropy

The idea that there are fundamental "laws of form" that explain the organization of living structures at different levels of reality underlies much of Piaget's biological theorizing. This basic idea explains his penchant for analogies and "partial isomorphisms" between cognitive and biological processes. If such fundamental laws of form really exist, then the basic principles of cognitive organization will be reflected in biological organization, and vice versa. Piaget's theory of the phenocopy, for example, would appear to be based almost entirely on models drawn from analyses of cognitive processes. Just as trial-and-error learning is not a purely random process, because repeated trials are to some extent "directed from the beginning," so natural selection is not a *purely* random process, because the variations subject to selection are likewise directed to some extent from the beginning. The difference is that the repeated trials leading to trial-and-error learning are directed by a goal pursued by the organism, but the variations subject to natural selection are directed instead by an environmental challenge or disequilibrium of some kind. Common to both models is the idea that *"randomness" is relative to a certain range of variation,* and this range of variation can change depending on the boundary conditions governing the respective processes. Both behavioral "trials" and genetic mutations can be generated "at random" (with respect to a given range of possible variation) and still be "directed" (with respect to a wider range of variation). Piaget did not argue that either the theory of trial-and-error learning or neo-Darwinist theories of natural selection were totally *wrong,* only that they were *insufficient* for explaining certain aspects of the phenomena they seek to explain.

With respect to biological evolution, Piaget argued that the phenomenon of the phenocopy (or what most biologists call the "genocopy") cannot easily be explained by simple neo-Darwinist models. In such cases, a phenotypic adaptation is followed by a genotypic adaptation having the same external form. In effect, the genotype "copies" the phenotypic adaptation. The reason why this process is difficult to explain solely in terms of natural selection is that selection operates at the level of the phenotype. There is no reason to expect that selection will favor a genotypic adaptation over a purely phenotypic adaptation if the phenotypes are identical in each case.

Against this general argument, the following points can be made: (a) The phenomenon of the genocopy apparently can be explained in a manner consistent with sophisticated neo-Darwinist models. (b) Piaget's particular theory of directed variation in response to environmental challenge may not be necessary to explain the phenomenon. (c) Some difficulties exist with respect to the mechanisms of his theory. Thus, Waddington (1975) explained Piaget's data on the genetic adaptation of alpine mollusks to their lacustrine environments in terms of what he called "genetic assimilation" – the selection of a capacity to be modified in a certain way by the environment. Piaget (1967/1971c) explicitly rejected this sort of argument, but he may have had an overly simplistic view of what was involved in genetic assimilation (Jablonka Tavory, 1985). The main problem with Piaget's own model is explaining how adaptations occurring at the somatic level can affect the germ cells. Such a mechanism would be required if those somatic adaptations were to be passed to the organism's progeny in the form of hereditary adaptations (ibid.). Perhaps the most that can be said for this model at the moment is that it is not impossible. McClintock (1984), for example, reported cases of genetic variations in plants produced as a response to certain kinds of environmental challenges or "shocks." But the transmission of somatic adaptations to the germ cells is considerably more problematic in sexually reproducing animal species than it is in plants, and how such environmental feedback to the genome could function as a general mechanism in organic evolution remains to be explained.

For these reasons, the worth of Piaget's biological ideas probably lies less in his specific speculations and hypotheses than in his more general vision. As in the case of his theories of logic, one can distinguish between his more basic intuitions and their realization in particular models. One may expect that Piaget's own models and hypotheses might not be the best possible, but this need not invalidate the general approach. As Apostel (1982) hinted in the passage quoted earlier, Piaget's basic intuitions in biology involved the anticipation of a general theory of self-organization applicable to both biological and cognitive levels. In short, the general question raised by Piaget's biological theories is to what extent theories of self-organization might be applicable to both biological and cognitive functioning.

One way of approaching theories of self-organization in biology is through the problems raised by attempts to reconcile biological and physical laws (Schrödinger, 1944/1967). According to the second law of thermodynamics, entropy increases with time; matter tends irreversibly toward a state of maximal disorganization. Organic development and evolution, however, appear to behave differently insofar as they are accompanied by *increasing* order. Yet all living organisms are ultimately composed of physical matter. How can one reconcile this contradiction?

Strictly speaking, the second law of thermodynamics holds without qualification only for closed systems – systems that do not interact with their environments. Organisms, however, are open systems engaged in active exchanges with their environments (von Bertalanffy, 1968). For this reason, organisms can (temporarily) evade the consequences of the second law either by assimilating order from the environment (Schrödinger, 1944/1967) or by "dissipating" their entropy into the environment (Prigogine, Nicolis, & Babloyantz, 1972). In this way, the capacity of organisms and other open systems for organization and development can be reconciled with the principles of thermodynamics. Because this capacity results from interactions among the components of the system and/or between the system and its environment (rather than from an external agent), it has been called a capacity for self-organization (Atlan, 1972, 1979; Brooks & Wiley, 1986; Eigen, 1971; Eigen & Schuster, 1977; Madore & Freedman, 1987; Prigogine, 1980; Prigogine & Stengers, 1984; Roth & Schwegler, 1981) or *autopoiesis,* meaning "self-creating" (Maturana & Varela, 1980; Varela, Maturana, & Uribe, 1974; Zeleny, 1977; Zeleny & Pierre, 1976). A review of existing theories of self-organization is beyond the scope of this chapter (Jantsch, 1981); instead, the general relevance of Piaget's ideas for such theories will be illustrated with some selected examples.

Piaget had already broached the problem of the relations between biological and physical laws in *Recherche* by way of contrasting the "equilibrium of genera" with purely mechanical equilibria (Piaget, 1918, pp. 152–153). The organization of living forms was viewed as being based on the equilibrium of genera, characterized by a balance between the parts and the whole and the conservation of the latter across momentary disequilibria resulting from interactions with the environment. In contrast, mechanical or material equilibria were characterized simply by an equilibrium between the parts. These intuitive speculations can be retrospectively reconstructed as an incipient theory of self-organization. As we have had occasion to see in the preceding chapters of this book, Piaget remained true to these intuitions in the course of his intellectual development.

In the conclusion to "The mechanism of mental development," for example, Piaget (1941) compared cognitive equilibria, such as those embodied in the groupings of concrete operations, to thermodynamic equilibria governing physical systems. Despite some superficial resemblances, Piaget concluded that cognitive and thermodynamic systems probably evolve in different directions. Thermodynamic systems are characterized by an irreversible increase in entropy, but cognitive systems evolve toward greater reversibility. In his haste to underscore the differences between cognitive development and entropy production, he overlooked some parallels: Like thermodynamic processes, cognitive development is "irreversible" in the sense that transitions from one stage to another normally occur in one direction only. And if the reversibility of cognitive operations is considered in terms of a symmetry between direct and inverse operations (Piaget, 1924/1928b, pp. 171–172), then both cognitive and thermodynamic systems can be said to evolve toward increasing symmetry.

After his encounter with the concept of open systems, Piaget realized that organic development and evolution need not contradict the second law of thermodynamics (Piaget, 1964/1967a, pp. 103–104, 1967/1971c, p. 359), although they might appear to do so at first glance. Even more significant for evaluating the contemporary relevance of Piaget's theory of equilibration was his encounter with the ideas of Prigogine during the 1970s. In the opening pages of *The equilibration of cognitive structures*, Piaget (1975/1985) likened cognitive structures to what Prigogine (1980) had called "dissipative structures" (i.e., structures capable of dissipating entropy into the environment). This comparison was spelled out in greater detail on the final page of *Psychogenèse et histoire des sciences*, where Piaget and Garcia (1983) wrote that cognitive structures resemble dissipative structures in five different respects: (a) They both involve dynamic equilibria in regard to exchanges with the environment. (b) These exchanges stabilize the structures. (c) The equilibria in question constitute a form of "self-organization." (d) Each successive structure can be understood only in terms of its predecessors. (e) Their stability is a function of their complexity. However, the two types of structures differ in one important respect: Unlike dissipative structures in general, cognitive structures always integrate within them the preceding structures that they have surpassed in the course of development. Although Piaget and Prigogine differed with respect to their understanding of "equilibrium" and "reversibility," a difference that Piaget believed to be only terminological (Inhelder et al., 1977), they both recognized the potential relevance of their ideas for each other's work (Piaget, 1975/1985; Piaget & Garcia,

1983; Prigogine, 1975, 1976, 1982). Piaget went so far as to proclaim: "Correct or not, I have the conviction of prolonging in constructivist epistemology the way opened by Prigogine" (Inhelder et al., 1977, p. 41).

Thus, Piaget's writings provide a substantial basis for interpreting the equilibration theory as a first attempt at a general theory of self-organization with specific applications to cognitive development. As such, it must be considered alongside other attempts to apply principles of self-organization to psychological processes (Brent, 1978; Goodwin, 1977, 1978, 1982; Maturana, 1980); Thelen, Kelso, & Fogel, 1987). Just as Piaget's specific models of logic can be understood as fragments toward a general theory of operatory logic (Apostel, 1982), so his equilibration theory can be understood as fragments toward a general theory of self-organization.

BEING AND VALUE

In our attempt to understand Piaget's theory in its own terms, one question remains. In chapter 1 we saw how he was inspired as a young man by the problem of reconciling science and religion, or, as he put it in *Recherche,* the order of being and the order of value (Piaget, 1918, pp. 22–23). This was the problem for which the science of genera was to provide a solution. And as our review of his life's work has indicated, his epistemological theory was a vast elaboration of the science of genera as originally outlined in *Recherche.* One may therefore ask to what extent he succeeded in his original task of reconciling science and value.

One difficulty in any attempt to answer this question is the fact that he wrote little on this topic after the last essay on "immanentism" (Piaget, 1930). Most of his later and more familiar works do not deal with problems of value at all. Several interpretations of this fact are possible:

1. Although inspired by the problem of science and religion as a young man, Piaget eventually lost interest in it, having become preoccupied with his psychological and epistemological work. One finds this interpretation in his discussion of his youthful writings in his autobiography and in his description of his "deconversion" from philosophy in *Insights and illusions of philosophy.*

2. Believing that he had solved the problem of science and value to his own satisfaction, Piaget saw no reason to dwell on it in his writings. Once it ceased to be a personal issue, he no longer considered it a theoretical problem. Having defined scientific research as a life-affirming value in its own right, he *lived* his particular solution to the problem in his activities as a scientist.

3. Because his religious and ethical views found little acceptance (and indeed met with strong public criticism), Piaget ceased to discuss these views openly, while continuing to hold them in private. Publicly, he concentrated his efforts in the fields of psychology and epistemology, where his views had met with greater understanding and acceptance. Thus, the problem of science and value was a "personal preoccupation" that may have motivated him as a scientist, but was

"filtered out" of his scientific work by professional and institutional demands. (On the "filtering out" of scientists' "personal preoccupations" from their work, see Toulmin, 1972.)

No choice among alternative interpretations of the mature Piaget's reticence about problems of science and value is possible on the basis of his writings alone. The evidence is ambiguous and complex: (a) Piaget's (1952a) attitude toward his juvenile writings in his autobiography was highly ambivalent: He called them "crude" and "immature," while hinting that they contained the "single personal idea" that had motivated his entire work. One has the impression that he was still very attracted by the ideas they contained, but wanted to minimize their apparent relevance for his scientific theories. One cannot in any case consider his autobiography as unequivocal evidence that he abandoned his interests in ethical and religious questions as a young man. (b) The "deconversion" from philosophy described in *Insights and illusions of philosophy* does not necessarily entail any lack of interest in the problem of science and value; in fact, he had already stated in *Recherche* that the new science of genera – his solution to the problem of science and value – made philosophy as such unnecessary (Piaget, 1918, p. 98). (c) The fact that he wrote about religious topics until 1930 indicates that he continued to consider problems of value as theoretical problems long after he had begun his professional life and presumably had resolved the conflict between science and religion on a purely personal level.

Further, a number of seemingly incidental remarks from his later works can be cited suggesting that he had not totally abandoned his early views. In the conversations with Bringuier, for example, he stated that he still believed in immanence, in the sense that "to believe in the subject is to believe in the spirit" (Piaget in Bringuier, 1977/1980, p. 51). He added, however, that such a belief requires no articulated metaphysics, nor a belief in God as such. Asked by Bringuier if metaphysics and religion did not satisfy a basic human need for unity, Piaget replied that the search (*la recherche*) for unity is more substantial than the mere *affirmation* of unity (ibid.). In his scientific works, one also finds occasional echoes of his youthful writings. In *Biology and knowledge,* for example, he argued against the notion of a transcendental subject with the argument that the epistemological subject is first of all a biological organism, and one should investigate the "immanent organization" of the subject as organism before appealing to any "transcendent organization" (Piaget, 1967/1971c, p. 362). And in the book on equilibration, he defended himself against the argument that the integrating power of relational totalities functions as a kind of deus ex machina in psychological explanation with the remark that if the assimilatory function is a deus, it is the deus "of life [in general] in all its manifestations, not just of cognitive functions" (Piaget, 1975/1985, p. 27; correction based on original text). These marginal comments and parenthetical remarks do not add up to any clear statement of Piaget's views, but they suggest that in some limited sense his earlier immanentist ideas continued to influence his thinking.

Instead of speculating about what the mature Piaget may or may not have thought about his earlier views on religious and ethical matters, a more productive approach might be to reconstruct the *potential* relevance of his life work for such "cosmological" questions using his early writings as a guide. As early as *The mission of the idea* (Piaget, 1916), Piaget expressed his belief that value and meaning in life were provided by the directionality of development and evolution. Similar views were expressed in *Recherche* (Piaget, 1918) and in his religious writings (Piaget, 1922a, 1928a, 1929a, 1930). In this respect, he resembled many other "progressivists," from Comte and Spencer to their latter-day counterparts (Midgley, 1985). But the distinctiveness of Piaget's position deserves to be underscored. To begin with, his constructivism implies that the directionality of development is not teleological. For each stage of development, a higher form of equilibrium exists toward which development tends. There is no final stage of development, nor any foreseeable "omega point" as the goal of evolution. Like other contemporary theories of self-organization (Brooks & Wiley, 1986; Prigogine & Stengers, 1984), Piaget's constructive evolution is open toward the future. Although one can affirm the existence of an ideal equilibrium as an immanent tendency in present reality, one cannot know the ultimate shape of the future nor even assert that it is determined in advance. Behind any present tendencies toward an ideal equilibrium, even higher forms of equilibrium may in time emerge. Such emergent tendencies may not preexist in the present even as concrete possibilities, for constructive evolution is characterized by the emergence of *new possibilities,* not merely the realization of existing ones. In this spirit, Piaget (1950/1973a) consistently denied the possibility of extrapolating developmental trends indefinitely into the future.

This conception of an "ideal equilibrium" is in fact the key to Piaget's reconciliation of the "is" and the "ought," the order of being and the order of value. As we have seen, Piaget (1918, 1952a) believed that a tendency toward the emergence of ever more inclusive relational totalities could be observed on all levels of reality, from the lowest forms of organic matter to the highest forms of human thought and action. In terms of their part–whole structure, such totalities can be described as forms of equilibrium, and the tendency toward emergence as a process of equilibration. This tendency can be observed and described by human beings as an objective phenomenon. At the level of the relational totalities themselves, however, the tendency toward equilibrium also possesses an implicit value in the sense that integrity and conservation of form are intrinsically "better" than disintegration and dissolution. Moreover, the evolutionary continuity between levels implies that each relational totality is implicated in both "higher" and "lower" values: its own integrity as a totality, and the integrity of the next higher totality of which it is a part. In this respect, Piaget's theory of constructive evolution is reminiscent of Koestler's (1978) hierarchy of "holons," defined as systems of relations that constitute both totalities in themselves and components of higher-order totalities.

The hierarchy of values implied by emerging forms of equilibria also exists at the level of human life and consciousness. The integrity of the human organism as a totality of cells, organs, and organ systems is thus valued above its disintegration, as is the unity of human consciousness above its dissolution. But human beings, like other relational totalities in nature, are themselves implicated in relational totalities greater than themselves. The integrity of these greater totalities presents human beings with certain "higher values." Piaget's reconciliation of being and value would seem to consist in the argument that even such higher values can be objects of scientific investigation and, further, that such investigation can, in principle, provide grounds for a relative ordering of values.

For example, one may affirm the norm of reciprocity as a higher value than social constraint, because the former represents a higher-order and (therefore) more stable form of equilibrium than the latter (Piaget, 1932/1965a). The norm of reciprocity is the equilibrium form of relationship among members of an ideal community of equals. To the extent that this norm is realized in the interactions among persons, a higher-order system tends to emerge in which the interests and perspectives of all its members are represented. In the language of Piaget's (1975/ 1985) later equilibration theory, the reciprocal character of interpersonal relations provides the community as a system with built-in regulatory mechanisms by which momentary disequilibria (i.e., conflicts of interests) may be compensated (Piaget, 1965/1977a). In contrast, social constraint results in a form of equilibrium in which the interests of some of its members predominate over those of others. The stability of this form of equilibrium depends on the continued domination by one component of the system over the others. The integrity of the system as a whole is threatened by a constant tendency to dissolve into its opposing component parts. It lacks the regulatory mechanisms of the ideal community of equals.

Obviously, any attempt to apply this method of relative valuation would immediately encounter a variety of problems. Human beings are involved in multiple higher-order totalities that may involve conflicting obligations. Further, the distinction between reciprocity and constraint might not be as clear in practice as it is in theory; as Marx (1849/1952) argued in his analysis of surplus value in the capitalist mode of production, the exploitive character of some social relations is not necessarily apparent on the surface. But the purpose of the present discussion is not to determine how practical Piaget's approach would be in making relative judgments of moral values, but rather to understand his approach as a theoretical solution to the problem of being and value.

In Piaget's (reconstructed) view, the problem arises in two ways at once: (a) from a positivistic science that recognizes only existing reality, not the tendencies toward organization that exist *within* reality, and (b) from a metaphysical religion that cognizes emerging ideals with the categories of the real. Piaget's (1928a, 1929a, 1930) early conception of "immanence" was advanced as an explicit alternative to both of these one-sided views. Against mechanistic science, he argued that a tendency toward higher forms of organization exists at all levels of reality, that this tendency is consistent with natural laws, and that it imbues nature with a hierarchy of values corresponding to the respective levels of organization. Against metaphysical religion, he argued that this same tendency toward higher forms of organization provides human beings with "higher values" in the form of ideals, that these ideals affect reality only insofar as they are embodied in human thought and action, and that, consequently, "God" cannot be identified with any supernatural force that affects the natural world from outside. Instead, God is identified with supreme values and universal norms of thought (Piaget, 1929b, 1930). "God is not a Being who imposes Himself upon us from without: His reality consists only in the intimate effort of the seeking mind [la pensée qui cherche]" (Piaget, 1930, p. 37). Our knowledge of the spirit derives from successive acts of reflection in which a universal normative activity is grasped in particular acts of thought, and a supreme value is recognized in individual acts of valuation. This normative activity is above all evident in its *directionality*, and the latter is manifest in the spontaneous development of thought itself, not in any final goal determined in advance. Individual human beings can find fulfillment by allying themselves with this tendency to realize the ideal. "To struggle for the good and the true is thus, in the fullest sense of the word, to collaborate with God" (ibid., p. 43). Nor is this "struggle" purely intellectual, for "every act of love makes man a collaborator of God's" (Piaget, 1929a, p. 152). This conception would further seem to imply that our struggle to realize such normative ideals is the primary means by which the Deity is active in the world.

The "immanentist" identification of the spirit with supreme values and norms of thought does not mean that it is reduced to the merely human. A God who is immanent in *supreme* values and *universal* norms of thought transcends the individual (Piaget, 1930, p. 45) as well as the norms and values imposed on the individual by any particular social collective. In *this* sense, Piaget (1929b) agreed that God is both immanent and transcendent. Indeed, the immanentist view would appear to imply that the spirit *in its fullness* transcends human knowledge, for like "reality itself," it is known only through successive approximations, as a "limit" that can be approached but never reached (on reality as a "limit," see Piaget, 1983, pp. 41, 173).

"Immanentism" is thus Piaget's resolution of the conflict between science and religion; it is a dialectical synthesis that transcends both positivistic science and metaphysical religion. The conflict occurs only because metaphysical religion, in conceiving the spirit in the categories of the real (especially causality and existence in space and time), asserts propositions that subsequently are found to be false or unnecessary by science. For Laplace, God was an unnecessary hypothesis. But such a statement makes sense only if God is first considered *as a hypothesis*.

Piaget's argument is not that science and religion have their own separate spheres of activity, for the boundaries of science are not fixed (Piaget, 1930, pp. 21ff.). His position is more radical. Instead of limiting oneself to the facts in the manner of positivism or positing a separate realm of metaphysical knowledge beyond that of science, knowledge of the absolute is to be sought *in the very conditions of scientific activity* (ibid., p. 18). Through critical reflection on scientific thought and its underlying values, the existence of the spirit in the form of an "intimate relation" between thought and reality can be inferred (ibid., pp. 30–31). Far from conflicting with each other or reserving exclusive rights to independent territories, science and religion actually interpenetrate one another without losing their respective identities. The successive *prises de conscience* that constitute scientific progress in fact provide one means by which the spirit comes to know itself. Thus, Piaget argued that the views of philosophers from Plato to Kant (and down to the present) on the nature of thought can be shown to have been influenced by the state of scientific knowledge of their day (ibid., pp. 22ff.).

Without claiming to be able to penetrate Piaget's private thoughts on this subject, one can easily imagine how his own scientific activities could have acquired spiritual connotations according to such a view. Genetic epistemology, in particular, acquires a special status as the research of stages in the development of the spirit and of the directionality of this development. In becoming aware in this way of its own progress, the spirit might even be said to have reached a new stage in its knowledge of itself. And in bringing this knowledge to light, the genetic epistemologist becomes the collaborator of the spirit.

Whether or not Piaget's "immanentism" possesses any general validity as a reconciliation of science and religion beyond whatever private significance it may have had for him personally is another question. The criteria for judging any such "reconciliation" cannot be determined in the abstract, but are relative to the concrete historical circumstances in which the problem itself arises. As Piaget might have said, oppositions are overcome through the coordination of perspectives. But social and historical circumstances determine what perspectives exist to be coordinated at a given time. The fact that evolutionary theory continues to be challenged by religiously motivated conceptions of natural origins (Ruse, 1982) and that some evolutionary theories themselves appear to aspire to the status of religion (Midgley, 1985) suggests that questions of the proper relation between science and religion have lost none of their relevance in the present. Piaget's thoughts on this topic place him in the rank of other eminent scientists who have discussed the implications of contemporary science for questions of meaning and value (Barrow & Tipler, 1986; Bohm, 1980; Capra, 1975; Davies, 1983, 1984; Jantsch, 1981; Orlov, 1982). His particular conception of constructive evolution allies him with other thinkers who have sought meaning in human life in the process of evolutionary change (Bergson, 1907/1944; Teilhard de Chardin, 1955/1965; Jantsch & Waddington, 1976; Polanyi, 1958, 1966; Whitehead, 1929/1978). But his ideas were distinctive in a number of respects and deserve to be considered alongside other contributions to contemporary debate on humanity's place in the universe revealed by modern science.

References

Adams, H. (1959). *Mont-Saint-Michel and Chartres*. Garden City, NY: Doubleday. (Original work published 1913)

Anderson, A. R., & Belnap, L. (1975). *Entailment: The logic of relevance and necessity*. Princeton University Press.

Apostel, L. (1982). The future of Piagetian logic. *Revue Internationale de Philosophie, 142–143*, 567–611.

Apostel, L. (1986). The unknown Piaget: From the theory of exchange and co-operation toward the theory of knowledge. *New Ideas in Psychology, 4*, 3–22.

Armstrong, D. M. (1978a). *Nominalism and realism*. Cambridge University Press.

Armstrong, D. M. (1978b). *A theory of universals*. Cambridge University Press.

Ascher, E. (1981). Psychogenèse de l'intelligence et histoire des sciences: Quelques considerations concernant leur modelisation. *Archives de Psychologie, 49*, 231–246.

Atkinson, C. (1983). *Making sense of Piaget*. London: Routledge & Kegan Paul.

Atlan, H. (1972). *L'organisation biologique et la théorie de l'information*. Paris: Hermann.

Atlan, H. (1979). *Entre le cristal et la fumée*. Paris: Editions du Seuil.

Baldwin, J. M. (1896). A new factor in evolution. *American Naturalist, 30*, 441–553.

Bambrough, J. R. (1960–1961). Universals and family resemblance. *Proceedings of the Aristotelian Society, 61*, 205–222. (Reprinted in Van Iten, 1970)

Barrow, J. D., & Tipler, F. J. (1986). *The anthropic cosmological principle*. Oxford: Clarendon Press.

Bartley, W. W., III (1984). *The retreat to commitment* (2nd ed.). La Salle, IL: Open Court.

Beilin, H. (1980). Piaget's theory: Refinement, revision or rejection? In R. Kluwe & H. Spada (Eds.), *Developmental models of thinking* (pp. 245–261). New York: Academic Press.

Beilin, H. (1983). The new functionalism and Piaget's program. In E. K. Scholnick (Ed.), *New trends in conceptual representation* (pp. 3–40). Hillsdale, NJ: Erlbaum.

Beilin, H. (1985). Dispensable and core elements in Piaget's research program. *The Genetic Epistemologist, 13*(3), 1–16.

Bergson, H. (1944). *Creative evolution*. New York: Modern Library. (Original work published 1907)

Beth, E. W., & Piaget, J. (1966). *Mathematical epistemology and psychology*. Dordrecht: Reidel. (Original work published 1961)

Bettelheim, B. (1983). Scandal in the family. *New York Review of Books, 30*(11), 39–44.

Bohm, D. (1980). *Wholeness and the implicate order*. London: Ark.

Borke, H. (1975). Piaget's mountains revisited: Changes in the egocentric landscape. *Developmental Psychology, 11*, 240–243.

Braine, M. D. S. (1959). The ontogeny of certain logical operations: Piaget's formulation examined by nonverbal methods. *Psychological Monographs: General and Applied, 73*(5, Whole No. 475), 1–43.

Braine, M. D. S. (1964). Development of a grasp of transitivity of length: A reply to Smedslund. *Child Development, 35,* 799–810.

Brainerd, C. J. (1973a). Judgments and explanations as criteria for the presence of cognitive structures. *Psychological Bulletin, 79,* 172–179.

Brainerd, C. J. (1973b). Order of acquisition of transitivity, conservation, and class inclusion of length and weight. *Developmental Psychology, 8,* 105–116.

Brainerd, C. J. (1973c). The origins of number concepts. *Scientific American, 228*(3), 101–109.

Brainerd, C. J. (1974). Training and transfer of transitivity, conservation, and class inclusion of length. *Child Development, 45,* 324–334.

Brainerd, C. J. (1977). Response criteria in concept development. *Child Development, 48,* 360–366.

Brainerd, C. J. (1978a). *Piaget's theory of intelligence.* Englewood Cliffs, NJ: Prentice-Hall.

Brainerd, C. J. (1978b). The stage question in cognitive-developmental theory. *The Behavioral and Brain Sciences, 2,* 173–182.

Brainerd, C. J. (1979). *The origins of the number concept.* New York: Praeger.

Brainerd, C. J., & Fraser, M. (1975). A further test of the ordinal theory of number development. *Journal of Genetic Psychology, 127,* 21–33.

Brainerd, C. J., & Kingma, J. (1984). Do children have to remember to reason? A fuzzy-trace theory of transitivity development. *Developmental Review, 4,* 311–377.

Brainerd, C. J., & Kingma, J. (1985). On the independence of short-term memory and working memory in cognitive development. *Cognitive Psychology, 17,* 210–247.

Brent, S. B. (1978). Prigogine's model for self-organization in nonequilibrium systems: Its relevance for developmental psychology. *Human Development, 21,* 374–387.

Bringuier, J.-C. (1980). *Conversations with Jean Piaget.* University of Chicago Press. (Original work published 1977)

Brooks, D. R., & Wiley, E. O. (1986). *Evolution as entropy.* University of Chicago Press.

Broughton, J. (1981). Piaget's structural developmental psychology. IV. Knowledge without a self and without a history. *Human Development, 24,* 320–346.

Brown, T., & Weiss, L. (1987). Structures, procedures, heuristics, and affectivity. *Archives de Psychologie, 55,* 59–94.

Bruner, J. S. (1964). The course of cognitive growth. *American Psychologist, 19,* 1–15.

Bruner, J. S. (1973). *Beyond the information given.* New York: Norton.

Bruner, J. S. (1983). State of the child. *New York Review of Books, 30*(16), 83–89.

Bryant, P. E. (1974). *Perception and understanding in young children.* London: Methuen.

Bryant, P. E., & Trabasso, T. (1971). Transitive inferences and memory in young children. *Nature, 232,* 456–458.

Buck-Morss, S. (1975). Socio-economic bias in Piaget's theory and its implications for cross-culture studies. *Human Development, 18,* 35–49.

Bullinger, A., & Chatillon, J.-F. (1983). Recent theory and research of the Genevan school. In P. H. Mussen (Ed.), *Handbook of child psychology* (4th ed., Vol. 3, pp. 231–262). New York: Wiley.

Bunge, M. (1963). *Causality* (2nd ed.). Cleveland: Meridian.

Bunge, M. (1971). Conjonction, succession, détermination, causalité. In M. Bunge, F. Halbwachs, T. S. Kuhn, J. Piaget, & L. Rosenfeld (Eds.), *Les théories de la causalité* (pp. 112–132). Paris: Presses Universitaires de France.

Burger, J.-D. (1929). Pour le transcendance. *Revue de Théologie et de Philosophie, 17,* 33–40.

Buss, A. R. (1978). Causes and reasons in attribution theory: A conceptual critique. *Journal of Personality and Social Psychology, 11,* 1311–1321.

Capra, F. (1975). *The tao of physics.* New York: Bantam.

Carotenuto, A. (1982). *A secret symmetry: Sabina Spielrein between Jung and Freud.* New York: Pantheon.

Case, R. (1985). *Intellectual development: Birth to adulthood.* Orlando, FL: Academic Press.

Chapman, M. (1986). The structure of exchange: Piaget's sociological theory. *Human Development, 29,* 181–194.

Chapman, M. (1987a). Piaget, attentional capacity, and the functional implications of formal structure. In H. W. Reese (Ed.), *Advances in child development and behavior* (Vol. 20, pp. 229–334). Orlando, FL: Academic Press.

Chapman, M. (1987b). Inner processes and outward criteria. Wittgenstein's importance for psychology. In M. Chapman & R. A. Dixon (Eds.), *Meaning and the growth of understanding: Wittgenstein's significance for developmental psychology* (pp. 103–127). Berlin: Springer-Verlag.

Chapman, M. (1987c). A longitudinal study of cognitive representation in symbolic play, self-recognition, and object permanence during the second year. *International Journal for Behavioral Development, 10,* 151–170.

Chapman, M., & Lindenberger, U. (1988). Functions, operations, and decalage in the development of transitivity. *Developmental Psychology,* in press.

Churchland, P. M. (1979). *Scientific realism and the plasticity of mind.* Cambridge University Press.

Cohen, D. (1983). *Piaget: Critique and reassessment.* London: Croom Helm.

Cooper, R. G., Jr. (1984). Early number development: Discovering number space with addition and subtraction. In C. Sophian (Ed.), *Origins of cognitive skills* (pp. 157–192). Hillsdale, NJ: Erlbaum.

Corrigan, R. (1979). Cognitive correlates of language: Differential criteria yield differential results. *Child Development, 50,* 617–631.

Cowan, P. A. (1978). *Piaget: With feeling.* New York: Holt, Rinehart & Winston.

Dancy, J. (1985). *An introduction to contemporary epistemology.* Oxford: Blackwell.

Davies, P. (1983). *God and the new physics.* Harmondsworth, Middlesex: Penguin.

Davies, P. (1984). *Superforce.* London: Unwin.

De Rivera, J. (1976). *A structural theory of the emotions.* New York: International Universities Press.

Ducret, J.-J. (1984). *Jean Piaget, savant et philosophe* (2 vols.). Geneva: Librairie Droz.

Durkheim, E. (1973). *Moral education.* New York: Free Press. (Original work published 1925)

Edelstein, W. (1983). Cultural constraints on development and the vicissitudes of progress. In F. S. Kessel & A. W. Siegel (Eds.), *The child and other cultural inventions* (pp. 49–81). New York: Praeger.

Eigen, M. (1971). Selforganization of matter and the evolution of biological macromolecules. *Die Naturwissenschaften, 58,* 465–523.

Eigen, M., & Schuster, P. (1977). The hypercycle. *Die Naturwissenschaften, 64,* 541–565, *65,* 7–41, 341–369.

Ennis, R. H. (1975). Children's ability to handle propositional logic. *Review of Educational Research, 45,* 1–41.

Erikson, E. K. (1968). *Identity, youth and crisis.* New York: Norton.

Ewing, A. C. (1952). *The fundamental questions of philosophy.* London: Routledge & Kegan Paul.

Fetz, R. L. (1982). Pour une ontologie génétique: Jean Piaget et la philosophie moderne. *Revue Internationale de Philosophie, 142–143,* 409–434.

Fetz, R. L. (1980). Histoire des sciences et épistémologie génétique: A propos des thèses de Kuhn et de leur "reconstruction logique" (Non Statement View). *Archives de Psychologie, 48,* 201–214.

Feyerabend, P. K. (1970). Consolations for the specialist. In I. Lakatos & A. Musgrove (Eds.), *Criticism and the growth of knowledge* (pp. 197–230). Cambridge University Press.

Feyerabend, P. K. (1975). *Against method.* London: NLB.

Feyerabend, P. K. (1977). Changing patterns of reconstruction. *British Journal for the Philosophy of Science, 28,* 351–382.

Feyerabend, P. K. (1978). *Science in a free society.* London: Verso.

Feyerabend, P. K. (1981). More clothes from the emperor's bargain basement: A review of Laudan's *Progress and its problems.* In P. K. Feyerabend, *Problems of empiricism* (pp. 231–246). Cambridge University Press.

Fischer, K. W. (1978). Open peer commentary. *Behavioral and Brain Sciences, 2,* 186–187.

Fischer, K. W. (1980). A theory of cognitive development: The control and construction of hierarchies of skills. *Psychological Review, 87,* 477–531.

Flavell, J. H. (1963). *The developmental psychology of Jean Piaget.* Princeton, NJ: Van Nostrand.

Flavell, J. H. (1971). Stage-related properties of cognitive development. *Cognitive Psychology, 2,* 421–452.

Flavell, J. H. (1977). *Cognitive development.* Englewood Cliffs, NJ: Prentice-Hall.

Flavell, J. H., & Wohlwill, J. F. (1969). Formal and functional aspects of cognitive development. In D. Elkind & J. H. Flavell (Eds.), *Studies in cognitive development* (pp. 67–120). New York: Oxford University Press.

Furth, H. G. (1980). *The world of grown-ups: Children's conceptions of society.* New York: Elsevier.

Furth, H. G. (1986). The social function of Piaget's theory: A response to Apostel. *New Ideas in Psychology, 4,* 23–29.

Garcia, R. (1980). Dialectique, psychogenèse et histoire des sciences. In J. Piaget, *Les formes élémentaires de la dialectique* (pp. 229–249). Paris: Gallimard.

Gelman, R. (1972). Logical capacity of very young children: Number invariance rules. *Child Development, 43,* 75–90.

Gelman, R., & Baillargeon, R. (1983). A review of some Piagetian concepts. In P. H. Mussen (Ed.), *Handbook of child psychology* (4th ed., Vol. 3, pp. 167–230). New York: Wiley.

Gesell, A., & Ilg, F. L. (1943). *Infant and child in the culture of today.* New York: Harper.

Gesell, A., & Ilg, F. L. (1946). *The child from five to ten.* New York: Harper.

Gibson, E. J. (1969). *Principles of perceptual learning and development.* New York: Appleton-Century-Crofts.

Gibson, J. J. (1979). *The ecological approach to visual perception.* Boston: Houghton Mifflin.

Goldmann, L. (1959). *Recherches dialectiques.* Paris: Gallimard.

Goodwin, B. C. (1977). Cognitive biology. *Communication and Cognition, 10,* 87–91.

Goodwin, B. C. (1978). A cognitive view of biological process. *Journal of Social and Biological Structures, 1,* 117–125.

Goodwin, B. C. (1982). Genetic epistemology and constructivist biology. *Revue Internationale de Philosophie, 142–143,* 527–548.

Gréco, P., Grize, J.-B., Papert, S., & Piaget, J. (1960). *Problèmes de la construction du nombre.* Paris: Presses Universitaires de France.

Green, D. R. (Ed.). (1971). *Measurement and Piaget*. New York: McGraw-Hill.

Grize, J.-B., Henry, K., Meylan-Backs, M., Orsini, F., Piaget, J., & Van Den Bogaert-Rombouts, N. (1966). *L'épistémologie du temps*. Paris: Presses Universitaires de France.

Gruber, H. E. (1982). Piaget's mission. *Social Research, 49*, 239–264.

Gruber, H. E., & Vonèche, J. J. (Eds.). (1977). *The essential Piaget*. New York: Basic Books.

Halford, G. (1982). *The development of thought*. Hillsdale, NJ: Erlbaum.

Hamlyn, D. (1978). *Experience and the growth of understanding*. London: Routledge & Kegan Paul.

Harré, R. (1985). *The philosophies of science* (2nd ed.). New York: Oxford University Press.

Hegel, G. W. F. (1967). *The phenomenology of mind*. New York: Harper Torchbooks. (Original work published 1807)

Hegel, G. W. F. (1982). *Vorlesungen über die Geschichte der Philosophie* (3 vols.). Leipzig: Reclam. (Original work published 1833)

Hooper, F. H., Toniolo, T. A., & Sipple, T. S. (1978). A longitudinal analysis of logical reasoning relationships: Conservation and transitive inference. *Developmental Psychology, 14*, 674–682.

Hume, D. (1957). A treatise of human nature. In T. V. Smith & M. Grene (Eds.), *Philosophers speak for themselves: Berkeley, Hume, and Kant*. (pp. 102–252). University of Chicago Press. (Original work published 1739)

Hutchins, R. M. (Ed.). (1952). *Great books of the Western world* (54 vols.). Chicago: Encyclopaedia Britannica.

Huttner, J. (1982). Egocentrism: A defense of pre-reflexive experience. *Revue Internationale de Philosophie, 142–143*, 508–526.

Inhelder, B., Garcia, R., & Vonèche, J. (Eds.). (1977). *Epistémologie génétique et équilibration*. Neuchâtel: Delachaux et Niestlé.

Inhelder, B., & Piaget, J. (1958). *The growth of logical thinking from childhood to adolescence*. New York: Basic Books. (Original work published 1955)

Inhelder, B., & Piaget, J. (1969). *The early growth of logic in the child*. New York: Norton. (Original work published 1959)

Inhelder, B., & Piaget, J. (1979). Procedures et structures. *Archives de Psychologie, 47*, 165–176.

Inhelder, B., Sinclair, H., & Bovet, M. (1974). *Learning and the development of cognition*. London: Routledge & Kegan Paul.

Jablonka Tavory, E. (1985, July). *Piagetian ambiguities and problems in biology*. Paper presented at a meeting of the International Society for the Study of Behavioural Development, Tours.

Jamison, W. (1973). Developmental interrelationships among concrete operational tasks: An investigation of Piaget's stage concept. *Journal of Experimental Child Psychology, 24*, 235–253.

Jantsch, E. (1981). *The self-organizing universe*. New York: Praeger.

Jantsch, E., & Waddington, C. (1976). *Evolution and consciousness*. Reading, MA: Addison-Wesley.

Jaspers, K. (1954). *Way to wisdom*. New Haven: Yale University Press. (Original work published 1950)

Kemper, T. D. (1978). *A social interactional theory of emotions*. New York: Wiley.

Kesselring, T. (1982). *Entwicklung und Widerspruch*. Frankfurt: Suhrkamp.

Kitchener, R. F. (1981). Piaget's social psychology. *Journal of the Theory of Social Behaviour, 11*, 253–277.

Kitchener, R. F. (1985). Holistic structuralism, elementarism and Piaget's theory of 'relationalism.' *Human Development, 28*, 281–294.

Kitchener, R. F. (1986). *Piaget's genetic epistemology*. New York, CT: Yale University Press.

Kitcher, P. (1984). *The nature of mathematical knowledge*. New York: Oxford University Press.

Klein, D. B. (1970). *A history of scientific psychology*. New York: Basic Books.

Kline, M. (1972). *Mathematical thought from ancient to modern times*. New York: Oxford University Press.

Kline, M. (1980). *Mathematics: The loss of certainty*. New York: Oxford University Press.

Koestler, A. (1978). *Janus*. New York: Vintage Books.

Kohlberg, L. (1969). Stage and sequence: The cognitive developmental approach to socialization. In D. A. Goslin (Ed.), *Handbook of socialization theory and research* (pp. 347–480). Chicago: Rand McNally.

Köhler, W. (1925). *The mentality of apes* (2nd ed.). New York: Harcourt, Brace. (Original work published 1917)

Kuhn, T. S. (1965). *The structure of scientific revolutions*. Chicago University Press.

Kuhn, T. S. (1970). Reflections on my critics. In I. Lakatos & A. Musgrave (Eds.), *Criticism and the growth of knowledge* (pp. 231–278). Cambridge University Press.

Kuhn, T. S. (1971). Les notions de causalité dans le développement de la physique. In M. Bunge, F. Halbwachs, T. S. Kuhn, J. Piaget, & L. Rosenfeld, *Les théories de la causalité* (pp. 7–18). Paris: Presses Universitaires de France.

Kuhn, T. S. (1976). Theory-change as structure-change: Comments on the Sneed formalism. *Erkenntnis, 10,* 179–199.

Lakatos, I. (1970). Falsification and the methodology of scientific research programmes. In I. Lakatos & A. Musgrave (Eds.), *Criticism and the growth of knowledge* (pp. 91–196). Cambridge University Press.

Langer, J. (1969). *Theories of development*. New York: Holt, Rinehart & Winston.

Laudan, L. (1977). *Progress and its problems*. Berkeley: University of California Press.

Leiser, D. (1982). Piaget's logical formalism for formal operations: An interpretation in context. *Developmental Review, 2,* 87–99.

Longeot, F. (1978). *Les stades opératoires de Piaget et les facteurs de l'intelligence*. Grenoble: Presses Universitaires de Grenoble.

McClintock, B. (1984). The significance of responses of the genome to challenge. *Science, 226,* 792–801.

McCloskey, H. J. (1964). The philosophy of linguistic analysis and the problem of universals. *Philosophy and Phenomenological Research, 24,* 329–338. (Reprinted in Van Iten, 1970)

MacLane, S. (1972). *Categories for the working mathematician*. New York: Springer-Verlag.

McLaughlin, G. H. (1963). Psycho-logic: A possible alternative to Piaget's formulation. *British Journal of Educational Psychology, 33,* 61–67.

Madore, B. F., & Freedman, W. L. (1987). Self-organizing structures. *American Scientist, 75,* 252–259.

Marx, K. (1952). Capital. In R. M. Hutchins (Ed.), *Great books of the Western world* (Vol. 50). Chicago: Encyclopaedia Britannica. (Original work published 1849)

Maturana, H. R. (1980). Biology of cognition. In H. R. Maturana & F. J. Varela, *Autopoiesis and cognition*. Dordrecht: Reidel.

Maturana, H. R., & Varela, F. J. (1980). *Autopoiesis and cognition*. Dordrecht: Reidel.

Mays, W. (1982). Piaget's sociological theory. In S. Modgil & C. Modgil (Eds.), *Jean Piaget: Consensus and controversy* (pp. 31–50). London: Holt, Rinehart & Winston.

Meacham, J. A., & Riegel, K. F. (1978). Dialektische Perspektiven in Piaget's Theorie.

In G. Steiner (Ed.), *Die Psychologie des 20. Jahrhunderts, Vol. 7: Piaget und die Folgen* (pp. 172–183). Zürich: Kindler.

Medawar, P. B. (1969). *Induction and intuition in scientific thought.* London: Methuen.

Midgley, M. (1985). *Evolution as a religion.* London: Methuen.

Mill, J. (1869). *Analysis of the phenomena of the human mind* (2 vols.). London: Longmans, Green, Reader and Dyer. (Original work published 1829)

Mill, J. S. (1875). *A system of logic* (2 vols., 9th ed.). London: Longmans, Green, Reader and Dyer. (Original work published 1843)

Moessinger, P. (1979). Interpersonal comparisons in Piaget's interpersonal equilibrium. *Canadian Journal of Behavioral Science, 11,* 153–159.

Murray, F. B. (Ed.). (1979). *The impact of Piagetian theory.* Baltimore: University Park Press.

Murray, F. B. (1983). Cognition of physical and social events. In W. F. Overton (Ed.), *The relationship between social and cognitive development* (pp. 91–101). Hillsdale, NJ: Erlbaum.

Murray, J. P., & Youniss, J. (1968). Achievement of inferential transitivity and its relation to serial ordering. *Child Development, 39,* 1259–1268.

Olson, D. R. (1978). Open peer commentary. *Behavioral and Brain Sciences, 2,* 197–199.

Orlov, Y. F. (1982). The wave logic of consciousness: A hypothesis. *International Journal of Theoretical Physics, 21,* 37–53.

Osherson, D. N. (1974). *Logical abilities in children* (Vol. 2). Potomac, MD: Erlbaum.

Osterrieth, P., Piaget, J., de Saussure, R., Tanner, J. M., Wallon, H., Zazzo, R., Inhelder, B., & Rey, A. (1956). *Le problème des stades en psychologie de l'enfant.* Paris: Presses Universitaires de France.

Overton, W. F. (1985). Scientific methodologies and the competence-moderator-performance issue. In E. D. Neimark, R. DeLisi, & J. L. Newman (Eds.), *Moderators of competence* (pp. 15–41). Hillsdale, NJ: Erlbaum.

Overton, W. F., & Reese, H. W. (1973). Models of development: Methodological implications. In J. R. Nesselroade & H. W. Reese (Eds.), *Life-span developmental psychology: Methodological issues* (pp. 65–86). New York: Academic Press.

Parsons, C. (1960). Inhelder and Piaget's *The growth of logical thinking. II. A logician's viewpoint. British Journal of Psychology, 51,* 75–84.

Pascual-Leone, J. (1970). A mathematical model for the transition rule in Piaget's developmental stages. *Acta Psychologica, 32,* 301–345.

Pascual-Leone, J. (1984). Attention, dialectic, and mental effort: Toward an organismic theory of life stages. In M. L. Commons, F. A. Richards, & C. Armon (Eds.), *Beyond formal operations* (pp. 182–215). New York: Plenum.

Piaget, J. (1914). L'espèce mendelienne a-t-elle une valeur absolue? *Zoologischer Anzeiger, 42,* 328–331.

Piaget, J. (1916). *La mission de l'idée.* Lausanne: La Concorde.

Piaget, J. (1918). *Recherche.* Lausanne: La Concorde.

Piaget, J. (1921a). *Introduction à la malacologie valaisanne.* Sion: F. Aymon.

Piaget, J. (1921b). Essai sur quelques aspects du développement de la notion de partie chez l'enfant. *Journal de Psychologie, 18,* 449–480.

Piaget, J. (1922a). La psychologie et les valeurs religieuses. In M. DuPasquier (Ed.), *Les raisons d'espérer et de persévérer* (pp. 38–82). Lausanne: La Concorde.

Piaget, J. (1922b). Essai sur la multiplication logique et les débuts de la pensée formelle chez l'enfant. *Journal de Psychologie, 19,* 222–261.

Piaget, J. (1923a). La pensée symbolique et la pensée de l'enfant. *Archives de Psychologie, 18,* 273–304.

Piaget, J. (1923b). Une forme verbale de la comparaison chez l'enfant: Un cas de transition entre le jugement prédicatif et le jugement de relation. *Archives de Psychologie, 18*, 141–172.

Piaget, J. (1928a). Immanence et transcendance. In J. Piaget & J. de La Harpe, *Deux types d'attitudes religieuses: Immanence et transcendance* (pp. 7–40). Geneva: Editions de l'Association Chrétienne d'Etudiants de Suisse Romande.

Piaget, J. (1928b). *Judgment and reasoning in the child*. London: Routledge & Kegan Paul. (Original work published 1924)

Piaget, J. (1929a). Pour l'immanence. *Revue de Théologie et de Philosophie, 17*, 146–152.

Piaget, J. (1929b). Encore 'immanence et transcendance.' *Cahiers Protestants, 13*, 325–330.

Piaget, J. (1929c). Les races lacustres de la ''Limnaea stagnalis'' L. Recherches sur les rapports de l'adaptation héréditaires avec le milieu. *Bulletin Biologique de la France et la Belgique, 63*, 424–455.

Piaget, J. (1929d). L'adaptation de la limnaea stagnalis aux milieux lacustres de la Suisse romande. *Revue Suisse de Zoologie, 36*, 263–531.

Piaget, J. (1930). *Immanentisme et foi religieuse*. Geneva: Groupe romand des Anciens Membres de l'Association Chrétienne d'Etudiants.

Piaget, J. (1937). Les relations d'égalité résultant de l'addition et de la soustraction logiques constituents-elles un groupe? *L'Enseignement Mathématique, 36*, 99–108.

Piaget, J. (1938). La réversibilité des opérations et l'importance de la notion de ''groupe'' pour la psychologie de la pensée. In H. Piéron & I. Meyerson (Eds.), *Onzième congrès international de psychologie, Paris, 25–31 Juillet, 1937: Rapports et comptes rendus* (pp. 433–435). Paris: Alcan.

Piaget, J. (1941). Le mécanisme du développement mental et les lois du groupement des opérations. *Archives de Psychologie, 28*, 215–285.

Piaget, J. (1942). *Classes, relations et nombres*. Paris: Vrin.

Piaget, J. (1950a). *Introduction à l'épistémologie génétique, 3: La pensée biologique, la pensée psychologique, et la pensée sociologique*. Paris: Presses Universitaires de France.

Piaget, J. (1950b). *The psychology of intelligence*. New York: Harcourt, Brace. (Original work published 1947)

Piaget, J. (1952a). [Autobiography]. In E. G. Boring (Ed.), *A history of psychology in autobiography* (Vol. 4, pp. 237–256). New York: Russell & Russell.

Piaget, J. (1952b). *Essai sur les transformations des opérations logiques*. Paris: Presses Universitaires de France.

Piaget, J. (1952c). *The child's conception of number*. London: Routledge & Kegan Paul. (Abridged translation of Piaget & Szeminska, 1941/1964)

Piaget, J. (1952d). Equilibre et structures d'ensemble. *Bulletin de Psychologie, 6*, 4–10.

Piaget, J. (1955). *The language and thought of the child*. Cleveland: Meridian. (Original work published 1923)

Piaget, J. (1957a). *Logic and psychology*. New York: Basic Books.

Piaget, J. (1957b). Logique et équilibre dans les comportements du sujet. In L. Apostel, B. Mandelbrot, & J. Piaget (Eds.), *Logique et équilibre* (pp. 27–117). Paris: Presses Universitaires de France.

Piaget, J. (1960a). Introduction. In P. Gréco, J.-B. Grize, S. Papert, & J. Piaget (Eds.), *Problèmes de la construction du nombre*. Paris: Presses Universitaires de France.

Piaget, J. (1960b). The general problems of the psychobiological development of the child. In J. M. Tanner & B. Inhelder (Eds.), *Discussions on child development* (Vol. 4, pp. 3–27). London: Tavistock.

Piaget, J. (1962). *Play, dreams and imitation in childhood*. New York: Norton. (Original work published 1945)

Piaget, J. (1963). *The origins of intelligence in children.* New York: Norton. (Original work published 1936)

Piaget, J. (1965a). *The moral judgment of the child.* New York: Free Press. (Original work published 1932)

Piaget, J. (1965b). Note sur des *Limnaea stagnalis* L. *var. lacustris* Stud. élevées dans une mare du plateau vaudois. *Revue Suisse de Zoologie, 72,* 769–787.

Piaget, J. (1966a). *The child's conception of physical causality.* London: Routledge & Kegan Paul. (Original work published 1927)

Piaget, J. (1966b). Observations sur le mode d'insertion et la chute des rameaux secondaires chez les Sedum. *Candolla, 21,* 137–239.

Piaget, J. (1966c). Need and significance of cross-cultural studies in genetic psychology. *International Journal of Psychology, 1,* 3–13.

Piaget, J. (1967a). *Six psychological studies.* New York: Vintage. (Original work published 1964)

Piaget, J. (Ed.). (1967b). *Logique et connaissance scientifique.* Paris: Gallimard.

Piaget, J. (1968a). *On the development of memory and identity.* Barre, MA: Clark University Press.

Piaget, J. (1968b). Explanation in psychology and psychophysiological parallelism. In P. Fraise & J. Piaget (Eds.), *Experimental psychology, its scope and method* (pp. 153–191). London: Routledge & Kegan Paul. (Original work published 1963)

Piaget, J. (1969). *The mechanisms of perception.* London: Routledge & Kegan Paul. (Original work published 1961)

Piaget, J. (1970a). *The child's conception of movement and speed.* London: Routledge & Kegan Paul. (Original work published 1946)

Piaget, J. (1970b). *Epistémologie des sciences de l'homme.* Paris: Gallimard.

Piaget, J. (1970c). *Structuralism.* New York: Basic Books. (Original work published 1968)

Piaget, J. (1970d). *Genetic epistemology.* New York: Norton.

Piaget, J. (1971a). *The construction of reality in the child.* New York: Ballantine. (Original work published 1937)

Piaget, J. (1971b). *The child's conception of time.* New York: Ballantine. (Original work published 1946)

Piaget, J. (1971c). *Biology and knowledge.* University of Chicago Press. (Original work published 1967)

Piaget, J. (1971d). The theory of stages in cognitive development. In D. R. Green (Ed.), *Measurement and Piaget* (pp. 1–11). New York: McGraw-Hill.

Piaget, J. (1972a). *Essai de logique opératoire.* Paris: Dunod. (2nd ed., *Traité de logique,* 1949)

Piaget, J. (1972b). *Insights and illusions of philosophy.* London: Routledge & Kegan Paul. (Original work published 1965)

Piaget, J. (1972c). *The principles of genetic epistemology.* London: Routledge & Kegan Paul. (Original work published 1970)

Piaget, J. (1972d). *La transmissions des mouvements.* Paris: Presses Universitaires de France.

Piaget, J. (1972e). *La directions des mobiles lors de chocs et de poussées.* Paris: Presses Universitaires de France.

Piaget, J. (1972f). Intellectual evolution from adolescence to adulthood. *Human Development, 15,* 1–12.

Piaget, J. (1972g). *Psychology and epistemology.* London: Penguin. (Original work published 1970)

Piaget, J. (1972–1973). The role of imitation in the development of representational thought. *International Journal of Mental Health, 1*(4), 67–74. (Original work published 1962; reprinted in Gruber & Vonèche, 1977)

Piaget, J. (1973a). *Introduction à l'épistémologie génétique, 1: La pensée mathématique.* Paris: Presses Universitaires de France. (Original work published 1950)

Piaget, J. (1973b). *The child's conception of the world.* London: Granada. (Original work published 1926)

Piaget, J. (1973c). *Main trends in psychology.* London: Allen & Unwin. (Original work published 1970)

Piaget, J. (1973d). *La formation de la notion de force.* Paris: Presses Universitaires de France.

Piaget, J. (1973e). *La compositions des forces et le problème des vecteurs.* Paris: Presses Universitaires de France.

Piaget, J. (1973f). Bref témoignage. *Revue de l'Institut de Sociologie,* (No. 3–4), 544–547.

Piaget, J. (1974a). *Introduction à l'épistémologie génétique, 2: La pensée physique.* Paris: Presses Universitaires de France. (Original work published 1950)

Piaget, J. (1974b). *Understanding causality.* New York: Norton. (Original work published 1971)

Piaget, J. (1976a). Autobiographie. *Revue Européenne des Sciences Sociales, 14*(38–39), 1–43.

Piaget, J. (1976b). *The grasp of consciousness.* Cambridge, MA: Harvard University Press. (Original work published 1974)

Piaget, J. (1976c). Postface. *Archives de Psychologie, 44,* 223–228.

Piaget, J. (1977a). *Etudes sociologiques* (3rd ed.). Geneva: Librairie Droz. (Original work published 1965)

Piaget, J. (1977b). Some recent research and its link with a new theory of groupings and conservations based on commutability. *Annals of the New York Academy of Sciences, 291,* 350–358.

Piaget, J. (1977c). *Recherches sur l'abstraction réfléchissante* (2 vols.). Paris: Presses Universitaires de France.

Piaget, J. (1978a). *Le jugement et le raisonnement chez l'enfant* (3rd ed.). Paris: Delachaux et Niestlé. (Original work published 1924)

Piaget, J. (1978b). *Success and understanding.* London: Routledge & Kegan Paul. (Original work published 1974)

Piaget, J. (1978c). *Behavior and evolution.* New York: Pantheon. (Original work published 1974)

Piaget, J. (1978d). *Recherches sur la généralisation.* Paris: Presses Universitaires de France.

Piaget, J. (1979). Correspondences and transformations. In F. B. Murray (Ed.), *The impact of Piagetian theory* (pp. 17–27). Baltimore: University Park Press.

Piaget, J. (1980a). *Experiments in contradiction.* University of Chicago Press. (Original work published 1974)

Piaget, J. (1980b). *Recherches sur les correspondances.* Paris: Presses Universitaires de France.

Piaget, J. (1980c). *Adaptation and intelligence.* University of Chicago Press. (Original work published 1974)

Piaget, J. (1980d). *Les formes élémentaires de la dialectique.* Paris: Gallimard.

Piaget, J. (1980e). Recent studies in genetic epistemology. *Cahiers de la Fondation Archives Jean Piaget, 1,* 3–7.

Piaget, J. (1981a). *Le possible et le nécessaire, Vol. 1: L'évolution des possibles chez l'enfant.* Paris: Presses Universitaires de France.

Piaget, J. (1981b). *Intelligence and affectivity.* Palo Alto: Annual Reviews, Inc. (Original work published 1954)

Piaget, J. (1983). *Le possible et le nécessaire, Vol. 2: L'évolution du nécessaire chez l'enfant*. Paris: Presses Universitaires de France.

Piaget, J. (1985). *The equilibration of cognitive structures*. University of Chicago Press. (Original work published 1975)

Piaget, J. (1986). Essay on necessity. *Human Development, 29*, 301–314.

Piaget, J., & Garcia, R. (1983). *Psychogenèse et histoire des sciences*. Paris: Flammarion.

Piaget, J., & Garcia, R. (1987). *Vers une logique des significations*. Geneva: Murionde.

Piaget, J., Grize, J.-B., Szeminska, A., & Vinh Bang (1977). *Epistemology and psychology of functions*. Dordrecht: Reidel. (Original work published 1968)

Piaget, J., & Inhelder, B. (1967). *The child's conception of space*. New York: Norton. (Original work published 1948)

Piaget, J., & Inhelder, B. (1969). *The psychology of the child*. New York: Basic Books. (Original work published 1966)

Piaget, J., & Inhelder, B. (1971). *Mental imagery in the child*. London: Routledge & Kegan Paul. (Original work published 1966)

Piaget, J., & Inhelder, B. (1973). *Memory and intelligence*. London: Routledge & Kegan Paul. (Original work published 1968)

Piaget, J., & Inhelder, B. (1974). *The child's construction of quantities*. London: Routledge & Kegan Paul. (Original work published 1941)

Piaget, J., & Inhelder, B. (1975). *The origin of the idea of chance in children*. London: Routledge & Kegan Paul. (Original work published 1951)

Piaget, J., & Inhelder, B. (1977). Mental images. In H. E. Gruber & J. J. Vonèche (Eds.), *The essential Piaget* (pp. 652–684). New York: Basic Books. (Original work published 1963)

Piaget, J., Inhelder, B., & Szeminska, A. (1960). *The child's conception of geometry*. New York: Harper Torchbooks. (Original work published 1948)

Piaget, J., & Szeminska, A. (1964). *La genèse du nombre chez l'enfant* (3rd ed.). Neuchâtel: Delachaux et Niestlé. (Original work published 1941)

Piaget, J., & Voyat, G. (1979). The possible, the impossible, and the necessary. In F. B. Murray (Ed.), *The impact of Piagetian theory* (pp. 65–85). Baltimore: University Park Press.

Piattelli-Palmarini, M. (Ed.). (1980). *Language and learning: The debate between Jean Piaget and Noam Chomsky*. London: Routledge & Kegan Paul.

Pinard, A., & Laurendeau, M. (1969). "Stage" in Piaget's cognitive-developmental theory: Exegesis of a concept. In D. Elkind & J. H. Flavell (Eds.), *Studies in cognitive development* (pp. 121–170). New York: Oxford University Press.

Poincaré, H. (1914). *La valeur de la science*. Paris: Flammarion.

Polanyi, M. (1958). *Personal knowledge*. London: Routledge & Kegan Paul.

Polanyi, M. (1966). *The tacit dimension*. Gloucester, MA: Peter Smith.

Popper, K. (1979). *Objective knowledge* (rev. ed.). New York: Oxford University Press.

Prigogine, I. (1975). Physique et métaphysique. In *Connaissance scientifique et philosophie* (pp. 291–319). Brussels: L'academie Royale des Sciences, de Lettres et des Beaux-Arts de Belgique.

Prigogine, I. (1976). Genèse des structures en physico-chimie. In B. Inhelder, R. Garcia, & J. Vonèche (Eds.), *Epistémologie génétique et équilibration* (pp. 29–38). Neuchâtel: Delachaux et Niestlé.

Prigogine, I. (1980). *From being to becoming*. San Francisco: W. H. Freeman.

Prigogine, I. (1982). Dialogue avec Piaget sur l'irréversible. *Archives de psychologie, 50*, 7–16.

Prigogine, I., Nicolis, G., & Babloyantz, A. (1972). Thermodynamics of evolution. *Physics Today, 25*(11), 23–28, *25*(12), 38–44.

Prigogine, I., & Stengers, I. (1984). *Order out of chaos*. New York: Bantam.

Quine, W. V. O. (1980). On what there is. In W. V. O. Quine, *From a logical point of view* (2nd ed., rev., pp. 1–19). Cambridge, MA: Harvard University Press. Reprinted in Van Iten, 1970)

Reese, H. W., & Overton, W. F. (1970). Models of development and theories of development. In L. R. Goulet & P. B. Baltes (Eds.), *Life-span developmental psychology: Research and theory* (pp. 115–145). New York: Academic Press.

Reymond, A. (1929). Transcendance et immanence. *Cahiers Protestants, 13,* 161–170, 331–333.

Rosch, E. (1987). Wittgenstein and categorization research in cognitive psychology. In M. Chapman & R. A. Dixon (Eds.), *Meaning and the growth of understanding: Wittgenstein's significance for developmental psychology* (pp. 151–166). Berlin: Springer-Verlag.

Ross, W. D. (Ed.). *The works of Aristotle* (Vols. 1 & 2). London: Oxford University Press.

Roth, G., & Schwegler, H. (Eds.). (1981). *Self-organizing systems: An interdisciplinary approach.* Frankfurt: Campus.

Rotman, B. (1977). *Jean Piaget: Psychologist of the real.* Hassocks, Sussex: Harvester Press.

Ruse, N. (1982). *Darwinism defended.* Reading, MA: Addison-Wesley.

Russell, B. (1960). *An introduction to mathematical philosophy.* London: Allen & Unwin. (Original work published 1919)

Russell, B. (1967). *The problems of philosophy.* New York: Oxford University Press. (Original work published 1912)

Russell, J. (1978). *The acquisition of knowledge.* London: Macmillan.

Sandler, A.-M. (1975). Comments on the significance of Piaget's work for psychoanalysis. *International Review of Psycho-analysis, 2,* 365–377.

Sartre, J.-P. (1953). *Being and nothingness.* New York: Washington Square Press. (Original work published 1943)

Schlipp, P. A. (1974). *The philosophy of Karl Popper.* La Salle, IL: Open Court.

Schöfthaler, T., & Goldschmidt, D. (Eds.). (1984). *Soziale Struktur und Vernunft: Jean Piaget's Modell entwickelten Denkens in der Diskussion kulturvergleichenden Forschung.* Frankfurt: Suhrkamp.

Schrödinger, E. (1967). *What is life?* Cambridge University Press. (Original work published 1944)

Schulman, V. I., Restaino-Baumann, L. C. R., & Butler, L. (Eds.). (1985). *The future of Piagetian theory.* New York: Plenum.

Shapere, D. (1984). *Reason and the search for knowledge.* Dordrecht: Reidel.

Siegler, R. S. (1983). Information processing approaches to development. In P. H. Mussen (Ed.), *Handbook of child psychology* (4th ed., Vol. 1, pp. 129–211). New York: Wiley.

Sigel, I. E. (1981). Social experience in the development of representational thought: Distancing theory. In I. E. Sigel, D. M. Brodzinsky, & R. M. Golinkoff (Eds.), *New directions in Piagetian theory and practice* (pp. 203–217). Hillsdale, NJ: Erlbaum.

Sinclair de Zwart, H. (1967). *Acquisition du langage et développement de la pensée.* Paris: Dunod.

Skinner, B. F. (1953). *Science and human behavior.* New York: Macmillan.

Smedslund, J. (1963). Development of concrete transitivity of length in children. *Child Development, 34,* 389–405.

Smedslund, J. (1964). Concrete reasoning: A study of intellectual development. *Monographs of the Society for Research in Child Development, 29*(2, Serial No. 93).

Smedslund, J. (1965). The development of transitivity of length: A comment on Braine's reply. *Child Development, 36,* 577–580.

Smedslund, J. (1977). Piaget's psychology in practice. *British Journal of Educational Psychology, 4,* 1–6.

Smith, L. (1982). Piaget and the solitary knower. *Philosophy of the Social Sciences, 12,* 173–182.

Sneed, J. D. (1971). *The logical structure of mathematical physics.* Dordrecht: Reidel.

Staniland, H. (1972). *Universals.* London: Macmillan.

Stegmüller, W. (1956). Das Universalienproblem einst und jetzt. *Archiv für Philosophie, 6,* 192–225.

Stegmüller, W. (1976). *The structure and dynamics of theories.* New York: Springer-Verlag.

Stegmüller, W. (1979). *The structuralist view of theories.* Berlin: Springer-Verlag.

Steiner, R. (1963). *Goethes Weltanschauung.* Dornach, Switzerland: Rudolf Steiner Verlag. (Original work published 1897)

Suarez, A. (1980). Connaissance et action. *Revue Suisse de Psychologie, 39,* 177–199.

Tanner, M., & Inhelder, B. (Eds.). (1960). *Discussions on child development* (Vol. 4). London: Tavistock.

Teilhard de Chardin, P. (1965). *The phenomenon of man* (2nd ed.). New York: Harper Torchbooks. (Original work published 1955)

Thelen, E., Kelso, J. A. S., & Fogel, A. (1987). Self-organizing systems and infant motor development. *Developmental Review, 7,* 39–65.

Toulmin, S. (1972). *Human understanding.* Princeton, NJ: Princeton University Press.

Toulmin, S. (1982). *The return to cosmology.* Berkeley: University of California Press.

Van Iten, R. J. (Ed.). (1970). *The problem of universals.* New York: Appleton-Century-Crofts.

Varela, F. G., Maturana, H. R., & Uribe, R. (1974). Autopoiesis: The organization of living systems, its characterization and a model. *BioSystems, 5,* 187–196.

Vidal, F. (1984). *La vanité de la nomenclature:* un manuscrit inédit de Jean Piaget. *History and Philosophy of the Life Sciences, 6,* 75–106.

Vidal, F. (1987). Jean Piaget and psychoanalysis: A historical and biographical note (up to the 1930s). In S. Bem, H. Rappard, & W. van Hoorn (Eds.), *Studies in the history of psychology and the social sciences* (Vol. 4, pp. 315–329). Leiden: Psychologisch Institut van de Rijksuniversiteit Leiden.

Vidal, F. (1987). Jean Piaget and the liberal protestant tradition. In M. G. Ash & W. R. Woodward (Eds.), *Psychology in twentieth-century thought and society* (pp. 271–294). Cambridge University Press.

von Bertalanffy, L. (1968). *General system theory.* New York: George Braziller.

von Glasersfeld, E. (1982). An interpretation of Piaget's constructivism. *Revue Internationale de Philosophie, 142–143,* 612–635.

Vurpillot, E. (1959). Piaget's law of relative centrations. *Acta Psychologica, 16,* 403–430.

Vuyk, R. (1980). *Overview and critique of Piaget's genetic epistemology, 1965–1980* (2 vols.). New York: Academic Press.

Vygotsky, L. S. (1962). *Thought and language.* Cambridge, MA: MIT Press.

Waddington, C. H. (1975). *The evolution of an evolutionist.* Edinburgh University Press.

Wallon, H. (1947). L'étude psychologique et sociologique de l'enfant. *Cahiers Internationaux de Sociologie, 3,* 3–23.

Wallon, H. (1970). *De l'acte à la pensée.* Paris: Flammarion. (Original work published 1942)

Wartofsky, M. W. (1982). Piaget's genetic epistemology and the Marxist theory of knowledge. *Revue Internationale de Philosophie, 142–143,* 470–507.

Weinberg, J. R. (1964). *A short history of medieval philosophy.* Princeton, NJ: Princeton University Press.

Whitehead, A. N. (1978). *Process and reality* (corrected ed.). New York: Free Press. (Original work published 1929)

Whitehead, A. N., & Russell, B. (1910–1913). *Principia mathematica* (3 vols.). Cambridge University Press.

Winer, G. A. (1980). Class-inclusion reasoning in children: A review of the empirical literature. *Child Development, 51,* 309–328.

Wittgenstein, L. (1958). *Philosophical investigations.* New York: Macmillan.

Wittgenstein, L. (1966). *Tractatus logico-philosophicus.* London: Routledge & Kegan Paul. (Original work published 1922)

Wittman, E. (1973). The concept of grouping in Jean Piaget's psychology: Formalization and applications. *Educational Studies in Mathematics, 5,* 125–146.

Wittman, E. (1982). Groupings. *Cahiers de la Fondation Archives Jean Piaget, 2–3,* 275–293.

Wohlwill, J. F. (1973). *The study of behavioral development.* New York: Academic Press.

Youniss, J. (1980). *Parents and peers in social development.* Chicago University Press.

Youniss, J., & Murray, J. P. (1970). Transitive inference with nontransitive solutions controlled. *Developmental Psychology, 2,* 169–175.

Zeleny, M. (1977). Self-organization of living systems: A formal model of autopoiesis. *International Journal of General Systems, 4,* 13–28.

Zeleny, M., & Pierre, N. A. (1976). Simulation of self-renewing systems. In E. Jantsch & C. Waddington (Eds.), *Evolution and consciousness* (pp. 150–165). Reading, MA: Addison-Wesley.

Author index

Abelard, P., 388–9, 390
Adams, H., 388
Agassiz, L., 58
Anderson, A. R., 329–30
Apostel, L., 239n.,264, 368n., 369, 371, 374, 400, 425–8, 430
Aristotle, 27–8, 58, 226–7, 259, 267, 382–3, 386–8, 393, 417n.
Armstrong, D. M., 403–4
Ascher, E., 418
Atkinson, C., 369
Atlan, H., 280, 430

Babloyantz, A., 430
Bachelard, G., 225
Baillargeon, R., 156, 333, 342, 347
Baldwin, J. M., 68, 276
Bambrough, J. R., 403, 413
Barrow, J. D., 437
Bartley, W. W., III., 405
Beilin, H., 10, 281, 328, 330, 334, 336, 368n., 369, 425
Belnap, L., 329–30
Bergson, H., 4–5, 9, 13–15, 19–20, 28–9, 33, 37, 44, 169, 191, 213, 227, 259, 260, 412, 437
Berkeley, G., 256, 394–5, 401
Beth, E. W., 145, 193, 327
Bettelheim, B., 122n.
Binet, A., 31, 34, 42–3
Bleuler, E., 17, 31
Bohm, D., 437
Bohr, N., 223
Boring, E. G., 13
Borke, H., 348, 352–3, 365–6
Bovet, M., 195
Bovet, P., 68–9, 76
Bowlby, J., 282
Braine, M. D. S., 341, 349, 353–4, 363, 367
Brainerd, C. J., 158, 190, 333–5, 337, 339, 341–2, 347, 349, 351, 352n., 355–7, 359, 364
Brent, S. B., 432

Bringuier, J.-C., 18, 122n., 264, 285, 375–6, 376n., 377, 417, 433
Brooks, D. R., 430, 434
Broughton, J., 180, 342, 369
Brouwer, L. E. J., 204, 410
Brown, T., 280n., 379
Bruner, J. S., 168, 193, 340, 369, 423
Brunschvicg, L., 31, 199, 225
Bryant, P. E., 349, 351–2, 369
Buck-Morss, S., 369, 374
Bullinger, A., 379
Bunge, M., 334
Burger, J.-D., 70
Burt, C., 31f., 34
Buss, A. R., 334
Butler, L., 379

Capra, F., 437
Carotenuto, A., 122n.
Case, R., 33n., 367
Chapman, M., 181, 343, 350–5, 359, 362, 364–5, 367, 371–2
Chatenay, V., 34
Chatillon, J.-F., 379
Chomsky, N., 372
Churchland, P. M., 417–18
Claparède, E., 34–5, 37, 39, 76, 102–3, 133, 189
Cohen, D., 333, 369
Comte, A., 225, 400, 434
Cooper, R. G., Jr., 350
Cornut, S., 14
Corrigan, R., 344–5
Cournot, A. A., 39
Cowan, P. A., 369, 378
Cuvier, G., 58

Dancy, J., 414
Darwin, C., 23, 267
Davies, P., 437
Dedekind, R., 205
De Rivera, J., 379
Descartes, R., 197, 211, 391–2
Ducret, J.-J., 46

Subject index

2810